SO-AXK-636

PROSE IN BRIEF
READING AND WRITING ESSAYS

PROSE IN BRIEF
READING AND WRITING ESSAYS

EDWARD PROFFITT
MANHATTAN COLLEGE

HARCOURT BRACE JOVANOVICH, PUBLISHERS
SAN DIEGO NEW YORK CHICAGO AUSTIN WASHINGTON, D.C.
LONDON SYDNEY TOKYO TORONTO

For Tom Broadbent,
whose voice informs every word.

Cover: "Moonlit Pears." Copyright © 1990, Will Crocker.

Copyright © 1991 by Harcourt Brace Jovanovich, Inc.

All rights reserved. No part of this publication may be reproduced or transmitted in any form or by any means, electronic or mechanical, including photocopy, recording or any information storage and retrieval system, without permission in writing from the publisher.

Requests for permission to make copies of any part of the work should be mailed to: Permissions Department, Harcourt Brace Jovanovich, Inc., 8th Floor, Orlando, Florida 32887.

ISBN: 0-15-572262-X

Library of Congress Catalog Card Number: 90-84205

Printed in the United States of America

Copyrights and Acknowledgments appear on pages 707–12, which constitute a continuation of the copyright page.

PREFACE

THIS BOOK PROVIDES AN INTRODUCTION TO WRITING AND TO THE ESSAY and an anthology of one hundred essays, seven by students. The introductory material is contained in the two opening chapters. Both chapters are concerned with reading and writing; the first focuses on writing essays, the second on reading them. Chapter 1 deals with the principles and process of writing both the paragraph and the essay. This chapter uses a professional work, E. M. Forster's "My Wood," as well as many student samples, to demonstrate essay structure (beginning/middle/end) and rewriting. The focus is on what is always most troublesome in student writing — transition, unity, and coherence. The meaning of these three topics, the difference they make, and the ways they can be attained are exemplified by showing how two student papers were revised. Chapter 2 deals with the various rhetorical elements of the essay, using professional samples to exemplify.

The anthology that follows, organized alphabetically for ease of locating titles, is wide-ranging in both theme and rhetorical strategy. The study questions that follow each essay are primarily concerned with structure and rhetoric. For the most part, these questions have definite answers; these answers are discussed in an Instructor's Manual.

The organization of this book into two basic parts — introduction and anthology — allows students to study essays in their entirety rather than piecemeal, element by element. Because students must learn to go beyond exercises to write whole essays, treating essays whole seems the best approach. However, by using the "Groupings by Elements and Other Formal Features" (pages 679–98), an instructor may discuss an element in the second chapter and exemplify it with essays from the anthology. This organization also underscores the book's uniqueness. Most reader/rhetorics stress either technique or purpose; because they are of equal importance to the writer, this book stresses both equally. Furthermore, most textbooks are concerned either with reading essays or with writing them; this book is concerned with both.

Another significant feature of this book is the average length of the essays. Most of the selections in the anthology are short; only twelve are more than six pages. This concentration on short essays offers a wide range of selections, and thereby a chance to demonstrate the many possible uses of various elements. Also, student essays are generally short, and short essays provide a better model for writing. However, the book contains enough longer essays to provide breadth of selection, and three authors — Joan Didion, Stephen Jay Gould, and Lewis Thomas — are represented at length.

Students will find help with terminology in the "Glossary of Terms" on pages 699–712. The "Groupings by Theme/Thesis and Mode" and the "Groupings by Elements and Other Formal Features" suggest some of the many connections, thematic and formal, that can be made among the essays. Appendix 1, "Using Metaphors," should aid students in mastering this most essential figure of speech. And "Appendix 2, "A Brief Guide to the Use and Documentation of Sources and Related Matters" offers advice on quoting, paraphrasing, summarizing, and documenting sources; it adheres to the style adopted by the Modern Language Association (MLA) in 1988.

ACKNOWLEDGMENTS

As always, I am indebted to Marie Duchon, my favorite librarian; to my wife, Nancy, for reading and rereading drafts and proof; and to my students, some of whose essays appear hereafter. I also owe thanks to Stuart Miller, my acquisitions editor, who saw this book through its several drafts; to Niamh Foley-Homan and Sheila Spahn, production editors; to Eleanor Garner, permissions editor; to Linda Miller, designer; to Cindy Simpson, manuscript editor; and to Mandy Van Dusen, production manager. Finally, I wish to express my appreciation to the following manuscript reviewers: Robert Bentley, Lansing Community College; Christine Cetrulo, University of Kentucky; Henry Morgenstein, Northwestern Michigan College; Robert Peterson, Middle Tennessee State University; Paula Ross, Gadsden State Community College; and Frank Weihs, Tacoma Community College.

CONTENTS

❖ 2 ❖

WORKING WITH THE ELEMENTS OF THE ESSAY

ESSAYS FOR STUDY AND WRITING ASSIGNMENTS

READING AND WRITING

READING FOR WRITING

"HOW CAN I KNOW WHAT I THINK TILL I SEE WHAT I SAY," SAYS A character in an E. M. Forster novel. Exactly so. In large part, we write in order to know our own minds. Of course, we write as well to let others know what we think, and as writers we must never forget the audience we are addressing. Still, the most wonderful potential of writing is that it can show us ourselves.

For the purposes of writing, at least the kind of writing that college students are most often called upon to write — that is, expository prose (which is what you are reading now) — the study of essays is particularly apt. For essays are expository themselves and so can help teach you the objectives and strategies of exposition. Also, because they are like what you have to write, they provide models for imitation, the classic way of mastering what was once called *the art of rhetoric*. Writing on essays — especially on their form — or writing in imitation of an essay — especially of some aspect of its form — should help you to improve your writing and to make it truly bear and communicate your ideas.

READING ESSAYS

Before we move to a discussion of writing, however, a brief consideration of reading essays might prove helpful. Note that what we are going to consider about reading essays by others applies equally to your reading of your own work in progress. After all, you must be able to read your own writing critically during the writing process, and to read *critically* means that you must be able to perceive the structures you are working with as well as all of the other elements of a piece of exposition. In that, for your purposes, how essays are constructed is of primary importance, we shall focus on essay construction, or the building blocks from which all essays are composed. To be fleshed out as we move along, a summation of these elements follows together with suggestions as to the kind of questions you should ask of the composition of essays, your own in progress no less than those by professional writers.

A Note on Procedure

Chapters 1 and 2 of this textbook are packed with information, much more than anyone could absorb on first reading. So do not try to remember everything your first time through. Just try to retain the main concepts. Then, when reading essays in the anthology and especially when writing papers yourself, come back and reread appropriate sections in these introductory chapters. In other words, use them to help guide yourself through reading, writing, and rewriting. I am sure you will find that by going about your study thus, you will ultimately both understand and retain more than you would by trying to grasp everything up front.

Of Audience: Who was this essay written for? In what way(s) does its implied audience account for its various features — its style, for instance, or its structure? To what extent does the judgment of the essay's success or failure depend on the prior judgment of its audience?

Of Narration: Is the essay narrative, either wholly or in part? That is, does it tell a story? If the essay is wholly narrative, what does it communicate? What is its theme? If the essay is narrative only in part, what is the function of the narration? How does it relate to the essay's main point?

Of Tone and Voice: What tone of voice does the essay convey? For instance, is it warm and friendly, or aloof and condescending? Are there any shifts in tone? If so, to what effect? Voice refers to the sense of a person speaking and is in large measure created by tone. What kind of a voice do you hear in the essay overall? How do tone and thence voice contribute to the essay's effect and meaning?

Of the Character Sketch: Does the essay delineate something about a specific person or perhaps a type of person generally? What is revealed about the one or the other? How is this revelation brought about? What is the point of the character sketch?

Of Setting: Does the essay present a setting? That is, is it located as to time and/or place? If so, what is the function of the description of the one and/or the other? For instance, might some aspect of the setting be symbolic? If so, what is symbolized and why? Or does the setting help establish mood? How so?

Of Examples and Other Concretions: What examples does the essay contain? How do they support the general point? What other concrete details do you find — for instance, metaphors, imagery, even the sound of an essay? How do they relate to the essay's point and help convey it?

Of Figurative Language: What figures of speech — such as similes and personification — are used in the essay? To what effect? Especially, what metaphors are used and how? Are these metaphors used just in passing, or is metaphor a central means of the essay? If the latter, how does metaphor help structure the essay?

Of Sound and Rhythm: Are there any patterns of sound and/or any rhythms that seem significant? What do they signify? In particular, what of the rhythm of the end of the essay? Does the rhythm of the ending help lend a sense of completion? How so?

Of Style: What kind of words and sentence patterns are marked in the essay? Is its vocabulary formal, slangy, conversational, childish? Are its sentences long and complex or short and simple? What is the effect of its kind of vocabulary and sentence structure in general, and, specifically, how do both affect tone and voice? What is the relation, finally, between style and meaning?

Of Means of Support: How is the point of the essay backed up and developed paragraph by paragraph? Does the author appeal to the authority of experts or statistics or immediate experience? What examples are used? What other means are incorporated? Are they convincing?

Of Structural Elements: How is the essay structured, its disparate materials made to cohere? Does it exhibit chronological organization, for instance — its materials organized according to their relationship in time? What about the material lends itself to the type of structure used? How does the author let the reader know the way the essay is organized, and how is the reader kept in mind of its overall structure?

Of Titles: What does the title do? What bearing does it have on the essay? Does it have symbolic weight, perhaps? Or does it emphasize a point or direct the reader to the essay's thesis or conclusion?

Of Theme or Thesis: What is the essay's point, that which is defined, exemplified, or argued? Note that the theme or thesis of an essay is not another element but the end to which the elements are means. How well do the means employed serve this end?

READING IN STEPS

Questions like these are what you should ask as you read. But read an essay *first* for pleasure, for its effect. Let it sink in. After your first reading, note down your reaction and any ideas and questions that come to mind. Then read the essay again, testing your response and ideas, seeking answers to your questions, and determining the essay's key elements in whatever order the essay itself suggests or simply in whatever order they come to mind. Be sure, too, to note down anything you observe about how the essay coheres. These step-by-step activities fall under the heading of *prewriting.* By following through on them, you should arrive at a pretty good understanding of the essay in question — especially of its construction — along with an articulation of your feelings about it, some relevant ideas that you could use in a paper focused on the essay, and perhaps also a sense of direction in which your thoughts and feelings might take you when writing. As you turn to E. M. Forster's "My Wood," go through the steps just specified. Then follow me as I go through them myself.

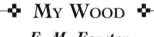

✜ MY WOOD ✜
E. M. Forster

A FEW YEARS AGO I WROTE A BOOK WHICH DEALT IN PART WITH THE   1 difficulties of the English in India. Feeling that they would have had no difficulties in India themselves, the Americans read the book freely. The more they read it the better it made them feel, and a cheque to the author was the result. I bought a wood with the cheque. It is not a large wood — it contains scarcely any trees, and it is intersected, blast it, by a public footpath. Still, it is the first property that I have owned, so it is right that other people should participate in my shame, and should ask themselves, in accents that will vary in horror, this very important question: What is the effect of property upon the character? Don't let's touch economics; the effect of private ownership upon the community as a whole is another question — a more important question, perhaps, but another one. Let's keep to psychology. If you own things, what's their effect on you? What's the effect on me of my wood?

In the first place, it makes me feel heavy. Property does 2 have this effect. Property produces men of weight, and it was a man of weight who failed to get into the Kingdom of Heaven. He was not wicked, that unfortunate millionaire in the parable, he was only stout; he stuck out in front, not to mention behind, and as he wedged himself this way and that in the crystalline entrance and bruised his well-fed flanks, he saw beneath him a comparatively slim camel passing through the eye of a needle and being woven into the robe of God. The Gospels all through couple stoutness and slowness. They point out what is perfectly obvious, yet seldom realized: that if you have a lot of things you cannot move about a lot, that furniture requires dusting, dusters require servants, servants require insurance stamps, and the whole tangle of them makes you think twice before you accept an invitation to dinner or go for a bathe in the Jordan. Sometimes the Gospels proceed further and say with Tolstoy that property is sinful; they approach the difficult ground of asceticism here, where I cannot follow them. But as to the immediate effects of property on people, they just show straightforward logic. It produces men of weight. Men of weight cannot, by definition, move like the lightning from the East unto the West, and the ascent of a fourteen-stone bishop into a pulpit is thus the exact antithesis of the coming of the Son of Man. My wood makes me feel heavy.

In the second place, it makes me feel it ought to be larger. 3

The other day I heard a twig snap in it. I was annoyed at 4 first, for I thought that someone was blackberrying, and depreciating the value of the undergrowth. On coming nearer, I saw it was not a man who had trodden on the twig and snapped it, but a bird, and I felt pleased. My bird. The bird was not equally pleased. Ignoring the relation between us, it took fright as soon as it saw the shape of my face, and flew straight over the boundary hedge into a field, the property of Mrs. Henessy, where it sat down with a loud squawk. It had become Mrs. Henessy's bird. Something seemed grossly amiss here, something that would not have occurred had the wood been larger. I could not afford to buy Mrs. Henessy out, I dared not murder her, and limitations of this sort beset me on every side. Ahab did not want that vineyard — he only needed it to round off his property, preparatory to plotting a new curve — and all the land around my wood has become necessary to me in order to round off the wood. A boundary protects. But — poor little thing — the boundary ought in its turn to be protected. Noises on the edge of it. Children throw stones. A little more, and then a little more, until we reach the sea. Happy Canute! Happier Alexander! And after all, why should even the world be the limit of possession? A rocket containing a Union Jack, will, it is hoped, be shortly fired at the moon. Mars. Sirius. Beyond which . . . But these immensities ended by saddening me. I could not suppose that my wood was the destined nucleus of universal dominion — it is so very small and contains no mineral wealth beyond the blackberries. Nor was I comforted when Mrs. Henessy's bird took alarm for the second time and flew clean away from us all, under the belief that it belonged to itself.

In the third place, property makes its owner feel that he 5 ought to do something to it. Yet he isn't sure what. A restlessness comes over him, a vague sense that he has a personality to express — the same sense which, without any vagueness, leads the artist to an act of creation. Sometimes I think I will cut down such trees as remain in the wood, at other times I want to fill up the gaps between them with new trees. Both impulses are pretentious and empty. They are not honest movements towards money-making or beauty. They spring from a foolish desire to express myself and from an inability to enjoy what I have got. Creation, property, enjoyment form a sinister trinity in the human mind. Creation and enjoyment are both very, very good, yet they are often unattainable without a material basis, and at such moments property pushes itself in as a substitute, saying, "Accept me instead — I'm good enough for all three." It is not enough. It is, as Shakespeare said of lust, "The expense of spirit in a waste of shame": it is "Before, a joy proposed; behind, a dream." Yet we don't know how to shun it. It is forced on us by our economic system as the alternative to starvation. It is also forced on us by an internal defect in the soul, by the feeling that in property may lie the germs of self-development and of exquisite or heroic deeds. Our life on earth is, and ought to be, material and carnal. But we have not yet learned to manage our materialism and carnality properly; they are still entangled with the desire for ownership, where (in the words of Dante) "Possession is one with loss."

And this brings us to our fourth and final point: the 6 blackberries.

Blackberries are not plentiful in this meagre grove, but they 7 are easily seen from the public footpath which traverses it, and all too easily gathered. Foxgloves, too — people will pull up the foxgloves, and ladies of an educational tendency even grub for toadstools to show them on the Monday in class. Other ladies, less educated, roll down the bracken in the arms of their gentlemen friends. There is paper, there are tins. Pray, does my wood belong to me or doesn't it? And, if it does, should I not own it best by allowing no one else to walk there? There is a wood near Lyme Regis, also cursed by a public footpath, where the owner has not hesitated on this point. He had built high stone walls each side of the path, and has spanned it by bridges, so that the public circulate like termites while he gorges on the blackberries unseen. He really does own his wood, this able chap. Dives in Hell did pretty well, but the gulf dividing him from Lazarus could be traversed by vision, and nothing traverses it here. And perhaps I shall come to this in time. I shall wall in and fence out until I really taste the sweets of property. Enormously stout, endlessly avaricious, pseudo-creative, intensely selfish, I shall weave upon my forehead the quadruple crown of possession until those nasty Bolshies come and take it off again and thrust me aside into the outer darkness.

[1936 — Great Britain]

First Reading: I like this essay. I especially like its speaker, who seems warm and friendly. A sentence of Thoreau's comes to mind: "The more one has, the less one is." Is this what Forster meant his little story about his wood to exemplify? Might the essay also have larger significance, the small world of the wood and its effects giving shape to something in the large world outside?

Second Reading: I like the essay even more and see that my initial intuition that it might have larger implication is correct: as well as concerning the effect of owning property on the author, it concerns the effect of ownership on people generally ("Possession is one with loss") and, by not too large a leap, the effect of the possession of colonies on the part of the British or any other imperial power. Upon second reading, I also see clearly the key elements that go into the making of the essay:

1. *Setting:* Clearly, the wood (a place) is an important means in the essay, both putting it in motion and coming to embody concretely the large abstractions *property* and *possession*.

2. *Exemplification/Narration:* In other words, the setting provides "My Wood" with its central example of the effects of owning property. The essay proceeds by a development of this example and so is partially narrative, telling the story of the wood and its effects. Its narrative example makes concrete ideas about property and possession that otherwise would be hard to get a handle on.

3. *Tone and Voice:* With respect to persuasion, the single most important element here is voice. The warmth of the essay's tone, along with the reasonable-sounding voice that the tone helps create, sways the reader to accept its point and point of view.

4. *Style:* Its straightforward sentence patterns and everyday vocabulary preclude condescension, for instance, and help to lend a sense of sincerity to the essay's voice.

5. *Structure:* Forster's structure also conditions voice by lending the essay a sense of reasonableness. Structured by enumeration (four reasons why — first, second, third, and finally), the essay is orderly and perfectly clear in its design, which is

high-lighted by the paragraphing. Therefore, the essay seems the product of a lucid mind, one we can trust and so one to which we are likely to assent.

6. *Audience:* Audience is a crucial consideration as to understanding the essay in full. The essay was not written immediately for us, after all, but for an audience of literate Britishers living in the 1930s. Realizing this, we have access to Forster's larger meaning. Britain still had a colonial empire in the 1930s, during which Britain's right to its Empire was hotly debated; and Forster had written a great novel —*A Passage to India*— about the ill effects of the Empire on the British themselves, a novel referred to in the first paragraph of the essay and that Forster's immediate audience would have known. His readers would have known, then, that Forster was anti-Empire. In other words, an assessment of Forster's intended audience leads us to see that much more is at stake in the essay than just one man and his patch of woods.

Now I think I grasp the essay — both its meanings and the thrust of its argument, and — more important from the point of view of studying writing — how it is constructed and the way it gains its effect. Now I am ready to write.

From Reading to Writing

Well, almost ready. For I still have to decide what to write. As you can see from the foregoing text, Forster's essay has generated ideas aplenty. But what and how to choose? The first principle of decision is *look to yourself.* What do you want to write? What most moves you or stimulates in you anger, delight, or whatever? Decent writing demands personal commitment. Then, what you choose must be feasible with respect to the length of what you are going to write: that is, just as your idea cannot be so narrow that you are left nothing to write, it must not be so broad as to require you to write a book, unless you are planning to write a book. For instance, " 'My Wood' concerns a patch of woods owned by the author" is too narrow; "property and the man" is too broad and unfocused. Though the phrase might serve as a title, it needs to be limited to, say, "In 'My Wood,' E. M. Forster illustrates the adverse effects of possession in general and, specifically, of owning property." This would be a viable thesis for either a paragraph or a whole essay. The difference between the two is not a matter of thesis but of the number of supporting ideas brought to bear and the depth of the discussion of each.

Topic/Opinion/Thesis

But let's pause for a moment over the word "thesis." You might be wondering, "What exactly is a thesis? Is it the same thing as the topic of a paper? Or is it just an opinion?" No, a thesis is neither a topic nor merely an opinion, and the distinctions are important. As to the first, a topic is the general area from which a thesis is drawn. Consider the following examples of topics: Owning and Being, Friendly Persuasion, We've Lost India!, A Miracle of Design. I have deliberately cast these phrases in the form of titles because each could be a title. In fact, the title of many an essay indicates its topic, stimulating in the reader the question, "What about it?" Having a topic in mind, the writer needs to ask the same question. So "what about" each of the four possible topics just enumerated? Here are my answers.

1. Owning and Being: "The more one has, the less one is," Thoreau declared. E. M. Forster would agree. Indeed, a major point of his essay "My Wood" is that ownership — specifically of property — is bad for the soul.
2. Friendly Persuasion: E. M. Forster's "My Wood" is an especially persuasive essay, in large part because of its congenial voice and tone.
3. We've Lost India!: E. M. Forster would not consider the loss of India or of any other colony something to grieve. The overriding point of "My Wood," indeed, is that Britain's Empire has done it no good. Therefore, the loss of India, say, would be a moral victory.

4. A Miracle of Design: The overall design of E. M. Forster's "My Wood" is a little miraculous. For its structure — that of enumeration, unabashedly emphasized by the paragraphing — is as mundane as it could be, yet it is turned into a vehicle for something like poetic insight.

Here are four possible theses, stated in at least one complete sentence each. (Note: If you don't have at least one complete sentence — that is, a complete statement of an idea — then you don't have a thesis.) Each thesis statement, notice, suggests how the writer might proceed. For instance, after an introductory paragraph, "A Reasonable Design" would move to a consideration of the enumerative structure of "My Wood," a consideration that would embrace a discussion of the essay's paragraphing, and then go on to consider the use and effect of that structure, ending with a concluding statement as to why the structure of Forster's essay is "a little miraculous." Note that the whole projected paper flows from the thesis statement, broad enough to leave something to be said yet narrow enough to keep what is said specific and directed toward a specific end.

So a thesis is not a topic. Nor is it an opinion, at least not a "mere" opinion, though the two might superficially resemble each other. "Oranges are the best fruit there is" is not a thesis but merely an opinion, as unarguable as it is uninteresting. In contrast, "Oranges may prove a treatment for cancer" is a thesis, for it can be argued, demonstrated, and so forth by way of facts, statements by experts, and so on. But if you wish to think of a thesis as an opinion, think of it as a *kind* of opinion that can be supported by facts and informed judgments. And that, of course, is one of the primary purposes of exposition in the first place. The thesis provides the controlling idea, and everything else in a paper goes to argue and support it.

In sum, in deciding what to write, let your feelings guide you to a topic. Then decide what it is *about the topic* you have to say. Write down your answer in at least one complete sentence. Then judge what you have written: is your statement still too broad, or is it too narrow to be of any help to you or your reader? If either seems the case, ask "What about it?" of your topic again and come up with another answer. Once you are satisfied that your statement is both one you feel committed to and one that will serve as a springboard for the work to come, you are ready to write. Before we get to the writing stage, however, there are a few more considerations — which you should have in mind as you begin to write — that need attention. The first, which many rhetoricians regard as being of primary importance, is the nature of your audience.

CONSIDERING YOUR AUDIENCE

Though what was said at the beginning of this chapter about writing and self-discovery is true, it is also true that one usually writes for other people as well as for oneself. Because many decisions one makes when writing depend (or should depend) on whom one is writing for, it is important to judge one's audience at the outset and to keep that audience in mind throughout the writing stage. To take an analogy, suppose you have to give a speech on some technical matter that you know thoroughly to a high school audience that knows nothing about your subject area. You would realize, no doubt, that you would have to simplify your presentation and define all terms. If you didn't, your audience would either fall asleep or boo you off the stage. But if you were giving the speech to a group of experts in your field, you could rely on their knowing your terminology and being able to deal with the subject matter in its complexity. This second audience wouldn't know your approach to the subject — if they did, there would be no point in your giving the speech — but they would have a good knowledge of the subject area. For this audience, therefore, you would not want to define most terms — if you did, your listeners might think you condescending — and you would want to treat your subject as fully as possible. In each case, your audience would be your measuring rod.

The same is true of writing in general, and, as we have seen, true for professional writers no less than for college students: The audience must be assessed and kept in mind. Forster's obvious assessment of the audience of "My Wood" is a clear example. But how is the student's audience to be sounded? To some extent, that depends on the type of course in question, but what I am now going to say about writing for an English class applies to most other courses as well. You should think of your audience as consisting of your instructor and fellow students. It is, then, a knowledgeable audience, one familiar with the essay you are discussing and the terminology of rhetorical analysis but not, of course, with your specific approach or thesis, or with the arguments you will use in supporting your ideas. In other words, you need not define terms or summarize the content of an essay that has been assigned to fill your readers in. Rather, use your limited space to exemplify and argue your thesis. That is where your focus should be. By keeping your audience in view in this way, you should find that the problem of deciding what need not be said and, conversely, what must be said is greatly reduced. Remembering your audience, then, should facilitate your writing process.

EXPOSITORY PROSE

Before we consider the process of writing exposition and its stages, you should bear in mind a further consideration as you sit down to write: the nature of exposition, or expository prose, itself, its function and types. As to function, exposition — which is what college students are most often called upon to write — is prose designed to *expose*, that is, to expose facts, ideas, and informed opinions in an orderly fashion to the scrutiny of others so that both writer and reader come to a greater understanding of something. "In an orderly fashion" is the key phrase. Because exposition has ready understanding as its goal, its greatest asset is clarity, and clarity demands that facts, ideas, and informed opinions be set forth point by point, with each clearly related to the next and with some plan of movement from one to another clearly followed. Perhaps this seems forbidding. But take heart: the more one writes, the less difficult writing becomes, just as the more time one puts in practicing a sport, the less difficult the sport becomes and the greater one's facility. One must know the ground rules to begin with, of course, as well as the purposes and ways of handling whatever equipment the sport entails. The same is true of writing. To continue the analogy, this whole chapter is aimed at acquainting you with the ground rules of exposition. As to equipment, we have the types of exposition, each type being a different piece of equipment you need to learn how to handle. Again, expository prose is designed to set forth facts, ideas, and informed opinions in an orderly fashion. Accordingly, there are three fundamental types of exposition, any of which a college student might encounter on assignments: informational, analytic, and persuasive.

Informational

As its name implies, *informational prose* delivers information. If, for instance, you became interested in E. M. Forster, you might do some research on his life and write up what you find. Or you might write a paper about the background of "My Wood" with regard to its larger significance — on, that is, the British Empire and how it altered the British way of life. Informational prose places two demands on the writer: first, it must be well-researched and factual; second, like the other kinds of exposition, it must proceed in an orderly fashion. The writer must consciously choose some way of organizing according to the nature of the material and follow through. Supported with reference to pertinent documents, the writings of experts, and so forth, the theses of informational essays are generally statements of fact: that a, b, and c are what happened to Forster when growing up, or that x, y, and z are the ways the empire altered the British. Interpretation of such facts is the business of analytic prose.

Analytic

From the Greek meaning "to break up," analysis entails first the breaking of a subject into its components and then a detailed examination component by component. If asked to write a piece of *analytic prose* on "My Wood," for example, I might choose to examine how Forster supports his overriding thesis that owning property is detrimental to the human spirit. *My* thesis would be that Forster supports *his* thesis by reference to human psychology and by a subtle appeal to authority. In other words, my thesis would be interpretative, which is the nature of all analytic theses. I would proceed by examining each of Forster's four supports *in turn*, showing first how each is psychologically apt and then the relevance and implications of Forster's references to Dante and the bible (his appeal to authority). Or I might write on how in large measure the way Forster treats the essay's elements is responsible for its persuasiveness. Here, too, I would have to think into my material and break it into its constituents — for instance, voice, style, and enumerative structure. Then I would examine each in relation to my controlling thesis about the persuasiveness of "My Wood," moving in an orderly way from one to the next and using evidence from the text for support point by point. Analytic prose, note, can incorporate informational prose. In my first hypothetical essay, for example, I might wish to cite one or another statistical study on the psychological effects of owning property. But analytic prose is different in purpose from prose designed primarily to impart information. The purpose of analytic prose is not to set forth facts but, by way of facts, to uncover and clarify meaning. For this reason, analytic prose is more complex than informational. Of the three broad types of exposition, it is analytic that you will most often be called upon to write in college, because the ability to analyze is perhaps the main mark of an educated mind.

Persuasive

Analytic prose overlaps with persuasive in that when writing an analysis, we wish the reader to accept our ideas; and when trying to persuade a reader, we must analyze in detail the reasons for the position we wish the reader to accept. And both analytic and persuasive prose incorporate information. Yet *persuasive prose*, or prose that entails evaluation, is a valid category unto itself, for it is not so much ideas as judgments, feelings, and informed opinions that the writer of such prose wishes to make the reader accept. "My Wood" provides an example of persuasive prose at its best, for its main concern is to persuade (gently) the reader of the truth of its thesis, which here involves judgment and evaluation. To take another example, should your thesis be that "My Wood" is a great essay, a true work of art, or, conversely, that it fails to convince the reader and so fails in its primary task, then you would be engaged in persuasion, your object now being to convince your reader of the rightness of your judgment. You would be writing criticism in the purest sense of the word. Book or movie reviews are of this order. Aimed at convincing readers of the merit or lack of merit of a book or movie, a review proceeds to lay out why the reviewer concludes that the movie or book is or is not worth bothering with. To be sure, analysis of the movie or book is how the reviewer supports his or her contention. But the goal is persuasion. Indeed, the differences between the three types of exposition can be summed up in terms of goal: setting forth of factual material (informational), interpreting facts and delving into ideas (analytic), defending judgments aroused by ideas (persuasive).

WRITING THE COLLEGE ESSAY

Whatever you write in whatever kind of format, you should divide the work into stages and proceed step by step. To exemplify, I will tell you what I do when I write. After I have done all of my preparations, thought out all that I can beforehand (finished, in other words, the prewriting stage), I wind up with a good many notes, one note per slip of paper. Sitting down to my word processor, I look through these notes carefully, dividing them into categories and trying to pull out something for the beginning and something for the end. My notes direct my thought and ease my mind, for they give me something to focus on and words with which to face the terrible blankness of the first page. With some plan of organization in mind, at any rate, I begin to write. Generally, my notes help me to organize my thoughts and to stay on target more or less. But I don't restrain myself too much as I write my first draft. I let things flow as much as they will. Then, however, I become a critic, looking closely at what I have written. I usually feel a moment of despair, but it passes as I get down to the real work of writing, which is rewriting. I pinpoint what doesn't flow easily, where more support is necessary, where I have digressed from my topic or included material that is redundant. Next, I do a second draft, rearranging material and providing transitions when necessary, adding the supports that seem needed, and deleting what seems digressive or repetitive. I am usually left with a draft that can be checked for grammar, spelling, and the nuances of style. After checking and correcting, I am ready to print out the final draft. Such is my writing process, which proceeds in steps because the mind cannot do everything at once. Note that what is crucial in the whole process is the matter of organization. Comprehensible organization is of primary importance if communication is to take place. So we shall go into the business of organization in some detail.

When you sit down to write, you probably have a number of things to say. How can they be brought together in an organized way? Everyone has this difficulty, and there are no rules to go by. But there are guidelines that can help in organizing, guidelines perhaps best exemplified by the one-paragraph essay, a form often required on examinations. The one-paragraph essay — hereafter called the discrete paragraph — is in its organization a model of the multiparagraph essay. To master the structure of the discrete paragraph, therefore, is to go far toward mastering the structure of the essay proper.

THE DISCRETE PARAGRAPH

Like the larger essay, the discrete paragraph has a beginning, a middle, and an end. The thesis statement — usually a sentence, though sometimes two or even three sentences — normally comes at the beginning. A thesis statement is necessary so that your reader will know what you will be talking about, and so that you will too. When my own students' writing goes wrong, it usually does so because there is no thesis statement to guide them as they

write and me as I read what they have written. So their work
rambles on, making unrelated points but not conveying anything
in particular. Getting a clear thesis statement and keeping it in
mind is half the battle of writing. The middle consists of a series
of sentences designed to support that statement: to expand upon
it, to lend it credence, to develop its implications, to fill in the
details. And the end concludes, ideally lending the paragraph a
sense of wholeness and completion. Here is a sample discrete
paragraph, which stays to "My Wood" as topic.

We've Lost India!

Lead-in

> To me, the stereotypical Britisher
wears a top hat and peers out through a
monocle as he exclaims in a highly
cultivated British accent, "Why, we've lost
India!" E. M. Forster, however, would not

Thesis
Statement

consider this any great loss, for the point
of his essay "My Wood" is that Britain's
colonies have done it no good. To be sure,

Support

the essay seems at first to concern only
one man and his feelings about the effects
on him of his owning a small piece of land.
But when carefully read, the essay implies

Support

a good deal more. The allusion in the
first paragraph to Forster's
anti–colonialist novel A Passage to India,
for instance, intimates a point of greater
scope than the essay declares overtly. The

Support

same is true of the references to Christ's
parable about the camel and the needle, to
Dante, to the biblical Ahab, to Canute and
Alexander, and to Shakespeare. These
weighty references, it seems to me, would
not be appropriate if Forster had not had
something of large significance in mind,
something of which his discussion of his

Support
wood is an example. That something is suggested by the statement about "A rocket containing a Union Jack" attaining "universal dominion." In light of this sentence, it's easy to see that the effects listed by Forster of his owning a piece of land—spiritual stoutness, selfishness, and so forth—are to be seen as the traits of the British people at large, the marks of

Ending: Summary and Conclusion
its possession of an Empire. In sum, "My Wood" is built on an unstated analogy: that the possession of property—even a wood, much less an Empire—is bad for the soul, whether that of an individual or of an entire nation.

Notice that the first sentence of the sample paragraph acts as a lead-in to the thesis statement, which here is the second sentence. Note, too, that the last two supports can be subdivided into *major support* and *minor support,* the latter serving to back up, clarify, enlarge upon the former, which in turn demonstrates, develops, lends credence to the thesis. For instance, the sentence beginning "These weighty references" in the third support block is minor support clarifying the major support offered in the preceding sentence as well as its relation to the paragraph's thesis. Like all sentences in a well-organized paragraph, then, the sentences here form a hierarchy of means, with minor support supporting major support supporting the thesis.

But what is most important to grasp about the sample paragraph is how the paragraph proceeds. The main writing problem we all face, whether writing a paragraph, a paper, or a book, is the arrangement of parts. What should come first, what second, what third, and so on? To decide, the writer must think into the material at hand and determine what plan is best suited for it. Having made a determination, the writer then must follow through, providing whatever markers are needed between the various segments of a piece both to delineate them and to show

how they are related. Material can be organized in many ways, but the five ways discussed immediately hereafter are the basic ones. For conveyance's sake, I shall exemplify with sample paragraphs, but be mindful that what is said applies to the organization of whole papers as well.

WAYS OF ORGANIZING

Chronology

Whenever something occurs in time, you can write about it in *chronological sequence.* That is, in describing or analyzing an event, for instance, you could arrange the material at hand according to the sequence of the event itself. Whatever happened first comes first, what happened second comes second, and so forth. Perhaps the most psychologically ingrained of patterns, chronological sequence is a particularly easy way of organizing once its possibility is recognized. All the writer must do is follow the sequence of whatever it is that is being written about, making sure that the sequence is clear by providing time markers, or transitions, between each of its segments. Here is an example of a paragraph organized chronologically, with all transitions put in italics.

Not long ago, I found myself ambling down Fifth Avenue. I had no place in particular to go, so I just took in the sights as I took my time. *Then,* something happened to change the character of my day: as I casually watched the cars going by, a woman in a fur coat darted out into the traffic mid-block and was struck by a green Mercedes. I stuck around because, though there were hundreds of people on both sides of the street, I was the only one, it seemed, who had actually witnessed the accident. In any case, the police arrived *shortly after* the accident, and maybe *a half an hour later* an ambulance appeared. *By then,* however, it was too late: the woman had died a good *ten minutes earlier. Once* she had been hauled off, the police told me to come to the station to make a report. *After* that, I went home, arriving *late* for dinner but fed up with the world. *Now, when* I reflect on the incident, I can only think of all of those people and me the only witness.

[Mary Pat Burke]

Spatial Sequence

Whenever something being written about exists in space or can be thought of in terms of physical extension, *spatial sequence* can be a good way of organizing: left to right or right to left, upward or downward, inward or outward, far to near or near to far, and so on. With regard both to the segments of a paragraph and to the paragraphs of an essay, the writer's fundamental task always is to find some plan of order, some kind of organization that will solve the problem of what to put first, second, third, fourth. If spatial sequence is possible, then that would provide a viable plan: for instance, first a distanced view of something from the outside, then a closer view, and then a shot of the inside (this sequence being far to near). The point is that the order of first to second to third cannot be random; every paragraph and every essay must proceed by a plan, which must be clear to the reader. Thus, a spatial sequence, like a chronological sequence, must have markers between segments that make the sequence clear. Now, however, the transitions will be spatial in character rather than temporal.

> *From a distance of a few hundred yards,* the old Newberry castle, which sits atop a rather steep hill, seems like something out of Camelot. With its turrets and terraces, it looks as splendid as it must have looked in its heyday at the turn of the century. Even from a *few hundred feet* the castle keeps its secret, like an aging movie star in a veil. But *close up* it shows its age. Because of years of neglect, its slate shingles have become loose and many have fallen; most of its window panes are cracked or missing; and its cement balustrades and gargoyles, some of which lie on the ground, have eroded and decayed. *Inside* the story is the same. The place is a shambles. But *from a few hundred yards away,* it still looks like a castle where King Arthur might be presiding over the round table.
>
> [Alfred J. Reiner]

Comparison and Contrast

The *comparison and contrast* method of organization offers a prime way of understanding: in everyday life we frequently come to grasp something by seeing how it is like and/or unlike something else. No less is true when we write. For the writer, comparison and contrast is a tool of analysis that also suggests ways in which a paragraph or a whole paper can be organized.

Technically, comparison emphasizes similarity and contrast emphasizes difference. In practice, however, the distinction is not so clear-cut, for comparison involves contrast and contrast entails comparison. This is so because what usually makes a comparison meaningful is that the like things being compared actually have some significant difference, and what gives a contrast point is that the unlike things being contrasted actually share some fundamental likeness. For instance, one might compare stainless steel and sterling silver knives, forks, and spoons. They have the same shapes, they both can be attractive, and they both wear well. But oh! how much nicer sterling is in its heft and silkiness on the lips. Finally, it could be concluded, there is no comparison at all. The point of the comparison, then, would be to highlight difference and thereby to make a point about silver flatware.

We can organize comparisons and contrasts in a number of ways. The two most common are *point by point* (A/B, A/B, A/B — or some variant) and *blocked* (all of A and then all of B, with the comparison/contrast drawn in the B block). The following paragraphs, the first entailing comparison and the second contrast, exemplify each of these two ways of organizing in turn.

> Stainless and sterling flatware are alike in many ways. Obviously, they look alike as to form: forks, knives, spoons have the same shape whatever they're made of. *Also*, a set of good stainless can be just about as attractive on a table as sterling. *Further*, both wear well: silver flatware can be handed down for generations, and stainless is practically indestructible. *However*, stainless lacks the two most wonderful qualities of silver: its heft in the hand and its silkiness on the lips. *Finally*, therefore, there is no comparison at all.

> Stainless steel makes a fine material for flatware. It is cheap, it can be brought to a high polish, and it is almost indestructable. *Further*, it is dishwasher safe and never needs polishing. Yes, for most people's daily needs, stainless is the flatware of choice. *In contrast with* stainless, sterling silver is expensive and is not dishwasher safe. *Moreover*, *unlike* stainless, sterling needs

to be polished frequently and stored carefully so that the sulphur in the air doesn't get at it. *To be sure,* sterling has a wonderful heft and silkiness that stainless lacks, and sterling is also durable. The two are alike, *then,* in having both pluses and minuses. One's choice must depend on one's circumstance and inclinations.

The first sample (the comparison) moves point by point, from a consideration of stainless and silver together to silver/stainless (A/B), to stainless/silver (B/A), to stainless/silver (B/A), ending with two crucial points of difference. The second sample (the contrast) moves from a discussion of stainless (A) to a discussion of sterling (B), with the contrast drawn in the second (B) segment. The paragraph ends with a likeness, which serves to give the contrast point.

These two basic ways of making a comparison/contrast can also work in combination to form a third way: for instance, one paragraph constructed point by point and the next blocked. And we can structure a comparison/contrast in other ways as well. For instance, we could arrange material by topics and make the comparison/contrast topic by topic. This could be a good way to organize a whole paper devoted to a comparison and/or contrast. Take, for instance, the material of the last sample paragraphs. Into what topics could we divide it? Well, durability could be one and price another, as well as maintenance and innate qualities. If you were writing such a paper, you could devote a paragraph or more to each of these topics, comparing and/or contrasting stainless and silver topic by topic. To be sure, you would have to develop the material much more than it is developed in the sample paragraphs. In the paragraph(s) on durability, for instance, you might present examples, and in the paragraph(s) on maintenance you might bring up different types of silver, some of which are dishwasher safe and require little polishing. But the point now is organization, procedure. That understood, everything else will fall into place.

A fourth way — this one quite elegant but hard to pull off — of handling a comparison/contrast is to discuss all of A in and of itself and — making sure to provide a bridge — all of B in and of itself, and then move to the comparison/contrast in a C section. Keeping to our stainless/silver comparison/contrast, you could discuss everything you have to say about stainless first, then, bridging with a statement like "Of course, many people prefer sterling silver," you could go on to discuss the merits of sterling. Then you could move to the comparison/contrast in a third (C) section. That would be your plan of organization, the plan being at least as important to communication as anything specific you have to say in clarifying your general point.

In deciding among these various ways of handling a comparison/contrast, you should consider the effect you desire along with the length of what it is you are writing. If you wish your pace to be quick, use the point-by-point type of arrangement; if you wish your pace to be more leisurely, use the block type. If you are writing a longish paper, it might be best to move point by point, each paragraph or paragraph cluster concerning one point of comparison or contrast (for a block organization in a longer paper runs the risk that readers will forget what is said in the paragraphs that constitute the A block by the time they get to those that constitute the B block). If the paper you are doing is short, however, then blocking might be ideal, as might the A-B-C kind of structure. A topic organization, on the other hand, is best reserved for longer papers.

Whatever the case, what should come first, what second, what third, and so on is still a pressing consideration. Let's say that you have decided to move point by point, A/B, A/B, A/B. But which A/B to put first, which second, which third? Always the prime judgment to be made, this decision should stem as much as possible from the material at hand. If what you are writing about is temporal or spatial, say, then the points in your comparison/contrast could be arranged accordingly. For instance, comparing Western and Eastern values, you might move chronologically, taking up ancient values first, then values from the period that we call the Middle Ages, and then modern values. (Note that the various ways of organizing considered here often overlap, with two or more ways working together to lend structure and coherence.) Or order of climax — the last mode of organizing that we will consider — might provide a rationale. Whatever the case, you should have a reason for the order you choose and you must somehow make the reader aware of that reason.

Enumeration

In *enumerating,* the writer lists in the thesis statement the points to be made in the paragraph or paper to follow, or at least suggests that a certain number of points will be taken up, and then goes on to develop them one by one. The transitions that enumeration calls for are, for example, *first, second, third, finally; to begin with, then, then again, last; at first, however, then, third, and finally.* The next sample paragraph exemplifies enumeration in an entirely straight-forward way.

> According to E. M. Forster in his essay "My Wood," there are four reasons why property is dangerous to the soul. *In the first place,* property makes one pompous and spiritually stout. In support of this contention, Forster argues that "Property produces men of weight," that is, people who are self-important and self-satisfied. *Then,* property tends to make one "avaricious": even a little bit of property tends to foster a desire for more and more. *Third,* ownership leads to a "pseudo-creativity," like the maintaining of lawns in the suburbs (my example), and, thus, leads away from genuine creativity and life-affirming values. *Last, and most important,* owning property makes one "intensely selfish." "Keep off the Grass," "Keep Out," "Private Property" — these are the property owner's mottos. Indeed, Forster's very title reflects this fourth charge if we hear the stress on the first word: *"My* Woods." It is no wonder that, quoting Dante, Forster concludes that " 'Possession is one with loss.' "
>
> [Marge Markey]

We move from part to part here by way of transitions appropriate to enumeration. But why the order of the four parts — spiritual stoutness to avariciousness to pseudo-creativity to selfishness? Again, the writer should always have a reason for ordering parts as they are ordered. Like comparison/contrast, enumeration can incorporate a chronological or spatial sequence to order points if either is possible. For instance, a thesis statement concerning the four interesting sights to see on the way from Cleveland to St. Louis could proceed by enumeration with the points ordered spatially: *first along the road; then we come to; about*

five hundred miles further; finally, almost at the door of St. Louis. As to
the sample paragraph, its points follow the order of Forster's
points in his essay. (Essays are easy to write about with regard to
our own organization because usually all we need do is follow the
sequence of the essay under consideration.) But why did Forster
arrange the parts of his essay thus? The answer is suggested in the
sample paragraph by the phrase "Last and most important."
Forster's essay moves from point to point in an order of climax,
our last category of organization.

Order of Climax

I have saved *order of climax* — that is, building to the most
important point — for last because of its special importance.
Climactic arrangement is of particular importance because it has
application to all of the other ways of organizing. Should you be
enumerating, for instance, or comparing and contrasting, order of
climax could help you decide how to arrange the parts of your
composition, the most important always coming last. Even spatial
and chronological sequences, though having their own sequential
logic, can move climactically, from a cause in the past, say, to its
subsequent result, or from a false appearance at a distance to the
reality up close. And should your material suggest no other kind
of order, remember that climactic order is always possible: simply
decide which of your points is the most important, which the least,
and which in between; then arrange the parts accordingly — that
is, from least to most important — making sure to let your reader
know how you are proceeding. But even if you are working with
some other pattern, order of climax should not be wholly out of
mind. If for no other reason than to avoid the possibility of
anticlimax, order of climax should be checked when it comes to
arranging parts into paragraphs and then paragraphs into an
essay. The last sample paragraph of this chapter exemplifies how
order of climax can structure material that does not suggest
innately any other kind of order. As you read the paragraph,
observe how the writer demarks his various points and informs us
point by point of how the material before us is organized.

Of the many ill effects of alcohol, perhaps *the least important* —
though this might sound odd at first — is its effect on the body.
To be sure, alcohol rots the liver and destroys the brain. But
that's the business of the individual. This is a free country, and
the choice to destroy oneself is an individual matter. Or it would
be if there were not other considerations involved. However,
there are other considerations, the family being one. *More
important* than what alcohol does to the individual is what it does
to the family of the alcoholic. In the majority of cases, it leads to
the dissolution of the alcoholic's family, with all of the misery
that divorce entails, especially for children. And even if
alcoholism doesn't lead finally to divorce, it still inevitably
causes misery to the other family members, who are guilty only
of tolerating the behavior of the drunken mother or father. *But
most important by far* — at least from society's point of view — is
the collective effect of alcoholism on the nation at large.
Statistics show that, taken together, the nation's alcoholics
significantly reduce American productivity on the one hand
(because of days absent and work done shoddily) and significantly increase the cost of medical insurance and care on the
other. For all of these reasons, *but especially the last*, it seems to
me that we should not tolerate excessive drinking one day more.

[Barry J. Gillin]

The Essay

Like the discrete paragraph, the essay has a beginning, a middle,
and an end. And, again, the beginning usually entails a statement
of thesis, the middle renders support and demonstration of the
thesis, and the ending gives a sense of an ending. As we now look
at each in turn, keep in mind this brief outline of their functions.
For the shape each takes depends on its function.

The Beginning

The beginning of any essay is special, and, or so most people find,
especially difficult to write. The problem the beginning poses is
how to present or lead to the thesis statement. Simply to state the
thesis in the first sentence would seem too abrupt for most
purposes. Most often, it is better to lead readers gently from

wherever they are mentally to where one wants them to be. For this reason, an especially useful kind of beginning is the *funnel,* which leads the reader to the thesis statement gently and with a sense of inevitability. Also, of the many ways to begin, the funnel has the advantage of being the only kind of beginning that will *always* work. Therefore, I shall stress the funnel kind of beginning as we move on.

But, you probably and rightly wonder, if the thesis statement should usually come at the end of the beginning, what should come before it? What exactly should be done to funnel down? Let me say first what one should not do. In the opening paragraph(s), *do not* overtly argue, support, or refer to your thesis. Your material, of course, must be related to your thesis and may implicitly exemplify or support it in some way. But if you present overt arguments here, what you go on to say in the body of your paper will almost assuredly seem redundant. Save all overt arguments, supports, and so forth for your middle paragraphs. That said, we still have the question before us of what one can and should do to funnel down to the thesis statement. There are a number of answers, in fact, or a number of different ways of accomplishing the task at hand. Though different, however, they are analogous, and often two, three, even four ways come into play simultaneously. I shall briefly describe the main modes of leading to the thesis and exemplify each as we go.

1. It is possible to lead to a thesis by way of analogy, or some striking comparison that touches on some aspect of the thesis it leads to and so naturally narrows to the explicit statement of that thesis.

   Everyone knows the story of the little engine that could. It seemed too small for the task it undertook — pulling a great big train over a mountain — but it succeeded because of its positive thinking ("I think I can, I think I can, I think I can") and sheer guts. Like the little engine, our varsity basketball team seems small (the average height is only 5'11"). But it has the guts to wind up on top. *All it needs is to think positively about itself. There are at least four good reasons for it to do so.*

   [James Stroh]

Note how easily the analogy here leads to the italicized thesis statement, which lays out the rest of the paper by virtue of the phrase "four good reasons." These the author went on to analyze reason by reason.

2. Contrast can also be a good way to move, perhaps from something that you consider wrong to a statement (your thesis statement) of what you consider right, or from a negative to a positive way of viewing something, or whatever.

This summer, I had the good fortune of getting the opportunity to taste high-class living — or so I thought at the outset. I was hired as a waitress in a ritzy "members only" country club on Long Island. Thinking that I would somehow acquire millions by, for instance, helping an old dowager and consequently being left her estate, or simply by marrying a member of the club, I walked into this job with a dazzling smile. However, my fantasy was cut short, for I soon realized that *working for the rich brings no benefits at all,* much less fringe benefits.

[Claire McMahon]

"Terry, that TV is going to rot your mind. Shut it off and get to your homework." While growing up, I became all too familiar with these words of my mother's. Fearing that my mind might be rotting — and fearing my mother's wrath as well — I would reluctantly turn off my favorite show and dutifully do my arithmetic. Now, looking back, I disagree with my mother. I have come to believe that *television can play a positive role in a person's development.*

[Terence Mulgrew]

The first paragraph moves by way of contrast between what was expected and what actually happened. The second moves from a negative view of television to a positive view. Notice how in each paragraph the thesis seems one with the lead-in, the two forming a seamless web drawing the reader on. In this regard, consider one more example of a thesis paragraph that moves by way of contrast — this one from a generally held view that the writer rejects to a contrasting view that he means to argue.

With thirty seconds left in the game, Toronto had to kill off a penalty to beat the Flyers. Marcel Demeres, the Toronto coach, screamed at his players to go out, hit hard, and bang the puck out of the zone. The crowd screamed its assent to this bad advice, which allowed the Flyers to come back and win the game. Neither the coach nor the fans understood that *it is not intimidation that kills penalties, but aggressive forechecking, instant clearing out of the front of the net, and good goal tending.*

[Edward Bendernagle]

The writer went on to argue his case by analyzing the importance to hockey of each of the three things enumerated at the end of this thesis paragraph.

3. While moving by contrast, this last piece also exemplifies another way of beginning — beginning with an anecdote of some sort or with reference to some personal experience related to one's thesis.

Laughing, my sister told me that she heard our mother say to our dog in the most serious tone of voice, "Milang, don't you remember what I told you this morning? We're having company tonight. So, if you want to stay inside, you must stay out of the living room." Now, isn't that silly? Not only do dogs not understand language but they have no memory and can't distinguish between the living room and the bedroom much less between yesterday and today. In his poem "The Animals," Edwin Muir expresses my feelings about dogs and other such creatures exactly. *Through the abstractions of "space," "time," and "language," he contrasts man and the rest of the animal kingdom, thereby delineating the nature of what is human and what is not.*

[Siu Lau]

This paragraph moves by contrast between the mother's view and the writer's as well as the poet's (analogy is also operative here). Its other kind of movement — from anecdote to thesis — is made possible by the fact that the anecdote bears directly on the thesis. What is particularly charming about this paragraph is how the anecdote relates to the specific terms of the thesis (which the author went on to explore)—

space relates to the living room, time to the mother's reference to "this morning" and "tonight," and language to talking to the dog in the first place. At one with the thesis, the anecdote leads to it seamlessly. The next sample thesis paragraph exemplifies how the recounting of one's experience can lead easily and smoothly to a thesis statement.

With every essay I write, I am faced with a serious dilemma. What will I title the damned thing? For me, the most torturous task when it comes to writing is thinking up an effective title. After a paper is finished, I sometimes find myself sitting in my room for hours trying to think of a title that will suite my purposes and meet my ethical demands. It takes hours of hard thought because a really good title — or so it seems to me — must satisfy two very different criteria: first, it should not mislead the reader (this is the ethical demand); yet, second, it should be imaginative. In other words, *a good title should both inform and delight.*

[Rae Cazzola]

4. Another way to set up a funnel paragraph is to move from the familiar to the unfamiliar, that is, from something related to your thesis that you know your reader knows to your thesis statement, which ostensibly is new to your reader. This is an especially good setup for a thesis that is markedly original or that goes against the grain, for it allows the audience to get its bearings before being asked to strike out into uncharted territory. While moving by way of analogy, the first sample paragraph of this subsection (the one that begins with reference to the little engine that could — page 29) also moves from the familiar (the story of the little engine) to the unfamiliar (the thesis about the basketball team). Here is another example of this kind of structuring.

Almost everybody knows what it's like to have a pet — namely, a dog or a cat. These most popular of animals populate some two-thirds of American homes. What accounts for their prevalence? I think the answer is *fur:* for whatever reason — perhaps because they're cuddly — people like furry creatures, even though their hair gets all over everything. But for an occasional cuddle, dog and cat owners pay a high price: they must feed their pet once or twice a day, walk the dog two or three times a day (and use a "pooper-scooper" in most cities) or clean out the litter box (ugh!), clean up the presents left by the pet, put up with scratched furniture (in the case of cats) or chewed upholstery (in the case of dogs), and live with the allergies their pets aggravate or cause. No, I'll take a snake any day. *Snakes make perfect pets.*

[Arais Matesich]

As I have said, a funnel paragraph can incorporate two or more modes of structuring at once. This paragraph, for instance, moves both from the negative (in the author's view) to the positive (again, in the author's view) and from the familiar to the unfamiliar. The latter is particularly apt here because of the nature of the thesis, which the student went on to argue point by point — that is, the feeding of snakes as compared the feeding of dogs and cats, the cleanliness of snakes as compared with the messiness of dogs and cats, and so forth. In other words, this thesis paragraph not only leads naturally to the thesis (because everything in the paragraph concerns pets) but also lays out the paper as a whole.

5. Finally, many essays begin with a movement from the general to the particular: from a generalization related to the thesis to the specific thesis statement. The following paragraph, which begins with material that bears on the thesis but *not with the thesis per se,* moves thus.

Possessions have a way of controlling their owners. Taking time, money, and energy to accumulate — and money itself, of course, takes time and energy to earn — possessions can come, indeed, to dominate a life: for once acquired, they continue to take time, money, and energy to maintain. And the more we own, it seems, the more we desire to own. Wordsworth points to this cycle of acquisition and its sad consequence in the second line of his sonnet "The World Is Too Much With Us": "Getting and spending, we lay waste our power." Thoreau meant much the same when he declared, "The more one has, the less one is." E. M. Forster makes a third, *the basic point of his essay "My Wood" being that possession is bad for the soul.*

Now the paper to follow should not be so hard to write: subsequent paragraphs or clusters of paragraphs would concern the effects of possession — specifically of property — that Forster enumerates, effect by effect, with each section of the middle of the paper showing why "possession is bad for the soul," or why Forster believes it to be so. The end could generalize out to all possessions, with property a prime example. Much of the work of writing lies in writing a strong beginning, one that lays out the paper to come, though the beginning might not be put into final shape until later in the writing process or even until the end.

For rarely do writers get things right the first time. The manuscripts of even (or especially) the greatest writers show them revising again and again. Writing entails just too many variables for anyone to bypass rewriting and still produce something that is readable. Beginnings in particular almost always require rewriting, for the beginning of any essay is too important not to be gotten right. The three paragraphs that follow demonstrate rewriting in action: the first is the student's original beginning, tentative and out of focus; the second shows her revising and suggests what she was thinking in making her revisions; and the third is the revised beginning as it headed the paper she turned in.

```
      It is painful and difficult to
   consider the all too possible consequences
   of the nuclear build-up.  But we all must
   face the frightening specter that the earth
   could be no more.  In the past, your
   greatest fear may have been that your
   parents might die and leave you alone.
   Now, that fear may be for your own safety
   and the destruction of humanity by a
   nuclear holocaust.  Who doesn't have great
   difficulty with the thought of the
   blackness that would descend with war, the
   blackness of despair, the blackness of
   death? Blasted, raw, charred, sterile might
   be all that once was greening over roundly.
```

———————◆———————

```
    It is painful and difficult to
consider the all too possible consequences
of the nuclear build-up. But we all must
face the frightening specter that the earth
could be no more. In the past, your
greatest fear may have been that your
parents might die and leave you alone. Now,
that fear may be for your own safety and
the destruction of humanity by a nuclear
holocaust. Who doesn't have great
difficulty with the thought of the
blackness that would descend with war, the
blackness of despair, the blackness of
death? Blasted, raw, charred, sterile
might be all that once was greening over
roundly.
```

```
    It is painful and difficult to
consider the all too possible consequences
of the nuclear build-up. Who doesn't have
great difficulty with the thought of the
blackness that would descend with war, the
blackness of despair, the blackness of
death? Blasted, raw, charred, sterile
might be all that once was greening over
roundly. But we all must face the
frightening specter that the earth could be
no more.
```

[MaryAnn McCarra]

Two of the sentences in the first draft here are irrelevant, serving only to blur the focus. And the thesis as stated in the first draft is obscured by its position. MaryAnn saw both problems and revised accordingly. The final paragraph, I think you will agree, is right on target for a paper concerned with why we each must face what the consequences of a nuclear exchange would be.

The process that led to the final version of this paper is typical. First came a halting attempt at a beginning, the first draft of which needed work but was good enough for the moment to allow the student to write on and complete a first draft of the paper. Then the whole paper was revised, with special attention at some point — whether before or after the revision of the rest — paid to the beginning. That is generally how I work, too. Of course, you might work in some other way. But however you go about things, remember that beginnings are of crucial importance and that they must be hammered into shape.

Middle Paragraphs

Middle paragraphs contain the meat of an essay. Here is where the thesis is exemplified, argued, demonstrated, or whatever. With the exception of paragraphs whose purpose is to provide transition only, each middle paragraph comes from and is somehow related to the thesis. That is, each develops some central idea (one per paragraph) that backs up, demonstrates, exemplifies, or otherwise expands upon the thesis statement of the essay. The central idea of each middle paragraph is usually stated in a single sentence, often called a "topic sentence," which, though it may be found anywhere in the paragraphs, is most commonly found at its beginning.

Like the discrete paragraph, each middle paragraph must be organized internally according to an appropriate plan — the ways of organizing discussed previously all apply to middle paragraphs. In addition, like individual sentences in a paragraph, the individual paragraphs in a paper must be arranged into some comprehensible sequence. Just as we must decide what to put first, what second, and so on within a single paragraph, we must do so with the middle paragraphs in the essay as a whole. Should you be writing a narrative essay, chronology might serve; if your thesis entails comparison and contrast, then that would be your governing strategy; or perhaps enumeration is called for because your thesis involves a list of steps, say, or effects. And, of course, order of climax is always to be considered, now with respect to the arrangement of paragraphs as they move one to the next.

Having a suitable design in the first place and following through on it will provide a coherent foundation for whatever paper you write. But transitional links between middle paragraphs are often needed, just as they are within paragraphs. Whenever a particular progression or relationship is not self-evident — even when the overall structure of the paper is — some phrase, sentence, or even a whole transitional paragraph must be supplied to make the relationship clear and the movement fluid. When you read the sample essays on pages 46–51, note the transitions used within and especially between paragraphs, and observe how, because of these transitions, both the supports within each paragraph and the paragraphs themselves move easily one from the last.

But how do we go about developing a middle paragraph and supporting its topic statement? The answer is that there are many ways. Here is a list of the most common.

Explanation — for instance, of how something works or why one believes x, y, or z.

Consideration of cause and effect — exploring the former and detailing the latter.

Presentation of facts — when facts, statistics, data of whatever sort can be brought to bear.

Description — of a person, a place, or whatever under consideration.

Evaluation — giving reasons for a value judgment, for instance.

Comparison/contrast — development by comparing/contrasting an idea with some other idea, usually one familiar to the reader.

Classification — breaking something into its classes or types and then discussing each in turn. Classification always proceeds by enumeration.

Exemplification — by way of narrative, like an anecdote, statistics, or whatever.

Definition — of terms or concepts related to a thesis.

Appeal to authority — whether to experts, statistics, or the authority of our own experience.

Conclusion — the drawing thereof.

Analogy — drawing inferences based on similarity.

These methods or modes of development or support are not, of course, mutually exclusive. Any may be used in combination with any other(s), though, obviously, the nature of the topic of a given paragraph must allow for the method(s) chosen. Some methods, that is, will be more appropriate to the nature of a topic than others.

But an example, no doubt, is in order at this point (notice *my* mode of procedure). Here is a sample middle paragraph in which fully six different methods of development or support are used.

Topic Sentence	No words could capture the bleakness of the dust bowl in the great depression.
Comparison	We have never seen anything like it except, perhaps, the landscape we've come to know
Comparison	of the moon. It was totally barren, devoid of a single living creature. Deserts are
Example	more alive in comparison. Just to give a minor example, not one stalk of corn grew in the five counties of Kansas that form
Authority	the buckle of the corn-belt. As Harrison Snowberry has said, "The dust bowl was the greatest disaster of an age of disasters."
Description	Just try to picture it: light-brown dust everywhere—the color of the land, the color of the air, the color of the sky. Nothing but grit to see, to breathe, to taste with
Cause and effect	every waking minute. But you naturally wonder about the cause. What could be the cause for so great an effect? Irrigation, or the lack of it, is the answer. Once the depression struck, farmers could not afford to irrigate their land, which required irrigation to bend to man's needs. Cause and effect were irremediable once the cause—the lack of irrigation—took hold. Thus, the land became barren, and, thus—as

Statistics   [
```
the Bureau of Statistics has estimated—
three million farm families had to take to
the road.
```

Of course, most paragraphs do not incorporate as many ways of development, or methods of support or procedure, as this one. Now, therefore, let's look at some selected methods and see how each can generate a paragraph by itself.

Exemplification: Exemplification is of special importance in exposition. Indeed, examples are the lifeblood of essays. Illustration by way of concrete instances animates the abstractions of a piece of exposition (like the thesis of a paper or the topic of a paragraph) by showing how they relate to the everyday world, which we rightly take as our measuring rod. Exemplification, then, is both a means of development and a way of solidifying and bringing home a point. Note how the abstraction of the topic sentence of the following paragraph is given shape by way of example (which here entails contrast) and that, given shape, the idea is much more forceful than it would be if not exemplified.

> There are many conflicts between what the Catholic Church teaches and the attitudes — upon which people act — of society at large. For example, my church teaches that one should be a virgin until marriage, that sex is appropriate only in marriage, and that marriage is for life. Marriage is a sacrament, a holy institution, and should be entered upon with great gravity. About such things, we have no choice; we must do as taught. In contrast, society holds that we must decide such matters for ourselves. Moreover, most people seem to think that virginity is something to be corrected as fast as possible, that marriage is nothing but a legal formality, and that the purpose of sex is merely pleasure, to be had as much and as often as possible. All you need do is to tune into TV or go to a few movies to see how different society's attitudes are from those of the church. How, then, can there be a reconciliation of the two? [The last sentence is a transition to the next paragraph.]
>
> [Scott Dinnell]

Definition: Definition, which can give rise to a thesis that such and such is so and so, is also a way of developing and supporting a point. Definition, note, usually incorporates examples, as do, for instance, most definitions in a dictionary. The next paragraph, from a paper defining the meaning of liberty, proceeds by definition (along with examples).

> But what is freedom? Does freedom mean that anyone can do anything that he or she likes? No, that's not freedom; that's anarchy. Or is freedom "just a word for having nothing left to lose," as Janis Joplin put it? If so, then not only are most people not free but the American ideal of "the pursuit of happiness" is a sham. At least it is a sham if we view happiness, as most of us do, as tied to "having" — not just things, but relationships, children, intellectual attainments. However different, these definitions share something fundamental, something that invalidates both equally: they both define freedom in such a way as to make it external to the self. In contrast, my definition of freedom is internal: freedom is the ability to act appropriately in the present. To take a negative instance, how many men respond to their wives or wives to their husbands as though they were their mothers or fathers? We keep reliving the past and so do not live in the present. Laying down the baggage of the past and living now, in the present — that is what freedom is. Freedom, then, is psychological, a state of being having nothing to do with externals.
>
> [Joanne de la Cruz]

Appeal to Authority: Appeal to authority is just that — the developing and supporting of a point by quoting, paraphrasing, or summarizing (the distinction between paraphrasing and summarizing is discussed in the Appendix on research papers, page 644) experts in a field or, simply, by referring to one's own irrefutable experience. The following paragraph incorporates both kinds of appeal.

> People seem always in such a rush, chasing from appointment to appointment, from party to party, never allowing themselves the peaceful moments that come in self-reflection when one is alone. As for me, I agree with Thoreau:

> I love to be alone. I never found the companion that
> was so companionable as solitude. We are for the most
> part more lonely when we go abroad among men than
> when we stay in our chambers.

How true that last sentence is! At a party I went to last year, for
instance, only three or four people knew each other. Everyone
else just stood around looking stupid. I felt terribly alone, as I'm
sure everyone else did except those few I mentioned. In
contrast, I never feel alone at home in my chair reading. My
thoughts provide all the company I need.

[Judy Carifto]

Analogy: Analogy is a type of inference based on the assumption
that if things are alike in some significant way, they are probably
alike in other ways as well. It is a means of support, as well as a
method of development, in that, by invoking the similarities of A
and B, one means to demonstrate some thesis about A. Here is a
clear example involving an analogy of gun-control laws and
prohibition.

> Gun-control laws don't work. Thousands of them already
> clutter the books of local and state governments, yet no one has
> found that these laws have prevented even one crime. It is
> indeed, however trite, the person and not the gun who commits
> a crime. But we Americans, who made alcohol illegal for a
> decade (I'm speaking of prohibition) should know better. What
> was the effect of prohibition? It was to create — and that's
> exactly the right word — organized crime in America. Why?
> Because people would not obey such a silly law. It was the law
> itself, then, that fostered crime. So, too, gun-control laws: they
> will only take guns out of the hands of the innocent citizen and
> put them solely into the hands of the criminal. In a word, gun
> laws will be about as effective as prohibition. They will do little
> but foster organized crime.

[Thomas Novak]

Note: The use of an analogy like that in the last sample does
not prove a point but, rather, helps clarify it. In fact,
none of the methods of development, or ways of
supporting a thesis or a paragraph topic, are exactly
proofs. Even the bringing of facts to bear is not. For

facts, like statistics, are tricky, and they can be used equally to argue opposite contentions. The methods of development enumerated earlier, therefore, should be thought of as rhetorical means of developing ideas, clarifying them, and supporting them in that development and clarification allow the reader to understand why the writer holds, concludes, espouses what he or she does.

The Ending

Like beginnings, endings are psychological in function. Also like beginnings, endings are particularly difficult, or so many people find them. The difficulty of ending is eased, however, by remembering what an ending should do: whereas the beginning should draw the reader in, the ending should wrap things up, tie everything together, and create thereby a sense of completion. That is why a single sentence telling the reader that the essay is finished would be no better in most cases than a single sentence at the beginning announcing the thesis. For the most part, a single sentence would simply not be satisfying. But there should be no arguing at the end, just as there should be none at the beginning. Argument is the function of the middle.

What, then, can be done to bring things to a point and thus to impart the sense of an ending? A summary is one possibility. The summary has the advantage of pulling ideas together and of reminding the reader of the main points made in the essay, some of which the reader may have lost sight of. Especially when writing a longer paper, consider the summary as a possible way of ending. A full summary, however, is not generally as well-suited to the short essay, for readers can be counted upon to retain the points of an argument through, say, five to ten paragraphs. But a brief summary in a sentence or two in combination with, perhaps, a concluding statement can serve the needs of any kind of paper. The two samples that follow, both the endings of papers whose beginnings are on page 31, exemplify this kind of ending.

In sum, for a team to kill off a powerplay successfully, the players must forecheck aggressively, clear out the front of the net, and get good goal-tending from the goalie. In other words, winning takes a concerted effort from all the players on the ice. And the effort must be one to win, not just to intimidate the opposing team.

[Edward Bendergale]

Memory, language, and a sense of space or boundary are the vehicles that Muir uses to show that man and beast are worlds apart. While many human beings will always relate to animals in human terms, to do so is in fact both futile and silly, Muir suggests. The lecturing of pets on their failure to observe household rules, for instance, or to distinguish one room from another is not only pointless but downright absurd.

[Siu Lau]

Look back to page 31 and compare the sample beginnings found there with these sample endings. Note, especially, how each ending refers to each sample beginning. This referring back by way of a restatement of the thesis or a key phrase in the thesis paragraph or even just a few prominent words helps to give an essay a sense of roundness — because the end rounds back to the beginning — and thus a satisfying sense of closure.

Or one might end with an analogy that both summarizes (albeit indirectly) the argument of an essay and widens its scope. Here, for instance, is an ending of a paper whose thesis is that "television can play a positive role in one's development" (page 30, second sample paragraph in point 2):

In a movie I remember seeing when I was little, a witch with a crystal ball could see anywhere in the world and anyone. She could summon up whatever person she had in mind and whatever place — past, present, or future. Her ability, of course, was deemed miraculous and magical. But, the future excepted (they're working on it, though), we each have that magic ball: we call it TV. Like the gypsy's crystal, TV shows us everyday the whole panorama of present and past. If viewed with discrimination, therefore, television is truly a window on the world, and as such it can be a positive force in one's development.

[Terence Mulgrew]

Or the writer might ask a question of some central point raised in the middle of the essay and end by answering it. This is the pattern of the next sample ending, which also makes reference to the sample beginning on page 33 (point 5) while fanning out to generalization.

> But why, one might ask, does owning property or anything else of substantial proportions bring about these psychological effects — of spiritual stoutness, avariciousness, pseudo-creativity, and intense selfishness? The answer, I think, is that ownership takes time and especially energy, or takes time and energy away from other pursuits and from human relationships. Remember Scrooge. Ownership leads one to become centered on things, a centeredness that leads away from true creativity, spirituality, and human concern. One's vital self shrinks as one becomes more and more acquisitive, leaving only a hard core of selfishness in its stead. It is thus that the more one has, the less one is. Possession is indeed one with loss.

While providing a quick summary as it moves from question to answer, this sample ending also moves from the particular to the general. Called the *reverse funnel*, though *megaphone* might be more apt metaphorically, this kind of an ending can be used along with any other kind. It is especially satisfying in that it links the concerns of an essay to the world at large and thus suggests the relevance of the essay's thesis to the reader's life.

One more word about endings: like beginnings, endings must be carefully worded. For instance, when writing an ending, pick up some words from the beginning of your paper. If you think carefully about your words, this picking up should be easy enough. Then, be sure to put things in terms that *your* thesis and *your* own logic require. You should do no less, of course, throughout your paper, but an error in statement is particularly noticeable and particularly damaging at the end. Here is an instance of misstatement:

> Television can teach us about and familiarize us with our world. To be sure, our education, families, and friends are undoubtedly

the main influences that shape the people we become. However, practically every person in the U.S. watches television every day; therefore, television is very educational.

The last sentence, the climax, of this ending does not deliver what it should. For one thing, it begs the question (just because people watch television does not make it educational); moreover, it does not really follow from the sentences that precede. Consequently, the reader is left dangling, without a sense that things have been tied up, without a sense of an ending. Now compare this paragraph with the following, in which the last sentence is restated to fit the context:

> Television can teach us about and familiarize us with our world. To be sure, our education, families, and friends are undoubtedly the main influences that shape the people we become. However, because practically every person in the U.S. watches television every day, it, too, must influence us in one way or another, and that influence should not be minimized.

As restated, the paragraph now comes to a logical conclusion and a firm ending. It doesn't take much: just a few words dropped and added. But those few words make all the difference.

The Whole Essay

Let us now draw the whole thing together — beginning, middle and end — by way of a couple of sample essays. Intimate in tone and informal in style, the first is a personal essay, one that I am sure you will find amusing. An expansion of the discrete paragraph found on page 33, the second is more academic and thus more formal. But both exemplify the things we have been considering. When reading them, therefore, be mindful of where the thesis statement of each comes and how it is led to; watch to see how the middle paragraphs of both essays are related to their thesis statements and to each other, as well as how the middle paragraphs are internally organized and arranged with regard to the paper as a whole; and mark how each paper achieves that sense of an ending I have spoken of.

My Dog
Sandra Calvi

Funnel
Beginning

Thesis

A dog is a man's best friend, as they
say, and a woman's, too. Yes, a canine can
be a true companion whatever one's
sex—playful, loyal, and selfless, never
asking anything in return for its
friendship. My dog, Smokey, is all of this
and more. Sometimes he cheers me up more
than any person can, even my boyfriend.
Indeed, in comparing my dog to my
boyfriend, I often think that a dog is a
better companion than a man.

Transition
and Topic
Sentences

Support
by Con-
trast

In the first place, a dog can't talk.
Consequently, it can't scream or ask
questions. My boyfriend, on the other
hand, often sounds like he's hosting a game
of twenty-one questions: "Where were you?
Why are you late? Who were you talking
with?" It's enough to drive anyone crazy.

Support

Moreover, his little game usually results
in a screaming match between the two of us.
In contrast, should I get home late, Smokey
just sits and wags his tail, just as he

Support

does when I'm on time. And when I talk to
him, he listens—unlike my boyfriend—and
never gives me a headache—again, unlike my
boyfriend.

Transition
and Sup-
port

In the second place, Smokey doesn't
watch television. So I never find him in a
comatose state watching a Yankee or a Rams
game. When I come home, Smokey always
greets me as though I were the most

Support
by Con-
trast

important person on earth. His excitement
is infectious. My boyfriend, on the other

hand, thinks it is a criminal offense to leave the television set during any sports event. More often than not, he greets me with a grunt when I go to his house and makes a beeline back to the TV. For companionship, I'll take a dog anytime.

Topic Sentence

Transition and Topic Sentence

    In the third place, Smokey asks for nothing more than People Snacks—little dog treats in the shape of doctors, mailmen, and so forth—on occasion. Boyfriends, in contrast, need to be catered to twenty-four hours a day. Sometimes I think that my boyfriend is just a grown child looking for a mother. There he sits in front of the TV and bids me get a snack—oh, nothing like People Snacks; no, he will settle for nothing less than a home-made pizza or two or three Reuben sandwiches. So, while he watches a game, I'm in the kitchen fixing a feast for his highness.

Support by Contrast

    What I don't understand is, if a dog is a man's best friend, how come they're nothing alike? I can't puzzle that one out. But I know one thing for sure: the next time my boyfriend wants a snack, he's going to get People Snacks. If they're good enough for Smokey, they're sure as hell good enough for him!

Ending by Conclusion

The thesis of this essay is that "a dog is a better companion than a man." That thesis is argued (with tongue in cheek in part) point by point. Each paragraph after the first adheres to the thesis and backs it up, giving reasons why the writer feels as she does. Nothing that does not bear on the thesis and support it, notice, is allowed in. Thus, the paper is coherent as it moves with a sense of inevitably to its conclusion.

Big Game or Small?

Funnel

Beginning

Thesis

Topic
Sentence

Support

Support

If you're out for big game, E. M.
Forster's "My Wood" might not seem like
much. It appears to be a little, cuddly
thing, not a weighty creature to be tracked
with patience and care. In fact, however,
the more steadily one looks at Forster's
"little" essay, the more it seems to
concern large, weighty issues, however,
miniature its example and seemingly slight
its scope. That is, the effects of
ownership enumerated by Forster are
analogous to and examples of the more
elusive effects of a far more insidious (or
so Forster would move the reader to feel)
type of ownership on the British public.

The date of the essay and a knowledge
of its intended audience are key to an
understanding of its full range. Dating
from the 1930s (when the British Empire was
still intact) and aimed at literate
Britishers, the essay assumes that its
targeted readers would be concerned with
the issue of Empire (a pressing political
concern in the 1930s) and would grasp that
Forster's novel A Passage to India is the
book alluded to in the first paragraph.
The intended audience would also have known
that this novel—Forster's most widely
celebrated single work—depicts British
imperialism and its adverse effects on the
British themselves. Once understood, this
allusion alone suggests that "My Wood"
concerns something rather more embracing
than the ownership of a small patch of
woods in some byway in Great Britain. It

suggests that the wood and the effects on the speaker of his ownership as described in the essay should be taken as part of an unstated analogy: that his wood is to Forster what the Empire is to the British. So the essay concerns "the effect of property upon the character" not only of the individual but of the nation at large.

Transition and Topic Sentence

The effects enumerated by Forster of his owning a piece of property, therefore, are also to be understood as the effects he sees in the British of their possession of

Support

colonies. Like him, they have become heavy—heavy by being weighed down by an empire ("if you have a lot of things you cannot move about a lot") and heavy by having become like the rich man in Christ's parable ("It is easier for a camel to go through the eye of a needle, than for a rich man to enter into the kingdom of God"). Physical heaviness here is symbolic of spiritual heaviness, of a pompous and self-satisfied state of soul. It is this that Forster sees in his countrymen—a profound spiritual heaviness stemming from their colonial power and rule.

Topic Sentence

As indirectly depicted by Forster, the British are also seen as expansionist and

Support

all but damnably acquisitive. Such is what his analogy suggests with respect to the second effect of owning property enumerated: just as Forster would extend the boundaries of his wood, acquiring property without end, so the British actually did extend the boundaries of the Empire in their avariciousness. The

Support

reference to Ahab, the infidel Old

Testament king who married Jezebel, suggests that the desire to expand—whether on the part of an individual or a nation—is as treacherous and immoral as Ahab and Jezebel themselves. (The reference is to 1 Kings 21:1—7).

Topic Sentence

The third charge against colonization is exemplified by Forster's desire to "express" his personality through doing something to his piece of property.

Support

Most suburbs bear witness to this expressive fallacy in their proliferating lawn ornaments, not to mention the lawns themselves and the energy wasted in a vain attempt at self—expression through lawn maintenance. Property surely does "push . . . itself in as a substitute" for true

Support

"creation and enjoyment." The implication of this expressive fallacy when extended to the Empire is that the energies of the British have been misdirected into and sapped by their colonial expansion. Thoreau's dictum that "The more one has, the less one is" applies to mighty nations no less than to private citizens.

Topic Sentence

Finally, there is selfishness—whether with regard to blackberries or colonies.

Support

Put in climactic order, this evil in particular redounds against the property owner and colonist alike by making them petty and mean—spirited. Such is what Forster's last example declares, as subtly does his title if we put the stress on its first word. The "sweets of property," whether a wood or an empire, are the sweets of sin.

To be sure, Forster does not refer to the British Empire directly; except for the pointed comment about "A rocket containing a Union Jack" attaining "universal dominion," he tells us only about himself and his wood. But his various references— to the Bible, for instance, and to Dante— intimate that he has something bigger in mind, something of the scope of those references, and that the effects detailed of the ownership of a small piece of property exemplify something more far-reaching. No, Forster does not take us after small game. It is big game he's after. In the course of his essay, that is, his little wood comes to stand for the British Empire itself and, further, for the very idea of possession; and the enumerated effects of Forster's ownership come to be those of the colonies on Britain and of ownership in general. Through his concrete example, then, Forster shows us the full meaning of the sentence he quotes from Dante: " 'Possession is one with loss.' "

Reverse
Funnel
Ending

WRITING TO REWRITING

Writing is difficult, so don't think that there is something wrong with you if you have difficulty doing it. Everyone does. What helps is to understand that, because the mind can't do everything at once, writing must proceed in stages, as I suggested when discussing the writing process: first a few jottings; then some thought about how to structure ideas; then a rough draft; then, usually, extensive revision; and finally proofreading and final typing. We will now turn to revision, or rewriting, which many writers consider to be the crucial stage of the writing process.

Revision, too, entails a number of steps. First of all, check what you have written, paragraph by paragraph, against your thesis statement. Should you find that you have wandered away from the point, then either bring the suspect passage into line or cut it out. You may even find that most of a paper does not go with the thesis as stated. One solution here would be to change the thesis. Because writing is a dynamic process, one never truly knows what one has to say until it is said. It is not surprising, therefore, that writers sometimes discover somewhere along the way that they actually have something other to say than what they initially thought they were going to say. Second, check the arrangement of your paragraphs to make sure that they move easily one to the next. You might find that some paragraphs should be repositioned. So reposition, making sure to change any transitional words or phrases as necessary. Third, check each paragraph internally for unity and coherence (see below), and check that you have provided whatever transitions are necessary between paragraphs. Finally, every time you look over what you have written, keep an eye out for what can be polished — a better word here, a more felicitous expression there — and polish as you go along.

Transition, unity, and coherence — you have encountered these key words before in this text. One can hardly talk about writing without using them. But here is where we shall focus in on them, for they are matters to be attended to mainly when rewriting, or, to put this the other way round, rewriting mainly entails attending to matters of transition, unity, and coherence. The following discussion of this trio should help you see what to do in the rewriting phase of the writing process.

TRANSITION

The word *transition* refers to anything in a written text that both demarcates points, thereby signaling a progression from one point to the next, and simultaneously glues material together, sentence to sentence and paragraph to paragraph, by showing how these parts of a composition are related. Sometimes, of course, the relationship between sentences or paragraphs is self-evident, and so nothing additional is needed to make the relationship clear. More often, however, something is needed — a word, a phrase, a sentence or two, or even a whole paragraph in longer essays — for the reader to understand exactly what the writer had in mind. Once again, you must remember your audience. As you read a draft of a paper, put yourself in the position of your readers. That is, put out of mind what you intended to say and read what you actually have said, checking that the relationship of each sentence and each paragraph to the one before and the one after is clear. If it is not, then provide whatever is necessary to make it so. From the reader's perspective, writing lacking the necessary transitions is simply unreadable. Except for your teachers, whose job it is to read what you write, no one will read your writing if it has to be mentally revised to make sense. And you probably would not persevere through somebody else's writing if you had to supply the necessary linkage between ideas. Besides, readers can't be trusted to get things right. And in any case, it is up to the writer to get things right in the first place.

Here is a good example of writing that is unreadable because of the lack of transitions, the lack of a thesis statement compounding the problem. By revising this paper, I think I can demonstrate what transitions are and do. On the left is the original paper, with a line through everything deleted in the revision; on the right is the revision, with all additions underlined.

The Jaspers

First of all you might be wondering, "What is a Jasper?" We get our name from a man named Jasper, who was the head of athletics at Manhattan College a number of years ago. What is a Jasper

1   What is a Jasper? Broadly, a Jasper—the name comes from a man named Jasper, who was the head of athletics at Manhattan College a number of years ago—is anyone who goes to Manhattan College. More

today? A Jasper is anyone who contributes to the college community. A Jasper is anyone who goes to Manhattan College.

meaningfully defined, a Jasper is someone who contributes to the college community. [This, now, is the thesis statement.]

Many students are avid athletes whether they are in league or intramural sports. The cross-country and the track teams ~~do extremely well each year.~~ The Lady J's basketball team ~~is also a very impressive team.~~ Swimming ~~is a~~ team ~~that holds its own each year.~~ The men's basketball team ~~has a long way to go, baby. Club~~ basketball ~~does well.~~ ~~Club sports such as~~ golf, tennis, football, volleyball, and hockey ~~can be fun. The gym is open for those who would like to run, take an aerobics class, swim, or organize their own game.~~

2   Student athletes, for instance, contribute much to the spirit of the college. They do so whether they are on such league teams as the cross-country and track teams, the Lady J's basketball team, the swimming team, and the men's basketball team; or such club teams as basketball, golf, tennis, football, volleyball, and hockey. All such students deserve the name "Jasper."*

*[Sometimes a point is implicit; sometimes it must be made explicit. The three sentences marked with an * here accomplish the latter.]

There are many other extra-curricular activities, ~~such as:~~ Social Action, Amnesty International, Young Republicans, Young Democrats, Peace Club, Student Government, Folk Singers' Club. ~~And it is~~

3   There are many other extracurricular activities through which a student can participate in campus life. They include Social Action, Amnesty International, Young Republicans, Young Democrats, Peace Club,

~~always possible for anyone~~
~~to start a club.~~

    Student Government, Folk
Singers' Club. <u>Those who
join such clubs are true
Jaspers.</u>*

Honor societies   4
~~reward excellent students.~~
~~There are general~~
~~excellence and individual~~
~~honor societies.~~ The
activities of ~~honor~~
~~societies~~ range from
printing a journal to
sponsoring a speaker. ~~The~~
~~school sponsors many~~
~~mixers, movies, and~~
~~cultural events. There~~
~~are two semiformals held~~
~~each year, the Jasper~~
~~Jingle and the Spring~~
~~Fling. Senior week is a~~
~~special time for seniors.~~
~~It is filled with a variety~~
~~of activities, from the~~
~~honors convention to the~~
~~prom.~~

<u>Those students
elected to</u> honor
societies, the activities
of <u>which</u> range from
printing a journal to
sponsoring a speaker,
<u>equally deserve the name
"Jasper." For they, too,
contribute.</u>*

Of course, who could   5
be a Jasper without going
to the bars below campus on
Broadway now and again.
~~All of~~ this ~~and so much~~
~~more make~~ a Jasper.

Of course, who could
be a Jasper without going
to the bars below campus on
Broadway now and again.
This, <u>too, defines what</u> a
Jasper <u>is.</u>

To be sure, I have done more than simply add transitions. I
have rewritten the first paragraph so that it has a thesis and
followed through on that thesis in the paper, paragraph by
paragraph. I have also deleted everything that is irrelevant to the

thesis as it now stands. Both the additions and the deletions, observe, give the revised paper focus and point. But most of all, observe how transition is gained, or how sentences and paragraphs are related in the revision:

¶1 —*Broadly* and *more meaningfully defined* are transitional. In relation to each other, they structure the paragraph and bring its ideas into relationship.

¶2 —*For instance* relates the first and second paragraphs and gives the second paragraph point. Taken together, *on such* and *or such* provide transition as they help to structure the paragraph.

¶3 —*Other* is the key transition here, linking paragraphs 2 and 3 by suggesting that the material of the one is an extension of that of the other.

¶4 —*Equally* and *too* are both transitional, relating paragraphs 2 and 3 to paragraph 4 and thereby giving point to paragraph 4.

¶5 —Here, again, *too* is transitional, relating the last paragraph to the rest of the paper.

Transition, then, frequently can be attained simply by the addition of a word or short phrase. The most common are such *conjunctive adverbs* as *however, therefore, consequently, moreover, thus, also, besides, furthermore, nevertheless, still, for example,* and *for instance.* Notice that each shows a specific kind of relationship: *for instance* says that what follows is a specific case of a generalization stated before; *however* and *nevertheless* show contrary movement; and *therefore, thus,* and *consequently* all say that what follows is a result of what precedes. Then there are *subordinating conjunctions,* the primary function of which is grammatical: to subordinate one element of a sentence to another. But in so doing, these conjunctions also show relationship. *Because,* for example, shows a cause and effect relationship between what is said in the main clause of a sentence and what is said in the subordinate clause that it (the subordinating conjunction *because*) heads; *although* shows a contrary relationship between main and subordinate clauses; words like *after* and *when* show a time relationship; and *if* and *unless* say that what is said in the clause headed by the one or the other is a condition for what is stated in the main clause.

With regard to how coherence is affected by the use of transitions, consider the following sentences and their revisions, in which things are tied together by subordinating conjunctions (and so, by subordination) and conjunctive adverbs.

Molly said she wants you to stay home. She wants you to watch the baby. I can't take you with me.

Molly said that she wants you to stay home *because* she wants you to watch the baby. *Therefore,* I can't take you with me.

I would love to have come. I wanted to see the chickens. My mother wouldn't let me. I had work to do.

I would love to have come, *since* I wanted to see the chickens. *However,* my mother wouldn't let me *because* I had work to do.

Harry was late. He got to his seat just before the curtain went up. The play was over. He was left with many feelings. He felt sad and yet somehow elated.

Although Harry was late, he got to his seat just before the curtain went up. *When* the play was over, he was left with many feelings. *For instance,* he felt sad and yet somehow elated.

Many other words and phrases can also serve as transitions. For example, in the rewrite of "The Jaspers," as we have seen, the adjective *other* and the adverb *equally* both are transitional. The seven coordinating conjunctions, too, are transitional, each showing a specific kind of relationship: *and* (similarity), *but* and *yet* (contrast), *for* and *so* (result, cause and effect), *or* (equivalence or alternate possibility), and *nor* (equality in negation). Repetition of a word or phrase from one sentence to the next can also effect transition, as can the use of pronouns in that they refer back. And often a whole sentence might be transitional or even a whole paragraph. For instance, let's say that you are going to write a short paper on the Pilgrims, your thesis falling into two parts — that the female Pilgrims were essential for the survival of the colony in its first year here and that they continued to be essential thereafter. After your thesis paragraph, you would devote a paragraph to the first half of the thesis, supporting it with whatever evidence you could bring to bear. Then, you would tackle the second half of the thesis in your third paragraph. But how would you get from the one to the other? A full sentence at the start of the third paragraph would probably be needed, a sentence something like this:

> It is clear, then, that women were essential during the colony's first year; that they remained essential during the years to come can be just as easily shown.

Having finished your argument and written a conclusion, you would have a short paper in hand. But now, say that you are going to write a much longer paper with the same thesis, with five or six paragraphs devoted to the first part of the thesis and an equal number to the second. In this case, you might need a short transitional paragraph between the two segments of the paper, a paragraph something like this:

> There is no question, then, that women were essential to the survival of the colony during its first year. As I have shown, it was the women, and not the Pilgrim Fathers, who knew how to find and prepare the roots and berries that fed the colony during that long first winter. But I have also stated that the women remained essential to the colony after its first year in America. So now, let us turn to the later history of the Pilgrim Mothers.

This whole paragraph would be transitional, serving to link the two halves of the paper and to make it one.

Whether a word or a phrase, a sentence or a paragraph, transitions are the mark of thoughtful and mature writing. Linking sentences as well as larger segments within paragraphs, linking paragraphs as well as larger divisions of a piece of writing, transitions more than anything else make writing readable. While demarcating points, they also serve as sign posts that tell the reader where the writer is going; they are what structure a piece of writing, or reveal to the reader how it is structured and so keep the reader from getting lost. Thus, transition and organization go hand in glove. Comprehensible organization requires transitions, and that's all there is to that.

UNITY AND COHERENCE

Earlier, I said that "the primary business of rewriting is to make sure that everything is to the point and follows as logically and gracefully as possible." In other words, a finished piece of writing should be both unified and coherent, unity and coherence being intimately related to transition and organization, and thus, along with transition and organization, the marks always of readable prose. Prose that does not show unity and coherence is like the rambling of one of those radio talk-show callers who go on and on aimlessly, and who never really come to the point or make a point. They are painful to listen to, just as the original version of "The Jaspers" — which lacks both unity (because much is irrelevant in it) and coherence (because nothing relates to anything else) is painful to read. Readers, too, want the writer to make a point and to stick to it by relating all supporting points both to the main point (a matter of unity) and to each other (a matter of coherence).

To be more specific, unity means that everything in a paper is to the same burden, or that everything somehow or other points back to and supports the governing thesis (the thesis, note, and not the topic). We might think of the relationship of thesis and supporting material as being vertical:

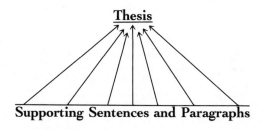

But what if something is not related thus? You can rewrite to gain unity in one of several ways. First, and most obvious, anything that seems irrelevant, and so breaks the sense of unity, can be deleted. For example, the second sentence of the following passage is totally irrelevant as stated and therefore destroys the sense of unity and coherence as well:

> Standardized tests do not really measure one's abilities. The most hated tests are the ones from our friends at Princeton. Standardized tests do not measure one's abilities, but only one's test-taking skills.

What does the fact that the SAT's are hated have to do with the thesis that standardized tests don't really measure one's abilities? Nothing. After all, tests that measure abilities well might well be equally hated. No necessary relationship exists between the two statements and none is drawn as the passage stands. The two derive from the same topic, of course, but, remember, everything in a paper must relate to its specific thesis and not merely to its general topic. One way to revise is simply to delete the second sentence:

> Standardized tests do not really measure one's abilities. These exams measure only one's test-taking skills.

Now there is nothing extraneous; now the passage has unity.

Another way to revise for unity is to take anything that is irrelevant as stated and to state it in terms of the thesis. The second sentence of the original passage on standardized testing, for instance, could be retained by restating it thus:

> Standardized tests do not really measure one's abilities. Certainly, those most hated tests from our friends at Princeton don't. All these and other such tests measure is one's test-taking skills.

Yet another way of gaining unity — one, indeed, suggested by the last revision (in which "our friends at Princeton" is subordinated) — is subordination. A typical cause for both disunity and incoherence is the putting of every thought into an independent clause or sentence. Only prime information should go into prime positions; all else should be subordinated by being put into a phrase or a subordinate clause. Note how unity can be gained by subordination:

> Standardized tests, like those most hated tests from our friends at Princeton, do not really measure one's abilities. All such tests measure is one's test-taking skills.

Here, the business about the "most hated tests" as well as about "our friends at Princeton" is put into a prepositional phrase, the preposition in each phrase acting as a link (a transition) from thought to thought. To be sure, one usually finds some material that got into one's first draft that is simply irrelevant and must simply be deleted. More often, however, one or another sentence that breaks unity because of how it is stated can be salvaged by restatement in terms of the thesis or by subordination. And sometimes, the point of a sentence or a paragraph must be spelled out so that its relationship to the thesis is clear. In this regard, look again at the revision of "The Jaspers," which, as I point out in my bracketed note on page 00, contains three such spellings-out.

Disunity and incoherence always go together. A passage that lacks unity will also lack coherence, for *coherence* means *relationship*, and something that is disunified is by definition unrelated. Unity and coherence are at one, too, with regard to focus and point. A passage that lacks unity and a passage that is incoherent (even if unified) will seem off the point and thus blurred as to intent (or out of focus). But coherence is different from unity, as is suggested by the fact that it is quite possible to write a unified paper that is incoherent. Unity, as we have seen, is a matter of vertical relationship, or the relation of everything in a paper to its thesis. Coherence, on the other hand, is a matter of horizontal relationship, or the relation of every sentence and every paragraph to what comes immediately before and immediately after:

$$\longrightarrow \quad \longleftrightarrow \quad \longleftrightarrow \quad \longleftrightarrow \quad \longleftrightarrow \quad \longleftarrow$$

So, I sometimes have occasion to say to one of my students, "Yes, all of your sentences and paragraphs relate to your thesis. But how do they relate to each other?" Here is a quick example of what I mean:

> The summer of 1989 is over, but not forgotten. Once again, I spent my vacation at the Jersey shore with my friends and relatives. The highlight of many teenage girls' first day back always proves to be finding out which lifeguards have returned for another season. Lifeguards go on duty at 8:00 A.M.

The first two sentences are OK, linked, as they are, by the phrase "once again." The second two, however, are badly incoherent, both in relationship (or lack thereof) to each other and to the sentences that begin the passage. What to do? Well, one could try subordination, for subordination is a way of gaining coherence as well as unity. When sentences do not follow readily, the problem can often be solved by subordinating one to another, thereby grammatically expressing the relationship of ideas. The second two sentences of the present sample, for instance, can be made coherent by subordination:

> The highlight of many teenage girls' first day back always proves to be finding out which lifeguards have returned for another season, even though that means getting up before 8:00 A.M., when the lifeguards go on duty.

Coherence can also be gained, as can unity, by overt explanation of how a support relates to another support if the relationship is not inherently clear. And, most of all, coherence is gained by the use of transitions, whose sole purpose is to spell out the kind of relationship that exists between sentences and paragraphs when that relationship is not self-evident (which more often than not proves to be the case). The incoherence of the second to third sentences of the present sample passage can be corrected by these two means:

> The summer of 1989 is over, but not forgotten. Once again, I spent my vacation at the Jersey shore with my friends and relatives. And once again [transition], the highlight of many teenage girls' first day back proved to be finding out which

lifeguards had returned for another season, even though that meant getting up before 8:00 A.M., when the lifeguards go on duty. As usual, I was one of those girls. [spelling out]

Finally, we can gain coherence by simply restating a sentence so as to incorporate something from the preceding sentence or from the thesis itself. For instance, the incoherence of the first pair of sentences that follows is easily rectified by the italicized addition in the second pair:

> The psychological and emotional scars of divorce are traumatic and long-lasting. A child who is witness to a constant bombardment of volatile arguments is apt to be left with the warped impression that such arguments are normal.

> The psychological and emotional scars of divorce can be traumatic and long-lasting. A child who is witness to the constant bombardment of volatile arguments *that almost always precedes a divorce* is apt to be left with the warped impression that such arguments are normal.

Every sentence within a paragraph, then, and every paragraph in a paper must somehow relate both to the thesis and to the previous sentence or paragraph and the following sentence or paragraph. And if one or another element does not so relate, then incoherence looms and the reader is sure to get lost. When writing, and especially when rewriting, therefore, be careful to watch that the relationship of your sentences and paragraphs is clear at all points. And if at any point it is not clear, then delete, subordinate, supply a transition, explain yourself in a sentence or two, or restate. You might also try doing what I do — indeed, I urge you to. When I write, I look back and back again: I never write a sentence without reading the sentence before it over and over, nor do I ever begin a paragraph without rereading at least the end of the preceding paragraph several times. In this way, I get my brain into the groove of coherence, as it were, and create the situation whereby sentence gives rise to sentence, paragraph to paragraph. Coherence, thus, is all but assured, though in the rewriting stage I still check that what I have written is coherent and make the necessary adjustments when I feel that the coherence here or there can be tightened. In fact, I have just made one such adjustment by adding the sentence "You might also try doing what I do — indeed, I urge you to" a few sentences back. On rereading, I felt there to be a gap at that point; I had jumped from thought to thought, leaving the reader behind. Linking what comes before to what comes after, the added sentence fills that gap.

Though "The Jaspers," or its revision, well exemplifies what I have been saying, one more example wouldn't hurt. But this time let's take a basically sound paper and, indeed, quite a nice paper in most respects. However, the paper needs a bit of work with regard to transition and some pruning, for it goes out of focus here and there and thus loses point. Also, some muddy sentences need restating and the end of the paper is not very satisfying. Compare, now, the original essay, on the left, with a line through everything deleted in the rewrite, and the rewrite, in which anything added is underlined. I think you will find that, though the original is not far from being a really good paper, it needs what is done in the rewrite to get there.

Entertaining a Child

Entertaining a child can be a difficult task. Parents spend hundreds of dollars on toys only to find their children bored after ten minutes. Having babysat my brother, I have discovered many games that will entertain any child for hours.

1

Entertaining a child can be a difficult task. How many parents spend hundreds of dollars on toys only to find their children bored after ten minutes? Toys, we can conclude, aren't the answer. Interaction is what is needed. Having babysat my brother, I have discovered many interactive games that will entertain any child for hours.

This first game I call "I've got your nose." This game is played by placing the thumb between the middle and index fingers and then pulling on the child's nose. I then tell my brother that I have his nose in my hand. ~~He's such a good kid. I really love him. He's so easy to get along with. And he's so easy to take in.~~ He spends twenty minutes trying to devise a plan to get back his nose. ~~He loves to plan sneck attacks on me to get his nose back.~~ When he feels desperate, he pretends to have my nose and offers to make a trade. By the time I give his nose back, we've played for more than an hour.

We play a game I call "Why are you hitting yourself?" I take Teddy's arms and lightly hit him in the face with his own hands. ~~Teddy is his name. I love that name, because he is a little Teddy Bear.~~ I then repeat "Why are you hitting yourself?" approximately a hundred times. He struggles to overpower me, but of

2   The first game I call "I've got your nose." This game is played by placing the thumb between the middle and index fingers and then pulling on the child's nose. I <u>do this and</u> then tell my brother that I have his nose in my hand. He spends twenty minutes trying to devise a plan to get back his nose. When he feels desperate, he pretends to have my nose and offers to make a trade. By the time I give his nose back, we've played for more than an hour.

3   <u>Another</u> game we play I call "Why are you hitting yourself." I take Teddy's arms and lightly hit him in the face with his own hands. I then repeat "Why are you hitting yourself?" approximately a hundred times. He struggles to overpower me, but of course I'm too strong for him. He may not admit that he loves the game, but he

course I'm too strong for
him. He may not admit that
he loves the game, but he
does. His squeals of
laughter fill the room
every time we play it. ~~The
laughter of kids is the
best. I love to hear kids
laugh. I think it's a
show.~~

    The third game we
play I call "The lazy man's
hide-and-seek." My
brother hides while I sit
on the couch. I then call
out places he might be.
"Are you in the bathroom?"
I ask. "No," he answers.
"The closet." "No."
"The kitchen." "Aw, you
found me." Teddy will
then come out laughing and
proceed to find a
different hiding place.
~~My favorite part of~~ this
game is that, while he is
hiding, I get to watch TV
~~and see some of my favorite
shows. I like reruns of
"Lucy" especially, and
some of the soaps.~~

    I entertain Teddy for
hours with these games.
He doesn't need toys, just
attention.

does. His squeals of
laughter fill the room
every time we play it. <u>And
when we do, another hour
flies by before we know it.</u>

4   The third game we
play I call "The lazy man's
hide-and-seek." My
brother hides while I sit
on the couch. I then call
out places he might be.
"Are you in the bathroom?"
I ask. "No," he answers.
"The closet?" "No." "The
kitchen." "Aw, you found
me." Teddy will then come
out laughing and proceed
to find a different hiding
place. <u>What I like best
about</u> this game is that,
while he is hiding, I get
to watch TV.

5   As I said, I
entertain Teddy for hours
with these games. He
doesn't need toys, just
attention. <u>And that, I
believe, is exactly what
all children need.</u>

<u>Expensive toys, which get</u>
<u>broken as soon as they're</u>
<u>opened anyway, will never</u>
<u>take the place of time</u>
<u>spent with a child. But</u>
<u>there's another good</u>
<u>reason I haven't mentioned</u>
<u>yet for spending time with</u>
<u>your younger brother or</u>
<u>sister or your own</u>
<u>children: entertaining a</u>
<u>child is entertaining.</u>
<u>Try it, you'll like it, I</u>
<u>guarantee.</u>

[Terence Mulgrew]   [Terence Mulgrew]

PROOFREADING AND TITLING

After you have gone through all of the steps outlined thus far in this section and have revised accordingly, you should have a final draft in hand. You are close to the end. What is left is careful proofreading. Because, once more, the mind cannot do everything at once, proofreading should also be done in steps. As I always suggest to my own students (and this is my own practice), read your final draft checking for subject-verb agreement only. Then read it again checking only for pronoun reference and agreement. These are potential problem spots of our language and therefore they require careful attention. Next, read your paper for spelling, punctuation, and other matters of mechanics, preferably aloud so that you can also check the sound of your prose. Watch especially for errors that you know you are prone to make.

After you have finished these steps, give your paper a title. To be sure, you may have a tentative title in mind from the beginning. But it is best to wait until the last to make a final decision about the title, for one cannot be sure of what one has to say until it is said. A good title, note, usually points to the thesis without exactly stating it: for example, the title "Possession and Being" would point to the thesis that the more one has, the less one is, but would leave the full statement to the essay's beginning. (As we will see in Chapter 2, however, there are other types of title, and *sometimes* a title may serve as the thesis statement.) Once you have decided on a title — which is, remember, the first thing the reader sees and so a tool for focusing the reader's attention and drawing the reader into your discourse — you are ready for the final typing, after which you should check your work one last time for typographical errors.

We return to where we began. As you read essays in this textbook, read with an eye toward writing. The reading should help stimulate ideas; the writing will help concretize those ideas and so help you better understand both the essay under consideration and yourself in relationship to it. Reading and writing alike should bring both the world and the self into play. Into play — the phrase leads me to my final point. Don't forget that reading and even writing can be wonderful fun. The play of the mind is full of delight if the mind allows itself the freedom to play.

Working with the
Elements of the
Essay

Essay Construction

Every essay is constructed of various elements. To understand an essay fully, therefore, one must understand the elements of which it is composed. Equally important, to come to write well, one must have a good grasp of the elements one is working with. As you read this chapter, then — and as you read essays subsequently — be mindful of your own writing. If you read with your own writing in mind, you should stand a good chance of improving it and even making it a pleasure to read. What follows is a consideration of the elements of the essay as listed toward the beginning of Chapter 1. Essay construction entails these elements, which every writer of exposition who hopes to reach and inform or influence an audience must master.

The Sense of an Audience

More than any other literary type, the essay is tailored to a specific audience. What this means to you as a reader of a given essay — a reader not probably a member of the audience addressed in the essay — is that you must determine the audience intended as you read and then read accordingly.

Take Alice Walker's book review, "Nuclear Madness: What You Can Do" (pages 572–75). Her essay begins and ends as follows:

> *Nuclear Madness* is a book you should read immediately. Before brushing your teeth. Before making love. Before lunch. . . .
>
> ───────────────◆───────────────
>
> But first, read Caldicott's book [*Nuclear Madness*], and remember: the good news may be that Nature is phasing out the white man, but the bad news is that's who She thinks we all are.

Walker's targeted audience is educated American blacks, whom she addresses directly in hopes of having a personal impact — an intent also suggested by her title. It is this audience that accounts for Walker's word choice, or diction, and tone — that of an insider talking as only an insider can to other insiders. The essay's warm, chummy tone is established by the informality of its beginning and maintained by such sentences as: "Write letters to . . . senators and congressmen . . . : tell them if they don't change, 'cullud' are going to invade their fallout shelters." To understand the essay fully, then, and to account for its diction, tone, and phrasing as well as to judge the efficacy of Walker's approach to her subject, you as reader must determine Walker's intended audience and take it into account as you read. The writer's sense of audience is a pervasive element of exposition and so is an attribute of essays that the reader should never lose sight of.

The sense of audience that you will pick up as you read essays in this book should help you as a writer to sharpen your own sense of audience. Again, as I suggested in Chapter 1, good expository prose is shaped with the reader in mind. Seeing how this is so in the essays you read should help you apply the principle when you write, both in your courses now and in whatever occupation you pursue.

NARRATION

Many essays incorporate narrative passages, or passages in which the author tells a story to exemplify a point or flesh out an argument. For, carrying the authority of direct experience, narrative can be a powerful tool of exposition. Let me tell you the story of how I learned the power of narration: A teenager at the time, I was alone in a huge old house in a foreign city; it was midnight; unable to sleep, I went into the library and pulled a book from a shelf — Poe's *Murders in the Rue Morgue;* I read it through and was literally scared stiff; I couldn't move for terror; the next morning I awoke in the chair in which I had read Poe's tale. Now, there was a little narrative passage, whose purpose is to exemplify, in an otherwise nonnarrative context. This kind of passage is found in all types of essays.

Some essays, of course, are entirely narrative. Biographical, autobiographical, and historical essays, which tell stories of people moving through time, are usually of this sort. (Note: Narrative passages like mine in the last paragraph and narrative essays are almost always structured chronologically.) A typical historical essay, for instance, proceeds to tell the story of historical personages and events as they occurred, as does the following excerpt from Peter Steinfels's "History is Bunk" (pages 480–83):

> . . . in the midst of the . . . tumult, The King called a brash, 47-year-old nobleman, politician, and diplomat to head the government. This was Otto von Bismarck. . . . Mr. Bismarck was not well received. He immediately defied the Chamber, proclaiming that power — blood and iron — would resolve the great questions of the day. The moderates and liberals replied that the legal and moral order was not violated with impunity. The historian Treitschke termed Bismarck's defiance a shallow and ridiculous vulgarity. But government without a budget continued.
>
> Meanwhile, Bismarck dissolved the Chamber and called new elections. In the intervening period, when there was no Chamber to counter his moves, he attacked the press, obtaining a royal order allowing the suppression of critical newspapers.

He further maligned his opponents as unpatriotic and even as traitors. When the elected deputies wished to question Bismarck about a semi-secret agreement which allowed Russian troops to cross into Prussia to exterminate fugitive Polish rebels against the Czar, Bismarck refused even to explain his policy publicly.

Steinfels here speaks of other people of another time. Third-person narration like his is apt for this kind of recounting.

An autobiographical reminiscence, Langston Hughes's "Salvation" (pages 321–23) exemplifies a more personal kind of narration, one that concerns the narrator directly and is, thus, related in the first person. "Salvation" begins as follows:

I was saved from sin when I was going on thirteen. But not really saved. It happened like this. There was a big revival at my Auntie Reed's church. Every night for weeks there had been much preaching, singing, praying, and shouting, and some very hardened sinners had been brought to Christ, and the membership of the church had grown by leaps and bounds. Then just before the revival ended, they held a special meeting for children, "to bring the young lambs to the fold." My aunt spoke of it for days ahead. That night I was escorted to the front row and placed on the mourners' bench with all the other young sinners, who had not yet been brought to Jesus.

"It happened like this" — and we're off. Following the chronology of the events as they occurred, Hughes goes on to tell the story of "that night." The point of the story — its theme, in this case — has to do with what Hughes as a boy discovered: that in the adult world saying can be more important than believing, and that people can easily be fooled because of their own beliefs and desires. This is what the story exemplifies, its narrative being a means, finally, of definition.

Now see what you can do with narration. You have a world of experiences stored up. Tap them as you write, using incidents in your life to exemplify and argue your point. Beginning writers, I find, rarely make use of the wealth they possess — their experiences in the world and the knowledge that comes with experience. As a result, their writing, even if coherent, tends to be pallid, lacking a sense of immediacy and the vibrance that comes thereof. When you read essays in this book, see how professional writers draw on their experience and to what effect. Then, when you turn to write, incorporate relevant incidents from your own life to make your discussion come alive and to help move it forward. By doing so, you will find that your writing is more vivid and has much greater impact. Of course, when you do, be aware that an overuse of *I* is always tedious for the reader. Use it, but don't abuse it.

TONE AND VOICE

All essays convey a sense of voice — a sense of a particular person expressing a particular attitude through the kinds of words used (diction) and the way they are put together (syntax), or through the tone of voice established thereby. Instructive in this regard is the essay whose speaker is a character to whom we are *not* meant to assent, as opposed to the author speaking in all earnestness. To create such a speaker, the essayist must carefully manipulate diction and syntax, for instance (see "Style" later in this chapter), creating, thus, the appropriate tone and voice for the ends at hand — stuffy, perhaps, or naive, or malevolent, or insane. Consider, for instance, two paragraphs from Jonathan Swift's "A Modest Proposal" (pages 498–507), a classic example of an essay with an imaginary speaker:

> I have been assured by a very knowing American of my acquaintance in London, that a young healthy child well nursed is at a year old a most delicious, nourishing and wholesome food, whether stewed, roasted, baked, or boiled, and I make no doubt that it will equally serve in a fricassee, or a ragout.
>
> I do therefore humbly offer it to public consideration, that of the hundred and twenty thousand children already computed, twenty thousand may be reserved for breed, whereof only one fourth part to be males, which is more than we allow to sheep, black-cattle, or swine, and my reason is that these children are seldom the fruits of marriage, a circumstance not much regarded by our savages, therefore one male will be sufficient to serve four females. That the remaining hundred thousand may at a year old be offered in sale to the persons of quality, and

fortune, through the kingdom, always advising the mother to let them suck plentifully in the last month, so as to render them plump, and fat for a good table. A child will make two dishes at an entertainment for friends, and when the family dines alone, the fore or hind quarter will make a reasonable dish, and seasoned with a little pepper or salt will be very good boiled on the fourth day, especially in winter.

This passage is not meant to be taken as spoken by Swift. Rather, we are to hear the voice of an imaginary bureaucrat who has lost sight of human values in his abstract musings about governmental problems and solutions (bureaucrats in the eighteenth century were not unlike those of today). The point of the essay is ironic, opposite from the point its speaker makes. But my point is that the tone and voice of "A Modest Proposal" were crafted by Swift for a purpose. The ordinary diction of the passage and its simple (for the eighteenth century) phrasing help to produce a matter-of-fact tone, a tone reinforced by the lack of emotion in and understatement of the passage. But the tone is entirely wrong for the horrendous subject matter. Is this the voice of insanity, one wonders? Yes, it is, and that is the point: Swift carefully crafted the tone and voice of the essay to suggest dramatically the insanity that so often governs our lawmakers, who so often focus on expediency rather than rectitude.

What I have said about "A Modest Proposal" — that its tone and voice were crafted for a purpose — is no less true of any professional essay, though it is easy to lose sight of this fact. An accomplished writer chooses words, sentence patterns, and so forth with the aim of creating a tonal posture right for the subject matter and the purpose at hand. With this principle in mind, read the following paragraph from E. M. Forster's "Tolerance" (pages 242–46) and determine what its tone is and the qualities of its voice, or of the person speaking the passage. Determine, too, whether or not its tone and voice are appropriate and effective with respect to what is being said. Then read the second paragraph — my rewrite — and contrast it with Forster's as to effect. Why did Forster *choose* the style he did rather than the style of my rewrite?

The world is very full of people — appallingly full; it has never been so full before — and they are all tumbling over each other. Most of these people one doesn't know and some of them one doesn't like; doesn't like the colour of their skins, say, or the shapes of their noses, or the way they blow them or don't blow them, or the way they talk, or their smell, or their clothes, or their fondness for jazz or their dislike of jazz, and so on. Well, what is one to do? There are two solutions. One of them is the Nazi solution. If you don't like people, kill them, banish them, segregate them, and then strut up and down proclaiming that you are the salt of the earth. The other way is much less thrilling, but it is on the whole the way of the democracies, and I prefer it. If you don't like people, put up with them as well as you can. Don't try to love them; you can't, you'll only strain yourself. But try to tolerate them. On the basis of that tolerance a civilized future may be built. Certainly I can see no other foundation for the post-war world.

———————————◆———————————

The world is vastly overpopulated — appallingly so; grotesquely overburdened with multitudes of homo sapiens as never before — and they interfere with each other in their diurnal endeavors. One is acquainted with only a minuscule fraction of these hominoids, and some of those of whom one is cognizant, one does not care for; does not care for the hue of their skin-tones, perhaps, or the dimensions of their proboscises, or how they expel or do not expel air through their nostrils to clear them, or the way they expostulate, or their odors, or their garments, or their liking or disliking music of a popular cast, et cetera. What, one may well ponder, is one's response to this situation to be, this situation in which one finds oneself helplessly enmeshed, hopelessly mired, and, though one tries to keep one's sense of perspective, in which that sense seems impossible to maintain, eroding, as it does, in proportion to one's proximity to one or another population center? Having perused the problem carefully and for some duration, I find there to be — and believe the reader will assent to my conclusion — two possible resolutions to the situation with which we are confronted, nay, two and only two practicable solutions: We must either endure these hordes in patience or, in Conrad's memorable phrase, "Exterminate the brutes."[Which do you think the speaker of this passage would be for?]

Established by diction and syntax — the diction and syntax of ordinary good English — as well as a gently wry kind of humor — for example, "you'll only strain yourself" — the voice of Forster's passage is that of an open, friendly, engaging person speaking to the reader as a friend, a voice that itself seems tolerant and so one that lends Forster's argument credence and authority. In contrast, the voice of the rewrite is persnickety, aloof, frigid to the core. Content, note, has been held constant; the difference is solely a matter of diction throughout and syntax toward the end. But what a difference! Just compare Forster's "they are all tumbling over each other" and "they interfere with each other" of the rewrite. The latter abstraction sounds disengaged and official; because of the charming concretion "tumbling," the original seems warm and loving.

Differences like these are not accidental; they result from deliberation and choice on the part of authors, who shape our feelings in large measure by way of tone and voice. To read an essay well, therefore, is to be aware of the various qualities of its voice and how they are created.

Such an awareness is equally valuable to you as writer: when writing, try to be alert to the voice you are creating (anything you write will exhibit voice, whether or not under your control) and try to control those aspects of writing that shape voice (diction and syntax especially) in order to create the voice you want. To gain control takes time and practice. But if you keep questioning essays as to voice, you will come to grasp how voice is established and how it functions in essays; then, perhaps, you will get the element of voice under control in your writing. With this end in mind, you might try your hand at forging a speaker other than yourself. Writing an essay with a fictional speaker will help distance you and so help you see more clearly what you must do to fashion the voice you want.

The Character Sketch

Because more often than not essays concern people, the character sketch is a common element of the essay, one frequently used to provide an example or to flesh out an idea by giving us a sense of the person whose idea it is (or was). Indeed, because people are fascinating in themselves, an entire essay may be given over to a character sketch of a specific person, real or imagined, or, perhaps, of a type of person in general. Isak Dinesen's "Pooran Singh" (pages 217–19), for instance, is a character sketch of an Indian blacksmith who had been in Dinesen's employ in Africa. The essay paints a portrait of him in words, a portrait as full and immediate as any found in fiction:

> . . . the blacksmith's shop had a great power of attraction, and when I went down to watch Pooran Singh at work I always found people in it and round it. Pooran Singh worked at a superhuman pace, as if his life depended upon getting the particular job of work finished within the next five minutes, he jumped straight up in the air over the forge, he shrieked out his orders to his two young Kikuyu assistants in a high bird's voice and behaved altogether like a man who is himself being burnt at the stake, or like some chafed over-devil at work. But Pooran Singh was no devil, but a person of the meekest disposition; out of working hours he had a little maidenly affectation of manner. He was our Fundee of the farm, which means an artisan of all work, carpenter, saddler and cabinet-maker, as well as black-smith; he constructed and built more than one waggon for the farm, all on his own. But he liked the work of the forge best, and it was a very fine, proud sight, to watch him tiring a wheel.

When reading an essay like this, pay special attention to details and how they are used. Just like the characters in fiction, the people in essays are brought to life by the details. That is, it is not enough for a writer to describe a person abstractly: "Ever cheerful, Pooran Singh was a blacksmith and so did all of the metal work around the ranch." We as readers demand more: we want to feel the intense heat of the forge (here captured by the detail "burnt at the stake"), to see Pooran jumping "straight up in the air," to hear him shrieking his orders in his "high bird's voice." We want to know him as he knew himself, not just to be told things about him. What animates a character sketch is the details. By paying attention to detail when reading "Pooran Singh," say, you will see this for yourself; by paying attention to detail generally, you will develop a habit of mind that will keep your writing concrete and thus vivid and immediate.

SETTING

Though an essay need not indicate a setting, many essays are located in time and place. Narrative essays, for instance (see "Narration"), almost always entail setting, for stories concern people, and people exist only in a given place at a given time. In many such essays, the setting functions only as a necessary backdrop, though the specific time and place described often help to create a mood as well. In some essays, however, setting is integral to the meaning: in this type of essay, setting or some aspect thereof becomes symbolic. Consider the following excerpt from Joan Didion's "Bureaucrats" (pages 184–89) in this regard:

> The closed door upstairs at 120 South Spring Street in downtown Los Angeles is marked OPERATIONS CENTER. In the windowless room beyond the closed door a reverential hush prevails. From six A.M. until seven P.M. in this windowless room men sit at consoles watching a huge board flash colored lights. "There's the heart attack," someone will murmur, or "we're getting the gawk effect." 120 South Spring is the Los Angeles office of Caltrans, or the California Department of Transportation, and the Operations Center is where Caltrans engineers monitor what they call "the 42-Mile Loop." . . . The windowless room at 120 South Spring is where incidents get "verified." "Incident verification" is turning on the closed-circuit TV on the console and watching the traffic slow down to see (this is "the gawk effect") where the Camaro tore out the fence.

Caltrans is a closed system having nothing to do with the real world (and so, too, bureaucracy in general, according to Didion): this is what the "closed door" and especially the "windowless room" come to symbolize. Here, that is, the setting provides a backdrop and much more: it also provides mute commentary on Caltrans and all like bureaucracies.

When considering setting in an essay, ask what the setting is doing or what is being done with it. Does the setting create mood? What mood and why? Does the setting seem symbolic? How so and of what? Questions like these will lead you to the heart of an essay in which setting is a prominent element. And remember to look for and at details. The "habit of mind" I refer to at the end of the last subsection will develop by your attending to all the details of an essay — those of setting if a setting is indicated no less than those used to sketch a character or create a certain kind of voice — and should be exercised with respect to all its concretions.

EXAMPLES AND OTHER CONCRETIONS

Right in the middle of Bertrand Russell's essay "How I Write" (pages 454–58) comes the following passage:

> . . . Having, by a time of very intense concentration, planted the problem in my subconsciousness, it would germinate underground until, suddenly, the solution emerged with blinding clarity, so that it only remained to write down what had appeared as if in a revelation.
>
> The most curious example of this process, and the one which led me subsequently to rely upon it, occurred at the beginning of 1914. I had undertaken to give the Lowell Lectures at Boston, and had chosen as my subject "Our Knowledge of the External World." Throughout 1913 I thought about this topic. In term time in my rooms at Cambridge, in vacations in a quiet inn on the upper reaches of the Thames, I concentrated with such intensity that I sometimes forgot to breathe and emerged panting as from a trance. But all to no avail. To every theory that I could think of I could perceive fatal objections. At last, in despair, I went off to Rome for Christmas, hoping that a holiday would revive my flagging energy. I got back to Cambridge on the last day of 1913, and although my difficulties were still completely unresolved I arranged, because the remaining time was short, to dictate as best as I could to a stenographer. Next morning, as she came in at the door, I suddenly saw exactly what I had to say, and proceeded to dictate the whole book without a moment's hesitation.

The process referred to is an abstraction; the example is a concretion. This movement from the abstract to the concrete, or from what is formless — ideas, feelings — to what can be visualized or otherwise sensed in the imagination (like Russell's narrative example), is characteristic of well-written essays. Why?

The answer is that, having form and dimension, we are concrete beings in a concrete world who understand best when given concretions to which we can relate. Thus, "for example," "for instance," "to take an example," and other such phrases are frequent in essays. The example makes tangible what otherwise would be formless, whether idea or feeling. Among the many concretions found in essays are stories, character sketches, sounds and prose rhythms, and figures of speech of all kinds, as, for instance, Didion's symbolic "windowless room" in "Bureaucrats." With respect to concretion, essayists are much like poets: both understand that genuine communication takes place only when the whole being of the reader is engaged and not just his or her intellect alone.

As a reader, observe how writers make their thought concrete and, thus, immediate, never straying too far or staying away too long from examples, images, descriptions, or whatever. Good essayists, at least, always come back and back again to examples, or incorporate stories along the way, or use metaphors and symbols to give shape to their ideas. Once you have observed as much through your reading, apply the principle to your own writing: be as concrete as possible; never keep your reader in the thin air of abstraction for more than four or five sentences running. Note my metaphor and how it makes my thought about abstraction palpable and thus immediate. Such is the power of full-blooded concretions, which sustain the life of the intellect.

Figurative Language

The topic of concretion leads easily to that of figuration, for all figures of speech are concrete in that they all figure, or give shape to, otherwise formless ideas and feelings by tying them to sensory experience — visual, olfactory, auditory, gustatory, tactile, or kinesthetic. Though we tend to associate figures of speech with poetry, all can be found in essays. Personification, for instance, is used by Russell Baker in "The Plot against People" (pages 130–32):

With the cunning peculiar to its breed, the automobile never breaks down while entering a filling station which has a large staff of idle mechanics. It waits until it reaches a downtown intersection in the middle of the rush hour, or until it is fully loaded with family and luggage on the Ohio Turnpike. Thus it creates maximum inconvenience, frustration, and irritability, thereby reducing its owner's lifespan.

By imputing volition to the automobile — and who among us doesn't? — Baker personifies it and thereby turns it into an adversary. His lightly satirical theme — that inanimate objects have it in for us — is thus exemplified.

Symbols, too, are found in essays, as we saw when looking at Joan Didion's "Bureaucrats." But take another essay by Didion, this one entitled "On Morality" (pages 178–82), which begins as follows:

> As it happens I am in Death Valley, in a room at the Enterprise Motel and Trailer Park, and it is July, and it is hot. In fact it is 119°. I cannot seem to make the air conditioner work, but there is a small refrigerator, and I can wrap ice cubes in a towel and hold them against the small of my back. With the help of the ice cubes I have been trying to think, because *The American Scholar* asked me to, in some abstract way about "morality," a word I distrust more every day, but my mind veers inflexibly toward the particular.

Here, as throughout the essay, Didion makes us feel miserably hot and sticky, prickly, nervous, as she feels in the setting described. Arguing against abstract moral codes, Didion herself stays with concretions — the concretion of rhythm, for instance (see "Sound and Rhythm" in the next subsection), and especially of symbolic images. Everything we are made to feel in connection with the concrete desert imagery as described in the essay — hot, sticky, prickly, nervous — we are to carry over to "nature" in general. Here the desert comes to symbolize Didion's central theme: the hostility of nature, which necessitates the kind of morality — concrete and practical — that Didion believes in. Her symbolism works to communicate and support both contentions.

But the most pervasive figure in essays, just as in language, however used, is metaphor — any figurative expression entailing an analogy, whether explicit or implicit, between essentially unlike things. It is the essential unlikeness of the things compared, note, that makes the analogy figurative in the first place. Indeed, so pervasive is metaphor that I feel safe in saying, though I have not taken even a statistical sampling, that no essay in this book, however straightforward and informational, does not contain metaphors; and a great many contain centrally important metaphors, and some are even structured on metaphor. But I need not go outside my own text to exemplify, for there are metaphors throughout. For instance, at the end of the last subsection I speak of "the thin air of abstraction" and pick up on the metaphor shortly after by saying that concretions, like oxygen vis-à-vis the brain, "sustain the life of the intellect." To take a more elaborate example, in Chapter 1, I use a metaphor to bring home the fact that practice in writing is necessary for ultimate mastery:

> . . . the more one writes, the less difficult writing becomes, just as the more time one puts in practicing a sport, the less difficult the sport becomes and the greater one's facility. One must know the ground rules to begin with, of course, as well as the purposes and ways of handling whatever equipment the sport entails. The same is true of writing. To continue the analogy, this whole chapter is aimed at acquainting you with the ground rules of exposition. As to equipment, we have the types of exposition, each type being a different piece of equipment you need to learn how to handle. (pages 14–15)

In each passage, metaphor helps me make my thought concrete; to express it in terms that you, my intended audience, will grasp easily — for I assume that you don't know what I am getting at but that you do know something about breathing and about sports. The second example, in particular, helps me give structure to my ideas and, thus, to my writing. With regard to metaphor and structure specifically, turn back to "Big Game or Small?" (pages 48–51) and read it now to see how the metaphor set up by the essay's title is extended — that is, made to recur — and how the extension helps to structure the essay and make it cohere.

In sum, figurative language is as important to the essayist as to the poet. It is one of the main tools, figuratively speaking, of any writer who hopes to reach an audience and truly communicate ideas and feelings. For, once more, ideas and feelings are shapeless; but we only feel that we truly understand when we have, either physically or mentally, seen, smelled, heard, tasted, touched, or felt kinesthetically. So part of a writer's job is to tie thoughts and feelings to sensation, thereby making them palpable and real. This is your job as a writer, too. You must try to convince your audience — teachers, fellow students — of the validity of whatever position you take. You will stand a good chance of doing so if you can come to wield (metaphorically) a metaphor and with it strike home. For there is nothing like a well-tempered metaphor to capture the attention of readers and make them yield to the justice of your cause. (For a further consideration of metaphor, see "Appendix 1: Using Metaphors," pages 631–35.)

SOUND AND RHYTHM

Sound and rhythm are yet more immediate and concrete than figures of speech, for neither needs to be imagined: sounds we hear directly with our ears and rhythms we feel directly in our muscles. But what does either have to do with the writing of exposition? In that anything made of words has both sound and rhythm, both must be considerations of every writer, the essayist no less than the poet. To be sure, someone writing an essay cannot pay the kind of attention to them that the poet does. Nevertheless, the essayist must be concerned with the way his or her words move and how they sound together if for no other reason than to expunge sounds that unduly call attention to themselves and sounds as well as rhythms that are harsh or halting for no particular reason. Furthermore, now and again, most people who write expository prose use sounds or rhythms or both for special effects.

Take these two sentences from Langston Hughes's "Salvation": "Suddenly the whole room broke into a sea of shouting, as they saw me rise. Waves of rejoicing swept the place" (page 323). These sentences show much gleeful excitement, excitement underpinned by their sound: by the *s* alliteration — that is, the repetition of the *s* sound — in conjunction with the concentration of the high-pitched vowels *e (-ly, sea, me, re-), a (they, waves, place),* and *i (rise).* Up in feeling (with short wavelengths, high-pitched vowels in concentration often create a sense of excitement and glee), the sound of this passage as much as its denotative meaning conveys the thrill of the moment.

As to rhythm, listen again to the opening of Joan Didion's "On Morality":

> As it happens, I am in Death Valley, in a room at the Enterprise Motel and Trailer Park, and it is July, and it is hot. In fact, it is 119°. I cannot seem to make the air conditioner work. (page 178)

Because of their length and syntax, these sentences are rhythmically panting; and through their panting rhythm they communicate the feel of what they describe. Listen, too, to a sentence from Isak Dinesen's "Pooran Singh": "All day long the place resounded with the deafening noise of the forge, — iron on iron, on iron once more" (page 217). This last phrase beautifully captures in its rhythm the rhythm of the forge itself.

When reading essays, pay some attention to sounds and to rhythms like Didion's and to their effects, if, that is, the sound or rhythm of a sentence or passage seems to have some special function. You might also pay attention both when reading and writing to how paragraphs move and to rhythm overall. Granted, prose rhythms are difficult to analyze, for we just don't have the tools to do so. Still, different essays and passages within essays move in different ways and have different rhythmic feels. Some move rapidly, some ponderously, some evenly, some erratically. Syntax (see "Style," which follows) has much to do with such differences in movement: a passage or an essay composed mainly of short, syntactically simple sentences, say, will move much more rapidly than and so have a different effect from a passage or an essay composed mainly of long, syntactically complex sentences. For instance, contrast these two passages from Lewis Thomas's "Late Night Thoughts on Listening to Mahler's Ninth Symphony" as to syntax, rhythm, and rhythmic effect.

> I cannot listen to Mahler's Ninth Symphony with anything like the old melancholy mixed with the high pleasure I used to take from this music. There was a time, not long ago, when what I heard, especially in the final movement, was an open acknowledgment of death and at the same time a quiet celebration of the tranquillity connected to the process. I took this music as a metaphor for reassurance, confirming my own strong hunch that the dying of every living creature, the most natural of all experiences, has to be a peaceful experience. I rely on nature. The long passages on all the strings at the end, as close as music can come to expressing silence itself, I used to hear as Mahler's idea of leave-taking at its best. But always, I have heard this music as a solitary, private listener, thinking about death. (page 533)

> Now all that has changed. I cannot think that way anymore. Not while those things are still in place, aimed everywhere, ready for launching.
> This is a bad enough thing for the people in my generation. We can put up with it, I suppose, since we must. We are moving along anyway, like it or not. I can even set aside my private fancy about hanging around, in midair.
> What I cannot imagine, what I cannot put up with, the thought that keeps grinding its way into my mind, making the Mahler into a hideous noise close to killing me, is what it would be like to be young. How do the young stand it? How can they keep their sanity? If I were very young, sixteen or seventeen years old, I think I would begin, perhaps very slowly and imperceptibly, to go crazy. (page 534)

With its syntactically complex sentences — as long as the "passages on all the strings" in Mahler's Ninth are said to be — the first passage is slow, meditative, graceful in its forward motion. The mind here is at its ease. In contrast, the second passage, composed of very short simple sentences or sentences built from short compounded phrases and clauses, is choppy, halting, irritable in its movement as well as its sentiment. Take note of such general differences as you read essays and try to relate the way an essay moves to its meaning.

Look also at your own writing in this regard. Are most of your sentences simple and short? Why? To what effect? Or are they mainly long and complex? Again, why and to what effect? (Remember, of course, that normally sentences should be varied in length and syntactical construction.) Having observed thus, you might wish to rewrite a passage just for the sake of its rhythm (or for sound if the sound is unmeaningfully jarring) if its rhythm — which you should be able to hear if you read your writing aloud — seems somehow out of keeping with your meaning: for example, if your sentences are mainly short and so rhythmically quick, but you are discussing a tragic killing and a funeral.

Consider as well what I call the *rhythm of closure,* which can help make the end of an essay particularly satisfying. I can't define this rhythm exactly, I'm afraid, but maybe I can exemplify it. Take the last paragraph of Wendell Berry's "Horse-Drawn Tools and the Doctrine of Labor Saving" (pages 137–43):

> I am, I think, as enthusiastic about the principle of adaptation as Mr. Butz. We differ only on the question of what should be adapted. He believes that we should adapt to the machines, that humans should be forced to conform to technological conditions or standards. I believe that the machines should be adapted to us — to serve our *human* needs as our history, our heritage, and our most generous hopes have defined them.

Now read the paragraph again, but this time stop before the dash in the last sentence. To my ear, the paragraph and thus the essay would seem truncated if it ended, "I believe that machines should be adapted to us." The paragraph needs what follows after the dash to bring it to a halt rhythmically, to give the ending the sense of an ending. You can develop this sense yourself by paying special attention to the endings of the essays you read, which you should do for rhetorical reasons as well — for instance, by reading

closing paragraphs aloud and observing what syntactical config-
urations lead to a strong stop at the end. Once you have developed
this sense of closure, it will help you attain something that is
always difficult to accomplish but always of value in terms of an
essay's effect on its readers — an ending that feels like an ending.
(This last phrase, I think, has the feel I mean.)

STYLE (DICTION AND SYNTAX)

Generally speaking, style is the cumulative by-product of all the
choices made by a writer and their effects. One writer writes a
narrative essay full of descriptive details and metaphors, an essay
that, in effect, is rich and sensuous; another presents a thesis and
supports it with definitions and examples, this second essay being
highly intellectual in effect. These are all matters of style or
stylistic choice. Specifically, style is the cumulative result of the
choices a writer makes with regard to diction and to syntax — that
is, to the kinds of words chosen and the sentence patterns they are
used to form — along with their effects. Diction and syntax are
particularly significant because both are instrumental in shaping
tone and voice, and syntax is also by far the most important
operative in the creation of prose rhythms. These effects are
beautifully demonstrated by Lincoln's "Gettysburg Address,"
perhaps his best-remembered piece of writing.

> Four score and seven years ago our fathers brought forth on this
> continent, a new nation, conceived in Liberty, and dedicated to
> the proposition that all men are created equal. Now we are
> engaged in a great civil war, testing whether that nation or any
> nation so conceived and so dedicated, can long endure. We are
> met on a great battlefield of that war. We have come to dedicate
> a portion of that field, as a final resting place for those who here
> gave their lives that that nation might live. It is altogether fitting
> and proper that we should do this. But, in a larger sense, we can
> not dedicate — we can not consecrate — we can not hallow —
> this ground. The brave men, living and dead, who struggled
> here have consecrated it, far above our poor power to add or
> detract. The world will little note, nor long remember what we
> say here, but it can never forget what they did here. It is for us
> the living, rather, to be dedicated here to the unfinished work

which they who fought here have thus far so nobly advanced. It is rather for us to be here dedicated to the great task remaining before us — that from these honored dead we take increased devotion to that cause for which they gave the last full measure of devotion — that we here highly resolve that these dead shall not have died in vain — that this nation, under God, shall have a new birth of freedom — and that government of the people, by the people, for the people, shall not perish from the earth.

The diction of the beginning of the speech is worth remarking. Lincoln might have begun, "Eighty-seven years ago" or even "Awhile back." But the diction of the second phrase is too informal for the occasion, too relaxed, and therefore out of keeping with Lincoln's subject. And the first phrase, though unobjectionable, is rather bland, whereas "Four score and seven" has the ring of the Old Testament prophets, which perhaps explains why it is such an arresting beginning. At any rate, the religious tone of the phrase is right for someone speaking of the hallowed dead and wishing to impress upon his audience with all the authority he can muster the necessity of giving themselves over to the cause so that those commemorated should not have died in vain.

Standard in its diction and straightforward in its syntax, the rest of the address has a tone of earnestness and the voice of sincerity. Pomposity and self-aggrandizement are precluded by Lincoln's diction and phrasing. Further, their very simplicity lends a stateliness to the utterance as it moves quietly yet emphatically from point to point. In sum, the voice of Lincoln's speech is that of a simple man roused to passionate conviction by the gravity of the moment.

We would be wrong, of course, to think of Lincoln's address as indeed the spontaneous outpouring of a simple man speaking from the heart, with no thought of matters of rhetoric and style. Clearly, the diction of the opening sentence was carefully calculated. And so was that of the rest of the speech: Lincoln created the voice of his address deliberately in light of the effect he desired to have. Lincoln's artistry is demonstrated in particular by one aspect of the syntax of his speech — its parallelism (or grouping of like thoughts into like constructions and patterns), the most prominent syntactical feature of the Old Testament. The address contains a number of instances of parallel construction, two of which are especially striking: "we can not dedicate — we can not consecrate — we can not hallow" and "of the people, by the people, for the people." Stylistically, parallelism tends to lend emphasis as well as a sense of sureness to the voice of a piece of writing. It also creates a rhythm of balance and suggests, thereby, a balanced, reasoning mind at work. And these are very much the effects of Lincoln's address. Then, too, parallel phrases and sentences, and sometimes even paragraphs, are often memorable because of their parallelism, as Lincoln's "government of the people, by the people, for the people" has proved to be.

Clearly, Lincoln was a master of words and verbal patterns. He is rightly considered a great prose stylist, one who could control the element of style and make it serve his purposes. Any way of putting words together will exhibit style of some sort — whether mature or childish, arresting or vapid, lively or dull. The trick is to control style, to choose words (a matter of diction) and to put them together (a matter of syntax) deliberately to create the tone and thence voice best suited to the purpose at hand as well as the right pace, or rhythm, and movement overall. Granted, style is elusive and difficult to master. But the more you read, the better the chance that you will grasp what constitutes various styles and what distinguishes them from each other. Then, perhaps, you will begin to look at your own writing from a stylistic point of view.

The two paragraphs that follow should help you toward this end. (You might also look back at the contrasting paragraphs on page 75.) Contrast them as to diction and syntax, and judge them as to the effectiveness of their respective styles overall. I am not revealing too much, I think, when I say that the second paragraph is much the better of the two. But why? This is for you to ponder.

In the next few minutes, it is my intention to do three things. First will be a description of the features of greatest salience of what is popularly called medicalese. Second will be a description of two consequences of that style. And third will be the presentation of one rule of great simplicity which if followed about 75% of the time would result in the transformation of medicalese into a prose of greater clarity that merely happened to be about medicine. A further intention in the presentation of the following is the illustration of that greater clarity of style. You have in your hands another version of what I will read, a version expressly written for the illustration of the differences between the style in use in this speech and in a prose style of utter straightforwardness.

In the next few minutes, I intend to do three things. First, I will describe the most salient feature of what is popularly called medicalese. Second, I will describe two consequences of that style. And third, I will present one very simple rule which if followed about 75% of the time would almost entirely transform medicalese into clear prose that merely happened to be about medicine. Furthermore, I intend to illustrate what I consider to be that clearer style in the way I present what follows. You have in your hands another version of what I will read, a version expressly written to differ from the style I am using now in the same way that medicalese differs from utterly straightforward prose.

MEANS OF SUPPORT

We have already considered how ideas can be developed and supported (see pages 37–42). In doing so, we looked at four ways in particular —*exemplification, definition, appeal to authority,* and *analogy*— which I exemplified with student samples. Here, I shall exemplify these same ways with samples from essays found hereafter.

Exemplification

We have taken up the subject of exemplification a number of times, both in Chapter 1 and here, in Chapter 2 (see "Examples and Other Concretions" as well as "Narration"). But the subject is so important that it cannot be discussed enough. As I say in Chapter 1, "examples are the lifeblood of essays." Isak Dinesen's "The Iguana" (pages 214–15) is a case in point. Indeed, this essay consists almost entirely of examples, all of which serve to support Dinesen's concluding statement: " 'I have conquered them all, but I am standing amongst graves.' " Here is the first of her examples:

> Once I shot an Iguana. I thought that I should be able to make some pretty things from his skin. A strange thing happened then, that I have never afterwards forgotten. As I went up to him, where he was lying dead upon his stone, and actually while I was walking the few steps, he faded and grew pale, all colour died out of him as in one long sigh, and by the time that I touched him he was grey and dull like a lump of concrete. It was the live impetuous blood pulsating within the animal, which had radiated out all that glow and splendour. Now that the flame was put out, and the soul had flown, the Iguana was as dead as a sandbag.

"Possession is one with loss" — Dante's fine phrase sums up Dinesen's point, the truth of which she drives home by giving us concrete instances, which help validate and support the essay's abstract idea.

Definition

As I put it in Chapter 1, "Definition, which can give rise to a thesis — that such and such is so and so — is also a way of developing and supporting a point." Take George Orwell's "Politics and the English Language" (pages 402-16). Orwell argues in this essay that the English language is in a bad way; he supports this thesis with examples of poor prose followed by definitions of terms that point to what is wrong with the prose cited. Here is his lead-in sentence and the beginning of his first definitional support:

> I list below, with notes and examples, various of the tricks by means of which the work of prose construction is habitually dodged:
> *Dying metaphors.* A newly invented metaphor assists thought by evoking a visual image, while on the other hand a metaphor which is technically "dead" (e.g. *iron resolution*) has in effect reverted to being an ordinary word and can generally be used without loss of vividness. But in between these two classes there

is a huge dump of worn-out metaphors which have lost all evocative power and are merely used because they save people the trouble of inventing phrases for themselves. Examples are: *Ring the changes on, take up the cudgels for, toe the line, ride roughshod over, stand shoulder to shoulder with, play into the hands of, no axe to grind, grist to the mill, fishing in troubled waters, rift within the lute, on the order of the day, Achilles' heel, swan song, hotbed.*

In part by way of example, Orwell defines "Dying metaphors" in order to support his primary point about bad writing, for the use of such metaphors as defined is clearly a mark of the writer's inattention and mental sloppiness. Generally, then, definition as well as exemplification, which is usually used in defining, is a way in which writers back up their judgments and support their ideas.

Appeal to Authority

Appeal to authority, remember, is the supporting of a point by way of what experts or revered personages have said or by the authority of immediate experience. As to experts and revered personages, William Zinsser supplies a fine example in his essay "Simplicity" (pages 625–29), in which he argues that prose should be simple and straightforward. He enlists Thoreau, one of America's greatest writers, to help support his (Zinsser's) contention thus:

> Simplify, simplify. Thoreau said it, as we are so often reminded, and no American writer more consistently practiced what he preached. Open *Walden* to any page and you will find a man saying in a plain and orderly way what is on his mind:
>
>> I love to be alone. I never found the companion that was so companionable as solitude. We are for the most part more lonely when we go abroad among men than when we stay in our chambers. A man thinking or working is always alone, let him be where he will. Solitude is not measured by the miles of space that intervene between a man and his fellows. The really diligent student in one of the crowded hives of Cambridge College is as solitary as a dervish in the desert.

As to experience as authority, the paragraph from Dinesen's "The Iguana" quoted in the subsection on exemplification (page 91) is an excellent example. Her appeal to her immediate experience carries a weight of authority, for it is not to be denied. Because one can hardly argue with such support if it is credible, the appeal to actual experience can be persuasive in arguing a general contention.

Analogy

Analogy is well exemplified by the following passage from John Ciardi's "Of Writing and Writers" (pages 150–53):

> The artist writes compulsively, as a way of knowing himself, or of clarifying what he does not know about himself. He writes, let us say, for those glimpses of order that form can make momentarily visible. But add that he writes in about the way a drunkard drinks. His passion springs not from reason, but from thirst.
>
> The artist-writer and the drunkard are both aware — if only in moments of painful sobriety — that there are consequences to what they do, but for both of them the doing itself is the real consequence.

Ciardi's point about the artist-writer is given shape and brought home by the analogy he draws between such a writer and a drunkard. Few of us know much about artists, but almost everyone knows something about drunkards. Ciardi's analogy, then, like all analogies, is a way of making a point in terms that an audience will grasp, as well as a way of developing and supporting that point as a passage moves on.

STRUCTURAL ELEMENTS

Here again, I shall exemplify with excerpts from essays in the anthology. The basic structural elements, recall, are: *chronology, spatial sequence, comparison and contrast, enumeration,* and *order of climax.*

Chronology

In January 1845, after a week of cold but brilliantly clear weather, it began to snow in southern Wyoming. Snow accumulated on the flat in a dead calm to a depth of four feet in only a few days. The day following the storm was breezy and warm — chinook weather. A party of Cheyenne camped in a river bottom spent the day tramping the snow down, felling cottonwood trees for their horses, and securing game, in response to a dream by one of them, a thirty-year-old man called Blue Feather on the Side of His Head, that they would be trapped by a sudden freeze.

That evening the temperature fell fifty degrees and an ice crust as rigid, as easily broken, as sharp as window glass formed over the snow. The crust held for weeks. (page 369)

Barry Lopez, "Buffalo"

Spatial Sequence

. . .[O]n the outskirts of Kassel, . . . there stands a palace large and splendid enough to house a full-blown emperor. And from the main façade of this palace there rises to the very top of the neighbouring mountain one of the most magnificent architectural gardens in the world. This garden, which is like a straight wide corridor of formal stone-work driven through the hillside forest, climbs up to a nondescript building in the grandest Roman manner, almost as large as a cathedral and surmounted by a colossal bronze statue of Hercules. Between Hercules at the top and the palace at the bottom lies an immense series of terraces, with fountains and cascades, pools, grottos, spouting tritons, dolphins, nereids and all the other mythological fauna of an eighteenth-century water-garden. (page 345)

Aldous Huxley, "Waterworks and Kings"

Comparison and Contrast

So Grant and Lee were in complete contrast, representing two diametrically opposed elements in American life. Grant was the modern man emerging; beyond him, ready to come on the stage, was the great age of steel and machinery, of crowded cities and a restless burgeoning vitality. Lee might have ridden down from the old age of chivalry, lance in hand, silken banner fluttering over his head. Each man was the perfect champion of his cause, drawing both his strengths and his weaknesses from the people he led.

Yet it was not all contrast, after all. Different as they were — in background, in personality, in underlying aspiration — these two great soldiers had much in common. Under everything else, they were marvelous fighters. Furthermore, their fighting qualities were really very much alike. (pages 147–48)

Bruce Catton, "Grant and Lee: A Study in Contrasts"

Enumeration

I liked Pooran Singh's forge, and it was popular with the Kikuyus, for two reasons.

First, because of the iron itself, which is the most fascinating of all raw materials, and sets people's imagination travelling on long tracks. The plough, the sword and cannon and the wheel, — the civilization of man — man's conquest of Nature in a nut, plain enough to be understood or guessed by the primitive people, — and Pooran Singh hammered the iron.

Secondly, the Native world was drawn to the forge by its song. The treble, sprightly, monotonous, and surprising rhythm of the blacksmith's work has a mythical force. It is so virile that it appals and melts the women's hearts, it is straight and unaffected and tells the truth and nothing but the truth. (pages 217–18)

Isak Dinesen, "Pooran Singh"

Note: Classification, which entails the breaking of something into its classes or types, always proceeds by enumeration. For example, I classify titles into six types in the next subsection and then enumerate each in turn. Any thesis that specifies a given number of types — for example, "There are five primary structural elements" — springs from classification and calls for enumeration (first, second, and so on) as to essay structure.

Order of Climax

Yet the idea does not die. Americans are not passive under their faults. We expose them and combat them. Somewhere every day some group is fighting a public abuse — openly and, on the whole, notwithstanding the FBI, with confidence in the First Amendment. The U.S. has slid a long way from the original idea. Nevertheless, somewhere between Gulag Archipelago and the featherbed of cradle-to-the-grave welfare, it still offers a greater opportunity for social happiness — that is to say, for well-being combined with individual freedom and initiative — than is likely elsewhere. The ideal society for which mankind has been striving through the ages will remain forever beyond our grasp. But if the great question, whether it is still possible to reconcile democracy with social order and individual liberty, is to find a positive answer, it will be here. (page 561)

Barbara Tuchman, "On Our Birthday — America as Idea"

Most of the essays grouped after this introduction exhibit one or another of these structural elements or several at once. When reading the essays, you can gain a good deal if you are alert to matters of structure: to enumeration when points are enumerated, to comparison and contrast and how each is carried out, to order of climax and its effect. By seeing these basic structures used well, you should be in a good position to use them well yourself. To further this end, you may wish to do some of the essay writing assignments that involve the imitation of the structure of a given essay, a possibility I shall elaborate on shortly.

TITLES

The title of an essay is the first thing that a reader sees, the element that first focuses the reader's attention and thinking. Therefore, as I noted in Chapter 1, titles are important and should not be neglected by you as reader or writer. As you might suspect, titles fall into a number of categories — six by my reckoning, some of which overlap. In thinking about the titles of essays you read and in forging titles of your own, consider the following types of title with respect to how each is formed and what each does.

1. A title may indicate — and the majority of titles do — the topic of an essay: "On Morality," "Families," "The Iks." By raising the question "What about it?" this type of title draws the reader to the essay's thesis statement, which provides the answer.

2. It is possible, however, for a title to point directly to a thesis without exactly stating it or to the conclusion drawn from arguing the thesis: Stephen Jay Gould's title "The Non-science of Human Nature," for instance, points us to the essay's thesis that there is no such thing as a "science" of human nature; Katherine Anne Porter's title "The Necessary Enemy" sums up her conclusion that hate is as necessary to human life as love is. In each case, the title clarifies what the author deems central to the essay at hand.

3. Titles may also be used for emphasis (the second and third categories overlap). Forster's title "My Wood" provides a good example. Of the four ill effects of owning property that Forster enumerates, the fourth — selfishness — is regarded by him as the most damnable: thus, Forster emphasizes this fourth effect by way of order of climax and his title (which should be heard with the stress on the first word).

4. Then, some titles are "grabbers," grabbing our attention and piquing our curiosity: for instance, "The Blood Lust," "We Have No 'Right to Happiness,'" "The Necessary Enemy," and best of all, "Sex, Drugs, Disasters, and the Extinction of the Dinosaurs." Titles that prove to be ironic with respect to the essays they head are also grabbers, albeit in retrospect: Swift's "A Modest Proposal" is such a title.

5. Further, a title may be figurative — metaphorical or symbolic. This kind of title may establish a metaphor to be developed in the essay proper or, perhaps, distill its meaning into a single image: Nancy Hill's title "Teaching as Mountaineering," for example, sets going the metaphor that pervades her essay; and Lilian Ross's title "The Vinyl Santa" comes to have symbolic significance in context, distilling all that the essay suggests is wrong with the way Americans celebrate Christmas.

6. The final type of title serves as thesis statement and by so serving allows the writer to bypass the beginning and plunge right into the middle. This possibility is exemplified by Alice Walker's title "Nuclear Madness: What You Can Do."

Walker's title says it all; therefore, she can begin directly with her argument, the resultant feeling of abruptness serving in this case to communicate a sense of urgency. You should try this last type of title and its resultant essay structure, as you should try all the other types enumerated here; but be aware that the title-as-thesis will work only in certain circumstances and should not be used simply to avoid the work of getting a sound beginning. Only an accomplished writer can use — I'm tempted to say "get away with" — this sixth class of title well; and if you are to become accomplished, you must master thesis presentation, which means that you must master beginnings.

THEME AND THESIS

The elements of the essay as just laid out are not ends in themselves. Obviously, no one reads an essay simply to see what examples are used or to determine its structural modality. Rather, the elements are a means of embodying a theme or expounding a thesis, depending on the essay in question. You already know what a thesis is from your reading of Chapter 1. In sum: A thesis is what an essay that argues a thesis argues, what its support material supports, what gives such an essay point and focus. Everything said in connection with your writing in the last chapter about the stating and arguing of a thesis applies equally to professional essays in which a thesis is argued — and *most* do present and support a thesis. However, there is a second type of essay of which you should be aware, one that does not expound a thesis but instead conveys and supports a theme.

The difference between a theme and a thesis is overtness: themes are implied; theses are stated in so many words. In his "REMark: Software Wildcats" (pages 163–66), for instance, Alan Cooper begins with a clear statement of the thesis he goes on to argue, a statement presented at the end of his first (funnel) paragraph:

Listening to some software developers, you'd think it's a jungle out there: Competition is fierce, the good niches are occupied, and precious few products remain to be written. I don't agree. Opportunities for software authors — and therefore for the computing public — have never been better.

In contrast, Hughes's "Salvation" conveys a theme, embodied especially in the following excerpt:

> I heard the songs and the minister saying: "Why don't you come? My dear child, why don't you come to Jesus? Jesus is waiting for you. He wants you. Why don't you come? Sister Reed, what is this child's name?"
>
> "Langston," my aunt sobbed.
>
> "Langston, why don't you come? Why don't you come and be saved? Oh, Lamb of God! Why don't you come?"
>
> Now it was really getting late. I began to be ashamed of myself, holding everything up so long. . . . So I decided that maybe to save further trouble, I'd better lie . . . and say that Jesus had come, and get up and be saved.
>
> So I got up.
>
> Suddenly the whole room broke into a sea of shouting, as they saw me rise. Waves of rejoicing swept the place. Women leaped in the air. My aunt threw her arms around me. The minister took me by the hand and led me to the platform.

In the adult world, the narrative here suggests, saying is sometimes as important as believing, and people are often fooled because of their own beliefs and desires. Such is Hughes's theme, nowhere stated but clearly implied by his narrative as it unfolds. Russell Baker's "Little Red Riding Hood Revisited" (pages 133–35) provides another example, the theme of Baker's essay ("theme" because it is not stated) being that the characteristic prose style of our day is marked by abstract diction and involuted syntax, and that this style is laughable. This theme Baker's own ironic style establishes and supports, as the following passage demonstrates:

> In an effort to make the classics accessible to contemporary readers, I am translating them into the modern American language. Here is the translation of "Little Red Riding Hood":

Once upon a point in time, a small person named Little Red Riding Hood initiated plans for the preparation, delivery and transportation of foodstuffs to her grandmother, a senior citizen residing at a place of residence in a forest of indeterminate dimension.

In the process of implementing this program, her incursion into the forest was in mid-transportation process when it attained interface with an alleged perpetrator. This individual, a wolf, made inquiry as to the whereabouts of Little Red Riding Hood's goal as well as inferring that he was desirous of ascertaining the contents of Little Red Riding Hood's foodstuffs basket. . . .

Though both are thematic, these last two essays are quite different in feel and the direction of their concerns: Hughes delves into the inner world of memory and childhood; Baker tackles the external world of public language and its misuse. This difference suggests a way of classifying and thinking about essays other than in terms of theme or thesis. I like to think of essays as being either *centrifugal* or *centripetal,* their energies moving either outward or inward, their sights focused either on the world external to the self or on the self. Accordingly, the centrifugal essay — whether it presents a thesis or conveys a theme — can be argued with or against: it could be argued, for instance, that the software market is saturated or that the characteristic prose style of our time is not laughable. Because the centripetal essay, in contrast, is personal, it is not open to refutation. "This is what happened when I was a boy," Hughes's essay implicitly declares, "and this is what it meant to me." One can hardly argue with that. Naturally, these two directions of energy and focus are sometimes mixed together in a single essay.

But to return to the primary distinction — that is, between theme and thesis — in reading an essay, judge early on whether it has a thesis or a theme. If you find no statement of thesis, then the essay must have a theme, which you should try to articulate as you read on and relate to the essay's elements. If the essay has a thesis — and whether or not it does will almost always be immediately apparent — underscore its thesis statement and watch how the rest of the essay relates to it point by point. In either case, try always to come to an understanding of how an essay is constructed as well as what its language does stylistically, or what elements go into its making and how they are used to embody a theme or argue a thesis. Then carry over what you have learned to your own writing.

WRITING ON AND AFTER ESSAYS

Before even thinking of writing, however, read the essay you are going to focus on carefully and well. That is, follow the steps specified in Chapter 1 and which I follow myself in discussing Forster's "My Wood." Then you should be ready to write. But write what? That depends on whether you intend to write on or after the given essay. Let me explain each possibility.

Writing *on* an essay generally involves a discussion of its theme or thesis and how the one is established and supported or the other supported and argued. If the essay you are going to write on is thematic, you could, for instance, state what its theme is, your statement of theme being *your* thesis; then, by analyzing the essay's elements, show how that theme is made manifest and supported; and conclude with a consideration of the essay's significance in general. For example, take the passage from Hughes's "Salvation" quoted on page 99. Hughes's theme, again, is that in the adult world, saying is sometimes as important as believing. That this *is* Hughes's theme could be *your* thesis. But how do we know that this is the theme? How is it established and how supported in the passage quoted and elsewhere in the essay? Such would be the concern of the middle of your paper: here you would want to talk especially about why the boy's calculated lie was not caught by the adults, blinded by their own enthusiasm (which is reflected in the sound and rhythm of the last paragraph of the passage quoted, both of which you could use as evidence); with regard to the essay's support, you could, for instance, define its kind of narration (first person) and discuss the authority of experience. In closing, you might bear witness to the validity of Hughes's theme with a relevant incident from your life, suggesting, thus, that the essay is of wide significance and of relevance to each of us in our journey to adulthood.

As to the essay that expounds a thesis, I will return to Forster's "My Wood" (pages 5–8), which you may wish quickly to review, for illustration of what writing on such an essay entails. Much could be written about this essay. You could, for instance, analyze how Forster gets his point across and why the essay is persuasive. To do so, you would need to consider the essay's main elements and how they work toward convincing the reader of the merit of Forster's position. In particular, you would want to look at audience, style, tone and voice, structure, and Forster's use of example and analogy. This is done in the first sample essay that follows, which is meant to show how to analyze the elements of an essay. You could also write a paper on the general significance of Forster's essay, your thesis being that ultimately the essay concerns by way of analogy the British Empire and its unfortunate effects on the British nation at large. This, of course, is the argument of the sample essay in Chapter 1 (pages 48–51). Or you could evaluate the essay, both its premise and its effectiveness. And much more. There may even be as many topics and possible theses as there are readers. At any rate, when you come to write on an essay — whether one with a theme or a thesis — write what you honestly think and feel. By staying in touch with yourself, you will stand a good chance of writing something worth reading.

Because essays are similar to what you are called upon to write, they offer a further possibility with respect to writing: that of imitation, or of writing *after* as well as *on*. I mentioned this possibility when considering "Structural Elements" because structure is particularly valuable to imitate. But you could also imitate voice, style, rhythm, or any other element prominent in an essay. Or you could imitate an essay in toto, which is what the second sample essay that follows does: in imitation of "My Wood," the essay, like Forster's, proceeds via a developed example and is structured enumeratively, incorporating the same transitions as are used in the essay it imitates. When you read the second sample essay, be sure to compare it with the original essay (pages 5–8) point by point. By so doing, I think you will see the purpose and value of imitation: while making clear the craft of the writer imitated, it helps one acquire craft oneself.

Friendly Persuasion

Funnel Beginning

Probably all writers hope for assent from their readers, even if the writer's primary aim is not to persuade but to inform or analyze. But for the writer who seeks to persuade, assent is the primary aim. Such a writer needs to use all of the means possible to win us over, for the force of an argument depends in large measure on the skill of the writer in arguing the case at hand. E. M. Forster's "My Wood" provides a fine example of persuasive prose, or of how a writer who looks to persuade goes about the business of persuasion. Through a calculated treatment of voice, tone, and diction as well as through structuring and style,

Thesis

Forster sways us toward accepting his point of view.

Topic Sentence

One of the charms of Forster's essay, certainly, is its warm, congenial voice.

Support

Here is a reasonable man, one thinks, a man who is honest with both himself and his readers and who does not take himself too seriously. Such a revelation as "I dared not murder her" convinces one of the speaker's openness and self-depreciation. It does so because of its meaning, of course, but also because of its bluntness in terms of diction. Indeed, the

Support

congeniality of the essay's voice results

in large part from its diction—that of good conversational English, neither condescendingly pompous nor self-ingratiatingly chummy.

Support   The tone of the essay, too (for example, that of the very human and very British "Blast it"), contributes to a sense of openness and congeniality, or to a feeling that the speaker is likable, trustworthy, and truly dedicated to seeking the truth.

Support   All in all, the voice of "My Wood," created by diction and tone (as well as syntax, which I will turn to shortly), makes me, for one, want to agree with its argument. I like the speaker and feel that I can trust him; so liking and feeling, I am inclined to give my assent. And that is the point: "My Wood" is a remarkably persuasive essay in good part because of its appealing voice.

Transition and Topic Sentence   The essay's overall structure is also appealing and a little miraculous.

Support   It is appealing because it is completely clear, completely coherent. There are no gaps here, no sudden flights that leave the reader behind; everything follows one, two, three. The essay's structure, thus, is at one with its voice in creating a sense of a reasonable mind at work, or of a mind reasoning as opposed to merely asserting. This, too, inclines one to assent.

Support   Yet, as I have stated, the essay's structure is also a little miraculous, for Forster here turns one of the most mundane and purely expository of structures—enumeration, unabashedly emphasized by the paragraphing—into a vehicle for something like poetic insight. That is, the very clarity of the structure of "My Wood" communicates a sense of the personhood of its speaker, his sensibility and the workings of his mind. Because that mind shows itself to be capable of profound thought and yet is always orderly and direct, we are swayed still more toward giving our assent to Forster's arguments.

Topic Sentence

Finally, there is the style of "My Wood," style being specifically a matter of diction and syntax. I have characterized

Support

Forster's diction already as that of "good conversational English" and pointed to its effect on voice. But there is still more to be said about the diction of "My Wood." That of good conversational English, Forster's vocabulary produces a conversational tone. This is not the diction of a moral lecture or a formal treatise, but of a friend talking cheerfully, though earnestly, to friends. Consequently, we don't feel that our arm is being twisted to get our assent; the persuasion is gentle, friendly persuasion, adult to adult. Forster's syntax also

Support

contributes to the tone and thence voice of the essay. Syntactically straightforward (as well as of average length and grammatical complexity), Forster's sentences are a model of lucidity. Though his allusions and references might escape the beginning reader, even such a reader could not help but understand the meaning of Forster's sentences otherwise. These are the sentences of a man who respects his reader and who wishes to be understood. Elegant in its simplicity, Forster's

syntax, like his diction, is that of a
friend addressing friends. His is a style
well suited to persuasion.

A writer, like Forster, who seeks to
persuade must be a master of the craft of
persuasion, which means a master of the
elements that go into the making of an
essay. For of the three basic types of
expository writing (informational,
analytic, and persuasive), the third hangs
most on the reader's response. Whether
Forster was, in fact, a warm, friendly
human being who was totally open and
genuine I do not know. All I know is that
he was an excellent writer, one who could
create the voice of a warm, friendly human
being totally open and genuine. But this
is what persuasion is about: we are
persuaded as much by the skill of the
writer as by the truth of what is said. If
we realize as much, then we can better give
our assent when appropriate and withhold it
when rhetoric is simply a tool of
manipulation.

Reverse
Funnel
Ending

My Car
(After E. M. Forster)

Maíréad Mensching

Funnel
Beginning

Thesis

Two summers ago, I bought a 1973
Volkswagen Superbeetle with what little
money I had in savings. It was my first
car, so I was excited. Little did I
know what I was getting myself into. I
now realize that car ownership is a

responsibility I'm not ready for; it's just too stressful.

Transition
Topic
Sentence

Support

Support
(and
point)

Transition
Topic
Sentence

Support

Support

Support
(and
point)

Transition
Topic
Sentences

Support

Support
(and
point)

In the first place, owning a car made me feel terribly burdened. It had to be cleaned at least once a month, the gas tank always seemed to need filling, the coolant level had to be checked before every trip, and, of course, the oil needed to be changed frequently. Buy yourself a car, especially a used car, and run yourself ragged.

In the second place, owning a car made me want a better car. Since I had started with an old used car, my next car, I thought, should be a late model, maybe from the mid '80's. But, if it's going to be that new, I fantasized, why not buy one brand new, right off the assembly line? Although I could hardly afford my VW, I planned out which luxury options I would get, what shiny color I would choose, and what kind of dreamy interior. The thought of my dream car made me look at my VW with disgust. So, the more I daydreamed, the greater the stress I felt when I returned to the reality of what I was driving.

In the third place, owning my car made me feel that I should do something to it. After my initial excitement wore off, I looked at my VW and saw nothing but room for improvement. A paint job was a must—who wants to drive an orange car?—as was an AM/FM stereo—who wants plain old AM? Such things cost money, of course, and since I had spent all that I had left after buying the car in a splurge of creativity fixing it up, I had nothing left over to

pay for the brakes when they failed. So
much for self-expression, which is just
another name for increased stress.

**Transition
Topic
Sentence
Support
by
Contrast**

This brings me to my fourth and final
point: the engine, or its ingratitude.

I felt I had a real rapport with my
engine. I talked to it every morning and
showed sympathy when it stalled, rattled,
or made strange noises. I even prayed for

Support

it. And what did I get in return? One
cold December morning, I turned the key and
the ungrateful engine would not turn over!
It simply stopped responding to the
ignition key. There I was with fifteen

**Support
(and
point)**

minutes to get to my first class and no way
of getting there. Talk about stress! Talk
about ingratitude!

**Transition
Lead-in**

Oh, I know I should have taken the
damned thing to a mechanic and had it gone
over. But I just didn't have the time.

Summary

And that's my whole point. What with
burdensome errands, daydreaming, splurges
of creative effort, and praying, I didn't
have time for anything; and not having
time put me in a constant state of stress.

**Rounding
Back**

But that's all in the past. I had my
Superbeetle towed away, and I'm glad I did.
Now I can relax and enjoy life again as I
ride my bicycle. A bicycle, I find,
requires much less upkeep and far less
responsibility (not to mention stress).

ESSAYS FOR STUDY AND WRITING ASSIGNMENTS

SOME STUDENT ESSAYS

THE FIRST SIX ESSAYS BELOW ARE BY STUDENTS LIKE YOU. AS WELL written as any of the essays by professionals that follow thereafter, these student pieces should give you an idea of what at least some of your contemporaries are doing. Any of these essays could serve as a model for you to pattern something of your own after.

✤ THE GUIDETTE ✤
Lisa Donofrio

THERE SHE GOES, MY FAVORITE GUIDETTE ON CAMPUS. SHE MUST BE   1
a Gina, Maria, Luisa, Theresa — one of those names that end in
i-a and sound natural when their boyfriends preface them with
"Yo." Definitely not a Harriet or an Anne. She's a HOT
BABE. At least, that's what her T-shirt says. Oh, here it comes,
the true test of the perfect guidette: can she walk up the quad

steps while chewing gum and simultaneously applying purple eyeshadow without tripping on her three-inch white pumps or splitting her jeans? Whew, she made it! Oh, and look. . . . The back of her T-shirt says "BRONX GIRLS, BEST IN THE WORLD." The T-shirt is nice. But what will she do in the winter? I don't think they make sweaters in neon pink.

She is in my history class. I saw her there yesterday. I turned round because there was a deafening explosion in my left ear. I came face to face with fuchsia lipstick, foundation makeup lines, and a big pink bubble that popped in my face. I lost all sense of reality for a moment (at least my reality). She leaned back to admire her matching fuchsia nails. My hearing returned and I looked back at the professor once more.

Later I saw her in a Bon-Jovi T-shirt. She was telling her friend, named something *i-a*, about the concert the night before. According to her, it was a "pissa," the height of pop entertainment. But how could you expect anything but a great night from music idols who are the paragons of masculinity, stuffing socks down the crotch of their leather pants and looking prettier than half the girls on campus?

She was quite pleased with herself. She managed to push her way to the front row, she told her friend, and get onstage and into the backstage party. From the hundreds of Ginas, Marias, Luisas, and Theresas, she was picked to go to bed with the lead singer's head bodyguard. "I was smart, though. I made him use protection. He said he would get me backstage for the Madison Square Garden concert. Do you think he'll call? God! I hope Tony doesn't find out. He's so possessive. When he picked me up in his Trans-Am today, he wouldn't even kiss me because I wore these jeans. He would have made me go home and change except that we didn't have enough time because he had to drive back to his house because he forgot his brush and gold chain." I turned around and asked if she had heard about the red-alert hair spray shortage. A wave of terror overtook her. The bell rang for the next class — religion, for me, which I strolled to contemplating a vision of Jesus saving the world and bringing everyone to heaven in yellow Camaros.

I wonder what guidettes major in. I can't see them writing 5
a research paper; I can't see them reading anything besides
Cosmopolitan; I can't even imagine them driving a car, much
less designing an engine. But they graduate somehow. Some
enter the corporate world. Some even go on to medical or law
school. I can see it now, guidette lawyers suing their fathers for
depriving them of a sweet sixteen party with alcohol at
Leonard's or Vinny's Clam Bar. And oh, my goodness, these
guidettes will marry guidos and have little guidos and guidettes
who will go to school with my children. I'm seized by panic
when I think of a possible future: my eight-year-old son coming
home from school, saying, "Yo, ma, be a good broad and get me
a brew."

[1988 – U.S.A.]

Questions

1. What does Donofrio set out to do in "The Guidette" (gwē-dĕt',
   derived from "Guido")? In what way could this essay be thought of
   as a definition? What does it define?
2. Why did Donofrio not give her focal character a name? How does
   the Guidette's not having a name tie in with the purpose of the
   essay?
3. Contrast "The Guidette" with "Pooran Singh" (pages 217–19).
   Both are character sketches, but they are very different otherwise.
   How do they differ in mood and aim?
4. "The Guidette" is a satire. What makes it satirical? Why is it funny?

Writing Assignments

1. In two or more paragraphs, contrast "The Guidette" and "Pooran
   Singh" (pages 217–19). Focus on the difference in aim between the
   two essays, a difference that can be gotten at especially by a
   consideration of the fact that Donofrio does not give her focal
   character a name.
2. Write a paper in which you sketch your best friend. You will want
   to individuate with details and examples.
3. Write an essay in which you define a given type of character by way
   of a satirical portrait. Try to make your portrait as specific and
   detailed as Donofrio's, and see if you can't make it funny as well.

------------- ✣ PARTY BUDDIES ✣ -------------

Edward Hoyt

I BECAME A PARTY BUDDY LAST WEEKEND AT AN UPTOWN IRISH BAR. 1
For I possess the one virtue needed under the circumstance.

"Dude-man, you're Irish, aren't you?" I was asked.   2

"Uh, yeah, Irish-American," I answered.   3

"AWRIGHT!" my interrogator shot back. "What coun- 4
try?"

"Um, Nassau," I replied, referring to my parent's home on 5
Long Island.

As question marks appeared above my compatriot's head, I 6
kind of regretted my aloofness. He may have been ignorant, but
he was friendly. Hadn't he referred to me as "brother" in
between the repeated slaps on my back? So, though my impulse
was to bail out, I stuck around as he tried to explain to another
brother exactly where in Boston he came from.

"No, Dude, not there!" he yelled. "That's niggertown."   7

I hit the street, cursing myself for not trusting my first 8
instinct. As I walked, I wondered: Are any of these third and
fourth generation American Celtics any more Irish than the
basketball team that goes by that name? Does the mere fact that
we have ancestors from the same island make this racist my
brother? What is the nature of the bond between party
buddies?

As to the last question, I'm sure that they must have a like 9
ancestry, be it Italian, German, or Spanish. Party buddies are
not only Irish-Americans; they are found in all ethnic groups.
Then, to be a party buddy, one must be or at least appear to be
as stupid as one's buddy. If you seem stupid enough, you are
declared "brother." If you seem stupid and crack a beer, you
are "Bud brothers" (or Bud-dies). And if, in your stupidity, you
smoke a spliff, you are "doobie brothers." Third, then, you
must drink and/or smoke along with your buddy. This buddy
system always entails a false sense of camaraderie-induced-by-

mood-altering-substances. Finally, and most important, you must behave in such a way and say whatever is necessary to convince your "friend" that you share beliefs entirely and that your mutual world view is entirely correct. Party buddies want to believe that theirs is the only valid way of life.

And if that way is somehow questioned, they can turn on a 10 dime. For instance, take my "dude-man" buddy of the other night. As I got up to leave, he said, "Where ya going? You offended by something?" Lying through my teeth, I said, "Naw, I just gotta get home." "Bull," he said, "you took offense at what I said. I can see it now. You're a god damned . . . abolitionist!" He turned away and moved down the bar. "B-b-but aren't you my buddy?" I pleaded ironically. He didn't reply, but acted as though he had never seen me. So much for glad hands, good-time pals, and party buddies wherever they're found.

[1989 — U.S.A.]

Questions

1. What is defined in this essay? Contrast serves definition here. How so?
2. What is the chief means of support used in this essay? What structural elements does Hoyt employ?
3. What is the overall point of this essay? How does Hoyt make this point?
4. Is the essay effective? Why or why not?

Writing Assignments

1. Write an essay in definition in which you distinguish between two states: acquaintanceship, say, and friendship, or friends and best friends. Your object will be to clarify the meaning of the second term of your chosen contrast.
2. Take a survey of your classmates about their definitions of liberty, say, or happiness, or the "American dream." Then write up your findings with the intention of defining your chosen concept. Remember that your goal will be definition, though your definition, no doubt, will express your point of view, as Hoyt's does his.

————✤ ORGANIZATIONAL CULTURES: ✤————
A CONTRAST
Laura Lalaina

F OR THE PAST TWO AND ONE-HALF YEARS, I HAVE BEEN A PART-TIME   1
bank teller. For the first two years I was employed at Yorkville
Federal Savings and Loan; for the past six months I have been
at The American Savings Bank. Why did I leave Yorkville to do
the exact same job at American Savings? Not money, for the
salaries are comparable. What then? The answer is that I could
no longer stand the *culture* of Yorkville Savings. I changed jobs
in order to change organizational cultures.

As defined by H. Koontz and H. Weihrich, *organizational*   2
culture is "the general pattern of behavior, beliefs, and values
that members of an organization have in common" (*Management,* 9th ed.). Further, Koontz and Weihrich hold that there
are two types of organizational culture: weak and strong.

YFSL has a weak culture, which I came to understand a   3
few months after I started on the job. I was slow at first because
I didn't know the routine or how to work the computer, so I
didn't notice that the experienced tellers moved little faster than
I. After a few months, however, I became a speed demon on the
computer, but the other tellers moved at the same slow pace.
Jokingly, I made a comment to the teller next to me about her
speed. She shot back, "Listen, I'm not killing myself for
anyone. I get the same pay whether I work fast or slow. Let the
customers wait!"

The assistant managers, Liz Smith and Marge Mehr, were   4
no better. Many customers voiced complaints about them,
saying things like: "Those two are as slow as molasses." "Ms.
Smith must *still* be on her coffee break." "Smith and Mehr must
hold a record for goldbricking." At first I defended my bosses,
but then I realized that the customers were right. Whether
consciously or subconsciously, Marge and Liz felt that, since

they were the bosses, they could take long breaks whenever they wanted to. They preached speed, but their practice belied their preaching. And it was their practice that most of the tellers took to heart.

Unable to tolerate this "weak" culture any longer, I rang in 5 the new year by getting another job. Although you may think that a bank is a bank is a bank, and though what I do at American Savings is exactly what I did at YFSL, the difference in organizational culture between the two is dramatic. At ASB the tellers' motto is "Work fast and get the customers out promptly." And the assistant managers, Frank Olds, Allison Nigel, and Susan Wrobel, are nothing less than paragons of efficiency. All three are fully professional and, though warm and friendly, strict bosses when the bank is busy. I've not heard a single customer complain about them or about the service of the tellers under them. Consequently, the atmosphere at ASB is upbeat and positive.

In sum, my experience highlights the two types of 6 organizational culture, weak and strong. A weak culture is marked by an every-man-for-himself attitude. A weak culture sponsors the feeling that one should get away with as much as possible, or that one should not do any more than the minimum amount of work. In consequence, customers are dissatisfied and a negative atmosphere prevails. A strong culture, on the other hand, promotes camaraderie and a sense of pulling together to get a job done. A strong culture focuses on achievement and reinforces one's sense of self-worth when one works well. Most important, perhaps, a strong culture fosters a positive atmo- sphere, making work a pleasure and so inspiring people to do their best. Both types of culture, then, feed on themselves: a weak culture creates a negative atmosphere, causing employees to work slowly, at a minimum level, which only increases the negativity; a strong culture creates a positive atmosphere, causing employees to do their best and thereby engendering a sense of pride and so further accentuating the positive. Though a weak culture requires less effort, it is far less rewarding than a strong culture in terms of job satisfaction. I don't know about you, but I would rather work hard and feel satisfied than shirk and watch the clock all day waiting for quitting time.

[1989 — U.S.A.]

Questions

1. The first paragraph here exemplifies the funnel beginning. How so?
2. What is the two-part theme of this essay? How does its title help establish the theme? What structural element does it entail? Why this element?
3. What is the function of the second paragraph? What means of support used in the essay as a whole does the paragraph incorporate? What other means of support permeates the essay?
4. How does the contrast rendered here proceed?
5. This essay moves from exemplification to generalization. What is the rhetorical effect of this kind of procedure? Is it an effective strategy with regard to persuading a reader?

Writing Assignments

1. Write an essay *after* "Organizational Cultures: A Contrast." First, establish a contrast; then, dividing your material into blocks (A and B), present specific examples; finally, in a C section, make the contrast in general terms. Serving as your conclusion, your generalization, of course, must be based on the specification of blocks A and B.
2. Write an essay in which you reverse Lalaina's procedure: that is, begin with a generalization and move to specific examples that make the contrast implied by your theme or stated in your thesis. The focus of this paper should be on the difference between things generally deemed exactly alike.

✛ THREE MONTHS WITH THE ABOTO ✛
M. T. Masucci

HAVING LIVED AMONG SOUTHWEST AFRICA'S ABOTO PEOPLE FOR   1
three months, I have learned much about them. First, they are
a harmless people who subsist on the vegetation and animals
around them. Second, they are literal communists, sharing
everything they have with each other and doing whatever they
do for the good of the tribe. And third, though close knit, the
Aboto welcome strangers and coexist peacefully with the many
white settlers who surround their territory.

As to the first point, the Aboto are peaceful hunters and   2
gatherers. Each morning, Aboto villages are emptied as Aboto
men and women go off in separate directions to find food. The
women gather grasses, nuts, and berries, while the men hunt
down wild boars and iguanas. Hunting, however, is the only
aggressive action allowed in the tribe. On my first day with the
Aboto, I was given one rule: violence is never permissible;
violence of any kind leads automatically to expulsion from the
Aboto land.

Absence of aggression between tribal members fosters   3
tribal unity. "I am because we are, and because we are, I am"
is the creed by which every Aboto lives — lives peacefully with
his or her fellows. Like a well-oiled machine of many parts, the
tribe works because of this sense of unity. Everyone contributes
to the life of the community and everything is shared by all. As
a result of their creed, the Aboto have survived in the
Southwest African wilds for many centuries.

Although the Aboto are close knit, they are not closed-   4
minded when dealing with strangers. In the past eighty years,
French, English, and Dutch settlers have settled in territories
that surround Aboto land. And never once has there been
trouble between the settlers and these peaceful hunter-gather-
ers. The Aboto-Ka (tribal elder) told me that as long as "the
pale ones" act the way human beings should, the Aboto are
content to live next to them.

I myself was received most warmly by these people. When 5 I arrived at their main village, I was immediately surrounded by laughing children. And when, over the first meal I was given, I revealed that my plan was to study them by day while spending my nights at one of the settlements, they immediately invited me to live with them so as to get to know them better than a daytime guest ever could.

My three-month stay with the Aboto as an Aboto was one 6 of the best periods of my life. To be sure, the work was hard and the sun was hot. But such things pale to nothing when one feels that, as we say in Aboto, "Kwe-Ha" — life is good.

[1990 — U.S.A.]

Questions

1. How is this essay structured? What in the thesis paragraph accounts for its coherence?
2. Paragraphs 3, 4, 5, and 6 do not begin with transitions. Why? How *are* they related?
3. To what extent does Masucci use detail? What do the essay's details serve to do?
4. Is the way the essay ends satisfying? Why or why not?

Writing Assignments

1. Write a short essay in which you detail some experience you have had with people very different from yourself. Be as specific as possible in describing them and relating your reactions to them.
2. Write a thesis paragraph like that of this essay — that is, with three statements that will be expanded upon subsequently — and then write a paper accordingly. See if you can't write it without the need for paragraph transitions. Analyze "Three Months with the Aboto" in this regard and try to proceed as Masucci does. However, use transitions if your material does not hold together of its own accord.

✦ DIALECTICAL SPIRITUALITY ✦
MaryAnn McCarra

IN CHILDHOOD, WE HAVE LITTLE CHOICE BUT TO BELIEVE WHAT WE'RE   1
told, especially in matters of religion. For us Catholics, the idea
of God as Father — that is, as male — is ingrained as soon as we
can lisp and make the sign of the cross. Impressed upon even
the smallest of children is the maleness of the power that
controls the universe — the sun, the moon, and the dear green
earth. And the language of the Church has a distinctly male
bias. For instance, I remember being assured that one day I
would be "a soldier of Christ." To be sure, this emphasis on
God as Father, as male, is tempered somewhat by the Virgin
Mary, who, though less important, still merits two important
prayers. Saints and Martyrs, too, can be female. But I was
drawn to male power; so it was the spectacular though rather
cloudy picture of St. Sebastian in the *Lives of the Saints* that
haunted my imagination and not that of the Little Flower
quietly hemorrhaging to death. I was no young feminist,
however, seeking power for myself. I idolized my God as I
idolized my father. The strength and pain I was made to see in
Christ through my mother's vivid description of the crucifixion
caused love and pity to well up in me. I trusted in the love and
redeeming power of God as I trusted in the strength and
protective power of my father.

In my teenage years, my faith in God as well as in my father   2
diminished, though faith still remained, albeit somewhat
changed. The earth, eternally rolling in its appointed course,
took all my imagination. My falling away from many of the
religious conceptions of my childhood stemmed, I think, from a
desire to know God in a tangible way. I started to feel God in
nature — in storms, in the roll of the oceans, in all of the energy
of the world. The hope of resurrection subtly modulated into a
sense of the regeneration of all things in nature, the cycle of
birth and decay ever renewing the greening of the world. The

regeneration that I could witness all around gave me a sense of sustenance that rote prayer never had. I never felt alone in the presence of clouds, falling snow, or the green leaf-tips of early spring. Prayer was then the awareness of all of nature around me, stretching, winding, curving, growing. I was part of nature, too, a young thing growing into her own.

But now, this second phase of my spirituality seems 3 incomplete, for it now seems to lack the human presence and humanity of my childhood Redeemer. Yet I cannot return to the religion of my childhood, with all its fears and superstitions. What I need, I now see, is a sense of Christ *in this world*, of nature imbued with His presence. I need to feel God as Christ in all of the humanity of His life on this earth. Even thinking this thought makes Him seem nearer. I feel both the sanctity of creation and the presence of the Creator.

[1988 — U.S.A.]

Questions

1. What does "dialectical" mean as used here? (Check your dictionary for "Hegelian dialectic.") Why does this essay consist of three paragraphs? How do its title and last sentence sum up its structure and progression?

2. Why does "Dialectical Spirituality" seem authentic? What role does detail play in this regard?

3. What type of structure governs this essay aside from its dialectical pattern? What are the markers of this type? Where does it leave us at the end of the essay? How does where we are left effect a sense of an ending?

Writing Assignments

1. Write an essay tracing the history of your religious beliefs or of why you have rejected such beliefs. Be specific (use McCarra as a model in this regard) and end, as she does, with your present understanding of matters of religion.

2. Write an essay in imitation of the present essay's dialectical pattern — statement, counterstatement, and synthesis. Some topics that might be suitable for this kind of treatment are your views of your

parents as a child, a teenager, and now; your changing views of siblings; your coming to understand the growth process itself; what you were in the past, how you differ now, and what you can project becoming in the future in light of the interaction of past and present.

✤ My Summer Job ✤
Claire McMahon

THIS SUMMER, I HAD THE GOOD FORTUNE OF GETTING THE 1 opportunity to taste high-class living — or so I thought at the outset. I was hired as a waitress at a ritzy "members only" country club on Long Island. Thinking that I would somehow acquire millions by helping an old dowager and consequently being left her estate, say, or simply by marrying a member of the club, I walked into this job with a dazzling smile. However, my fantasy was cut short, for I soon realized that working for the rich brings no benefits at all, much less fringe benefits.

To begin with, the salary was terrible — five dollars for 2 bowing to bitches. As for tips, forget it! I soon found that the rich don't tip — for aren't tips taken care of in the members' dues? Dues or no dues, I got nothing from those greedy bastards, except, of course, for insults and complaints about my service.

In the second place, I gained ten pounds on the job. I had 3 thought that it would help me firm up my figure. Running from table to table, standing there taking orders, and cleaning up would surely get me in shape. No go. My tables were next to one another, I learned to memorize orders in a week, and all clean-up was done by a cleaning crew at night. The only exercise I got was hand-to-mouth, shoving in the gourmet food that the members only pecked at.

In the third place, I knew that I had turned sour, and I 4 didn't like myself like that. Disenchanted with millionaires, I struggled not to pour coffee into the laps of my assigned members. These members, *my* members, sat and ate at my tables day after day. I knew them by name, by dish, by perfume or after shave. In gratitude, they begged my attention by yelling, "Hey, Missey!" I would then trot over to their thrones like an obedient dog. I didn't like having turned sour, but I liked being an obedient dog (the cause) even less. The only enjoyment I had from this whole fiasco was dancing on bagel rounds in the kitchen, then tucking the chips into baskets and placing them on my favorite members' tables.

And then there's my last and greatest grievance: the 5 memories of my otherwise decrepit members.

Like elephants, they remembered everything, every spill, 6 every slip-up. One woman even had the gall to remind me of a saltshaker I tipped over on my very first day working at the club. And what do you think her husband was doing while she was engaged in this bit of nostalgia? "Hubby" was sneaking a squeeze of my newly-chubby behind. I had to quit this job for my sanity, not to mention my figure! Luckily, summer was just about over anyway. And now the new semester has begun. I never thought I'd say it, but it's nice to be back at school.

[1989 — U.S.A.]

Questions

1. What kind of a beginning does this essay have?
2. Comment on the diction here. What kind of tone does the diction help create?
3. There is much irony in "My Summer Job." What of the title in this regard? What of such words as "favorite" (paragraph 4) and "nostalgia" (paragraph 6)? How does irony here help mold tone and voice?
4. This essay has some interesting sound and rhythmic effects: for instance, "five dollars for bowing to bitches" and " 'Hubby' was sneaking a squeeze of my newly-chubby behind." How do these effects contribute to the making of tone and voice?
5. What is McMahon's main structural mode? How does she keep the essay's structure in mind? What other type of structure marks the essay overall?

6. Comment on McMahon's use of detail. What comic touches does she include? To what effect?

7. The ending of this essay seems particularly satisfying. Why?

Writing Assignments

1. Write a paragraph or more on the tone and thence voice of "My Summer Job." How are tone and voice established here? What effect do they have?

2. Have you ever had a job you hated? If so, write an essay about it patterned on McMahon's with regard to structure (and use the same transitions she uses). Use concrete details all along the way and try to make your essay as lively and engaging as the one at hand.

✤ COURT DAY ✤

William O'Connell

IF YOU WALK TO THE CORNER, YOU GET A PRETTY GOOD VIEW OF Yankee Stadium. If you walk around the corner, you get a pretty good view of police and corrections officers hustling bodies to trials or bookings. 251 West 161 Street is the address of Bronx Criminal Court and Bronx Central Booking.

It's not what I expected a courthouse to be like. It looks like a Greek temple, except, instead of priests and crowds of the devout, there are various court officers hanging around for security, I guess, and police officers hanging out waiting for their cases to be called.

I went to courtroom AR 9. There was no problem getting in: all that was needed was a quick explanation of my intention and the court officer admitted me. The court I was in was called by Police Officer Michael Cody of the Bronx Task Force "a court for minor offenses."

This is not Perry Mason's or even "The People's" court. It's more like the dean's office. The first thing anyone would notice is the judge's bench, which is totally out of proportion with the rest of the room and its contents. Surrounding the bench are several regular-sized desks: to the right, the court officer's desk; to the left, the stenographer's; and in front, a long desk the only purpose of which I could discern being to keep people as far away as possible from his majesty.

There's no room for a large audience because of the size of 5 the judge's bench. In all, about thirty people could fit in the room. I was sitting in the back as people filtered in. First about ten uniformed patrolmen came in in succession; then, some fifteen civilians — the motley crew of defendants — came in piecemeal. Some of them seemed not to have a care in the world while others, especially a father whose son was caught stealing fireworks, were overwrought. Again, especially the father — he was concerned not only about his son but also about his lawyer, who was busy associating himself with the gypsy cab driver in front of me.

Here we all waited together. And we waited and waited and 6 waited. Judge Felix — I learned his name from Court Officer O'Donnell — was the missing ingredient, the captain without whom the ship could not sail, the key without which the engine of the court could not run. He, we were informed, was in his chambers next to the courtroom, probably (I thought) on the phone making plans for his lunch.

Finally, we were graced with his presence. Everyone stood, 7 Court Officer O'Donnell mumbled something out, and we were on our way. First off was a young man with a summons for drinking in public. The man pleaded guilty and the judge promptly gave him a $25.00 fine. The teenager with his dad and lawyer also pleaded guilty and got his fine reduced after a long-winded statement from the lawyer. A tall man who had been caught with an ounce of marijuana pleaded guilty with an explanation. After his explanation he was summarily fined $100.00. Fifteen minutes had gone by and the judge had not looked up once. For a minute I even thought that he might have dozed off. But he was awake all right, but punch drunk from the whole scenario. He didn't really listen; he just went through the motions by rote.

Judge Felix finally did look up and looked annoyed as well. 8
The defendant who had been summoned to court for not having
a motor vehicle tax sticker in his gypsy cab couldn't speak
English. The judge motioned to the court officer and in a few
minutes he returned with a short, neatly dressed Spanish
woman. She was briefed on the situation and then the theatrics
began. The judge, the defendant, and the Spanish woman
began a web of discussion that was impossible to follow. And
the whole thing proved to be much ado in any case. The cab
driver produced the proper sticker and that was that: "Not
Guilty." As to the woman, she stayed and translated for one
more defendant, then went about her business, which I
assumed was translating in one and then another courtroom.
Later, my friend Cody told me that she is in fact a cleaning
woman in the building.

All in all, it was a frustrating and disappointing experience. 9
Many of the police I saw came to court poorly prepared — at
best with notes they couldn't decipher half of the time — and
spoke with as much authority as a bunch of ten-year-olds. The
judge just seemed to be a sour grape. But what most turned me
off was the motley crowd of defendants and their attitude
toward the court and the system of justice it represents. If I had
to face this bunch every day, I guess I'd turn sour too.

According to Police Officer Cody, upwards of fifty- 10
thousand cases come through this one building alone in a year.
That is a staggering load for society, for the judicial system, and
for that cleaning woman too.

[1989 — U.S.A.]

Questions

1. Why doesn't O'Connell tell us anything about his case? How does
   his attitude toward the judge change by the end of the essay? Why
   does it change? What theme does this narrative essay build to?

2. What tone(s) do you detect here? How does diction affect our sense
   of tone? What of the anti-climax in the last paragraph in this regard?
   How does tone help to establish the theme of the essay?

3. What metaphors do you find here? What function do they serve? What function do such details as the naming of names and the description of the setting have?

4. Account for the paragraphing here paragraph by paragraph. Is the paragraphing effective? How so? How does the paragraphing highlight the essay's primary structural mode? How does the last paragraph bring the essay to a firm close?

Writing Assignments

1. In a paragraph or short paper, write an evaluation of "Court Day." Address such questions as the following: Is the essay coherent? Does it have a discernible structure? Does O'Connell keep things in proper focus with regard to his theme? Does his essay communicate precisely or in some vague way if at all? What flaws (if any) does it have? All in all, is it a successful essay, one worth reading, or isn't it worth the bother?

2. Find a topic like O'Connell's ("my day at the races," for instance, or "the first time I visited a hospital"), and write a narrative essay in which you recount what happened to you but also what you learned. Use "Court Day" as a model, especially with regard to concreteness and particularity.

PROFESSIONAL ESSAYS

——✤ THE WARFARE IN THE FOREST ✤——
IS NOT WANTON
Brooks Atkinson

AFTER THIRTY-FIVE YEARS THE FOREST IN SPRUCE NOTCH IS TALL AND   1
sturdy. It began during the Depression when work gangs
planted thousands of tiny seedlings in abandoned pastures on
Richmond Peak in the northern Catskills. Nothing spectacular
has happened there since; the forest has been left undisturbed.

But now we have a large spread of Norway spruces a foot   2
thick at the butt and 40 or 50 feet high. Their crowns look like
thousands of dark crosses reaching into the sky.

The forest is a good place in which to prowl in search of   3
wildlife. But also in search of ideas. For the inescapable fact is
that the world of civilized America does not have such a clean
record. Since the seedlings were planted the nation has fought
three catastrophic wars, in one of which the killing of
combatants and the innocent continues.[1] During the lifetime of
the forest 350,000 Americans have died on foreign battlefields.

Inside America civilized life is no finer. A President, a   4
Senator, a man of God have been assassinated. Citizens are
murdered in the streets. Riots, armed assaults, looting, burning,
outbursts of hatred have increased to the point where they have
become commonplace.

Life in civilized America is out of control. Nothing is out of   5
control in the forest. Everything complies with the instinct for
survival — which is the law and order of the woods.

Although the forest looks peaceful it supports incessant   6
warfare, most of which is hidden and silent. For thirty-five

---

[1] The Vietnam War.

years the strong have been subduing the weak. The blueberries that once flourished on the mountain have been destroyed. All the trees are individuals, as all human beings are individuals; and every tree poses a threat to every other tree. The competition is so fierce that you can hardly penetrate some of the thickets where the lower branches of neighboring trees are interlocked in a blind competition for survival.

Nor is the wildlife benign. A red-tailed hawk lived there last   7 summer — slowly circling in the sky and occasionally drawing attention to himself by screaming. He survived on mice, squirrels, chipmunks and small birds. A barred owl lives somewhere in the depth of the woods. He hoots in midmorning as well as at sunrise to register his authority. He also is a killer. Killing is a fundamental part of the process. The nuthatches kill insects in the bark. The woodpeckers dig insects out. The thrushes eat beetles and caterpillars.

But in the forest, killing is not wanton or malicious. It is for   8 survival. Among birds of equal size most of the warfare consists of sham battles in which they go through the motions of warfare until one withdraws. Usually neither bird gets hurt.

Nor is the warfare between trees vindictive. Although the   9 spruces predominate they do not practice segregation. On both sides of Lost Lane, which used to be a dirt road, maples, beeches, ashes, aspens and a few red oaks live, and green curtains of wild grapes cover the wild cherry trees. In the depths of the forest there are a few glades where the spruces stand aside and birches stretch and grow. The forest is a web of intangible tensions. But they are never out of control. Although they are wild they are not savage as they are in civilized life.

For the tensions are absorbed in the process of growth, and 10 the clusters of large cones on the Norway spruces are certificates to a good future. The forest gives an external impression of discipline and pleasure. Occasionally the pleasure is rapturously stated. Soon after sunrise one morning last summer when the period of bird song was nearly over, a solitary rose-breasted grosbeak sat on the top of a tall spruce and sang with great resonance and beauty. He flew a few rods to another tree and continued singing: then to another tree where he poured out his matin again, and so on for a half hour. There was no practical motive that I was aware of.

After thirty-five uneventful years the spruces have created 11 an environment in which a grosbeak is content, and this one said so gloriously. It was a better sound than the explosion of bombs, the scream of the wounded, the crash of broken glass, the crackle of burning buildings, the shriek of the police siren.

The forest conducts its affairs with less rancor and 12 malevolence than civilized America.

[1986 — U.S.A.]

Questions

1. What age-old puzzle does Atkinson here meditate upon? What is his theme? What is the focus of his meditation and what his means of support?
2. What kind of structure governs this essay? What points of dissimilarity between the natural world and the human are brought out?
3. Given the historical setting (which is what, exactly?), did Atkinson have reason to "lament," as Wordsworth put it, "What man has made of man"? How so?
4. Paragraphs 8 and 12 make the same point. What is it? Why the repetition?

Writing Assignments

1. Write an essay addressed to the human quandary that of all of the species, we are the only one that is wantonly destructive. Why? Is there any hope that our destructive impulses can become constructive? Why or why not?
2. Have you ever meditated on the nature of human kind? If so, write a paper on your thinking. Provide concrete examples, with some, perhaps, involving contrast with the rest of creation as we see it.

✛The Plot Against People✛

Russell Baker

INANIMATE OBJECTS ARE CLASSIFIED SCIENTIFICALLY INTO THREE MAJOR   1
categories — those that break down, those that get lost, and
those that don't work.

The goal of all inanimate objects is to resist man and   2
ultimately to defeat him, and the three major classifications are
based on the method each object uses to achieve its purpose. As
a general rule, any object capable of breaking down at the
moment when it is most needed will do so. The automobile is
typical of the category.

With the cunning peculiar to its breed, the automobile   3
never breaks down while entering a filling station which has a
large staff of idle mechanics. It waits until it reaches a
downtown intersection in the middle of the rush hour, or until
it is fully loaded with family and luggage on the Ohio Turnpike.
Thus it creates maximum inconvenience, frustration, and
irritability, thereby reducing its owner's lifespan.

Washing machines, garbage disposals, lawn mowers, fur-   4
naces, TV sets, tape recorders, slide projectors — all are in
league with the automobile to take their turn at breaking down
whenever life threatens to flow smoothly for their enemies.

Many inanimate objects, of course, find it extremely   5
difficult to break down. Pliers, for example, and gloves and
keys are almost totally incapable of breaking down. Therefore,
they have had to evolve a different technique for resisting man.

They get lost. Science has still not solved the mystery of   6
how they do it, and no man has ever caught one of them in the
act. The most plausible theory is that they have developed a
secret method of locomotion which they are able to conceal
from human eyes.

It is not uncommon for a pair of pliers to climb all the way   7
from the cellar to the attic in its single-minded determination to

raise its owner's blood pressure. Keys have been known to burrow three feet under mattresses. Women's purses, despite their great weight, frequently travel through six or seven rooms to find hiding space under a couch.

Scientists have been struck by the fact that things that 8 break down virtually never get lost, while things that get lost hardly ever break down. A furnace, for example, will invariably break down at the depth of the first winter cold wave, but it will never get lost. A woman's purse hardly ever breaks down; it almost invariably chooses to get lost.

Some persons believe this constitutes evidence that inani- 9 mate objects are not entirely hostile to man. After all, they point out, a furnace could infuriate a man even more thoroughly by getting lost than by breaking down, just as a glove could upset him far more by breaking down than by getting lost.

Not everyone agrees, however, that this indicates a 10 conciliatory attitude. Many say it merely proves that furnaces, gloves and pliers are incredibly stupid.

The third class of objects — those that don't work — is the 11 most curious of all. These include such objects as barometers, car clocks, cigarette lighters, flashlights and toy-train locomotives. It is inaccurate, of course, to say that they *never* work. They work once, usually for the first few hours after being brought home, and then quit. Thereafter, they never work again.

In fact, it is widely assumed that they are built for the 12 purpose of not working. Some people have reached advanced ages without ever seeing some of these objects — barometers, for example — in working order.

Science is utterly baffled by the entire category. There are 13 many theories about it. The most interesting holds that the things that don't work have attained the highest state possible for an inanimate object, the state to which things that break down and things that get lost can still only aspire.

They have truly defeated man by conditioning him never to 14 expect anything of them. When his cigarette lighter won't light or his flashlight fails to illuminate, it does not raise his blood pressure. Objects that don't work have given man the only peace he receives from inanimate society.

[1968 — U.S.A.]

Questions

1. How is what Baker does in the first paragraph apt given the stance he takes (that is, as a scientist)? What kind of structure does the first paragraph inevitably give rise to?
2. What means of support is used here? What other kind of structure is operative in the essay?
3. Paragraph 5 is transitional. How so? What figure of speech dominates "The Plot Against People"? Why?
4. Characterize the voice of this essay. How does Baker make it clear from the outset that the essay is intended to be humorous?

Writing Assignments

1. How frustrating mechanical objects can be and how much they sometimes seem to have a life of their own! In a paragraph or more, write a narrative account of some humorous encounter you have had with some thing that seemed self-willed and utterly perverse.
2. Using Baker's essay as your model as to form, write an essay on "types of humor" or "types of laughter." What you write may be amusing, but it may also become earnest depending on the direction of your thought.

———✦ LITTLE RED RIDING HOOD ✦———
REVISITED
Russell Baker

IN AN EFFORT TO MAKE THE CLASSICS ACCESSIBLE TO CONTEMPORARY   1
readers, I am translating them into the modern American
language. Here is the translation of "Little Red Riding Hood":

Once upon a point in time, a small person named Little Red   2
Riding Hood initiated plans for the preparation, delivery and
transportation of foodstuffs to her grandmother, a senior citizen
residing at a place of residence in a forest of indeterminate
dimension.

In the process of implementing this program, her incursion   3
into the forest was in mid-transportation process when it
attained interface with an alleged perpetrator. This individual,
a wolf, made inquiry as to the whereabouts of Little Red Riding
Hood's goal as well as inferring that he was desirous of
ascertaining the contents of Little Red Riding Hood's foodstuffs basket, and all that.

"It would be inappropriate to lie to me," the wolf said,   4
displaying his huge jaw capability. Sensing that he was a mass
of repressed hostility intertwined with acute alienation, she
indicated.

"I see you indicating," the wolf said, "but what I don't see   5
is whatever it is you're indicating at, you dig?"

Little Red Riding Hood indicated more fully, making one   6
thing perfectly clear — to wit, that it was to her grandmother's
residence and with a consignment of foodstuffs that her mission
consisted of taking her to and with.

At this point in time the wolf moderated his rhetoric and   7
proceeded to grandmother's residence. The elderly person was
then subjected to the disadvantages of total consumption and
transferred to residence in the perpetrator's stomach.

"That will raise the old woman's consciousness," the wolf   8
said to himself. He was not a bad wolf, but only a victim of an

oppressive society, a society that not only denied wolves' rights, but actually boasted of its capacity for keeping the wolf from the door. An interior malaise made itself manifest inside the wolf.

"Is that the national malaise I sense within my digestive 9 tract?" wondered the wolf. "Or is it the old person seeking to retaliate for her consumption by telling wolf jokes to my duodenum?" It was time to make a judgment. The time was now, the hour had struck, the body lupine cried out for decision. The wolf was up to the challenge. He took two stomach powders right away and got into bed.

The wolf had adopted the abdominal-distress recovery 10 posture when Little Red Riding Hood achieved his presence.

"Grandmother," she said, "your ocular implements are of 11 an extraordinary order of magnitude."

"The purpose of this enlarged viewing capability," said the 12 wolf, "is to enable your image to register a more precise impression upon my sight systems."

"In reference to your ears," said Little Red Riding Hood, 13 "it is noted with the deepest respect that far from being underprivileged, their elongation and enlargement appear to qualify you for unparalleled distinction."

"I hear you loud and clear, kid," said the wolf, "but what 14 about these new choppers?"

"If it is not inappropriate," said Little Red Riding Hood, "it 15 might be observed that with your new miracle masticating products you may even be able to chew taffy again."

This observation was followed by the adoption of an 16 aggressive posture on the part of the wolf and the assertion that it was also possible for him, due to the high efficiency ratio of his jaw, to consume little persons, plus, as he stated, his firm determination to do so at once without delay and with all due process and propriety, notwithstanding the fact that the ingestion of one entire grandmother had already provided twice his daily recommended cholesterol intake.

There ensued flight by Little Red Riding Hood accompa- 17 nied by pursuit in respect to the wolf and a subsequent intervention on the part of a third party, heretofore unnoted in the record.

Due to the firmness of the intervention, the wolf's stomach 18 underwent ax-assisted aperture with the result that Red Riding Hood's grandmother was enabled to be removed with only minor discomfort.

The wolf's indigestion was immediately alleviated with 19 such effectiveness that he signed a contract with the intervening third party to perform with grandmother in a television commercial demonstrating the swiftness of this dramatic relief for stomach discontent.

"I'm going to be on television," cried grandmother.   20

And they all joined her happily in crying, "What a 21 phenomena!"

[1979 — U.S.A.]

Questions

1. Why should the classics need to be translated "into the modern American language"?
2. Comment on the overall diction of the present "translation." With respect to diction, what does the essay satirize?
3. What else is satirized here? For instance, what is the satiric point of paragraph 8? What is the satiric point of the error in the last three words of the essay?
4. What kind of voice does the diction here produce? Is the voice that of the author or of an imagined speaker? How do you know?
5. What contrasting type of diction is found in the essay? Where? Why?
6. What theme underlies this essay? Formulate it in a sentence or two and tell what leads you to this conclusion.

Writing Assignments

1. In brief, translate a fairy tale of your own choosing into language like Baker's. Then translate it again into slang. Finally, write a paragraph on the difference in effect between your two translations.
2. Rewrite the second to fifth paragraphs of "Little Red Riding Hood Revisited" in plain English. Then write a paragraph commenting on the difference between the two versions.

3. This essay is a satire. Write a paragraph or more on what it satirizes and how it does so.

4. An interesting question raised by this piece is, is it an essay? What, exactly, distinguishes an essay from, say, a short story? Write a paper considering this question and using "Little Red Riding Hood Revisited" as a case in point.

✤ HORSE-DRAWN TOOLS ✤
AND THE DOCTRINE OF LABOR SAVING
Wendell Berry

FIVE YEARS AGO, WHEN WE ENLARGED OUR FARM FROM ABOUT TWELVE   1 acres to about fifty, we saw that we had come to the limits of the equipment we had on hand: mainly a rotary tiller and a Gravely walking tractor; we had been borrowing a tractor and mower to clip our few acres of pasture. Now we would have perhaps twenty-five acres of pasture, three acres of hay, and the garden; and we would also be clearing some land and dragging the cut trees out for firewood. I thought for a while of buying a second-hand 8N Ford tractor, but decided finally to buy a team of horses instead.

I have several reasons for being glad that I did. One reason   2 is that it started me thinking more particularly and carefully than before about the development of agricultural technology. I had learned to use a team when I was a boy, and then had learned to use the tractor equipment that replaced virtually all the horse and mule teams in this part of the country after World War II. Now I was turning around, as if in the middle of my own history, and taking up the old way again.

Buying and borrowing, I gathered up the equipment I   3 needed to get started: wagon, manure spreader, mowing machine, disk, a one-row cultivating plow for the garden. Most of these machines had been sitting idle for years. I put them back into working shape, and started using them. That was 1973. In the years since, I have bought a number of other horse-drawn tools, for myself and other people. My own outfit now includes a breaking plow, a two-horse riding cultivator, and a grain drill.

As I have repaired these old machines and used them, I have seen how well designed and durable they are, and what good work they do. When the manufacturers modified them for use with tractors, they did not much improve either the machines or the quality of their work. (It is necessary, of course, to note some exceptions. Some horsemen, for instance, would argue that alfalfa sod is best plowed with a tractor. And one must also except such tools as hay conditioners and chisel plows that came after the development of horse-drawn tools had ceased. We do not know what innovations, refinements, and improvements would have come if it had continued.) At the peak of their development, the old horse tools were excellent. The coming of the tractor made it possible for a farmer to do more work, but not better. And there comes a point, as we know, when *more* begins to imply *worse*. The mechanization of farming passed that point long ago — probably, or so I will argue, when it passed from horse power to tractor power.

The increase of power has made it possible for one worker to crop an enormous acreage, but for this "efficiency" the country has paid a high price. From 1946 to 1976, because fewer people were needed, the farm population declined from thirty million to nine million; the rapid movement of these millions into the cities greatly aggravated that complex of problems which we now call the "urban crisis," and the land is suffering for want of the care of those absent families. The coming of a tool, then, can be a cultural event of great influence and power. Once that is understood, it is no longer possible to be simpleminded about technological progress. It is no longer possible to ask, What is a good tool? without asking at the same time, How *well* does it work? and, What is its influence?

One could say, as a rule of thumb, that a good tool is one that makes it possible to work faster *and* better than before. When companies quit making them, the horse-drawn tools fulfilled both requirements. Consider, for example, the

International High Gear No. 9 mowing machine. This is a horse-drawn mower that certainly improved on everything that came before it, from the scythe to previous machines in the International line. Up to that point, to cut fast and to cut well were two aspects of the same problem. Past that point the speed of the work could be increased, but not the quality.

I own one of these mowers. I have used it in my hayfield at 7 the same time that a neighbor mowed there with a tractor mower; I have gone from my own freshly cut hayfield into others just mowed by tractors; and I can say unhesitatingly that, though the tractors do faster work, they do not do it better. The same is substantially true, I think, of other tools: plows, cultivators, harrows, grain drills, seeders, spreaders, etc. Through the development of the standard horse-drawn equipment, quality and speed increased together; after that, the principal increase has been in speed.

Moreover, as the speed has increased, care has tended to 8 decline. For this, one's eyes can furnish ample evidence. But we have it also by the testimony of the equipment manufacturers themselves. Here, for example, is a quote from the public relations paper for one of the largest companies: "Today we have multi-row planters that slap in a crop in a hurry, putting down seed, fertilizer, insecticide and herbicide in one quick swipe across the field."

But good work and good workmanship cannot be accom- 9 plished by "slaps" and "swipes." Such language seems to be derived from the heman vocabulary of TV westerns, not from any known principles of good agriculture. What does the language of good agricultural workmanship sound like? Here is the voice of an old-time English farmworker and horseman, Harry Groom, as quoted in George Ewart Evans's *The Horse in the Furrow:* "It's all rush today. You hear a young chap say in the pub: 'I done thirty acres today.' But it ain't messed over, let alone done. You take the rolling, for instance. Two mile an hour is fast enough for a roll or a harrow. With a roll, the slower the better. If you roll fast, the clods are not broken up, they're just pressed in further. Speed is everything now; just jump on the tractor and way across the field as if it's a dirt-track. You see it when a farmer takes over a new farm: he goes in and plants straight-away, right out of the book. But if one of the old farmers took a new farm, and you walked round the land with him and asked him: 'What are you going to plant here and here?' he'd look at you some queer; because he wouldn't plant nothing much at first. He'd wait a bit and see what the land was like: he'd *prove* the land first. A good practical man would hold on for a few weeks, and get the feel of the land under his feet. He'd walk on it and feel it through his boots and see if it was in good heart, before he planted anything: he'd sow only when he knew what the land was fit for."

Granted that there is always plenty of room to disagree 10 about farming methods, there is still no way to deny that in the first quotation we have a description of careless farming, and in the second a description of a way of farming as careful — as knowing, skillful, and loving — as any other kind of high workmanship. The difference between the two is simply that the second considers where and how the machine is used, whereas the first considers only the machine. The first is the point of view of a man high up in the air-conditioned cab of a tractor described as "a beast that eats acres." The second is that of a man who has worked close to the ground in the open air of the field, who has studied the condition of the ground as he drove over it, and who has cared and thought about it.

If we had tools thirty-five years ago that made it possible to 11 do farm work both faster and better than before, then why did we choose to go ahead and make them no longer better, but just bigger and bigger and faster and faster? It was, I think, because we were already allowing the wrong people to give the wrong answers to questions raised by the improved horse-drawn machines. Those machines, like the ones that followed them, were *labor savers*. They may seem old-timey in comparison to today's "acre eaters," but when they came on the market they greatly increased the amount of work that one worker could do in a day. And so they confronted us with a critical question: How would we define labor saving?

We defined it, or allowed it to be defined for us by the 12 corporations and the specialists, as if it involved no human considerations at all, as if the labor to be "saved" were not human labor. We decided, in the language of some experts, to look on technology as a "substitute for labor." Which means that we did not intend to "save" labor at all, but to *replace* it, and to *displace* the people who once supplied it. We never asked what should be done with the "saved" labor; we let the "labor market" take care of that. Nor did we ask the larger questions of what values we should place on people and their work and on the land. It appears that we abandoned ourselves unquestioningly to a course of technological evolution, which would value the development of machines far above the development of people.

And so it becomes clear that, by itself, my rule-of-thumb 13 definition of a good tool (one that permits a worker to work both better and faster) does not go far enough. Even such a tool can cause bad results if its use is not directed by a benign and healthy social purpose. The coming of a tool, then, is not just a cultural event; it is also an historical crossroad — a point at which people must choose between two possibilities: to become more intensive or more extensive; to use the tool for quality or for quantity, for care or for speed.

In speaking of this as a choice, I am obviously assuming 14 that the evolution of technology is *not* unquestionable or uncontrollable; that "progress" and the "labor market" do *not* represent anything so unyielding as natural law, but are aspects of an economy; and that any economy is in some sense a "managed" economy, managed by an intention to distribute the benefits of work, land, and materials in a certain way. (The present agricultural economy, for instance, is slanted to give the greater portion of these benefits to the "agribusiness" corporations. If this were not so, the recent farmers' strike would have been an "agribusiness" strike as well.) If those assumptions are correct, we are at liberty to do a little historical supposing, not meant, of course, to "change history" or "rewrite it," but to clarify somewhat this question of technological choice.

Suppose, then, that in 1945 we had valued the human life 15
of farms and farm communities 1 percent more than we valued
"economic growth" and technological progress. And suppose
we had espoused the health of homes, farms, towns, and cities
with anything like the resolve and energy with which we built
the "military-industrial complex." Suppose, in other words,
that we had really meant what, all that time, most of us and
most of our leaders were saying, and that we had really tried to
live by the traditional values to which we gave lip service.

Then, it seems to me, we might have accepted certain 16
mechanical and economic limits. We might have used the
improved horse-drawn tools, or even the small tractor equipment that followed, not to displace workers and decrease care
and skill, but to intensify production, improve maintenance,
increase care and skill, and widen the margins of leisure,
pleasure, and community life. We might, in other words, by
limiting technology to a human or a democratic scale, have been
able to use the saved labor *in the same places where we saved it.*

It is important to remember that "labor" is a very crude, 17
industrial term, fitted to the huge economic structures, the
dehumanized technology, and the abstract social organization
of urban-industrial society. In such circumstances, "labor"
means little more than the sum of two human quantities, human
energy plus human time, which we identify as "man-hours."
But the nearer home we put "labor" to work, and the smaller
and more familiar we make its circumstances, the more we
enlarge and complicate and enhance its meaning. At work in a
factory, workers are only workers, "units of production"
expending "man-hours" at a task set for them by strangers. At
work in their own communities, on their own farms or in their
own households or shops, workers are *never* only workers, but
rather persons, relatives, and neighbors. They work *for* those
they work *among* and *with.* Moreover, workers tend to be
independent in inverse proportion to the size of the circumstance in which they work. That is, the work of factory workers
is ruled by the factory, whereas the work of housewives, small
craftsmen, or small farmers is ruled by their own morality, skill,

and intelligence. And so, when workers work independently and at home, the society as a whole may lose something in the way of organizational efficiency and economies of scale. But it begins to *gain* values not so readily quantifiable in the fulfilled humanity of the workers, who then bring to their work not just contracted quantities of "man-hours," but qualities such as independence, skill, intelligence, judgment, pride, respect, loyalty, love, reverence.

To put the matter in concrete terms, if the farm communi- 18 ties had been able to use the best horse-drawn tools to save labor in the true sense, then they might have used the saved time and energy, first of all, for leisure — something that technological progress has given to farmers. Second, they might have used it to improve their farms: to enrich the soil, prevent erosion, conserve water, put up better and more permanent fences and buildings; to practice forestry and its dependent crafts and economies; to plant orchards, vineyards, gardens of bush fruits; to plant market gardens; to improve pasture, breeding, husbandry, and the subsidiary enterprises of a local, small-herd livestock economy; to enlarge, diversify, and deepen the economies of households and homesteads. Third, they might have used it to expand and improve the specialized crafts necessary to the health and beauty of communities: carpentry, masonry, leatherwork, cabinetwork, metalwork, pottery, etc. Fourth, they might have used it to improve the homelife and the home instruction of children, thereby preventing the hardships and expenses now placed on schools, courts, and jails.

It is probable also that, if we *had* followed such a course, we 19 would have averted or greatly ameliorated the present shortages of energy and employment. The cities would be much less crowded; the rates of crime and welfare dependency would be much lower; the standards of industrial production would probably be higher. And farmers might have avoided their present crippling dependence on money lenders.

I am aware that all this is exactly the sort of thinking that 20 the technological determinists will dismiss as nostalgic or wishful. I mean it, however, not as a recommendation that we "return to the past," but as a criticism of the past; and my criticism is based on the assumption that we had in the past, and that we have now, a *choice* about how we should use technology and what we should use it for. As I understand it, this choice depends absolutely on our willingness to limit our desires as well as the scale and kind of technology we use to satisfy them. Without that willingness, there is no choice; we must simply abandon ourselves to whatever the technologists may discover to be possible.

The technological determinists, of course, do not accept 21 that such a choice exists — undoubtedly because they resent the moral limits on their work that such a choice implies. They speak romantically of "man's destiny" to go on to bigger and more sophisticated machines. Or they take the opposite course and speak the tooth-and-claw language of Darwinism.[1] Ex-secretary of agriculture Earl Butz speaks, for instance, of "Butz's Law of Economics" which is "Adapt or Die."

I am, I think, as enthusiastic about the principle of 22 adaptation as Mr. Butz. We differ only on the question of what should be adapted. He believes that we should adapt to the machines, that humans should be forced to conform to technological conditions or standards. I believe that the machines should be adapted to us — to serve our *human* needs as our history, our heritage, and our most generous hopes have defined them.

[1981 — U.S.A.]

Questions

1. What audience do you imagine Berry had in mind for this essay? What is its general tone? (Consider especially the long parenthesis in paragraph 4, the beginning of paragraph 10, and paragraph 20 as to tone.) How are tone and voice here audience-directed?

---

[1]*Darwinism:* The reference is to Darwin's theory of "the survival of the fittest," applied by Social Darwinists to all human endeavors.

2. This essay opens (paragraphs 1–4) with a personal anecdote leading to the thesis statement. What is that statement? Is this an effective way to begin?

3. What is the function of paragraph 5? What kind of appeal and what type of structure does Berry use in paragraph 18? What role does definition play in this essay?

4. What kind of evidence does Berry enumerate to support his contention about farm machinery? Is the evidence convincing? Why or why not?

5. Several paragraphs here contain unsupported assertions. What, for instance, of paragraph 5 in this regard? In paragraph 5, Berry intimates a secondary thesis. What is it? Does it help clarify or does it only complicate the issue unduly?

6. How is the essay structured overall? How does Berry handle this structure? Why this way rather than another?

7. What kind of ending does "Horse-Drawn Tools" have? Why this kind? (Consider the targeted audience in answering.) To what does Berry appeal in the last sentence? The essay could end with the phrase "to serve our *human* needs." Why doesn't it?

Writing Assignments

1. Are you convinced by Berry's argument? Write a paragraph or more telling why you are or aren't convinced.

2. Read Glenn Gould's "Music and Technology" (pages 256–61) and then write a paper contrasting Berry's and Gould's views on the subject of technological progress.

3. What is "progress"? Write an essay defining the word as you think it should be defined, weighing your definition against the way the word is actually used.

✠ GRANT AND LEE: ✠
A STUDY IN CONTRASTS
Bruce Catton

WHEN ULYSSES S. GRANT AND ROBERT E. LEE MET IN THE PARLOR   1
of a modest house at Appomattox Court House, Virginia, on
April 9, 1865, to work out the terms for the surrender of Lee's
Army of Northern Virginia, a great chapter in American life
came to a close, and a great new chapter began.

These men were bringing the Civil War to its virtual finish.   2
To be sure, other armies had yet to surrender, and for a few
days the fugitive Confederate government would struggle
desperately and vainly, trying to find some way to go on living
now that its chief support was gone. But in effect it was all over
when Grant and Lee signed the papers. And the little room
where they wrote out the terms was the scene of one of the
poignant, dramatic contrasts in American history.

They were two strong men, these oddly different generals,   3
and they represented the strengths of two conflicting currents
that, through them, had come into final collision.

Back of Robert E. Lee was the notion that the old   4
aristocratic concept might somehow survive and be dominant in
American life.

Lee was tidewater Virginia, and in his background were   5
family, culture, and tradition . . . the age of chivalry transplanted to a New World which was making its own legends and
its own myths. He embodied a way of life that had come down
through the age of knighthood and the English country squire.
America was a land that was beginning all over again, dedicated
to nothing much more complicated than the rather hazy belief
that all men had equal rights and should have an equal chance
in the world. In such a land Lee stood for the feeling that it was
somehow of advantage to human society to have a pronounced
inequality in the social structure. There should be a leisure
class, backed by ownership of land; in turn, society itself should

be keyed to the land as the chief source of wealth and influence. It would bring forth (according to this ideal) a class of men with a strong sense of obligation to the community; men who lived not to gain advantage for themselves, but to meet the solemn obligations which had been laid on them by the very fact that they were privileged. From them the country would get its leadership; to them it could look for the higher values — of thought, of conduct, of personal deportment — to give it strength and virtue.

Lee embodied the noblest elements of this aristocratic ideal.   6 Through him, the landed nobility justified itself. For four years, the Southern states had fought a desperate war to uphold the ideals for which Lee stood. In the end, it almost seemed as if the Confederacy fought for Lee; as if he himself was the Confederacy . . . the best thing that the way of life for which the Confederacy stood could ever have to offer. He had passed into legend before Appomattox. Thousands of tired, underfed, poorly clothed Confederate soldiers, long since past the simple enthusiasm of the early days of the struggle, somehow considered Lee the symbol of everything for which they had been willing to die. But they could not quite put this feeling into words. If the Lost Cause, sanctified by so much heroism and so many deaths, had a living justification, its justification was General Lee.

Grant, the son of a tanner on the Western frontier, was   7 everything Lee was not. He had come up the hard way and embodied nothing in particular except the eternal toughness and sinewy fiber of the men who grew up beyond the mountains. He was one of a body of men who owed reverence and obeisance to no one, who were self-reliant to a fault, who cared hardly anything for the past but who had a sharp eye for the future.

These frontier men were the precise opposite of the   8 tidewater aristocrats. Back of them, in the great surge that had taken people over the Alleghenies and into the opening Western country, there was a deep, implicit dissatisfaction with a past that had settled into grooves. They stood for democracy, not from any reasoned conclusion about the proper ordering of human society, but simply because they had grown up in the middle of democracy and knew how it worked. Their society might have privileges, but they would be privileges each man had won for himself. Forms and patterns meant nothing. No man was born to anything, except perhaps to a chance to show how far he could rise. Life was competition.

Yet along with this feeling had come a deep sense of   9 belonging to a national community. The Westerner who developed a farm, opened a shop, or set up in business as a trader, could hope to prosper only as his own community prospered — and his community ran from the Atlantic to the Pacific and from Canada down to Mexico. If the land was settled, with towns and highways and accessible markets, he could better himself. He saw his fate in terms of the nation's own destiny. As its horizons expanded, so did his. He had, in other words, an acute dollars-and-cents stake in the continued growth and development of his country.

And that, perhaps, is where the contrast between Grant 10 and Lee becomes most striking. The Virginia aristocrat, inevitably, saw himself in relation to his own region. He lived in a static society which could endure almost anything except change. Instinctively, his first loyalty would go to the locality in which that society existed. He would fight to the limit of endurance to defend it, because in defending it he was defending everything that gave his own life its deepest meaning.

The Westerner, on the other hand, would fight with an 11 equal tenacity for the broader concept of society. He fought so because everything he lived by was tied to growth, expansion, and a constantly widening horizon. What he lived by would survive or fall with the nation itself. He could not possibly stand by unmoved in the face of an attempt to destroy the Union. He would combat it with everything he had, because he could only see it as an effort to cut the ground out from under his feet.

So Grant and Lee were in complete contrast, representing 12 two diametrically opposed elements in American life. Grant was the modern man emerging; beyond him, ready to come on the stage, was the great age of steel and machinery, of crowded cities and a restless burgeoning vitality. Lee might have ridden down from the old age of chivalry, lance in hand, silken banner fluttering over his head. Each man was the perfect champion of his cause, drawing both his strengths and his weaknesses from the people he led.

Yet it was not all contrast, after all. Different as they were 13 — in background, in personality, in underlying aspiration — these two great soldiers had much in common. Under everything else, they were marvelous fighters. Furthermore, their fighting qualities were really very much alike.

Each man had, to begin with, the great virtue of utter 14 tenacity and fidelity. Grant fought his way down the Mississippi Valley in spite of acute personal discouragement and profound military handicaps. Lee hung on in the trenches at Petersburg after hope itself had died. In each man there was an indomitable quality . . . the born fighter's refusal to give up as long as he can still remain on his feet and lift his two fists.

Daring and resourcefulness they had, too; the ability to 15 think faster and move faster than the enemy. These were the qualities which gave Lee the dazzling campaigns of Second Manassas and Chancellorsville and won Vicksburg for Grant.

Lastly, and perhaps greatest of all, there was the ability, at 16 the end, to turn quickly from war to peace once the fighting was over. Out of the way these two men behaved at Appomattox came the possibility of a peace of reconciliation. It was a possibility not wholly realized, in the years to come, but which did, in the end, help the two sections to become one nation again . . . after a war whose bitterness might have seemed to make such a reunion wholly impossible. No part of either man's life became him more than the part he played in their brief meeting in the McLean house at Appomattox. Their behavior there put all succeeding generations of Americans in their debt. Two great Americans, Grant and Lee — very different, yet under everything very much alike. Their encounter at Appomattox was one of the great moments of American history.

[1956 — U.S.A.]

Questions

1. Clearly, this essay is structured upon comparison and contrast. How is the contrast made as to its organization? How the comparison?

2. Grant and Lee are here spoken of as private individuals with unique personal characteristics, yet both are also taken as exemplars of American cultural trends, or of our past and our future (from the standpoint of an observer in 1865). How so?

3. Why does Catton take the contrast first and then the comparison? What is suggested thereby as to the state of the union after the Civil War?

4. "Grant and Lee" exhibits another structural mode along with comparison and contrast. What is that? How does it work to the same end as the movement from contrast to comparison?

5. Why the two one-sentence paragraphs (3 and 4)? What is the function of each? What is the function of paragraph 12? How does the essay achieve a sense of an ending?

6. A good deal is covered in this short essay, yet it is thoroughly coherent. What accounts for its coherence?

Writing Assignments

1. In two or more paragraphs, discuss the structure of Catton's essay: how the contrast proceeds, how the comparison, and why Catton takes the comparison after the contrast.

2. Write an essay like "Grant and Lee" in overall design. Begin by discussing the differences between two books, say, or two television situation comedies, or two teachers, or what you will, and then move on to and conclude with a discussion of their similarities. Or, if you have reason, reverse the strategy, taking likeness first and then difference. Whatever you do, be sure to decide beforehand what method of organization you will use in contrasting and comparing, and then follow through.

✜ OF WRITING AND WRITERS ✜
John Ciardi

THERE IS NO FORMULA BY WHICH A MAN CAN BECOME A WRITER, AND   1
there is no end to the number of ways in which a man can be
one. Writing can be an art, a trade, a craft, or a hobby. The
artist writes compulsively, as a way of knowing himself, or of
clarifying what he does not know about himself. He writes, let
us say, for those glimpses of order that form can make
momentarily visible. But add that he writes in about the way a
drunkard drinks. His passion springs not from reason, but from
thirst.

The artist-writer and the drunkard are both aware — if only   2
in moments of painful sobriety — that there are consequences to
what they do, but for both of them the doing itself is the real
consequence. The happy difference between the writer's
compulsion and the drunkard's is that the drunkard hopes to
lose himself in his bottle, whereas the writer hopes to find
himself on his page. In his act of writing, the writer finds
himself wiser, more sentient, more pertinent to his own life,
perhaps more confused by it, but more meaningfully confused.
He is a language-haunted man and a cadence-haunted man and
a form-haunted man and an image-haunted man, and he knows
that whatever ghosts he gathers about him in the writing are,
finally, his best sense of himself. And he knows that those
ghosts are the shadowy tribesmen of every man's first-and-last
identity. The writer as artist does say things, but he does not
write for the sake of saying. The saying is inevitable but
secondary. He writes to be in the company of his necessary
ghosts, much as a man will trek halfway round the world to get
back home to the company of what names him.

The man who writes as a trade is simply an employed   3
person, a wage-earner. He may be more or less serious about
his trade. He may be good or bad at it. He may, at times,
confuse his own motives and try to write as an artist does. He

may even refuse easy assignments that could produce fat checks. Still, as a man practicing a trade, he must write, finally, to make a living. That is to say he must write not for himself (compelled) but for the check his writing will bring.

The difference between the craftsman and the hobbyist is, 4 as I see it, a matter of intensity. Or perhaps there is no real difference except that the word "craft" implies at root an agonizing exertion, whereas the word "hobby" carries no feeling with it but the sense of idle play. The craftsman works at his writing harder than does the hobbyist, whether for pay or not, and is likely to be more self-demanding without ever quite achieving the passion and the compulsion of the artist. I am tempted to think of Dr. Samuel Johnson,[1] lexicographer, as practicing the craft of writing without quite managing to make a trade of it. But who would dare call him a hobbyist? The hobbyist simply amuses himself. The center of what he does with his life is somewhere else. The writing, like a stamp collection, is a way of passing a quiet evening in a room somewhere off the center of the house.

In writing, trade blurs into craft, and craft blurs into hobby, 5 but there can be no blurring of the line between the artist-writer and every other kind of writer. Except, perhaps, that it is possible to write well on any of these four levels. Even the hobbyist might turn out an enduring if slight fragment — say, a memorable piece of light verse. Even a craftsman or a man plying a trade — say, a Daniel Defoe [2] — might turn out a piece of real or imagined journalism so firmly marshaled upon itself that it stays memorable and firm. But only the writer-as-artist, I believe, can write in a way that burns forever.

Combustion is, of course, the heart of it. And combustion in 6 art can be produced only by the passion of compulsive men. The artist is once more like the drunkard in that he cannot stop to count the cost of his compulsion. The writer may write

---

[1] *Dr. Johnson* (1709–1784): British critic, essayist, and poet who compiled the first English dictionary.

[2] *Daniel Defoe* (1660?–1731): British novelist, author of *Robinson Crusoe.*

himself (as the drunkard may drink himself) out of employment, family, social acceptance, and out of health and life itself. There is no help for it: the man *must* do what he does. There is no mercy in it: no page cares what it has cost the writer.

All writing is measured, in the long run, by its memorableness. A man either writes in forms that cling to human memory, and so become unforgettable; or he writes forgettably and is soon forgotten — with, perhaps, the temporary exception that the American school system often seems to be a conspiracy to keep some unflaggingly forgettable writing in student memory by forced feeding. 7

The fact is that language supremely used will survive the death of its own mother tongue. Latin and Greek are both dead languages, but the high moments of Greek and Latin writing are still alive in men's minds. Man needs language because he lives by it and knows himself by it, and because he lives in it and knows himself in it without recourse to logic, but as an act of identity he can never hope to reason out or do without. He will store great acts of language for the simple reason that he lives by them. 8

The combustion of the artist-writer springs from the passion with which he engages that mysterious act of identity, losing himself in it as his only hope of finding himself. The writer may be wrong, of course. And there is no mercy for the wrong. If a man ruins himself in his compulsion to write a dull book, I am left with no compulsion to read it. Another man may write, no, not easily, but joyously, thriving on his difficulties because he has an appetite for them, and that man may come in a glow of well-being to write a good book. The page has treated him kindly. 9

But the reader does not care what it costs the man. Why should he? The library is full of books, and he owes no duty to any but those that please him. He reads joyously through the happy man's good book without a thought for the self-ruined failure whose volume continues to gather dust until it becomes itself dust. Or, finished with the happy man's good book, the reader may lose himself next in the good book another man 10 killed himself to write. What should the reader care? He does not so much as see the corpse. There is no corpse in good writing: the writing is always a life. It is the writer who becomes the corpse, but never in his writing — not if it is of the memorable and burning.

And add one thing more about the writing — on whatever 11 level, the success of the writing is measured by the most democratic process in human experience. Whoever you are as a person, whoever you were, the writing lives or dies outside of you and apart from you. Whether you write from a throne or a dungeon, and whether or not you deserve to be on the one or in the other, the reader does not know you and does not care and has no reason to care. Take a piece of paper, put a life on it or a piece of a life, make that life burn to reality (that is to say, to the illusion of a reality) in the act of language in which you summon it — and the reader (always the unknown reader) is yours without a thought of who you are in yourself on the other side of that page.

[1964 — U.S.A.]

Questions

1. What is Ciardi's primary concern here? How does the focus of the first paragraph signal that concern?
2. How does Ciardi extend the artist/drunkard analogy — that is, what similarities does he note between them? What key point of contrast does the comparison lead to?
3. What is the thesis of this essay? How is it established and where is it stated? Why there?
4. In what way is the essay's thesis definitional? How does classification serve definition here?

Writing Assignments

1. At the end of the seventh paragraph, Ciardi charges our school system with perpetuating "forgettable writing." In a paragraph or more, discuss your own primary and secondary education in this regard and the merit or lack of merit of the charge.

2. Pick a topic area and get a thesis that lends itself to development like that of "Of Writing and Writers" — that is, by definition entailing classification. Now write a paper in which you proceed to define by way of classification, establishing what defines what you wish to define by contrast with other things in the same class. For instance, you could define one type of music or musician by classifying the various types of either (classical, jazz, pop) and holding the type you're interested in against the others.

✤ THE BLOOD LUST ✤
Eldridge Cleaver

THE BOXING RING IS THE ULTIMATE FOCUS OF MASCULINITY IN   1
America, the two-fisted testing ground of manhood, and the heavyweight champion, as a symbol, is the real Mr. America. In a culture that secretly subscribes to the piratical ethic of "every man for himself" -- the social Darwinism of "survival of the fittest" being far from dead, manifesting itself in our ratrace political system of competing parties, in our dog-eat-dog economic system of profit and loss, and in our adversary system of justice wherein truth is secondary to the skill and connections of the advocate — the logical culmination of this ethic, on a person-to-person level, is that the weak are seen as the natural and just prey of the strong. But since this dark principle violates our democratic ideals and professions, we force it underground, out of a perverse national modesty that reveals us as a nation of peep freaks who prefer the bikini to the naked body, the white lie to the black truth, Hollywood smiles and canned laughter to a soulful Bronx cheer. The heretical mailed fist of American reality rises to the surface in the velvet glove of our every institutionalized endeavor, so that each year we, as a nation, grind through various cycles of attrition, symbolically quenching the insatiable appetite of the *de facto* jungle law underlying our culture, loudly and unabashedly proclaiming to the world that "competition" is the law of life, getting confused, embar-

rassed, and angry if someone retorts: "Competition is the Law of the Jungle and Cooperation is the Law of Civilization."

Our mass spectator sports are geared to disguise, while affording expression to, the acting out in elaborate pageantry of the myth of the fittest in the process of surviving. From the Little League to the major leagues, through the orgiastic climax of the World Series; from high school football teams, through the college teams, to the grand finale of the annual bowl washouts; interspersed with the subcycles of basketball, track, and field meets — all of our mass spectator sports give play to the basic cultural ethic, harnessed and sublimated into national-communal pagan rituals.

But there is an aspect of the crystal of our nature that eschews the harness, scorns sublimation, and demands to be seen in its raw nakedness, crying out to us for the sight and smell of blood. The vehemence with which we deny this obvious fact of our nature is matched only by our Victorian hysteria on the subject of sex. Yet, we deny it in vain. Whether we quench our thirst from the sight of a bleeding Jesus on the Cross, from the ritualized sacrifice in the elevation of the Host and the consecration of the Blood of the Son, or from bullfighting, cockfighting, dogfighting, wrestling, or boxing, spiced with our Occidental memory and heritage of the gladiators of Rome and the mass spectator sport of the time of feeding Christians and other enemies of society to the lions in the Coliseum — whatever the mask assumed by the impulse, the persistent beat of the drum over the years intones the chant: Though Dracula and Vampira must flee the scene with the rising of the sun and the coming of the light, night has its fixed hour and darkness must fall. And all the lightbulbs ever fashioned, and all the power plants generating electricity, have absolutely no effect on the primeval spinning of the earth in its orbit.

In America, we give maximum expression to our blood lust in the mass spectator sport of boxing. Some of us are Roman enough to admit our love and need of the sport. Others pretend to look the other way. But when a heavyweight championship fight rolls around, the nation takes a moral holiday and we are all tuned in — some of us peeping out of the corner of our eye at the square jungle and the animal test of brute power unfolding there.

Every institution in America is tainted by the mystique of   5 race, and the question of masculinity is confused by the presence of both a "white" man and a "black" man here. One was the master and the other was the slave until a moment ago when they both were declared to be equal "men"; which leaves American men literally without a unitary, nationally viable self-image. Whatever dim vision of masculinity they have is a rough-and-ready, savage mishmash of violence and sexuality, a dichotomized exercise and worship of physical force/submission to and fear of physical force — which is only one aspect of the broken-down relationship between men and women in America. This is an era when the models of manhood and womanhood have been blasted to dust by social upheaval, as the most alienated males and females at the bottom of society move out of "their places" and bid for their right to be "man" and "woman" on an equal basis with the former masters and mistresses. These, in turn, are no longer seen by themselves and others as supermen and superwomen, but only as men and women like all other. And in this period of social change and sexual confusion, boxing, and the heavyweight championship in particular, serves as the ultimate test of masculinity, based on the perfection of the body and its use.

[1967 — U.S.A.]

Questions

1. This essay's theme is pointed to by its title. What is that theme? How does it account for each paragraph of the essay?
2. What analogy is suggested in the first two sentences by way of simple juxtaposition? What does boxing come to symbolize in Cleaver's essay? How does what boxing symbolizes tie in with the essay's theme?
3. What kind of diction marks "The Blood Lust"? What kind of syntax? What is the effect of both on voice? Describe the essay's voice. Why did Cleaver create this type of voice?

Writing Assignments

1. Write a paragraph or more in which you use some image or reference symbolically, as Cleaver does boxing in "The Blood Lust." Your symbol should be tied in with your theme or thesis and placed prominently — at the beginning and end, for example, or perhaps at the end of your introduction, where it could be used to help state your thesis or imply your theme.

2. In two or more paragraphs, discuss the style of "The Blood Lust" — that is, examine its diction and syntax and their effects. First describe each, making sure to give examples, and then consider the tone and voice that they help to fashion.

✠ "PREFACE" TO ✠
THE NIGGER OF THE NARCISSUS
Joseph Conrad

A WORK THAT ASPIRES, HOWEVER HUMBLY, TO THE CONDITION OF ART 1 should carry its justification in every line. And art itself may be defined as a single-minded attempt to render the highest kind of justice to the visible universe, by bringing to light the truth, manifold and one, underlying its every aspect. It is an attempt to find in its forms, in its colors, in its light, in its shadows, in the aspects of matter and in the facts of life, what of each is fundamental, what is enduring and essential — their one illuminating and convincing quality — the very truth of their existence. The artist, then, like the thinker or the scientist, seeks the truth and makes his appeal. Impressed by the aspect of the world, the thinker plunges into ideas, the scientist into facts — whence, presently, emerging they make their appeal to those qualities of our being that fit us best for the hazardous enterprise of living. They speak authoritatively to our common sense, to our intelligence, to our desire of peace or to our desire of unrest; not seldom to our prejudices, sometimes to our fears, often to our egoism — but always to our credulity. And their words are heard with reverence, for their concern is with weighty matters: with the cultivation of our minds and the proper care of our bodies, with the attainment of our ambitions, with the perfection of the means and the glorification of our precious aims.

It is otherwise with the artist.   2

Confronted by the same enigmatical spectacle, the artist   3 descends within himself, and in that lonely region of stress and strife, if he be deserving and fortunate, he finds the terms of his appeal. His appeal is made to our less obvious capacities: to that part of our nature which, because of the warlike conditions of existence, is necessarily kept out of sight within the more resisting and hard qualities — like the vulnerable body within a steel armor. His appeal is less loud, more profound, less distinct, more stirring — and sooner forgotten. Yet its effect endures forever. The changing wisdom of successive genera- tions discards ideas, questions facts, demolishes theories. But the artist appeals to that part of our being which is not dependent on wisdom: to that in us which is a gift and not an acquisition — and, therefore, more permanently enduring. He speaks to our capacity for delight and wonder, to the sense of mystery surrounding our lives; to our sense of pity, and beauty, and pain; to the latent feeling of fellowship with all creation — and to the subtle but invincible conviction of solidarity that knits together the loneliness of innumerable hearts, to the solidarity in dreams, in joy, in sorrow, in aspirations, in illusions, in hope, in fear, which binds men to each other, which binds together all humanity — the dead to the living and the living to the unborn.

It is only some such train of thought, or rather of feeling,   4 that can in a measure explain the aim of the attempt, made in the tale which follows, to present an unrestful episode in the obscure lives of a few individuals out of all the disregarded multitude of the bewildered, the simple, and the voiceless. For, if any part of truth dwells in the belief confessed above, it becomes evident that there is not a place of splendor or a dark corner of the earth that does not deserve if only a passing glance of wonder and pity. The motive, then, may be held to justify the matter of the work; but this preface, which is simply an avowal of endeavor, cannot end here — for the avowal is not yet complete.

Fiction — if it at all aspires to be art — appeals to temper- 5
ament. And in truth it must be, like painting, like music, like all art, the appeal of one temperament to all the other innumerable temperaments whose subtle and resistless power endows passing events with their true meaning, and creates the moral, the emotional, atmosphere of the place and time. Such an appeal to be effective must be an impression conveyed through the senses; and, in fact, it cannot be made in any other way, because temperament, whether individual or collective, is not amenable to persuasion. All art, therefore, appeals primarily to the senses, and the artistic aim when expressing itself in written words must also make its appeal through the senses, if its high desire is to reach the secret spring of responsive emotions. It must strenuously aspire to the plasticity of sculpture, to the color of painting, and to the magic suggestiveness of music — which is the art of arts. And it is only through complete, unswerving devotion to the perfect blending of form and substance; it is only through an unremitting never-discouraged care for the shape and ring of sentences that an approach can be made to plasticity, to color, and that the light of magic suggestiveness may be brought to play for an evanescent instant over the commonplace surface of words: of the old, old words, worn thin, defaced by ages of careless usage.

The sincere endeavor to accomplish that creative task, to go 6
as far on that road as his strength will carry him, to go undeterred by faltering, weariness or reproach, is the only valid justification for the worker in prose. And if his conscience is clear, his answer to those who in the fullness of a wisdom which looks for immediate profit, demand specifically to be edified, consoled, amused; who demand to be promptly improved, or encouraged, or frightened, or shocked, or charmed, must run thus: My task which I am trying to achieve is, by the power of the written word to make you hear, to make you feel — it is, before all, to make you see. That — and no more, and it is everything. If I succeed, you shall find there according to your

deserts: encouragement, consolation, fear, charm — all you demand — and, perhaps also that glimpse of truth for which you have forgotten to ask.

To snatch in a moment of courage, from the remorseless 7 rush of time, a passing phase of life, is only the beginning of the task. The task approached in tenderness and faith is to hold up unquestioningly, without choice and without fear, the rescued fragment before all eyes in the light of a sincere mood. It is to show its vibration, its color, its form; and through its movement, its form, and its color, reveal the substance of its truth — disclose its inspiring secret: the stress and passion within the core of each convincing moment. In a single-minded attempt of that kind, if one be deserving and fortunate, one may perchance attain to such clearness of sincerity that at last the presented vision of regret or pity, of terror or mirth, shall awaken in the hearts of the beholders that feeling of unavoidable solidarity; of the solidarity in mysterious origin, in toil, in joy, in hope, in uncertain fate, which binds men to each other and all mankind to the visible world.

It is evident that he who, rightly or wrongly, holds by the 8 convictions expressed above cannot be faithful to any one of the temporary formulas of his craft. The enduring part of them — the truth which each only imperfectly veils — should abide with him as the most precious of his possessions, but they all: Realism, Romanticism, Naturalism, even the unofficial sentimentalism (which like the poor, is exceedingly difficult to get rid of), all these gods must, after a short period of fellowship, abandon him — even on the very threshold of the temple — to the stammerings of his conscience and to the outspoken consciousness of the difficulties of his work. In that uneasy solitude the supreme cry of Art for Art itself loses the exciting ring of its apparent immorality. It sounds far off. It has ceased to be a cry, and is heard only as a whisper, often incomprehensible, but at times and faintly encouraging.

Sometimes, stretched at ease in the shade of a roadside tree, 9 we watch the motions of a laborer in a distant field, and, after a time, begin to wonder languidly as to what the fellow may be at. We watch the movements of his body, the waving of his arms, we see him bend down, stand up, hesitate, begin again. It may add to the charm of an idle hour to be told the purpose of his exertions. If we know he is trying to life a stone, to dig a ditch, to uproot a stump, we look with a more real interest at his efforts; we are disposed to condone the jar of his agitation upon the restfulness of the landscape; and even, if in a brotherly frame of mind, we may bring ourselves to forgive his failure. We understood his object, and, after all, the fellow has tried, and perhaps he had not the strength — and perhaps he had not the knowledge. We forgive, go on our way — and forget.

And so it is with the workman of art. Art is long and life is 10 short, and success is very far off. And thus, doubtful of strength to travel so far, we talk a little about the aim — the aim of art, which, like life itself, is inspiring, difficult — obscured by mists. It is not in the clear logic of a triumphant conclusion; it is not in the unveiling of one of those heartless secrets which are called the Laws of Nature. It is not less great, but only more difficult.

To arrest, for the space of a breath, the hands busy about 11 the work of the earth, and compel men entranced by the sight of distant goals to glance for a moment at the surrounding vision of form and color, of sunshine and shadows; to make them pause for a look, for a sigh, for a smile — such is the aim, difficult and evanescent, and reserved only for a very few to achieve. But sometimes, by the deserving and the fortunate, even that task is accomplished. And when it is accomplished — behold! — all the truth of life is there: a moment of vision, a sigh, a smile — and the return to an eternal rest.

[1897 — Great Britain]

Questions

1. The first paragraph of Conrad's "Preface" proceeds by way of a comparison — of the artist with the scientist and the thinker. What point does this comparison lead to? Why is the point surprising?

2. Why the one-sentence paragraph (paragraph 2)? What is its effect? What question does this sentence raise? What, then, is the essay's thesis?

3. Definition is the basic goal of this essay. What is Conrad trying to define? To what extent is he successful? How so? Why might he not be fully successful?

4. In the first paragraph, Conrad says: "The artist, then, like the thinker and the scientist, seeks the truth and makes his appeal. Impressed by the aspect of the world, the thinker plunges into ideas, the scientist into facts. . ."; and in the tenth paragraph, Conrad says of art: "It is not in the clear logic of a triumphant conclusion; it is not in the unveiling of one of those heartless secrets which are called the Laws of Nature." How are these statements related? How do they help to unify the essay?

5. "All art," Conrad says in the fifth paragraph, "appeals primarily to the senses, and the artistic aim when expressing itself in written words must also make its appeal through the senses. . . ." Is Conrad true to his understanding of art in the present essay? What sense words does he use? Where and how?

Writing Assignments

1. In two or more paragraphs, compare and/or contrast Conrad's view of the art of writing and John Ciardi's (see "Of Writing and Writers," pages 150–53). Your thesis should be that their views are similar or dissimilar, or similar in some ways and dissimilar in others. Give examples from each essay to back up your conclusion (that is, your thesis).

2. Write an essay in which you set out to define some large abstraction — home, democracy, paradise. See if you can work in an effective one-sentence paragraph, as Conrad does in his "Preface." Try, too, to use concretions to tie down each part of your definition.

——✤ REMark: Software Wildcats ✤——
Alan Cooper

Listening to some software developers, you'd think it's a jungle out there: Competition is fierce, the good niches are occupied, and precious few products remain to be written. I don't agree. Opportunities for software authors — and therefore for the computing public — have never been better.

My view of the software development world is a good deal more sanguine than that proffered by many of my partners in programming. I see that world as a vast plain populated with software authors who can drink at any number of watering holes. What's disconcerting is the startling number of these pools of opportunity that are deserted — programmers are crowding around only a half-dozen or so oases. Personal-computer-based word processing programs, spreadsheets, and data base managers now number in the hundreds, yet among them, new ideas and implementations are rare. *ThinkTank's* ingenuity caught many by surprise, as did *LisaProject*. In software development, success inspires imitation. The result: we now have a bombardment of outline processors and graphics-oriented project planners.

Software development is tough, and the obstacles are invisible to all but the developer. Fortunately, the rewards are great, and the breadth of opportunity surpasses that offered by any other business endeavor. The rising mortality rate in the software industry has nothing to do with market shrinkage or "windows of opportunity" that have abruptly slammed shut. Aside from a few spectacularly badly managed companies, failures have occurred where developers ignored yawning market gaps while trying to occupy already crowded niches. It boils down to this: We don't need another integrated productivity package. The sweetest watering hole on the veld will eventually dry up if it's drained by too many thirsty artists.

The craft or art or science (take your pick) of writing   4
personal computer software is not unlike the creative process
behind any other commercial product. Programming itself is
easy; it's certainly no harder than carpentry. Commercial
software development, however, is brutal. Programming differs
from product development in the same way that carpentry
differs from architecture. If a building collapses, it's generally a
function of the quality of its design, not the quality of its
workmanship. If a building succeeds, it does so on the merits of
its concept and design — not because of exceptional construction. In the same way, a software product can't succeed without
an innovative idea at its heart. Elegant code alone won't send a
program to the top of the charts.

Among computer industry cognoscenti, horror stories   5
abound. People groan about *WordStar*'s spaghetti-like maze of
indecipherable code, *VisiCalc*'s ridiculous — and frequently
imitated — "slash command" structure, and CP/M's notorious
omissions. But these programs did not prosper because of their
carpentry — their code. Rather, they achieved their considerable success because of innovative design. Each did something
unprecedented and did it well enough that complaints didn't
surface until the product was firmly entrenched as a market
leader.

Business graphics programs, on the other hand, represent a   6
triumph of creative inertia. Virtually every graphing package
depends for its data on numbers entered in a spreadsheet; the
program then draws a graph from the numbers. Why not be a
little outrageous and create a program that reverses the action?
Let a user sketch a line on a video screen and then translate that
into a spreadsheet full of proportional numbers.

This kind of rethinking — of divining fresh solutions to old   7
problems — is as rare as geese that lay golden eggs, and it's
nearly as profitable. For perhaps the first time since Gutenberg,
an invention — the personal computer — has enabled software
developers to reach a mass audience cheaply. This opportunity
attracts mainstream thinkers, sure, but eccentrics and prodigies
are still in their heyday. In accounting, precocious 22-year-old

bookkeepers don't make millions, but in software, the "high-school dropout makes a fortune" saga is not unheard of. Because the cost of entry is so low, the field continues to stimulate innovation. A kid weaned on a Commodore PET in junior high school can turn personal computing on its ear with an original program idea.

The flip side of this astonishing opportunity is the hidden 8 cost of software development. The discipline moves ahead by bounds, leaving gaps in the knowledge base. Indeed, the personal computer software field lacks an information infra-structure and a shared pool of expertise from which successful new PC software can be fashioned. Few of today's hits are based on another developer's success; instead, they're from-the-ground-up monuments to self-expression.

The qualities that breed success in the marketplace are 9 intangible and ill-defined: friendliness, performance, respon-siveness, and metaphor. Little has been written about these elusive essentials. And despite their indisputable value, these attributes receive scant attention from university researchers, corporations, and think tanks. Academia continues to be enthralled with such details as pattern recognition and sorting algorithms, but in the real world of PC software development, technical tricks don't ensure a high-performance product — or money in the bank. *1-2-3* may contain dozens of fancy algorithms, but rest assured that they are not the cause of its success.

Universities channel creativity in a way that encourages 10 advances in small increments rather than in giant strides. Academic research is firmly based on previous research and boasts undeniable advantages: thoroughness, comprehensive documentation, avoidance of duplication of effort, and rela-tive independence from market forces and individual personal-ities. Academia suffers, however, from its sloth — making innovations rare. The private sector shares that trait. The enormous capital investment required to address a mass audience invariably means the players move at an elephantine pace.

That's why so many successful products are generated by 11 iconoclastic authors in their garages or back rooms or mountain cabins. They're the creative stock who benefit from the absence of a knowledge base — they thrive on being on the cutting edge, alone. Like catamounts on a savanna, they're solo hunters wandering from watering hole to watering hole, sizing up opportunities invisible to the grazing herd. Powerful, lazy, brilliant, unpredictable, and of course, very rare, they can count on abundant pools remaining, and thus need not be an endangered species.

[1985 — U.S.A.]

Questions

1. How does Cooper get to his thesis statement? What is that statement? What type of introduction is exemplified here?

2. How does the essay's thesis statement control the essay? That is, how is each subsequent idea related to the initial statement of purpose?

3. What audience was this essay written for? Do its diction and voice seem appropriate for this audience? How so?

4. What analogy is drawn in paragraph 4? What metaphor is extended in this essay? How does this metaphor help Cooper achieve an ending?

5. Though about opportunities for software development, "REMark: Software Wildcats" has application to other fields and to human behavior in general. What does it tell us when generalized about ourselves and our endeavors?

Writing Assignments

1. If you are knowledgable with respect to software, write two or more paragraphs on the meaning of "metaphor" as applied by Cooper to software (paragraph 9) and how that meaning relates to the linguistic meaning (see the Glossary).

2. "In software development, success inspires imitation," Cooper states in paragraph 2, and suggests later that imitation leades to failure. Write a paper addressed to this paradoxical phenomenon. Where else can it be witnessed (movies, TV programing, contemporary building design)? Why is imitation so common when it rarely leads to success? Why is there so little genuine creativity in the world?

3. If you know what Cooper is talking about in the first sentence of paragraph 9, write an essay defining each of the four intangibles he enumerates and discuss how it is that they "breed success."

❖ OVERCOMING AN ❖
INVISIBLE HANDICAP
Thomas J. Cottle

ON HER 30TH BIRTHDAY, LUCILLE ELMORE INFORMED HER HUSBAND   1
that she was going through a crisis. "I was 30 years old, active, in good health — and I was illiterate," she recalls. "I didn't know books. I didn't know history, I didn't know science. I had the barest understanding of the arts. Like a physical condition, my knowledge limped, my intelligence limped."

She was not only the mother of two young children but also   2
was working full time as an administrative assistant in a business-consulting firm. Nevertheless, at age 30, with her husband's agreement, Lucille Elmore enrolled in college. "I thought getting in would be difficult," she says. "It was easy. I thought I couldn't discipline myself, but that came. Half the people in the library the first day thought I was the librarian, but that didn't deter me."

For Lucille, the awareness of her invisible limp came only   3
gradually. As a young woman, she had finished high school, but she had chosen not to go on with her education. Her parents, who had never completed high school themselves, urged her to go to college, but she refused. At the time, she was perhaps a bit timid and lacked a certain confidence in her own intellectual or academic abilities. Besides, a steady job was far more important at that point to Lucille than schooling: she felt she could read on her own to make up for any lack of education.

At 20, working full time, she married Ted Elmore, a   4
salesman for a food-store chain, a man on his way to becoming more than modestly successful. There was no need for her to work, but she did so until her first child was born; she was then

22. A second child was born two years later, and three years after that, she went back to work. With her youngest in a day-care program, she felt no reservations about working, but her lack of education began to nag at her as she approached the age of 30. She thus gave up her job, entered a continuing-education program at a nearby university, and began what she likens to a love affair.

"I'm carrying on an open affair with books, but like a 5 genuinely good lover, I'm being guided. Reading lists, suggested reading, recommended readings — I want them all. I must know what happened in the 12th, 13th, 18th centuries. I want to know how the world's major religions evolved. Papal history, I know nothing of papal history and succession, or the politics involved. I read the Bible, but I never studied it. It's like music: I listened, but it wasn't an informed listening. Now all of this is changing.

"I must tell you, I despise students when they talk about 6 'the real world,' as if college were a dream world. They simply don't understand what the accumulation of knowledge and information means. Maybe you have to be 30 at least, and going through a personal crisis, to fully appreciate what historical connections are.

"A line of Shakespeare challenges me more than half the 7 jobs I'll be equipped for when I'm finished. I'm having an affair with him, too, only it's called Elizabethan Literature 606. I think many people prefer the real world of everyday work because it's less frightening than the larger-than-life world of college.

"There's a much more important difference between the 8 rest of the students and me. We don't agree at all on what it means to be a success. They think in terms of money, material things. I suppose that's normal. They don't understand that with a nice home, and decent job prospects, and two beautiful children, I know I am a failure. I'm a failure because I am ignorant. I'm a failure until I have knowledge, until I can work with it, be excited by and play with ideas.

"I don't go to school for the rewards down the line. I want 9
to reach the point at which I don't measure knowledge by
anything but itself. An idea has value or it doesn't. This is how
I now determine success and failure."

" 'How can I use it?' That's what students ask. 'What good 10
will this do me?' They don't think about what the question says
about them, even without an answer attached to it. Questions
like that only build up competition. But competition is the
bottom line for so many students, I guess, getting ahead, getting
a bit of a step up on the other guy. I know, it's my husband's
life.

"I'll tell you what I think I like most about my work: the 11
library. I can think of no place so exclusive and still so open and
public. Millions of books there for the taking. A chair to sit in,
a row of books, and you don't need a penny. For me, the library
is a religious center, a shrine.

"Students talk about the real world out there. What about 12
the free world in here? Here, no one arrests you for what you're
thinking. In the library, you can't talk, so you have to think. I
never knew what it meant to think about something, to really
think it through. I certainly never understood what you had to
know to even begin to think. I always thought it was normal to
limp."

[1980 — U.S.A.]

Questions

1. After introducing us to Lucille Elmore at age 30 (paragraphs 1 and
2), Cottle traces her earlier life (paragraphs 3 and 4). What principle
of organization guides his sketch? Is the sketch necessary? Why or
why not? Is Elmore real or fictional? Does it matter? Why or why
not?

2. This essay presents us with two voices, the one of paragraphs 1–4
and the one of paragraphs 5–11. How is each established? Contrast
the two and the effect of each. What does Cottle gain by using two
voices instead of one?

3. Elmore gives us a character sketch of herself as student (paragraphs 5–11). How does she come off? In what ways does she differ from younger students?
4. What function(s) does the title of this essay have? How does the title relate to the essay's theme?
5. How does metaphor help concretize the main idea here? How does metaphor help tie the essay together?

Writing Assignments

1. Write a paragraph or more spoken by a person other than yourself (as paragraphs 5–11 of "Overcoming an Invisible Handicap" are spoken by Lucille Elmore), your object being character revelation (the piece will be a character sketch) through what your speaker says about himself or herself and how what is said is said. If possible, use a metaphor to help structure your piece, as Cottle does in the essay at hand.
2. Lucille Elmore seems to be an ideal student. If you agree, write an essay on what constitutes an ideal student, using Elmore to exemplify. If you do not agree, write an essay on what you believe an ideal student to be, using Elmore for contrast.

✤ WHO KILLED BENNY PARET? ✤

Norman Cousins

SOMETIME ABOUT 1935 OR 1936 I HAD AN INTERVIEW WITH MIKE   1
Jacobs, the prize-fight promoter. I was a fledgling newspaper reporter at that time; my beat was education, but during the vacation season I found myself on varied assignments, all the way from ship news to sports reporting. In this way I found myself sitting opposite the most powerful figure in the boxing world.

There was nothing spectacular in Mr. Jacobs's manner or   2
appearance; but when he spoke about prize fights, he was no longer a bland little man but a colossus who sounded the way Napoleon must have sounded when he reviewed a battle. You

knew you were listening to Number One. His saying something made it true.

We discussed what to him was the only important element 3 in successful promoting — how to please the crowd. So far as he was concerned, there was no mystery to it. You put killers in the ring and the people filled your arena. You hire boxing artists — men who are adroit at feinting, parrying, weaving, jabbing, and dancing, but who don't pack dynamite in their fists — and you wind up counting your empty seats. So you searched for the killers and sluggers and maulers — fellows who could hit with the force of a baseball bat.

I asked Mr. Jacobs if he was speaking literally when he 4 said people came out to see the killer.

"They don't come out to see a tea party," he said evenly. 5 "They come out to see the knockout. They come out to see a man hurt. If they think anything else, they're kidding themselves."

Recently a young man by the name of Benny Paret was 6 killed in the ring. The killing was seen by millions; it was on television. In the twelfth round he was hit hard in the head several times, went down, was counted out, and never came out of the coma.

The Paret fight produced a flurry of investigations. 7 Governor Rockefeller was shocked by what happened and appointed a committee to assess the responsibility. The New York State Boxing Commission decided to find out what was wrong. The District Attorney's office expressed its concern. One question that was solemnly studied in all three probes concerned the action of the referee. Did he act in time to stop the fight? Another question had to do with the role of the examining doctors who certified the physical fitness of the fighters before the bout. Still another question involved Mr. Paret's manager; did he rush his boy into the fight without adequate time to recuperate from the previous one?

In short, the investigators looked into every possible cause 8 except the real one. Benny Paret was killed because the human fist delivers enough impact, when directed against the head, to produce a massive hemorrhage in the brain. The human brain is the most delicate and complex mechanism in all creation. It has a lacework of millions of highly fragile nerve connections. Nature attempts to protect this exquisitely intricate machinery by encasing it in a hard shell. Fortunately, the shell is thick enough to withstand a great deal of pounding. Nature, however, can protect man against everything except man himself. Not every blow to the head will kill a man — but there is always the risk of concussion and damage to the brain. A prize fighter may be able to survive even repeated brain concussions and go on fighting, but the damage to his brain may be permanent.

In any event, it is futile to investigate the referee's role and seek to determine whether he should have intervened to stop the fight earlier. This is not where the primary responsibility lies. The primary responsibility lies with the people who pay to see a man hurt. The referee who stops a fight too soon from the crowd's viewpoint can expect to be booed. The crowd wants the knockout; it wants to see a man stretched out on the canvas. This is the supreme moment in boxing. It is nonsense to talk about prize fighting as a test of boxing skills. No crowd was ever brought to its feet screaming and cheering at the sight of two men beautifully dodging and weaving out of each other's jabs. The time the crowd comes alive is when a man is hit hard over the heart or the head, when his mouthpiece flies out, when blood squirts out of his nose or eyes, when he wobbles under the attack and his pursuer continues to smash at him with poleax impact.

Don't blame it on the referee. Don't even blame it on the fight managers. Put the blame where it belongs — on the prevailing mores that regard prize fighting as a perfectly proper enterprise and vehicle of entertainment. No one doubts that many people enjoy prize fighting and will miss it if it should be thrown out. And that is precisely the point.

[1967 — U.S.A.]

Questions

1. Cousins attributes Paret's death to two causes. What are they? Which, finally, is the primary cause?
2. What is the thesis of this essay? Where does the thesis statement come? How is Cousins's title related to his thesis?
3. What functions does the first block of paragraphs (1-5) have? How is this block of paragraphs related to paragraphs 6-9?
4. Why didn't Cousins provide transition between paragraphs 5 and 6? Is a transition necessary and, therefore, the essay incoherent? Why or why not?
5. How do you respond to the last paragraph here? Is this a satisfying ending or does it leave us hanging for no apparent reason? In either case, why or why not?

Writing Assignments

1. a) Write a paragraph addressed to the two-part structure of Cousins's essay (paragraphs 1-5 and 6-9). What are the functions of the first part? How are the two parts related? Is there really a gap between paragraphs 5 and 6 or is there a principle of coherence operative here that precludes the need for a transition?

   b) In a separate paragraph, state what your response to this essay is and then discuss why you respond thus.
2. Write a short paper beginning with an anecdote with a point and, without transition, moving on to an example of that point. See if you can make your material cohere in and of itself, thus precluding the need for transition between your major blocks.
3. Read Eldridge Cleaver's "The Blood Lust" (pages 154-56) and then write an essay contrasting Cleaver's view of boxing and Cousins's. Since contrast is not an end in itself, use the contrast you draw to support a thesis of your own.

✤ DISCRIMINATION BY CREED ✤

Alan M. Dershowitz

I REMEMBER, AS A KID, READING IN SUPERMAN COMICS THAT IT WAS   1
un-American to judge a person on the basis of race, creed,
religion or national origin. I always understood why it was
wrong to judge on the basis of factors beyond a person's
control, but people should be judged by their creeds, if that
means by the beliefs they have chosen to govern their behavior.

Adherents of the Ku Klux Klan, or of Stalinism, or of   2
Nazism should be judged by the abhorrent principles for which
they stand. I would never choose a friend on the basis of race,
religion or origin. But I would most certainly reject any
friendship with a segregationist or a misogynist. Superman was
wrong to equate discrimination on the basis of heritage with the
very different concept of judging people by their voluntary
beliefs and actions. The California branch of the American Civil
Liberties Union seems to be making that same equation in a
troubling case now pending before the Los Angeles Superior
Court.

The case grows out of an incident last October after four   3
men wearing swastikas walked into the Alpine Inn, a German
restaurant in Torrance, and sat down for dinner. When the
jukebox played a German marching song, the Nazis rose and
gave a "Heil Hitler" salute. After they left, the restrooms were
found papered with anti-Semitic stickers.

A week later, the Nazis returned. This time the restaurant   4
was filled with more than 1000 customers for a large Oktober-
fest celebration. There was concern that violence might ensue,
and the Nazis were asked either to leave or to remove their
swastikas. They refused and were arrested.

Now they are suing the restaurant under a California civil   5
rights statute that bars discrimination by business establishments on the basis of "sex, race, color, religion, ancestry or
national origin." Creed is not specifically mentioned, but the

California courts have interpreted the law to bar "all arbitrary discrimination," while allowing businesses to exclude customers who are "disruptive" or fail to comply with "reasonable deportment regulations." The ACLU[1] of California is representing the Nazis.

The issues raised by this case are far more complex than those raised by cases involving discrimination on the basis of race, gender or heritage. At one level, there are obvious similarities. Some restaurant customers are genuinely offended, even outraged, by a wide range of activities, including interracial or homosexual hand holding, cigaret and cigar smoking or informal dress. Restaurants quite properly have the power to establish some rules for their patrons. 6

But federal, state and local laws impose limits. Even if every white patron would be offended to the point of leaving by the restaurant serving black or interracial guests, no restaurant may discriminate on the basis of race. The same is generally true — and should be true — for sexual preference, religious background and national origin. 7

But what about political expression? The issue would be simple if the restaurant enforced an across-the-board policy of refusing admission to anyone wearing any political symbol, or anyone standing up to make any kind of salute during the meal, or anyone posting any sign in the bathroom, or anyone engaging in disruptive conduct of any kind. And perhaps that is how this case will eventually be decided. 8

But that would not quite be an intellectually honest way of confronting the difficult issues posed here. The content of what these customers were wearing, saying, saluting and postering was critical to why they were excluded. And therein lies the rub. 9

Imagine the outrage if the owner of a restaurant refused to serve only those people who wore anti-apartheid pins, or anti-war armbands, but willingly served customers who sported 10

---

[1]*ACLU:* The American Civil Liberties Union, which is usually identified with liberal causes.

pro-apartheid and "nuke the reds" signs. Consider the case of a previously segregated restaurant being frustrated in its attempt to comply with the equal accommodation law by a group of KKK members eating at the establishment wearing sheets and hoods. Obviously, this would be the functional equivalent of a sign at the door reading "Blacks not welcome." Most of us probably would applaud a restaurant owner who ordered the Klansmen to remove their paraphernalia or leave.

A German restaurant frequented by patrons wearing 11 swastikas and making "Heil Hitler" salutes certainly would not encourage Jewish or black patronage. Indeed, it might effectively exclude them, in violation of the very law invoked by the Nazis.

The issue is a difficult one with no knee-jerk solution. 12 Several distinctions must be kept in mind. This is not the Skokie case; there is an enormous difference between public thoroughfares and private restaurants. I supported the ACLU's opposition to the efforts of Skokie, Ill., to bar a Nazi march through town. I feel much more conflict about the ACLU's defense of the rights of Nazis to practice their offensive politics during the dinner hour at a private restaurant.

Nor is this a case of discrimination based on race, religion, 13 gender or national origin. It is a question of people being judged for their political beliefs. I hope these distinctions are kept in mind when the courts confront this complex case.

[1986 — U.S.A.]

Questions

1. What kind of title is "Discrimination by Creed"? What does the title lead you to ask?
2. What kind of beginning does this essay have? How does Dershowitz get down to his thesis statement? What is that statement?
3. What extension of meaning does the reference in paragraph 1 to Superman suggest? What other function(s) does the reference have?
4. In paragraph 2, Dershowitz picks up the reference to Superman. How does the second reference help him gain coherence?

5. How does Dershowitz proceed in arguing his case? In paragraph 12, he asserts that "there is an enormous difference between public thoroughfares and private restaurants." We can say from what's been said previously that he does not mean that private restaurants have the right to discriminate at will. But what exactly does he mean? Is there some confusion here? Might it be deliberate? How so?

6. How does the last paragraph here glance back to the first? Why does it do so? To what effect?

Writing Assignments

1. Write a paragraph or more suggesting why the ACLU — a champion of civil rights — would file for the Nazis in the case Dershowitz discusses. Is its position consistent with its history as a liberal organization? Could it be argued that those who would deny civil rights to others have no right to make use of civil rights laws themselves?

2. In a short paper, evaluate Dershowitz's argument. What does he argue? Does he do so succinctly and clearly? What evidence does he bring to bear? Is the evidence convincing? Why or why not? Are there any points of confusion in the essay? If so, what are they, and can they be justified? Is the essay well written? How so?

3. Write an essay explaining how you would decide the case at hand and why. Establish what the case is, the issues it involves, and what your judgment of it would be. Then, step by step, detail your reasons for so deciding. End with a paragraph that verbally echoes your beginning.

✤ ON MORALITY ✤

Joan Didion

As it happens I am in Death Valley, in a room at the 1
Enterprise Motel and Trailer Park, and it is July, and it is hot.
In fact it is 119°. I cannot seem to make the air conditioner
work, but there is a small refrigerator, and I can wrap ice cubes
in a towel and hold them against the small of my back. With the
help of the ice cubes I have been trying to think, because *The
American Scholar* asked me to, in some abstract way about
"morality," a word I distrust more every day, but my mind
veers inflexibly toward the particular.

Here are some particulars. At midnight last night, on the 2
road in from Las Vegas to Death Valley Junction, a car hit a
shoulder and turned over. The driver, very young and
apparently drunk, was killed instantly. His girl was found alive
but bleeding internally, deep in shock. I talked this afternoon to
the nurse who had driven the girl to the nearest doctor, 185
miles across the floor of the Valley and three ranges of lethal
mountain road. The nurse explained that her husband, a talc
miner, had stayed on the highway with the boy's body until the
coroner could get over the mountains from Bishop, at dawn
today. "You can't just leave a body on the highway," she said.
"It's immoral."

It was one instance in which I did not distrust the word, 3
because she meant something quite specific. She meant that if a
body is left alone for even a few minutes on the desert, the
coyotes close in and eat the flesh. Whether or not a corpse is
torn apart by coyotes may seem only a sentimental consideration, but of course it is more: one of the promises we make to
one another is that we will try to retrieve our casualties, try not
to abandon our dead to the coyotes. If we have been taught to
keep our promises — if, in the simplest terms, our upbringing is
good enough — we stay with the body, or have bad dreams.

I am talking, of course, about the kind of social code that is   4
sometimes called, usually pejoratively, "wagon-train morality."
In fact that is precisely what it is. For better or worse, we are
what we learned as children: my own childhood was illuminated by graphic litanies of the grief awaiting those who failed
in their loyalties to each other. The Donner-Reed Party,
starving in the Sierra snows, all the ephemera of civilization
gone save that one vestigial taboo, the provision that no one
should eat his own blood kin. The Jayhawkers, who quarreled
and separated not far from where I am tonight. Some of them
died in the Funerals and some of them died down near
Badwater and most of the rest of them died in the Panamints.
A woman who got through gave the Valley its name. Some
might say that the Jayhawkers were killed by the desert
summer, and the Donner Party by the mountain winter, by
circumstances beyond control; we were taught instead that they
had somewhere abdicated their responsibilities, somehow
breached their primary loyalties, or they would not have found
themselves helpless in the mountain winter or the desert
summer, would not have given way to acrimony, would not
have deserted one another, would not have *failed*. In brief, we
heard such stories as cautionary tales, and they still suggest the
only kind of "morality" that seems to me to have any but the
most potentially mendacious meaning.

You are quite possibly impatient with me by now; I am   5
talking, you want to say, about a "morality" so primitive that it
scarcely deserves the name, a code that has as its point only
survival, not the attainment of the ideal good. Exactly.
Particularly out here tonight, in this country so ominous and
terrible that to live in it is to live with antimatter, it is difficult
to believe that "the good" is a knowable quantity. Let me tell
you what it is like out here tonight. Stories travel at night on the
desert. Someone gets in his pickup and drives a couple of
hundred miles for a beer, and he carries news of what is
happening, back wherever he came from. Then he drives

another hundred miles for another beer, and passes along stories from the last place as well as from the one before; it is a network kept alive by people whose instincts tell them that if they do not keep moving at night on the desert they will lose all reason. Here is a story that is going around the desert tonight: over across the Nevada line, sheriff's deputies are diving in some underground pools, trying to retrieve a couple of bodies known to be in the hole. The widow of one of the drowned boys is over there; she is eighteen, and pregnant, and is said not to leave the hole. The divers go down and come up, and she just stands there and stares into the water. They have been diving for ten days but have found no bottom to the caves, no bodies and no trace of them, only the black 90° water going down and down and down, and a single translucent fish, not classified. The story tonight is that one of the divers has been hauled up incoherent, out of his head, shouting — until they got him out of there so that the widow could not hear — about water that got hotter instead of cooler as he went down, about light flickering through the water, about magma, about underground nuclear testing.

That is the tone stories take out here, and there are quite a   6
few of them tonight. And it is more than the stories alone. Across the road at the Faith Community Church a couple of dozen old people, come here to live in trailers and die in the sun, are holding a prayer sing. I cannot hear them and do not want to. What I can hear are occasional coyotes and a constant chorus of "Baby the Rain Must Fall" from the jukebox in the Snake Room next door, and if I were also to hear those dying voices, those Midwestern voices drawn to this lunar country for some unimaginable atavistic rites, *rock of ages cleft for me*, I think I would lose my own reason. Every now and then I imagine I hear a rattlesnake, but my husband says that it is a faucet, a paper rustling, the wind. Then he stands by a window, and plays a flashlight over the dry wash outside.

What does it mean? It means nothing manageable. There is   7
some sinister hysteria in the air out here tonight, some hint of the monstrous perversion to which any human idea can come.

"I followed my own conscience." "I did what I thought was right." How many madmen have said it and meant it? How many murderers? Klaus Fuchs said it, and the men who committed the Mountain Meadows Massacre said it, and Alfred Rosenberg said it. And, as we are rotely and rather presumptuously reminded by those who would say it now, Jesus said it. Maybe we have all said it, and maybe we have been wrong. Except on that most primitive level — our loyalties to those we love — what could be more arrogant than to claim the primacy of personal conscience? ("Tell me," a rabbi asked Daniel Bell when he said, as a child, that he did not believe in God. "Do you think God cares?") At least some of the time, the world appears to me as a painting by Hieronymous Bosch;[1] were I to follow my conscience then, it would lead me out onto the desert with Marion Faye, out to where he stood in *The Deer Park*[2] looking east to Los Alamos and praying, as if for rain, that it would happen: ". . . *let it come and clear the rot and the stench and the stink, let it come for all of everywhere, just so it comes and the world stands clear in the white dead dawn.*"

Of course you will say that I do not have the right, even if   8
I had the power, to inflict that unreasonable conscience upon you; nor do I want you to inflict your conscience, however reasonable, however enlightened, upon me. ("We must be aware of the dangers which lie in our most generous wishes," Lionel Trilling once wrote. "Some paradox of our nature leads us, when once we have made our fellow men the objects of our enlightened interest, to go on to make them the objects of our pity, then of our wisdom, ultimately of our coercion.") That the ethic of conscience is intrinsically insidious seems scarcely a revelatory point, but it is one raised with increasing infrequency; even those who do raise it tend to *segue* with troubling readiness into the quite contradictory position that the ethic of

---

[1]*Bosch* (1450?–1516): Dutch painter of weird, hellish scenes, which we would call "surrealistic."

[2]*The Deer Park:* A novel by Norman Mailer, in which Marion Faye is a prominent character.

conscience is dangerous when it is "wrong," and admirable when it is "right."

You see I want to be quite obstinate about insisting that we 9 have no way of knowing — beyond that fundamental loyalty to the social code — what is "right" and what is "wrong," what is "good" and what "evil." I dwell so upon this because the most disturbing aspect of "morality" seems to me to be the frequency with which the word now appears; in the press, on television, in the most perfunctory kinds of conversation. Questions of straightforward power (or survival) politics, questions of quite indifferent public policy, questions of almost anything: they are all assigned these factitious moral burdens. There is something facile going on, some self-indulgence at work. Of course we would all like to "believe" in something, like to assuage our private guilts in public causes, like to lose our tiresome selves; like, perhaps, to transform the white flag of defeat at home into the brave white banner of battle away from home. And of course it is all right to do that; that is how, immemorially, things have gotten done. But I think it is all right only so long as we do not delude ourselves about what we are doing, and why. It is all right only so long as we remember that all the *ad hoc* committees, all the picket lines, all the brave signatures in *The New York Times*, all the tools of agitprop straight across the spectrum, do not confer upon anyone any *ipso facto* virtue. It is all right only so long as we recognize that the end may or may not be expedient, may or may not be a good idea, but in any case has nothing to do with "morality." Because when we start deceiving ourselves into thinking not that we want something or need something, not that it is a pragmatic necessity for us to have it, but that it is a *moral imperative* that we have it, then is when we join the fashionable madmen, and then is when the thin whine of hysteria is heard in the land, and then is when we are in bad trouble. And I suspect we are already there.

[1965 — U.S.A.]

Questions

1. Analyze the sentences of the first paragraph syntactically. What kind of rhythm does the syntax here produce? Why this rhythm?
2. The essay's thesis, which entails definition, is suggested at the end of the first paragraph. How? What is that thesis? Where in the essay is it stated overtly?
3. What audience was this essay written for? What does the reference to *The American Scholar* suggest? What in the essay is accounted for by its intended audience?
4. Why the emphasis on setting here? How does this emphasis tie in with the essay's thesis? How does the particularity of the setting contrast with the "ethic of conscience," which we are told "is intrinsically insidious" (paragraph 8)?
5. Much disparate material is brought together here coherently. How does Didion achieve coherence? For instance, how does she make the transition between paragraphs?
6. The image of the deputies diving to recover the two bodies is an emblem of Didion's understanding of morality. How so? What does the image say about the relation of humans and the natural world? How else is the nature of this relationship intimated in the essay? How does Didion's view of the relationship account for her sense of morality?

Writing Assignments

1. a) In a paragraph, write a critique of "On Morality." State its thesis; then consider the validity of the thesis as well as how it is argued and how well the case is made.

   b) In a separate paragraph, state your response to the essay and why you so respond.
2. Write an essay like "On Morality." For topic, choose an abstraction about which you feel you have something to say — democracy, duty, salvation, good, evil, or whatever. Then develop a thesis and argue it entirely by way of particulars — for instance, the particulars of concrete examples, of the details of a specified setting, of imagery. You may draw on disparate areas, as does Didion, as long as you are coherent and provide all transitions necessary, again, as does Didion.
3. Read the three essays by Didion that follow. Then write a paper analyzing her characteristic voice, her style, and the relationship between the two.

————————✤ Bureaucrats ✤————————

Joan Didion

The closed door upstairs at 120 South Spring Street in [1] downtown Los Angeles is marked OPERATIONS CENTER. In the windowless room beyond the closed door a reverential hush prevails. From six A.M. until seven P.M. in this windowless room men sit at consoles watching a huge board flash colored lights. "There's the heart attack," someone will murmur, or "we're getting the gawk effect." 120 South Spring is the Los Angeles office of Caltrans, or the California Department of Transportation, and the Operations Center is where Caltrans engineers monitor what they call "the 42-Mile Loop." The 42-Mile Loop is simply the rough triangle formed by the intersections of the Santa Monica, the San Diego and the Harbor freeways, and 42 miles represents less than ten per cent of freeway mileage in Los Angeles County alone, but these particular 42 miles are regarded around 120 South Spring with a special veneration. The Loop is a "demonstration system," a phrase much favored by everyone at Caltrans, and is part of a "pilot project," another two words carrying totemic weight on South Spring.

The Loop has electronic sensors embedded every half-mile [2] out there in the pavement itself, each sensor counting the crossing cars every twenty seconds. The Loop has its own mind, a Xerox Sigma V computer which prints out, all day and night, twenty-second readings on what is and is not moving in each of the Loop's eight lanes. It is the Xerox Sigma V that makes the big board flash red when traffic out there drops below fifteen miles an hour. It is the Xerox Sigma V that tells the Operations crew when they have an "incident" out there. An "incident" is the heart attack on the San Diego, the jackknifed truck on the Harbor, the Camaro just now tearing out the Cyclone fence on the Santa Monica. "Out there" is where incidents happen. The windowless room at 120 South Spring is where incidents get "verified." "Incident verification" is turning on the closed-circuit TV on the console and watching the traffic slow down to see (this is "the gawk effect") where the Camaro tore out the fence.

As a matter of fact there is a certain closed-circuit aspect to 3 the entire mood of the Operations Center. "Verifying" the incident does not after all "prevent" the incident, which lends the enterprise a kind of tranced distance, and on the day recently when I visited 120 South Spring it took considerable effort to remember what I had come to talk about, which was that particular part of the Loop called the Santa Monica Freeway. The Santa Monica Freeway is 16.2 miles long, runs from the Pacific Ocean to downtown Los Angeles through what is referred to at Caltrans as "the East-West Corridor," carries more traffic every day than any other freeway in California, has what connoisseurs of freeways concede to be the most beautiful access ramps in the world, and appeared to have been transformed by Caltrans, during the several weeks before I went downtown to talk about it, into a 16.2-mile parking lot.

The problem seemed to be another Caltrans "demonstra- 4 tion," or "pilot," a foray into bureaucratic terrorism they were calling "The Diamond Lane" in their promotional literature and "The Project" among themselves. That the promotional literature consisted largely of schedules for buses (or "Diamond Lane Expresses") and invitations to join a car pool via computer ("Commuter Computer") made clear not only the putative point of The Project, which was to encourage travel by car pool and bus, but also the actual point, which was to eradicate a central Southern California illusion, that of individual mobility, without anyone really noticing. This had not exactly worked out. "FREEWAY FIASCO," the *Los Angeles Times* was headlining page-one stories. "THE DIAMOND LANE: ANOTHER BUST BY CALTRANS." "CALTRANS PILOT EFFORT ANOTHER IN LONG LIST OF FAILURES." "OFFICIAL DIAMOND LANE STANCE: LET THEM HOWL."

All "The Diamond Lane" theoretically involved was reserv- 5 ing the fast inside lanes on the Santa Monica for vehicles carrying three or more people, but in practice this meant that 25 per cent of the freeway was reserved for 3 per cent of the cars, and there were other odd wrinkles here and there suggesting that Caltrans had dedicated itself to making all movement around Los Angeles as arduous as possible. There was for example the matter of surface streets. A "surface street" is anything around Los Angeles that is not a freeway ("going surface" from one part of town to another is generally regarded as idiosyncratic), and surface streets do not fall directly within the Caltrans domain, but now the engineer in charge of surface streets was accusing Caltrans of threatening and intimidating him. It appeared that Caltrans wanted him to create a "confused and congested situation" on his surface streets, so as to force drivers back to the freeway, where they would meet a still more confused and congested situation and decide to stay home, or take a bus. "We are beginning a process of deliberately making it harder for drivers to use freeways," a Caltrans director had in fact said at a transit conference some months before. "We are prepared to endure considerable public outcry in order to pry John Q. Public out of his car. . . . I would emphasize that this is a political decision, and one that can be reversed if the public gets sufficiently enraged to throw us rascals out."

Of course this political decision was in the name of the   6
greater good, was in the interests of "environmental improvement" and "conservation of resources," but even there the figures had about them a certain Caltrans opacity. The Santa Monica normally carried 240,000 cars and trucks every day. These 240,000 cars and trucks normally carried 260,000 people. What Caltrans described as its ultimate goal on the Santa Monica was to carry the same 260,000 people, "but in 7,800 fewer, or 232,200 vehicles." The figure "232,200" had a visionary precision to it that did not automatically create confidence, especially since the only effect so far had been to disrupt traffic throughout the Los Angeles basin, triple the number of daily accidents on the Santa Monica, prompt the initiation of two lawsuits against Caltrans, and cause large numbers of Los Angeles County residents to behave, most

uncharacteristically, as an ignited and conscious proletariat. Citizen guerrillas splashed paint and scattered nails in the Diamond Lanes. Diamond Lane maintenance crews expressed fear of hurled objects. Down at 120 South Spring the architects of the Diamond Lane had taken to regarding "the media" as the architects of their embarrassment, and Caltrans statements in the press had been cryptic and contradictory, reminiscent only of old communiqués out of Vietnam.

To understand what was going on it is perhaps necessary to 7 have participated in the freeway experience, which is the only secular communion Los Angeles has. Mere driving on the freeway is in no way the same as participating in it. Anyone can "drive" on the freeway, and many people with no vocation for it do, hesitating here and resisting there, losing the rhythm of the lane change, thinking about where they came from and where they are going. Actual participants think only about where they are. Actual participation requires a total surrender, a concentration so intense as to seem a kind of narcosis, a rapture-of-the-freeway. The mind goes clean. The rhythm takes over. A distortion of time occurs, the same distortion that characterizes the instant before an accident. It takes only a few seconds to get off the Santa Monica Freeway at National-Overland, which is a difficult exit requiring the driver to cross two new lanes of traffic streamed in from the San Diego Freeway, but those few seconds always seem to me the longest part of the trip. The moment is dangerous. The exhilaration is in doing it. "As you acquire the special skills involved," Reyner Banham observed in an extraordinary chapter about the freeways in his 1971 *Los Angeles: The Architecture of Four Ecologies*, "the freeways become a special way of being alive . . . the extreme concentration required in Los Angeles seems to bring on a state of heightened awareness that some locals find mystical."

Indeed some locals do, and some nonlocals too. Reducing 8 the number of lone souls careering around the East-West Corridor in a state of mechanized rapture may or may not have seemed socially desirable, but what it was definitely not going to seem was easy. "We're only seeing an initial period of unfamiliarity," I was assured the day I visited Caltrans. I was talking to a woman named Eleanor Wood and she was thoroughly and professionally grounded in the diction of "planning" and it did not seem likely that I could interest her in considering the freeway as regional mystery. "Any time you try to rearrange people's daily habits, they're apt to react impetuously. All this project requires is a certain rearrangement of people's daily planning. That's really all we want."

It occurred to me that a certain rearrangement of people's 9 daily planning might seem, in less rarefied air than is breathed at 120 South Spring, rather a great deal to want, but so impenetrable was the sense of higher social purpose there in the Operations Center that I did not express this reservation. Instead I changed the subject, mentioned an earlier "pilot project" on the Santa Monica: the big electronic message boards that Caltrans had installed a year or two before. The idea was that traffic information transmitted from the Santa Monica to the Xerox Sigma V could be translated, here in the Operations Center, into suggestions to the driver, and flashed right back out to the Santa Monica. This operation, in that it involved telling drivers electronically what they already knew empirically, had the rather spectral circularity that seemed to mark a great many Caltrans schemes, and I was interested in how Caltrans thought it worked.

"Actually the message boards were part of a larger pilot 10 project," Mrs. Wood said. "An ongoing project in incident management. With the message boards we hoped to learn if motorists would modify their behavior according to what we told them on the boards."

I asked if the motorists had.   11

"Actually no," Mrs. Wood said finally. "They didn't react 12 to the signs exactly as we'd hypothesized they would, no. *But.* If we'd *known* what the motorist would do . . . then we wouldn't have needed a pilot project in the first place, would we."

The circle seemed intact. Mrs. Wood and I smiled, and 13 shook hands. I watched the big board until all lights turned green on the Santa Monica and then I left and drove home on it, all 16.2 miles of it. All the way I remembered that I was watched by the Xerox Sigma V. All the way the message boards gave me the number to call for CAR POOL INFO. As I left the freeway it occurred to me that they might have their own rapture down at 120 South Spring, and it could be called Perpetuating the Department. Today the California Highway Patrol reported that, during the first six weeks of the Diamond Lane, accidents on the Santa Monica, which normally range between 49 and 72 during a six-week period, totaled 204. Yesterday plans were announced to extend the Diamond Lane to other freeways at a cost of $42,500,000.

[1979 – U.S.A.]

Questions

1. In the first two paragraphs, the phrases "the closed door" and "the windowless room" repeat several times. Why? What might the two images symbolize?

2. There are many references to and images of circularity here. Pick out three or four. What does circularity come to symbolize in "Bureaucrats"? How does it tie in with the images of "closed door" and "windowless room"?

3. There is much repetition in "Bureaucrats." Why? What does Didion achieve through repetition?

4. Throughout the essay, words associated with religion are used in connection with Caltrans and the freeway (the oft repeated "rapture," for example). What is the point of such diction? In what way is the analogy implied by the diction ironic?

5. Didion makes few direct comments about Caltrans. How, then, is her attitude conveyed? What is the tone of the essay? How is tone established and maintained here?

6. What is the theme of this essay? In what way is it about diction?

Writing Assignments

1. Have you ever been caught in a bureaucratic tangle? If so, describe and discuss it in a paragraph or more. You might end with a consideration of the general significance of the incident if you feel it says something about, for instance, the educational establishment, or the military, or society at large.

2. In a paper, discuss some group with which you are familiar that has its own special jargon. Establish what that jargon is and then discuss why it is used by the group and why plain English is eschewed.

3. Didion lets the facts speak for themselves, though she loads her language to communicate an ironic perspective on those facts. Choose something that interests you and write an essay in which you report on what you have chosen *without direct comment.* Imply your attitude (and thus your thesis), as does Didion, through strategic repetition, diction, tone, and so on.

✤ In Bed ✤

Joan Didion

THREE, FOUR, SOMETIMES FIVE TIMES A MONTH, I SPEND THE DAY IN   1
bed with a migraine headache, insensible to the world around me. Almost every day of every month, between these attacks, I feel the sudden irrational irritation and flush of blood into the cerebral arteries which tell me that migraine is on its way, and I take certain drugs to avert its arrival. If I did not take the drugs, I would be able to function perhaps one day in four. The physiological error called migraine is, in brief, central to the given of my life. When I was 15, 16, even 25, I used to think that I could rid myself of this error by simply denying it, character over chemistry. "Do you have headaches *sometimes? frequently? never?*" the application forms would demand. "Check one." Wary of the trap, wanting whatever it was that the successful circumnavigation of that particular form could bring (a job, a scholarship, the respect of mankind and the grace of God), I would check one. *"Sometimes,"* I would lie. That in fact I spent one or two days a week almost unconscious with pain seemed a shameful secret, evidence not merely of some chemical inferiority but of all my bad attitudes, unpleasant tempers, wrongthink.

For I had no brain tumor, no eyestrain, no high blood   2
pressure, nothing wrong with me at all: I simply had migraine

headaches, and migraine headaches were, as everyone who did not have them knew, imaginary. I fought migraine then, ignored the warnings it sent, went to school and later to work in spite of it, sat through lectures in Middle English and presentations to advertisers with involuntary tears running down the right side of my face, threw up in washrooms, stumbled home by instinct, emptied ice trays onto my bed and tried to freeze the pain in my right temple, wished only for a neurosurgeon who would do a lobotomy on house call, and cursed my imagination.

It was a long time before I began thinking mechanistically 3 enough to accept migraine for what it was: something with which I would be living, the way some people live with diabetes. Migraine is something more than the fancy of a neurotic imagination. It is an essentially hereditary complex of symptoms, the most frequently noted but by no means the most unpleasant of which is a vascular headache of blinding severity, suffered by a surprising number of women, a fair number of men (Thomas Jefferson had migraine, and so did Ulysses S. Grant, the day he accepted Lee's surrender), and by some unfortunate children as young as two years old. (I had my first when I was eight. It came on during a fire drill at the Columbia School in Colorado Springs, Colorado. I was taken first home and then to the infirmary at Peterson Field, where my father was stationed. The Air Corps doctor prescribed an enema.) Almost anything can trigger a specific attack of migraine: stress, allergy, fatigue, an abrupt change in barometric pressure, a contretemps over a parking ticket. A flashing light. A fire drill. One inherits, of course, only the predisposition. In other words I spent yesterday in bed with a headache not merely because of my bad attitudes, unpleasant tempers and wrongthink, but because both my grandmothers had migraine, my father has migraine and my mother has migraine.

No one knows precisely what it is that is inherited. The 4 chemistry of migraine, however, seems to have some connection with the nerve hormone named serotonin, which is naturally present in the brain. The amount of serotonin in the blood falls sharply at the onset of migraine, and one migraine drug, methysergide, or Sansert, seems to have some effect on serotonin. Methysergide is a derivative of lysergic acid (in fact Sandoz Pharmaceuticals first synthesized LSD-25 while looking for a migraine cure), and its use is hemmed about with so many contraindications and side effects that most doctors prescribe it only in the most incapacitating cases. Methysergide, when it is prescribed, is taken daily, as a preventive; another preventive which works for some people is old-fashioned ergotamine tartrate, which helps to constrict the swelling blood vessels during the "aura," the period which in most cases precedes the actual headache.

Once an attack is under way, however, no drug touches it. 5 Migraine gives some people mild hallucinations, temporarily blinds others, shows up not only as a headache but as a gastrointestinal disturbance, a painful sensitivity to all sensory stimuli, an abrupt overpowering fatigue, a strokelike aphasia, and a crippling inability to make even the most routine connections. When I am in a migraine aura (for some people the aura lasts fifteen minutes, for others several hours), I will drive through red lights, lose the house keys, spill whatever I am holding, lose the ability to focus my eyes or frame coherent sentences, and generally give the appearance of being on drugs, or drunk. The actual headache, when it comes, brings with it chills, sweating, nausea, a debility that seems to stretch the very limits of endurance. That no one dies of migraine seems, to someone deep into an attack, an ambiguous blessing.

My husband also has migraine, which is unfortunate for 6 him but fortunate for me: perhaps nothing so tends to prolong an attack as the accusing eye of someone who has never had a headache. "Why not take a couple of aspirin," the unafflicted will say from the doorway, or "I'd have a headache, too, spending a beautiful day like this inside with all the shades drawn." All of us who have migraine suffer not only from the attacks themselves but from this common conviction that we are perversely refusing to cure ourselves by taking a couple of aspirin, that we are making ourselves sick, that we "bring it on ourselves." And in the most immediate sense, the sense of why we have a headache this Tuesday and not last Thursday, of course we often do. There certainly is what doctors call a "migraine personality," and that personality tends to be ambitious, inward, intolerant of error, rather rigidly organized, perfectionist. "You don't look like a migraine personality," a doctor once said to me. "Your hair's messy. But I suppose you're a compulsive housekeeper." Actually my house is kept even more negligently than my hair, but the doctor was right nonetheless: perfectionism can also take the form of spending most of a week writing and rewriting and not writing a single paragraph.

But not all perfectionists have migraine, and not all 7 migrainous people have migraine personalities. We do not escape heredity. I have tried in most of the available ways to escape my own migrainous heredity (at one point I learned to give myself two daily injections of histamine with a hypodermic needle, even though the needle so frightened me that I had to close my eyes when I did it), but I still have migraine. And I have learned now to live with it, learned when to expect it, how to outwit it, even how to regard it, when it does come, as more friend than lodger. We have reached a certain understanding, my migraine and I. It never comes when I am in real trouble. Tell me that my house is burned down, my husband has left me, that there is gunfighting in the streets and panic in the banks, and I will not respond by getting a headache. It comes instead when I am fighting not an open but a guerrilla war with my own life, during weeks of small household confusions, lost laundry, unhappy help, canceled appointments, on days when the telephone rings too much and I get no work done and the wind is coming up. On days like that my friend comes uninvited.

And once it comes, now that I am wise in its ways, I no 8 longer fight it. I lie down and let it happen. At first every small apprehension is magnified, every anxiety a pounding terror. Then the pain comes, and I concentrate only on that. Right there is the usefulness of migraine, there in that imposed yoga, the concentration on the pain. For when the pain recedes, ten or twelve hours later, everything goes with it, all the hidden resentments, all the vain anxieties. The migraine has acted as a circuit breaker, and the fuses have emerged intact. There is a pleasant convalescent euphoria. I open the windows and feel the air, eat gratefully, sleep well. I notice the particular nature of a flower in a glass on the stair landing. I count my blessings.

[1979 — U.S.A.]

Questions

1. This essay has many figures of speech. What are a few? What do they serve to do in this context?
2. Didion is always rewarding to read and to study with respect to tone. This essay contains two contrasting tones. What are they? Why does the tone shift around the middle of paragraph 7?
3. What is Didion's primary aim through paragraph 6? Her essay, however, goes beyond this aim. How so? What is Didion's theme?
4. Didion's procedure is unusual in that her main theme does not announce itself until the end. Why? What is gained by this procedure? How does Didion hold our attention before we get to her main idea?

Writing Assignments

1. Have you ever had an illness that led people to treat you in a way you didn't like, as Didion says she was treated (paragraph 6)? If so, write a paragraph or two describing how they treated you and why they acted so inappropriately.
2. Write an essay on how something good can come from something bad. Structure your essay as Didion does hers, beginning with the bad and then surprising your reader with the unexpected good.

✤ Miami: The Cuban Presence ✤
Joan Didion

On the 150th anniversary of the founding of Dade County, 1
in February of 1986, the Miami *Herald* asked four prominent
amateurs of local history to name "the ten people and the ten
events that had the most impact on the county's history." Each
of the four submitted his or her own list of "The Most
Influential People in Dade's History," and among the names
mentioned were Julia Tuttle ("pioneer businesswoman"),
Henry Flagler ("brought the Florida East Coast Railway to
Miami"), Alexander Orr, Jr. ("started the research that saved
Miami's drinking water from salt"), Everest George Sewell
("publicized the city and fostered its deepwater seaport"). . . .
There was Dr. James M. Jackson, an early Miami physician.
There was Napoleon Bonaparte Broward, the governor of
Florida who initiated the draining of the Everglades. There
appeared on three of the four lists the name of the developer of
Coral Gables, George Merrick. There appeared on one of the
four lists the name of the coach of the Miami Dolphins, Don
Shula.

On none of these lists of "The Most Influential People in 2
Dade's History" did the name Fidel Castro appear, nor for that
matter did the name of any Cuban, although the presence of
Cubans in Dade County did not go entirely unnoted by the
Herald panel. When it came to naming the Ten Most Important
"Events," as opposed to "People," all four panelists mentioned
the arrival of the Cubans, but at slightly off angles ("Mariel
Boatlift of 1980" was the way one panelist saw it), and as if this
arrival had been just another of those isolated disasters or
innovations which deflect the course of any growing community, on an approximate par with the other events mentioned,
for example the Freeze of 1895, the Hurricane of 1926, the
opening of the Dixie Highway, the establishment of Miami
International Airport, and the adoption, in 1957, of the

metropolitan form of government, "enabling the Dade County Commission to provide urban services to the increasingly populous unincorporated area."

This set of mind, in which the local Cuban community was 3 seen as a civic challenge determinedly met, was not uncommon among Anglos to whom I talked in Miami, many of whom persisted in the related illusions that the city was small, manageable, prosperous in a predictable broad-based way, southern in a progressive Sunbelt way, American, and belonged to them. In fact 43 percent of the population of Dade County was by that time "Hispanic," which meant mostly Cuban. Fifty-six percent of the population of Miami itself was Hispanic. The most visible new buildings on the Miami skyline, the Arquitectonica buildings along Brickell Avenue, were by a firm with a Cuban founder. There were Cubans in the board rooms of the major banks, Cubans in clubs that did not admit Jews or blacks, and four Cubans in the most recent mayoralty campaign, two of whom, Raul Masvidal and Xavier Suarez, had beaten out the incumbent and all other candidates to meet in a runoff, and one of whom, Xavier Suarez, a thirty-six-year-old lawyer who had been brought from Cuba to the United States as a child, was by then mayor of Miami.

The entire tone of the city, the way people looked and 4 talked and met one another, was Cuban. The very image the city had begun presenting of itself, what was then its newfound glamour, its "hotness" (hot colors, hot vice, shady dealings under the palm trees), was that of prerevolutionary Havana, as perceived by Americans. There was even in the way women dressed in Miami a definable Havana look, a more distinct emphasis on the hips and décolletage, more black, more veiling, a generalized flirtatiousness of style not then current in American cities. In the shoe departments at Brudine's and Jordan Marsh there were more platform soles than there might have been in another American city, and fewer displays of the running shoe ethic. I recall being struck, during an afternoon spent at La Liga Contra el Cancer, a prominent exile charity which raises money to help cancer patients, by the appearance of the volunteers who had met that day to stuff envelopes for a benefit. Their hair was sleek, of a slightly other period, immaculate pageboys and French twists. They wore Bruno Magli pumps, and silk and linen dresses of considerable expense. There seemed to be a preference for strictest gray or black, but the effect remained lush, tropical, like a room full of perfectly groomed mangoes.

This was not, in other words, an invisible 56 percent of the 5 population. Even the social notes in *Diario Las Americas* and in *El Herald,* the daily Spanish edition of the *Herald* written and edited for *el exilio,* suggested a dominant culture, one with money to spend and a notable willingness to spend it in public. La Liga Contra el Cancer alone sponsored, in a single year, two benefit dinner dances, one benefit ball, a benefit children's fashion show, a benefit telethon, a benefit exhibition of jewelry, a benefit presentation of Miss Universe contestants, and a benefit showing, with Saks Fifth Avenue and chicken *vol-au-vent,* of the Adolfo (as it happened, a Cuban) fall collection.

One morning *El Herald* would bring news of the gala at the 6 Pavillon of the Amigos Latinamericanos del Museo de Ciencia y Planetarium; another morning, of an upcoming event at the Big Five Club, a Miami club founded by former members of five fashionable clubs in prerevolutionary Havana: a *coctel,* or cocktail party, at which tables would be assigned for yet another gala, the annual "Baile Imperial de las Rosas" of the American Cancer Society, Hispanic Ladies Auxiliary. Some members of the community were honoring Miss America Latina with dinner dancing at the Doral. Some were being honored themselves, at the Spirit of Excellence Awards Dinner at the Omni. Some were said to be enjoying the skiing at Vail; others to prefer Bariloche, in Argentina. Some were reported unable to attend (but sending checks for) the gala at the Pavillon of the Amigos Latinamericanos del Museo de Ciencia y Planetarium because of a scheduling conflict, with *el coctel de* Paula Hawkins.

Fete followed fete, all high visibility. Almost any day it was 7 possible to drive past the limestone arches and fountains which marked the boundaries of Coral Gables and see little girls being photographed in the tiaras and ruffled hoop skirts and maribou-trimmed illusion capes they would wear at their *quinces,* the elaborate fifteenth-birthday parties at which the community's female children came of official age. The favored facial expression for a *quince* photograph was a classic smolder. The favored backdrop was one suggesting Castilian grandeur, which was how the Coral Gables arches happened to figure. Since the idealization of the virgin implicit in the *quince* could exist only in the presence of its natural foil, *machismo,* there was often a brother around, or a boyfriend. There was also a mother, in dark glasses, not only to protect the symbolic virgin but to point out the better angle, the more aristocratic location. The *quinceanera* would pick up her hoop skirts and move as directed, often revealing the scuffed Jellies she had worn that day to school. A few weeks later there she would be, transformed in *Diario Las Americas,* one of the morning battalion of smoldering fifteen-year-olds, each with her arch, her fountain, her borrowed scenery, the gift if not exactly the intention of the late George Merrick, who built the arches when he developed Coral Gables.

Neither the photographs of the Cuban *quinceaneras* nor the   8 notes about the *coctel* at the Big Five were apt to appear in the newspapers read by Miami Anglos, nor, for that matter, was much information at all about the daily life of the Cuban majority. When, in the fall of 1986, Florida International University offered an evening course called "Cuban Miami: A Guide for Non-Cubans," the *Herald* sent a staff writer, who covered the classes as if from a distant beat. "Already I have begun to make some sense out of a culture, that, while it totally surrounds us, has remained inaccessible and alien to me," the *Herald* writer was reporting by the end of the first meeting, and, by the end of the fourth:

> What I see day to day in Miami, moving through mostly Anglo corridors of the community, are just small bits and pieces of that other world, the tip of something much larger than I'd imagined. . . . We may frequent the restaurants here, or wander into the occasional festival. But mostly we

try to ignore Cuban Miami, even as we rub up against this teeming, incomprehensible presence.

Only thirteen people, including the *Herald* writer, turned up 9 for the first meeting of "Cuban Miami: A Guide for Non-Cubans" (two more appeared at the second meeting, along with a security guard, because of telephone threats prompted by what the *Herald* writer called "somebody's twisted sense of national pride"), an enrollment which suggested a certain willingness among non-Cubans to let Cuban Miami remain just that, Cuban, the "incomprehensible presence." In fact there had come to exist in South Florida two parallel cultures, separate but not exactly equal, a key distinction being that only one of the two, the Cuban, exhibited even a remote interest in the activities of the other. "The American community is not really aware of what is happening in the Cuban community," an exiled banker named Luis Botifoll said in a 1983 *Herald* Sunday magazine piece about ten prominent local Cubans. "We are clannish, but at least we know who is whom in the American establishment. They do not." About another of the ten Cubans featured in this piece, Jorge Mas Canosa, the *Herald* had this to say:

> He is an advisor to US Senators, a confidant of federal bureaucrats, a lobbyist for anti-Castro US policies, a near unknown in Miami. When his political group sponsored a luncheon speech in Miami by Secretary of Defense Caspar Weinberger, almost none of the American business leaders attending had ever heard of their Cuban host.

The general direction of this piece, which appeared under 10 the cover line "THE CUBANS: *They're ten of the most powerful men in Miami. Half the population doesn't know it,* " was, as the *Herald* put it,

> to challenge the widespread presumption that Miami's Cubans are not really Americans, that they are a foreign presence here, an exile community that is trying to turn South Florida into North Cuba. . . . The top ten are not separatists; they have achieved success in the most

traditional ways. They are the solid, bedrock citizens, hard-working humanitarians who are role models for a community that seems determined to assimilate itself into American society.

This was interesting. It was written by one of the few 11 Cubans then on the *Herald* staff, and yet it described, however unwittingly, the precise angle at which Miami Anglos and Miami Cubans were failing to connect: Miami Anglos were in fact interested in Cubans only to the extent that they could cast them as aspiring immigrants, "determined to assimilate," a "hard-working" minority not different in kind from other groups of resident aliens. (But had I met any Haitians, a number of Anglos asked when I said that I had been talking to Cubans.) Anglos (who were, significantly, referred to within the Cuban community as "Americans") spoke of cross-cultur- alization, and of what they believed to be a meaningful second-generation preference for hamburgers, and rock-and- roll. They spoke of "diversity," and of Miami's "Hispanic flavor," an approach in which 56 percent of the population was seen as decorative, like the Coral Gables arches.

Fixed as they were on this image of the melting pot, of 12 immigrants fleeing a disruptive revolution to find a place in the American sun, Anglos did not on the whole understand that assimilation would be considered by most Cubans a doubtful goal at best. Nor did many Anglos understand that living in Florida was still at the deepest level construed by Cubans as a temporary condition, an accepted political option shaped by the continuing dream, if no longer the immediate expectation, of a vindicatory return. *El exilio* was for Cubans a ritual, a respected tradition. *La revolución* was also a ritual, a trope fixed in Cuban political rhetoric at least since José Martí, a concept broadly interpreted to mean reform, or progress, or even just change. Ramón Grau San Martín, the president of Cuba during the autumn of 1933 and from 1944 until 1948, had presented himself as a revolutionary, as had his 1948 successor, Carlos Prío. Even Fulgencio Batista had entered Havana life calling for *la revolución,* and had later been accused of betraying it, even as Fidel Castro was now.

This was a process Cuban Miami understood, but Anglo 13 Miami did not, remaining as it did arrestingly innocent of even the most general information about Cuba and Cubans. Miami Anglos for example still had trouble with Cuban names, and Cuban food. When the Cuban novelist Guillermo Cabrera Infante came from London to lecture at Miami-Dade Community College, he was referred to by several Anglo faculty members to whom I spoke as "Infante." Cuban food was widely seen not as a minute variation on that eaten throughout both the Caribbean and the Mediterranean but as "exotic," and full of garlic. A typical Thursday food section of the *Herald* included recipes for Broiled Lemon-Curry Cornish Game Hens, Chicken Tetrazzini, King Cake, Pimiento Cheese, Raisin Sauce for Ham, Sauteed Spiced Peaches, Shrimp Scampi, Easy Beefy Stir-Fry, and four ways to use dried beans ("Those cheap, humble beans that have long sustained the world's poor have become the trendy set's new pet"), none of them Cuban.

This was all consistent, and proceeded from the original 14 construction, that of the exile as an immigration. There was no reason to be curious about Cuban food, because Cuban teenagers preferred hamburgers. There was no reason to get Cuban names right, because they were complicated, and would be simplified by the second generation, or even by the first. "Jorge L. Mas" was the way Jorge Mas Canosa's business card read. "Raul Masvidal" was the way Raul Masvidal y Jury ran for mayor of Miami. There was no reason to know about Cuban history, because history was what immigrants were fleeing.

Even the revolution, the reason for the immigration, could 15 be covered in a few broad strokes: "Batista," "Castro," "26 Julio," this last being the particular broad stroke that inspired the Miami Springs Holiday Inn, on July 26, 1985, the thirty-second anniversary of the day Fidel Castro attacked the Moncada Barracks and so launched his six-year struggle for power in Cuba, to run a bar special on Cuba Libres, thinking to attract local Cubans by commemorating their holiday. "It was a mistake," the manager said, besieged by outraged exiles. "The gentleman who did it is from Minnesota."

There was in fact no reason, in Miami as well as in 16 Minnesota, to know anything at all about Cubans, since Miami Cubans were now, if not Americans, at least aspiring Americans, and worthy of Anglo attention to the exact extent that they were proving themselves, in the *Herald's* words, "role models for a community that seems determined to assimilate itself into American society"; or, as George Bush put it in a 1986 Miami address to the Cuban American National Foundation, "the most eloquent testimony I know to the basic strength and success of America, as well as to the basic weakness and failure of Communism and Fidel Castro."

The use of this special lens, through which the exiles were 17 seen as a tribute to the American system, a point scored in the battle of the ideologies, tended to be encouraged by those outside observers who dropped down from the northeast corridor for a look and a column or two. George Will, in *Newsweek*, saw Miami as "a new installment in the saga of America's absorptive capacity," and Southwest Eighth Street as the place where "these exemplary Americans," the seven Cubans who had been gotten together to brief him, "initiated a columnist to fried bananas and black-bean soup and other Cuban contributions to the tanginess of American life." George Gilder, in *The Wilson Quarterly*, drew pretty much the same lesson from Southwest Eighth Street, finding it "more effervescently thriving than its crushed prototype," by which he seemed to mean Havana. In fact Eighth Street was for George Gilder a street that seemed to "percolate with the forbidden commerce of the dying island to the south . . . the Refrescos Cawy, the Competidora and El Cuño cigarettes, the *guayaberas*, [1] the Latin music pulsing from the storefronts, the pyramids of mangoes and tubers, gourds and plantains, the iced coconuts

---

[1]*Guayaberas:* Short, lightweight jackets.

served with a straw, the new theaters showing the latest anti-Castro comedies."

There was nothing on this list, with the possible exception 18 of the "anti-Castro comedies," that could not most days be found on Southwest Eighth Street, but the list was also a fantasy, and a particularly *gringo* fantasy, one in which Miami Cubans, who came from a culture which had represented western civilization in this hemisphere since before there was a United States of America, appeared exclusively as vendors of plantains, their native music "pulsing" behind them. There was in any such view of Miami Cubans an extraordinary element of condescension, and it was the very condescension shared by Miami Anglos, who were inclined to reduce the particular liveliness and sophistication of local Cuban life to a matter of shrines on the lawn and love potions in the *botanicas*, the primitive exotica of the tourist's Caribbean.

Cubans were perceived as most satisfactory when they 19 appeared most fully to share the aspirations and manners of middle-class Americans, at the same time adding "color" to the city on appropriate occasions, for example at their *quinces* (the *quinces* were one aspect of Cuban life almost invariably mentioned by Anglos, who tended to present them as evidence of Cuban extravagance, i.e., Cuban irresponsibility, or child-ishness), or on the day of the annual Calle Ocho Festival, when they could, according to the *Herald*, "samba" in the streets and stir up a paella for two thousand (ten cooks, two thousand mussels, two hundred and twenty pounds of lobster, and four hundred and forty pounds of rice), using rowboat oars as spoons. Cubans were perceived as least satisfactory when they "acted clannish," "kept to themselves," "had their own ways," and, two frequent flash points, "spoke Spanish when they didn't need to" and "got political"; complaints, each of them, which suggested an Anglo view of what Cubans should be at significant odds with what Cubans were.

This question of language was curious. The sound of 20 spoken Spanish was common in Miami, but it was also common in Los Angeles, and Houston, and even in the cities of the Northeast. What was unusual about Spanish in Miami was not that it was so often spoken, but that it was so often heard: In, say, Los Angeles, Spanish remained a language only barely registered by the Anglo population, part of the ambient noise, the language spoken by the people who worked in the car wash and came to trim the trees and cleared the tables in restaurants. In Miami Spanish was spoken by the people who ate in the restaurants, the people who owned the cars and the trees, which made, on the socio-auditory scale, a considerable difference. Exiles who felt isolated or declassed by language in New York or Los Angeles thrived in Miami. An entrepreneur who spoke no English could still, in Miami, buy, sell, negotiate, leverage assets, float bonds, and, if he were so inclined, attend galas twice a week, in black tie. "I have been after the *Herald* ten times to do a story about millionaires in Miami who do not speak more than two words in English," one prominent exile told me. " 'Yes' and 'no.' Those are the two words. They come here with five dollars in their pockets and without speaking another word of English they are millionaires."

The truculence a millionaire who spoke only two words of 21 English might provoke among the less resourceful native citizens of a nominally American city was predictable, and manifested itself rather directly. In 1980, the year of Mariel, Dade County voters had approved a referendum requiring that county business be conducted exclusively in English. Notwithstanding the fact that this legislation was necessarily amended to exclude emergency medical and certain other services, and notwithstanding even the fact that many local meetings continued to be conducted in that unbroken alternation of Spanish and English which had become the local patois ("I will be in Boston on Sunday and *desafortunadamente yo tengo un compromiso en* Boston *que no puedo romper y yo no podré estar con Vds.*," read the minutes of a 1984 Miami City Commission meeting I had occasion to look up. "*En espíritu, estaré, pero* the other members of the commission I am sure are invited . . ."),[2] the very existence of this referendum was seen by many as ground regained, a point made. By 1985 a St. Petersburg optometrist named Robert Melby was launching his third attempt in four years to have English declared the official language of the state of Florida, as it would be in 1986 of California. "I don't know why your legislators here are so, how should I put it? — spineless," Robert Melby complained about those South Florida politicians who knew how to count. "No one down here seems to want to run with the issue."

Even among those Anglos who distanced themselves from [22] such efforts, Anglos who did not perceive themselves as economically or socially threatened by Cubans, there remained considerable uneasiness on the matter of language, perhaps because the inability or the disinclination to speak English tended to undermine their conviction that assimilation was an ideal universally shared by those who were to be assimilated. This uneasiness had for example shown up repeatedly during the 1985 mayoralty campaign, surfacing at odd but apparently irrepressible angles. The winner of that contest, Xavier Suarez, who was born in Cuba but educated in the United States, a graduate of Harvard Law, was reported in a wire service story to speak, an apparently unexpected accomplishment, "flawless English."

A less prominent Cuban candidate for mayor that year had [23] unsettled reporters at a televised "meet the candidates" forum by answering in Spanish the questions they asked in English. "For all I or my dumbstruck colleagues knew," the *Herald* political editor complained in print after the event, "he was reciting his high school's alma mater or the ten Commandments over and over again. The only thing I understood was the

---

[2] *("I Will be in Boston . . .")*: An illustration of the mingling of English and Spanish in Miami speech. Fully in English, the statement reads: "I will be in Boston on Sunday and unfortunately I have an appointment in Boston that I can't break, so I won't be able to be with you. In spirit I will be, but the other members of the commission I'm sure are invited. . . ."

occasional *Cubanos vota Cubano* he tossed in." It was noted by another *Herald* columnist that of the leading candidates, only one, Raul Masvidal, had a listed telephone number, but: ". . . if you call Masvidal's 661–0259 number on Kiaora Street in Coconut Grove — during the day, anyway — you'd better speak Spanish. I spoke to two women there, and neither spoke enough English to answer the question of whether it was the candidate's number."

On the morning this last item came to my attention in the 24 *Herald* I studied it for some time. Raul Masvidal was at that time the chairman of the board of the Miami Savings Bank and the Miami Savings Corporation. He was a former chairman of the Biscayne Bank, and a minority stockholder in the M Bank, of which he had been a founder. He was a member of the Board of Regents for the state university system of Florida. He had paid $600,000 for the house on Kiaora Street in Coconut Grove, buying it specifically because he needed to be a Miami resident (Coconut Grove is part of the city of Miami) in order to run for mayor, and he had sold his previous house, in the incorporated city of Coral Gables, for $1,100,000.

The Spanish words required to find out whether the 25 number listed for the house on Kiaora Street was in fact the candidate's number would have been roughly these: *"¿Es la casa de Raul Masvidal?"* The answer might have been *"Sí,"* or the answer might have been *"No."* It seemed to me that there must be very few people working on daily newspapers along the southern borders of the United States who would consider this exchange entirely out of reach, and fewer still who would not accept it as a commonplace of American domestic life that daytime telephone calls to middle-class urban households will frequently be answered by women who speak Spanish.

Something else was at work in this item, a real resistance, 26 a balkiness, a coded version of the same message Dade County voters had sent when they decreed that their business be done only in English: WILL THE LAST AMERICAN TO LEAVE MIAMI PLEASE BRING THE FLAG, the famous bumper stickers had read the year of

Mariel. "It was the last American stronghold in Dade County," the owner of the Gator Kicks Longneck Saloon, out where Southwest Eighth Street runs into the Everglades, had said after he closed the place for good the night of Super Bowl Sunday, 1986. "Fortunately or unfortunately, I'm not alone in my inability," a *Herald* columnist named Charles Whited had written a week or so later, in a column about not speaking Spanish. "A good many Americans have left Miami because they want to live someplace where everybody speaks one language: theirs." In this context the call to the house on Kiaora Street in Coconut Grove which did or did not belong to Raul Masvidal appeared not as a statement of literal fact but as shorthand, a glove thrown down, a stand, a cry from the heart of a beleaguered raj.[3]

[1987 — U.S.A.]

Questions

1. Separated by spacing, Didion's beginning sets both the tone and the method of her essay as a whole. How so? What are the tone and method here?

2. Compare "Miami: The Cuban Presence" with "Bureaucrats" (pages 184–89) as to both tone and method. What can we conclude from the two essays about Didion's voice and stance generally?

3. What would you deduce Didion's thesis to be from the first two paragraphs alone? The thesis is not stated, however, until paragraph 9, and then only by the way. What is the thesis statement? Why is it placed so inconspicuously?

4. What kind of title is "Miami: The Cuban Presence"? How does it help focus the reader's mind and point to the thesis here?

5. What kind of evidence does Didion use? Is her evidence effective? Why or why not?

6. As the essay develops, its purview (or range, scope) widens. Where does it do so? What extension of meaning does this widening suggest?

---

[3]*Raj:* British rule in India.

7. Why does Didion save the subject of language for last? Why the word "curious"? (See the first sentence of paragraph 20.) What does her last sentence intimate about the future of Miami's white community? What kind of ending is this?

Writing Assignments

1. Has Didion changed your view of Miami? If so, write a paragraph or two contrasting your present view with your former notions.

2. Write a short paper in which you compare "Miami: The Cuban Presence" with "Bureaucrats" (pages 184–89) as to tone and method. Having established the points of comparison, go on to discuss the characteristics of a Didion essay.

3. Have you watched *Miami Vice?* If so, write an essay on the view taken in the show of Miami Cubans and the Cuban subculture, and how that view resembles or differs from Didion's view as well as that of the Anglos as she presents them.

4. Write an essay focused on details, chosen and arranged so as to speak for themselves. Make your title work for you, and build to a climax by putting your most salient and perhaps summary details last.

5. Didion clearly did a good deal of research to write this essay (just look at paragraph 17 alone). Do some research of your own on some controversial subject that interests you, and then, selecting quotations with which you *disagree,* demonstrate (as Didion does in paragraph 17) how narrow and one-sided some commentators' views can be.

6. If you have read all four essays by Didion in this book, write a review of the four essays together. Point out Didion's characteristics as a writer — of subject matter and approach as well as of diction/tone/voice, style, and so forth — and evaluate the effectiveness of her rhetoric and the worth of her work from what you conclude about it from the four essays you have read.

✤ LIVING LIKE WEASELS ✤
Annie Dillard

A WEASEL IS WILD. WHO KNOWS WHAT HE THINKS? HE SLEEPS IN HIS 1
underground den, his tail draped over his nose. Sometimes he
lives in his den for two days without leaving. Outside, he stalks
rabbits, mice, muskrats, and birds, killing more bodies than he
can eat warm, and often dragging the carcasses home. Obedient
to instinct, he bites his prey at the neck, either splitting the
jugular vein at the throat or crunching the brain at the base of
the skull, and he does not let go. One naturalist refused to kill
a weasel who was socketed into his hand deeply as a rattlesnake. The man could in no way pry the tiny weasel off, and he
had to walk half a mile to water, the weasel dangling from his
palm, and soak him off like a stubborn label.

And once, says Ernest Thompson Seton — once, a man shot 2
an eagle out of the sky. He examined the eagle and found the
dry skull of a weasel fixed by the jaws to his throat. The sup-
position is that the eagle had pounced on the weasel and the
weasel swiveled and bit as instinct taught him, tooth to neck,
and nearly won. I would like to have seen that eagle from the
air a few weeks or months before he was shot: was the whole
weasel still attached to his feathered throat, a fur pendant? Or
did the eagle eat what he could reach, gutting the living weasel
with his talons before his breast, bending his beak, cleaning the
beautiful airborne bones?

I have been reading about weasels because I saw one last 3
week. I startled a weasel who startled me, and we exchanged a
long glance.

Twenty minutes from my house, through the woods by the 4
quarry and across the highway, is Hollins Pond, a remarkable
piece of shallowness, where I like to go at sunset and sit on a
tree trunk. Hollins Pond is also called Murray's Pond; it covers
two acres of bottomland near Tinker Creek with six inches of

water and six thousand lily pads. In winter, brown-and-white steers stand in the middle of it, merely dampening their hooves; from the distant shore they look like miracle itself, complete with miracle's nonchalance. Now, in summer, the steers are gone. The water lilies have blossomed and spread to a green horizontal plane that is terra firma to plodding blackbirds, and tremulous ceiling to black leeches, crayfish, and carp.

This is, mind you, suburbia. It is a five-minute walk in three 5 directions to rows of houses, though none is visible here. There's a 55 mph highway at one end of the pond, and a nesting pair of wood ducks at the other. Under every bush is a muskrat hole or a beer can. The far end is an alternating series of fields and woods, fields and woods, threaded everywhere with motorcycle tracks — in whose bare clay wild turtles lay eggs.

So. I had crossed the highway, stepped over two low 6 barbed-wire fences, and traced the motorcycle path in all gratitude through the wild rose and poison ivy of the pond's shoreline up into high grassy fields. Then I cut down through the woods to the mossy fallen tree where I sit. This tree is excellent. It makes a dry, upholstered bench at the upper, marshy end of the pond, a plush jetty raised from the thorny shore between a shallow blue body of water and a deep blue body of sky.

The sun had just set. I was relaxed on the tree trunk, 7 ensconced in the lap of lichen, watching the lily pads at my feet tremble and part dreamily over the thrusting path of a carp. A yellow bird appeared to my right and flew behind me. It caught my eye; I swiveled around — and the next instant, inexplicably, I was looking down at a weasel, who was looking up at me.

Weasel! I'd never seen one wild before. He was ten inches 8 long, thin as a curve, a muscled ribbon, brown as fruitwood, soft-furred, alert. His face was fierce, small and pointed as a lizard's; he would have made a good arrowhead. There was just a dot of chin, maybe two brown hairs' worth, and then the pure white fur began that spread down his underside. He had two black eyes I didn't see, any more than you see a window.

The weasel was stunned into stillness as he was emerging 9
from beneath an enormous shaggy wild rose bush four feet
away. I was stunned into stillness twisted backward on the tree
trunk. Our eyes locked, and someone threw away the key.

Our look was as if two lovers, or deadly enemies, met 10
unexpectedly on an overgrown path when each had been
thinking of something else: a clearing blow to the gut. It was
also a bright blow to the brain, or a sudden beating of brains,
with all the charge and intimate grate of rubbed balloons. It
emptied our lungs. It felled the forest, moved the fields, and
drained the pond; the world dismantled and tumbled into that
black hole of eyes. If you and I looked at each other that way,
our skulls would split and drop to our shoulders. But we don't.
We keep our skulls. So.

He disappeared. This was only last week, and already I 11
don't remember what shattered the enchantment. I think I
blinked, I think I retrieved my brain from the weasel's brain,
and tried to memorize what I was seeing, and the weasel felt the
yank of separation, the careening splash-down into real life and
the urgent current of instinct. He vanished under the wild rose.
I waited motionless, my mind suddenly full of data and my
spirit with pleadings, but he didn't return.

Please do not tell me about "approach-avoidance conflicts." 12
I tell you I've been in that weasel's brain for sixty seconds, and
he was in mine. Brains are private places, muttering through
unique and secret tapes — but the weasel and I both plugged
into another tape simultaneously, for a sweet and shocking
time. Can I help it if it was a blank?

What goes on in his brain the rest of the time? What does 13
a weasel think about? He won't say. His journal is tracks in
clay, a spray of feathers, mouse blood and bone: uncollected,
unconnected, loose-leaf, and blown.

I would like to learn, or remember, how to live. I come to 14
Hollins Pond not so much to learn how to live as, frankly, to
forget about it. That is, I don't think I can learn from a wild
animal how to live in particular — shall I suck warm blood, hold

my tail high, walk with my footprints precisely over the prints of my hands? — but I might learn something of mindlessness, something of the purity of living in the physical sense and the dignity of living without bias or motive. The weasel lives in necessity and we live in choice, hating necessity and dying at the last ignobly in its talons. I would like to live as I should, as the weasel lives as he should. And I suspect that for me the way is like the weasel's: open to time and death painlessly, noticing everything, remembering nothing, choosing the given with a fierce and pointed will.

I missed my chance. I should have gone for the throat. I 15 should have lunged for that streak of white under the weasel's chin and held on, held on through mud and into the wild rose, held on for a dearer life. We could live under the wild rose wild as weasels, mute and uncomprehending. I could very calmly go wild. I could live two days in the den, curled, leaning on mouse fur, sniffing bird bones, blinking, licking, breathing musk, my hair tangled in the roots of grasses. Down is a good place to go, where the mind is single. Down is out, out of your ever-loving mind and back to your careless senses. I remember muteness as a prolonged and giddy fast, where every moment is a feast of utterance received. Time and events are merely poured, unremarked, and ingested directly, like blood pulsed into my gut through a jugular vein. Could two live that way? Could two live under the wild rose, and explore by the pond, so that the smooth mind of each is as everywhere present to the other, and as received and as unchallenged, as falling snow?

We could, you know. We can live any way we want. People 16 take vows of poverty, chastity, and obedience — even of silence — by choice. The thing is to stalk your calling in a certain skilled and supple way, to locate the most tender and live spot and plug into that pulse. This is yielding, not fighting. A weasel doesn't "attack" anything; a weasel lives as he's meant to, yielding at every moment to the perfect freedom of single necessity.

I think it would be well, and proper, and obedient, and 17 pure, to grasp your one necessity and not let it go, to dangle from it limp wherever it takes you. Then even death, where you're going no matter how you live, cannot you part. Seize it and let it seize you up aloft even, till your eyes burn out and drop; let your musky flesh fall off in shreds, and let your very bones unhinge and scatter, loosened over fields, over fields and woods, lightly, thoughtless, from any height at all, from as high as eagles.

[1982 – U.S.A.]

Questions

1. What means of support are used in paragraphs 1 and 2? What part of this essay is narrative? How is this segment organized?
2. Why are paragraphs 3 and 13 printed as paragraphs? What function do they have?
3. What tone does Dillard strike here with respect to her audience? Why this tone?
4. Dillard turns the image of the eagle with the weasel (paragraph 2) into metaphor and symbol. What should put us in mind of the image in paragraph 14? What is the metaphor? What does the image symbolize in the last paragraph (17)? How is a sense of closure achieved here?
5. What is the thesis of this essay? Where is it stated? Why there?
6. Dillard uses parallelism and repetition frequently and meaningfully. What of the parallelism at the end of paragraph 7 and the repetition in paragraph 9? What function does each have? How are syntax and sense related in each case?
7. This essay contains some surprising effects created by sound and rhythm. What kind of sound patterns, for instance, mark the last sentence of paragraph 2? What do these concretions suggest? What is remarkable about the last sentence of paragraph 13 as to both sound and rhythm? What meanings do the sound and rhythm here suggest? How are they related to the prose sense of the passage?

Writing Assignments

1. In a paragraph or more, interpret this essay as to its main idea and discuss how Dillard arrives at this idea.
2. In a short paper, discuss the images used throughout this essay that involve a contrast between wild nature and civilization. Establish

five or six such images; then consider what their function is in the essay overall.

3. Write a discrete paragraph or paper with your thesis presented at the end as a conclusion. Begin, as Dillard begins, with a narration of something of note that has happened to you and work down to what you have concluded (which will be your thesis) from this incident. Along the way, you might try to turn the sound of some key passage to your advantage.

4. Our feelings about civilization seem ever problematic. Read *Civilization and Its Discontents* — Sigmund Freud's short treatise on the subject — and then write an essay interpreting "Living Like Weasels" in light of what Freud has to say. For help with quoting and noting, see Appendix 2: A Brief Guide to the Use and Documentation of Sources.

✢ THE IGUANA ✢
Isak Dinesen

IN THE RESERVE I HAVE SOMETIMES COME UPON THE IGUANA, THE BIG   1
lizards, as they were sunning themselves upon a flat stone in a riverbed. They are not pretty in shape, but nothing can be imagined more beautiful than their colouring. They shine like a heap of precious stones or like a pane cut out of an old church window. When, as you approach, they swish away, there is a flash of azure, green and purple over the stones, the colour seems to be standing behind them in the air, like a comet's luminous tail.

Once I shot an Iguana. I thought that I should be able to   2
make some pretty things from his skin. A strange thing happened then, that I have never afterwards forgotten. As I went up to him, where he was lying dead upon his stone, and actually while I was walking the few steps, he faded and grew pale, all colour died out of him as in one long sigh, and by the time that I touched him he was grey and dull like a lump of concrete. It was the live impetuous blood pulsating within the animal, which had radiated out all that glow and splendour.

Now that the flame was put out, and the soul had flown, the Iguana was as dead as a sandbag.

Often since I have, in some sort, shot an Iguana, and I have 3 remembered the one of the Reserve. Up at Meru I saw a young Native girl with a bracelet on, a leather strap two inches wide, and embroidered all over with very small turquoise-coloured beads which varied a little in colour and played in green, light blue and ultramarine. It was an extraordinarily live thing; it seemed to draw breath on her arm, so that I wanted it for myself, and made Farah buy it from her. No sooner had it come upon my own arm than it gave up the ghost. It was nothing now, a small, cheap, purchased article of finery. It had been the play of colours, the duet between the turquoise and the "nègre",— that quick, sweet, brownish black, like peat and black pottery, of the Native's skin, — that had created the life of the bracelet.

In the Zoological Museum of Pietermaritzburg, I have 4 seen, in a stuffed deep-water fish in a showcase, the same combination of colouring, which there had survived death; it made me wonder what life can well be like, on the bottom of the sea, to send up something so live and airy. I stood in Meru and looked at my pale hand and at the dead bracelet, it was as if an injustice had been done to a noble thing, as if truth had been suppressed. So sad did it seem that I remembered the saying of the hero in a book that I had read as a child: "I have conquered them all, but I am standing amongst graves."

In a foreign country and with foreign species of life one 5 should take measures to find out whether things will be keeping their value when dead. To the settlers of East Africa I give the advice: "For the sake of your own eyes and heart, shoot not the Iguana."

[1937 — Denmark]

Questions

1. The voice of this essay has the ring of authority. What gives it this quality? Why is it necessary for Dinesen to establish an authoritative voice?

2. Why is the beginning of paragraph 2 startling? How are paragraphs 2 and 3 related? What accounts for the tight coherence of the essay?

3. What is Dinesen's thesis? Where is it stated? Why there? Is the statement necessary?

4. Toward what audience is the essay directed? How is its belated statement of thesis accounted for by its intended audience together with Dinesen's evident intent vis-à-vis that audience?

5. E. M. Forster's quotation from Dante — "Possession is one with loss" (see page 8) — could serve as a statement of the larger meaning of "The Iguana," of its theme as distinguished from its belatedly articulated thesis. How so?

Writing Assignments

1. The richness of its detail gives "The Iguana" weight and authority. Pick some creature or object that you have lived with and really know. Then, in a paragraph or more, describe it in detail so that your reader will see it imaginatively, as one can see Dinesen's iguana and bracelet.

2. Do what is suggested in the first assignment, only now set your descriptive paragraphs in a framework that will make them something more than simply descriptive. You could provide a thesis, for instance, that would make an example out of the creature or object presented, or you could frame your description in such a way that a theme emerges, or perhaps you could do both at once, as Dinesen does. In any case, let the details of your paper say most of what you have to say.

✤ Pooran Singh ✤
Isak Dinesen

Pooran Singh's little blacksmith's shop down by the mill was 1
a miniature Hell on the farm, with all the orthodox attributes of
that place. It was built of corrugated iron, and when the sun
shone down upon the roof of it, and the flames of the furnace
rose inside it, the air itself, in and around the hut, was
white-hot. All day long, the place resounded with the deafening
noise of the forge, — iron on iron, on iron once more, — and the
hut was filled with axes, and broken wheels, that made it look
like some ancient gruesome picture of a place of execution.

All the same the blacksmith's shop had a great power of 2
attraction, and when I went down to watch Pooran Singh at
work I always found people in it and round it. Pooran Singh
worked at a superhuman pace, as if his life depended upon
getting the particular job of work finished within the next five
minutes, he jumped straight up in the air over the forge, he
shrieked out his orders to his two young Kikuyu assistants in a
high bird's voice and behaved altogether like a man who is
himself being burnt at the stake, or like some chafed over-devil
at work. But Pooran Singh was no devil, but a person of the
meekest disposition; out of working hours he had a little
maidenly affectation of manner. He was our Fundee of the
farm, which means an artisan of all work, carpenter, saddler
and cabinet-maker, as well as blacksmith; he constructed and
built more than one waggon for the farm, all on his own. But he
liked the work of the forge best, and it was a very fine, proud
sight, to watch him tiring a wheel.

Pooran Singh, in his appearance, was something of a fraud. 3
When fully dressed, in his coat and large folded white turban,
he managed, with his big black beard, to look a portly,
ponderous man. But by the forge, bared to the waist, he was
incredibly slight and nimble, with the Indian hour-glass torso.

I liked Pooran Singh's forge, and it was popular with the 4
Kikuyus, for two reasons.

First, because of the iron itself, which is the most 5
fascinating of all raw materials, and sets people's imagination
travelling on long tracks. The plough, the sword and cannon
and the wheel, — the civilization of man — man's conquest of
Nature in a nut, plain enough to be understood or guessed by
the primitive people, — and Pooran Singh hammered the iron.

Secondly, the Native world was drawn to the forge by its 6
song. The treble, sprightly, monotonous, and surprising rhythm
of the blacksmith's work has a mythical force. It is so virile that
it appals and melts the women's hearts, it is straight and
unaffected and tells the truth and nothing but the truth.
Sometimes it is very outspoken. It has an excess of strength and
is gay as well as strong, it is obliging to you and does great
things for you, willingly, as in play. The Natives, who love
rhythm, collected by Pooran Singh's hut and felt at their ease.
According to an ancient Nordic law a man was not held
responsible for what he had said in a forge. The tongues were
loosened in Africa as well, in the blacksmith's shop, and the talk
flowed freely; audacious fancies were set forth to the inspiring
hammer-song.

Pooran Singh was with me for many years and was a 7
well-paid functionary of the farm. There was no proportion
between his wages and his needs, for he was an ascetic of the
first water. He did not eat meat, he did not drink, or smoke, or
gamble, his old clothes were worn to the thread. He sent his
money over to India for the education of his children. A small
silent son of his, Delip Singh, once came over from Bombay on
a visit to his father. He had lost touch with the iron, the only
metal that I saw about him was a fountain pen in his pocket.
The mythical qualities were not carried on in the second
generation.

But Pooran Singh himself, raging above the forge, kept his 8
halo as long as he was on the farm, and I hope as long as he
lived. He was the servant of the gods, heated through,
white-hot, an elemental spirit. In Pooran Singh's blacksmith's
shop the hammer sang to you what you wanted to hear, as if it
was giving voice to your own heart. To me myself the hammer

was singing an ancient Greek verse, which a friend had translated:

> "Eros struck out, like a smith with his hammer,
> So that the sparks flew from my defiance.
> He cooled my heart in tears and lamentations,
> Like red-hot iron in a stream."

[1937 — Denmark]

Questions

1. Read the first paragraph aloud. Can you spot where Dinesen creates a rhythm to match her subject? Where does it come? How do her words match the rhythm of the forge?

2. What other concretions — for instance, visual, aural, tactile, or gustatory images — does Dinesen use? To what effect? What purpose is served by the repetition of the epithet "white-hot," used in both paragraph 1 and paragraph 8?

3. "Pooran Singh" is basically a character sketch, though somewhat more indirect than most such sketches. Nevertheless, we learn a good deal about Pooran Singh. What exactly do we learn? People, we have reason to believe, are many-faceted and therefore usually inconsistent in one way or another. What inconsistency does Dinesen's portrait of the blacksmith underscore?

4. What kinds of organization do paragraphs 5 and 6 follow? Why is the material of the sixth paragraph put second?

5. "Pooran Singh" is a character sketch and more. How does the mythic element here extend the meaning of the essay? How does the mythic element tie in with the erotic element? How does Pooran Singh's son with his "fountain pen" stand against everything else in the essay? What might we take as its theme with respect to Delip Singh's pen?

Writing Assignments

1. Choose someone you know fairly well, someone whose occupation or life history or eccentricities make him or her particularly interesting, and write a character sketch of the person. Try to capture the person's contradictions no less than the surface that he or she presents. Try, too, to make your portrait vivid by using concrete details all along the way. Study Dinesen's essay in this

regard and model your essay after hers with regard to imagistic detail and specificity.

2. Dinesen refers or alludes to various mythologies and mythological figures: the Christian heaven and hell, the Norse god Vulcan, the Greek gods Hephaistos and Prometheus. Research these concepts and figures; then write a paper using your research to explicate (that is, to make clear) their function and meaning in the essay at hand.

✦ I Wish They'd Do It Right ✦
Jane Doe

My son and his wife are not married. They have lived together for seven years without benefit of license. Though occasionally marriage has been a subject of conjecture, it did not seem important until the day they announced, jubilantly, that they were going to have a child. It was happy news. I was ready and eager to become a grandmother. Now, I thought, they will take the final step and make their relationship legal. 1

I was appraised of the Lamaze method of natural child-birth. I was prepared by Leboyer for birth without violence. I admired the expectant mother's discipline. She ate only organic foods, abstained from alcohol, avoided insecticides, smog and trauma. Every precaution was taken to insure the arrival of a healthy, happy infant. No royal birth had been prepared for more auspiciously. All that was lacking was legitimacy. 2

Finally, when my grandson was two weeks old, I dared to question their intentions. 3

"We don't believe in marriage," was all that was volunteered. 4

"Not even for your son's sake?" I asked. "Maybe he will." 5

Their eyes were impenetrable, their faces stiffened to masks. "You wouldn't understand," I was told. 6

And I don't. Surely they cannot believe they are pioneering, making revolutionary changes in society. That frontier has long been tamed. Today marriage offers all the options. Books and 7 talk shows have surfeited us with the freedom offered in open marriage. Lawyers, psychologists and marriage counselors are growing rich executing marriage contracts. And divorce, should it come to that, is in most states easy and inexpensive.

On the other hand, living together out of wedlock can be 8 economically impractical as well as socially awkward. How do I present her — as my son's roommate? his spouse? his spice, as one facetious friend suggested? Even my son flounders in these waters. Recently, I heard him refer to her as his girl friend. I cannot believe that that description will be endearing to their son when he is able to understand.

I have resolved that problem for myself, bypassing their 9 omission, introducing her as she is, my daughter-in-law. But my son, in militant support of his ideology, refutes any assumption, however casual, that they have taken vows.

There are economic benefits which they are denying 10 themselves. When they applied for housing in the married-students dormitory of the university where he is seeking his doctorate, they were asked for their marriage certificate. Not having one, they were forced to find other, more expensive quarters off campus. Her medical insurance, provided by the company where she was employed, was denied him. He is not her husband. There have been and will be other inconveniences they have elected to endure.

Their son will not enjoy the luxury of choice about the 11 inconveniences and scurrility to which he will be subject from those of his peers and elders who dislike and fear society's nonconformists.

And if in the future, his parents should decide to separate, 12 will he not suffer greater damage than the child of divorce, who may find comfort in the knowledge that his parents once believed they could live happily ever after, and committed themselves to that idea? The child of unwed parents has no sanctuary. His mother and father have assiduously avoided a pledge of permanency, leaving him drifting and insecure.

I know my son is motivated by idealism and honesty in his 13 reluctance to concede to what he considers mere ceremony. But he is wise enough to know that no one individual can fight all of society's foibles and frauds. Why does he persist in this, a battle already lost? Because though he rejects marriage, California, his residence, has declared that while couples living together in imitation of marriage are no longer under the jurisdiction of the family court, their relationship is viewed by the state as an implicit contract somewhat like a business agreement. This position was mandated when equal property rights were granted a woman who had been abandoned by the man she had lived with for a number of years.

Finally, the couple's adamancy has been depriving to all the rest of the family. There has been no celebration of wedding or anniversaries. There has been concealment from certain family elders who could not cope with the situation. Its irregularity has put constraint on the grandparents, who are stifled by one another's possible embarrassment or hurt. 14

I hope that one day very soon my son and his wife will acknowledge their cohabitation with a license. The rest of us will not love them any more for it. We love and support them as much as possible now. But it will be easier and happier for us knowing that our grandson will be spared the continued explanation and harassment, the doubts and anxieties of being a child of unmarried parents. 15

[1977 – U.S.A.]

Questions

1. What assumption underlies the title of this essay? What is its thesis?
2. How does the tone of both the title and the essay reflect this thesis?
3. What is the structural mode of the essay as a whole? What is suggested by the positioning of the material in paragraph 14? What does the positioning suggest about the speaker's motivation?
4. Does marriage in fact offer "all the options"? What arguments could be made on the other side with respect to economics, say? What other points of Doe's argument could be brought into question?
5. The point made in paragraph 8 might better have been left out. Why? Doe seems to undercut her own argument in paragraph 13. How so?

6. Does Doe argue her case with factual evidence or back it up with assertions based on assumptions that she does not see? How so? Is her evidence, therefore, sound or questionable? Again, how so?

Writing Assignments

1. Write an open letter from the son in answer to his mother's criticism. Answer her point by point, using evidence based on fact and not just assumption.
2. Write a short paper analyzing the speaker here. What kind of a person is she? How does she see herself? How do you see her? Why? Use the essay's tone, the ways the speaker backs up her argument, her assumptions, and so forth as evidence in your analysis.
3. Might this essay be satirical? Take it as so being and write a short satirical paper after it spoken by a speaker whom you wish to expose as haughty, self-serving, and thoroughly illogical.

✣ No Home in Africa ✣
Annette Dula

I HAVE NO CULTURAL ROOTS IN AFRICA NOR DO I WANT ANY. I HAVE discovered that Egypt is not black Africa. The skin isn't black enough and the hair isn't kinky enough. An Egyptian merchant put his light brown arm next to my black arm and said, "My skin isn't black but I'm African, too." Sincerity was not in his voice.

In Khartoum, the Sudan, a near-riot developed when I appeared to be an African woman walking down the street in a leather miniskirt. I liked melting into the anonymity of hundreds of black faces, but I also wanted the freedom that tourists enjoy.

I went to Ethiopia with Kay, who is white. The people were hostile. They pelted me with rotten tomatoes. They did not bother Kay. Didn't they realize that I was black like them?

In East Africa, the Africans were too servile toward whites. I got extremely angry when a gnarled little old man would bow down and call my friend "Mensaab." An African woman would not become angry.

I hated the mercenary Indians of East Africa more than the   5 Africans hated them. Two years after the incident, I can still taste the bitterness. I wanted to buy material for a blouse. At the time, most shopkeepers in East Africa were Indians. I had walked in ahead of Kay. The shopkeeper continued talking to another Indian. Kay walked in. The shopkeeper rushed up to her.

"Can I help you, madam?" he asked, with the proper   6 servility.

"My friend wants to buy material," she said.   7

"How much does she want to pay for it?" he asked.   8

"Perhaps you'd better talk to her, sir."   9

Completely ignoring her suggestion, he continued explain-   10 ing to Kay the virtues of expensive imported materials over cheaper native ones. "You know, these Africans are lazy. They just aren't capable of the superior quality you get in Western work!"

I walked out. I knew what prejudice was — but not this   11 kind. This was the type my parents had known in North Carolina 25 years ago. I rejoiced when the Indians were kicked out of Uganda.

I do have the appearance of a black African. I have even   12 been asked by Africans, "To what tribe do you belong?" And, "From what part of Africa do you come?" When it was to my advantage to be considered African, it pleased me. At other times, embarrassing situations could develop.

Once when I was walking from a restaurant at around 9:30   13 P.M., four or five policemen jumped out of a squad car, surrounded me, and pointed their loaded guns at me. Though they were speaking in Swahili, I soon gathered that I was being arrested on prostitution charges. The more I protested in English, the more incensed they became. I reacted as any American woman would. "Who do you think you are? Get those guns out of my face. I am an American. I want to call the Ambassador." (Later, I learned that Kenya had a new law making it illegal for unescorted African women to be on the street after 9:30 P.M.).

More often than not, I resented being treated as an African 14 by Africans. I was truly galled at the customs station between Zaire and the Central African Republic. Tourists usually pass customs by merely showing their passports. Africans are subjected to a thorough search. As I was about to move along with other tourists, I was roughly grabbed from behind and thrust back into the crowd. I had to be freed by other tourists. The mob attitude was: "Who do you think you are? You're not a tourist! You're one of us." Why didn't I protest the preferential treatment that tourists receive? Because I felt as the American tourists do: "We are entitled to these consider- ations."

When I understood that the average African male has little 15 respect for the female intellect, I was surprised. Ngimbus, a close friend of mine, decided that I was a militant feminist when I lectured him on male-female equality!

"She looks like an African, but she talks nonsense," he said 16 later.

Often, I found myself defending black Americans to 17 nationalist West-Africans. A favorite question was "Why do you call yourselves *Afro*-American?" I usually answered in terms of cultural heritage, identity oppression, and other nebulous words that explain nothing. The conversation would continue: "You have forfeited the right to call yourselves *Afro*-Americans. If you were worthy of the name *Afro-*, your people would never have taken all those years of such treatment. We sympathize with you, but you're too docile for us."

"What about South Africa and Mozambique?" I would 18 always ask.

The question was usually ignored or if answered, the time 19 factor was brought in: "We have accomplished more in eighty years than you have accomplished in 400 years." The conver- sation always left me with a need to explain our differences. But there never were acceptable explanations.

My experiences in Africa typify the reciprocal misunder- 20
standings between black Americans and Africans. Our common
color is not enough. Too much time has passed.

I am not patriotic, but I am a product of America. I believe 21
in freedom of speech, even if it is only token. I take education
for granted though we may not receive it equally. I believe in
the working of democracy even though it never seems to work.
I am forced to accept that I am an American and that here in
America lie my cultural roots — whether I like it or not.

[1975 — U.S.A.]

Questions

1. The first sentence of this essay might be printed as a separate
   paragraph. What might be gained by printing it thus?
2. Dula reports some incidents and uses dialogue to recreate others. In
   what way(s) is each technique appropriate to the nature of the event
   that the technique is used to unfold?
3. What means of support does Dula use? Does she do so effectively?
   Is hers a good way to argue in general? Why or why not?
4. What generalization does the title point to? What is the theme of this
   essay? Is the generalization well supported? Does it seem like a just
   conclusion drawn from the facts given? Why or why not?

Writing Assignments

1. Did you ever feel the odd man out? Were you ever in a strange place
   where you felt misunderstood by people who reacted only to your
   race, sex, style of dress or hair, or something else equally superficial?
   If so, write a paragraph or more on the incident. Describe it, using
   dialogue if you like, and move to a reflection on its meaning.
2. What experiences of your own could be used to support a thesis or
   embody a theme? Write an essay incorporating these experiences as
   examples. If you have a thesis in mind, state it and then marshal your
   examples behind it. But if you think that the material speaks for
   itself, then let it, making sure, however, that your theme clearly
   binds together the incidents you report.

✚ A MORAL LITTLE TALE ✚

Lord Dunsany

THERE WAS ONCE AN EARNEST PURITAN WHO HELD IT WRONG TO 1
dance. And for his principles he labored hard; his was a zealous
life. And there loved him all of those who hated the dance; and
those that loved the dance respected him too; they said, "He is
a pure, good man and acts according to his lights."

He did much to discourage dancing and helped to close 2
several Sunday entertainments. Some kinds of poetry, he said,
he liked, but not the fanciful kind, as that might corrupt the
thoughts of the very young. He always dressed in black.

He was interested in morality and was quite sincere, and 3
there grew to be much respect on Earth for his honest face and
his flowing purewhite beard.

One night the Devil appeared unto him in a dream and 4
said, "Well done."

"Avaunt," said that earnest man. 5

"No, no, friend," said the Devil. 6

"Dare not to call me 'friend,' " he answered bravely. 7

"Come, come, friend," said the Devil. "Have you not done 8
my work? Have you not put apart the couples that would
dance? Have you not checked their laughter and their accursed
mirth? Have you not worn my livery of black? O friend, friend,
you do not know what a detestable thing it is to sit in hell and
hear people being happy, and singing in theatres, and singing in
the fields, and whispering after dances under the moon," and he
fell into cursing fearfully.

"It is you," said the Puritan, "that put into their hearts the 9
evil desire to dance; and black is God's own livery, not yours."

And the Devil laughed contemptuously and spoke. 10

"He only made the silly colors," he said, "and useless dawns 11
on hill-slopes facing South, and butterflies flapping along them
as soon as the sun rose high, and foolish maidens coming out to
dance, and the warm mad West wind, and worst of all that
pernicious influence Love."

And when the Devil said that God made Love that earnest 12
man sat up in bed and shouted, "Blasphemy! Blasphemy!"

"It's true," said the Devil. "It isn't I that sends the village 13
fools muttering and whispering two by two in the woods when
the harvest moon is high. It's as much as I can bear even to see
them dancing."

"Then," said the man, "I have mistaken right for wrong; 14
but as soon as I wake I will fight you yet."

"O, no you don't," said the Devil. "You don't wake up out 15
of this sleep."

And somewhere far away Hell's black steel doors were 16
opened, and arm in arm those two were drawn within, and the
doors shut behind them, and still they went arm in arm,
trudging further and further into the deeps of Hell. And it was
that Puritan's punishment to know that those that he cared for
on Earth would do evil as he had done.

[1915 — Great Britain]

Questions

1. What is the main element (voice, setting, rhythm, or whatever) that
   Dunsany works with here? To what end? (That is, what is his
   purpose?)
2. How is God portrayed as opposed to the devil? Why? What does
   what we are told exemplify? What is Dunsany's theme?
3. Why may this piece be considered an essay rather than a short
   story?

Writing Assignments

1. Write a little story of your own from which a clear-cut conclusion
   can be drawn. Then, in a discrete paragraph, specify what the
   conclusion is and how your story exemplifies it.
2. Write an essay that satirically points out some conceptual idiocy
   — in your view, of course — of one or more of your college
   classmates. Use "The Guidette" (pages 109–111) and "A Moral
   Little Tale" as models.

✚ ELVIRA'S STORY ✚
Flora Mancuso Edwards

O<small>VER</small> 150 <small>YEARS AGO THE</small> E<small>NGLISH HISTORIAN</small> T<small>HOMAS</small> C<small>ARLYLE</small>   1
had this to say about Victorian society:

> It is not to die, or even to die of hunger, that makes a man
> wretched; many men have died; all men must die. . . . But
> it is to live miserable we know not why; to work sore and yet
> gain nothing; to be heartworn, weary, yet isolated, unrelated,
> girt in with a cold, universal Laissezfaire.[1]

There are over 4 million people in the United States today   2
who still live miserable and know not why, who still "work sore
and yet gain nothing." They are our laboring poor.

Elvira Ramirez is just one example of those who must sell   3
their labor so cheaply that the necessities of life are just barely
met. Elvira is a soft-spoken, cheerful, well-mannered woman
who works in a luxurious East Side beauty salon doing
shampoos and manicures. Her average day is filled by serving
New York's well-to-do matrons who spend spring in New
York, winter in Miami, and summer on Cape Cod. Elvira
listens sympathetically to their problems in getting "reliable
help" or to their last-minute preparations for a child's wedding
in Switzerland.

For her services and good company she receives $0.25 to   4
$0.50 from each one and occasionally $1.00 from a more
generous customer. These tips bring up her total salary of
$90.00 to approximately $110.00 a week. On this salary, Elvira
supports herself, her son, a teen-age daughter, and her mother
in a one-bedroom apartment in the Nathan Strauss Housing
Projects in the Chelsea section on Manhattan's West Side.

---

[1]Quoted in Robert Hunter, *Poverty*. ed. Peter d'A. Jones (New York: Macmillan, 1904;
Harper & Row, 1965), p. 1 [Author's note] . *Laissez-faire:* Literally meaning "let things
alone," *Laissez-faire* is the old-line capitalist doctrine that government should stay out of the
private sector, leaving business to govern itself.

Her apartment is on the third floor of a building whose 5
elevators are as offensive as they are nonfunctioning. Elvira,
her mother, her daughter, and her son all used to sleep in one
room, but now the boy is older and has inherited the sofa in the
living room, which doubles as his bedroom. The apartment has
no closets, and there is little room even for the metal
Woolworth's wardrobes. The kitchen is so small that there is no
place for a table, so when the family must eat together, the sofa
is moved and a table set up in the living room.

Elvira receives no health insurance from her job, nor does 6
she receive a vacation or overtime pay. Her mother is only sixty
and neither blind nor technically disabled, so she receives no
social security or public assistance. Elvira's income — marginal
as it may be — is too high for Medicaid, so Elvira works
fourteen to sixteen hours a day, six days a week, and prays that
no one will get sick. But, because the windows of the third-floor
apartment keep getting broken, New York's winter always
seems to take its toll in doctor bills, which each year are
increasingly hard to pay.

When Elvira was hospitalized several years ago, the 7
Department of Social Services came to her rescue. But it did
not take long for Elvira to realize that the benefits came at a
high price.

> No, the welfare is all waiting with the children crying,
> waiting outside the office for hours in the freezing cold, sick
> hungry waiting all day in the clinic, waiting to be looked
> down on, insulted, and humiliated. No, I'm not earning much
> more — but it's better than waiting.
> God willing, I don't get sick again.[2]

Elvira has no savings and therefore cannot move to larger 8
quarters. As it is, rent is her biggest expenditure. Her hopes?

> Maybe I go back to the Island[3] when Michele finish school.
> You know, I guess I didn't do so bad after all. Michele finish

---

[2]Personal interviews conducted between May and December 1973. [Author's note. Ditto the next quotation.]

[3]*Island*: Puerto Rico.

fourth in her class. Now she goes to Harpur College. She got a scholarship, you know. I thought when she finish high school she would get a job and help out, but maybe it's better like this. Now she'll be somebody. . . . You know, like a teacher or a nurse or something. That's the most important thing — the kids. Sure I work hard — but the kids — they're going to be something.

Am I poor? No, not really. Really poor people take the welfare. Most of the time we manage to get by.

Elvira receives no benefits, no medical coverage, no public 9 assistance. She earns $6,000 a year before taxes. She works harder and longer than most people and earns considerably less. She eats little meat and indulges herself in no luxuries. She does not own a car, goes on no vacations, eats in few restaurants, and buys a minimum of clothing.

Elvira's job is similar to almost one-third of all the jobs in 10 New York, and Elvira is one of 600,000 New Yorkers who live below the poverty line and struggle on day by day, eking out a marginal existence in New York, one of the richest cities in the world.

On a national level, over 4.5 million people (not counting 11 rural sharecroppers) are employed full time and are still poor. In almost half of these families, two people work full time in order to reap the bitter rewards of poverty and want.

[1978 — U.S.A.]

Questions

1. What is Edwards' purpose here? What kind of an essay is this (informative, analytic, persuasive)? What is her theme? Why didn't she state it as a thesis?
2. What kind of a voice does this essay present? Why this kind?
3. What means of support does Edwards use at the beginning and at the end of the essay? What does the initial quotation from Carlyle suggest? Why does Edwards suggest rather than state?
4. What is the primary means of support here? How does it serve Edwards' purpose?
5. Why the statistics at the end? What purpose do they serve?
6. How does this essay end? (See paragraphs 10 and 11.) Why is this particular kind of ending apt given Edwards overriding purpose?

Writing Assignments

1. Write a paragraph or more beginning with a generalization, moving to a specific case, and ending with a generalization. Try to fashion a voice that is objective, yet to evoke sympathy from your reader with regard to the specific case you present.

2. Write an essay focused on a story from your own experience, or that of someone you know or have read about, that illustrates a general point — for instance, "Nature can be capricious," "Politicians make good (or bad) role models," "We value money too much," "It's hard to move from one stage in life to the next." Let your story convey your point as much as possible. Indeed, you may not even have to make the point overtly. This, of course, you must judge for yourself.

✦ DESPERATION WRITING ✦

Peter Elbow

I KNOW I AM NOT ALONE IN MY RECURRING TWINGES OF PANIC THAT I   1
won't be able to write something when I need to, I won't be able to produce coherent speech or thought. And that lingering doubt is a great hindrance to writing. It's a constant fog or static that clouds the mind. I never got out of its clutches till I discovered that it was possible to write something — not something great or pleasing but at least something usable, workable — when my mind is out of commission. The trick is that you have to do all your cooking out on the table: Your mind is incapable of doing any inside. It means using symbols and pieces of paper not as a crutch but as a wheel chair.

The first thing is to admit your condition: Because of some   2
mood or event or whatever, your mind is incapable of anything that could be called thought. It can put out a babbling kind of speech utterance, it can put a simple feeling, perception, or sort-of-thought into understandable (though terrible) words. But it is incapable of considering anything in relation to anything else. The moment you try to hold that thought or feeling up against some other to see the relationship, you simply

lose the picture — you get nothing but buzzing lines or waving colors.

So admit this. Avoid anything more than one feeling, 3 perception, or thought. Simply write as much as possible. Try simply to steer your mind in the direction or general vicinity of the thing you are trying to write about and start writing and keep writing.

Just write and keep writing. (Probably best to write on 4 only one side of the paper in case you should want to cut parts out with scissors — but you probably won't.) Just write and keep writing. It will probably come in waves. After a flurry, stop and take a brief rest. But don't stop too long. Don't think about what you are writing or what you have written or else you will overload the circuit again. Keep writing as though you are drugged or drunk. Keep doing this till you feel you have a lot of material that might be useful; or, if necessary, till you can't stand it any more — even if you doubt that there's anything useful there.

Then take a pad of little pieces of paper — or perhaps 3 × 5 5 cards — and simply start at the beginning of what you were writing, and as you read over what you wrote, every time you come to any thought, feeling, perception, or image that could be gathered up into one sentence or one assertion, do so and write it by itself on a little sheet of paper. In short, you are trying to turn, say, ten or twenty pages of wandering mush into twenty or thirty hard little crab apples. Sometimes there won't be many on a page. But if it seems to you that there are none on a page, you are making a serious error — the same serious error that put you in this comatose state to start with. You are mistaking lousy, stupid, second-rate, wrong, childish, foolish, worthless ideas for no ideas at all. Your job is not to pick out *good* ideas but to pick out ideas. As long as you were conscious, your words will be full of things that could be called feelings, utterances, ideas — things that can be squeezed into one simple sentence. This is your job. Don't ask for too much.

After you have done this, take those little slips or cards, 6 read through them a number of times — not struggling with them, simply wandering and mulling through them; perhaps shifting them around and looking through them in various sequences. In a sense these are cards you are playing solitaire with, and the rules of this particular game permit shuffling the unused pile.

The goal of this procedure with the cards is to get them to 7 distribute themselves in two or three or ten or fifteen different piles on your desk. You can get them to do this almost by themselves if you simply keep reading through them in different orders; certain cards will begin to feel like they go with other cards. I emphasize this passive, thoughtless mode because I want to talk about desperation writing in its pure state. In practice, almost invariably at some point in the procedure, your sanity begins to return. It is often at this point. You actually are moved to have thoughts or — and the difference between active and passive is crucial here — to *exert* thought; to hold two cards together and *build* or *assert* a relationship. It is a matter of bringing energy to bear.

So you may start to be able to do something active with 8 these cards, and begin actually to think. But if not, just allow the cards to find their own piles with each other by feel, by drift, by intuition, by mindlessness.

You have now engaged in the two main activities that will 9 permit you to get something cooked out on the table rather than in your brain: writing out into messy words, summing up into single assertions, and even sensing relationships between assertions. You can simply continue to deploy these two activities.

If, for example, after that first round of writing, assertion- 10 making, and pile-making, your piles feel as though they are useful and satisfactory for what you are writing — paragraphs or sections or trains of thought — then you can carry on from there. See if you can gather each pile up into a single assertion. When you can, then put the subsidiary assertions of that pile into their best order to fit with that single unifying one. If you *can't* get the pile into one assertion, then take the pile as the basis for doing some more writing out into words. In the course of this writing, you may produce for yourself the single unifying assertion you were looking for; or you may have to go through the cycle of turning the writing into assertions and piles and so forth. Perhaps more than once. The pile may turn out to want to be two or more piles itself; or it may want to become part of a pile you already have. This is natural. This kind of meshing into one configuration, then coming apart, then coming together and meshing into a different configuration — this is growing and cooking. It makes a terrible mess, but if you can't do it in your head, you have to put up with a cluttered desk and a lot of confusion.

If, on the other hand, all that writing *didn't* have useful 11 material in it, it means that your writing wasn't loose, drifting, quirky, jerky, associative enough. This time try especially to let things simply remind you of things that are seemingly crazy or unrelated. Follow these odd associations. Make as many metaphors as you can — be as nutty as possible — and explore the metaphors themselves — open them out. You may have all your energy tied up in some area of your experience that you are leaving out. Don't refrain from writing about whatever else is on your mind: how you feel at the moment, what you are losing your mind over, randomness that intrudes itself on your consciousness, the pattern on the wallpaper, what those people you see out the window have on their minds — though keep coming back to the whateveritis you are supposed to be writing about. Treat it, in short, like ten-minute writing exercises. Your best perceptions and thoughts are always going to be tied up in whatever is really occupying you, and that is also where your energy is. You may end up writing a love poem — or a hate poem — in one of those little piles while the other piles will finally turn into a lab report on data processing or whatever you have to write about. But you couldn't, in your present state of having your head shot off, have written that report without also writing the poem. And the report will have some of the juice of the poem in it and vice versa.

[1973 — U.S.A.]

Questions

1. What is Elbow's thesis? Where does it come? What kind of a beginning does this essay have?

2. What type of structure is used here? What transitions keep us in mind of the essay's overall structure? Given that the essay describes a process, why is this type of structure appropriate?

3. In light of what Elbow says about metaphor in paragraph 11, it is not surprising that a number of metaphors dot his essay. What are three or four? What metaphor is extended?

4. Who was "Desperation Writing" written for? How does its style (its diction and syntax) along with the rhythm, tone, and voice created by this style point toward this audience?

5. What is the function of paragraphs 8 and 9? How does Elbow achieve a sense of closure?

6. According to Elbow, you should be looking for two things when dividing cards into piles. What are they? Why these two?

Writing Assignments

1. The conscious mind, finally, must be the arbiter of anything we write. But during the writing process, the unconscious plays a key role. Write a paragraph or more on the role of the unconscious in this process as analyzed by Elbow. Does what Elbow suggests tally with your own experience? If so, how so?

2. Approach the next paper you have to write for any subject exactly as Elbow suggests. Then write the paper. Subsequently, write a paper on the process you went through in writing the first paper. Quickly summarize the process; then evaluate Elbow's method in light of your experience with it. Did the method work? Did it lead to some good ideas? Did it help you to find what you had to say (that is, lead you to a "single unifying assertion") and help you find relationships (and, thus, to write coherently)? Did the method lead to anything surprising? These are some of the questions you should address in your evaluation.

✛ How to Talk ✛
about the World
Peter Farb

I f HUMAN BEINGS PAID ATTENTION TO ALL THE SIGHTS, SOUNDS, AND   1
smells that besiege them, their ability to codify and recall
information would be swamped. Instead, they simplify the
information by grouping it into broad verbal categories. For
example, human eyes have the extraordinary power to discriminate some ten million colors, but the English language reduces
these to no more than four thousand color words, of which only
eleven basic terms are commonly used. That is why a driver
stops at all traffic lights whose color he categorizes as *red*, even
though the lights vary slightly from one to another in their hues
of redness. Categorization allows people to respond to their
environment in a way that has great survival value. If they hear
a high-pitched sound, they do not enumerate the long list of
possible causes of such sounds: a human cry of fear, a scream
for help, a policeman's whistle, and so on. Instead they become
alert because they have categorized high-pitched sounds as
indicators of possible danger.

Words, therefore, are more than simply labels for specific   2
objects; they are also parts of sets of related principles. To a
very young child, the word *chair* may at first refer only to his
highchair. Soon afterward, he learns that the four-legged object
on which his parents sit at mealtimes is also called a *chair*. So is
the thing with only three legs, referred to by his parents as a
broken chair, and so is the upholstered piece of furniture in the
living room. These objects form a category, *chair*, which is set
apart from all other categories by a unique combination of
features. A *chair* must possess a seat, legs, and back; it may also,
but not necessarily, have arms; it must accommodate only one
person. An object that possesses these features with but a single
exception — it accommodates three people — does not belong to

the category *chair* but rather to the category *couch,* and that category in turn is described by a set of unique features.

Furthermore, Americans think of *chairs* and *couches* as being   3 related to each other because they both belong to a category known in English as *household furniture.* But such a relationship between the category *chair* and the category *couch* is entirely arbitrary on the part of English and some other speech communities. Nothing in the external world decrees that a language must place these two categories together. In some African speech communities, for example, the category *chair* would most likely be thought of in relation to the category *spear,* since both are emblems of ruler's authority.

The analysis of words by their categories for the purpose of   4 determining what they mean to speakers of a particular language — that is, what the native speaker, and not some visiting linguist, feels are the distinguishing features or components of that word — is known as "componential analysis" or "formal semantic analysis." The aim, in brief, is to determine the components or features that native speakers use to distinguish similar terms from one another so that more exact meanings can be achieved.

Anyone who visits an exotic culture quickly learns that the   5 people are linguistically deaf to categories he considers obvious, yet they are extraordinarily perceptive in talking about things he has no easy way to describe. An English-speaking anthropologist studying the Koyas of India, for example, soon discovers that their language does not distinguish between dew, fog, and snow. When questioned about these natural phenomena, the Koyas can find a way to describe them, but normally their language attaches no significance to making such distinctions and provides no highly codable words for the purpose. On the other hand, a Koya has the linguistic resources to speak easily about seven different kinds of bamboo — resources that the visiting anthropologist utterly lacks in his own language. More important than the significance, or the lack of it, that a language places on objects and ideas is the way that language categorizes the information it does find significant. A *pig,* for example, can be categorized in several ways: a mammal with cloven hoofs and bristly hairs and adapted for digging with its snout; a mold in which metal is cast; a British sixpence coin. The Koyas categorize the pig in none of these ways; they simply place it in the category of animals that are edible. Their neighbors, Muslims, think of it in a different way by placing it in the category of defiled animals.

Everyone, whether he realizes it or not, classifies the items 6 he finds in his environment. Most speakers of English recognize a category that they call *livestock,* which is made up of other categories known as *cattle, horses, sheep,* and *swine* of different ages and sexes. An English speaker who is knowledgeable about farm life categorizes a barnyardful of these animals in a way that establishes relationships based on distinguishing features. For example, he feels that a *cow* and a *mare,* even though they belong to different species, are somehow in a relationship to each other. And of course they are, because they both belong to the category of Female Animal under the general category of Livestock. The speaker of English unconsciously groups certain animals into various sub-categories that exclude other animals:

LIVESTOCK				
	Cattle	*Horses*	*Sheep*	*Swine*
Female	cow	mare	ewe	sow
Intact Male	bull	stallion	ram	boar
Castrated Male	steer	gelding	wether	barrow
Immature	heifer	colt/filly	lamb	shoat/gilt
Newborn	calf	foal	yearling	piglet

A table such as this shows that speakers of English are 7 intuitively aware of certain contrasts. They regard a *bull* and a *steer* as different — which they are, because one belongs to a category of Intact Males and the other to a category of Castrated Males. In addition to discriminations made on the basis of livestock's sex, speakers of English also contrast mature and immature animals. A *foal* is a newborn horse and a *stallion* is a mature male horse.

The conceptual labels by which English-speaking peoples 8 talk about barnyard animals can now be understood. The animal is defined by the point at which two distinctive features intersect: sex (male, female, or castrated) and maturity (mature, immature, or newborn). A *stallion* belongs to a category of horse that is both intact male and mature; a *filly* belongs to a category of horse that is both female and immature. Nothing in external reality dictates that barnyard animals should be talked about in this way; it is strictly a convention of English and some other languages.

In contrast, imagine that an Amazonian Indian is brought 9 to the United States so that linguists can intensively study his language. When the Indian returns to his native forests, his friends and relatives listen in disbelief as he tells about all the fantastic things he saw. He summarizes his impressions of America in terms of the familiar categories his language has accustomed him to. He relates that at first he was bewildered by the strange animals he saw on an American farm because each animal not only looked different but also seemed to represent a unique concept to the natives of the North American tribe. But after considerable observation of the curious folkways of these peculiar people, at last he understood American barnyard animals. He figured out that some animals are good for work and that some are good for food. Using these two components — rather than the Americans' features of sex and maturity — his classification of livestock is considerably different. He categorized *stallion, mare,* and *gelding* as belonging to both the Inedible and Work (Riding) categories. The *bull* also belonged to the Inedible category but it was used for a different kind of Work as a draught animal. He further placed a large number of animals — *cow, ewe, lamb, sow,* and so on — in the category of Edible but Useless for Work. Since his method of categorizing the barnyard failed to take into account the breeding process, which depends upon the categories of sex and maturity, he no doubt found it inexplicable that some animals —*ram, colt, boar,* and so on — were raised even though they could not be eaten or used for work.

To an American, the Amazonian Indian's classification of barnyard animals appears quite foolish, yet it is no more foolish than the American's system of classification by the features of sex and maturity. Speakers of each language have the right to recognize whatever features they care to. And they have a similar right to then organize these features according to the rules of their own speech communities. No one system is better than another in making sense out of the world in terms that can be talked about; the systems are simply different. A speaker of English who defines a *stallion* as a mature, male horse is no wiser than the Amazonian who claims it is inedible and used for riding. Both the speaker of English and the speaker of the Amazonian language have brought order out of the multitudes of things in the environment — and, in the process, both have shown something about how their languages and their minds work.

[1973 — U.S.A.]

Questions

1. What is Farb's purpose in this essay? What is its thesis? The thesis here is unfolded step by step in paragraphs 6, 8, and 10. What specific sentences when taken together form the thesis statement?

2. Why did Farb not state his thesis all at once at the beginning? Is his method effective? How so?

3. Farb moves from colors to furniture to livestock. What accounts for this order of his enumerated items? Why colors first and livestock last?

4. The material of paragraph 4 is somewhat extraneous. How does Farb make the paragraph coherent — that is, how does it relate to paragraphs 3 and 5?

5. At the end of the essay, Farb states as a conclusion the final part of his thesis. Does his evidence support his statement? Is it indeed drawn from the evidence or is it simply a prejudice slipped in, in such a way as to seem logical?

Writing Assignments

1. Make a chart like Farb's classifying some group of people, animals, or things: teachers, dogs, clothing. Then, in a paragraph or more, explain your criteria for so classifying and justify your categories on some basis (for instance, their usefulness).

2. Look over the titles of the essays you have read in this book. Classify them according to some system appropriate to the material: prosaic versus poetic, elaborate versus simple, to-the-point versus tangential, descriptive versus intriguing, or any combination of these or other categories. Now write a paper on what makes for a good title. Does your classification shed light on why some titles are more effective than others? How? Or do good titles cut across categories? If so, what can be concluded from that?

3. Farb would have us believe that all systems of classification are equal. But couldn't it be argued on some basis or other that this is not so? Write an essay specifying why one system might be preferable to another. To do so convincingly, you will have to find cogent reasons and exemplify them clearly and well.

✦ TOLERANCE ✦

E. M. Forster

EVERYBODY IS TALKING ABOUT RECONSTRUCTION. OUR ENEMIES HAVE   1
their schemes for a new order in Europe, maintained by their secret police, and we on our side talk of rebuilding London or England, or western civilization, and we make plans how this is to be done. Which is all very well, but when I hear such talk, and see the architects sharpening their pencils and the contractors getting out their estimates, and the statesmen marking out their spheres of influence, and everyone getting down to the job, a very famous text occurs to me: "Except the Lord build the house, they labour in vain that build it." Beneath the poetic imagery of these words lies a hard scientific truth, namely, unless you have a sound attitude of mind, a right psychology, you cannot construct or reconstruct anything that will endure. The text is true, not only for religious people, but

for workers whatever their outlook, and it is significant that one of our historians, Dr. Arnold Toynbee, should have chosen it to preface his great study of the growth and decay of civilizations. Surely the only sound foundation for a civilization is a sound state of mind. Architects, contractors, international commissioners, marketing boards, broadcasting corporations will never, by themselves, build a new world. They must be inspired by the proper spirit, and there must be the proper spirit in the people for whom they are working. For instance, we shall never have a beautiful new London until people refuse to live in ugly houses. At present, they don't mind; they demand more comfort, but are indifferent to civic beauty; indeed they have no taste. I live myself in a hideous block of flats, but I can't say it worries me, and until we are worried all schemes for reconstructing London beautifully must automatically fail.

What, though, is the proper spirit? We agree that the basic   2 problem is psychological, that the Lord must build if the work is to stand, that there must be a sound state of mind before diplomacy or economics or trade conferences can function. But what state of mind is sound? Here we may differ. Most people, when asked what spiritual quality is needed to rebuild civilization, will reply "Love". Men must love one another, they say; nations must do likewise, and then the series of cataclysms which is threatening to destroy us will be checked.

Respectfully but firmly, I disagree. Love is a great force in   3 private life; it is indeed the greatest of all things; but love in public affairs does not work. It has been tried again and again: by the Christian civilizations of the Middle Ages, and also by the French Revolution, a secular movement which reasserted the Brotherhood of Man. And it has always failed. The idea that nations should love one another, or that business concerns or marketing boards should love one another, or that a man in Portugal should love a man in Peru of whom he has never heard — it is absurd, unreal, dangerous. It leads us into perilous and vague sentimentalism. "Love is what is needed," we chant, and then sit back and the world goes on as before. The fact is, we can only love what we know personally. And we cannot know much. In public affairs, in the rebuilding of civilization, something much less dramatic and emotional is needed, namely tolerance. Tolerance is a very dull virtue. It is boring. Unlike love, it has always had a bad press. It is negative. It merely means putting up with people, being able to stand things. No one has ever written an ode to tolerance, or raised a statue to her. Yet this is the quality which will be most needed after the war. This is the sound state of mind which we are looking for. This is the only force which will enable different races and classes and interests to settle down together to the work of reconstruction.

The world is very full of people — appallingly full; it has 4 never been so full before — and they are all tumbling over each other. Most of these people one doesn't know and some of them one doesn't like; doesn't like the colour of their skins, say, or the shapes of their noses, or the way they blow them or don't blow them, or the way they talk, or their smell, or their clothes, or their fondness for jazz or their dislike of jazz, and so on. Well, what is one to do? There are two solutions. One of them is the Nazi solution. If you don't like people, kill them, banish them, segregate them, and then strut up and down proclaiming that you are the salt of the earth. The other way is much less thrilling, but it is on the whole the way of the democracies, and I prefer it. If you don't like people, put up with them as well as you can. Don't try to love them; you can't, you'll only strain yourself. But try to tolerate them. On the basis of that tolerance a civilized future may be built. Certainly I can see no other foundation for the post-war world.

For what it will most need is the negative virtues: not being 5 huffy, touchy, irritable, revengeful. I have lost all faith in positive militant ideals; they can so seldom be carried out without thousands of human beings getting maimed or imprisoned. Phrases like "I will purge this nation", "I will clean up this city", terrify and disgust me. They might not have mattered when the world was emptier; they are horrifying now, when one nation is mixed up with another, when one city cannot be organically separated from its neighbours. And another point:

reconstruction is unlikely to be rapid. I do not believe that we are psychologically fit for it, plan the architects never so wisely. In the long run, yes, perhaps; the history of our race justifies that hope. But civilization has its mysterious regressions, and it seems to me that we are fated now to be in one of them, and must recognize this and behave accordingly. Tolerance, I believe, will be imperative after the establishment of peace. It's always useful to take a concrete instance; and I have been asking myself how I should behave if, after peace was signed, I met Germans who had been fighting against us. I shouldn't try to love them; I shouldn't feel inclined. They have broken a window in my little ugly flat for one thing. But I shall try to tolerate them, because it is common sense, because in the post-war world we shall have to live with Germans. We can't exterminate them, any more than they have succeeded in exterminating the Jews. We shall have to put up with them, not for any lofty reason, but because it is the next thing that will have to be done.

I don't then, regard tolerance as a great eternally estab- 6 lished divine principle, though I might perhaps quote "In my Father's house are many mansions" in support of such a view. It is just a makeshift, suitable for an overcrowded and overheated planet. It carries on when love gives out, and love generally gives out as soon as we move away from our home and our friends, and stand among strangers in a queue for potatoes. Tolerance is wanted in the queue; otherwise we think, "Why will people be so slow?"; it is wanted in the tube, or "Why will people be so fat?"; it is wanted at the telephone, or "Why are they so deaf?" or, conversely, "Why do they mumble?" It is wanted in the street, in the office, at the factory, and it is wanted above all between classes, races and nations. It's dull. And yet it entails imagination. For you have all the time to be putting yourself in someone else's place. Which is a desirable spiritual exercise.

This ceaseless effort to put up with other people seems 7 tame, almost ignoble, so that it sometimes repels generous natures, and I don't recall many great men who have recommended tolerance. St. Paul certainly did not. Nor did Dante. However, a few names occur. Going back over two thousand years, and to India, there is the great Buddhist Emperor Asoka, who set up inscriptions recording not his own exploits but the need for mercy and mutual understanding and peace. Going back about four hundred years, to Holland, there is the Dutch scholar Erasmus, who stood apart from the religious fanaticism of the Reformation and was abused by both parties in consequence. In the same century there was the Frenchman Montaigne, subtle, intelligent, witty, who lived in his quiet country house and wrote essays which still delight and confirm the civilized. And England: there was John Locke, the philosopher; there was Sydney Smith, the Liberal and liberal-izing divine; there was Lowes Dickinson, writer of *A Modern Symposium*, which might be called the Bible of Tolerance. And Germany — yes, Germany: there was Goethe. All these men testify to the creed which I have been trying to express: a negative creed, but necessary for the salvation of this crowded jostling modern world.

Two more remarks. First, it is very easy to see fanaticism in   8 other people, but difficult to spot in oneself. Take the evil of racial prejudice. We can easily detect it in the Nazis; their conduct has been infamous ever since they rose to power. But we ourselves — are we guiltless? We are far less guilty than they are. Yet is there no racial prejudice in the British Empire? Is there no colour question? I ask you to consider that, those of you to whom tolerance is more than a pious word. My other remark is to forestall a criticism. Tolerance is not the same as weakness. Putting up with people does not mean giving in to them. This complicates the problem. But the rebuilding of civilization is bound to be complicated. I only feel certain that unless the Lord builds the house they will labour in vain who build it. Perhaps, when the house is completed, love will enter it, and the greatest force in our private lives will also rule in public life.

[1942 — Great Britain]

Questions

1. What is Forster's thesis? How do you know? Where is it stated?

2. "Tolerance" was written as a speech. How does Forster's style reflect this?

3. Look at the sentences in the second and third paragraphs with respect to length and syntax. Forster adeptly varies both. How? Why?

4. What means of support does Forster use in paragraph 7? Is this type of support effective here? Why or why not?

5. What kind of voice do you hear when reading "Tolerance"? What is the essay's tone? How are its tone and sense of voice created? In what way is the essay's tone (a matter of form) at one with its content?

Writing Assignments

1. Choose a thesis and, in a paragraph or more, argue it by referring to authorities who have held the same view (as Forster does in paragraph 7). Be sure to have a reason for the arrangement of the authorities you enumerate.

2. Forster presents tolerance as a "state of mind," and then argues for it in a tone that is his best example. Pick another state of mind — serenity, say, or joy — and, in an essay focused on the virtues of the attitude you choose, discuss it in a tone (created by diction and syntax as well as the epithets you use and other aspects of your verbal structure) that itself conveys the attitude you name.

---------- ✤ WHY GUN-CONTROL ✤ ----------
LAWS DON'T WORK
Barry Goldwater

LET ME SAY IMMEDIATELY THAT IF I THOUGHT MORE GUN-CONTROL 1
laws would help diminish the tragic incidence of robberies,
muggings, rapes and murders in the United States, I would be
the first to vote for them. But I am convinced that making more
such laws approaches the problem from the wrong direction.

It is clear, I think, that gun legislation simply doesn't work. 2
There are already some 20,000 state and local gun laws on the
books, and they are no more effective than was the prohibition
of alcoholic beverages in the 1920s. Our most recent attempt at
federal gun legislation was the Gun Control Act of 1968,
intended to control the interstate sale and transportation of
firearms and the importation of uncertified firearms; it has done
nothing to check the availability of weapons. It has been
bolstered in every nook and cranny of the nation by local gun-
control laws, yet the number of shooting homicides per year has
climbed steadily since its enactment, while armed robberies
have increased 60 percent.

Some people, even some law-enforcement officials, contend 3
that "crimes of passion" occur because a gun just happens to be
present at the scene. I don't buy that. I can't equate guns with
the murder rate, because if a person is angry enough to kill, he
will kill with the first thing that comes to hand — gun, a knife,
an ice pick, a baseball bat.

I believe our *only* hope of reducing crime in this country is 4
to control not the weapon but the user. We must reverse the
trend toward leniency and permissiveness in our courts — the
plea bargaining, the pardons, the suspended sentences and
unwarranted paroles — and make the lawbreaker pay for what
he has done by spending time in jail. We have plenty of statutes
against killing and maiming and threatening people with
weapons. These can be made effective by strong enforcement

and firm decisions from the bench. When a man knows that if he uses a potentially deadly object to rob or do harm to another person he is letting himself in for a mandatory, unparolable stretch behind bars, he will think twice about it.

Of course, no matter what gun-control laws are enacted 5 — including national registration — the dedicated crook can always get a weapon. So, some people ask, even if national registration of guns isn't completely airtight, isn't it worth trying? Sure, it would cause a little inconvenience to law-abiding gun owners. And it certainly wouldn't stop all criminals from obtaining guns. But it might stop a few, maybe quite a few. What's wrong with that?

There are several answers. The first concerns enforcement. 6 How are we going to persuade the bank robber or the street-corner stickup artist to register his means of criminal livelihood? Then there is the matter of expense. A study conducted eight years ago showed a cost to New York City of $72.87 to investigate and process one application for a pistol license. In mid-1970 dollars, the same procedure probably costs over $100. By extrapolation to the national scale, the cost to American taxpayers of investigating and registering the 40 to 50 million handguns might reach $4 billion or $5 billion. On top of that, keeping the process in operation year after year would require taxpayer financing of another sizable federal bureau. We ought to have far better prospects of success before we hobble ourselves with such appalling expenditures.

Finally, there are legal aspects based on the much- 7 discussed Second Amendment to the Bill of Rights, which proclaims that "A well regulated Militia, being necessary to the security of a free State, the right of the people to keep and bear Arms, shall not be infringed." The anti-gun faction argues that this right made sense in the days of British oppression but that it has no application today. I contend, on the other hand, that the Founding Fathers conceived of an armed citizenry as a necessary hedge against tyranny from within as well as from without, that they saw the right to keep and bear arms as basic and perpetual, the one thing that could spell the difference between freedom and servitude. Thus I deem most forms of gun control unconstitutional in intent.

Well, then, I'm often asked, what kind of gun laws *are* you 8 for? I reply that I am for laws of common sense. I am for laws that prohibit citizen access to machine guns, bazookas and other military devices. I am for laws that are educational in nature. I believe that before a person is permitted to buy a weapon he should be required to take a course that will teach him how to use it, to handle it safely and keep it safely about the house.

Gun education, in fact, can actually reduce lawlessness in a 9 community, as was demonstrated in an experiment conducted in Highland Park, Mich. City police launched a program to instruct merchants in the use of handguns. The idea was to help them protect themselves and their businesses from robbers, and it was given wide publicity. The store-robbery rate dropped from an average of 1.5 a day to none in four months.

Where do we go from here? My answer to this is based on 10 the firm belief that we have a crime problem in this country, not a gun problem, and that we must meet the enemy on his own terms. We must start by making crime as unprofitable for him as we can. And we have to do this, I believe, by getting tough in the courts and corrections systems.

A recent news story in Washington, D.C., reports that, of 11 184 persons convicted of gun possession in a six-month period, only 14 received a jail sentence. Forty-six other cases involved persons who had previously been convicted of a felony or possession of a gun. Although the maximum penalty for such repeaters in the District of Columbia is ten years in prison, half of these were not jailed at all. A study last year revealed that in New York City, which has about the most prohibitive gun legislation in the country, only one out of six people convicted of crimes involving weapons went to jail.

This sorry state of affairs exists because too many judges 12 and magistrates either don't know the law or are unwilling to apply it with appropriate vigor. It's time to demand either that they crack down on these criminals or be removed from office. It may even be time to review the whole system of judicial appointments, to stop weakening the cause of justice by putting men on the bench who may happen to be golfing partners of Congressmen and too often lack the brains and ability for the job. In Arizona today we elect our judges, and the system is working well, in part because we ask the American and local bar associations to consider candidates and make recommendations. In this way, over the last few years, we have replaced many weaklings with good jurists.

We have long had all the criminal statutes we need to turn 13 the tide against the crime wave. There is, however, one piece of proposed legislation that I am watching with particular interest. Introduced by Sen. James McClure (R., Idaho), it requires that any person convicted of a federal crime in which a gun is used serve five to ten years in jail automatically on top of whatever penalty he receives for the crime itself. A second conviction would result in an extra ten-year-to-life sentence. These sentences would be mandatory and could not be suspended. It is, in short, a "tough" bill. I think that this bill would serve as an excellent model for state legislation.

And so it has in California which, last September, signed 14 into law a similar bill requiring a mandatory jail sentence for any gun-related felony.

Finally, it's important to remember that this is an area of 15 great confusion; an area in which statistics can be juggled and distorted to support legislation that is liable to be expensive, counter-productive or useless. The issue touches upon the freedom and safety of all of us, whether we own firearms or not. The debate over gun control is an adjunct to the war against crime, and that war must be fought with all the intelligence and tenacity we can bring to it.

[1976 — U.S.A.]

Questions

1. What does the last sentence of paragraph 1 imply? What is Goldwater's thesis in full?
2. How does this thesis, which falls into two parts, govern the essay? To answer, make a paragraph outline of it, giving a label to each

paragraph according to its topic and showing the relationship of each to the thesis.

3. What kinds of evidence does Goldwater use? Why is what he includes about the judicial system essential to his argument? Which of his points are strong and which weak?

4. Is Goldwater's analogy between gun control and prohibition (paragraph 2) a strong argument, or does the analogy, when carried out, actually hurt his case? How so?

5. What is the function of the first sentence of paragraph 6 and of paragraph 14?

6. Contrast Goldwater's method here with Joan Didion's in "Miami: The Cuban Presence" (pages 195–207). Didion, too, has a thesis and a very definite point of view. The essays differ radically, however, in the ways in which they communicate the points of view of their respective authors. How so? Which way, if either, is better suited for the job of persuasion?

Writing Assignments

1. Write a paper in which you argue for or against gun control using what Goldwater says either as evidence supporting your view or as a foil against which to highlight your dissenting view by way of contrast.

2. Do some research into the area of gun control and, using your research to back you up, write an essay in which you support or attack the idea that further legislation is the way to cure the problem of handguns. Because the secondary literature seems to be open to interpretation one way or the other, be sure to suggest what validates your interpretation of it and your reading of whatever statistics are available.

✢ THE JUST-RIGHT WIFE ✢

Ellen Goodman

THE UPPER-MIDDLE-CLASS MEN OF ARABIA ARE LOOKING FOR JUST THE 1
right kind of wife. Arabia's merchant class, reports the
Associated Press, finds the women of Libya too backward, and
the women of Lebanon too forward, and have therefore gone
shopping for brides in Egypt.

Egyptian women are being married off at the rate of thirty 2
a day — an astonishing increase, according to the Egyptian
marriage bureau. It doesn't know whether to be pleased or
alarmed at the popularity of its women. According to one recent
Saudi Arabian groom, the Egyptian women are "just right."

"The Egyptian woman is the happy medium," says Aly 3
Abdul el-Korrary of his bride, Wafaa Ibrahiv (the happy
medium herself was not questioned). "She is not too inhibited
as they are in conservative Moslem societies, and not too liberal
like many Lebanese."

Is this beginning to sound familiar? Well, the upper- 4
middle-class, middle-aged, merchant-professional-class man of
America also wants a "happy medium" wife. He is confused.
He, too, has a problem and he would like us to be more
understanding.

If it is no longer chic for a sheik to marry a veiled woman, 5
it is somehow no longer "modern" for a successful member of
the liberal establishment to be married to what he used to call
a "housewife" and what he now hears called a "household
drudge."

As his father once wanted a wife who had at least started 6
college, now he would like a wife who has a mind, and even a
job, of her own. The younger men in his office these days wear
their wives' occupations on their sleeves. He thinks he, too,
would like a wife — especially for social occasions — whose
status would be his status symbol. A lady lawyer would be nice.

These men, you understand, now say (at least in private to   7
younger working women in their office) that they are bored
with women who "don't do anything." No matter how much
some of them conspired in keeping them at home Back Then,
many are now saying, in the best Moslem style, "I divorce
thee." They are replacing them with more up-to-date models. A
Ph.D. candidate would be nice.

The upper-middle-class, middle-aged man of today wants a   8
wife who won't make him feel guilty. He doesn't want to worry
if she's happy. He doesn't want to hear her complain about her
dusty American history degree. He doesn't want to know if
she's crying at the psychiatrist's office. He most definitely
doesn't want to be blamed. He wants her to fulfill herself
already! He doesn't mean that maliciously.

On the other hand, Lord knows, he doesn't want a wife   9
who is too forward. The Saudi Arabian merchant believes that
the Egyptian woman adapts more easily to his moods and
needs. The American merchant also wants a woman who adapts
herself to his moods and needs — his need for an independent
woman and a traditional wife.

He doesn't want to live with a "household drudge," but it   10
would be nice to have an orderly home and well-scrubbed
children. Certainly he wouldn't want a wife who got high on
folding socks — he is not a Neanderthal — but it would be nice
if she arranged for these things to get done. Without talking
about marriage contracts.

He wants a wife who agreed that "marriage is a matter of   11
give and take, not a business deal and 50–50 chores." It would
help if she had just enough conflict herself (for not being her
mother) to feel more than half the guilt for a full ashtray.

Of course, he sincerely would like her to be involved in her   12
own work and life. But on the other hand, he doesn't want it to
siphon away her energy for him. He needs to be taken care of,
nurtured. He would like her to enjoy her job, but be ready to
move for his, if necessary (after, of course, a long discussion in
which he feels awful about asking and she ends up comforting
him and packing).

He wants a wife who is a sexually responsive and satisfied 13
woman, and he would even be pleased if she initiated sex with
him. Sometimes. Not too often, however, because then he
would get anxious.

He is confused, but he does, in all sincerity (status symbols 14
aside), want a happy marriage to a happy wife. A happy
medium. He is not sure exactly what he means, but he, too,
would like a wife who is "just right."

The difference is that when the upper-middle-class, middle- 15
aged man of Arabia wants his wife he goes out and buys one.
His American "brother" can only offer himself as the prize.

[1984 — U.S.A.]

Questions

1. Paragraph 4 begins with a question: "Is this beginning to sound
   familiar?" To whom is this question addressed? Who is the intended
   audience? With respect to this audience, do you think that
   Goodman's satire is effective? Why or why not?

2. "The Just-Right Wife" is full of verbal fun. What of "chic for a
   sheik" (paragraph 5) in this regard? What is the effect of the last
   sentence of paragraph 6 and of paragraph 7? Comment on the
   diction of "already" at the end of paragraph 8.

3. Goodman is not really interested in "upper-middle-class men of
   Arabia." What is her interest, which is to say, what is her theme?

4. Since her interest lies elsewhere, why does Goodman refer to "men
   of Arabia" at all? The essay is built on an analogy. What is it? What
   is its basis? Why this particular analogy? What does it convey? (In
   answering, consider American attitudes about the Middle East.)

5. What passages extend the analogy? How does it help to bring the
   essay to a conclusion?

Writing Assignments

1. Write a few paragraphs — satirical if you wish — defining the
   "just-right" something or other. One of the following topics would
   do: the just-right teenager, the just-right mother or father, the
   just-right sister or brother, the just-right college instructor. If you
   mean to be satirical, then you must find a way of informing your
   reader that you are expressing (satirically) your mother's views

about the just-right teenager, for instance, or your sister's on the just-right brother.

2. Write an essay "after" Goodman's. That is, whatever your thesis, proceed by way of analogy. Establish your analogy early on (indeed, it could help form your thesis statement) and then, exploiting as many points of similarity as you can, extend the analogy in some way paragraph by paragraph. You might conclude, as does Goodman, with a notable point of difference.

✚ MUSIC AND TECHNOLOGY ✚
Glenn Gould[1]

ONE SUNDAY MORNING IN DECEMBER 1950, I WANDERED INTO A 1 living-room-sized radio studio, placed my services at the disposal of a single microphone belonging to the Canadian Broadcasting Corporation, and proceeded to broadcast "live" (tape was already a fact of life in the recording industry, but in those days radio broadcasting still observed the first-note-to-last-and-damn-the-consequences syndrome of the concert hall) two sonatas: one by Mozart, one by Hindemith. It was my first network broadcast, but it was not my first contact with the microphone; for several years I'd been indulging in experiments at home with primitive tape recorders — strapping the mikes to the sounding board of my piano, the better to emasculate Scarlatti sonatas, for example, and generally subjecting both instruments to whichever imaginative indignities came to mind.

But the CBC occasion, as I've hinted already, was a 2 memorable one: not simply because it enabled me to communicate without the immediate presence of a gallery of witnesses (though the fact that in most forms of broadcasting a

---

[1]*Gould:* Glenn Gould (1932–1982) was a great, though eccentric, classical pianist. The three classical composers he mentions — Scarlatti, Mozart, and Hindemith — are from the early and late 18th century and the 20th century respectively.

microphone six feet away stands as surrogate for an audience has always been, for me, prominent among the attractions of the medium) but rather because later the same day I was presented with a soft-cut "acetate," a disc which dimly reproduced the felicities of the broadcast in question and which, even today, a quarter-century after the fact, I still take down from the shelf on occasion in order to celebrate that moment in my life when I first caught a vague impression of the direction it would take, when I realized that the collected wisdom of my peers and elders to the effect that technology represented a compromising, dehumanizing intrusion into art was nonsense, when my love affair with the microphone began.

I suspect, indeed, that if I were to assign an absolute time 3 to the moment of recognition, that time would relate to the occasion when, later in the day, rehearing the acetate for the third or fourth time, I discovered that if I gave it a bass cut at a hundred cycles or thereabouts and a treble boost at approximately five thousand, the murky, unwieldy, bass-oriented studio piano with which I had had to deal earlier in the day could be magically transformed on playback into an instrument seemingly capable of the same sonic perversions to which I had already introduced Maestro Scarlatti.

"A plausible approach qua Mozart," you say, "but entirely 4 inappropriate for Hindemith!" Perhaps; perhaps not. I'm reluctant to argue the case on musical grounds, for my intentions, of course, were only secondarily musical; they were primarily theatrical and illusory. I had prevailed upon the most primitive technology to sponsor a suggestion of that which was not; my own contribution as artist was no longer the be-all and end-all of the project at hand, no longer a fait accompli. Technology had positioned itself between the attempt and the realization; the "charity of the machine," to quote the theologian Jean Le Moyne, had interposed itself between "the frailty of nature and the vision of the idealized accomplishment." "Remarkable clarity — must have been an incredible piano," friends would say. "Believe me, you simply can't imagine," I would respond. I had learned the first lesson of technology; I had learned to be creatively dishonest.

Let me say straight off that I admit to no inherent 5 contradiction in those terms. Technology, in my view, is not primarily a conveyor belt for the dissemination of information; it is not primarily an instantaneous relay system; it is not primarily a memory bank in whose vaults are deposited the achievements and shortcomings, the creative credits and documented deficits, of man. It is, of course, or can be, any of those things, if required, and perhaps you will remind me that "the camera does not lie," to which I can only respond, "Then the camera must be taught to forthwith." For technology should not, in my view, be treated as a noncommittal, noncommitted voyeur; its capacity for dissection, for analysis — above all, perhaps, for the idealization of an impression — must be exploited, and no area with which it is currently occupied better demonstrates the philosophical conflicts with which its practitioners and theorists have been too long preoccupied than the aims and techniques of recording.

I believe in "the intrusion" of technology because, essen- 6 tially, that intrusion imposes upon art a notion of morality which transcends the idea of art itself. And before, as in the case of "morality," I use some other old-fashioned words, let me explain what I mean by that one. Morality, it seems to me, has never been on the side of the carnivore — at least not when alternative life-styles are available. And evolution, which is really the biological rejection of inadequate moral systems — and particularly the evolution of man in response to his technology — has been anticarnivorous to the extent that, step by step, it has enabled him to operate at increasing distances from, to be increasingly out of touch with, his animal response to confrontation.

A war, for instance, engaged in by computer-aimed missiles 7 is a slightly better, slightly less objectionable war than one fought by clubs or spears. Not much better, and unquestionably more destructive, statistically, but better to the extent, at least, that, all things being equal, the adrenal response of the participants (we had better forget about the bystanders or the argument collapses) is less engaged by it. Well, Margaret Mead, if I read her rightly, disapproves of that distancing factor, of that sense of disengagement from biological limitation. But I do believe in it, and recordings, though they're rarely understood as such, are one of the very best metaphors we have for it.

A few months back, for instance, I was listening to the broadcast memoirs of the very distinguished and very venerable British conductor Sir Adrian Boult. At one point Sir Adrian was asked what he thought of recording, and he said, predictably enough, something to the effect that "Well, of course, it's fair game to make them, especially for those who can't get out to the concert hall, but they're never going to take the place of the concert, are they? I always say to my producer at the outset of the session, 'Look here, old man, it's my job to get the very best I can out of the band, and I shall strive to do that even if we need two or three takes. But I don't want any of this patching! That's all you young chaps seem to think of these days — patching. Should the horn fluff his part — well, bad luck, I say, and if time permits, we'll let him have another go at it. But I don't want you to repair the warts by patching, d'you see, because at all costs I must have the long line intact.' " (I hasten to add that I do not have Sir Adrian's transcript at hand, but the paraphrase is as accurate as memory can make it.)

In any case, Sir Adrian's attitude toward "patching" — which we call "editing" or "splicing" on this side of the water — and toward recording technology in general represents one of the more unbreachable sectors of the generation gap. He's wrong, of course — splicing doesn't damage lines. Good splices build good lines, and it shouldn't much matter if one uses a splice every two seconds or none for an hour so long as the result *appears* to be a coherent whole. After all, if one buys a new car, it doesn't really matter how many assembly-line hands are involved in its production. The more the better, really, insofar as they can help to ensure the security of its operation.

But what really bothers Sir Adrian, I suspect, is that since 10 the splice divides the elements of a particular problem, it transcends the physical anxieties, the coordinative challenges, represented by that problem. It seems to preclude the possibility that man unaided is his own best advocate — the most unwarranted assumption of the post-Renaissance era — and for that reason to be, in some way, antihuman.

Of course, we very often tend to confuse a sense of 11 humanity with the way in which human concerns are traditionally resolved. Traditionally, they're resolved by individual moments of enlightenment, of vision, and it's that almost mystical faith in the omnipotence of the enlightened moment, in the challenge honorably overcome, which makes people of Sir Adrian's generation distrust recording technology.

I mentioned already the generation gap, but there's also a 12 geographical gap involved. The farther east you go, the more likely you are to find recordings which are in effect taped concerts. Of course, if you go far enough east, you get to Japan, and in that country, which has no inhibiting Westernized concert-hall tradition to reckon with, recordings are understood as indigenous experiences. But in general, as one heads east from the Rhine, the perspective becomes more distant, as in a concert hall, usually more reverberant, and less precise, for that reason, and the whole operation functions mainly as an exercise in memory.

Of course, there is nothing really wrong with making 13 records for that purpose. Fifty years ago, most people thought that recording was essentially an archival operation, [2] the better to remember Grandpapa's generation by. And, as I've said, that's part of what it does, but not at all what the process is about.

---

[2]*Archival operation:* Something that keeps the *record* of an event.

I do quite a bit of fancy editorial footwork with the voices 14
of characters that I interview for radio documentaries, and if I
do it well, I defy anyone to find in my editorial "patching"
something other than a tauter, more coherent character
synthesis. It is of course true that the amount of work one does
is often relative to the value of what's being said by the
character in question, and that if virtually nothing is being said,
the sense of portraiture could conceivably be enhanced by
leaving the material uncut. If, for instance, one stumbled into
an interview with a character who said, "Well, like, man, I sorta
don't wanna go out on a limb to, like, answer da question, you
know, because, like, well, it takes all kinds, you know, and,
well, either you dig it or maybe not, am I right? But, like, man,
if I were to give a real conclusive answer, I'd say that — well,
could be, you know." If he said that, it might be tempting not
to cut it, to keep it intact as a portrait. If, however, one
happened to deduce that what he was really saying was "To be
or — like, uh — not to be," and those words were bound within
that quote, then I really think that "like, uh" should go.

[1974 — Canada]

Questions

1. What in paragraph 1 reveals Gould's attitude about technology,
   though that attitude is not stated until later?
2. Whom did Gould envision as his audience and what kind of a
   relationship did he mean to establish with this audience? What role
   does diction play in both regards?
3. Is voicing the view of the other side, as Gould does in paragraph 8,
   an effective ploy in an argument? Why or why not?
4. Definition is an important means of support in this essay. How so?
   What does Gould define? In what way does definition along with
   diction shape our attitude toward the speaker and thus the way we
   relate to him?
5. What means of support does paragraph 14 exemplify? Is this an
   effective way of ending? How so?
6. Paragraph 12 is a model of coherence. Analyze this paragraph to see
   how its disparate statements are brought together coherently.

Writing Assignments

1. Read paragraph 12 carefully. Then write a paragraph on how its diverse materials have been made to cohere. Strive for the same level of coherence yourself.

2. Gould believes that we are overly concerned with the anti-human aspects of technology. Do you agree or disagree? Whichever, write a paper supporting your view on the matter. For your ending, imitate Gould's last paragraph; that is, end with an extended analogy that sums up your main point.

✤ THE NONSCIENCE OF ✤ HUMAN NATURE
Stephen Jay Gould

WHEN A GROUP OF GIRLS SUFFERED SIMULTANEOUS SEIZURES IN THE   1
presence of an accused witch, the justices of seventeenth century Salem could offer no explanation other than true demonic possession. When the followers of Charlie Manson attributed occult powers to their leader, no judge took them seriously. In nearly three hundred years separating the two incidents, we have learned quite a bit about social, economic, and psychological determinants of group behavior. A crudely literal interpretation of such events now seems ridiculous.

An equally crude literalism used to prevail in interpreting   2
human nature and the differences among human groups. Human behavior was attributed to innate biology; we do what we do because we are made that way. The first lesson of an eighteenth-century primer stated the position succinctly: In Adam's fall, we sinned all. A movement away from this biological determinism has been a major trend in twentieth-century science and culture. We have come to see ourselves as a learning animal; we have come to believe that the influences of class and culture far outweigh the weaker predispositions of our genetic constitution.

Nonetheless, we have been deluged during the past decade 3
by a resurgent biological determinism, ranging from "pop
ethology" to outright racism.

With Konrad Lorenz[1] as godfather, Robert Ardrey as 4
dramatist, and Desmond Morris as raconteur, we are presented
with man, "the naked ape," descended from an African
carnivore, innately aggressive and inherently territorial.

Lionel Tiger and Robin Fox try to find a biological basis for 5
outmoded Western ideals of aggressive, outreaching men and
docile, restricted women. In discussing cross-cultural differences between men and women, they propose a hormonal
chemistry inherited from the requirements of our supposed
primal roles as group hunters and child rearers.

Carleton Coon offered a prelude of events to come with his 6
claim (*The Origin of Races*, 1962) that five major human races
evolved independently from *Homo erectus* ("Java" and "Peking"
man) to *Homo sapiens*, with black people making the transition
last. More recently, the IQ test has been (mis)used to infer
genetic differences in intelligence among races (Arthur Jensen
and William Shockley) and classes (Richard Herrnstein)
— always, I must note, to the benefit of the particular group to
which the author happens to belong (see next essay).

All these views have been ably criticized on an individual 7
basis; yet they have rarely been treated together as expressions
of a common philosophy — a crude biological determinism. One
can, of course, accept a specific claim and reject the others. A
belief in the innate nature of human violence does not brand
anyone a racist. Yet all these claims have a common underpin-
ning in postulating a direct genetic basis for our most
fundamental traits. If we are programmed to be what we are,
then these traits are ineluctable. We may, at best, channel them,
but we cannot change them, either by will, education, or
culture.

---

[1]*Lorenz et al.*: Scientists and popular writers who have argued for biological determinism,
or the idea that biology and biological history are a kind of fate determining human
character and destiny. Some of the people and ideas referred to here are discussed at
greater length later in the essay.

If we accept the usual platitudes about "scientific method" 8
at face value, then the coordinated resurgence of biological
determinism must be attributed to new information that refutes
the earlier findings of twentieth-century science. Science, we
are told, progresses by accumulating new information and
using it to improve or replace old theories. But the new
biological determinism rests upon no recent fund of information
and can cite in its behalf not a single unambiguous fact. Its
renewed support must have some other basis, most likely social
or political in nature.

Science is always influenced by society, but it operates 9
under a strong constraint of fact as well. The Church eventually
made its peace with Galileo because, after all, the earth does go
around the sun. In studying the genetic components of such
complex human traits as intelligence and aggressiveness,
however, we are freed from the constraint of fact, for we know
practically nothing. In these questions, "science" follows (and
exposes) the social and political influences acting upon it.

What then, are the nonscientific reasons that have fostered 10
the resurgence of biological determinism? They range, I
believe, from pedestrian pursuits of high royalties for best
sellers to pernicious attempts to reintroduce racism as respectable science. Their common denominator must lie in our
current malaise. How satisfying it is to fob off the responsibility
for war and violence upon our presumably carnivorous
ancestors. How convenient to blame the poor and the hungry
for their own condition — lest we be forced to blame our
economic system or our government for an abject failure to
secure a decent life for all people. And how convenient an
argument for those who control government and, by the way,
provide the money that science requires for its very existence.

Deterministic arguments divide neatly into two groups 11
— those based on the supposed nature of our species in general
and those that invoke presumed differences among "racial
groups" of *Homo sapiens*. I discuss the first subject here and treat
the second in my next essay.

Summarized briefly, mainstream pop ethology contends 12 that two lineages of hominids inhabited Pleistocene Africa. One, a small, territorial carnivore, evolved into us; the other, a larger, presumably gentle herbivore, became extinct. Some carry the analogy of Cain and Abel to its full conclusion and accuse our ancestors of fratricide. The "predatory transition" to hunting established a pattern of innate violence and engendered our territorial urges: "With the coming of the hunting life to the emerging hominid came the dedication to territory" (Ardrey, *The Territorial Imperative*). We may be clothed, citified, and civilized, but we carry deep within us the genetic patterns of behavior that served our ancestor, the "killer ape." In *Africa Genesis* Ardrey champions Raymond Dart's contention that "the predatory transition and the weapons fixation explained man's bloody history, his eternal aggression, his irrational, self-destroying, inexorable pursuit of death for death's sake."

Tiger and Fox extend the theme of group hunting to 13 proclaim a biological basis for the differences between men and women that Western cultures have traditionally valued. Men did the hunting; women stayed home with the kids. Men are aggressive and combative, but they also form strong bonds among themselves that reflect the ancient need for cooperation in the killing of big game and now find expression in touch football and rotary clubs. Women are docile and devoted to their own children. They do not form intense bonds among themselves because their ancestors needed none to tend their homes and their men: sisterhood is an illusion. "We are wired for hunting. . . . We remain Upper Paleolithic hunters, fine-honed machines designed for the efficient pursuit of game" (Tiger and Fox, *The Imperial Animal*).

The story of pop ethology has been built on two lines of 14 supposed evidence, both highly disputable:

1. Analogies with the behavior of other animals (abundant 15 but imperfect data). No one doubts that many animals (including some, but not all, primates) display innate patterns of aggression and territorial behavior. Since we exhibit similar

behavior, can we not infer a similar cause? The fallacy of this assumption reflects a basic issue in evolutionary theory. Evolutionists divide the similarities between two species into *homologous* features shared by common descent and a common genetic constitution, and *analogous* traits evolved separately.

Comparisons between humans and other animals lead to   16 causal assertions about the genetics of our behavior only if they are based on homologous traits. But how can we know whether similarities are homologous or analogous? It is hard to differentiate even when we deal with concrete structures, such as muscles and bones. In fact, most classical arguments in the study of phylogeny involve the confusion of homology and analogy, for analogous structures can be strikingly similar (we call this phenomenon evolutionary convergence). How much harder it is to tell when similar features are only the outward motions of behavior! Baboons may be territorial; their males may be organized into a dominance hierarchy — but is our quest for Lebensraum[2] and the hierarchy of our armies an expression of the same genetic makeup or merely an analogous pattern that might be purely cultural in origin? And when Lorenz compares us with geese and fish, we stray even further into pure conjecture; baboons, at least, are second cousins.

2. Evidence from hominid fossils (scrappy but direct data).   17 Ardrey's claims for territoriality rest upon the assumption that our African ancestor *Australopithecus africanus*, was a carnivore. He derives his "evidence" from accumulations of bones and tools at the South African cave sites and the size and shape of teeth. The bone piles are no longer seriously considered; they are more likely the work of hyenas than of hominids.

Teeth are granted more prominence, but I believe that the   18 evidence is equally poor if not absolutely contradictory. The argument rests upon relative size of grinding teeth (premolars and molars). Herbivores need more surface area to grind their

---

[2]*Lebensraum:* "living space"; additional territory felt necessary by a nation for its economic well-being.

gritty and abundant food. *A. robustus,* the supposed gentle herbivore, possessed grinding teeth relatively larger than those of its carnivorous relative, our ancestor *A. africanus.*

But *A. robustus* was a larger creature than *A. africanus.* As 19 size increases, an animal must feed a body growing as the cube of length by chewing with tooth areas that increase only as the square of length if they maintain the same relative size (see essays of section 6). This will not do, and larger mammals must have differentially larger teeth than smaller relatives. I have tested this assertion by measuring tooth areas and body sizes for species in several groups of mammals (rodents, piglike herbivores, deer, and several groups of primates). Invariably, I find that larger animals have relatively larger teeth — not because they eat different foods, but simply because they are larger.

Moreover, the "small" teeth of *A. africanus* are not at all 20 diminutive. They are *absolutely larger* than ours (although we are three times as heavy), and they are about as big as those of gorillas weighing nearly ten times as much! The evidence of tooth size indicates to me that *A. africanus* was primarily herbivorous.

The issue of biological determinism is not an abstract 21 matter to be debated within academic cloisters. These ideas have important consequences, and they have already permeated our mass media. Ardrey's dubious theory is a prominent theme in Stanley Kubrick's film *2001.* The bone tool of our apelike ancestor first smashes a tapir's skull and then twirls about to transform into a space station of our next evolutionary stage — as the superman theme of Richard Strauss' *Zarathustra* yields to Johann's *Blue Danube.* Kubrick's next film, *Clockwork Orange,* continues the theme and explores the dilemma inspired by claims of innate human violence. (Shall we accept totalitarian controls for mass deprogramming or remain nasty and vicious within a democracy?) But the most immediate impact will be felt as male privilege girds its loins to battle a growing women's movement. As Kate Millett remarks in *Sexual Politics:*

"Patriarchy has a tenacious or powerful hold through its successful habit of passing itself off as nature."

[1977 – U.S.A.]

Questions

1. Clear thinking produces clear writing. Nowhere is this maxim better exemplified than in the work of Stephen Jay Gould. To see how splendidly coherent the essay at hand is, outline its progression of ideas. In doing so, note all transitional material from paragraph 2 on; indicate the topic sentence of each paragraph or paragraph cluster; and write a sentence or so summarizing the point of each paragraph or cluster of paragraphs. Also, note where the thesis is presented and what it is, and indicate what paragraphs are transitional in nature (the point of these paragraphs is transition). Finally, note any familiar structures you find in the essay – for example, order of climax or enumeration.

2. Gould's title does a good deal of work. How so? How, for instance, does his title allow Gould to delay his thesis statement?

3. Why does the thesis statement come where it comes?

4. The essay begins with a contrast that leads to an analogy in paragraph 2. What rhetorical function does this beginning have? How might it predispose the reader to accept Gould's argument against the new determinists? Is Gould's an effective way to begin? Why?

5. The last paragraph here is a reverse funnel. How so? What Gould says in the last two sentences could have been said in the second half of paragraph 10. Why did Gould save this material for last? Is the end of the essay effective in its appeal to authority? Why or why not?

Writing Assignments

1. Write a paragraph or more in imitation of "The Nonscience of Human Nature." Find a topic that lends itself to enumeration. Then begin with some striking contrast or analogy or both in sequence (as does Gould), enumerate your points according to some plan, and conclude with a quotation from someone of note that backs you up.

2. Much of Gould's essay entails the drawing of a clear distinction – specifically, between science and masquerade science. Write a paper yourself involving distinction. For instance, there are different

types of laughter, though we usually don't distinguish among them. To do so could make an excellent paper, as could a discussion of the different types of tears or smiles. In this paper you will be categorizing first and then enumerating as you draw your distinction(s). Be sure to provide transitions between all major blocks of material.

3. Write an essay like Gould's in general structure. Begin by summarizing in a few paragraphs a position opposed to your own on the given topic (which you must somehow specify); then, in a paragraph, state your thesis (which basically will be that the position you sum up in the beginning of your paper is in error); and then argue your case, bringing as much evidence to bear as is necessary. In your conclusion you might suggest various ramifications of your hypothetical opponent's position and indicate why, in light of these ramifications, that position not only is in error but is potentially downright harmful.

———✤ SEX, DRUGS, DISASTERS, ✤———
AND THE EXTINCTION OF DINOSAURS
Stephen Jay Gould

SCIENCE, IN ITS MOST FUNDAMENTAL DEFINITION, IS A FRUITFUL MODE   1
of inquiry, not a list of enticing conclusions. The conclusions are the consequence, not the essence.

My greatest unhappiness with most popular presentations   2
of science concerns their failure to separate fascinating claims from the methods that scientists use to establish the facts of nature. Journalists, and the public, thrive on controversial and stunning statements. But science is, basically, a way of knowing — in P. B. Medawar's apt words, "the art of the soluble." If the growing corps of popular science writers would focus on *how* scientists develop and defend those fascinating claims, they would make their greatest possible contribution to public understanding.

Consider three ideas, proposed in perfect seriousness to   3
explain that greatest of all titillating puzzles — the extinction of

dinosaurs. Since these three notions invoke the primally fascinating themes of our culture — sex, drugs, and violence — they surely reside in the category of fascinating claims. I want to show why two of them rank as silly speculation, while the other represents science at its grandest and most useful.

Science works with testable proposals. If, after much 4 compilation and scrutiny of data, new information continues to affirm a hypothesis, we may accept it provisionally and gain confidence as further evidence mounts. We can never be completely sure that a hypothesis is right, though we may be able to show with confidence that it is wrong. The best scientific hypotheses are also generous and expansive: They suggest extensions and implications that enlighten related, and even far distant, subjects. Simply consider how the idea of evolution has influenced virtually every intellectual field.

Useless speculation, on the other hand, is restrictive. It 5 generates no testable hypothesis, and offers no way to obtain potentially refuting evidence. Please note that I am not speaking of truth or falsity. The speculation may well be true; still, if it provides, in principle, no material for affirmation or rejection, we can make nothing of it. It must simply stand forever as an intriguing idea. Useless speculation turns in on itself and leads nowhere; good science, containing both seeds for its potential refutation and implications for more and different testable knowledge, reaches out. But, enough preaching. Let's move on to dinosaurs, and the three proposals for their extinction.

1. *Sex.* Testes function only in a narrow range of temperature (those of mammals hang externally in a scrotal sac because internal body temperatures are too high for their proper function). A worldwide rise in temperature at the close of the Cretaceous period caused the testes of dinosaurs to stop functioning and led to their extinction by sterilization of males.

2. *Drugs.* Angiosperms (flowering plants) first evolved toward the end of the dinosaurs' reign. Many of these plants contain

psychoactive agents, avoided by mammals today as a result of their bitter taste. Dinosaurs had neither means to taste the bitterness nor livers effective enough to detoxify the substances. They died of massive overdoses.

3. *Disasters*. A large comet or asteroid struck the earth some 65 million years ago, lofting a cloud of dust into the sky and blocking sunlight, thereby suppressing photosynthesis and so drastically lowering world temperatures that dinosaurs and hosts of other creatures became extinct.

Before analyzing these three tantalizing statements, we must establish a basic ground rule often violated in proposals for the dinosaurs' demise. *There is no separate problem of the extinction of dinosaurs*. Too often we divorce specific events from their wider contexts and systems of cause and effect. The fundamental fact of dinosaur extinction is its synchrony with the demise of so many other groups across a wide range of habitats, from terrestrial to marine.

The history of life has been punctuated by brief episodes of   6 mass extinction. A recent analysis by University of Chicago paleontologists Jack Sepkoski and Dave Raup, based on the best and most exhaustive tabulation of data ever assembled, shows clearly that five episodes of mass dying stand well above the "background" extinctions of normal times (when we consider all mass extinctions, large and small, they seem to fall in a regular 26-million-year cycle). The Cretaceous debacle, occurring 65 million years ago and separating the Mesozoic and Cenozoic eras of our geological time scale, ranks prominently among the five. Nearly all the marine plankton (single-celled floating creatures) died with geological suddenness; among marine invertebrates, nearly 15 percent of all families perished, including many previously dominant groups, especially the ammonites (relatives of squids in coiled shells). On land, the dinosaurs disappeared after more than 100 million years of unchallenged domination.

In this context, speculations limited to dinosaurs alone   7 ignore the larger phenomenon. We need a coordinated explanation for a system of events that includes the extinction of dinosaurs as one component. Thus it makes little sense, though it may fuel our desire to view mammals as inevitable inheritors of the earth, to guess that dinosaurs died because small mammals ate their eggs (a perennial favorite among untestable speculations). It seems most unlikely that some disaster peculiar to dinosaurs befell these massive beasts — and that the debacle happened to strike just when one of history's five great dyings had enveloped the earth for completely different reasons.

8   The testicular theory, an old favorite from the 1940s, had its root in an interesting and thoroughly respectable study of temperature tolerances in the American alligator, published in the staid *Bulletin of the American Museum of Natural History* in 1946 by three experts on living and fossil reptiles — E. H. Colbert, my own first teacher in paleontology; R. B. Cowles; and C. M. Bogert.

9   The first sentence of their summary reveals a purpose beyond alligators: "This report describes an attempt to infer the reactions of extinct reptiles, especially the dinosaurs, to high temperatures as based upon reactions observed in the modern alligator." They studied, by rectal thermometry, the body temperatures of alligators under changing conditions of heating and cooling. (Well, let's face it, you wouldn't want to try sticking a thermometer under a 'gator's tongue.) The predictions under test go way back to an old theory first stated by Galileo in the 1630s — the unequal scaling of surfaces and volumes. As an animal, or any object, grows (provided its shape doesn't change), surface areas must increase more slowly than volumes — since surfaces get larger as length squared, while volumes increase much more rapidly, as length cubed. Therefore, small animals have high ratios of surface to volume, while large animals cover themselves with relatively little surface.

10   Among cold-blooded animals lacking any physiological mechanism for keeping their temperatures constant, small creatures have a hell of a time keeping warm — because they lose so much heat through their relatively large surfaces. On

the other hand, large animals, with their relatively small surfaces, may lose heat so slowly that, once warm, they may maintain effectively constant temperatures against ordinary fluctuations of climate. (In fact, the resolution of the "hot-blooded dinosaur" controversy that burned so brightly a few years back may simply be that, while large dinosaurs possessed no physiological mechanism for constant temperature, and were not therefore warm-blooded in the technical sense, their large size and relatively small surface area kept them warm.)

Colbert, Cowles, and Bogert compared the warming rates 11 of small and large alligators. As predicted, the small fellows heated up (and cooled down) more quickly. When exposed to a warm sun, a tiny 50-gram (1.76-ounce) alligator heated up one degree Celsius every minute and a half, while a large alligator, 260 times bigger at 13,000 grams (28.7 pounds), took seven and a half minutes to gain a degree. Extrapolating up to an adult 10-ton dinosaur, they concluded that a one-degree rise in body temperature would take eighty-six hours. If large animals absorb heat so slowly (through their relatively small surfaces), they will also be unable to shed any excess heat gained when temperatures rise above a favorable level.

The authors then guessed that large dinosaurs lived at or 12 near their optimum temperatures; Cowles suggested that a rise in global temperatures just before the Cretaceous extinction caused the dinosaurs to heat up beyond their optimal tolerance — and, being so large, they couldn't shed the unwanted heat. (In a most unusual statement within a scientific paper, Colbert and Bogert then explicitly disavowed this speculative extension of their empirical work on alligators.) Cowles conceded that this excess heat probably wasn't enough to kill or even to enervate the great beasts, but since testes often function only within a narrow range of temperature, he proposed that this global rise might have sterilized all the males, causing extinction by natural contraception.

The overdose theory has recently been supported by UCLA 13 psychiatrist Ronald K. Siegel. Siegel has gathered, he claims, more than 2,000 records of animals who, when given access, administer various drugs to themselves — from a mere swig of alcohol to massive doses of the big H. Elephants will swill the equivalent of twenty beers at a time, but do not like alcohol in concentrations greater than 7 percent. In a silly bit of anthropocentric speculation, Siegel states that "elephants drink, perhaps, to forget . . . the anxiety produced by shrinking rangeland and the competition for food."

Since fertile imaginations can apply almost any hot idea to 14 the extinction of dinosaurs, Siegel found a way. Flowering plants did not evolve until late in the dinosaurs' reign. These plants also produced an array of aromatic, amino-acid-based alkaloids — the major group of psychoactive agents. Most mammals are "smart" enough to avoid these potential poisons. The alkaloids simply don't taste good (they are bitter); in any case, we mammals have livers happily supplied with the capacity to detoxify them. But, Siegel speculates, perhaps dinosaurs could neither taste the bitterness nor detoxify the substances once ingested. He recently told members of the American Psychological Association: "I'm not suggesting that all dinosaurs OD'd on plant drugs, but it certainly was a factor." He also argued that death by overdose may help explain why so many dinosaur fossils are found in contorted positions. (Do not go gentle into that good night.)[1]

Extraterrestrial catastrophes have long pedigrees in the 15 popular literature of extinction, but the subject exploded again in 1979, after a long lull, when the father-son, physicist-geologist team of Luis and Walter Alvarez proposed that an asteroid, some 10 km in diameter, struck the earth 65 million years ago (comets, rather than asteroids, have since gained favor. Good science is self-corrective).

The force of such a collision would be immense, greater by 16 far than the megatonnage of all the world's nuclear weapons. In trying to reconstruct a scenario that would explain the simultaneous dying of dinosaurs on land and so many creatures

---

[1]*Do not go gentle.* . . : The title and one of the two refrains of a poem by Dylan Thomas.

in the sea, the Alvarezes proposed that a gigantic dust cloud, generated by particles blown aloft in the impact, would so darken the earth that photosynthesis would cease and temperatures drop precipitously. (Rage, rage against the dying of the light.)[2] The single-celled photosynthetic oceanic plankton, with life cycles measured in weeks, would perish outright, but land plants might survive through the dormancy of their seeds (land plants were not much affected by the Cretaceous extinction, and any adequate theory must account for the curious pattern of differential survival). Dinosaurs would die by starvation and freezing; small, warm-blooded mammals, with more modest requirements for food and better regulation of body temperature, would squeak through. "Let the bastards freeze in the dark," as bumper stickers of our chauvinistic neighbors in sunbelt states proclaimed several years ago during the Northeast's winter oil crisis.

All three theories, testicular malfunction, psychoactive 17 overdosing, and asteroidal zapping, grab our attention mightily. As pure phenomenology, they rank about equally high on any hit parade of primal fascination. Yet one represents expansive science, the others restrictive and untestable speculation. The proper criterion lies in evidence and methodology; we must probe behind the superficial fascination of particular claims.

How could we possibly decide whether the hypothesis of 18 testicular frying is right or wrong? We would have to know things that the fossil record cannot provide. What temperatures were optimal for dinosaurs? Could they avoid the absorption of excess heat by staying in the shade, or in caves? At what temperatures did their testicles cease to function? Were late Cretaceous climates ever warm enough to drive the internal temperatures of dinosaurs close to this ceiling? Testicles simply don't fossilize, and how could we infer their temperature tolerances even if they did? In short, Cowles's hypothesis is

---

[2]*Rage, rage against.* . . *:* The second refrain of Thomas's "Do Not Go Gentle into That Good Night."

only an intriguing speculation leading nowhere. The most damning statement against it appeared right in the conclusion of Colbert, Cowles, and Bogert's paper, when they admitted: "It is difficult to advance any definite arguments against this hypothesis." My statement may seem paradoxical — isn't a hypothesis really good if you can't devise any arguments against it? Quite the contrary. It is simply untestable and unusable.

Siegel's overdosing has even less going for it. At least 19 Cowles extrapolated his conclusion from some good data on alligators. And he didn't completely violate the primary guideline of setting dinosaur extinction in the context of a general mass dying — for rise in temperature could be the root cause of a general catastrophe, zapping dinosaurs by testicular malfunction and different groups for other reasons. But Siegel's speculation cannot touch the extinction of ammonites or oceanic plankton (diatoms make their own food with good sweet sunlight; they don't OD on the chemicals of terrestrial plants). It is simply a gratuitous, attention-grabbing guess. It cannot be tested, for how can we know what dinosaurs tasted and what their livers could do? Livers don't fossilize any better than testicles.

The hypothesis doesn't even make any sense in its own 20 context. Angiosperms were in full flower ten million years before dinosaurs went the way of all flesh. Why did it take so long? As for the pains of a chemical death recorded in contortions of fossils, I regret to say (or rather I'm pleased to note for the dinosaurs' sake) that Siegel's knowledge of geology must be a bit deficient: Muscles contract after death and geological strata rise and fall with motions of the earth's crust after burial — more than enough reason to distort a fossil's pristine appearance.

The impact story, on the other hand, has a sound basis in 21 evidence. It can be tested, extended, refined and, if wrong, disproved. The Alvarezes did not just construct an arresting guess for public consumption. They proposed their hypothesis after laborious geochemical studies with Frank Asaro and Helen Michael had revealed a massive increase of iridium in rocks deposited right at the time of extinction. Iridium, a rare metal of the platinum group, is virtually absent from indigenous rocks of the earth's crust; most of our iridium arrives on extraterrestrial objects that strike the earth.

The Alvarez hypothesis bore immediate fruit. Based origi- 22 nally on evidence from two European localities, it led geochemists throughout the world to examine other sediments of the same age. They found abnormally high amounts of iridium everywhere — from continental rocks of the western United States to deep sea cores from the South Atlantic.

Cowles proposed his testicular hypothesis in the mid- 23 1940s. Where has it gone since then? Absolutely nowhere, because scientists can do nothing with it. The hypothesis must stand as a curious appendage to a solid study of alligators. Siegel's overdose scenario will also win a few press notices and fade into oblivion. The Alvarezes' asteroid falls into a different category altogether, and much of the popular commentary has missed this essential distinction by focusing on the impact and its attendant results, and forgetting what really matters to a scientist — the iridium. If you talk just about asteroids, dust, and darkness, you tell stories no better and no more entertaining than fried testicles or terminal trips. It is the iridium — the source of testable evidence — that counts and forges the crucial distinction between speculation and science.

The proof, to twist a phrase, lies in the doing. Cowles's 24 hypothesis has generated nothing in thirty-five years. Since its proposal in 1979, the Alvarez hypothesis has spawned hundreds of studies, a major conference, and attendant publications. Geologists are fired up. They are looking for iridium at all other extinction boundaries. Every week exposes a new wrinkle in the scientific press. Further evidence that the Cretaceous iridium represents extraterrestrial impact and not indigenous volcanism continues to accumulate. As I revise this essay in November 1984 (this paragraph will be out of date when [it] is published), new data include chemical "signatures" of other isotopes indicating unearthly provenance, glass spherules of a size and sort produced by impact and not by volcanic eruptions, and high-pressure varieties of silica formed (so far as we know) only under the tremendous shock of impact.

My point is simply this: Whatever the eventual outcome (I 25 suspect it will be positive), the Alvarez hypothesis is exciting, fruitful science because it generates tests, provides us with things to do, and expands outward. We are having fun, battling back and forth, moving toward a resolution, and extending the hypothesis beyond its original scope.

As just one example of the unexpected, distant cross- 26 fertilization that good science engenders, the Alvarez hypothesis made a major contribution to a theme that has riveted public attention in the past few months — so-called nuclear winter. In a speech delivered in April 1982, Luis Alvarez calculated the energy that a ten-kilometer asteroid would release on impact. He compared such an explosion with a full nuclear exchange and implied that all-out atomic war might unleash similar consequences.

This theme of impact leading to massive dust clouds and 27 falling temperatures formed an important input to the decision of Carl Sagan[3] and a group of colleagues to model the climatic consequences of nuclear holocaust. Full nuclear exchange would probably generate the same kind of dust cloud and darkening that may have wiped out the dinosaurs. Temperatures would drop precipitously and agriculture might become impossible. Avoidance of nuclear war is fundamentally an ethical and political imperative, but we must know the factual consequences to make firm judgments. I am heartened by a final link across disciplines and deep concerns — another criterion, by the way, of science at its best:[4] A recognition of the very phenomenon that made our evolution possible by exterminating the previously dominant dinosaurs and clearing a way for the evolution of large mammals, including us, might actually

---

[3]*Carl Sagan:* See "The Nuclear Winter," pages 459–67.

[4]This quirky connection so tickles my fancy that I break my own strict rule about eliminating redundancies from [my writing] . . . [author's note].

help to save us from joining those magnificent beasts in contorted poses among the strata of the earth.

[1984 — U.S.A.]

Questions

1. What is Gould's thesis and where is it stated? What allows him to state his thesis as he does? What kind of pace does the way the thesis is stated help establish?

2. What is the tone of the essay? How is this tone created? What is the effect of tone and pacing together on voice, on the way the essay reads, and on the reader's reception? (Incidentally, what audience is targeted here?)

3. What three means of support does Gould use? Identify an instance of each. Identify as well an instance of each of the three structural elements used here.

4. Why are the three theories arranged as they are: "Sex," then "Drugs," then "Disasters"? How does the arrangement in paragraph 5 carry over to the rest of the essay and help make it coherent?

5. What is the function of paragraph 17? Why does Gould remind us of his thesis here?

6. What crucial ideas are introduced toward the beginning and the end of paragraph 5? Why are they crucial? How do they tie in with what is said later in the essay? How do they relate to the thesis and its demonstration?

Writing Assignments

1. This essay is remarkably coherent. To see as much, write a paragraph stating Gould's thesis and describing the steps of his demonstration. Or, if you like, do this in outline form.

2. According to Gould, science is a "mode of inquiry." Some other modes of inquiry are philosophy, criticism, historical analysis, and psychoanalysis. Pick one of these or take a mode of inquiry of your own choosing and write an essay on what the goals of the mode in question are and how it goes about reaching these goals (its methodology). Your task is to *define* the mode clearly and, if possible, with verve.

3. Choose a subject (an intellectual discipline like English, perhaps, or a sport, or even a hobby) that you feel quite serious about, though

it is something that brings you great pleasure, and write an essay about it — what it is, what it entails, how it works, or whatever. Now the trick: communicate your pleasure not by mere statement but by your pace and tone. Study Gould in this regard and see how he makes a potentially somber and even dull subject (science, or the definition thereof) come alive and seem full of joy.

✛ IN A JUMBLED DRAWER ✛

Stephen Jay Gould

Old, bad arguments never die (they don't fade away either).[1]

As MY SON GROWS, I HAVE MONITORED THE CHANGING FASHIONS IN kiddie culture for words expressing deep admiration — what I called "cool" in my day, and my father designated "swell." The half-life seems to be about six months, as "excellent" (with curious lingering emphasis on the first syllable) gave way to "bad" (extended, like a sheep bleat, long enough to turn into its opposite), to "wicked," to "rad" (short for radical). The latest incumbent — "awesome" — possesses more staying power, and has been reigning for at least two years. My only objection, from the fuddy-duddy's corner, lies in kiddie criteria for discernment. Ethan's buddies require such a tiny extension beyond the ordinary to proclaim something "awesome" — just a little bit bigger, brighter, and especially, louder will do. This or that is proclaimed awesome every second sentence — and we have lost a wonderful English word.

Now let me tell you about awesome — the real thing, when adults still held possession of the concept. I collected fossils all my youthful life, or at least on those rare occasions of departure from the asphalt of New York City. I had amassed, by the end of college, five cartonfuls, all ordered and labeled — and I was

---

[1]*Epigraph:* An altered version of General Douglas MacArthur's "Old soldiers never die, they just fade away."

pretty proud of both quantity and quality. Then I got my present job as curator of fossil invertebrates at Harvard's Museum of Comparative Zoology. I came to Cambridge with my five cartons and discovered that my new stewardship extended to 15,000 drawers of fossils, including some of the world's finest and oldest specimens, brought from Europe by Louis Agassiz more than a century ago. I put the cartons in a back corner of my office twenty years ago this month. I have never opened them. Me with my five cartons facing those 15,000 drawers — that is awe.

But when awe subsides, ecstasy creeps in. For I had 15,000   3 drawers to open, each harboring a potential discovery or insight. Raise to the nth power any simile you ever heard for "as happy as" — a boy in a candy store, a pig in . . . well, you know what. I spent two weeks pulling out every last drawer, and I found a cornucopia of disparate objects that have fueled my aesthetic and intellectual pleasure ever since.

The fossils were sublime, but I found as much fascination in   4 the odd paraphernalia of culture that, for various reasons, ends up in museum drawers. Late eighteenth century apothecary boxes, thread cases from the mills of Lawrence, Victorian cigar boxes of gaudy Cuban design — all the better to house fossils. Tickets to Lowell Institute lecture series by Gray, Agassiz, and Lyell, invitations to a ball honoring Napoleon III, merchants' calling cards from Victorian Cincinnati — all the better (on their blank obverses) to label fossils. Pages from the Sears catalog for 1903, snippets of nineteenth-century newspapers — all the better to wrap fossils. The most interesting news item, a headline from a Cincinnati paper for July 11, 1881, read, "Garfield's Grit" and announced that the president, though severely wounded in the recent assassination attempt, "is now on the sunny side of life again," and would almost surely recover — the flip side to a happy Harry Truman holding that 1948 *Chicago Tribune* headline announcing Dewey's victory.

For my most interesting discovery, I opened a drawer late   5 one night and found only a jumble of specimens inside. Someone had obviously overturned the drawer and dumped the contents. But the thick layer of dust identified the disordered pile as a very old jumble. Inside, I found the following note:

> This incident was the result of the carelessness of the Janitor Eli Grant who managed to overturn about half a dozen drawers of specimens by undertaking to move certain trays which he was not authorized to touch. The accident happened during my absence but I judge that it arose from an excess of zeal rather than from any recklessness. I have deemed it best to leave the specimens exactly as I found them awaiting an opportunity to have them arranged by Mr. Hartt.

I developed an immediate dislike for this pusillanimous 6
assistant — fingering the janitor, distancing himself even further from responsibility by assuring the boss that he hadn't been there at the time, then feeling a bit guilty for placing Mr. Grant's job in jeopardy and praising him for zeal through the back door. I then looked at the date and signature — Cambridge, April 26, 1869, N. S. Shaler.

David lamented over Saul: "How are the mighty fallen." 7
But one might look the other way in ontogeny[2] and observe, "How meek are the mighty when young and subservient." Nathaniel Southgate Shaler became one of the greatest and most popular teachers in the history of Harvard University. He was a giant among late nineteenth century American naturalists. But in 1869, Shaler was just a junior professor without tenure, and his superior was the most powerful and imperious biologist in America — none other than Louis Agassiz himself. Obviously, Shaler had written that note in mortal fear of Agassiz's celebrated wrath. Equally obviously, Agassiz had never found out — for Shaler became professor of paleontology later that year, while a century of undisturbed dust still lies atop the jumbled specimens.

N. S. Shaler reaped the rewards of his unflinching loyalty 8
to Agassiz. The path of devotion was not smooth. Agassiz was

---

[2]*Ontogeny:* The word refers specifically to the course of development of an organism. This meaning is extended here to apply to the general course of things in human affairs.

a transplanted European with an Old World sense of professorial authority. He told students what they would study, awarded degrees by oral examination and direct assessment of competence, and insisted upon personal approval for any publication based on material at his museum. He never failed in encouragement, warmth, and enthusiasm — and he was a beloved teacher. But he never relinquished one iota of authority. These attitudes might only have yielded a tightly run ship in times of intellectual quiescence, but Agassiz was captain on the most troubled waters of biological history. Agassiz opened his museum in 1859, the same year that Darwin published *The Origin of Species*. He gathered around himself the most promising, and therefore most independently minded, group of young zoologists in America, Shaler included. Inevitably, evolution became the chief subject of discussion. With equal inevitability, students flocked eagerly to this beacon of intellectual excitement and became enthusiastic converts. But Agassiz had built both a career and a coherent philosophy upon the creationist premise that species are ideas in God's mind, made incarnate by his hand in a world of material objects. Sooner shall a camel pass through the eye of a needle than the old lion and young wolf cubs shall dwell in harmony amidst such disagreement.

And so, inevitably once more, Agassiz's students revolted 9 — against both his overweening authority and his old-fashioned ideas. In 1863, they formed what they called, in half-jest, a committee for the protection of American students from foreign-born professors. Agassiz, however, held all the cards in a hierarchical world, and he chucked the rebels out, much to the benefit of American science, as they formed departments and centers at other great universities. Agassiz then staffed his museum with older and uncontroversial professionals, bringing peace and mediocrity once again to Harvard.

Of his truly excellent students, only Shaler remained loyal. 10 And Shaler reaped his earthly reward. He received his bachelor of science in geology, *summa cum laude,* in July 1862. After a spell of service in the Civil War, fighting for the Union from his native Kentucky, Shaler returned to Harvard in 1864. Agassiz, describing Shaler as "the one of my American students whom I love the best," appointed him assistant in paleontology at the Museum of Comparative Zoology. In 1869, soon after he penned the guilty note that would lie unread for exactly 100 years (I found it in 1969), Shaler received his lifetime appointment as professor of geology, succeeding Agassiz (who continued to lecture in zoology until he died in 1873). There Shaler remained until his death in 1906, writing numerous treatises on everything from the geology of Martha's Vineyard to the nature of morality and immortality. He also became, by far, Harvard's most popular professor. His classes overflowed, and his students poured forth praise for his enthusiasm, his articulateness, and the comfort, optimism, and basic conventionality of his words, spoken to the elite at the height of America's gilded age. On the day of his funeral, flags in city buildings and student fraternities flew at half-mast, and many shops closed. Thirty years later, at the Harvard tercentenary of 1936, Shaler was named twelfth among the fifty people most important to the history of Harvard. To this day, his bust rests, with only fourteen others, including Franklin's, Longfellow's, and of course, Agassiz's in the faculty room of Bullfinch's University Hall.

Shaler's loyalty to Agassiz, and to comfortable convention 11 in general, held as strongly in ideology as in practice. Shaler wrote these words of condolence to Agassiz's widow, Elizabeth Cary, founder of Radcliffe College, when Louis died in 1873: "He never was a greater teacher than now. He never was more truly at his chosen work. . . . While he lived I always felt myself a boy beside him." (See David N. Livingstone, *Nathaniel Southgate Shaler and the Culture of American Science,* University of Alabama Press, 1987, for the source of this quotation and an excellent account of Shaler's intellectual life.)

I don't think that Shaler, in his eulogy to Elizabeth, either 12 erred or exaggerated in his chosen metaphor of subservience to Agassiz's vision. While Shaler remained subordinate, he followed Agassiz's intellectual lead, often with the epigone's style of exaggerating his master's voice. Shaler's very first publication provides an interesting example ("Lateral Symmetry in Brachiopoda," 1861, *Proceedings of the Boston Society of Natural History*, vol. 8, pp. 274–79). Here Shaler supports both Agassiz's creationism and his zoological classification. Brachiopods, once a dominant group in the fossil record of marine invertebrates, are now a minor component of oceanic faunas. With their bivalved shells, they look superficially like clams, but their soft anatomy is entirely distinct, and they are now classified as a separate phylum. But Georges Cuvier, Agassiz's great mentor, had placed brachiopods with clams and snails in his phylum Mollusca — and Agassiz, whose loyalty to Cuvier matched any devotion of Shaler's, wished both to uphold Cuvier's classification and to use his concept of Mollusca as an argument against Darwin.

Shaler obliged in his first public performance. He affirmed 13 Cuvier and Agassiz's inclusion of brachiopods in the Mollusca by demonstrating a bilateral symmetry of soft parts similar enough to the symmetry of such "standard" forms as clams and squids to justify a conclusion of common plan in design. But he then took a swipe at Darwin's reason for including separate groups in a single phylum by arguing that no evolutionary transition could possibly link adult brachiopod and clam. (Shaler was quite right about this, but not for his stated reason. You cannot transform a brachiopod into a clam, but then nature never did because brachiopods aren't mollusks and the two groups are entirely separate — contrary to Shaler's first conclusion.) The planes of bilateral symmetry are different for the two groups, Shaler argued correctly, and no transition could occur because any smooth intermediate would have to pass through a nonbilateral stage entirely inconsistent with molluscan design. Shaler wrote:

> Such a transition would require a series of forms, each of which must present a negation of that very principle of bilateral symmetry which we have found of so much

importance. And must we not, therefore, conclude that the series which united these two orders is a series of thought, which is itself connected, though manifested by two structures which have no genetic relations.

Now if you're holding a nineteenth-century scorecard, and 14 therefore know the players, only one man could be lurking behind this statement. Only one real Platonist of this ilk operated in America, only one leading biologist still willing to designate species as thoughts of a Creator, and taxonomic relationships as the interconnections within His mind — Louis Agassiz. Shaler, with the true zeal of the acolyte, even out-Agassized Agassiz in referring to the central character of bilateral symmetry as "the fundamental thought of the type" and then designating animal taxonomy as "a study of personified thought." Even Agassiz was not so explicit in specifying the attributes of his God.

When the winds of inevitability blew strongly enough, and 15 when Shaler's own position became secure in the late 1860s, he finally embraced evolution, but ever so gently, and in a manner that would cause minimal offense to Agassiz and to any Brahmin member of the old Boston order. After Agassiz's death, Shaler continued to espouse a version of evolution with maximal loyalty to Agassiz's larger vision of natural harmony, and marked aversion to all Darwinian ideas of chanciness, contingency, unpredictability, opportunism, and quirkiness. He led the American Neo-Lamarckian[3] school — a powerful group of anti-Darwinian evolutionists who held out for order, purpose, and progress in nature through the principle of inheritance for features acquired by the effort of organisms. Progress in mentality might be predictably ordained if some organisms strove for such improvement during their lives and

---

[3]*Lamarckian:* Refers to the theory of how physical changes occur in species held by Chevalier de Lamarck (1744–1829). Lamarck believed that adaptive responses of organisms to their environment cause such changes and that these can be inherited. This view is opposed to Darwinian evolution.

passed their achievements to their offspring. No waiting for the Darwinian chanciness of favorable environments and fortuitous variations.

Shaler's loyalty to Agassiz persisted right through this 16 fundamental change from creationism to evolution. For example, though he could scarcely deny the common origin of all humans in the light of evolutionary theory, Shaler still advocated Agassiz's distinctive view (representing the "polygenist" school of pre-Darwinian anthropology) that human races are separate species, properly and necessarily kept apart both on public conveyances and in bedrooms. Shaler argued for an evolutionary separation of races so long ago that accumulated differences had become, for all practical purposes, permanent.

Practical purposes, in the genteel racism of patrician 17 Boston, abetted by a slaveholding Kentucky ancestry, meant "using biology as an accomplice" (in Condorcet's words) to advocate a "nativist" social policy (where "natives" are not the truly indigenous American Indians, but the earliest immigrants from Protestant western and northern Europe). Shaler reserved his lowest opinion for black Americans, but invested his social energies in the Immigration Restriction League and its attempts to prevent dilution of American whites (read WASPs) by the great Catholic and Jewish unwashed of southern and eastern Europe.

One can hardly fathom the psychological and sociological 18 complexities of racism, but the forced intellectual rationales are always intriguing and more accessible. Shaler's own defense merged his two chief interests in geography and zoology. He argued that we live in a world of sensible and optimal pattern, devoid of quirk or caprice. People differ because they have adapted by Lamarckian means to their local environments; our capacities are a map of our dwelling places — and we really oughtn't be elsewhere (hence the biological rectitude of restricting immigration). The languid tropics cannot inspire genius, and you cannot contemplate the Pythagorean absolute while trying to keep body and soul together in an igloo. Hence the tough, but tractable, lands of northern Europe yielded the best of humanity. Shaler wrote:

> Our continents and seas cannot be considered as physical accidents in which, and on which, organic beings have found an everperilous resting place, but as great engines operating in a determined way to secure the advance of life.

Shaler then applied this cardinal belief in overarching order 19 (against the Darwinian specter of unpredictable contingency) to the largest question of all — the meaning of human life as a proof of God's existence and benevolence. In so doing, he completed the evolutionary version of Agassiz's dearest principle — the infusion of sensible, progressive, divine order into the cosmos, with the elevation of "man" (and I think they really meant only half of us) to the pinnacle of God's intent. Shaler could not deny his generation's proof of evolution, and had departed from his master in this conviction, but he had been faithful in constructing a vision of evolution so mild that it left all cosmic comfort intact, thereby affirming the deepest principle of Agassiz's natural theology.

Shaler rooted his argument in a simple claim about 20 probability. (Shaler often repeated this line of reasoning. My quotations come from his latest and most widely read book — *The Individual: A Study of Life and Death,* New York: D. Appleton and Company, 1901.) Human life is the end result of an evolutionary sequence stretching back into the immensity of time and including thousands of steps, each necessary as a link in the rising sequence:

> The possibility of man's development has rested on the successive institution of species in linked order. . . . If, in this succession of tens of thousands of species, living through a series of millions of years, any of these links of the human chain had been broken; if any one of the species had failed to give birth to its successor, the chance of the development of man would have been lost.

Human evolution, Shaler holds, would have been "unat- 21 tainable without the guidance of a controlling power intent on the end." If this sequence alone could have engendered us, and if the world be ruled by Darwinian caprice and contingency, our appearance would have been "essentially impossible." For surely, one link would have failed, one step in ten thousand aborted, thus ending forever the ascent toward consciousness. Only divine watchfulness and intent could have produced the human mind (not a direct finger in the pot, perhaps, but at least an intelligent construction of nature's laws with a desired end in view):

> The facts connected with the organic approach to man afford what is perhaps the strongest argument, or at least the most condensed, in favor of the opinion that there is an intelligent principle in control of the universe.

Nathaniel Southgate Shaler was one of the most influential 22 American intellectuals of his time. Today, he is unknown. I doubt that one in a thousand readers of this essay (geologists and Harvardians excepted) has ever heard of him. His biography rates thirteen lines in the *Encyclopedia Britannica*, more than half devoted to a listing of book titles. Why has he faded, and what does his eclipse teach us about the power and permanence of human thought? We can, perhaps, best approach this question by considering one of Shaler's best friends, a man also influenced by Agassiz, but in a different way — William James. In their day, Shaler and James were peas in a pod of Harvard fame. Now Shaler is a memory for a few professionals, and James is one of America's great gifts to the history of human thought. Why the difference?

William James also came under Agassiz's spell as an 23 undergraduate. Agassiz decided to take six undergraduates along on his famous Thayer Expedition to Brazil (1866). They would help the trained scientists in collecting specimens and, in return, hear lectures from Agassiz on all aspects of natural history. William James, among the lucky six, certainly appreciated the value of Agassiz's formidable intellect and pedagogical skill. He wrote to his father: "I am getting a pretty valuable training from the Prof. who pitches into me right and left and makes me [own] up to a great many of my imperfections. This morning he said I was 'totally uneducated.' "

But James maintained his critical perspective, while Shaler 24 became an acolyte and then an epigone. James wrote:

> I have profited a great deal by hearing Agassiz talk, not so much by what he says, for never did a man utter a greater amount of humbug, but by learning the way of feeling of such a vast practical engine as he is. . . . I delight to be with him. I only saw his defects at first, but now his wonderful qualities throw them quite in the background. . . . I never saw a man work so hard.

Was James "smarter" than Shaler? Does their differential 25 in renown today reflect some basic disparity in amount of intellectual power? This is a senseless question for many reasons. Intelligence is too complex and multifaceted a thing to reduce to any single dimension. What can we say? Both men had certain brilliance, but they used their skills differently. Shaler was content to follow Agassiz throughout his career, happy to employ his formidable intellect in constructing an elaborate rationale for contemporary preferences, never challenging the conservative truths of his class and culture. James questioned Agassiz from day one. James probed and wondered, reached and struggled every day of his life. Shaler built pretty buildings to house comfortable furniture. Intelligence or temperament; brains or guts? I don't know. But I do know that oblivion was one man's reward, enduring study and respect the other's.

As a dramatic illustration of the difference, consider 26 James's critique of Shaler's "probability argument" for God's benevolence from the fact of human evolution. James read Shaler's *The Individual,* and wrote a very warm, though critical, letter to his dear friend. He praised "the gravity and dignity and peacefulness" of Shaler's thoughts, but singled out the probability argument for special rebuttal.

James points out that the actual result of evolution is the 27 only sample we have. We cannot compute a "probability" or even speak in these terms. Any result in a sample of one would appear equally miraculous when you consider alternative possibilities. But something had to happen. We may only talk of odds if we could return to stage 1, list a million possible outcomes, and then lay cold cash upon one possibility alone:

> We never know what ends may have been kept from realization, for the dead tell no tales. The surviving witness would in any case, and whatever he were, draw the conclusion that the universe was planned to make him and the like of him succeed, for it actually did so. But your argument that it is millions to one that it didn't do so by chance doesn't apply. It would apply if the witness had preexisted in an independent form and framed his scheme, and then the world had realized it. Such a coincidence would prove the world to have a kindred mind to his. But there has been no such coincidence. The world has come but once, the witness is there after the fact and simply approves. . . . Where only one fact is in question, there is no relation of "probability" at all. [James's letter is reprinted, in full, in *The Autobiography of Nathaniel Southgate Shaler*, Boston: Houghton Mifflin, 1909.]

Old, bad arguments never die (they don't fade away either), particularly if they match our hopes. Shaler's false probability argument is still a favorite among those who yearn to find a cosmic rationale for human importance. And James's retort is as brilliant and as valid now as when he first presented it to Shaler. We could save ourselves from a lot of nonsense today if every devotee of the anthropic principle (strong version), every fan of Teilhard's noosphere, simply read and understood James's letter to Shaler.

James then continues with the ultimate Darwinian riposte to Shaler's doctrine of cosmic hope and importance. Human intellect is a thing of beauty — truly awesome. But its evolution need not record any more than a Darwinian concatenation of improbabilities:

> I think, therefore, that the excellence we have reached and now approve may be due to no general design, but merely to a succession of the short designs we actually know of, taking advantage of opportunity, and adding themselves together from point to point.

Which brings us back to Mr. Eli Grant. (I do hope, 30 compassionate reader, that you have been worrying about this poor man's fate while I temporized in higher philosophical realms.) The young Shaler tried to cover his ass by exposing Grant's. Obviously, he succeeded, but what happened to the poor janitor, left to take the rap?

This story has a happy ending, based on two sources of 31 evidence: one inferential; the other direct. Since Agassiz never found out, never saw the note, and since Mr. Hartt, like Godot, never arrived, we may assume that Grant's zealous accident eluded Agassiz's watchful eye. More directly, I am delighted to report that I found (in yet another drawer) a record book for the Department of Invertebrate Paleontology in 1887. Mr. Eli Grant was still listed as janitor.

Was Mr. Grant meant to survive because he did? Does his 32 tenure on the job indicate the workings of a benevolent and controlling mind? (Why not, for I can envisage 100 other scenarios, all plausible but less happy.) Or was Mr. Grant too small to fall under God's direct providence? But if so, by what hubris do we consider ourselves any bigger in a universe of such vastness? Such unprofitable, such unanswerable questions. Let us simply rejoice in the happy ending of a small tale, and give the last word to William James, still trying to set his friend Shaler straight:

> What if we did come where we are by chance, or by mere fact, with no one general design? What is gained, is gained, all the same. As to what may have been lost, who knows of it, in any case?

[1988 – U.S.A.]

Questions

1. Compare and contrast "In a Jumbled Drawer" and "Sex, Drugs, Disasters" (pages 269–79). How do they differ as to pacing and thesis presentation? How do they differ as to the ways each unfolds and the sense of centeredness or the lack thereof? Yet they are both by the same author. How are they alike with regard to diction, tone, and voice? In what way are the two endings similar? How are the two essays alike in intellection?

2. Given the disparateness of its materials, the present essay is remarkably coherent with respect to the movement from paragraph to paragraph. To see as much, do a quick topic outline of the first third of the essay (say, paragraphs 1–12). Just note the topic sentence of each paragraph and observe the strong linkage of each paragraph to the next.

3. We don't get to Gould's main point (his thesis) until late in the essay. What keeps us reading? Consider the essay's forward momentum; what we might feel about its author from having read other essays by him; the effect of the little points he makes all along the way; the fact that the essay is geared to a general audience (how so?); Gould's way with phrases and the diction, tone, and voice here; the essay's epigraph; and, finally, Gould's sheer brilliance.

4. How does Gould make use of comparison and contrast in presenting his thesis? What is that thesis?

5. With what means of support does the essay end? How does the end sum up Gould's thesis? I find Gould's ending to be strong and satisfying, for it has the feel of an ending and clinches the essay's main point to boot. Do you agree or dissent? Why?

6. Why might both the end of "In a Jumbled Drawer" and its beginning be called "crafty"? How has Gould engineered his getting in and getting out of this essay?

Writing Assignments

1. Write a paper addressing question number 1 above. Follow the progression of the question as given, beginning with contrast and ending with comparison.

2. Write an essay addressing Gould's rhetorical mastery. In a series of middle paragraphs designed to demonstrate this mastery, discuss Gould's use of the character sketch; comparison and contrast; diction, tone, and voice; exemplification; and analogy, as well as his clear sense of audience. Conclude with a statement about the relation of rhetoric and verbal communication generally.

3. Read or reread Joan Didion's "Miami: The Cuban Presence" (pages 195–207). Then write an essay comparing and contrasting Didion's method of "objective" reporting with Gould's method of juxtaposing quotations and thereby having James answer Shaler. To what extent does Gould, like Didion, let the facts speak for themselves? To what extent does he, unlike Didion, intrude himself? What is the difference in effect between intrusion and nonintrusion? What other similarities and differences do you see? A good way to organize this essay would be to begin with comparison and end with contrast.

4. If you have read all three essays by Stephen Jay Gould in this book,
   write a review of the three essays together. Point out Gould's
   characteristics as a writer — of subject matter and approach as well
   as of diction/tone/voice, style, and so forth — and evaluate the
   effectiveness of his rhetoric and the worth of his work from the three
   essays you've read.

✦ THE BLACK AND WHITE TRUTH ✦
ABOUT BASKETBALL
Jeff Greenfield

THE DOMINANCE OF BLACK ATHLETES OVER PROFESSIONAL BASKETBALL   1
is beyond dispute. Two-thirds of the players are black, and the
number would be greater were it not for the continuing practice
of picking white bench warmers for the sake of balance. Over
the last two decades, no more than three white players have
been among the ten starting players on the National Basketball
Association's All-Star team, and in the last quarter century,
only two white players — Dave Cowens and Larry Bird of the
Boston Celtics — have ever been chosen as the NBA's Most
Valuable Player.

And at a time when a baseball executive could lose his job   2
for asserting that blacks lacked "the necessities" to become pro
sports executives and when the National Football League still
has not hired a single black head coach, the NBA stands as a
pro sports league that hired its first black head coach in 1968
(Bill Russell) and its first black general manager in the early
1970s (Wayne Embry of the Milwaukee Bucks). What
discrimination remains — lack of equal opportunity for speaking engagements and product endorsements — has more to do
with society than with basketball.

This dominance reflects a natural inheritance: Basketball is   3
a pastime of the urban poor. The current generation of black
athletes are heirs to a tradition more than half a century old. In
a neighborhood without the money for bats, gloves, hockey

sticks and ice skates, or shoulder pads, basketball is an eminently accessible sport. "Once it was the game of the Irish and Italian Catholics in Rockaway and the Jews on Fordham Road in the Bronx," writes David Wolf in his brilliant book, *Foul!* "It was recreation, status, and a way out." But now the ethnic names have been changed: Instead of the Red Holzmans, Red Auerbachs, and the McGuire brothers, there are Julius Ervings and Michael Jordans, Ralph Sampsons and Kareem Abdul-Jabbars. And professional basketball is a sport with national television exposure and million-dollar salaries.

But the mark on basketball of today's players can be   4 measured by more than money or visibility. It is a question of style. For there is a clear difference between "black" and "white" styles of play that is as clear as the difference between 155th Street at Eighth Avenue and Crystal City, Missouri. Most simply (remembering we are talking about culture, not chromosomes), "black" basketball is the use of superb athletic skill to adapt to the limits of space imposed by the game. "White" ball is the pulverization of that space by sheer intensity.[1]

It takes a conscious effort to realize how constricted the   5 space is on a basketball court. Place a regulation court (ninety-four by fifty feet) on a football field, and it will reach from the back of the end zone to the twenty-one-yard line; its width will cover less than a third of the field. On a baseball diamond, a basketball court will reach from home plate to first base. Compared to its principal indoor rival, ice hockey, basketball covers about one-fourth the playing area. Moreover, during the normal flow of the game, most of the action takes place on the third of the court nearest the basket. It is in this dollhouse space that ten men, each of them half a foot taller than the average man, come together to battle each other.

---

[1]This distinction has nothing to do with the question of whether whites can play as "well" as blacks. In 1987, the Detroit Pistons' Isaiah Thomas quipped that the Celtics' Larry Bird was "a pretty good player," but would be much less celebrated and wealthy if he were black. As Thomas later said, Bird is one of the greatest pro players in history. Nor is this distinction about "smart," although the Los Angeles Lakers' Magic Johnson is right in saying that too many journalists ascribe brilliant strategy by black players to be solely due to "innate" ability. [Author's note.]

There is, thus, no room; basketball is a struggle for the 6
edge: the half step with which to cut around the defender for a
lay-up, the half second of freedom with which to release a jump
shot, the instant a head turns allowing a pass to a teammate
breaking for the basket. It is an arena for the subtlest of skills:
the head fake, the shoulder fake, the shift of body weight to the
right and the sudden cut to the left. Deception is crucial to
success; and to young men who have learned early and
painfully that life is a battle for survival, basketball is one of the
few pursuits in which the weapon of deception is a legitimate
tactic rather than the source of trouble.

If there is, then, the need to compete in a crowd, to battle 7
for the edge, then the surest strategy is to develop the
unexpected: to develop a shot that is simply and fundamentally
different from the usual methods of putting the ball in the
basket. Drive to the hoop, but go under it and come up the
other side; hold the ball at waist level and shoot from there
instead of bringing the ball up to eye level; leap into the air, but
fall away from the basket instead of toward it. All these tactics,
which a fan can see embodied in the astonishing play of the
Chicago Bulls' Michael Jordan, take maximum advantage of
the crowding on the court. They also stamp uniqueness on
young men who may feel it nowhere else.

"For many young men in the slums," David Wolf writes, 8
"the school yard is the only place they can feel true pride in
what they do, where they can move free of inhibitions and
where they can, by being spectacular, rise for the moment
against the drabness and anonymity of their lives. Thus, when
a player develops extraordinary 'school yard' moves and shots
. . . [they] become his measure as a man."

So the moves that begin as tactics for scoring soon become 9
calling cards. You don't just lay the ball in for an uncontested
basket; you take the ball in both hands, leap as high as you can,
and slam the ball through the hoop. When you jump in the air,
fake a shot, bring the ball back to your body, and throw up a
shot, all without coming back down, you have proven your
worth in uncontestable fashion.

This liquid grace is an integral part of "black" ball, almost 10
exclusively the province of the playground player. Some white
stars like Bob Cousy, Billy Cunningham, and Doug Collins had
it, and the Celtics' Kevin McHale has it now: the body control,
the moves to the basket, the free-ranging mobility. Most of
them also possessed the surface ease that is integral to the
"black" style; an incorporation of the ethic of mean streets — to
"make it" is not just to have wealth but to have it without strain.
Whatever the muscles and organs are doing, the face of the
"black" star almost never shows it. Magic Johnson of the
Lakers can bring the ball down court with two men on him,
whip a pass through an invisible opening, cut to the basket,
take a return pass, and hit the shot all with no more emotion
than a quick smile. So stoic was San Antonio Spurs' great
George Gervin that he earned the nickname "Ice Man."
(Interestingly, a black coach like Boston's K. C. Jones exhibits
far less emotion on the bench than a white counterpart like
Dick Motta or Jack Ramsey.)

If there is a single trait that characterizes "black" ball it is 11
leaping ability. Bob Cousy, ex-Celtic great and former pro
coach, says that "when coaches get together, one is sure to say,
'I've got the one black kid in the country who can't jump.'
When coaches see a white boy who can jump or who moves
with extraordinary quickness, they say, 'He should have been
born black, he's that good.' "

Don Nelson, now a top executive with the Golden State 12
Warriors, recalls that back in 1970, Dave Cowens, then a
relatively unknown graduate of Florida State, prepared for his
rookie pro season by playing in the Rucker League, an outdoor
competition in Harlem playgrounds that pits pros against
college kids and playground stars. So ferocious was Cowens'
leaping ability, Nelson says, that "when the summer was over,
everyone wanted to know who the white son of a bitch was who
could jump so high." That's another way to overcome a crowd
around the basket — just go over it.

Speed, mobility, quickness, acceleration, "the moves" — all 13
of these are catch-phrases that surround the "black" playground

athlete, the style of play. So does the most racially tinged of attributes, "rhythm." Yet rhythm is what the black stars themselves talk about: feeling the flow of the game, finding the tempo of the dribble, the step, the shot. It is an instinctive quality (although it stems from hundreds of hours of practice), and it is one that has led to difficulty between system-oriented coaches and free-form players.

"Cats from the street have their own rhythm when they 14 play," said college dropout Bill Spivey, onetime New York high school star. "It's not a matter of somebody setting you up and you shooting. You *feel* the shot. When a coach holds you back, you lose the feel and it isn't fun anymore."

When legendary Brooklyn playground star Connie Hawk- 15 ins was winding up his NBA career under Laker coach Bill Sharman, he chafed under the methodical style of play. "He's systematic to the point where it begins to be a little too much. It's such an action-reaction type of game that when you have to do everything the same way, I think you lose something."

There is another kind of basketball that has grown up in 16 America. It is not played on asphalt playgrounds with a crowd of kids competing for the court; it is played on macadam driveways by one boy with a ball and a backboard nailed over the garage; it is played in gyms in the frigid winter of the rural Midwest and on Southern dirt courts. It is a mechanical, precise development of skills (when Don Nelson was an Iowa farm boy, his incentive to make his shots was that an errant rebound would land in the middle of chicken droppings). It is a game without frills, without flow, but with effectiveness. It is "white" basketball: jagged, sweaty, stumbling, intense. Where a "black" player overcomes an obstacle with finesse and body control, a "white" player reacts by outrunning or overpowering the obstacle.

By this definition, the Boston Celtics are a classically 17 "white" team. They rarely suit up a player with dazzling moves; indeed such a player would probably make Red Auerbach swallow his cigar. Instead, the Celtics wear you down with execution, with constant running, with the same play run again and again and again. The rebound by Robert Parrish triggers the fast break, as everyone races downcourt; the ball goes to Larry Bird, who pulls up and takes the shot or who drives and then finds Danny Ainge or Kevin McHale free for an easy basket.

Perhaps the most definitively "white" position is that of the [18] quick forward, one without great moves to the basket, without highly developed shots, without the height and mobility for rebounding effectiveness. So what does he do?

He runs. He runs from the opening jump to the final [19] buzzer. He runs up and down the court, from base line to base line, back and forth under the basket, looking for the opening, the pass, the chance to take a quick step, the high percentage shot. To watch San Antonio's Mark Olberding or Detroit's Bill Lambeer, players without speed or obvious moves, is to wonder what they are doing in the NBA — until you see them swing free and throw up a shot that, without demanding any apparent skill, somehow goes in the basket more frequently than the shots of many of their more skilled teammates. And to have watched the New York Knicks' (now U.S. Senator) Bill Bradley, or the Celtics' John Havlicek, is to have watched "white" ball at its best.

Havlicek or Lambeer, or the Lakers' Kurt Rambis, stand in [20] dramatic contrast to Michael Jordan or to the Philadelphia 76ers' legend, Julius Erving. Erving had the capacity to make legends come true, leaping from the foul line and slam-dunking the ball on his way down; going up for a lay-up, pulling the ball to his body, and driving under and up the other side of the rim, defying gravity and probability with impossible moves and jumps. Michael Jordan of the Chicago Bulls has been seen by thousands spinning a full 360 degrees in midair before slamming the ball through the hoop.

When John Havlicek played, by contrast, he was the living [21] embodiment of his small-town Ohio background. He would bring the ball downcourt, weaving left, then right, looking for a path. He would swing the ball to a teammate, cut behind the pick, take the pass, and release the shot in a flicker of time. It looked plain, unvarnished. But it was a blend of skills that not more than half a dozen other players in the league possessed.

To former pro Jim McMillian, a black who played quick 22
forward with "white" attributes, "it's a matter of environment.
Julius Erving grew up in a different environment from
Havlicek. John came from a very small town in Ohio. There
everything was done the easy way, the shortest distance
between two points. It's nothing fancy; very few times will he
go one-on-one. He hits the lay-up, hits the jump shot, makes the
free throw, and after the game you look up and say, 'How did
he hurt us that much?' "

"White" ball, then, is the basketball of patience, method 23
and sometimes brute strength. "Black" ball is the basketball of
electric self-expression. One player has all the time in the world
to perfect his skills, the other a need to prove himself. These are
slippery categories, because a poor boy who is black can play
"white" and a white boy of middle-class parents can play
"black." Bill Cartwright of the New York Knicks and Steve
Alford of the Dallas Mavericks are athletes who seem to defy
these categories.

And what makes basketball the most intriguing of sports is 24
how these styles do not necessarily clash; how the punishing
intensity of "white" players and the dazzling moves of the
"blacks" can fit together, a fusion of cultures that seems more
and more difficult in the world beyond the out-of-bounds line.

[1988 — U.S.A.]

Questions

1. Where is the essay's thesis stated and what is it?
2. What is the function of paragraphs 1–3? What is the function of the
   last sentence of paragraph 3 and the first sentence of paragraph 4?
3. What does Greenfield do in paragraphs 5–7? What audience does
   his means of support here suggest?
4. What does Greenfield do in paragraphs 8–15? What in 16–22?
   What means of support is used in both 8–15 and 16–22? What is
   the structural mode of 16–22? How is it treated?
5. Greenfield makes some rather sweeping generalizations here
   — always a potentially dangerous thing to do. How does he guard

himself against the criticism that he is stereotyping? How does his use of authority help guard him in this regard?

6. What is the function of paragraph 23? What kind of an ending does paragraph 24 provide? Is it effective? How so?

Writing Assignments

1. In a paragraph or more, consider how (by what means) Greenfield tries to check the potential criticism that he is merely stereotyping. Does he succeed or fail in your view? How so?

2. Write four paragraphs modeled on paragraphs 1–4 of Greenfield's essay. Your first three paragraphs should serve as an introduction leading to your fourth paragraph, in which you will state your thesis fully. Obviously, your thesis will have to be of some complexity to need a whole paragraph for statement.

3. Write an essay contrasting two styles of doing something of people in the same profession — two singers, two teachers, two athletes in the same sport, two priests or ministers, and so on. Along the way, try to account for the differences, as Greenfield accounts for why the styles of black and white basketball differ. What you say in this regard could be your thesis.

✙ IF YOU HAD TO KILL ✙ YOUR OWN HOG
Dick Gregory

MY MOMMA COULD NEVER UNDERSTAND HOW WHITE FOLKS COULD   1
twist the words of the Bible around to justify racial segregation. Yet she could read the Ten Commandments, which clearly say, "Thou shalt not kill," and still justify eating meat. Momma couldn't read the newspaper very well, but she sure could interpret the Word of God. "God meant you shouldn't kill people," she used to say. But I insisted, "Momma, He didn't say that. He said, 'Thou shalt not kill.' If you leave that statement alone, a whole lot of things would be safe from killing. But if you are going to twist the words about killing to mean what you

want them to mean, then let white folks do the same thing with justifying racial segregation."

"You can't live without eating meat," Momma would   2
persist. "You'd starve." I couldn't buy that either. You get milk from a cow without killing it. You do not have to kill an animal to get what you need from it. You get wool from the sheep without killing it. Two of the strongest animals in the jungle are vegetarians — the elephant and the gorilla. The first two years are the most important years of a man's life, and during that period he is not involved with eating meat. If you suddenly become very ill, there is a good chance you will be taken off a meat diet. So it is a myth that killing is necessary for survival. The day I decide that I must have a piece of steak to nourish my body, I will also give the cow the same right to nourish herself on human beings.

There is so little basic difference between animals and   3
humans. The process of reproduction is the same for chickens, cattle, and humans. If suddenly the air stopped circulating on the earth, or the sun collided with the earth, animals and humans would die alike. A nuclear holocaust will wipe out all life. Life in the created order is basically the same and should be respected as such. It seems to me the Bible says it is wrong to kill — period.

If we can justify *any* kind of killing in the name of religion,   4
the door is opened for all kinds of other justifications. The fact of killing animals is not as frightening as our human tendency to justify it — to kill and not even be aware that we are taking life. It is sobering to realize that when you misuse one of the least of Nature's creatures, like the chicken, you are sowing the seed for misusing the highest of Nature's creatures, man.

Animals and humans suffer and die alike. If you had to kill   5
your own hog before you ate it, most likely you would not be able to do it. To hear the hog scream, to see the blood spill, to see the baby being taken away from its momma, and to see the look of death in the animal's eye would turn your stomach. So you get the man at the packing house to do the killing for you.

In like manner, if the wealthy aristocrats who are perpetrating conditions in the ghetto actually heard the screams of ghetto suffering, or saw the slow death of hungry little kids, or witnessed the strangulation of manhood and dignity, they could not continue the killing. But the wealthy are protected from such horror. They have people to do the killing for them. The wealthy profit from the daily murders of ghetto life but they do not see them. Those who immerse themselves in the daily life of the ghetto see the suffering — the social workers, the police, the local merchants, and the bill collectors. But the people on top never really see.

By the time you see a piece of meat in the butcher shop   6 window, all the blood and suffering have been washed away. When you order a steak in the restaurant, the misery has been forgotten and you see the finished product. You see a steak with butter and parsley on it. It looks appetizing and appealing and you are pleased enough to eat it. You never even consider the suffering which produced your meal or the other animals killed that day in the slaughterhouse. In the same way, all the wealthy aristocrats ever see of the black community is the finished product, the window dressing, the steak on the platter — Ralph Bunche and Thurgood Marshall. The United Nations or the Supreme Court bench is the restaurant and the ghetto street corner is the slaughterhouse.

Life under ghetto conditions cuts short life expectancy. The   7 Negro's life expectancy is shorter than the white man's. The oppressor benefits from continued oppression financially; he makes more money so that he can eat a little better. I see no difference between a man killing a chicken and a man killing a human being, by overwork and forcing ghetto conditions upon him, both so that he can eat a little better. If you can justify killing to eat meat, you can justify the conditions of the ghetto. I cannot justify either one.

Every time the white folks made my momma mad, she   8 would grab the Bible and find something bitter in it. She would come home from the rich white folks' house, after they had just called her "nigger," or patted her on the rump or caught her stealing some steaks, open her Bible and read aloud, "It is easier for a camel to pass through the eye of a needle than for a rich man to get into Heaven." When you get involved with distorting the words of the Bible, you don't have to be bitter. The same tongue can be used to bless and curse men.

[1968 — U.S.A.]

Questions

1. Who do you think did Gregory envision his audience to be?
2. Gregory attempts to make two different points by presenting them as analogous. What are they? Are they really analogous? Why or why not?
3. Which way is the analogy here supposed to work? What is its primary term? Might the analogy be detrimental to one or both of Gregory's points?
4. Several assertions are made in this essay about "wealthy aristocrats" and "the oppressor." Are these assertions just? Are they backed up or demonstrated somehow? Do they further or impede the essay's argument? How so?

Writing Assignments

1. Write a short critique of the essay judging how well its statements are supported and the efficacy of its structural analogy (that is, eating meat is like the treatment of blacks). Whatever your judgment, conclude with a consideration of what can be learned from this essay about writing exposition.
2. Write a short paper addressing question 4 above. You might introduce your paper with a statement about the potential trickiness of analogies and then go on to exemplify by your analysis of the specific analogy in question. Answer the questions given and end, perhaps, with a statement about the need to be cautious when using analogy.

✦ How to Write "Official" ✦
Gerald Grow

1. Start with a simple statement: We quit. Why? Nobody knew how to program the computer.
2. Put it in the passive voice and dilute the responsibility: *It was decided to* quit.
3. Expand with terminology that does not add meaning: It was decided to *terminate.*
4. Build in noun strings: It was decided to terminate *project processes.*[1]
5. Add a qualifier of uncertain relation to the original statement: *On account of the status of the computer,* it was decided to terminate project processes.
6. Add noun strings and terminology to the qualifier: On account of the status of the *computer program assessment planning development effort,* it was decided to terminate project processes.
7. Separate related words: On account of the status of the computer program assessment planning development effort, it was decided to terminate *until a later date* project processes.
8. Equivocate: On account of the *uncertain* status of the computer program assessment planning development effort, it was *proposed and tentatively accepted* to terminate until a later date project processes.
9. Obfuscate: Due to uncertainties in the status of the computer program assessment planning development effort, *proposals were carefully considered and tentatively adopted to suspend temporarily* until a later date project processes.

---

[1]Also, build in strings of prepositional phrases, like the string in number 5: "*On* account *of* the status *of* the computer."

10. Cover your tracks; make yourself look good: Due to 10
    unavoidable uncertainties in the status of the computer
    program assessment planning development effort, *a number
    of contingency* proposals were carefully considered and one
    was tentatively adopted to suspend on a temporary basis
    until a later date those project processes *deemed unessential to
    the expeditious fulfillment of contract requirements.*

[1982 — U.S.A.]

Questions

1. Why is the title of this essay essential?
2. What is the ostensible purpose of the essay? How do we come to
   know that this is not its real purpose?
3. What is the essay's tone? How is this tone established? What, then,
   is the essay's real purpose and what is its theme?

Writing Assignments

1. Take a simple sentence and carry it through the steps that Grow
   enumerates. Then write a paragraph suggesting why you will never
   let such a sentence as the one you wind up with into your writing.
2. In two or more paragraphs, contrast the styles (the diction and
   syntax) of the sentences and phrases in bold type here with those in
   italics. What tone does this contrast help establish? Why are the
   instructions far better than the examples as to style?

❖ WHAT DOES IT MEAN ❖
TO BE CREATIVE?
S. I. Hayakawa

WHAT DISTINGUISHES THE CREATIVE PERSON? BY CREATIVE PERSON I   1
don't mean only the great painter or poet or musician. I also
want to include the creative housewife, teacher, warehouse-
man, sales manager — anyone who is able to break through
habitual routines and invent new solutions to old problems,
solutions that strike people with their appropriateness as well as
originality, so that they say, "Why didn't I think of that?"

A creative person, first, is not limited in his thinking to   2
"what everyone knows." "Everyone knows" that trees are
green. The creative artist is able to see that in certain lights
some trees look blue or purple or yellow. The creative person
looks at the world with his or her own eyes, not with the eyes
of others. The creative individual also knows his or her own
feelings better than the average person. Most people don't
know the answer to the question, "How are you? How do you
feel?" The reason they don't know is that they are so busy
feeling what they are supposed to feel, thinking what they are
supposed to think, that they never get down to examining their
own deepest feelings.

"How did you like the play?" "Oh, it was a fine play. It was   3
well reviewed in *The New Yorker*."

With authority figures like drama critics and book review-   4
ers and teachers and professors telling us what to think and
how to feel, many of us are busy playing roles, fulfilling other
people's expectations. As Republicans, we think what other
Republicans think. As Catholics, we think what other Catholics
think. And so on. Not many of us ask ourselves, "How do I
feel? What do I think?" — and wait for answers.

Another characteristic of the creative person is that he is   5
able to entertain and play with ideas that the average person
may regard as silly, mistaken, or downright dangerous. All new

ideas sound foolish at first, because they are new. (In the early days of the railroad, it was argued that speeds of twenty-five mph or over were impractical because people's brains would burst.) A person who is afraid of being laughed at or disapproved of for having "foolish" or "unsound" ideas will have the satisfaction of having everyone agree with him, but he will never be creative, because creativity means being willing to take a chance — to go out on a limb.

The person who would be creative must be able to endure loneliness — even ridicule. If he has a great and original idea that others are not yet ready to accept, there will be long periods of loneliness. There will be times when his friends and relatives think he is crazy, and he'll begin to wonder if they are right. A genuinely creative person, believing in his creation, is able to endure this loneliness — for years if necessary.   6

Another trait of the creative person is idle curiosity. Such a person asks questions, reads books, conducts investigations into matters apparently unrelated to job or profession — just for the fun of knowing. It is from these apparently unrelated sources that brilliant ideas often emerge to enrich one's own field of work.   7

Finally, the creative person plays hunches. "Pure intellect," says Dr. Hans Selye, the great medical researcher at the University of Montreal, "is largely a quality of the middle-class mind. The lowliest hooligan and the greatest creator in the fields of science are activated mainly by imponderable instincts and emotions, especially faith. Curiously, even scientific research, the most intellectual creative effort of which man is capable, is no exception in this respect."   8

Alfred Korzybski also understood well the role of undefinable emotions in the creative life. He wrote, "Creative scientists know very well from observation of themselves that all creative work starts as a feeling, inclination, suspicion, intuition, hunch, or some other nonverbal affective state, which only at a later date, after a sort of nursing, takes the shape of verbal expression worked out later in a rationalized, coherent . . . theory."   9

Creativity is the act of bringing something new into the 10
world, whether a symphony, a novel, an improved layout for a
supermarket, a new and unexpected casserole dish. It is based
first on communication with oneself, then testing that communication with experience and the realities one has to contend
with. The result is the highest, most exciting kind of learning.

[1979 – U.S.A.]

Questions

1. In a sentence, summarize Hayakawa's understanding of the meaning
   of "creative." What examples does he use in defining the concept?
2. We're told as much about noncreative people here as we are about
   creative people. Why? Why are the three short sentences of
   paragraph 3 separated into a paragraph?
3. What is the main structural type here? What transitions suggest this
   kind of a structure and keep it in mind?
4. Where does Hayakawa appeal to authority? Why these authorities
   in particular?
5. Why is "creative person" defined before "creativity"? Why is the
   definition of "creativity" saved till the end? What kind of an ending
   does the essay have?

Writing Suggestions

1. Using Hayakawa's definition of "creative," write a paragraph or
   more telling why you believe someone you know to be creative even
   though this person is not in an occupation usually thought of as
   creative — a housewife, perhaps, or a salesman, a plumber, a
   teacher.
2. Write an essay in definition, using "What Does It Mean to Be
   Creative" as a model. Enumerate your points, perhaps make use of
   some comparison and/or contrast, and provide plenty of examples.

———✦ TEACHING AS MOUNTAINEERING ✦———
Nancy K. Hill

JUST RECENTLY A COMMITTEE MEETING AT THE UNIVERSITY OF 1
Colorado was interrupted by the spectacle of a young man
scaling the wall of the library just outside the window.
Discussion of new interdisciplinary courses halted as we
silently hoped he had discipline enough to return safely to the
earth. Hope was all we could offer from our vantage point in
Ketchum Hall, the impulse to rush out and catch him being
checked by the realization of futility.

The incident reinforced my sense that mountaineering 2
serves as an apt analogy for the art of teaching. The excitement,
the risk, the need for rigorous discipline all correspond, though
the image I have in mind is not that of the solitary adventurer
rappelling off a wall, but that of a Swiss guide leading an
expedition.

I remember a mountaineer named Fritz who once led a 3
group up the Jungfrau at the same time a party was climbing
the north face of the Eiger. My own mountaineering skill was
slender, and my enthusiasm would have faltered had I not felt
Fritz was capable of hauling not only me but all the rest of us
off that mountain. Strong, self-assured, calm, he radiated that
solid authority that encouraged me to tie on to his rope. But I
soon realized that my presence on his line constituted a risk for
Fritz. Had I been so foolhardy as to try to retrieve my glove
which went tumbling off a precipice, or had I slipped into one
of those inexplicably opening crevasses, I might well have
pulled the noble Fritz down with me. It was a sobering
realization. I, the novice, and he, the expert, were connected by
the same lifeline in an experience of mutual interdependence.
To give me that top of the world exaltation he, too, was taking
a risk.

The analogy to teaching seems to me apt, and not just for 4
professors who happen to live in Colorado, for the analogy

implies an active acceptance of responsibility for one's own fate, whereas most other analogies to teaching suggest passivity. What is needed to restore teachers' confidence that the profession is significant is a new analogy, a new metaphor (I shy away from the PR word, "image") that conveys more of the essence of teaching than the worn-out analogies we have known. Most previous analogies are seriously inadequate, for while they may describe a part of the teaching activity, they also suggest patterns that are not fully applicable to teaching. It is not a simple matter, for those faulty analogies create misunderstandings about the professor's role, not only in the lay public, but in the professoriate itself. These wrong analogies have contributed to growing demoralization within the profession, and have confused the difficult issue of proper evaluation.

The most common analogies to the teacher are the   5
preacher, the shepherd, the curator, the actor, the researcher, and, most insidiously, the salesman. None captures the special relationship between teacher and students, a relationship better described by Socrates as a coming together of friends. Rather than emphasizing the mutuality of the endeavor, each of these common analogies turns on a separation between the professional and his clients. Each leads to a certain kind of evaluation.

The preacher exhorts, cajoles, pleads with a congregation   6
often so benighted as to exist in a state of somnolence. He measures his success by the number of souls so stirred as either to commit themselves to his cause, or vehemently to reject it. Somewhat like the preacher is the shepherd who gathers and watches over a flock clearly inferior to himself. The analogy may be apt for the Lord and his subangelic followers, but it will not do for teacher and students, or, especially, for Socrates and his friends. The Shepherd is likely to be evaluated by the gulf separating his wisdom from that of his flock.

If the poor country curate has often furnished an analogy to   7
the bleating professor, so has the curator of a museum. Lips pursed so as to distill a purer essence of hauteur, the curator as connoisseur points out the rarities of classical cultures to the uninitiated who can scarcely be expected to appreciate these

finer things. Since they cannot understand him anyway, the curator has no compunction about sprinkling his presentation with Latin and Greek and with English so esoteric as to sound foreign. Chances are high that the professor as connoisseur will succeed in convincing most of the class that the subject is really the province of a secret society with its own arcane practices and language, best left behind its own inaccessible walls. Indeed, colleagues of the connoisseur measure his success by the paucity of devotees allowed in to the society through this winnowing process.

The teacher as actor also plays to a passive audience, but he 8 measures success by larger numbers. A certain aura of the magician clings to him as he lures spectators into witnessing his academic sleight-of-hand without their ever really getting in on the trick. A certain tinge of the stand-up comedian colors the performance as the actor plays to the audience to register laughs big enough to drown out the lecturer droning on next door.

A bastardized version of the actor is that figure now 9 thought so apt an analogy in our consumer-conscious society: the salesman. His predecessors include the snake-oil man and the door-to-door purveyor of anything from brushes to Britannicas. He or she takes the product to the people, wherever they are, and tailors the pitch to their pockets. While all of these analogies create a certain level of despair in the professoriate either struggling to pattern themselves in a particular mode or hopelessly realizing they can never achieve it, the salesman analogy has the most deleterious effects. No longer adhering even to a prepared script, the salesman shamelessly alters his or her presentation so it will draw the largest number of contented consumers.

The researcher as teacher differs from the previous 10 analogies, and that very distinction is often thought to make him or her a good teacher. Taciturn, solitary, he disdains the performing arts and is content merely to mutter out an assortment of scattered facts to the young only dimly perceived beyond his clouded trifocals. His measure of success is his students' capacity to regurgitate factual data.

None of these analogies comes close enough to the essential 11 magic and majesty of a real learning experience. None even dimly anticipates that self-eradicating feature that is built in to the teaching process, for those who have truly mastered what their teacher has presented no longer need him or her. None accepts as a necessary ingredient in the learning process, activity, the sense of an intellectual excitement so compelling that one's whole being is caught up in it. None acknowledges the peril, and the joy, of encountering those mental deeps Hopkins described.

> . . . the mind, mind has mountains; cliffs of fall
> Frightful, sheer, no-man-fathomed. Hold them cheap
> May who ne'er hung there.

Mountaineering furnishes the needed analogy. The Swiss 12 mountain guide, like the true teacher, has a quiet authority about his very person. He or she engenders trust and confidence so that one is willing to join the endeavor. The mountaineer accepts his leadership role, yet recognizes that the success of the journey (measured by the scaling of the heights) depends upon close cooperation and active participation by each member of the group. He has crossed the terrain before and is familiar with the landmarks, but each trip is new, and generates its own anxiety and excitement. Essential skills must be mastered if the trip is to be successful; lacking them, disaster looms as an ominous possibility. The very precariousness of the situation necessitates keen focus and rapt attention; slackness, misjudgment, or laziness can bring doom.

The teacher as mountaineer learns, as E. M. Forster urged, 13 to connect. The guide rope links mountaineers together so that they may assist each other in the ascent. The effective teacher does something similar by using the oral and written contributions of the students as instructional materials. The teacher also makes other connections, locating the text in its historical setting, forging inter- and intradisciplinary links where plausible, joining the material of the course with the lives of the students, where possible, and with the wider national life beyond the classroom where pertinent.

Teaching as mountaineering does not encourage the yellowed lecture note syndrome. Indeed, the analogy does not really encourage lecturing at all. If the student as mountaineer is to be challenged, the student must come to each class session ready and prepared to assist in scaling the next peak, ready to test his or her own abilities against those of the master teacher. Only by arduous and sustained effort does the student approach the mastery of the teacher, and only then is the student ready to assume the role of guide — well-trained in the art of mountaineering, able to take controlled risks, ready to lead others to a mountain-top experience. Not a huckster, not a performer, not a pleader, but a confident, exuberant guide on expeditions of shared responsibility. 14

To encourage and further such mountain-top experiences the society must recognize teaching for the sublime art it is — not merely an offshoot of research, not merely a performance before a passive audience, but a guided expedition into the most exciting and least understood terrain on earth — the mind itself. 15

[1980 — U.S.A.]

Questions

1. Do a quick outline of this essay, noting the topics of paragraphs 1, 2, 3, 4, 5, 6–11, 12–14, and 15. Now account for the ordering of topics here.
2. What is the function of paragraph 3? What is the function of paragraph 12?
3. Hill spends a good deal of time on faulty analogies. Why?
4. Can't we just call a spade a spade? Why should we bother with analogies at all?
5. This essay closes with a metaphor. What is it? What purpose does it serve? How is it related to the analogy of the teacher as mountaineer?

Writing Assignments

1. Analogy can inform, but it can also distract. With this in mind, write two or more paragraphs comparing and contrasting Hill's use of analogy with Dick Gregory's in "If You Had to Kill Your Own

Hog" (pages 301–304). Which essay is more successful as to analogy? Why?

2. Many people remember "that one great teacher who. . . ." If you have had such a teacher, write a paper on what you remember about and how you were influenced by him or her. Conclude with a consideration of what your experience with this teacher reveals about great teachers and teaching generally.

3. Write a short essay in which you define something by way of an extended analogy. Your mode of procedure will be analogy; your structural mode will be enumeration. If you find a good analogy to begin with, your paper should all but write itself.

4. Write an essay in answer to the question, "Why do we need analogies?" By way of preparation, you might read "Concepts We Live By," by George Lakoff and Mark Johnson (pages 358–60).

✤ FAMILIES ✤

Jane Howard

EACH OF US IS BORN INTO ONE FAMILY NOT OF OUR CHOOSING. IF   1
we're going to go around devising new ones, we might as well have the luxury of picking their members ourselves. Clever picking might result in new families whose benefits would surpass or at least equal those of the old. The new ones by definition cannot spawn us — as soon as they do that, they stop being new — but there is plenty they can do. I have seen them work wonders. As a member in reasonable standing of six or seven tribes in addition to the one I was born to, I have been trying to figure which earmarks are common to both kinds of families.

(1) Good families have a chief, or a heroine, or a founder   2
— someone around whom others cluster, whose achievements as the Yiddish word has it, let them *kvell*, and whose example spurs them on to like feats. Some blood dynasties produce such figures regularly; others languish for as many as five generations between demigods, wondering with each new pregnancy whether this, at last, might be the messianic baby who will redeem us. Look, is there not something gubernatorial about

her footstep, or musical about the way he bangs with his spoon on his cup? All clans, of all kinds, need such a figure now and then. Sometimes clans based on water rather than blood harbor several such personages at one time. The Bloomsbury Group in London six decades ago was not much hampered by its lack of a temporal history.

(2) Good families have a switchboard operator — someone 2 like my mother who cannot help but keep track of what all the others are up to, who plays Houston Mission Control to everyone else's Apollo. This role, like the foregoing one, is assumed rather than assigned. Someone always volunteers for it. That person often also has the instincts of an archivist, and feels driven to keep scrapbooks and photograph albums up to date, so that the clan can see proof of its own continuity.

(3) Good families are much to all their members, but 4 everything to none. Good families are fortresses with many windows and doors to the outer world. The blood clans I feel most drawn to were founded by parents who are nearly as devoted to whatever it is they do outside as they are to each other and their children. Their curiosity and passion are contagious. Everybody, where they live, is busy. Paint is spattered on eyeglasses. Mud lurks under fingernails. Person-to-person calls come in the middle of the night from Tokyo and Brussels. Catchers' mitts, ballet slippers, overdue library books and other signs of extrafamilial concerns are everywhere.

(4) Good families are hospitable. Knowing that hosts need 5 guests as much as guests need hosts, they are generous with honorary memberships for friends, whom they urge to come early and often and to stay late. Such clans exude a vivid sense of surrounding rings of relatives, neighbors, teachers, students and godparents, any of whom at any time might break or slide into the inner circle. Inside that circle a wholesome, tacit emotional feudalism develops: you give me protection, I'll give you fealty. Such treaties begin with, but soon go far beyond, the jolly exchange of pie at Thanksgiving for cake on birthdays. It means you can ask me to supervise your children for the fortnight you will be in the hospital, and that however

inconvenient this might be for me, I shall manage to. It means
I can phone you on what for me is a dreary, wretched Sunday
afternoon and for you is the eve of a deadline, knowing you will
tell me to come right over, if only to watch you type. It means
we need not dissemble. ("To yield to seeming," as Buber wrote,
"is man's essential cowardice, to resist it is his essential courage
. . . one must at times pay dearly for life lived from the being,
but it is never too dear.")

(5) Good families deal squarely with direness. Pity the 6
tribe that doesn't have, and cherish, at least one flamboyant
eccentric. Pity too the one that supposes it can avoid for long
the woes to which all flesh is heir. Lunacy, bankruptcy, suicide
and other unthinkable fates sooner or later afflict the noblest of
clans with an undertow of gloom. Family life is a set of givens,
someone once told me, and it takes courage to see certain givens
as blessings rather than as curses. Contradictions and inconsis-
tencies are givens, too. So is the war against what the Oregon
patriarch Kenneth Babbs calls malarkey. "There's always
malarkey lurking, bubbles in the cesspool, fetid bubbles that
pop and smell. But I don't put up with malarkey, between my
stepkids and my natural ones or anywhere else in the family."

(6) Good families prize their rituals. Nothing welds a 7
family more than these. Rituals are vital especially for clans
without histories, because they evoke a past, imply a future,
and hint at continuity. No line in the Seder service at Passover
reassures more than the last: "Next year in Jerusalem!" A clan
becomes more of a clan each time it gathers to observe a fixed
ritual (Christmas, birthdays, Thanksgiving, and so on), grieve
at a funeral (anyone may come to most funerals; those who do
declare their tribalness), and devises a new rite of its own.
Equinox breakfasts and all-white dinners can be at least as
welding as Memorial Day parades. Several of us in the old *Life*
magazine years used to meet for lunch every Pearl Harbor Day,
preferably to eat some politically neutral fare like smorgasbord,
to "forgive" our only ancestrally Japanese colleague Irene
Kubota Neves. For that and other reasons we became, and
remain, a sort of family.

"Rituals," a California friend of mine said, "aren't just   8
externals and holidays. They are the performances of our lives.
They are a kind of shorthand. They can't be decreed. My
mother used to try to decree them. She'd make such a goddamn
fuss over what we talked about at dinner, aiming at Topics of
Common Interest, topics that celebrated our cohesion as a
family. These performances were always hollow, because the
phenomenology of the moment got sacrificed for the *idea* of the
moment. Real rituals are discovered in retrospect. They emerge
around constitutive moments, moments that only happen once,
around whose memory meanings cluster. You don't choose
those moments. They choose themselves." A lucky clan
includes a born mythologizer, like my blood sister, who has the
gift of apprehending such a moment when she sees it, and who
cannot help but invent new rituals everywhere she goes.

(7) Good families are affectionate. This of course is a   9
matter of style. I know clans whose members greet each other
with gingerly handshakes or, in what pass for kisses, with
hurried brushes of side jawbones, as if the object were to touch
not the lips but the ears. I don't see how such people manage.
"The tribe that does not hug," as someone who has been part of
many *ad hoc* families recently wrote to me, "is no tribe at all.
More and more I realize that everybody, regardless of age,
needs to be hugged and comforted in a brotherly or sisterly way
now and then. Preferably now."

(8) Good families have a sense of place, which these days   10
is not achieved easily. As Susanne Langer wrote in 1957, "Most
people have no home that is a symbol of their childhood, not
even a definite memory of one place to serve that purpose . . .
all the old symbols are gone." Once I asked a roomful of supper
guests who, if anyone, felt any strong pull to any certain spot on
the face of the earth. Everyone was silent, except for a visitor
from Bavaria. The rest of us seemed to know all too well what
Walker Percy means in *The Moviegoer* when he tells of the
"genie-soul of the place which every place has or else is not a
place [and which] wherever you go, you must meet and master

or else be met and mastered." All that meeting and mastering saps plenty of strength. It also underscores our need for tribal bases of the sort which soaring real estate taxes and splintering families have made all but obsolete.

So what are we to do, those of us whose habit and pleasure 11 and doom is our tendency, as a Georgia lady put it, to "fly off at every other whipstitch?" Think in terms of movable feasts, for a start. Live here, wherever here may be, as if we were going to belong here for the rest of our lives. Learn to hallow whatever ground we happen to stand on or land on. Like medieval knights who took their tapestries along on Crusades, like modern Afghanis with their yurts, we must pack such totems and icons as we can to make short-term quarters feel like home. Pillows, small rugs, watercolors can dispel much of the chilling anonymity of a sublet apartment or motel room. When we can, we should live in rooms with stoves or fireplaces or anyway candlelight. The ancient saying still is true: Extinguished hearth, extinguished family. Round tables help, too, and as a friend of mine once put it, so do "too many comfortable chairs, with surfaces to put feet on, arranged so as to encourage a maximum of eye contact." Such rooms inspire good talk, of which good clans can never have enough.

(9) Good families, not just the blood kind, find some way 12 to connect with posterity. "To forge a link in the humble chain of being, encircling heirs to ancestors," as Michael Novak has written, "is to walk within a circle of magic as primitive as humans knew in caves." He is talking of course about babies, feeling them leap in wombs, giving them suck. Parenthood, however, is a state which some miss by chance and others by design, and a vocation to which not all are called. Some of us, like the novelist Richard P. Brickner, "look on as others name their children who in turn name their own lives, devising their own flags from their parents' cloth." What are we who lack children to do? Build houses? Plant trees? Write books or symphonies or laws? Perhaps, but even if we do these things, there still should be children on the sidelines, if not at the

center, of our lives. It is a sadly impoverished tribe that does not allow access to, and make much of, some children. Not too much, of course: it has truly been said that never in history have so many educated people devoted so much attention to so few children. Attention, in excess, can turn to fawning, which isn't much better than neglect. Still, if we don't regularly see and talk to and laugh with people who can expect to outlive us by twenty years or so, we had better get busy and find some.

(10) Good families also honor their elders. The wider the 13 age range, the stronger the tribe. Jean-Paul Sartre and Margaret Mead, to name two spectacularly confident former children, have both remarked on the central importance of grandparents in their own early lives. Grandparents now are in much more abundant supply than they were a generation or two ago when old age was more rare. If actual grandparents are not at hand, no family should have too hard a time finding substitute ones to whom to give unfeigned homage. The Soviet Union's enchantment with day care centers, I have heard, stems at least in part from the state's eagerness to keep children away from their presumably subversive grandparents. Let that be a lesson to clans based on interest as well as to those based on genes.

[1978 — U.S.A.]

Questions

1. "Families" begins with a funnel thesis paragraph. What is the thesis? How does Howard work down to it?
2. Clearly, this essay proceeds by enumeration. What advantages does the list structure afford? What are its potential pitfalls? How well does it work in "Families"? Why?
3. "Families" exhibits *structural parallelism*. That is, each section runs parallel to every other section in structure. What is the basic structural pattern repeated here?
4. This essay lacks a concluding paragraph. But its last sentence gives it a sense of an ending. How so?

Writing Assignments

1. Write a paragraph or more suggesting how your own experience of family life either confirms or runs counter to Howard's definition of a viable family. Quickly summarize her ten points first; then discuss your experience in light of them.

2. Choose a topic that can entail enumeration and be treated in a list structure: for instance, "a good student," "an effective parent," "a compatible roommate." Then write an essay enumerating and defining the qualities of such a student, parent, roommate, or whomever in a list structure like Howard's. Try to make each paragraph parallel every other paragraph in outline and movement.

 **SALVATION**

Langston Hughes

I WAS SAVED FROM SIN WHEN I WAS GOING ON THIRTEEN. BUT NOT   1 really saved. It happened like this. There was a big revival at my Auntie Reed's church. Every night for weeks there had been much preaching, singing, praying, and shouting, and some very hardened sinners had been brought to Christ, and the membership of the church had grown by leaps and bounds. Then just before the revival ended, they held a special meeting for children, "to bring the young lambs to the fold." My aunt spoke of it for days ahead. That night I was escorted to the front row and placed on the mourners' bench with all the other young sinners, who had not yet been brought to Jesus.

My aunt told me that when you were saved you saw a light,   2 and something happened to you inside! And Jesus came into your life! And God was with you from then on! She said you could see and hear and feel Jesus in your soul. I believed her. I had heard a great many old people say the same thing and it seemed to me they ought to know. So I sat there calmly in the hot, crowded church, waiting for Jesus to come to me.

The preacher preached a wonderful rhythmical sermon, all 3
moans and shouts and lonely cries and dire pictures of hell, and
then he sang a song about the ninety and nine safe in the fold,
but one little lamb was left out in the cold. Then he said: "Won't
you come? Won't you come to Jesus? Young lambs, won't you
come?" And he held out his arms to all us young sinners there
on the mourners' bench. And the little girls cried. And some of
them jumped up and went to Jesus right away. But most of us
just sat there.

A great many old people came and knelt around us and 4
prayed, old women with jet-black faces and braided hair, old
men with work-gnarled hands. And the church sang a song
about the lower lights are burning, some poor sinners to be
saved. And the whole building rocked with prayer and song.

Still I kept waiting to *see* Jesus.   5

Finally all the young people had gone to the altar and were 6
saved, but one boy and me. He was a rounder's[1] son named
Westley. Westley and I were surrounded by sisters and deacons
praying. It was very hot in the church, and getting late now.
Finally Westley said to me in a whisper: "God damn! I'm tired
o' sitting here. Let's get up and be saved." So he got up and was
saved.

Then I was left all alone on the mourners' bench. My aunt 7
came and knelt at my knees and cried, while prayers and songs
swirled all around me in the little church. The whole congregation prayed for me alone, in a mighty wail of moans and
voices. And I kept waiting serenely for Jesus, waiting, waiting
— but he didn't come. I wanted to see him, but nothing
happened to me. Nothing! I wanted something to happen to
me, but nothing happened.

I heard the songs and the minister saying: "Why don't you 8
come? My dear child, why don't you come to Jesus? Jesus is
waiting for you. He wants you. Why don't you come? Sister
Reed, what is this child's name?"

---

[1]*rounder:* a dissolute and/or dishonest person.

"Langston," my aunt sobbed.   9

"Langston, why don't you come? Why don't you come and 10
be saved? Oh, Lamb of God! Why don't you come?"

Now it was really getting late. I began to be ashamed of 11
myself, holding everything up so long. I began to wonder what
God thought about Westley, who certainly hadn't seen Jesus
either, but who was now sitting proudly on the platform,
swinging his knickerbockered legs and grinning down at me,
surrounded by deacons and old women on their knees praying.
God had not struck Westley dead for taking his name in vain or
for lying in the temple. So I decided that maybe to save further
trouble, I'd better lie, too, and say that Jesus had come, and get
up and be saved.

So I got up.   12

Suddenly the whole room broke into a sea of shouting, as 13
they saw me rise. Waves of rejoicing swept the place. Women
leaped in the air. My aunt threw her arms around me. The
minister took me by the hand and led me to the platform.

When things quieted down, in a hushed silence, punctuated 14
by a few ecstatic "Amens," all the new young lambs were
blessed in the name of God. Then joyous singing filled the
room.

That night, for the last time in my life but one — for I was 15
a big boy twelve years old — I cried. I cried, in bed alone, and
couldn't stop. I buried my head under the quilts, but my aunt
heard me. She woke up and told my uncle I was crying because
the Holy Ghost had come into my life, and because I had seen
Jesus. But I was really crying because I couldn't bear to tell her
that I had lied, that I had deceived everybody in the church,
that I hadn't seen Jesus, and that now I didn't believe there was
a Jesus any more, since he didn't come to help me.

[1940 — U.S.A.]

Questions

1. The title of this essay is ironic. How so? How does the irony,
   underscored by the second sentence of the first paragraph, lend
   dramatic tension to the essay overall?

2. Aside from the reasons given at the end, why did the boy remembered here cry the night he lied? What is the theme of the essay?

3. There are many details involving setting in "Salvation." Why? What purpose do they serve?

4. Varying between the poetic and the mundane, Hughes's diction is worth looking at. Find examples of each kind of diction. What effects does the diction have? How does the diction tie in with the essay's theme?

5. How would you describe the general style of "Salvation"? Why is it appropriate to the subject matter? What is the effect on pace of the one-sentence paragraphs? There are other fine rhythmic effects here. Locate two or three and describe them.

6. From Hughes's autobiography, *The Big Sea*, "Salvation" is close to being a story. What makes it an essay? Consider intent and reader psychology.

Writing Assignments

1. Write two paragraphs on the same subject but opposite in diction (poetic versus mundane, for instance, or technical versus slangy) and/or syntax (sentence length and sentence type). Then sum up the difference in effect between your two paragraphs.

2. Were you ever pressured into doing something as a child that you believed wrong? If so, write an essay on the incident. Try to make your narration immediate by your descriptive details, and dramatic by the way you pace it and build to a climax.

3. In a paper, compare and contrast Lord Dunsany's "A Moral Little Tale" (pages 227 – 28) and "Salvation." Both are narratives and can be considered essays, yet they are very different and are essays for very different reasons. Focus especially on the differences as to why each is an essay.

✛ THE BEAT GOES OFF: ✛
HOW TECHNOLOGY HAS GUMMED UP ROCK'S GROOVES
Mark Hunter

NOT LONG AGO I BORROWED A CAR, LOADED IT WITH 211   1
phonograph albums that had been sent to me by record
companies over the past three years, and drove to a secondhand
record store, where I sold them for about $150. This was illegal;
the albums were plainly marked "demonstration — not for sale"
(though every record company knows that many of the critics
on its mailing list derive a sizable share of their income by
selling these albums). I didn't set out to break the law; but I'd
offered a dozen or so people as many records as they could
carry away, and I'd gotten no takers. Selling the records
seemed somehow better than simply dumping them in the
street — or keeping them.

Of the roughly 500 albums I've received in the past five   2
years, maybe thirty were worth keeping. It's not easy for me to
say that. Since the age of thirteen — that's twenty-one years ago
— I have lived with and for rock-and-roll. I have spent
incalculable hours around stereos and in rock clubs, listening,
dancing, performing, falling in and out of love. I believed, as a
California dance-hall queen told me once, that "rock-and-roll
will keep you young." That the music itself would one day grow
old was beyond imagining. Yet from what I hear, and I have
heard an awful lot, the great creative period of this music is
over.

What has aged rock music isn't merely or mainly laziness or   3
a lack of imagination — though there has been more than
enough of that. The overwhelming problem is the new
technology behind the backbeat and the changes it has set in
motion, changes that demand an entirely different approach to
music from the one that initially made rock a fresh and exciting
form. Technology, in music as in every other field, has its

imperatives as well as its possibilities. For rock, the imperatives have proved deadly.

I am fully aware that most rock fans, let alone most critics, 4 could care less about the technology involved in making records. But given the extraordinary extent to which rock music has penetrated our lives — a number-one pop hit today could be defined as a song that nearly everyone in the world will hear at least once — one might well take an interest in how it was recorded, and how this in turn shapes the kind of music being made. The fact is that what might be called the *content* of rock — the songs, the sound — follows to a great extent from formulas *imposed* by recording techniques. And these formulas are giving us music that is murderously dull.

The worldwide rock explosion began in 1963 when the 5 Beatles set off what would become, within a decade, a doubling of global record and tape sales (to about $2 billion worth). The Beatles represented something new in pop music, but it was not their beat that was new so much as the fact that they were a self-contained composing, arranging, and performing unit. In this way they were quite different from the stars of the 1950s, who recorded material written by pop composers and arranged by record label "A&R" (artist and repertoire) directors. The great bands of the "British Invasion" of the mid-1960s — the Who, the Animals, the Rolling Stones — were similarly self-reliant, as were the literally thousands of rock bands that sprang up in England and the United States in the wake of their success.

The Beatles and the other great British bands arrived on 6 the scene just ahead of a profound change in recording techniques — the move from monophonic taping, in which all the instruments used in a composition are recorded simultaneously on the entire width of the tape, to "multitracking," in which each instrument is recorded on a separate band of tape and then "mixed down" into the final product. The shift to multitracking took time, and its progress was reflected in the argot of the recording studio. In the 1960s, when a recording artist or engineer spoke of a "track," he meant an entire song (as in the Stones' Keith Richards's famous description of a typical pop album as "a hit single and ten tracks of shit"). Since the mid-1970s, "track" has been used to describe *one* instrumental or vocal part of a composition.

In the monophonic era, recording a song meant gathering   7 an ensemble in a room, putting out one or more microphones, and recording the music in one "take," live. If you didn't like the take, you did it over, period. This was how Elvis Presley's epochal first recordings for the Sun label were made in the early fifties, and it remained the standard technique (there were some exceptions) through the mid-sixties.

The advantage of this method, in retrospect — at the time,   8 engineers and producers simply had no other methods available — was that players could inspire one another to the kind of extra effort that comes only in ensemble work. If you have ever played in a good group, you know what those moments are like: Suddenly, each musician seems to be hearing the music *before it is played*. That's what happens on Elvis's "Mystery Train"; Scotty Moore (on guitar) and Elvis (singing) anticipate each other's phrases, arriving together just ahead of where the ear would expect the beat to fall, driving the song toward a mounting excitement. There is no drummer on "Mystery Train," but that doesn't keep you from dancing to it.

The disadvantages of this method were considerable,   9 however, and evident even at the time — in particular, the difficulty in getting a distinct sound color, or timbre, for each instrument, and in capturing a performance in which every musician and singer was at a peak. Producers went crazy when one verse on a take was poorly sung but the rest were superb, because there was no way to cut out the bad and keep the good. Engineers went crazy trying to keep the sounds of drums and amplified guitars from ending up in the singer's microphone. It could be done, but it was hard, and it became even harder in the 1960s, when the electric bass came into wide use and made possible a rhythm-section sound of extraordinary power.

Engineers developed techniques that ameliorated these   10 problems, but they could not solve them entirely. By recording the instruments first, for example, and then rerecording this tape onto another, simultaneously with a live take of the singer, the problem of instruments fouling up a brilliant vocal could be eliminated. Unfortunately, every time sounds are transferred from one tape to another, there is a loss in quality. Producers tried to get as much of the sound on tape in a single take as possible, and to limit the number of times they made additions to the original performance. That is why Phil Spector introduced bigger rhythm sections to pop, and why he used such innovations as "massed pianos" on the sessions he produced for the Crystals in 1961 and 1962. The only way to achieve orchestral depth was to record an orchestra.

All this changed with the invention of stereo machines with 11 three recording heads (or "capstans") in the early sixties. Now an engineer could not only record the vocals and instruments on separate tracks. He could "punch in" a performer at a given moment on a recording, and then "punch out" in confidence that the new, punched-in sounds would be in sequence with the rest of the composition. Simply put, it was no longer necessary to record a song from beginning to end. "Synchronization" opened the way to true multitrack recording.

The pop album that most profoundly signaled this shift was 12 the Beatles' *Sgt. Pepper's Lonely Hearts Club Band,* released in 1967. The album was recorded on a four-track machine, the best then available, and the shock it caused when it was released, for rock musicians and listeners alike, was manifold.

To start with, all the lyrics are comprehensible on first 13 listening — this was a rock rarity in 1967. Moreover, by recording the various parts — bass, drums, vocals, horns, guitars — on separate tracks, stopping periodically for "premixes" in order to combine several parts on one track, then "mixing down" to the final stereo product, the Beatles achieved a precision and clarity of each instrument and effect that was unprecedented in pop. When next you hear that album, note how McCartney's bass line on "Being for the Benefit of Mr. Kite!" is distinct from the rest of the sound; on the Beatles' earlier records, the bass blends in with the drums and rhythm guitars, an angry roar at the bottom of the sound.

In essence, the techniques used to make *Sgt. Pepper* allowed 14
the Beatles to *compose* an album, instead of performing it as they
would onstage. When it soared to number one on the charts,
those techniques became a commercial imperative. (Think of
the Stones, who rushed onto the market the slipshod *Their
Satanic Majesties Request* — a hash of psychedelic effects and
chopped-up song structures.) In the wake of *Sgt. Pepper,* rock
performance and rock recording became sharply divided
domains. Eventually, that gap became the gulch where rock
ran dry.

With multitracking, all the musicians involved in making a 15
record no longer had to be present at the same time (a point
underlined by the Beatles in 1969 in the making of *Abbey Road;*
rarely were all of them in the studio together). Once the bass
line was on tape, the bass player could go home. Conversely, if
one player made a mistake, only his part needed to be
rerecorded. Moreover, thanks to the process of overdubbing,
which allows the engineer to record over selected portions of a
track, the performance of a given player on a song no longer
had to be continuous. If one verse was no good, the singer
could retake it. And the engineer could "treat" the sounds
electronically during recording or mixing to alter their timbre.

These techniques all but eliminated what had always been 16
an essential element in rock, the concept of ensemble spontaneity. Cream's marvelous recording of Robert Johnson's
"Crossroads," for example, contains some notes that might as
well not have been played, but one hardly notices them because
the three musicians (Eric Clapton on guitar, Jack Bruce on
bass, and Ginger Baker on drums) adapt their individual
intensity and attack to one another's work, moving in and out
of the lead as the moment demands. In multitrack work, where
musicians take turns recording their parts, it is nearly impossible for an individual player to alter the ensemble's direction in
this manner. A mistake will sound like a mistake, instead of a
cue for the rest of the ensemble to incorporate an accident into
a large effect.

Multitracking also changed the dynamic flow of individual 17
performances. All music achieves its effects through contrast;
soft moments set up the tough ones, which in turn give way,
relax. This follows naturally from performing a song in its
entirety. In the version of "Try a Little Tenderness" that Otis
Redding and his backup band, the Bar-Kays, recorded in the
mid-sixties, Redding keeps a certain power in reserve until the
final measures, when he pleads outright with the listener to
"love her, please her, never leave her," while the band rises
behind him to a frenzied crescendo. In the multitrack era, when
a musician will cut an entire track and then go back to "correct"
certain passages, often phrase by phrase, performances tend to
settle at a single dynamic level. Vocalists in particular seem to
lose a sense of overall dynamic flow. Listen to Madonna's
"Material Girl": the final chorus sounds just like the first.

Along with this loss of dynamism there is, on an over- 18
whelming number of records, an absence of rhythmic invention. On one disc after another there is the "boom-BOOM" of
a thudding bass drum followed by a snare enveloped in
reverberation — a "handclap" effect. Part of the reason for this
awful sameness is that multitracking has led musicians and
producers to think of rhythm as a domain unto itself, which it
decidedly is not. When you listen to the records Marvin Gaye
made for Motown in the monophonic era, records like "Ain't
That Peculiar," you can't help but notice that piano, bass,
guitar, and drum sounds blend into a single timbre. It is
practically impossible to hear the sound of the bass drum
separately from the sound of the bass guitar on this record,
which is no doubt why the drummer chose to rely on his
sharply percussive snare drum to set the beat. The way the
timbres of their instruments would eventually come through on
tape forced the musicians to think of rhythm as being the
domain of no one instrument, but rather as an element
emerging from a dynamic equilibrium among the members of
the ensemble.

When multitracking made it possible to record the bass and 19
drums separately, and to hear them distinctly even at high
volumes, the role of rhythm musicians was deeply altered.

Their sound was no longer far back in a percussive cloud, but could be moved right to the front of the mix — which works just fine in discos and dance clubs, where you listen mostly with your feet, but not at home in front of the stereo. You can hear the difference on a collection of "never before released masters" recorded by Gaye in the mid-sixties and early seventies and put on the market last year under the title *Motown Remembers Marvin Gaye.* Some remembrance: On nearly every song new bass and drum parts have been added through multitrack overdubs and mixed into the forefront. You can follow the beat more easily — even a deaf person could feel the impact of the bass drum — but its texture has been impoverished, cut off from the rest of the sound.

Before multitracking came along, a "groove" meant the 20 sense of swing inherent in an entire arrangement. On Wilson Pickett's "Midnight Mover," for example, the bass guitar opens with a four-measure pattern, constantly shifting in accent, that first descends an octave, then holds firm around the root chord while the rhythm guitar knocks out a two-bar phrase that counterpoints both halves of the bass line, in time and harmonically. Today, bass and drums are typically recorded first, and are thus obliged to play in a way that will not complicate the recording of subsequent tracks. A groove now means a two-bar phrase of bass and drum notes (often "played" by an electronic drum box) that repeats without changing, as on David Bowie's tiresome single "Let's Dance." Rhythm, once the backbone, has simply become the flat bottom.

Multitracking has flattened rock in other ways. For one 21 thing, it cut short a revolution in the creative politics of the music industry. The people who rose to the top of the industry in the sixties, people like Clive Davis of Columbia, believed in letting rock bands "do their own thing" in the studio. That made sense when what counted on a record was the ensemble creation. It no longer made sense with multitrack machines.

Aside from the fact that the entire ensemble is no longer 22 needed to finish a record, multitracking has made bands more dependent on producers and engineers, who understand the new techniques better than most musicians do. Moreover, anyone who has recorded both monophonically and multitrack will tell you that it takes far longer to make a record one sound at a time. In the studio, time is money, and in the multitrack era time costs more money than ever: Studios have to update their equipment constantly to remain competitive, and the price of the investment is passed on to musicians and their record companies. In the early sixties, the cost of recording a typical "commercial" album — that is, one whose sound quality appeals to radio programmers and the average record buyer — was a few thousand dollars; the cost rose to $100,000 in the mid-seventies, and now often reaches twice that figure. With that much money at stake, most contracts now specify that the record company has the right to choose the producer; and, to an extent unmatched since the pre-Beatles days, those producers tend to impose proven commercial styles on artists.

An exception here proves the rule: In 1979, when the 23 Police made their first and, in terms of dynamic variation, perhaps their best album, *Outlandos d'Amour*, they recorded each song as an ensemble, overdubbing only vocals and a few lead parts. In an attempt to retain control of their sound and hold down costs the group recorded the songs in a sixteen-track studio. (The standard number of tracks is now twenty-four; Yoko Ono has actually recorded on ninety-six tracks.) In effect, the Police made a multitrack record by a monophonic method. (By contrast, consider the fate of the Humans, an idiosyncratic Santa Cruz band whose first — twenty-four-track — album, *Happy Hour*, has a flat, compressed sound quite unlike the group's roaring surf-meets-psychedelia live sound, but quite like their producer's last hit. Not surprisingly, it bombed, taking the Humans down with it.)

Multitrack technology long ago altered the terms of live 24 performance as well as audience expectations. In the sixties, rock bands typically amplified each instrument individually; this was true whether you were talking about the neighborhood garage band or the Jimi Hendrix Experience. The result was a charged, erratic, stormy sound. But when multitracking took hold, the rock public began to demand that live concerts sound as "clean" as studio recordings, and so stage amplification moved in the direction of complex live-mixing systems that could faithfully reproduce studio sound. These mixing systems sent the cost of concert production through the roof. And, in doing so, they drove a wedge between the thousands of local groups that constitute the amateur base of the rock movement and its better-heeled professional practitioners, who are the only ones who can afford the new equipment.

The punk movement of the mid-seventies angrily attempted 25 to restore sonic amateurism to rock. When you listen to the Sex Pistols' *Never Mind the Bollocks,* it is like having hot metal poured over your head. But punk didn't sell — not much, anyway — and the New Wave music that followed (and drew on punk) confirmed the takeover of the technicians. New Wave, above all, was a clean-sounding music.

And as went music, so went the clubs where it was played. 26 Rock club owners began to realize that their expensive sound systems could be amortized — without the hassles and expense of hiring musicians — simply by using them to play records for people who didn't care how the sound was made, so long as they could dance to the beat. The result was that the club scene sharply declined. Today, no major city boasts more than a few live-rock clubs of any distinction. And almost all rockers now mix records for dance clubs, which have become a crucial promotional route. The most pronounced sound on these "disco mixes" is the monotonous domination of bass and drums.

The decline of the club scene has wiped out the major 27 training ground for rock musicians, and destroyed whatever claims rock had to the status of modern-day folk music. Folk music is, above all, local music, made by musicians playing their own arrangements of a broad standard repertoire as well as their own compositions. That is precisely how the Beatles, the Rolling Stones, or Bruce Springsteen, for that matter, got their start. These artists began by copying songs from records, then changed the arrangements to suit their own ideas and talents. A good example is the way the Band rearranged "Mystery Train," substituting Rick Danko's stuttering bass for the guitar that drives Elvis's classic. By the time these musicians started writing their own material, they had already developed large repertoires and coherent, instantly recognizable ensemble styles. And they had been able to refine their styles over time before live audiences.

In the mid-1980s, such an apprenticeship is no longer 28 possible for new bands. With club space reduced to a few showcases in major cities, most bands don't have the opportunity to play four sets a night in the same club for a week. They have to play forty-five minutes' worth of music — enough to prove to any record company executives in the audience that they can make an album. When Spandau Ballet, one of the aurally anonymous "New Romantic" English bands of the early 1980s, was awarded its first recording contract, the members of the group had been playing together for six months, and knew one set of material. (Not coincidentally, instead of touring, the group promoted the album with disco singles.)

It should not surprise us, then, that we have "rock bands" 29 today that are made up of as many machines — synthesizers and drum boxes — as young men and women, or that the audience for rock *watches* their favorites on TV.

Many recent rock movements, like the New Romantics, 30 have been based not on a distinct musical style or, better yet, the ability to create new styles — the Beatles were masters at this — but on a *look*, in the fashion sense of the term. There is even a term for this, "visual bands." No one would deny, of course, that the visual aspect has always been crucial to a pop star's success; that was true for the young Frank Sinatra as well as for the Beatles. But these artists' visual presence served mainly to dramatize their music, rather than to distract from its hollowness.

Close your eyes the next time you watch an MTV video, 31 and you'll realize that the band could be anyone, which is to say *no one*. What rock video has confirmed is that rock music no longer requires an emotional — let alone physical — engagement on the part of its audience. It is merely something one watches, passively, without noticing its constituent elements. It is no longer worth *listening* to.

[1986 — U.S.A.]

Questions

1. How does paragraph 1 function? What is Hunter's thesis and where is it stated? What kind of a movement (for example, negative to positive) marks paragraphs 1 and 2? What kind of a beginning is this?

2. What is the function of paragraphs 5–14? What kind of an audience is suggested by 5–14 as well as by Hunter's defining most terms?

3. This essay abounds with transitions, many of which are of the same type. Pick out a half dozen used between paragraphs and try to find a classification that will fit most of them. Why should so many be of the same type?

4. How does Hunter make use of comparison and contrast? What kind of evidence does he use to support his statements? What is his purpose overall? How does his tone serve that purpose?

5. Hunter's argument is based on personal judgment. What are the merits of this kind of argument? What are its problems? Aside from merely contradicting Hunter (for instance, by a counterstatement like "Spontaneity isn't dead"), how might you take his thesis to task? Where does he leave himself open to attack?

Writing Assignments

1. If you disagree with Hunter, write a critique of his essay in which you take him to task point by point. What you write will be based on personal judgment, but your argument should incorporate facts and a good number of examples.

2. Write a paper comparing and contrasting "The Beat Goes On" and Glenn Gould's "Music and Technology" (pages 256–61). Focus on how the two (Hunter and Gould) differ in their views of the benefits of technology and, perhaps, why they differ.

✤ How It Feels to ✤
Be Colored Me
Zora Neale Hurston

I AM COLORED BUT I OFFER NOTHING IN THE WAY OF EXTENUATING   1
circumstances except the fact that I am the only Negro in the
United States whose grandfather on the mother's side was *not*
an Indian chief.

I remember the very day that I became colored. Up to my   2
thirteenth year I lived in the little Negro town of Eatonville,
Florida. It is exclusively a colored town. The only white people
I knew passed through the town going to or coming from
Orlando. The native whites rode dusty horses, the Northern
tourists chugged down the sandy village road in automobiles.
The town knew the Southerners and never stopped cane
chewing when they passed. But the Northerners were something else again. They were peered at cautiously from behind
curtains by the timid. The more venturesome would come
out on the porch to watch them go past and got just as
much pleasure out of the tourists as the tourists got out of the
village.

The front porch might seem a daring place for the rest of   3
the town, but it was a gallery seat to me. My favorite place was
atop the gate-post. Proscenium box for a born first-nighter. Not
only did I enjoy the show, but I didn't mind the actors knowing
that I liked it. I usually spoke to them in passing. I'd wave at
them and when they returned my salute, I would say something
like this: "Howdy-do-well-I-thank-you-where-you-goin'?" Usually the automobile or the horse paused at this, and after a
queer exchange of compliments, I would probably "go a piece
of the way" with them, as we say in farthest Florida. If one of
my family happened to come to the front in time to see me, of
course negotiations would be rudely broken off. But even so, it
is clear that I was the first "welcome-to-our-state" Floridian,
and I hope the Miami Chamber of Commerce will please take
notice.

During this period, white people differed from colored to 4
me only in that they rode through town and never lived there.
They liked to hear me "speak pieces" and sing and wanted to
see me dance the parse-me-la, and gave me generously of their
small silver for doing these things, which seemed strange to me
for I wanted to do them so much that I needed bribing to stop.
Only they didn't know it. The colored people gave no dimes.
They deplored any joyful tendencies in me, but I was their Zora
nevertheless. I belonged to them, to the nearby hotels, to the
county — everybody's Zora.

But changes came in the family when I was thirteen, and I 5
was sent to school in Jacksonville. I left Eatonville, the town of
the oleanders, as Zora. When I disembarked from the
river-boat at Jacksonville, she was no more. It seemed that I
had suffered a sea change. I was not Zora of Orange County
any more, I was now a little colored girl. I found it out in certain
ways. In my heart as well as in the mirror, I became a fast
brown — warranted not to rub nor run.

But I am not tragically colored. There is no great sorrow 6
dammed up in my soul, nor lurking behind my eyes. I do not
mind at all. I do not belong to the sobbing school of Negrohood
who hold that nature somehow has given them a lowdown dirty
deal and whose feelings are all hurt about it. Even in the
helter-skelter skirmish that is my life, I have seen that the world
is to the strong regardless of a little pigmentation more or less.
No, I do not weep at the world — I am too busy sharpening my
oyster knife.

Someone is always at my elbow reminding me that I am the 7
granddaughter of slaves. It fails to register depression with me.
Slavery is sixty years in the past. The operation was successful
and the patient is doing well, thank you. The terrible struggle
that made me an American out of a potential slave said "On the
line!" The Reconstruction said "Get set!"; and the generation
before said "Go!" I am off to a flying start and I must not halt
in the stretch to look behind and weep. Slavery is the price I
paid for civilization, and the choice was not with me. It is a
bully adventure and worth all that I have paid through my

ancestors for it. No one on earth ever had a greater chance for glory. The world to be won and nothing to be lost. It is thrilling to think — to know that for any act of mine, I shall get twice as much praise or twice as much blame. It is quite exciting to hold the center of the national stage,[1] with the spectators not knowing whether to laugh or to weep.

The position of my white neighbor is much more difficult. 8 No brown specter pulls up a chair beside me when I sit down to eat. No dark ghost thrusts its leg against mine in bed. The game of keeping what one has is never so exciting as the game of getting.

I do not always feel colored. Even now I often achieve the 9 unconscious Zora of Eatonville before the Hegira.[2] I feel most colored when I am thrown against a sharp white background.

For instance at Barnard. "Beside the waters of the Hudson" 10 I feel my race. Among the thousand white persons, I am a dark rock surged upon, overswept by a creamy sea. I am surged upon and overswept, but through it all, I remain myself. When covered by the waters, I am; and the ebb but reveals me again.

Sometimes it is the other way around. A white person is set 11 down in our midst, but the contrast is just as sharp for me. For instance, when I sit in the drafty basement that is The New World Cabaret with a white person, my color comes. We enter chatting about any little nothing that we have in common and are seated by the jazz waiters. In the abrupt way that jazz orchestras have, this one plunges into a number. It loses no time in circumlocutions, but gets right down to business. It constricts the thorax and splits the heart with its tempo and narcotic harmonies. This orchestra grows rambunctious, rears on its hind legs and attacks the tonal veil with primitive fury, rending it, clawing it until it breaks through to the jungle

---

[1]*stage:* Associated with the Harlem Renaissance, Hurston was becoming a well-known writer at this time.

[2]*Hegira:* The flight of Mohammed from Mecca in 622 A.D.; thus, the beginning of the Moslem era.

beyond. I follow those heathen — follow them exultingly. I dance wildly inside myself; I yell within, I whoop; I shake my assegai[3] above my head, I hurl it true to the mark *yeeeeooww!* I am in the jungle and living in the jungle way. My face is painted red and yellow and my body is painted blue. My pulse is throbbing like a war drum. I want to slaughter something — give pain, give death to what, I do not know. But the piece ends. The men of the orchestra wipe their lips and rest their fingers. I creep back slowly to the veneer we call civilization with the last tone and find the white friend sitting motionless in his seat, smoking calmly.

"Good music they have here," he remarks, drumming the 12 table with his fingertips.

Music! The great blobs of purple and red emotion have not 13 touched him. He has only heard what I felt. He is far away and I see him but dimly across the ocean and the continent that have fallen between us. He is so pale with his whiteness then and I am *so* colored.

At certain times I have no race, I am *me*. When I set my hat 14 at a certain angle and saunter down Seventh Avenue, Harlem City, feeling as snooty as the lions in front of the Forty-Second Street Library, for instance. So far as my feelings are concerned, Peggy Hopkins Joyce[4] on the Boule Mich with her gorgeous raiment, stately carriage, knees knocking together in a most aristocratic manner, has nothing on me. The cosmic Zora emerges. I belong to no race nor time. I am the eternal feminine with its string of beads.

I have no separate feeling about being an American citizen 15 and colored. I am merely a fragment of the Great Soul that surges within the boundaries. My country, right or wrong.

Sometimes, I feel discriminated against, but it does not 16 make me angry. It merely astonishes me. How *can* any deny themselves the pleasure of my company! It's beyond me.

---

[3]*assegai:* A light spear used by Southern African tribesmen.

[4]*Peggy Hopkins Joyce:* Socialite and patron of the arts who spent the 1920s in Paris.

But in the main, I feel like a brown bag of miscellany 17
propped against a wall. Against a wall in company with other
bags, white, red and yellow. Pour out the contents, and there is
discovered a jumble of small things priceless and worthless. A
first-water diamond, an empty spool, bits of broken glass,
lengths of string, a key to a door long since crumbled away, a
rusty knife-blade, old shoes saved for a road that never was and
never will be, a nail bent under the weight of things too heavy
for any nail, a dried flower or two, still a little fragrant. In your
hand is the brown bag. On the ground before you is the jumble
it held — so much like the jumble in the bags, could they be
emptied, that all might be dumped in a single heap and the bags
refilled without altering the content of any greatly. A bit of
colored glass more or less would not matter. Perhaps that is
how the Great Stuffer of Bags filled them in the first place
— who knows?

[1928 – U.S.A.]

Questions

1. The title of this essay gives it point and focus. How so?
2. What is the effect of the paragraphing of paragraphs 12 and 13?
   Might the contrast drawn in paragraphs 11–13 be open to the
   charge of stereotyping on both sides, white and black? Why or why
   not?
3. In paragraph 7, Hurston says: "Slavery is the price I paid for
   civilization." What implications does this have as to her African
   heritage? Later in the essay (specifically, paragraphs 11–13),
   Hurston seems to contradict herself on this score. How so? Is there
   any point to the contradiction, or is it just a flaw? Why do you
   conclude what you do here?
4. This essay contains many figures of speech. Pick out an example of
   personification. Pick out a paragraph other than paragraph 17 that
   proceeds by metaphorical extension. What is accomplished by each
   figure?
5. What metaphor underlies paragraph 17? The imagery here is meant
   to summarize Hurston's sense of herself. Does it succeed? Is this a
   good way of ending an essay, at least an essay that is primarily
   personal in nature?

Writing Assignments

1. Write a paper comparing and/or contrasting how Hurston sees herself and how you see yourself. As much as possible, follow the order of the present essay point by point.

2. In her essay "In Search of Our Mothers' Gardens," Alice Walker says that Hurston's autobiography shows "evidence of 'contrary instincts'" and that Hurston's "loyalties were completely divided, as was, without question, her mind." Could the same be said of "How It Feels to Be Colored Me"? Write an essay either refuting Walker with evidence from the essay at hand or reading it in light of Walker's comments, thus finding it to reveal more, perhaps, than Hurston herself understood. Before beginning, consider questions 2 and 3 above.

✛ A Crime of Compassion ✛

Barbara Huttmann

"**M**URDERER," A MAN SHOUTED. "GOD HELP PATIENTS WHO GET *YOU*   1
for a nurse."

"What gives you the right to play God?" another one asked.   2

It was the Phil Donahue show where the guest is a fatted   3
calf and the audience a 200-strong flock of vultures hungering to pick at the bones. I had told them about Mac, one of my favorite cancer patients. "We resuscitated him 52 times in just one month. I refused to resuscitate him again. I simply sat there and held his hand while he died."

There wasn't time to explain that Mac was a young, witty,   4
macho cop who walked into the hospital with 32 pounds of attack equipment, looking as if he could single-handedly protect the whole city, if not the entire state. "Can't get rid of this cough," he said. Otherwise, he felt great.

Before the day was over, tests confirmed that he had lung   5
cancer. And before the year was over, I loved him, his wife, Maura, and their three kids as if they were my own. All the nurses loved him. And we all battled his disease for six months

without ever giving death a thought. Six months isn't such a long time in the whole scheme of things, but it was long enough to see him lose his youth, his wit, his macho, his hair, his bowel and bladder control, his sense of taste and smell, and his ability to do the slightest thing for himself. It was also long enough to watch Maura's transformation from a young woman into a haggard, beaten old lady.

When Mac had wasted away to a 60-pound skeleton kept 6 alive by liquid food we poured down a tube, i.v. solutions we dripped into his veins, and oxygen we piped to a mask on his face, he begged us: "Mercy . . . for God's sake, please just let me go."

The first time he stopped breathing, the nurse pushed the 7 button that calls a "code blue" throughout the hospital and sends a team rushing to resuscitate the patient. Each time he stopped breathing, sometimes two or three times in one day, the code team came again. The doctors and technicians worked their miracles and walked away. The nurses stayed to wipe the saliva that drooled from his mouth, irrigate the big craters of bedsores that covered his hips, suction the lung fluids that threatened to drown him, clean the feces that burned his skin like lye, pour the liquid food down the tube attached to his stomach, put pillows between his knees to ease the bone-on-bone pain, turn him every hour to keep the bedsores from getting worse, and change his gown and linen every two hours to keep him from being soaked in perspiration.

At night I went home and tried to scrub away the smell of 8 decaying flesh that seemed woven into the fabric of my uniform. It was in my hair, the upholstery of my car — there was no washing it away. And every night I prayed that Mac would die, that his agonized eyes would never again plead with me to let him die.

Every morning I asked his doctor for a "no-code" order. 9 Without that order, we had to resuscitate every patient who stopped breathing. His doctor was one of several who believe we must extend life as long as we have the means and knowledge to do it. To not do it is to be liable for negligence, at least in the eyes of many people, including some nurses. I thought about what it would be like to stand before a judge, accused of murder, if Mac stopped breathing and I didn't call a code.

And after the fifty-second code, when Mac was still lucid 10 enough to beg for death again, and Maura was crumbled in my arms again, and when no amount of pain medication stilled his moaning and agony, I wondered about a spiritual judge. Was all this misery and suffering supposed to be building character or infusing us all with the sense of humility that comes from impotence?

Had we, the whole medical community, become so arrogant 11 that we believed in the illusion of salvation through science? Had we become so self-righteous that we thought meddling in God's work was our duty, our moral imperative and our legal obligation? Did we really believe that we had the right to force "life" on a suffering man who had begged for the right to die?

Such questions haunted me more than ever early one 12 morning when Maura went home to change her clothes and I was bathing Mac. He had been still for so long, I thought he at last had the blessed relief of coma. Then he opened his eyes and moaned, "Pain . . . no more . . . Barbara . . . do something . . . God, let me go."

The desperation in his eyes and voice riddled me with guilt. 13 "I'll stop," I told him as I injected the pain medication.

I sat on the bed and held Mac's hands in mine. He pressed 14 his bony fingers against my hand and muttered, "Thanks." Then there was one soft sigh and I felt his hands go cold in mine. "Mac?" I whispered, as I waited for his chest to rise and fall again.

A clutch of panic banded my chest, drew my finger to the 15 code button, urged me to do something, anything . . . but sit there alone with death. I kept one finger on the button, without pressing it, as a waxen pallor slowly transformed his face from person to empty shell. Nothing I've ever done in my 47 years has taken so much effort as it took *not* to press that code button.

Eventually, when I was as sure as I could be that the code 16 team would fail to bring him back, I entered the legal twilight zone and pushed the button. The team tried. And while they

were trying, Maura walked into the room and shrieked, "No
. . . don't let them do this to him . . . for God's sake . . .
please, no more."

Cradling her in my arms was like cradling myself, Mac, and 17
all those patients and nurses who had been in this place before,
who do the best they can in a death-denying society.

So a TV audience accused me of murder. Perhaps I am 18
guilty. If a doctor had written a no-code order, which is the
only *legal* alternative, would he have felt any less guilty? Until
there is legislation making it a criminal act to code a patient who
has requested the right to die, we will all of us risk the same fate
as Mac. For whatever reason, we developed the means to
prolong life, and now we are forced to use it. We do not have
the right to die.

[1983 — U.S.A.]

Questions

1. By and large, this essay is a narrative recounting of the stages of
   Mac's illness. What is Huttmann's main structural mode? What
   three large segments does the narrative fall into? (Specify by
   paragraph numbers and content.) Why is the longest segment the
   longest? What other type of support is operative here?

2. What is the function of paragraph 11? Why are the questions that it
   is comprised of placed here?

3. What is the effect of the opening? What kind of ending does the
   essay have? What is suggested by its paradoxical title?

4. When Huttmann speaks of ours as "a death-denying society" and
   states that "We do not have the right to die," is she overstating for
   rhetorical emphasis or is she speaking the simple truth? In either
   case, what is the effect of these bold statements?

5. What does Huttmann mean to persuade us of? How is her style
   — her diction and syntax — suited to the job? (With regard to style,
   note especially Huttmann's verbs and her use of short declarative
   sentences.)

Writing Assignments

1. Huttmann tells us about a terribly difficult decision she made.
   Narrate an episode in your life that faced you with an important and
   difficult decision. Be sure to detail why the decision was significant
   to you and why it was difficult to make.

2. Write an essay on something that you feel as much urgency about as Huttmann does about mercy killing. To engender that sense of urgency, try to make your style as vivid as Huttmann's. Before starting, study her diction (especially her verbs) and syntax; then, use her style as a model.

✛ WATERWORKS AND KINGS ✛
Aldous Huxley

In THE CHANCELLERIES OF EIGHTEENTH-CENTURY EUROPE NOBODY 1 bothered very much about Hesse. Its hostility was not a menace, its friendship brought no positive advantages. Hesse was only one of the lesser German states — a tenth-rate Power.

Tenth-rate: and yet, on the outskirts of Kassel, which was 2 the capital of this absurdly unimportant principality, there stands a palace large and splendid enough to house a full-blown emperor. And from the main façade of this palace there rises to the very top of the neighbouring mountain one of the most magnificent architectural gardens in the world. This garden, which is like a straight wide corridor of formal stone-work driven through the hillside forest, climbs up to a nondescript building in the grandest Roman manner, almost as large as a cathedral and surmounted by a colossal bronze statue of Hercules. Between Hercules at the top and the palace at the bottom lies an immense series of terraces, with fountains and cascades, pools, grottos, spouting tritons, dolphins, nereids and all the other mythological fauna of an eighteenth-century water-garden. The spectacle, when the waters are flowing, is magnificent. There must be the best part of two miles of neo-classic cataract and elegantly canalized foam. The water-works at Versailles are tame and trivial in comparison.

It was Whit Sunday when I was at Kassel. With almost the 3 entire population of the town I had climbed up to the shrine of Hercules on the hilltop. Standing there in the shadow of the god, with the waters in full splash below me and the sunshine brilliant on the green dome of the palace at the long cataract's foot, I found myself prosaically speculating about ways and means and motives. How could a mere prince of Hesse run to such imperial splendours? And why, having somehow raised the money, should he elect to spend it in so fantastically wasteful a fashion? And, finally, why did the Hessians ever put up with his extravagance? The money, after all, was theirs; seeing it all squandered on a house and garden, why didn't they rise up against their silly, irresponsible tyrant?

The answer to these last questions was being provided, even as I asked them, by the good citizens of Kassel around me. *Schön, herrlich, prachtvoll* [roughly: beautiful, magnificent, splendid]— their admiration exploded emphatically on every side. Without any doubt, they were thoroughly enjoying themselves. In six generations, humanity cannot undergo any fundamental change. There is no reason to suppose that the Hessians of 1750 were greatly different from those of 1932. Whenever the prince allowed his subjects to visit his water-works, they came and, I have no doubt, admired and enjoyed their admiration just as much as their descendants do today. The psychology of revolutionaries is apt to be a trifle crude. The magnificent display of wealth does not necessarily, as they imagine, excite a passion of envy in the hearts of the poor. Given a reasonable amount of prosperity, it excites, more often, nothing but pleasure. The Hessians did not rise up and kill their prince for having wasted so much money on his house and garden; on the contrary, they were probably grateful to him for having realized in solid stone and rainbow-flashing water their own vague day-dreams of a fairy-tale magnificence. One of the functions of royalty is to provide people with a vicarious, but none the less real, fulfilment of their wishes. Kings who make a fine show are popular; and the people not only forgive, but actually commend, extravagances which, to the good Marxian, must seem merely criminal. Wise kings always ear-marked a certain percentage of their income for display. Palaces and waterworks were good publicity for kingship, just as an impressive office building is good publicity for a business corporation. Business, indeed, has inherited many of the responsibilities of royalty. It shares with the State and the municipality the important duty of providing the common people with vicarious wish-fulfilments. Kings no longer build palaces; but newspapers and insurance companies do. Popular restaurants are as richly marbled as the mausoleum of the Escorial; hotels are more splendid than Versailles. In every society there must always be some person or some organization whose task it is to realize the day-dreams of the masses. Life in a perfectly sensible, utilitarian community would be intolerably dreary. Occasional explosions of magnificent folly are as essential to human well-being as a sewage system. More so, probably. Sanitary plumbing, it is significant to note, is a very recent invention; the splendours of kingship are as old as civilization itself.

[1937 — Great Britain]

Questions

1. There is a certain playfulness in Huxley's title if one recalls Lewis Carroll. What is the allusion here? What light does it shed on Huxley's attitude?
2. What is the topic sentence of paragraph 4? How does this sentence give unity to the paragraph and the essay as a whole?
3. What is the essay's theme? Where is it implied?
4. What examples does Huxley use? What is the main example and what are the subsidiary examples?

Writing Assignments

1. If you had to choose between a sewer system and "occasional explosions of magnificent folly," which would it be? Write a paragraph or more stating your reasoning.
2. Write a paper based on one solid example of whatever your thesis is. State your thesis, and then proceed in your argument by developing your example point by point.

——————————✤ THE NEED FOR ✤——————————
HANDGUN CONTROL
Edward M. Kennedy

THE WOUNDING OF PRESIDENT REAGAN HAS STUNNED THE WORLD   1
and stirred a vast reaction. Yet he is only the most famous
casualty of an endless guerrilla war inside this country waged
with a growing arsenal of handguns in the wrong hands. Every
day others less famous are wounded or killed; their families
worry and suffer. They weep and, too often, they mourn.

Every 50 minutes an American is killed by a handgun; 29   2
Americans who are alive today will be shot dead tomorrow. In
the streets of our cities, the arms race of Saturday-night specials
and cheap handguns will take 10,000 lives this year and will
threaten or wound another 250,000 citizens. In the past year
alone, we have seen a 13 percent rise in violent crime, the
greatest increase in a decade.

Today the clear and present danger to our society is the   3
midnight mugger and the deranged assassin. And their weapons are as close as the nearest pawnshop. There are 55 million
handguns in circulation. The lethal number rises by two and a
half million each year. By the year 2000, there will be 100
million handguns in America.

The shooting of President Reagan was frightening, but not   4
surprising. Are we now too accustomed to the repeated carnage
of our national leaders? Are we ready to accept the neighbor-
hoods of our cities as permanent free-fire zones? That sort of
fatalism insures more fatalities.

But handgun control is hardly the whole answer to   5
lawlessness. That is why we must adopt other measures as well.

We can, and we must, set more stringent conditions on bail,   6
because no suspect charged with violent crime should be free to
rape or to rob again. We can, and we must, demand that
juveniles who shoot, stab and assault should not be allowed to
misuse their youth as an automatic excuse for their offenses.

We can, and we must, provide sufficient resources for law enforcement. No police officer should ever have to jeopardize his life for a subsistence salary that cannot support his family.

All of this is important — but none of it is enough. In the 7 truest sense, law enforcement is part of our national defense. And in the effort to defend ourselves, we must not duck the question of gun control. No sane society should stand by while its enemies arm themselves — whether those enemies are adversaries abroad or criminals and assassins at home.

For America in 1981, crime control means gun control. This 8 is not an easy issue for any officeholder or candidate. In 1980, in the presidential primaries, I constantly met voters who opposed me because they thought I favored confiscation of hunting rifles, shotguns and sporting pistols. It was not true, but it was believed — because the gun lobby had repeated it over and over.

Other senators and representatives faced a similar assault 9 in 1980. The political action committees opposing gun control spent $2.2 million for their candidates, while those on the other side had less than a tenth as much to contribute. This is why we cannot control the plague of handguns even though two-thirds of the American people have favored such control ever since 1963.

Perhaps this latest tragedy will challenge us to put away 10 past apprehensions and appeals which have treated handgun control as a sinister plot or a subversion of civil liberties. I hope we can now agree that the first civil liberty of all citizens is freedom from fear of violence and sudden death on the streets of their communities.

In this session of congress, I will join again with Rep. Peter 11 Rodino (D-N.J.) to introduce a bill to control handguns. It will be a moderate bill. It will be a sensible bill. It is all I will seek on this issue — and it is something all Americans should be able to support.

All Americans, including sportsmen and hunters, should be 12 able to support a ban on Saturday-night specials and cheap handguns. Those guns are not accurate beyond a range of 10 or

15 feet. They are meant to maim or kill another human being. Saturday-night specials can be purchased now because of a loophole in the law that allows their lethal parts to be imported from abroad, to be assembled and sold in this country. And last week, one of those weapons almost killed our President.

All Americans, including all liberals, should be able to 13 support a mandatory minimum prison sentence for any felon who commits a crime with a handgun. And all Americans, including the National Rifle Assn., should be able to support a waiting period for the purchase of handguns to prevent them from falling into the hands of criminals and psychopaths.

The question is not whether we will disarm honest citizens, 14 as some gun lobbyists have charged. The question is whether we will make it harder for those who break the law to arm themselves.

Gun control is not an easy issue. But, for me, it is a 15 fundamental issue. My family has been touched by violence; too many others have felt the same terrible force. Too many children have been raised without a father or a mother. Too many widows have lived out their lives alone. Too many people have died.

We all know the toll that has been taken in this nation. We 16 all know the leaders of our public life and of the human spirit who have been lost or wounded year after year: My brother, John Kennedy, and my brother, Robert Kennedy; Medgar Evers, who died so that others could live free; Martin Luther King, the apostle of nonviolence who became the victim of violence; George Wallace, who has been paralyzed for nearly nine years, and George Moscone, the mayor of San Francisco, who was killed in his office. Last year alone, we lost Allard Lowenstein and we almost lost Vernon Jordan. Four months ago, we lost John Lennon, that gentle soul who challenged us in song to "give peace a chance." We had two attacks on President Ford and now the attack on President Reagan.

It is unacceptable that all these good men have been shot 17 down. They all sought, each in their own way, to make ours a better world. And, too often, too soon, their own world came to an end.

It is unacceptable that a man who has been arrested before, 18 who has been apprehended carrying loaded guns through an airport security check, who apparently has psychiatric problems as well as a criminal record should be able to go to a pawnshop and buy a cheap handgun imported because of a loophole in the law, and then use that gun to attempt murder against the President of the United States.

It is unacceptable that there are states in the American 19 union where the accused attacker of President Reagan could today buy another Saturday night special.

The day after Martin Luther King's assassination, Robert 20 Kennedy said: "The victims of violence are black and white, rich and poor, young and old, famous and unknown. They are, most important of all, human beings whom other human beings loved and needed. No one, no matter where he lives or what he does, can be certain who next will suffer from some senseless act of bloodshed. And yet it goes on, and on, and on, in this country of ours. Why?"

Thirteen years later, that same tragic question must be 21 raised again.

It is for us to answer it. We must resolve that the next 22 generation of Americans will not have to witness the carnage next time and ask — "Why?"

[1981 – U.S.A.]

Questions

1. Why does Kennedy begin with the "wounding of President Reagan" (who was shot by John Hinckley in the spring of 1981) and not with the assassinations of his brothers? Indeed, he underplays those assassinations when they come up in paragraphs 15 and 16. Why?

2. Is Kennedy's use of statistics (paragraphs 2 and 3) persuasive? Why or why not? Why does he use statistics at all?

3. What is the function of paragraphs 5 and 6? What is the function of paragraph 12? Why does Kennedy use the analogy he does in paragraph 7?

4. Repetition and parallelism are common in political speeches. What words and phrases does Kennedy repeat? What contrast does this repetition set up and emphasize? How does the repetition forestall

the arguments of the gun lobbyists? What are some examples of parallelism here? What effect do repetition and parallelism have as the essay progresses?

Writing Assignments

1. Write a critique of Kennedy's essay stating its strengths with respect to persuasiveness and any weaknesses you detect in this regard. What techniques of persuasion does Kennedy use? To what extent are they effective? Especially if you are in favor of gun control, you must look at the essay as objectively as you can to judge the effectiveness of its argumentation.

2. Write an essay like Kennedy's in which you argue against gun control or for it with arguments other than his. In either case, think about how you might best persuade your reader and then go about doing so.

3. Read or reread Goldwater's "Why Gun-Control Laws Don't Work" (pages 248–51), and then write an essay comparing and contrasting Goldwater's and Kennedy's views. About what do they agree? On what do their views diverge? Which view seems better supported? Why? Which *essay* is more persuasive? How so?

✦ I Have a Dream ✦
Martin Luther King, Jr.

FIVE SCORE YEARS AGO, A GREAT AMERICAN, IN WHOSE SYMBOLIC   1
shadow we stand,[1] signed the Emancipation Proclamation. This momentous decree came as a great beacon light of hope to millions of Negro slaves who had been seared in the flames of withering injustice. It came as a joyous daybreak to end the long night of captivity.

But one hundred years later, we must face the tragic fact   2
that the Negro is still not free. One hundred years later, the life of the Negro is still sadly crippled by the manacles of

---

[1] *shadow we stand:* Commemorating the centennial of Lincoln's signing the Emancipation Proclamation, this speech was given from the steps of the Lincoln Memorial in Washington, D.C.

segregation and the chains of discrimination. One hundred years later, the Negro lives on a lonely island of poverty in the midst of a vast ocean of material prosperity. One hundred years later, the Negro is still languishing in the corners of American society and finds himself an exile in his own land. So we have come here today to dramatize an appalling condition.

In a sense we have come to our nation's capital to cash a 3 check. When the architects of our republic wrote the magnificent words of the Constitution and the Declaration of Independence, they were signing a promissory note to which every American was to fall heir. This note was a promise that all men would be guaranteed the unalienable rights of life, liberty, and the pursuit of happiness.

It is obvious today that America has defaulted on this 4 promissory note insofar as her citizens of color are concerned. Instead of honoring this sacred obligation, America has given the Negro people a bad check; a check which has come back marked "insufficient funds." But we refuse to believe that the bank of justice is bankrupt. We refuse to believe that there are insufficient funds in the great vaults of opportunity of this nation. So we have come to cash this check — a check that will give us upon demand the riches of freedom and the security of justice. We have also come to this hallowed spot to remind America of the fierce urgency of *now*. This is no time to engage in the luxury of cooling off or to take the tranquilizing drugs of gradualism. *Now* is the time to make real the promises of Democracy. *Now* is the time to rise from the dark and desolate valley of segregation to the sunlit path of racial justice. *Now* is the time to open the doors of opportunity to all of God's children. *Now* is the time to lift our nation from the quicksands of racial injustice to the solid rock of brotherhood.

It would be fatal for the nation to overlook the urgency of 5 the moment and to underestimate the determination of the Negro. This sweltering summer of the Negro's legitimate discontent will not pass until there is an invigorating autumn of freedom and equality. 1963 is not an end, but a beginning. Those who hope that the Negro needed to blow off steam and will now be content will have a rude awakening if the nation returns to business as usual. There will be neither rest nor tranquillity in America until the Negro is granted his citizenship rights. The whirlwinds of revolt will continue to shake the foundations of our nation until the bright day of justice emerges.

But there is something that I must say to my people who 6 stand on the warm threshold which leads into the palace of justice. In the process of gaining our rightful place we must not be guilty of wrongful deeds. Let us not seek to satisfy our thirst for freedom by drinking from the cup of bitterness and hatred. We must forever conduct our struggle on the high plane of dignity and discipline. We must not allow our creative protest to degenerate into physical violence. Again and again we must rise to the majestic heights of meeting physical force with soul force. The marvelous new militancy which has engulfed the Negro community must not lead us to a distrust of all white people, for many of our white brothers, as evidenced by their presence here today, have come to realize that their destiny is tied up with our destiny and their freedom is inextricably bound to our freedom. We cannot walk alone.

And as we walk, we must make the pledge that we shall 7 march ahead. We cannot turn back. There are those who are asking the devotees of civil rights, "When will you be satisfied?" We can never be satisfied as long as the Negro is the victim of the unspeakable horrors of police brutality. We can never be satisfied as long as our bodies, heavy with the fatigue of travel, cannot gain lodging in the motels of the highways and the hotels of the cities. We cannot be satisfied as long as the Negro's basic mobility is from a smaller ghetto to a larger one. We can never be satisfied as long as a Negro in Mississippi cannot vote and a Negro in New York believes he has nothing for which to vote. No, no, we are not satisfied, and we will not be satisfied until justice rolls down like waters and righteousness like a mighty stream.

I am not unmindful that some of you have come here out of 8 great trials and tribulations. Some of you have come fresh from narrow jail cells. Some of you have come from areas where your quest for freedom left you battered by the storms of persecution and staggered by the winds of police brutality. You have been the veterans of creative suffering. Continue to work with the faith that unearned suffering is redemptive.

Go back to Mississippi, go back to Alabama, go back to 9 South Carolina, go back to Georgia, go back to Louisiana, go back to the slums and ghettos of our northern cities, knowing that somehow this situation can and will be changed. Let us not wallow in the valley of despair.

I say to you today, my friends, that in spite of the difficulties 10 and frustrations of the moment I still have a dream. It is a dream deeply rooted in the American dream.

I have a dream that one day this nation will rise up and live 11 out the true meaning of its creed: "We hold these truths to be self-evident; that all men are created equal."

I have a dream that one day on the red hills of Georgia the 12 sons of former slaves and the sons of former slaveowners will be able to sit down together at the table of brotherhood.

I have a dream that one day even the state of Mississippi, 13 a desert state sweltering with the heat of injustice and oppression, will be transformed into an oasis of freedom and justice.

I have a dream that my four little children will one day live 14 in a nation where they will not be judged by the color of their skin but by the content of their character.

I have a dream today. 15

I have a dream that one day the state of Alabama, whose 16 governor's lips are presently dripping with the words of interposition and nullification, will be transformed into a situation where little black boys and black girls will be able to join hands with little white boys and white girls and walk together as sisters and brothers.

I have a dream today. 17

I have a dream that one day every valley shall be exalted, 18 every hill and mountain shall be made low, the rough places will be made plain, and the crooked places will be made straight, and the glory of the Lord shall be revealed, and all flesh shall see it together.

This is our hope. This is the faith with which I return to the 19 South. With this faith we will be able to hew out of the mountain of despair a stone of hope. With this faith we will be able to transform the jangling discords of our nation into a beautiful symphony of brotherhood. With this faith we will be able to work together, to pray together, to struggle together, to go to jail together, to stand up for freedom together, knowing that we will be free one day.

This will be the day when all of God's children will be able 20 to sing with new meaning

> My country, 'tis of thee,
> Sweet land of liberty,
>   Of thee I sing:
> Land where my fathers died,
> Land of the pilgrims' pride,
> From every mountain-side
>   Let freedom ring.

And if America is to be a great nation this must become true. So 21 let freedom ring from the prodigious hilltops of New Hampshire. Let freedom ring from the mighty mountains of New York. Let freedom ring from the heightening Alleghenies of Pennsylvania!

Let freedom ring from the snowcapped Rockies of Colo- 22 rado!

Let freedom ring from the curvaceous peaks of California! 23

But not only that; let freedom ring from Stone Mountain of 24 Georgia!

Let freedom ring from Lookout Mountain of Tennessee! 25

Let freedom ring from every hill and molehill of Missis- 26 sippi. From every mountainside, let freedom ring.

When we let freedom ring, when we let it ring from every 27 village and every hamlet, from every state and every city, we will be able to speed up that day when all of God's children, black men and white men, Jews and Gentiles, Protestants and

Catholics, will be able to join hands and sing in the words of the old Negro spiritual, "Free at last! free at last! thank God almighty, we are free at last!"

[1963 — U.S.A.]

Questions

1. What suggests that "I Have a Dream" was written to be spoken and heard rather than read? But is it not also effective in the reading? Why or why not? Comment on its parallelism and the rhythm that its parallelism creates in both regards (that is, the piece as spoken or written).

2. What is the overall purpose of King's speech? What thesis is developed in paragraphs 2–7? Why did King feel the need to expound this thesis? What is the function of the rest of the essay (paragraphs 8–27)?

3. Why the first four words of the essay? King begins with the past and refers to it a number of times in the first half of the essay. Where, for instance? Why these references? Yet he spends much more time speaking of the future. Where does he do so? Why?

4. What analogy is developed in paragraphs 3 and 4? How is it appropriate to modern America? Does it carry any Biblical overtones for you? If so, what are they? What function do they serve?

5. What figures of speech does King use here? To what effect?

6. Is "I Have a Dream" more specific or general in its observations? Why the one or the other? What is King's rhetoric aimed at? Is it persuasive? Why or why not? Under what conditions is the kind of appeal that King makes effective and when is it not?

Writing Assignments

1. Have we as a nation moved any closer to the realization of King's dream? Write an essay arguing that we have or that we have not. Support your reasoning with specific examples and with facts.

2. Write a speech meant primarily to uplift and inspire the audience you have in mind — your classmates, the student body, a scout troop, or whomever. In doing so, try to use some of the techniques found in King's speech — especially repetition and parallelism.

❖ Concepts We Live By ❖

George Lakoff and Mark Johnson

METAPHOR IS FOR MOST PEOPLE A DEVICE OF THE POETIC IMAGINA- 1
tion and the rhetorical flourish — a matter of extraordinary
rather than ordinary language. Moreover, metaphor is typically
viewed as characteristic of language alone, a matter of words
rather than thought or action. For this reason, most people
think they can get along perfectly well without metaphor. We
have found, on the contrary, that metaphor is pervasive in
everyday life, not just in language but in thought and action.
Our ordinary conceptual system, in terms of which we both
think and act, is fundamentally metaphorical in nature.

The concepts that govern our thought are not just matters 2
of the intellect. They also govern our everyday functioning,
down to the most mundane details. Our concepts structure
what we perceive, how we get around in the world, and how we
relate to other people. Our conceptual system thus plays a
central role in defining our everyday realities. If we are right in
suggesting that our conceptual system is largely metaphorical,
then the way we think, what we experience, and what we do
every day is very much a matter of metaphor.

But our conceptual system is not something we are 3
normally aware of. In most of the little things we do every day,
we simply think and act more or less automatically along
certain lines. Just what these lines are is by no means obvious.
One way to find out is by looking at language. Since
communication is based on the same conceptual system that we
use in thinking and acting, language is an important source of
evidence for what that system is like.

Primarily on the basis of linguistic evidence, we have found 4
that most of our ordinary conceptual system is metaphorical in
nature. And we have found a way to begin to identify in detail
just what the metaphors are that structure how we perceive,
how we think, and what we do.

To give some idea of what it could mean for a concept to be   5
metaphorical and for such a concept to structure an everyday
activity, let us start with the concept ARGUMENT and the
conceptual metaphor ARGUMENT IS WAR. This metaphor is
reflected in our everyday language by a wide variety of
expressions:

ARGUMENT IS WAR

Your claims are *indefensible*.
He *attacked every weak point* in my argument.
His criticisms were *right on target*.
I *demolished* his argument.
I've never *won* an argument with him.
You disagree? Okay, *shoot!*
If you use that *strategy*, he'll *wipe you out*.
He *shot down* all of my arguments.

It is important to see that we don't just *talk* about   6
arguments in terms of war. We can actually win or lose
arguments. We see the person we are arguing with as an
opponent. We attack his positions and we defend our own. We
gain and lose ground. We plan and use strategies. If we find a
position indefensible, we can abandon it and take a new line of
attack. Many of the things we *do* in arguing are partially
structured by the concept of war. Though there is no physical
battle, there is a verbal battle, and the structure of an
argument — attack, defense, counterattack, etc. — reflects this.
It is in this sense that the ARGUMENT IS WAR metaphor is one that
we live by in this culture; it structures the actions we perform
in arguing.

Try to imagine a culture where arguments are not viewed in   7
terms of war, where no one wins or loses, where there is no
sense of attacking or defending, gaining or losing ground.
Imagine a culture where an argument is viewed as a dance, the
participants are seen as performers, and the goal is to perform
in a balanced and aesthetically pleasing way. In such a culture,
people would view arguments differently, experience them

differently, carry them out differently, and talk about them differently. But *we* would probably not view them as arguing at all: they would simply be doing something different. It would seem strange even to call what they were doing "arguing." Perhaps the most neutral way of describing this difference between their culture and ours would be to say that we have a discourse form structured in terms of battle and they have one structured in terms of dance.

This is an example of what it means for a metaphorical   8 concept, namely, ARGUMENT IS WAR, to structure (at least in part) what we do and how we understand what we are doing when we argue. *The essence of metaphor is understanding and experiencing one kind of thing in terms of another.* It is not that arguments are a subspecies of war. Arguments and wars are different kinds of things — verbal discourse and armed conflict — and the actions performed are different kinds of actions. But ARGUMENT is partially structured, understood, performed, and talked about in terms of WAR. The concept is metaphorically structured, the activity is metaphorically structured, and, consequently, the language is metaphorically structured.

Moreover, this is the *ordinary* way of having an argument   9 and talking about one. The normal way for us to talk about attacking a position is to use the words "attack a position." Our conventional ways of talking about arguments presuppose a metaphor we are hardly ever conscious of. The metaphor is not merely in the words we use — it is in our very concept of an argument. The language of argument is not poetic, fanciful, or rhetorical; it is literal. We talk about arguments that way because we conceive of them that way — and we act according to the way we conceive of things.

[1980 — U.S.A.]

Questions

1. How does the first paragraph funnel down to the essay's thesis statement? Given the thesis as stated, what is the purpose of the essay and consequently its mode of argumentation?

2. "Arguments and wars," say Lakoff and Johnson, "are different kinds of things" (paragraph 8). How does this observation and what is said in the rest of paragraph 8 square with the definition of metaphor given in chapter 2 (page 82)?

3. Define "conceptual metaphor" in your own words and give an example or two. In "Politics and the English Language," George Orwell also discusses metaphor (see pages 404–405). But Orwell's point of focus differs from that of Lakoff and Johnson. How so? Would Orwell agree or disagree with Lakoff and Johnson? In either case, why?

4. There is a sharp break between paragraphs 6 and 7. How might this break be seen as functional rather than merely disruptive?

5. The authors make use of both exemplification and contrast. Where do they do so (that is, in what paragraphs)? Why do they do so?

6. What kind of an ending does this essay have? Given the nature of the discussion, this kind is apt. Why?

Writing Assignments

1. If, as the authors state, "argument is *partially* [italics mine] structured . . . in terms of war" (paragraph 8), then the conceptual metaphor "argument is war" does not structure the concept entirely. Write a discrete paragraph or short paper considering the ways in which our underlying concept of argument does not entail the metaphor of war. Does our concept of argument involve some other metaphor(s) as well as that of war, or is it at some level of intellection purely literal, naked, without metaphorical clothing at all?

2. The following are some other possible conceptual metaphors:
   competitive sports as wars;
   time as money;
   intellect, understanding, ideas as light;
   happy as up and sad as down;
   flying (as in "I'm flying high");
   versus falling (as in "falling in love").
Take one of these conceptual metaphors or find one of your own and write an essay showing how your chosen metaphor governs everyday thought and action. You will need to find at least five or six verbal expressions of the metaphor and to exemplify fairly extensively. Use "Concepts We Live By" as a model with regard to exemplification.

✠ WE HAVE NO ✠ "RIGHT TO HAPPINESS"

C. S. Lewis

"AFTER ALL," SAID CLARE, "THEY HAD A RIGHT TO HAPPINESS." 1

We were discussing something that once happened in our 2 own neighborhood. Mr. A. had deserted Mrs. A. and got his divorce in order to marry Mrs. B., who had likewise got her divorce in order to marry Mr. A. And there was certainly no doubt that Mr. A. and Mrs. B. were very much in love with one another. If they continued to be in love, and if nothing went wrong with their health or their income, they might reasonably expect to be very happy.

It was equally clear that they were not happy with their old 3 partners. Mrs. B. had adored her husband at the outset. But then he got smashed up in the war. It was thought he had lost his virility, and it was known that he had lost his job. Life with him was no longer what Mrs. B. had bargained for. Poor Mrs. A., too. She had lost her looks — and all her liveliness. It might be true, as some said, that she consumed herself by bearing his children and nursing him through the long illness that overshadowed their earlier married life.

You mustn't, by the way, imagine that A. was the sort of 4 man who nonchalantly threw a wife away like the peel of an orange he'd sucked dry. Her suicide was a terrible shock to him. We all knew this, for he told us so himself. "But what could I do?" he said. "A man has a right to happiness. I had to take my one chance when it came."

I went away thinking about the concept of a "right to 5 happiness."

At first this sounds to me as odd as a right to good luck. For 6 I believe — whatever one school of moralists may say — that we depend for a very great deal of our happiness or misery on circumstances outside all human control. A right to happiness doesn't, for me, make much more sense than a right to be six feet tall, or to have a millionaire for your father, or to get good weather whenever you want to have a picnic.

I can understand a right as a freedom guaranteed me by the 7 laws of the society I live in. Thus, I have a right to travel along the public roads because society gives me that freedom; that's what we mean by calling the roads "public." I can also understand a right as a claim guaranteed me by the laws, and correlative to an obligation on someone else's part. If I have a right to receive £100 from you, this is another way of saying that you have a duty to pay me £100. If the laws allow Mr. A. to desert his wife and seduce his neighbor's wife, then, by definition, Mr. A. has a legal right to do so, and we need bring in no talk about "happiness."

But of course that was not what Clare meant. She meant 8 that he had not only a legal but a moral right to act as he did. In other words, Clare is — or would be if she thought it out — a classical moralist after the style of Thomas Aquinas, Grotius, Hooker, and Locke. She believes that behind the laws of the state there is a Natural Law.

I agree with her. I hold this conception to be basic to all 9 civilization. Without it, the actual laws of the state become an absolute, as in Hegel. They cannot be criticized because there is no norm against which they should be judged.

The ancestry of Clare's maxim, "They have a right to 10 happiness," is august. In words that are cherished by all civilized men, but especially by Americans, it has been laid down that one of the rights of man is a right to "the pursuit of happiness." And now we get to the real point.

What did the writers of that august declaration mean?   11

It is quite certain what they did not mean. They did not 12 mean that man was entitled to pursue happiness by any and every means — including, say, murder, rape, robbery, treason, and fraud. No society could be built on such a basis.

They meant "to pursue happiness by all lawful means"; that 13 is, by all means which the Law of Nature eternally sanctions and which the laws of the nation shall sanction.

Admittedly this seems at first to reduce their maxim to the 14
tautology that men (in pursuit of happiness) have a right to do
whatever they have a right to do. But tautologies, seen against
their proper historical context, are not always barren tautologies. The declaration is primarily a denial of the political
principles which long governed Europe: a challenge flung
down to the Austrian and Russian empires, to England before
the Reform Bills, to Bourbon France. It demands that whatever
means of pursuing happiness are lawful for any should be
lawful for all; that "man," not men of some particular caste,
class, status, or religion, should be free to use them. In a
century when this is being unsaid by nation after nation and
party after party, let us not call it a barren tautology.

But the question as to what means are "lawful" — what 15
methods of pursuing happiness are either morally permissible
by the Law of Nature or should be declared legally permissible
by the legislature of a particular nation — remains exactly
where it did. And on that question I disagree with Clare. I don't
think it is obvious that people have the unlimited "right to
happiness" which she suggests.

For one thing, I believe that Clare, when she says 16
"happiness," means simply and solely "sexual happiness."
Partly because women like Clare never use the word "happiness" in any other sense. But also because I never heard Clare
talk about the "right" to any other kind. She was rather leftist
in her politics, and would have been scandalized if anyone had
defended the actions of a ruthless man-eating tycoon on the
ground that his happiness consisted in making money and he
was pursuing his happiness. She was also a rabid teetotaler; I
never heard her excuse an alcoholic because he was happy
when he was drunk.

A good many of Clare's friends, and especially her female 17
friends, often felt — I've heard them say so — that their own
happiness would be perceptibly increased by boxing her ears. I
very much doubt if this would have brought her theory of a
right to happiness into play.

Clare, in fact, is doing what the whole western world seems 18
to me to have been doing for the last forty-odd years. When I
was a youngster, all the progressive people were saying, "Why
all this prudery? Let us treat sex just as we treat all our other
impulses." I was simple-minded enough to believe they meant
what they said. I have since discovered that they meant exactly
the opposite. They meant that sex was to be treated as no other
impulse in our nature has ever been treated by civilized people.
All the others, we admit, have to be bridled. Absolute
obedience to your instinct for self-preservation is what we call
cowardice; to your acquisitive impulse, avarice. Even sleep
must be resisted if you're a sentry. But every unkindness and
breach of faith seems to be condoned provided that the object
aimed at is "four bare legs in a bed."

It is like having a morality in which stealing fruit is 19
considered wrong — unless you steal nectarines.

And if you protest against this view you are usually met 20
with chatter about the legitimacy and beauty and sanctity of
"sex" and accused of harboring some Puritan prejudice against
it as something disreputable or shameful. I deny the charge.
Foam-born Venus . . . golden Aphrodite . . . Our Lady of
Cyprus . . . I never breathed a word against you. If I object to
boys who steal my nectarines, must I be supposed to disapprove
of nectarines in general? Or even of boys in general? It might,
you know, be stealing that I disapproved of.

The real situation is skillfully concealed by saying that the 21
question of Mr. A.'s "right" to desert his wife is one of "sexual
morality." Robbing an orchard is not an offense against some
special morality called "fruit morality." It is an offense against
honesty. Mr. A.'s action is an offense against good faith (to
solemn promises), against gratitude (toward one to whom he
was deeply indebted), and against common humanity.

Our sexual impulses are thus being put in a position of 22
preposterous privilege. The sexual motive is taken to condone
all sorts of behavior which, if it had any other end in view,
would be condemned as merciless, treacherous, and unjust.

Now though I see no good reason for giving sex this 23
privilege, I think I see a strong cause. It is this.

It is part of the nature of a strong erotic passion — as 24
distinct from a transient fit of appetite — that it makes more
towering promises than any other emotion. No doubt all our
desires make promises, but not so impressively. To be in love
involves the almost irresistible conviction that one will go on
being in love until one dies, and that possession of the beloved
will confer, not merely frequent ecstasies, but settled, fruitful,
deep-rooted, lifelong happiness. Hence *all* seems to be at stake.
If we miss this chance we shall have lived in vain. At the very
thought of such a doom we sink into fathomless depths of
self-pity.

Unfortunately these promises are found often to be quite 25
untrue. Every experienced adult knows this to be so as regards
all erotic passions (except the one he himself is feeling at the
moment). We discount the world-without-end pretensions of
our friends' amours easily enough. We know that such things
sometimes last — and sometimes don't. And when they do last,
this is not because they promised at the outset to do so. When
two people achieve lasting happiness, this is not solely because
they are great lovers but because they are also — I must put it
crudely — good people; controlled, loyal, fairminded, mutually
adaptable people.

If we establish a "right to (sexual) happiness" which 26
supersedes all the ordinary rules of behavior, we do so not
because of what our passion shows itself to be in experience but
because of what it professes to be while we are in the grip of it.
Hence, while the bad behavior is real and works miseries and
degradations, the happiness which was the object of the
behavior turns out again and again to be illusory. Everyone
(except Mr. A. and Mrs. B.) knows that Mr. A. in a year or so
may have the same reason for deserting his new wife as for
deserting his old. He will feel again that all is at stake. He will
see himself again as the great lover, and his pity for himself will
exclude all pity for the woman.

Two further points remain.   27

One is this. A society in which conjugal infidelity is   28
tolerated must always be in the long run a society adverse to
women. Women, whatever a few male songs and satires may
say to the contrary, are more naturally monogamous than men;
it is a biological necessity. Where promiscuity prevails, they
will therefore always be more often the victims than the
culprits. Also, domestic happiness is more necessary to them
than to us. And the quality by which they most easily hold a
man, their beauty, decreases every year after they have come to
maturity, but this does not happen to those qualities of
personality — women don't really care twopence about our
looks — by which we hold women. Thus in the ruthless war of
promiscuity women are at a double disadvantage. They play for
higher stakes and are also more likely to lose. I have no
sympathy with moralists who frown at the increasing crudity of
female provocativeness. These signs of desperate competition
fill me with pity.

Secondly, though the "right to happiness" is chiefly claimed   29
for the sexual impulse, it seems to me impossible that the matter
should stay there. The fatal principle, once allowed in that
department, must sooner or later seep through our whole lives.
We thus advance toward a state of society in which not only
each man but every impulse in each man claims *carte blanche.*
And then, though our technological skill may help us survive a
little longer, our civilization will have died at heart, and
will — one dare not even add "unfortunately" — be swept away.

[1947 — Great Britain]

Questions

1. What is the thesis of this essay? What advantages are afforded by its
   placement? What is the essay's main example used to back up the
   thesis?

2. What is the tone of paragraph 4? What is the tone of the essay as a
   whole? What kind of voice does it create? Does the voice here
   incline you to accept or reject Lewis's thesis?

3. This essay contains a number of one-sentence paragraphs. What function do they serve? Consider paragraphs 1 and 19 in particular — What effect do they have?

4. The story or narrative of Mr. and Mrs. A and Mr. and Mrs. B along with the references to Claire is an important element here. Why? What function does it have?

5. In paragraph 19, Lewis introduces a simile. In what way is the simile apt? Trace its extension in the next two paragraphs. How does the extension help Lewis make his point?

6. Lewis's last paragraph fans out to suggest wide reaches of meaning. What meaning? Why is this an effective way to end an essay?

Writing Assignments

1. In a paragraph or more, discuss the tone and consequent voice of the present essay and how its tone and voice help persuade the reader of the merit of the essay's thesis.

2. Are there any "natural" rights? Write an essay detailing what rights you believe people have according to nature and why these rights are indisputable. If you like, you might incorporate some dialogue in your essay, as Lewis does in his, and even an imagined scene or situation to help make concrete this completely abstract topic.

3. Choose any topic you like and write an essay on it in which you extend a metaphor, as Lewis does in paragraphs 19–21. Establish your metaphor firmly in the reader's mind (perhaps by using it in your title and/or thesis statement) and then, paying careful attention to your diction, bring it back to mind (that is, extend it) at key points. Remember the dual purpose for doing what you are asked here: to help structure your material and to give your ideas shape and solidity.

✤ BUFFALO ✤
Barry Lopez

IN JANUARY 1845, AFTER A WEEK OF COLD BUT BRILLIANTLY CLEAR   1
weather, it began to snow in southern Wyoming. Snow
accumulated on the flat in a dead calm to a depth of four feet in
only a few days. The day following the storm was breezy and
warm — chinook weather. A party of Cheyenne camped in a
river bottom spent the day tramping the snow down, felling
cottonwood trees for their horses, and securing game, in
response to a dream by one of them, a thirty-year-old man
called Blue Feather on the Side of His Head, that they would
be trapped by a sudden freeze.

That evening the temperature fell fifty degrees and an ice   2
crust as rigid, as easily broken, as sharp as window glass
formed over the snow. The crust held for weeks.

Access across the pane of ice to game and pasturage on the   3
clear, wind-blown slopes of the adjacent Medicine Bow
Mountains was impossible for both Indian hunters and a
buffalo herd trapped nearby. The buffalo, exhausted from
digging in the deep snow, went to their knees by the thousands,
their legs slashed by the razor ice, glistening red in the bright
sunlight. Their woolly carcasses lay scattered like black
boulders over the blinding white of the prairie, connected by a
thin crosshatching of bloody red trails.

Winds moaned for days in the thick fur of the dead and   4
dying buffalo, broken by the agonized bellows of the animals
themselves. Coyotes would not draw near. The Cheyenne
camped in the river bottom were terrified. As soon as they were
able to move they departed. No Cheyenne ever camped there
again.

The following summer the storm and the death of the herd   5
were depicted on a buffalo robe by one of the Cheyenne, a man
called Raven on His Back. Above the scene, in the sky, he drew
a white buffalo. The day they had left camp a man was

supposed to have seen a small herd of buffalo, fewer than twenty, leaving the plains and lumbering up the Medicine Bow River into the mountains. He said they were all white, and each seemed to him larger than any bull he had ever seen. There is no record of this man's name, but another Cheyenne in the party, a medicine man called Walks Toward the Two Rivers, carried the story of the surviving white buffalo to Crow and Teton Sioux in an effort to learn its meaning. In spite of the enmity among these tribes their leaders agreed that the incident was a common and disturbing augury. They gathered on the Box Elder River in southeastern Montana in the spring of 1846 to decipher its meaning. No one was able to plumb it, though many had fasted and bathed in preparation.

Buffalo were never seen again on the Laramie Plains after 1845, in spite of the richness of the grasses there and the size of the buffalo herds nearby in those days. The belief that there were still buffalo in the Medicine Bow Mountains, however, survivors of the storm, persisted for years, long after the disappearance of buffalo (some 60 million animals) from Wyoming and neighboring territories by the 1880s. 6

In the closing years of the nineteenth century, Arapaho and Shoshoni warriors who went into the Medicine Bow to dream say they did, indeed, see buffalo up there then. The animals lived among the barren rocks above timberline, far from any vegetation. They stood more than eight feet at the shoulder; their coats were white as winter ermine and their huge eyes were light blue. At the approach of men they would perch motionless on the granite boulders, like mountain goats. Since fogs are common in these high valleys in spring and summer it was impossible, they say, to tell how many buffalo there were. 7

In May 1887 a Shoshoni called Long Otter came on two of these buffalo in the Snowy Range. As he watched they watched him. They began raising and lowering their hooves, started drumming softly on the rocks. They began singing a death song, way back in the throat like the sound of wind 8 moaning in a canyon. The man, Long Otter, later lost his mind and was killed in a buckboard accident the following year. As far as I know this is the last report of living buffalo in the Medicine Bow.

It is curious to me that in view of the value of the hides no 9 white man ever tried to find and kill one of these buffalo. But that is the case. No detail of the terrible storm of that winter, or of the presence of a herd of enormous white buffalo in the Medicine Bow, has ever been found among the papers of whites who lived in the area or who might have passed through in the years following.

It should be noted, however, by way of verification, that a 10 geology student from Illinois called Fritiof Fryxell came upon two buffalo skeletons in the Snowy Range in the summer of 1925. Thinking these barren heights an extraordinary elevation at which to find buffalo, he carefully marked the location on a topographic map. He measured the largest of the skeletons, found the size staggering, and later wrote up the incident in the May 1926 issue of the *Journal of Mammalogy*.

In 1955, a related incident came to light. In the fall of 1911, 11 at the request of the Colorado Mountain Club, a party of Arapaho Indians were brought into the Rocky Mountains in the northern part of the state to relate to white residents the history of the area prior to 1859. The settlers were concerned that during the years when the white man was moving into the area, and the Indian was being extirpated, a conflict in historical records arose such that the white record was incomplete and possibly in error.

The Arapaho were at first reluctant to speak; they made up 12 stories of the sort they believed the whites would like to hear. But the interest and persistence of the white listeners made an impression upon them and they began to tell what had really happened.

Among the incidents the Arapaho revealed was that in the 13 winter of 1845 (when news of white settlers coming in covered wagons first reached them) there was a terrible storm. A herd of buffalo wintering in Brainard Valley (called then Bear in the Hole Valley) began singing a death song. At first it was barely audible, and it was believed the wind was making the sound until it got louder and more distinct. As the snow got deeper the buffalo left the valley and began to climb into the mountains. For four days they climbed, still singing the moaning death song, followed by Arapaho warriors, until they reached the top of the mountain. This was the highest place but it had no name. Now it is called Thatchtop Mountain.

14 During the time the buffalo climbed they did not stop singing. They turned red all over; their eyes became smooth white. The singing became louder. It sounded like thunder that would not stop. Everyone who heard it, even people four or five days' journey away, was terrified.

15 At the top of the mountain the buffalo stopped singing. They stood motionless in the snow, the wind blowing clouds around them. The Arapaho men who had followed had not eaten for four days. One, wandering into the clouds with his hands outstretched and a rawhide string connecting him to the others, grabbed hold of one of the buffalo and killed it. The remaining buffalo disappeared into the clouds; the death song began again, very softly, and remained behind them. The wind was like the singing of the buffalo. When the clouds cleared the men went down the mountain.

16 The white people at the 1911 meeting said they did not understand the purpose of telling such a story. The Arapaho said this was the first time the buffalo tried to show them how to climb out through the sky.

17 The notes of this meeting in 1911 have been lost, but what happened there remained clear in the mind of the son of one of the Indians who was present. It was brought to my attention by accident one evening in the library of the university where I teach. I was reading an article on the introduction of fallow deer in Nebraska in the August 1955 issue of the *Journal of Mammalogy* when this man, who was apparently just walking by, stopped and, pointing at the opposite page, said, "This is

not what this is about." The article he indicated was called "An Altitudinal Record for Bison in Northern Colorado." He spoke briefly of it, as if to himself, and then departed.

Excited by this encounter I began to research the incident. 18 I have been able to verify what I have written here. In view of the similarity between the events in the Medicine Bow and those in Colorado, I suspect that there were others in the winter of 1845 who began, as the Arapaho believe, trying to get away from what was coming, and that subsequent attention to this phenomenon is of some importance.

I recently slept among weathered cottonwoods on the 19 Laramie Plains in the vicinity of the Medicine Bow Mountains. I awoke in the morning to find my legs broken.

[1981 — U.S.A.]

Questions

1. Combining fiction and nonfiction, scholarly research and imagination, "Buffalo" is both a story and an essay. In what way is it a story? In what way is it an essay?

2. The narrator here should be taken as fictional and not as Lopez himself. Considering the narrator's diction, the way he approaches things, and his general cast of mind, characterize him. Why this narrator? What is his function? What irony arises out of the narrator's approach to the Indian stories and the truth they reveal?

3. History is history and myth is myth. But in "Buffalo" they merge. What is the point of this blurring of distinction between fact and fiction?

4. "Buffalo" implicitly involves a criticism of our world view, that of the modern West. How so? What is that criticism? What is Lopez's theme? In light of this theme, what is the meaning of the broken legs referred to in the last paragraph?

Writing Assignments

1. In a few paragraphs, contrast the Indian view of animals as portrayed in "Buffalo" with ours, especially with regard to our pets. Which view is more wholesome, finally?

2. We cannot be sure what is fact and what fiction in "Buffalo." Does it matter? Write a paper defending Lopez's blurring of the two and

showing how it serves his purposes or, on some rational ground, condemning the mixture and showing why it fails to persuade the reader. In either case, you will need to articulate the theme of "Buffalo" and consider the meaning of the narrator's broken legs mentioned at the end.

———————✣ A ROSE-COLORED MAP ✣———————

Ben Marsh

COUNTRY MUSIC PRESENTS TWO IMAGES OF LIFE — LIFE AS IT SHOULD   1
be, and life as it should not be. The conflict between these two themes is the force that drives country music; it is this dialectic of right and wrong that makes country music exciting to the millions who listen to it. Perhaps the melodies are formulaic, but it is the lyrics that sell the songs, the descriptions of everyday people facing problems and making right or wrong decisions about them. The right decision is the one that lets people be honest, faithful, moral, and therefore happy.

Right and wrong in country music are not distributed   2
randomly across the American landscape. Goodness is concentrated in the South and in the countryside, while badness is far more common in cities and in the North. If the lyrics of country songs were all someone knew about America, he would think that everything of value was in the rural South. Country music contains a clear, if incidental, regional geography of the South, describing its terrain, its climate, its agriculture, and its natural resources. Everybody in country songs grew up on a farm in the South, where their parents still live. The normal city in country music is Nashville, the normal river is the Mississippi, the normal beer is Lone Star, the normal crop is cotton, the normal dog is a hound, and the normal food is black-eyed peas. And if the directions given in various songs are treated like a road map, that map says it is "up" to Chicago and Cincinnati, "down" to New Orleans and Georgia, "over" or "across" to the Carolinas, and "out" to Texas or California, while it is "back"

to Tennessee or Kentucky, "back" to the mountains, and "back" to the farm. The center of country music's map of America is clearly the rural South, especially the mountain states.

The South, as it is presented in country music, is the best 3 possible place to live, the standard for comparing all other places, especially the Northern city. The North, in general, is a cold, gray, hazy area at the periphery of country music's map, as far from home as one can get. Listen to one song or a hundred, the pattern is the same. If a song is about someone being unfaithful, drunken, jobless, or lonely, it will be in a city, probably in the North. If a song is about family, security, childhood, love, or other pleasant things, it will be in the South, probably on a farm. Texas usually appears as a land of heroic men and romantic women. Canada and Alaska show up as our new frontiers, important places for individualists. And California is an ambiguous place with both Southern and Northern characteristics, perhaps a reflection of the conflict between the agricultural and urban parts of that state.

There are obvious advantages for the writers of allegorical 4 tales like country music's to have a conventionalized geography to reinforce the message. But why does country music use *this* image of America? Why is country music so pleased with the South and so upset with the North? The answer to this question lies not in the actual geography of the United States, but in how country music's audience perceives the geography of the United States. It is not a question of what America is, but of what America means to these people. As a result, the question has to do with far more than just a style of singing, it has to do with the attitudes of the millions of Americans who listen to country music — attitudes about regional differences in American society, about the role of the media as part of the American power structure, and about the value of progress in general.

One attractive explanation of the geography *in* country 5 music is that it is a reflection of the geography *of* country music. This argument holds that country music views the world from the South because most of the performers, or most of the audience, live in the South. However, this is untrue. Country music is not exclusively Southern in any sense but its history and its perspective. True, most of the older performers came from the South, but many were from Northern states like Illinois and Pennsylvania, or even from Canada. And modern country music stars are from all over the English-speaking world.

Country music's audience is even less Southern than its 6 performers. The music is indisputably popular in the South, but the evidence — from the distribution of country music radio stations, from performers' itineraries, and from the regional circulation of fan magazines — indicates that country music has more listeners outside the South than in it. Some suggest that this is because a large part of country music's audience is homesick expatriate Southerners living in Northern cities, but the data does not support this. For example, country music is not, as one would expect, especially popular in industrial cities such as Detroit, which traditionally has been a pole of South-North migration.

Country music's Southern perspective on the world must 7 be treated as symbolism, not reporting. Perhaps country music once glorified the South because it was parochial music about local places, but it is now popular nearly everywhere. In the United States country music is the typical music on stage at small-town high schools and county fairs all across America, and on the radio in machine shops and beauty parlors, on truckers' tape decks, and on jukeboxes in ten thousand little bars.

To understand how the vision of America in country music 8 is appropriate to this audience, it is necessary to look carefully at how country music functions in American culture. Country music comes to its audience through the media and must be viewed in that context. Country music's morality plays appear on records, in movies, in magazines, on syndicated television shows, and especially over the radio. The history of early country music is inseparable from the history of early radio, and there are now over 1,700 radio stations in the U.S. that play country music every day. Country music is a radio ministry, and the gospel it preaches — that we should all be moral, righteous, and Southern — makes sense when it is seen in this context.

Country music's view of America must be compared with 9 another view, as distinctive as country music's but offering a different perspective — the image projected by network television, the wire services, and mass-circulation magazines. In these media virtually all the decisions about content are made in New York, Washington, Chicago, and Los Angeles. Accordingly, the brightest, most exciting, most memorable spots on these, our most frequently reinforced pictures of our land, are the big cities. Compared to them, the South and the rest of the country seem almost featureless, perhaps a little sinister, or maybe just boring.

Country music's image of America contradicts that of the 10 "mainstream" American media — and that is its appeal. The South is presented as a virtuous place to country music fans all over America not for what it is, but for what it is not. Unlike the North, the seat of the media, the South is not responsible for the shape we are in. According to the media's own reporting, the South has had nothing to do with inflation, taxes, shortages, abuses of federal power, Supreme Court rulings, and so forth. The same innocence of the sins of power that let Jimmy Carter go from ex-governor of Georgia to President in twenty-two months lets country music paint the South as a haven from the sins of the nation.

The South has escaped bad press mostly because it is 11 underreported, and this is why country music has been free to impose whatever meaning it chooses on the South. When the South has appeared in the national media, it has been protrayed as backward, ignorant, and reactionary. But country music can transform these attributes into virtues: backward easily becomes rustic, ignorant becomes simple and uncomplicated, and reactionary becomes old-fashioned.

The ability to see a region which is nearly ignored in the 12 media as the best part of America, and to see the centers of media power as the worst part, reflects deep displeasure by millions of Americans with the content of those media. Country music's gloomy image of the North is a reflection of what the audience feels about what is happening to America in general. The South, in contrast, is a picture of how the nation would be if it had not gone astray.

What country music's audience seeks to escape by vicarious 13 life in the rural South is, in a word, progress. Country music's South is above all old-fashioned. Life in the South means old-fashioned family, old-fashioned religion, old-fashioned values. Life in the South is life in the past, a laundered past without smallpox and without lynchings. This is what country music's rural Southern perspective is all about — the South has none of the problems of the North, and the country has none of the problems of the city, because the past has none of the problems of the present. Country music's South provides escape from modern America.

It seems extreme to suggest that millions of Americans feel 14 the need to escape from the land they live in, yet that is the clear message of country music's picture of the world. Escape is certainly a common enough theme in the rest of country music. Drinking, divorce, traveling, prison, and death can all be considered kinds of escape, and all are quite common in country music. To Freud the countryside itself symbolized escape. The rural South is just another kind of escape; it is a place where one avoids the problems of the modern world and lives the simple, friendly, old-fashioned country life.

Who are the people who feel they need country music's exit 15 and haven from the world we all live in? It is possible to construct a picture of an average country music listener from various kinds of television, radio, and magazine marketing data. The picture of this average person is entirely consonant with his expressed desire to avoid the wrongs of modern American life. Quite simply, the person who needs to escape into the mythically old-fashioned South is the one who is losing something as America progresses. It is not the rural-urban migrant, it is not the second- or third-generation European-

American, it is not the Black. All these people have gained as America industrializes, urbanizes, progresses. None of them fear the future and cherish the past. None of them could be as nostalgic as the country music fan for a South that never was.

Country music is for the small-town American. Country 16 music and its image of America pleases those millions of quiet people in traditional, socially conservative communities, who daily face erosion of the values that make their lives meaningful. America is moving from the nineteenth century into mass society not in a smooth glide, but in a series of painful little shocks, and the person most likely to appreciate country music is the person for whom those shocks hurt most. Country music's function is to replenish the system of values that we seem to be losing.

The image of America in country music may seem extreme 17 and one-sided, but it is in answer to what its audience perceives as an extreme and one-sided world. It is important to these threatened Americans everywhere to know that there is still a region in this land where life is lived as they know it should be, and where there is relief from the changes they fear. The fiction of the rural South in country music is that place.

By glorifying the South, country music departs radically 18 from nearly every other popular geography of the United States. But country music's message that America is taking drastically wrong directions is radical, too. Country music seems to have almost Marxian overtones in its treatment of the injuries of class. Poverty is ennobling, for example, while wealth imprisons its owners. And some recent songs have been surprisingly militant in their calls for greater social justice through rejection of illegitimate authority and through greater economic equity. Johnny Cash has produced several successful songs in the past few years about men's attempt to get more control on their jobs. In one an auto worker steals a Cadillac "one piece at a time" in his lunchbox; in another a hungry farmworker steals a strawberry cake from a fancy hotel, after spending weeks picking strawberries; and in a third song a machinist plots that on the day he retires he will punch out his boss as he leaves. The songs are meant to be ironic, yet they are portrayals of what would be acts of revolution if they occurred en masse. In content and even in style, these songs are reminiscent of Woody Guthrie's songs during the Depression.

Partly because of this radicalness, an odd convergence has 19 taken place between country music and the music descended from the folk/protest tradition of the Sixties, sometimes called "folk-rock." Both are displeased with modern urban America and each uses instrumentation and arrangements derived from their common Appalachian folk origins. The result is that the themes and the performances in the two genres are similar enough that performers like Kris Kristofferson or Commander Cody, who are virtually antithetical in politics, religion, and life-style to the average country fan, can compete in the same market with some performers so puritanical that they will not appear in clubs where liquor is served.

Country music shares its radically positive image of the 20 South with two other recent national movements. Neither the election of Jimmy Carter to the Presidency, nor those southward migrations of population, industry, and political power to the so-called Sun Belt, would have been possible in the face of strong anti-Southern sentiment. There are obvious differences between the motivations that determine how people vote, where they move to, and what kind of music they listen to, but perhaps all these events are best thought of as manifestations of a single change in attitude. In years to come we can only expect to see more reaction to the old alignment of power in America, power expressed through the government and the major media.

America was settled by immigrants, and we have never 21 stopped moving. From Plymouth Rock to the Cumberland Gap to the Oregon Trail, if a man did not like life where he was, he could move down the road and it would be different. But we have run out of frontiers. Today, if a new place is needed, an old place must be redefined. Country music is showing us this process in action, as a major American region acquires a new image. However, allegiance to this new South takes place at the expense of allegiance to the country as a whole. The irony of country music's audience considering itself to be an especially patriotic group is that it is loyal to a mythical earlier America as symbolized by the sunny, old-fashioned South of country music, not to America as it now exists.

[1977 — U.S.A.]

Questions

1. Marsh's title is symbolic. What does it symbolize with respect to the essay it heads?
2. What is the thesis of this essay and where is it stated? Though not generally the best way of placing a thesis, the placement here is apt because of the way the thesis is stated. How so?
3. How are the characteristics of country music that Marsh considers related to his thesis? Though many examples are provided, this essay is more general than specific. Why?
4. What is the primary means of support here? Paragraph 4 ends with three items: "attitudes about regional differences. . ., about the role of the media. . ., and about the value of progress." Paragraphs 5 – 17 concern these three items in this order. What, then, is the primary structural mode of the essay? Why is the last item taken up last? What paragraph clusters concern each of the three? (Specify by paragraph numbers.)
5. This essay points to a good many ironies. What, for instance? What is the essay's tone? How does irony affect tone here?
6. Marsh restates his thesis in the last paragraph. How so? What kind of an ending does the essay have? Is its ending effective?

Writing Assignments

1. a) Write a paragraph illustrating from your own knowledge of country music Marsh's conclusion that it is old-fashioned in its values and anti-progress, or contradicting Marsh and suggesting that country music is an integral aspect of America on the move.

   b) In a separate paragraph, state your response to this essay and tell why you respond to it as you do.

2. Write a short paper in which, somewhere after the beginning, you suggest that you will go on to enumerate three points and then go on to do so.

3. In an essay, analyze the cultural attitudes that underlie pop music and broadway musicals before 1960, rock music from 1955–1975, or rock music today. In doing so, you may wish to compare and/or contrast two or all three of these categories. Exemplify when appropriate and be sure to fill in necessary (with regard to the audience you project) background information and definitions.

✤ BEHIND THE ✤ FORMALDEHYDE CURTAIN
Jessica Mitford

THE DRAMA BEGINS TO UNFOLD WITH THE ARRIVAL OF THE CORPSE AT   1
the mortuary.

Alas, poor Yorick! How surprised he would be to see how   2
his counterpart of today is whisked off to a funeral parlor and is in short order sprayed, sliced, pierced, pickled, trussed, trimmed, creamed, waxed, painted, rouged, and neatly dressed — transformed from a common corpse into a Beautiful Memory Picture. This process is known in the trade as embalming and restorative art, and is so universally employed in the United States and Canada that the funeral director does it routinely, without consulting corpse or kin. He regards as eccentric those few who are hardy enough to suggest that it might be dispensed with. Yet no law requires embalming, no religious doctrine commends it, nor is it dictated by considerations of health, sanitation, or even of personal daintiness. In no part of the world but in Northern America is it widely used. The purpose of embalming is to make the corpse presentable for viewing in a suitably costly container; and here too the funeral director routinely, without first consulting the family, prepares the body for public display.

Is all this legal? The processes to which a dead body may be 3
subjected are after all to some extent circumscribed by law. In
most states, for instance, the signature of next of kin must be
obtained before an autopsy may be performed, before the
deceased may be cremated, before the body may be turned over
to a medical school for research purposes; or such provision
must be made in the decedent's will. In the case of embalming,
no such permission is required nor is it ever sought. A textbook,
The Principles and Practices of Embalming, comments on this:
"There is some question regarding the legality of much that is
done within the preparation room." The author points out that
it would be most unusual for a responsible member of a
bereaved family to instruct the mortician, in so many words, to
"embalm" the body of a deceased relative. The very term
"embalming" is so seldom used that the mortician must rely
upon custom in the matter. The author concludes that unless
the family specifies otherwise, the act of entrusting the body to
the care of a funeral establishment carries with it an implied
permission to go ahead and embalm.

Embalming is indeed a most extraordinary procedure, and 4
one must wonder at the docility of Americans who each year
pay hundreds of millions of dollars for its perpetuation,
blissfully ignorant of what it is all about, what is done, how it
is done. Not one in ten thousand has any idea of what actually
takes place. Books on the subject are extremely hard to come
by. They are not to be found in most libraries or bookshops.

In an era when huge television audiences watch surgical 5
operations in the comfort of their living rooms, when, thanks to
the animated cartoon, the geography of the digestive system has
become familiar territory even to the nursery school set, in a
land where the satisfaction of curiosity about almost all matters
is a national pastime, the secrecy surrounding embalming can,
surely, hardly be attributed to the inherent gruesomeness of the
subject. Custom in this regard has within this century suffered
a complete reversal. In the early days of American embalming,
when it was performed in the home of the deceased, it was
almost mandatory for some relative to stay by the embalmer's

side and witness the procedure. Today, family members who might wish to be in attendance would certainly be dissuaded by the funeral director. All others, except apprentices, are excluded by law from the preparation room.

A close look at what does actually take place may explain in large measure the undertaker's intractable reticence concerning a procedure that has become his major *raison d' être*. Is it possible he fears that public information about embalming might lead patrons to wonder if they really want this service? If the funeral men are loath to discuss the subject outside the trade, the reader may, understandably, be equally loath to go on reading at this point. For those who have the stomach for it, let us part the formaldehyde curtain. . . . 6

The body is first laid out in the undertaker's morgue — or rather, Mr. Jones is reposing in the preparation room — to be readied to bid the world farewell. 7

The preparation room in any of the better funeral establishments has the tiled and sterile look of a surgery, and indeed the embalmer-restorative artist who does his chores there is beginning to adopt the term "dermasurgeon" (appropriately corrupted by some mortician-writers as "demi-surgeon") to describe his calling. His equipment, consisting of scalpels, scissors, augers, forceps, clamps, needles, pumps, tubes, bowls, and basins, is crudely imitative of the surgeon's, as is his technique, acquired in a nine- or twelve-month post-high-school course in an embalming school. He is supplied by an advanced chemical industry with a bewildering array of fluids, sprays, pastes, oils, powders, creams, to fix or soften tissue, shrink or distend it as needed, dry it here, restore the moisture there. There are cosmetics, waxes, and paints to fill and cover features, even plaster of Paris to replace entire limbs. There are ingenious aids to prop and stabilize the cadaver: a Vari-Pose Head Rest, the Edwards Arm and Hand Positioner, the Repose Block (to support the shoulders during the embalming), and the Throop Foot Positioner, which resembles an old-fashioned stocks. 8

Mr. John H. Eckels, president of the Eckels College of 9
Mortuary Science, thus describes the first part of the embalming procedure: "In the hands of a skilled practitioner, this work
may be done in a comparatively short time and without
mutilating the body other than by slight incision — so slight that
it scarcely would cause serious inconvenience if made upon a
living person. It is necessary to remove the blood, and doing
this not only helps in the disinfecting, but removes the principal
cause of disfigurements due to discoloration."

Another textbook discusses the all-important time element: 10
"The earlier this is done, the better, for every hour that elapses
between death and embalming will add to the problems and
complications encountered. . . ." Just how soon should one
get going on the embalming? The author tells us, "On the basis
of such scanty information made available to this profession
through its rudimentary and haphazard system of technical
research, we must conclude that the best results are to be
obtained if the subject is embalmed before life is completely
extinct — that is, before cellular death has occurred. In the
average case, this would mean within an hour after somatic
death." For those who feel that there is something a little
rudimentary, not to say haphazard, about this advice, a
comforting thought is offered by another writer. Speaking of
fears entertained in early days of premature burial, he points
out, "One of the effects of embalming by chemical injection,
however, has been to dispel fears of live burial." How true;
once the blood is removed, chances of live burial are indeed
remote.

To return to Mr. Jones, the blood is drained out through 11
the veins and replaced by embalming fluid pumped in through
the arteries. As noted in *The Principles and Practices of Embalming*,
"every operator has a favorite injection and drainage point — a
fact which becomes a handicap only if he fails or refuses to
forsake his favorites when conditions demand it." Typical
favorites are the carotid artery, femoral artery, jugular vein,
subclavian vein. There are various choices of embalming fluid.

If Flextone is used, it will produce a "mild, flexible rigidity. The skin retains a velvety softness, the tissues are rubbery and pliable. Ideal for women and children." It may be blended with B. and G. Products Company's Lyf-Lyk tint, which is guaranteed to reproduce "nature's own skin texture . . . the velvety appearance of living tissue." Suntone comes in three separate tints: Suntan; Special Cosmetic Tint, a pink shade "especially indicated for female subjects"; and Regular Cosmetic Tint, moderately pink.

About three to six gallons of a dyed and perfumed solution 12
of formaldehyde, glycerin, borax, phenol, alcohol, and water is soon circulating through Mr. Jones, whose mouth has been sewn together with a "needle directed upward between the upper lip and gum and brought out through the left nostril," with the corners raised slightly "for a more pleasant expression." If he should be bucktoothed, his teeth are cleaned with Bon Ami and coated with colorless nail polish. His eyes, meanwhile, are closed with flesh-tinted eye caps and eye cement.

The next step is to have at Mr. Jones with a thing called a 13
trocar. This is a long, hollow needle attached to a tube. It is jabbed into the abdomen, poked around the entrails and chest cavity, the contents of which are pumped out and replaced with "cavity fluid." This done, and the hole in the abdomen sewn up, Mr. Jones's face is heavily creamed (to protect the skin from burns which may be caused by leakage of the chemicals), and he is covered with a sheet and left unmolested for a while. But not for long — there is more, much more, in store for him. He has been embalmed, but not yet restored, and the best time to start the restorative work is eight to ten hours after embalming, when the tissues have become firm and dry.

The object of all this attention to the corpse, it must be 14
remembered, is to make it presentable for viewing in an attitude of healthy repose. "Our customs require the presentation of our dead in the semblance of normality . . . unmarred by the ravages of illness, disease, or mutilation," says Mr. J. Sheridan

Mayer in his *Restorative Art.* This is rather a large order since few people die in the full bloom of health, unravaged by illness and unmarked by some disfigurement. The funeral industry is equal to the challenge: "In some cases the gruesome appearance of a mutilated or disease-ridden subject may be quite discouraging. The task of restoration may seem impossible and shake the confidence of the embalmer. This is the time for intestinal fortitude and determination. Once the formative work is begun and affected tissues are cleaned or removed, all doubts of success vanish. It is surprising and gratifying to discover the results which may be obtained."

The embalmer, having allowed an appropriate interval to 15 elapse, returns to the attack, but now he brings into play the skill and equipment of sculptor and cosmetician. Is a hand missing? Casting one in plaster of Paris is a simple matter. "For replacement purposes, only a cast of the back of the hand is necessary; this is within the ability of the average operator and is quite adequate." If a lip or two, a nose, or an ear should be missing, the embalmer has at hand a variety of restorative waxes with which to model replacements. Pores and skin texture are simulated by stippling with a little brush, and over this cosmetics are laid on. Head off? Decapitation cases are rather routinely handled. Ragged edges are trimmed, and head joined to torso with a series of splints, wires, and sutures. It is a good idea to have a little something at the neck — a scarf or a high collar — when time for viewing comes. Swollen mouth? Cut out tissue as needed from inside the lips. If too much is removed, the surface contour can easily be restored by padding with cotton. Swollen necks and cheeks are reduced by removing tissue through vertical incisions made down each side of the neck. "When the deceased is casketed, the pillow will hide the suture incisions . . . as an extra precaution against leakage, the suture may be painted with liquid sealer."

The opposite condition is more likely to present itself 16 — that of emaciation. His hypodermic syringe now loaded with massage cream, the embalmer seeks out and fills the hollowed and sunken areas by injection. In this procedure the backs of the hands and fingers and the under-chin area should not be neglected.

Positioning the lips is a problem that recurrently challenges 17 the ingenuity of the embalmer. Closed too tightly, they tend to give a stern, even disapproving expression. Ideally, embalmers feel, the lips should give the impression of being ever so slightly parted, the upper lip protruding slightly for a more youthful appearance. This takes some engineering, however, as the lips tend to drift apart. Lip drift can sometimes be remedied by pushing one or two straight pins through the inner margin of the lower lip and then inserting them between the two front upper teeth. If Mr. Jones happens to have no teeth, the pins can just as easily be anchored in his Armstrong Face Former and Denture Replacer. Another method to maintain lip closure is to dislocate the lower jaw, which is then held in its new position by a wire run through holes which have been drilled through the upper and lower jaws at the midline. As the French are fond of saying, *il faut souffrir pour être belle.*[1]

If Mr. Jones has died of jaundice, the embalming fluid will 18 very likely turn him green. Does this deter the embalmer? Not if he has intestinal fortitude. Masking pastes and cosmetics are heavily laid on, burial garments and casket interiors are color-correlated with particular care, and Jones is displayed beneath rose-colored lights. Friends will say "How *well* he looks." Death by carbon monoxide, on the other hand, can be rather a good thing from the embalmer's viewpoint: "One advantage is the fact that this type of discoloration is an exaggerated form of a natural pink coloration." This is nice because the healthy glow is already present and needs but little attention.

The patching and filling completed, Mr. Jones is now 19 shaved, washed, and dressed. Cream-based cosmetic, available in pink, flesh, suntan, brunette, and blond, is applied to his

---

[1] *il faut souffrir pour être belle:* It is necessary to suffer to be beautiful.

hands and face, his hair is shampooed and combed (and, in the case of Mrs. Jones, set), his hands manicured. For the horny-handed son of toil special care must be taken; cream should be applied to remove ingrained grime, and the nails cleaned. "If he were not in the habit of having them manicured in life, trimming and shaping is advised for better appearance — never questioned by kin."

Jones is now ready for casketing (this is the present 20 participle of the verb "to casket"). In this operation his right shoulder should be depressed slightly "to turn the body a bit to the right and soften the appearance of lying flat on the back." Positioning the hands is a matter of importance, and special rubber positioning blocks may be used. The hands should be cupped slightly for a more lifelike, relaxed appearance. Proper placement of the body requires a delicate sense of balance. It should lie as high as possible in the casket, yet not so high that the lid, when lowered, will hit the nose. On the other hand, we are cautioned, placing the body too low "creates the impression that the body is in a box."

Jones is next wheeled into the appointed slumber room 21 where a few last touches may be added — his favorite pipe placed in his hand or, if he was a great reader, a book propped into position. (In the case of little Master Jones a Teddy bear may be clutched.) Here he will hold open house for a few days, visiting hours 10 A.M. to 9 P.M.

All now being in readiness, the funeral director calls a staff 22 conference to make sure that each assistant knows his precise duties. Mr. Wilber Kriege writes: "This makes your staff feel that they are a part of the team, with a definite assignment that must be properly carried out if the whole plan is to succeed. You never heard of a football coach who failed to talk to his entire team before they go on the field. They have drilled on the plays they are to execute for hours and days, and yet the successful coach knows the importance of making even the bench-warming third-string substitute feel that he is important if the game is to be won." The winning of *this* game is predicated upon glass-smooth handling of the logistics. The funeral director has notified the pallbearers whose names were furnished by the family, has arranged for the presence of clergyman, organist, and soloist, has provided transportation for everybody, has organized and listed the flowers sent by friends. In *Psychology of Funeral Service* Mr. Edward A. Martin points out: "He may not always do as much as the family thinks he is doing, but it is his helpful guidance that they appreciate in knowing they are proceeding as they should. . . . The important thing is how well his services can be used to make the family believe they are giving unlimited expression to their own sentiment."

The religious service may be held in a church or in the 23 chapel of the funeral home; the funeral director vastly prefers the latter arrangement, for not only is it more convenient for him but it affords him the opportunity to show off his beautiful facilities to the gathered mourners. After the clergyman has had his say, the mourners queue up to file past the casket for a last look at the deceased. The family is *never* asked whether they want an open-casket ceremony; in the absence of their instruction to the contrary, this is taken for granted. Consequently well over 90 per cent of all American funerals feature the open casket — a custom unknown in other parts of the world. Foreigners are astonished by it. An English woman living in San Francisco described her reaction in a letter to the writer:

> I myself have attended only one funeral here — that of an elderly fellow worker of mine. After the service I could not understand why everyone was walking towards the coffin (sorry, I mean casket), but thought I had better follow the crowd. It shook me rigid to get there and find the casket open and poor old Oscar lying there in his brown tweed suit, wearing a suntan makeup and just the wrong shade of lipstick. If I had not been extremely fond of the old boy, I have a horrible feeling that I might have giggled. Then and there I decided that I could never face another American funeral — even dead.

The casket (which has been resting throughout the service 24
on a Classic Beauty Ultra Metal Casket Bier) is now
transferred by a hydraulically operated device called Porto-Lift
to a balloon-tired, Glide Easy casket carriage which will wheel
it to yet another conveyance, the Cadillac Funeral Coach. This
may be lavender, cream, light green — anything but black.
Interiors, of course, are color-correlated, "for the man who
cannot stop short of perfection."

At graveside, the casket is lowered into the earth. This 25
office, once the prerogative of friends of the deceased, is now
performed by a patented mechanical lowering device. A
"Lifetime Green" artificial grass mat is at the ready to conceal
the sere earth, and overhead, to conceal the sky, is a portable
Steril Chapel Tent ("resists the intense heat and humidity of
summer and the terrific storms of winter . . . available in Silver
Grey, Rose, or Evergreen"). Now is the time for the ritual
scattering of earth over the coffin, as the solemn words "earth
to earth, ashes to ashes, dust to dust" are pronounced by the
officiating cleric. This can today be accomplished "with a mere
flick of the wrist with the Gordon Leak-Proof Earth Dispenser.
No grasping of a handful of dirt, no soiled fingers. Simple,
dignified, beautiful, reverent! The modern way!" The Gordon
Earth Dispenser (at $5) is of nickel-plated brass construction.
It is not only "attractive to the eye and long wearing"; it is also
"one of the 'tools' for building better public relations" if
presented as "an appropriate non-commercial gift" to the
clergyman. It is shaped something like a saltshaker.

Untouched by human hand, the coffin and the earth are 26
now united.

It is in the function of directing the participants through 27
this maze of gadgetry that the funeral director has assigned to
himself his relatively new role of "grief therapist." He has
relieved the family of every detail, he has revamped the corpse
to look like a living doll, he has arranged for it to nap for a few
days in a slumber room, he has put on a well-oiled performance
in which the concept of *death* has played no part whatsoever

— unless it was inconsiderately mentioned by the clergyman who conducted the religious service. He has done everything in his power to make the funeral a real pleasure for everybody concerned. He and his team have given their all to score an upset victory over death.

[1963 — U.S.A.]

Questions

1. What is Mitford's theme? Why does she go into such grisly detail? Why does she switch from "corpse" and "body" to "Mr. Jones" in paragraph 7? What is her purpose overall?

2. How do we come to know what the theme of this essay is? With regard to how we come to know its theme, comment on the essay's tone and how it is established.

3. However ghastly the details, there is much that is humorous here. What, for instance? What ends does the humor serve?

4. How do the various quotations from journals and textbooks serve Mitford's purpose? What, in this regard, of the letter quoted in paragraph 23?

5. What is the effect of paragraphs 1 and 26? What structural value do these paragraphs have?

6. Mitford divides the process she analyzes (everything that happens from the time a body reaches a funeral home to graveside rites) into five stages. What are they? (Name each stage and give the inclusive paragraph numbers of each.) What is Mitford's primary mode of organization with respect to these stages? Specify the transitions used between each major block of paragraphs, each block concerning one stage.

7. What kind of ending does Mitford provide? Why is this kind appropriate? To what does the metaphor of the last sentence allude? What does the metaphor imply about American culture and the American public generally?

Writing Assignments

1. Does the American funeral establishment deserve Mitford's treatment of it? Write a paragraph defending morticians or Mitford, depending on your point of view.

2. How does this essay affect you? Write a paragraph or more stating your response and considering why the essay affects you thus.

3. With the help of your librarian, look into the new technique of "quick-freezing" corpses. Then write a paper describing the method step by step (using Mitford as a model), concluding with the long-range result looked for. What is your attitude about this new method of treating the dead? Try to convey your attitude by way of your tone instead of direct statement.

4. Do some research into the burial procedures of other cultures and other times. Then write an essay comparing and contrasting two or three of these other procedures with ours at present. What light does your research shed on our practices? What does our way of treating the dead and death itself reveal about our culture generally?

✚ DRINKING HEMLOCK AND ✚ OTHER NUTRITIONAL MATTERS
Harold J. Morowitz

IT WAS A RATHER DARK, BLEAK MORNING, AND AFTER RISING EARLY I thought it appropriate to turn on the television and communicate, unidirectionally to be sure, with the outside world. There to my great surprise was a famous movie star of a few years back discoursing on the evils of sugar. The former Hollywood idol was vehement in her denunciation of this hexose dimer particularly in its purified and crystallized form. She denounced it as an "unnatural food," an epithet that may well have bruised the egos of the photosynthesizing cane and beet plants. The mental image evoked was that of a solemn judge sentencing someone in perpetuity for an "unnatural act." In no time at all this great lady had me caught up in her crusade, and I kept muttering "hate sucrose" as I prepared an unnatural extract of coffee beans and dropped in a highly synthetic saccharin tablet.

A few minutes later, when the veil of sleep had lifted and the uncertainty of reason had replaced the assuredness of emotion, I began to wonder where my cinema heroine had acquired such self-righteous certainty about biochemical and nutritional matters that have eluded my colleagues for years.

Perhaps all this messy experimental work of grinding and extracting tissue and otherwise mucking about the laboratory is not the shortest road to truth at all, and we of the dirty white lab coat crowd are missing some mysterious pathway whereby true nutritional knowledge comes with blinding insight and transforms the lives of the faithful.

All of this recalled a frequent, painful experience that 3 haunts biomedical scientists like a recurring nightmare. One is at a cocktail party or other social gathering where someone appears in the crowd and begins an oratorical declamation on Good Nutrition. The "facts" being set forth are often inconsistent with everything one knows about metabolic pathways, cell and organ physiology, enzymology, and common sense. If the listener is so bold as to raise the question, "How do you know that?", he or she is greeted with a look that must have faced Columbus when he queried, "How do you know that the world is flat?"

Nutrition seems to be like politics; everyone is an expert. It 4 would appear that to the general public years of education are as naught compared to knowledge somehow painlessly available to everyone, regardless of his familiarity with innumerable facts and theories that constitute a complex discipline.

The situation described is by no means confined to the 5 choice of foods, and I certainly feel ill prepared to get involved in the sucrose controversy. Nevertheless, the field of nutrition is a good example of the many areas where we are constantly subjected to a host of dogmatic statements, some of which are true, some of which are false, and many of which are indeterminate. The response to each of these assertions should be the query, "How do you know that what you are saying is indeed a statement of fact?" At this level of question, I believe our educational system has been a total failure.

Asking how we know the things that we know is part of the 6 philosophical discipline of epistemology, the theory of knowledge, which is usually taught in upper-level and graduate philosophy courses and is therefore restricted to a small group of college students. But can there be any study that is more basic to education? Should not every high school graduate be prepared to cope with the many incorrect and misleading assertions that come his way every day? On the surface it seems strange that acquiring skills in assessing the validity of statements is not a core feature of the school curriculum.

Education, as conceived at present, is largely a matter of transferring subject matter from teacher to student, and uncertainty is usually settled by appeal to authority, the teacher, a textbook, or an encyclopedia. The methodological issue of how knowledge is obtained is rarely mentioned. Thus one of the most important analytical tools that an educated individual should possess is ignored. This is not to argue against the transfer of information but rather to assert that by itself it is insufficient protection in a real world containing demagogues and all kinds of charlatans and hucksters who have a free rein because almost no one is asking the appropriate questions.

On the issue of sorting out reality, most holders of doctoral degrees are almost as naive as grade-school graduates, and all manner of academic disciplines also expend effort on statements that would be quickly discarded if epistemological criteria were invoked. This takes us back briefly to the subject of nutrition, where methodological problems make it very difficult to obtain even pragmatically useful information. Statements are made on the basis of averaging over populations when we have no idea of the distribution functions that go into forming the averages. The impossibility of large-scale experiments with people requires extrapolation of animal or small-scale human determinations over ranges where the correctness of the extrapolation procedure is unknown. Nutrition is thus beset with difficulties that are clearly of an epistemological nature and, until these are resolved, careful scientists will be confined to very limited statements. Dogmatic assertions will remain the province of cocktail party orators.

The problem of why the theory of knowledge is not taught in the schools is relatively easy to see. Epistemology is, after all, a dangerous subject. If we start to question the validity of statements, then the teachers themselves come under question.

All assertions about education, established forms of religion, government, and social mores will also be subject to justification on the grounds of how they are known to be true. For parents and teachers who have not been through the experience of exploring how we determine facts, it would be unnerving to have their children continuously questioning the roots of knowledge. Inquiry is indeed a challenge to the acceptance of things as they are.

To realize the threat to established ways that is perceived in the type of analysis we are discussing, we need to go back to ancient Athens, where the philosopher Socrates taught his young followers by the technique of questioning everything and seeking answers. As Will Durant[1] has noted, "he went about prying into the human soul, uncovering assumptions and questioning certainties." This has come to be known as the Socratic method. The citizens of the Greek city-state condemned the inquiring teacher to death by poisoning with hemlock. One of the most serious charges against him was "corrupting the young." The fate of the first propounder of the Theory of Knowledge has perhaps served as a warning to keep the subject out of the school system.   10

There is still an objection that it is dangerous to teach the art and science of inquiry to the young; I would submit that it is more dangerous not to teach it to them, thus leaving them vulnerable to the quacks and phonies who now add mass communication to their bag of tricks. If we believe that rationality will lead the way to the solution of problems, then we must start by making the examination of what is "real" a part of everyone's thought. If challenging young people are a nuisance, think of how much more of a menace is presented by young people marching off in lock step and never questioning where they are going.   11

The solution seems clear. When we return education to the basics of reading, writing, and 'rithmetic, we should add a   12

---

[1] *Will Durant:* (1885–1971) American historian of ideas best known for his popularizations of history and philosophy.

fourth R, "reality." Starting at the first grade and continuing through graduate training we must see that students become sensitized to the meaning of what is said and the realization of how valid knowledge is established. If this seems radical, it is. Drinking hemlock may be less painful than swallowing some of the drivel that comes over the TV set every day.

[1979 – U.S.A.]

Questions

1. What kind of a title does this essay have? What does the title do?
2. What tone is struck in paragraphs 1 and 2 with respect to the television personage? What is the purpose of this tone?
3. How does Morowitz suggest his authority? Why does he do so?
4. What is Morowitz's thesis? Why doesn't he state it at the beginning of the essay? How does the essay move to its thesis statement (for example, from negative to positive, by analogy, from general to particular)?
5. "Drinking Hemlock" falls into five parts. Identify by paragraph number each of these parts and specify what each concerns.
6. What kind of an ending does this essay have? How does the essay's last sentence help impart a sense of closure?

Writing Assignments

1. Thinking back on your own secondary schooling, do you or do you not find that the "methodological issue of how knowledge is obtained [was] rarely mentioned" (paragraph 7)? In either case, write a paragraph or more on your secondary education with regard to instruction in epistemology.
2. Write a short paper beginning with an example related to your thesis, then moving to your thesis statement, and then arguing it. If you can, establish your authority obliquely, as does Morowitz in "Drinking Hemlock." Some possible topics are television testimonials, how we know what we know, reasons to study epistemology.
3. Is it reasonable to expect any culture to ask its young to question the "established forms of religion, government, and social mores"? Write an essay addressing this question. In so doing, you might consider why many (including Thomas Jefferson) have held that it is not only reasonable but essential for a democracy to encourage such questioning.

✤ Pedestrian Students and ✤ High-Flying Squirrels

Liane Ellison Norman

THE SQUIRREL IS CURIOUS. HE DARTS AND EDGES, PROFILE FIRST, ONE 1
bright black eye on me, the other alert for enemies on the other
side. Like a fencer, he faces both ways, for every impulse
toward me, an impulse away. His tail is airy. He flicks and
flourishes it, taking readings of some subtle kind.

I am enjoying a reprieve of warm sun in a season of rain and 2
impending frost. Around me today is the wine of the garden's
final ripening. On the zucchini, planted late, the flagrant
blossoms flare and decline in a day's time.

I am sitting on the front porch thinking about my students. 3
Many of them earnestly and ardently want me to teach them to
be hacks. Give us ten tricks, they plead, ten nifty fail-safe ways
to write a news story. Don't make us think our way through
these problems, they storm (and when I am insistent that
thinking *is* the trick, "You never listen to us," they complain.)
Who cares about the First Amendment? they sneer. What are
John Peter Zenger[1] and Hugo Black[2] to us? Teach us how to
earn a living. They will be content, they explain, with
know-how and jobs, satisfied to do no more than cover the
tedium of school board and weather.

Under the rebellion, there is a plaintive panic. What if, on 4
the job — assuming there is a job to be on — they fearlessly
defend the free press against government, grand jury, and
media monopoly, but don't know how to write an obituary.
Shouldn't obituaries come first?

I hope not, but even obituaries need good information and 5
firm prose, and both, I say, require clear thought.

---

[1]*John Peter Zenger:* (1697–1746) Printer who struggled for the freedom of the press.
[2]*Hugo Black:* (1886–1971) Supreme Court justice and proponent of civil rights.

The squirrel does not share my meditation. He grows tired 6
of inquiring into me. His dismissive tail floats out behind as he
takes a running leap into the tree. Up the bark he goes and onto
a branch, where he crashes through the leaves. He soars from
slender perch to slender perch, shaking up the tree as if he were
the west wind. What a madcap he is, to go racing from one twig
that dips under him to another at those heights!

His acrobatic clamor loosens buckeyes in their prickly 7
armor. They drop, break open, and he is down the tree in a
twinkling, picking, choosing. He finds what he wants and
carries it, an outsize nut which is burnished like a fine cello,
across the lawn, up a pole, and across the tightrope telephone
line to the other side, where he disappears in maple foliage.

Some inner clock or calendar tells him to stock his larder 8
against the deep snows and hard times that are coming. I have
heard that squirrels are fuzzy-minded, that they collect their
winter groceries and store them, and then forget where they are
cached. But this squirrel is purposeful; he appears to know he'd
better look ahead. Faced with necessity, he is prudent, but not
fearful. He prances and flies as he goes about his task of
preparation, and he never fails to look into whatever startles his
attention.

Though he is not an ordinary pedestrian, crossing the street 9
far above, I sometimes see the mangled fur of a squirrel on the
street, with no flirtation left. Even a highflying squirrel may zap
himself on an aerial live wire. His days are dangerous and his
winters are lean, but still he lays in provisions the way a trapeze
artist goes about his work, with daring and dash.

For the squirrel, there is no work but living. He gathers 10
food, reproduces, tends the children for a while, and stays out
of danger. Doing these things with style is what distinguishes
him. But for my students, unemployment looms as large as the
horizon itself. Their anxiety has cause. And yet, what good is
it? Ten tricks or no ten tricks, there are not enough jobs. The
well-trained, well-educated stand in line for unemployment
checks with the unfortunates and the drifters. Neither skill nor
virtue holds certain promise. This being so, I wonder, why

should these students not demand, for the well-being of their souls, the liberation of their minds?

It grieves me that they want to be pedestrians, earthbound 11 and always careful. You ask too much, they say. What you want is painful and unfair. There are a multitude of pressures that instruct them to train, not free, themselves.

Many of them are the first generation to go to college; 12 family aspirations are in their trust. Advisers and models tell them to be doctors, lawyers, engineers, cops, and public-relations people; no one ever tells them they can be poets, philosophers, farmers, inventors, or wizards. Their elders are anxious too; they reject the eccentric and the novel. And, realism notwithstanding, they cling to talismanic determination; play it safe and do things right and I, each one thinks, will get a job even though others won't.

I tell them fondly of my college days, which were a dizzy 13 time (as I think the squirrel's time must be), as I let loose and pitched from fairly firm stands into the space of intellect and imagination, never quite sure what solid branch I would light on. That was the most useful thing I learned, the practical advantage (not to mention the exhilaration) of launching out to find where my propellant mind could take me.

A luxury? one student ponders, a little wistfully. 14

Yes, luxury, and yet necessity, and it aroused that flight, a 15 fierce unappeasable appetite to know and to essay. The luxury I speak of is not like other privileges of wealth and power that must be hoarded to be had. If jobs are scarce, the heady regions of treetop adventure are not. Flight and gaiety cost nothing, though of course they may cost everything.

The squirrel, my frisky analogue, is not perfectly free. He 16 must go on all fours, however nimbly he does it. Dogs are always after him, and when he barely escapes, they rant up the tree as he dodges among the branches that give under his small weight. He feeds on summer's plenty and pays the price of strontium in his bones. He is no freer of industrial ordure than I am. He lives, mates, and dies (no obituary, first or last, for him), but still he plunges and balances, risking his neck because it is his nature.

I like the little squirrel for his simplicity and bravery. He 17 will never get ahead in life, never find a good job, never settle down, never be safe. There are no sure-fire tricks to make it as a squirrel.

[1978 — U.S.A.]

Questions

1. What is the setting here as to both time and place? Why does Norman indicate a setting at all? What purpose does it have?
2. What is the difference in tone between the paragraphs in which Norman contemplates the squirrel (for example, paragraphs 1, 9, and 17) and those concerning her students (for example, paragraphs 2 and 3)? How is tone established in each case?
3. What analogy lies at the heart of this essay? What contrast does this analogy help to make concrete? Contrast is the essay's structural mode. How so? How does its main contrast proceed?
4. What is this essay's theme? How does its central contrast symbolize that theme?

Writing Assignments

1. Are you a high-flying squirrel or a ground hog? In a short paper, discuss yourself and your present course in terms of one or the other. Is it better to be one as opposed to the other? If you think so, defend your judgment. If you think not, why not?
2. Write an essay evaluating "Pedestrian Students and High-Flying Squirrels." In your view, does the essay succeed in getting its point across? Why or why not? Is the main distinction it draws valid? Why or why not? What values underlie its speaker's judgments? Are they generally-accepted values or are they merely personal? What is your judgment of the essay's writing and construction? What leads you to this judgment?
3. Write a short paper in which you use a symbolic image like Norman's squirrel as your focal point. Be sure that the image you choose somehow suggests in and of itself the idea, quality, feeling, or whatever that you mean it to symbolize and that your context makes your symbolic meaning clear.

✤ Politics and the ✤
English Language
George Orwell

MOST PEOPLE WHO BOTHER WITH THE MATTER AT ALL WOULD ADMIT   1
that the English language is in a bad way, but it is generally
assumed that we cannot by conscious action do anything about
it. Our civilisation is decadent, and our language — so the
argument runs — must inevitably share in the general collapse.
It follows that any struggle against the abuse of language is a
sentimental archaism, like preferring candles to electric light or
hansom cabs to aeroplanes. Underneath this lies the half-
conscious belief that language is a natural growth and not an
instrument which we shape for our own purposes.

Now, it is clear that the decline of a language must   2
ultimately have political and economic causes: it is not due
simply to the bad influence of this or that individual writer. But
an effect can become a cause, reinforcing the original cause and
producing the same effect in an intensified form, and so on
indefinitely. A man may take to drink because he feels himself
to be a failure, and then fail all the more completely because he
drinks. It is rather the same thing that is happening to the
English language. It becomes ugly and inaccurate because our
thoughts are foolish, but the slovenliness of our language makes
it easier for us to have foolish thoughts. The point is that the
process is reversible. Modern English, especially written
English, is full of bad habits which spread by imitation and
which can be avoided if one is willing to take the necessary
trouble. If one gets rid of these habits one can think more
clearly, and to think clearly is a necessary first step towards
political regeneration: so that the fight against bad English is
not frivolous and is not the exclusive concern of professional
writers. I will come back to this presently, and I hope that by
that time the meaning of what I have said here will have become

clearer. Meanwhile, here are five specimens of the English language as it is now habitually written.

These five passages have not been picked out because they are especially bad — I could have quoted far worse if I had chosen — but because they illustrate various of the mental vices from which we now suffer. They are a little below the average, but are fairly representative samples. I number them so that I can refer back to them when necessary: 3

1. I am not, indeed, sure whether it is not true to say that the Milton who once seemed not unlike a seventeenth-century Shelley had not become, out of an experience ever more bitter in each year, more alien (sic) to the founder of that Jesuit sect which nothing could induce him to tolerate. Professor Harold Laski (Essay in *Freedom of Expression*).

2. Above all, we cannot play ducks and drakes with a native battery of idioms which prescribes such egregious collocations of vocables as the Basic *put up with* for *tolerate* or *put at a loss* for *bewilder*.
Professor Lancelot Hogben *(Interglossa)*.

3. On the one side we have the free personality: by definition it is not neurotic, for it has neither conflict nor dream. Its desires, such as they are, are transparent, for they are just what institutional approval keeps in the forefront of consciousness; another institutional pattern would alter their number and intensity; there is little in them that is natural, irreducible, or culturally dangerous. But *on the other side*, the social bond itself is nothing but the mutual reflection of these self-secure integrities. Recall the definition of love. Is not this the very picture of a small academic? Where is there a place in this hall of mirrors for either personality or fraternity?
Essay on psychology in *Politics* (New York).

4. All the "best people" from the gentlemen's clubs, and all the frantic Fascist captains, united in common hatred of Socialism and bestial horror of the rising tide of the mass revolutionary movement, have turned to acts of provocation, to foul incendiarism, to medieval legends of poisoned wells, to legalise their own destruction to proletarian organisations, and rouse the agitated petty-bourgeoisie to chauvinistic

fervour on behalf of the fight against the revolutionary way
out of the crisis.

Communist pamphlet.

5. If a new spirit *is* to be infused into this old country, there
is one thorny and contentious reform which must be tackled,
and that is the humanisation and galvanisation of the BBC.
Timidity here will bespeak canker and atrophy of the soul.
The heart of Britain may be sound and of strong beat, for
instance, but the British lion's roar at present is like that of
Bottom in Shakespeare's *Midsummer Night's Dream* — as
gentle as any sucking dove. A virile new Britain cannot
continue indefinitely to be traduced in the eyes, or rather
ears, of the world by the effete languors of Langham Place,
brazenly masquerading as "standard English". When the
Voice of Britain is heard at nine o'clock, better far and
infinitely less ludicrous to hear aitches honestly dropped than
the present priggish, inflated, inhibited, school-ma'amish
arch braying of blameless bashful mewing maidens!

Letter in *Tribune.*

Each of these passages has faults of its own, but, quite apart   4
from avoidable ugliness, two qualities are common to all of
them. The first is staleness of imagery: the other is lack of
precision. The writer either has a meaning and cannot express
it, or he inadvertently says something else, or he is almost
indifferent as to whether his words mean anything or not. This
mixture of vagueness and sheer incompetence is the most
marked characteristic of modern English prose, and especially
of any kind of political writing. As soon as certain topics are
raised, the concrete melts into the abstract and no one seems
able to think of turns of speech that are not hackneyed: prose
consists less and less of *words* chosen for the sake of their
meaning, and more of *phrases* tacked together like the sections
of a prefabricated hen-house. I list below, with notes and
examples, various of the tricks by means of which the work of
prose construction is habitually dodged:

Dying metaphors. A newly invented metaphor assists thought   5
by evoking a visual image, while on the other hand a metaphor
which is technically "dead" (e.g. *iron resolution*) has in effect

reverted to being an ordinary word and can generally be used without loss of vividness. But in between these two classes there is a huge dump of worn-out metaphors which have lost all evocative power and are merely used because they save people the trouble of inventing phrases for themselves. Examples are: *Ring the changes on, take up the cudgels for, toe the line, ride roughshod over, stand shoulder to shoulder with, play into the hands of, no axe to grind, grist to the mill, fishing in troubled waters, rift within the lute, on the order of the day, Achilles' heel, swan song, hotbed.* Many of these are used without knowledge of their meaning (what is a "rift", for instance?), and incompatible metaphors are frequently mixed, a sure sign that the writer is not interested in what he is saying. Some metaphors now current have been twisted out of their original meaning without those who use them even being aware of the fact. For example, *toe the line* is sometimes written *tow the line.* Another example is *the hammer and the anvil,* now always used with the implication that the anvil gets the worst of it. In real life it is always the anvil that breaks the hammer, never the other way about: a writer who stopped to think what he was saying would be aware of this, and would avoid perverting the original phrase.

Operators, or *verbal false limbs.* These save the trouble of picking out appropriate verbs and nouns, and at the same time pad each sentence with extra syllables which give it an appearance of symmetry. Characteristic phrases are: *render inoperative, militate against, prove unacceptable, make contact with, be subjected to, give rise to, give grounds for, have the effect of, play a leading part (rôle) in, make itself felt, take effect, exhibit a tendency to, serve the purpose of,* etc etc. The keynote is the elimination of simple verbs. Instead of being a single word, such as *break, stop, spoil, mend, kill,* a verb becomes a *phrase,* made up of a noun or adjective tacked on to some general-purposes verb such as *prove, serve, form, play, render.* In addition, the passive voice is wherever possible used in preference to the active, and noun constructions are used instead of gerunds *(by examination of* instead of *by examining).* The range of verbs is further cut down by means of the *-ise* and *de-* formations, and banal statements are given an appearance of profundity by means of the *not un-* formation. Simple conjunctions and prepositions are replaced by such phrases as *with respect to, having regard to, the fact that, by dint of, in view of, in the interests of, on the hypothesis that;* and the ends of sentences are saved from anticlimax by such resounding commonplaces as *greatly to be desired, cannot be left out of account, a development to be expected in the near future, deserving of serious consideration, brought to a satisfactory conclusion,* and so on and so forth.

Pretentious diction. Words like *phenomenon, element, individual* 7 (as noun), *objective, categorical, effective, virtual, basic, primary, promote, constitute, exhibit, exploit, utilise, eliminate, liquidate,* are used to dress up simple statements and give an air of scientific impartiality to biassed judgements. Adjectives like *epoch-making, epic, historic, unforgettable, triumphant, age-old, inevitable, inexorable, veritable,* are used to dignify the sordid processes of international politics, while writing that aims at glorifying war usually takes on an archaic colour, its characteristic words being: *realm, throne, chariot, mailed fist, trident, sword, shield, buckler, banner, jackboot, clarion.* Foreign words and expressions such as *cul de sac, ancien régime, deus ex machina, mutatis mutandis, status quo, Gleichschaltung, Weltanschauung,* are used to give an air of culture and elegance. Except for the useful abbreviations *i.e., e.g.,* and *etc,* there is no real need for any of the hundreds of foreign phrases now current in English. Bad writers, and especially scientific, political and sociological writers, are nearly always haunted by the notion that Latin or Greek words are grander than Saxon ones, and unnecessary words like *expedite, ameliorate, predict, extraneous, deracinated, clandestine, sub-aqueous* and hundreds of others constantly gain ground from their Anglo-Saxon opposite numbers.[1] The jargon peculiar to Marx-

---

1. An interesting illustration of this is the way in which the English flower names which were in use till very recently are being ousted by Greek ones, *snapdragon* becoming *antirrhinum, forget-me-not* become *myosotis,* etc. It is hard to see any practical reason for this change of fashion: it is probably due to an instinctive turning-away from the more homely word and a vague feeling that the Greek word is scientific. [Author's footnote.]

ist writing (*hyena, hangman, cannibal, petty bourgeois, these gentry, lacquey, flunkey, mad dog, White Guard,* etc) consists largely of words and phrases translated from Russian, German or French; but the normal way of coining a new word is to use a Latin or Greek root with the appropriate affix and, where necessary, the *-ise* formation. It is often easier to make up words of this kind (*deregionalise, impermissible, extramarital, non-fragmentatory* and so forth) than to think up the English words that will cover one's meaning. The result, in general, is an increase in slovenliness and vagueness.

Meaningless words. In certain kinds of writing, particularly in art criticism and literary criticism, it is normal to come across long passages which are almost completely lacking in meaning.[2] Words like *romantic, plastic, values, human, dead, sentimental, natural, vitality,* as used in art criticism, are strictly meaningless, in the sense that they not only do not point to any discoverable object, but are hardly even expected to do so by the reader. When one critic writes, "The outstanding features of Mr. X's work is its living quality", while another writes, "The immediately striking thing about Mr. X's work is its peculiar deadness", the reader accepts this as a simple difference of opinion. If words like *black* and *white* were involved, instead of the jargon words *dead* and *living,* he would see at once that language was being used in an improper way. Many political words are similarly abused. The word *Fascism* has now no meaning except in so far as it signifies "something not desirable". The words *democracy, socialism, freedom, patriotic, realistic, justice,* have each of them several different meanings which cannot be reconciled with one another. In the case of a word like *democracy,* not only is there no agreed definition, but the attempt to make one is resisted from all sides. It is almost

---

2. Example: "Comfort's catholicity of perception and image, strangely Whitmanesque in range, almost the exact opposite in aesthetic compulsion, continues to evoke that trembling atmospheric accumulative hinting at a cruel, an inexorably serene timelessness . . . Wrey Gardiner scores by aiming at simple bullseyes with precision. Only they are not so simple, and through this contented sadness runs more than the surface bitter-sweet of resignation." (*Poetry Quarterly.*) [Author's footnote.]

universally felt that when we call a country democratic we are praising it: consequently the defenders of every kind of régime claim that it is a democracy, and fear that they might have to stop using the word if it were tied down to any one meaning. Words of this kind are often used in a consciously dishonest way. That is, the person who uses them has his own private definition, but allows his hearer to think he means something quite different. Statements like *Marshal Pétain was a true patriot, The Soviet press is the freest in the world, The Catholic Church is opposed to persecution,* are almost always made with intent to deceive. Other words used in variable meanings, in most cases more or less dishonestly, are: *class, totalitarian, science, progressive, reactionary, bourgeois, equality.*

Now that I have made this catalogue of swindles and 9
perversions, let me give another example of the kind of writing that they lead to. This time it must of its nature be an imaginary one. I am going to translate a passage of good English into modern English of the worst sort. Here is a well-known verse from *Ecclesiastes:*

> I returned, and saw under the sun, that the race is not to the swift, nor the battle to the strong, neither yet bread to the wise, nor yet riches to men of understanding, nor yet favour to men of skill; but time and chance happeneth to them all.

Here it is in modern English: 10

> Objective consideration of contemporary phenomena compels the conclusion that success or failure in competitive activities exhibits no tendency to be commensurate with innate capacity, but that a considerable element of the unpredictable must invariably be taken into account.

This is a parody, but not a very gross one. Exhibit 3, above, 11
for instance, contains several patches of the same kind of English. It will be seen that I have not made a full translation. The beginning and ending of the sentence follow the original meaning fairly closely, but in the middle the concrete illustrations — race, battle, bread — dissolve into the vague

phrase "success or failure in competitive activities". This had to be so, because no modern writer of the kind I am discussing — no one capable of using phrases like "objective consideration of contemporary phenomena" — would ever tabulate his thoughts in that precise and detailed way. The whole tendency of modern prose is away from concreteness. Now analyse these two sentences a little more closely. The first contains 49 words but only 60 syllables, and all its words are those of everyday life. The second contains 38 words of 90 syllables: 18 of its words are from Latin roots, and one from Greek. The first sentence contains six vivid images, and only one phrase ("time and chance") that could be called vague. The second contains not a single fresh, arresting phrase, and in spite of its 90 syllables it gives only a shortened version of the meaning contained in the first. Yet without a doubt it is the second kind of sentence that is gaining ground in modern English. I do not want to exaggerate. This kind of writing is not yet universal, and outcrops of simplicity will occur here and there in the worst-written page. Still, if you or I were told to write a few lines on the uncertainty of human fortunes, we should probably come much nearer to my imaginary sentence than to the one from *Ecclesiastes*.

As I have tried to show, modern writing at its worst does 12 not consist in picking out words for the sake of their meaning and inventing images in order to make the meaning clearer. It consists in gumming together long strips of words which have already been set in order by someone else, and making the results presentable by sheer humbug. The attraction of this way of writing is that it is easy. It is easier — even quicker, once you have the habit — to say *In my opinion it is a not unjustifiable assumption that* than to say *I think.* If you use ready-made phrases, you not only don't have to hunt about for words; you also don't have to bother with the rhythms of your sentences, since these phrases are generally so arranged as to be more or less euphonious. When you are composing in a hurry — when you are dictating to a stenographer, for instance, or making a public speech — it is natural to fall into a pretentious, latinised style. Tags like *a consideration which we should do well to bear in mind* or *a conclusion to which all of us would readily assent* will save many a sentence from coming down with a bump. By using stale metaphors, similes and idioms, you save much mental effort, at the cost of leaving your meaning vague, not only for your reader but for yourself. This is the significance of mixed metaphors. The sole aim of a metaphor is to call up a visual image. When these images clash — as in *The Fascist octopus has sung its swan song, the jackboot is thrown into the melting-pot* — it can be taken as certain that the writer is not seeing a mental image of the objects he is naming; in other words he is not really thinking. Look again at the examples I gave at the beginning of this essay. Professor Laski (1) uses five negatives in 53 words. One of these is superfluous, making nonsense of the whole passage, and in addition there is the slip *alien* for akin, making further nonsense, and several avoidable pieces of clumsiness which increase the general vagueness. Professor Hogben (2) plays ducks and drakes with a battery which is able to write prescriptions, and, while disapproving of the everyday phrase *put up with,* is unwilling to look *egregious* up in the dictionary and see what it means. (3), if one takes an uncharitable attitude towards it, is simply meaningless: probably one could work out its intended meaning by reading the whole of the article in which it occurs. In (4) the writer knows more or less what he wants to say, but an accumulation of stale phrases chokes him like tea-leaves blocking a sink. In (5) words and meaning have almost parted company. People who write in this manner usually have a general emotional meaning — they dislike one thing and want to express solidarity with another — but they are not interested in the detail of what they are saying. A scrupulous writer, in every sentence that he writes, will ask himself at least four questions, thus: What am I trying to say? What words will express it? What image or idiom will make it clearer? Is this image fresh enough to have an effect? And he will probably ask himself two more: Could I put it more shortly? Have I said anything that is avoidably ugly? But you are not obliged to go to all this trouble. You can shirk it by simply throwing your mind open and letting the ready-made phrases come crowding in. They will construct your sentences for you — even think your thoughts for you, to a certain extent — and at need they will perform the important service of partially concealing your meaning even from yourself. It is at this point that the special connection between politics and the debasement of language becomes clear.

In our time it is broadly true that political writing is bad 13 writing. Where it is not true, it will generally be found that the writer is some kind of rebel, expressing his private opinions, and not a "party line". Orthodoxy, of whatever colour, seems to demand a lifeless, imitative style. The political dialects to be found in pamphlets, leading articles, manifestos, White Papers and the speeches of Under-Secretaries do, of course, vary from party to party, but they are all alike in that one almost never finds in them a fresh, vivid, home-made turn of speech. When one watches some tired hack on the platform mechanically repeating the familiar phrases — *bestial atrocities, iron heel, bloodstained tyranny, free peoples of the world, stand shoulder to shoulder* — one often has a curious feeling that one is not watching a live human being but some kind of dummy: a feeling which suddenly becomes stronger at moments when the light catches the speaker's spectacles and turns them into blank discs which seem to have no eyes behind them. And this is not altogether fanciful. A speaker who uses that kind of phraseology has gone some distance towards turning himself into a machine. The appropriate noises are coming out of his larynx, but his brain is not involved as it would be if he were choosing his words for himself. If the speech he is making is one that he is accustomed to make over and over again, he may be almost unconscious of what he is saying, as one is when one utters the responses in church. And this reduced state of consciousness, if not indispensable, is at any rate favourable to political conformity.

In our time, political speech and writing are largely the 14 defence of the indefensible. Things like the continuance of British rule in India, the Russian purges and deportations, the dropping of the atom bombs on Japan, can indeed be defended, but only by arguments which are too brutal for most people to face, and which do not square with the professed aims of political parties. Thus political language has to consist largely of euphemism, question-begging and sheer cloudy vagueness. Defenceless villages are bombarded from the air, the inhabitants driven out into the countryside, the cattle machine-gunned, the huts set on fire with incendiary bullets: this is called *pacification*. Millions of peasants are robbed of their farms and sent trudging along the roads with no more than they can carry: this is called *transfer of population* or *rectification of frontiers*. People are imprisoned for years without trial, or shot in the back of the neck or sent to die of scurvy in Arctic lumber camps: this is called *elimination of unreliable elements*. Such phraseology is needed if one wants to name things without calling up mental pictures of them. Consider for instance some comfortable English professor defending Russian totalitarianism. He cannot say outright, "I believe in killing off your opponents when you can get good results by doing so". Probably, therefore, he will say something like this:

> While freely conceding that the Soviet régime exhibits certain features which the humanitarian may be inclined to deplore, we must, I think, agree that a certain curtailment of the right to political opposition is an unavoidable concomitant of transitional periods, and that the rigours which the Russian people have been called upon to undergo have been amply justified in the sphere of concrete achievement.

The inflated style is itself a kind of euphemism. A mass of 15 Latin words falls upon the facts like soft snow, blurring the outlines and covering up all the details. The great enemy of clear language is insincerity. When there is a gap between one's real and one's declared aims, one turns as it were instinctively to long words and exhausted idioms, like a cuttlefish squirting out ink. In our age there is no such thing as "keeping out of politics". All issues are political issues, and politics itself is a mass of lies, evasions, folly, hatred and schizophrenia. When the general atmosphere is bad, language must suffer. I should expect to find — this is a guess which I have not sufficient knowledge to verify — that the German, Russian and Italian languages have all deteriorated in the last ten or fifteen years, as a result of dictatorship.

But if thought corrupts language, language can also corrupt 16 thought. A bad usage can spread by tradition and imitation, even among people who should and do know better. The debased language that I have been discussing is in some ways very convenient. Phrases like *a not unjustifiable assumption, leaves much to be desired, would serve no good purpose, a consideration which we should do well to bear in mind*, are a continuous temptation, a packet of aspirins always at one's elbow. Look back through this essay, and for certain you will find that I have again and again committed the very faults I am protesting against. By this morning's post I have received a pamphlet dealing with conditions in Germany. The author tells me that he "felt impelled" to write it. I open it at random, and here is almost the first sentence that I see: "(The Allies) have an opportunity not only of achieving a radical transformation of Germany's social and political structure in such a way as to avoid a nationalistic reaction in Germany itself, but at the same time of laying the foundations of a co-operative and unified Europe." You see, he "feels impelled" to write — feels, presumably, that he has something new to say — and yet his words, like cavalry horses answering the bugle, group themselves automatically into the familiar dreary pattern. This invasion of one's mind by ready-made phrases *(lay the foundations, achieve a radical transformation)* can only be prevented if one is constantly on guard against them, and every such phrase anaesthetises a portion of one's brain.

I said earlier that the decadence of our language is probably 17 curable. Those who deny this would argue, if they produced an argument at all, that language merely reflects existing social conditions, and that we cannot influence its development by any direct tinkering with words and constructions. So far as the general tone or spirit of a language goes, this may be true, but it is not true in detail. Silly words and expressions have often disappeared, not through any evolutionary process but owing to the conscious action of a minority. Two recent examples were *explore every avenue* and *leave no stone unturned*, which were killed by the jeers of a few journalists. There is a long list of fly-blown metaphors which could similarly be got rid of if enough people would interest themselves in the job; and it should also be possible to laugh the *not un-* formation out of existence,[3] to reduce the amount of Latin and Greek in the average sentence, to drive out foreign phrases and strayed scientific words, and, in general, to make pretentiousness unfashionable. But all these are minor points. The defence of the English language implies more than this, and perhaps it is best to start by saying what it does *not* imply.

To begin with, it has nothing to do with archaism, with the 18 salvaging of obsolete words and turns of speech, or with the setting-up of a "standard English" which must never be departed from. On the contrary, it is especially concerned with the scrapping of every word or idiom which has outworn its usefulness. It has nothing to do with correct grammar and syntax, which are of no importance so long as one makes one's meaning clear, or with the avoidance of Americanisms, or with having what is called a "good prose style". On the other hand it is not concerned with fake simplicity and the attempt to make written English colloquial. Nor does it even imply in every case preferring the Saxon word to the Latin one, though it does imply using the fewest and shortest words that will cover one's meaning. What is above all needed is to let the meaning choose the word, and not the other way about. In prose, the worst thing one can do with words is to surrender to them. When you think of a concrete object, you think wordlessly, and then, if you want to describe the thing you have been visualising, you probably hunt about till you find the exact words that seem to fit it. When you think of something abstract you are more inclined to use words from the start, and unless you make a

---

3. One can cure oneself of the *not un-* formation by memorising this sentence: *A not unblack dog was chasing a not unsmall rabbit across a not ungreen field.* [Author's footnote.]

conscious effort to prevent it, the existing dialect will come rushing in and do the job for you, at the expense of blurring or even changing your meaning. Probably it is better to put off using words as long as possible and get one's meaning as clear as one can through pictures or sensations. Afterwards one can choose — not simply *accept* — the phrases that will best cover the meaning, and then switch round and decide what impression one's words are likely to make on another person. This last effort of the mind cuts out all stale or mixed images, all prefabricated phrases, needless repetitions, and humbug and vagueness generally. But one can often be in doubt about the effect of a word or a phrase, and one needs rules that one can rely on when instinct fails. I think the following rules will cover most cases:

    i. Never use a metaphor, simile or other figure of speech which you are used to seeing in print.
   ii. Never use a long word where a short one will do.
  iii. If it is possible to cut a word out, always cut it out.
  iv. Never use the passive where you can use the active.
   v. Never use a foreign phrase, a scientific word or a jargon word if you can think of an everyday English equivalent.
  vi. Break any of these rules sooner than say anything outright barbarous.

These rules sound elementary, and so they are, but they demand a deep change of attitude in anyone who has grown used to writing in the style now fashionable. One could keep all of them and still write bad English, but one could not write the kind of stuff that I quoted in those five specimens at the beginning of this article.

    I have not here been considering the literary use of 19 language, but merely language as an instrument for expressing and not for concealing or preventing thought. Stuart Chase and others have come near to claiming that all abstract words are meaningless, and have used this as a pretext for advocating a kind of political quietism. Since you don't know what Fascism is, how can you struggle against Fascism? One need not swallow such absurdities as this, but one ought to recognise that the present political chaos is connected with the decay of language, and that one can probably bring about some improvement by starting at the verbal end. If you simplify your English, you are freed from the worst follies of orthodoxy. You cannot speak any of the necessary dialects, and when you make a stupid remark its stupidity will be obvious, even to yourself. Political language — and with variations this is true of all political parties, from Conservatives to Anarchists — is designed to make lies sound truthful and murder respectable, and to give an appearance of solidity to pure wind. One cannot change this all in a moment, but one can at least change one's own habits, and from time to time one can even, if one jeers loudly enough, send some worn-out and useless phrase — some *jackboot, Achilles' heel, hotbed, melting pot, acid test, veritable inferno* or other lump of verbal refuse — into the dustbin where it belongs.

[1946 — Great Britain]

Questions

1. "Politics and the English Language" covers much territory. Nevertheless, it is thoroughly coherent. To see as much, write down a word or two describing what happens in each of the five major divisions of the essay. Then list the paragraphs and paragraph clusters that fall within each division and write down the topic of each. For example,
      I. Thesis Presentation
         ¶1 — "The language is in a bad way."
         ¶2 —"The decline of a language must ultimately have political and economic causes"; "the process is reversible."
      II. [Etcetera]
   When finished, read over your outline to see the *progression* of ideas and how they cohere.
2. This essay is basically definitional. How so?
3. The three parts of Orwell's thesis are stated separately in the first two paragraphs, as is suggested in question 1. Why?
4. In paragraph 16, Orwell suggests that his own essay is less than what it should be and that it exhibits the very faults he protests

against. Is this really true, or only an ingratiating allowance on Orwell's part that he, too, can be in error? Can you find any such faults? If you can, why didn't Orwell catch them?

5. How does diction affect meaning as exemplified by Orwell? What is the diction of politics and what is its purpose? Is such diction still in evidence some 40 years after Orwell's essay was first published? If so, what accounts for its longevity?

Writing Assignments

1. Find a piece of run-of-the-mill prose — be it an advertisement, a blurb on a book or cassette, a letter to "Dear Abby" or to the editor — and write a paragraph or two pointing out the inadequacy of its language. Why does it fail to communicate the full weight of what it seems intended to communicate? What common problems with language as detailed by Orwell does it exemplify?

2. With Orwell's six guidelines (paragraph 18) for accurately using language in mind, dig out an old paper of yours and read it carefully and critically. Then revise it, rooting out all trite phrases, abstractions, and so forth, and making its language active and specific.

3. In a short paper, compare and contrast "Politics and the English Language" and Joan Didion's "Bureaucrats" (pages 184–89). Both essays concern the corruption of language on the part of government and concur in their analysis of how and why government officials abuse good sense and the mother tongue. However, the essays are quite different in style. First consider the agreement of Orwell and Didion in their separate analyses. Then consider the differences in effect of the essays attributable to the differences in style.

4. Write an essay on television and the English language. Has the effect of television's barrage of words been for the better or the worse with respect to how we write and speak? How so? To what extent does television dictate what sociologists call our "language behavior"? To what extent should we guard ourselves against being influenced by the tube (not to mention sociologists)?

——————————— ✤ A HANGING ✤ ———————————
George Orwell

It was in Burma, a sodden morning of the rains. A sickly light,   1
like yellow tinfoil, was slanting over the high walls into the jail
yard. We were waiting outside the condemned cells, a row of
sheds fronted with double bars, like small animal cages. Each
cell measured about ten feet by ten and was quite bare within
except for a plank bed and a pot for drinking water. In some of
them brown, silent men were squatting at the inner bars, with
their blankets draped round them. These were the condemned
men, due to be hanged within the next week or two.

One prisoner had been brought out of his cell. He was a   2
Hindu, a puny wisp of a man, with a shaven head and vague
liquid eyes. He had a thick, sprouting mustache, absurdly too
big for his body, rather like the mustache of a comic man on the
films. Six tall Indian warders were guarding him and getting
him ready for the gallows. Two of them stood by with rifles and
fixed bayonets, while the others handcuffed him, passed a chain
through his handcuffs and fixed it to their belts, and lashed his
arms tight to his sides. They crowded very close about him,
with their hands always on him in a careful, caressing grip, as
though all the while feeling him to make sure he was there. It
was like men handling a fish which is still alive and may jump
back into the water. But he stood quite unresisting, yielding his
arms limply to the ropes, as though he hardly noticed what was
happening.

Eight o'clock struck and a bugle call, desolately thin in the   3
wet air, floated from the distant barracks. The superintendent
of the jail, who was standing apart from the rest of us, moodily
prodding the gravel with his stick, raised his head at the sound.
He was an army doctor, with a gray toothbrush mustache and
a gruff voice. "For God's sake, hurry up, Francis," he said
irritably. "The man ought to have been dead by this time.
Aren't you ready yet?"

Francis, the head jailer, a fat Dravidian[1] in a white drill suit 4
and gold spectacles, waved his black hand. "Yes sir, yes sir," he
bubbled. "All iss satisfactorily prepared. The hangman iss
waiting. We shall proceed."

"Well, quick march, then. The prisoners can't get their 5
breakfast until this job's over."

We set out for the gallows. Two warders marched on either 6
side of the prisoner, with their rifles at the slope; two others
marched close against him, gripping him by the arm and
shoulder, as though at once pushing and supporting him. The
rest of us, magistrates and the like, followed behind. Suddenly,
when we had gone ten yards, the procession stopped short
without any order or warning. A dreadful thing had
happened — a dog, come goodness knows whence, had appeared in the yard. It came bounding among us with a loud
volley of barks and leapt round us wagging its whole body, wild
with glee at finding so many human beings together. It was a
large woolly dog, half Airedale, half pariah. For a moment it
pranced around us, and then, before anyone could stop it, it had
made a dash for the prisoner, and jumping up tried to lick his
face. Everybody stood aghast, too taken aback even to grab the
dog.

"Who let that bloody brute in here?" said the superinten- 7
dent angrily. "Catch it, someone!"

A warder detached from the escort, charged clumsily after 8
the dog, but it danced and gambolled just out of his reach,
taking everything as part of the game. A young Eurasian jailer
picked up a handful of gravel and tried to stone the dog away,
but it dodged the stones and came after us again. Its yaps
echoed from the jail walls. The prisoner, in the grasp of the two
warders, looked on incuriously, as though this was another
formality of the hanging. It was several minutes before someone
managed to catch the dog. Then we put my handkerchief
through its collar and moved off once more, with the dog still
straining and whimpering.

---

[1]*Dravidian:* A native speaker of a southern Indian language.

It was about forty yards to the gallows. I watched the bare 9
brown back of the prisoner marching in front of me. He walked
clumsily with his bound arms, but quite steadily, with that
bobbing gait of the Indian who never straightens his knees. At
each step his muscles slid neatly into place, the lock of hair on
his scalp danced up and down, his feet printed themselves on
the wet gravel. And once, in spite of the men who gripped him
by each shoulder, he stepped lightly aside to avoid a puddle on
the path.

It is curious; but till that moment I had never realized what 10
it means to destroy a healthy, conscious man. When I saw the
prisoner step aside to avoid the puddle, I saw the mystery, the
unspeakable wrongness, of cutting a life short when it is in full
tide. This man was not dying, he was alive just as we are alive.
All the organs of his body were working — bowels digesting
food, skin renewing itself, nails growing, tissues forming — all
toiling away in solemn foolery. His nails would still be growing
when he stood on the drop, when he was falling through the air
with a tenth-of-a-second to live. His eyes saw the yellow gravel
and the gray walls, and his brain still remembered, foresaw,
reasoned — even about puddles. He and we were a party of
men walking together, seeing, hearing, feeling, understanding
the same world; and in two minutes, with a sudden snap, one
of us would be gone — one mind less, one world less.

The gallows stood in a small yard, separate from the main 11
grounds of the prison, and overgrown with tall prickly weeds.
It was a brick erection like three sides of a shed, with planking
on top, and above that two beams and a crossbar with the rope
dangling. The hangman, a gray-haired convict in the white
uniform of the prison, was waiting beside his machine. He
greeted us with a servile crouch as we entered. At a word from
Francis the two warders, gripping the prisoner more closely
than ever, half led, half pushed him to the gallows and helped
him clumsily up the ladder. Then the hangman climbed up and
fixed the rope round the prisoner's neck.

We stood waiting, five yards away. The warders had 12
formed in a rough circle round the gallows. And then, when the

noose was fixed, the prisoner began crying out to his god. It was a high, reiterated cry of "Ram! Ram! Ram! Ram!"[2] not urgent and fearful like a prayer or cry for help, but steady, rhythmical, almost like the tolling of a bell. The dog answered the sound with a whine. The hangman, still standing on the gallows, produced a small cotton bag like a flour bag and drew it down over the prisoner's face. But the sound, muffled by the cloth, still persisted, over and over again: "Ram! Ram! Ram! Ram! Ram!"

The hangman climbed down and stood ready, holding the 13 lever. Minutes seemed to pass. The steady, muffled crying from the prisoner went on and on, "Ram! Ram! Ram!" never faltering for an instant. The superintendent, his head on his chest, was slowly poking the ground with his stick; perhaps he was counting the cries, allowing the prisoner a fixed number — fifty, perhaps, or a hundred. Everyone had changed color. The Indians had gone gray like bad coffee, and one or two of the bayonets were wavering. We looked at the lashed, hooded man on the drop, and listened to his cries — each cry another second of life; the same thought was in all our minds; oh, kill him quickly, get it over, stop that abominable noise!

Suddenly the superintendent made up his mind. Throwing 14 up his head he made a swift motion with his stick. "Chalo!"[3] he shouted almost fiercely.

There was a clanking noise, and then dead silence. The 15 prisoner had vanished, and the rope was twisting on itself. I let go of the dog, and it galloped immediately to the back of the gallows; but when it got there it stopped short, barked, and then retreated into a corner of the yard, where it stood among the weeds, looking timorously out at us. We went round the gallows to inspect the prisoner's body. He was dangling with his toes pointed straight downwards, very slowly revolving, as dead as a stone.

---

[2]*Ram:* Rama, an incarnation of Vishnu, the chief Hindu deity.
[3]*"Chalo!":* "Drop him!" in Hindi.

The superintendent reached out with his stick and poked 16
the bare brown body; it oscillated slightly. "*He's* all right," said
the superintendent. He backed out from under the gallows, and
blew out a deep breath. The moody look had gone out of his
face quite suddenly. He glanced at his wristwatch. "Eight
minutes past eight. Well, that's all for this morning, thank
God."

The warders unfixed bayonets and marched away. The 17
dog, sobered and conscious of having misbehaved itself, slipped
after them. We walked out of the gallows yard, past the
condemned cells with their waiting prisoners, into the big
central yard of the prison. The convicts, under the command of
warders armed with lathis,[4] were already receiving their
breakfast. They squatted in long rows, each man holding a tin
pannikin,[5] while two warders with buckets marched around
ladling out rice; it seemed quite a homely, jolly scene, after the
hanging. An enormous relief had come upon us now that the
job was done. One felt an impulse to sing, to break into a run,
to snigger. All at once everyone began chattering gaily.

The Eurasian boy walking beside me nodded towards the 18
way we had come, with a knowing smile: "Do you know, sir,
our friend" (he meant the dead man) "when he heard his appeal
had been dismissed, he pissed on the floor of his cell. From
fright. Kindly take one of my cigarettes, sir. Do you not admire
my new silver case, sir? From the boxwallah,[6] two rupees eight
annas. Classy European style."

Several people laughed — at what, nobody seemed certain. 19

Francis was walking by the superintendent, talking garru- 20
lously: "Well, sir, all has passed off with the utmost satisfac-
toriness. It was all finished —flick! Like that. It is not always
so — oah, no! I have known cases where the doctor was obliged to go beneath the gallows and pull the prisoner's legs to
ensure decease. Most disagreeable!"

---

[4]*lathis:* Police clubs.

[5]*pannikan:* A small pan.

[6]*boxwallah:* Merchant dealing in decorative boxes and cases.

"Wriggling about, eh? That's bad," said the superinten- 21
dent.

"Ach, sir, it iss worse when they become refractory! One 22
man, I recall, clung to the bars of hiss cage when we went to
take him out. You will scarcely credit, sir, that it took six
warders to dislodge him, three pulling at each leg. We reasoned
with him, 'My dear fellow,' we said, 'think of the all the pain
and trouble you are causing to us!' But no, he would not listen!
Ach, he wass very troublesome!"

I found that I was laughing quite loudly. Everyone was 23
laughing. Even the superintendent grinned in a tolerant way.
"You'd better all come out and have a drink," he said quite
genially. "I've got a bottle of whiskey in the car. We could do
with it."

We went through the big double gates of the prison into the 24
road. "Pulling at his legs!" exclaimed a Burmese magistrate
suddenly, and burst into a loud chuckling. We all began
laughing again. At that moment Francis' anecdote seemed
extraordinarily funny. We all had a drink together, native and
European alike, quite amicably. The dead man was a hundred
yards away.

[1950 — Great Britain]

Questions

1. What does the setting depicted in the first paragraph make you feel?
   How is what the setting makes you feel relevant to the essay as it
   unfolds?

2. Consider the following details: the generalized description of the
   prisoner in paragraph 2, the evident discomfort of the superintendent (what tells us of his discomfort?), the dog's response to the
   prisoner in paragraph 6 as everyone else stands aghast (why are the
   rest "aghast"?), the mention of the prisoner's footprints and his
   avoidance of the puddle (paragraph 9), the reference to "a party of
   men" in paragraph 10, the prisoner's chant and everyone's hearing
   it as an "abominable noise" (paragraph 13), and the "enormous
   relief" and laughter after the hanging (paragraphs 17 and 23). What
   is the common denominator running between these details? What
   together do they say?

3. How is the essay ordered? Why does Orwell interrupt his organizational scheme with paragraph 10? Why doesn't he tell us of the prisoner's trangression? What theme does all of this, together with the details enumerated in question 2, suggest?

4. Like the typical voice of most first-rate reportage, that of "The Hanging" is by and large detached. How, then, does Orwell get his point across? Consider irony, the intrusion and tone of paragraph 10, and especially the dog as described in paragraphs 6 and 15.

5. What makes Orwell's style as vivid as it is? Its vividness supplies indirect comment. How so?

6. Orwell himself spoke of this essay as being a mixture of fact and fiction. What might be fictional? After all, however, does it really matter? Why or why not?

Writing Assignments

1. a) Write a paragraph summing up the effect of "The Hanging" and the purpose that effect serves.

   b) In a separate paragraph, discuss your reaction to the essay and why you so react.

2. Write a short narrative essay about some memorable event you have witnessed — a wedding, a funeral, an induction, or whatever. Try to use concrete images in your description (Orwell can serve as a model), and somehow *imply* what made the event memorable, or what meaning it held for you.

3. Does an essay have to be factual or can an essayist, like a fiction writer, use invented details, scenes, conversations, and so forth? Critics can be found on either side of this issue. What about you? Write an essay arguing your position through a careful analysis of what you think the essay is and how it should be defined.

✛ What Is Poverty? ✛
Jo Goodwin Parker

You ask me what is poverty? Listen to me. Here I am, dirty, 1
smelly, and with no "proper" underwear on and with the stench
of my rotting teeth near you. I will tell you. Listen to me. Listen
without pity. I cannot use your pity. Listen with understanding.
Put yourself in my dirty, worn out, ill-fitting shoes, and hear
me.

Poverty is getting up every morning from a dirt- and 2
illness-stained mattress. The sheets have long since been used
for diapers. Poverty is living in a smell that never leaves. This
is a smell of urine, sour milk, and spoiling food sometimes
joined with the strong smell of long-cooked onions. Onions are
cheap. If you have smelled this smell, you did not know how it
came. It is the smell of the outdoor privy. It is the smell of
young children who cannot walk the long dark way in the
night. It is the smell of the mattresses where years of
"accidents" have happened. It is the smell of the milk which has
gone sour because the refrigerator long has not worked, and it
costs money to get it fixed. It is the smell of rotting garbage. I
could bury it, but where is the shovel? Shovels cost money.

Poverty is being tired. I have always been tired. They told 3
me at the hospital when the last baby came that I had chronic
anemia caused from poor diet, a bad case of worms, and that I
needed a corrective operation. I listened politely — the poor are
always polite. The poor always listen. They don't say that there
is no money for iron pills, or better food, or worm medicine.
The idea of an operation is frightening and costs so much that,
if I had dared, I would have laughed. Who takes care of my
children? Recovery from an operation takes a long time. I have
three children. When I left them with "Granny" the last time I
had a job, I came home to find the baby covered with fly
specks, and a diaper that had not been changed since I left.
When the dried diaper came off, bits of my baby's flesh came

with it. My other child was playing with a sharp bit of broken glass, and my oldest was playing alone at the edge of a lake. I made twenty-two dollars a week, and a good nursery school costs twenty dollars a week for three children. I quit my job.

Poverty is dirt. You say in your clean clothes coming from your clean house, "Anybody can be clean." Let me explain about housekeeping with no money. For breakfast I give my children grits with no oleo or cornbread without eggs and oleo. This does not use up many dishes. What dishes there are, I wash in cold water and with no soap. Even the cheapest soap has to be saved for the baby's diapers. Look at my hands, so cracked and red. Once I saved for two months to buy a jar of Vaseline for my hands and the baby's diaper rash. When I had saved enough, I went to buy it and the price had gone up two cents. The baby and I suffered on. I have to decide every day if I can bear to put my cracked, sore hands into the cold water and strong soap. But you ask, why not hot water? Fuel costs money. If you have a wood fire it costs money. If you burn electricity, it costs money. Hot water is a luxury. I do not have luxuries. I know you will be surprised when I tell you how young I am. I look so much older. My back has been bent over the wash tubs for so long, I cannot remember when I ever did anything else. Every night I wash every stitch my school age child has on and just hope her clothes will be dry by morning.   4

Poverty is staying up all night on cold nights to watch the fire, knowing one spark on the newspaper covering the walls means your sleeping children die in flames. In summer poverty is watching gnats and flies devour your baby's tears when he cries. The screens are torn and you pay so little rent you know they will never be fixed. Poverty means insects in your food, in your nose, in your eyes, and crawling over you when you sleep. Poverty is hoping it never rains because diapers won't dry when it rains and soon you are using newspapers. Poverty is seeing your children forever with runny noses. Paper handkerchiefs cost money and all your rags you need for other things. Even more costly are antihistamines. Poverty is cooking without food and cleaning without soap.   5

Poverty is asking for help. Have you ever had to ask for   6
help, knowing your children will suffer unless you get it? Think
about asking for a loan from a relative, if this is the only way
you can imagine asking for help. I will tell you how it feels. You
find out where the office is that you are supposed to visit. You
circle that block four or five times. Thinking of your children,
you go in. Everyone is very busy. Finally, someone comes out
and you tell her that you need help. That never is the person
you need to see. You go see another person, and after spilling
the whole shame of your poverty all over the desk between you,
you find that this isn't the right office after all — you must
repeat the whole process, and it never is any easier at the next
place.

You have asked for help, and after all it has a cost. You are   7
again told to wait. You are told why, but you don't really hear
because of the red cloud of shame and the rising black cloud of
despair.

Poverty is remembering. It is remembering quitting school   8
in junior high because "nice" children had been so cruel about
my clothes and my smell. The attendance officer came. My
mother told him I was pregnant. I wasn't but she thought that
I could get a job and help out. I had jobs off and on, but never
long enough to learn anything. Mostly I remember being
married. I was so young then. I am still young. For a time, we
had all the things you have. There was a little house in another
town, with hot water and everything. Then my husband lost his
job. There was unemployment insurance for a while and what
few jobs I could get. Soon, all our nice things were repossessed
and we moved back here. I was pregnant then. This house
didn't look so bad when we first moved in. Every week it gets
worse. Nothing is ever fixed. We now had no money. There
were a few odd jobs for my husband, but everything went for
food then, as it does now. I don't know how we lived through
three years and three babies, but we did. I'll tell you something,
after the last baby I destroyed my marriage. It had been a good
one, but could you keep on bringing children in this dirt? Did
you ever think how much it costs for any kind of birth control?

I knew my husband was leaving the day he left, but there were no good-byes between us. I hope he has been able to climb out of this mess somewhere. He never could hope with us to drag him down.

That's when I asked for help. When I got it, you know how   9
much it was? It was, and is, seventy-eight dollars a month for the four of us; that is all I ever can get. Now you know why there is no soap, no needles and thread, no hot water, no aspirin, no worm medicine, no hand cream, no shampoo. None of these things forever and ever and ever. So that you can see clearly, I pay twenty dollars a month rent, and most of the rest goes for food. For grits and cornmeal, and rice and milk and beans. I try my best to use only the minimum electricity. If I use more, there is that much less for food.

Poverty is looking into a black future. Your children won't   10
play with my boys. They will turn to other boys who steal to get what they want. I can already see them behind the bars of their prison instead of behind the bars of my poverty. Or they will turn to the freedom of alcohol or drugs, and find themselves enslaved. And my daughter? At best, there is for her a life like mine.

But you say to me, there are schools. Yes, there are schools.   11
My children have no extra books, no magazines, no extra pencils, or crayons, or paper and the most important of all, they do not have health. They have worms, they have infections, they have pinkeye all summer. They do not sleep well on the floor, or with me in my one bed. They do not suffer from hunger, my seventy-eight dollars keeps us alive, but they do suffer from malnutrition. Oh yes, I do remember what I was taught about health in school. It doesn't do much good. In some places there is a surplus commodities program. Not here. The county said it cost too much. There is a school lunch program. But I have two children who will already be damaged by the time they get to school.

But, you say to me, there are health clinics. Yes, there are   12
health clinics and they are in the towns. I live out here eight miles from town. I can walk that far (even if it is sixteen miles both ways), but can my little children? My neighbor will take

me when he goes; but he expects to get paid, *one way or another*. I bet you know my neighbor. He is that large man who spends his time at the gas station, the barbershop, and the corner store complaining about the government spending money on the immoral mothers of illegitimate children.

Poverty is an acid that drips on pride until all pride is worn 13 away. Poverty is a chisel that chips on honor until honor is worn away. Some of you say that you would do *something* in my situation, and maybe you would, for the first week or the first month, but for year after year after year?

Even the poor can dream. A dream of a time when there is 14 money. Money for the right kinds of food, for worm medicine, for iron pills, for toothbrushes, for hand cream, for a hammer and nails and a bit of screening, for a shovel, for a bit of paint, for some sheeting, for needles and thread. Money to pay *in money* for a trip to town. And, oh, money for hot water and money for soap. A dream of when asking for help does not eat away the last bit of pride. When the office you visit is as nice as the offices of other governmental agencies, when there are enough workers to help you quickly, when workers do not quit in defeat and despair. When you have to tell your story to only one person, and that person can send you for other help and you don't have to prove your poverty over and over and over again.

I have come out of my despair to tell you this. Remember 15 I did not come from another place or another time. Others like me are all around you. Look at us with an angry heart, anger that will help you help me. Anger that will let you tell of me. The poor are always silent. Can you be silent too?

[1971 – U.S.A.]

Questions

1. What is Parker's means of support? How does her argument proceed? What is her purpose?
2. Though nothing is known about this author, she surely seems to know what she is talking about. How does she establish her authority and thereby bring home her message?

3. Parker offers no dictionary definition of poverty, nor does she refer to any statistical studies. Why? Why is her essay more compelling than all the statistics on the poor that could be cited?
4. What is the tone of this essay? How is this tone established and maintained?
5. What kind of rhythm pervades the essay? How is it created? How does it serve Parker's purpose?

Writing Assignments

1. Using "What Is Poverty?" as a model, write an essay in definition. Choose something that you know — what it is to be handicapped, a child whose parents are divorced, a student who has to work part-time, or whatever — and define what you choose as vividly as you can. Your object will be to make your readers understand not just intellectually, but on their pulses, as does Parker.
2. Write a paper on the subject of poverty. You may focus on your own observations and experience, or you may research the topic and report on what you find. In either case, try to make your writing direct and immediate, as vivid as Parker's essay on what it is to be poor.

✤ THE NECESSARY ENEMY ✤
Katherine Anne Porter

SHE IS A FRANK, CHARMING, FRESH-HEARTED YOUNG WOMAN WHO   1
married for love. She and her husband are one of those gay, good-looking young pairs who ornament this modern scene rather more in profusion perhaps than ever before in our history. They are handsome, with a talent for finding their way in their world, they work at things that interest them, their tastes agree and their hopes. They intend in all good faith to spend their lives together, to have children and do well by them and each other — to be happy, in fact, which for them is the whole point of their marriage. And all in stride, keeping their wits about them. Nothing romantic, mind you; their feet are on the ground.

Unless they were this sort of person, there would be not 2
much point to what I wish to say; for they would seem to be an
example of the high-spirited, right-minded young whom the
critics are always invoking to come forth and do their duty and
practice all those sterling old-fashioned virtues which in every
generation seem to be falling into disrepair. As for virtues, these
young people are more or less on their own, like most of their
kind; they get very little moral or other aid from their society;
but after three years of marriage this very contemporary young
woman finds herself facing the oldest and ugliest dilemma of
marriage.

She is dismayed, horrified, full of guilt and forebodings 3
because she is finding out little by little that she is capable of
hating her husband, whom she loves faithfully. She can hate
him at times as fiercely and mysteriously, indeed in terribly
much the same way, as often she hated her parents, her
brothers and sisters, whom she loves, when she was a child.
Even then it had seemed to her a kind of black treacherousness
in her, her private wickedness that, just the same, gave her her
only private life. That was one thing her parents never knew
about her, never seemed to suspect. For it was never given a
name. They did and said hateful things to her and to each other
as if by right, as if in them it was a kind of virtue. But when they
said to her, "Control your feelings," it was never when she was
amiable and obedient, only in the black times of her hate. So it
was her secret, a shameful one. When they punished her,
sometimes for the strangest reasons, it was, they said, only
because they loved her — it was for her good. She did not
believe this, but she thought herself guilty of something worse
than ever they had punished her for. None of this really
frightened her: the real fright came when she discovered that at
times her father and mother hated each other; this was like
standing on the doorsill of a familiar room and seeing in a
lightning flash that the floor was gone, you were on the edge of
a bottomless pit. Sometimes she felt that both of them hated
her, but that passed, it was simply not a thing to be thought of,
much less believed. She thought she had outgrown all this, but

here it was again, an element in her own nature she could not control, or feared she could not. She would have to hide from her husband, if she could, the same spot in her feelings she had hidden from her parents, and for the same no doubt disreputable, selfish reason: she wants to keep his love.

Above all, she wants him to be absolutely confident that she loves him, for that is the real truth, no matter how unreasonable it sounds, and no matter how her own feelings betray them both at times. She depends recklessly on his love; yet while she is hating him, he might very well be hating her as much or even more, and it would serve her right. But she does not want to be served right, she wants to be loved and forgiven — that is, to be sure he would forgive her anything, if he had any notion of what she had done. But best of all she would like not to have anything in her love that should ask for forgiveness. She doesn't mean about their quarrels — they are not so bad. Her feelings are out of proportion, perhaps. She knows it is perfectly natural for people to disagree, have fits of temper, fight it out; they learn quite a lot about each other that way, and not all of it disappointing either. When it passes, her hatred seems quite unreal. It always did.

Love. We are early taught to say it. I love you. We are trained to the thought of it as if there were nothing else, or nothing else worth having without it, or nothing worth having which it could not bring with it. Love is taught, always by precept, sometimes by example. Then hate, which no one meant to teach us, comes of itself. It is true that if we say I love you, it may be received with doubt, for there are times when it is hard to believe. Say I hate you, and the one spoken to believes it instantly, once for all.

Say I love you a thousand times to that person afterward and mean it every time, and still it does not change the fact that once we said I hate you, and meant that too. It leaves a mark on that surface love had worn so smooth with its eternal caresses. Love must be learned, and learned again and again; there is no end to it. Hate needs no instruction, but waits only to be provoked . . . hate, the unspoken word, the unacknowledged presence in the house, that faint smell of brimstone among the roses, that invisible tongue-tripper, that unkempt finger in every pie, that sudden oh-so-curiously *chilling* look — could it be boredom? — on your dear one's features, making them quite ugly. Be careful: love, perfect love, is in danger.

If it is not perfect, it is not love, and if it is not love, it is   7
bound to be hate sooner or later. This is perhaps a not too exaggerated statement of the extreme position of Romantic Love, more especially in America, where we are all brought up on it, whether we know it or not. Romantic Love is changeless, faithful, passionate, and its sole end is to render the two lovers happy. It has no obstacles save those provided by the hazards of fate (that is to say, society), and such sufferings as the lovers may cause each other are only another word for delight: exciting jealousies, thrilling uncertainties, the ritual dance of courtship within the charmed closed circle of their secret alliance; all *real* troubles come from without, they face them unitedly in perfect confidence. Marriage is not the end but only the beginning of true happiness, cloudless, changeless to the end. That the candidates for this blissful condition have never seen an example of it, nor ever knew anyone who had, makes no difference. That is the ideal and they will achieve it.

How did Romantic Love manage to get into marriage at   8
last, where it was most certainly never intended to be? At its highest it was tragic; the love of Héloïse and Abélard. At its most graceful, it was the homage of the trouvère for his lady. In its most popular form, the adulterous strayings of solidly married couples who meant to stray for their own good reasons, but at the same time do nothing to upset the property settlements or the line of legitimacy; at its most trivial, the pretty trifling of shepherd and shepherdess.

This was generally condemned by church and state and a   9
word of fear to honest wives whose mortal enemy it was. Love within the sober, sacred realities of marriage was a matter of personal luck, but in any case, private feelings were strictly a private affair having, at least in theory, no bearing whatever on

the fixed practice of the rules of an institution never intended as a recreation ground for either sex. If the couple discharged their religious and social obligations, furnished forth a copious progeny, kept their troubles to themselves, maintained public civility and died under the same roof, even if not always on speaking terms, it was rightly regarded as a successful marriage. Apparently this testing ground was too severe for all but the stoutest spirits; it too was based on an ideal, as impossible in its way as the ideal Romantic Love. One good thing to be said for it is that society took responsibility for the conditions of marriage, and the sufferers within its bonds could always blame the system, not themselves. But Romantic Love crept into the marriage bed, very stealthily, by centuries, bringing its absurd notions about love as eternal springtime and marriage as a personal adventure meant to provide personal happiness. To a Western romantic such as I, though my views have been much modified by painful experience, it still seems to me a charming work of the human imagination, and it is a pity its central notion has been taken too literally and has hardened into a convention as cramping and enslaving as the older one. The refusal to acknowledge the evils in ourselves which therefore are implicit in any human situation is as extreme and unworkable a proposition as the doctrine of total depravity; but somewhere between them, or maybe beyond them, there does exist a possibility for reconciliation between our desires for impossible satisfactions and the simple unalterable fact that we also desire to be unhappy and that we create our own sufferings; and out of these sufferings we salvage our fragments of happiness.

Our young woman who has been taught that an important 10 part of her human nature is not real because it makes trouble and interferes with her peace of mind and shakes her self-love, has been very badly taught; but she has arrived at a most important stage of her re-education. She is afraid her marriage is going to fail because she has not love enough to face its difficulties; and this because at times she feels a painful hostility toward her husband, and cannot admit its reality because such an admission would damage in her own eyes her view of what love should be, an absurd view, based on her vanity of power. Her hatred is real as her love is real, but her hatred has the advantage at present because it works on a blind instinctual level, it is lawless; and her love is subjected to a code of ideal conditions, impossible by their very nature of fulfillment, which prevents its free growth and deprives it of its right to recognize its human limitations and come to grips with them. Hatred is natural in a sense that love, as she conceives it, a young person brought up in the tradition of Romantic Love, is not natural at all. Yet it did not come by hazard, it is the very imperfect expression of the need of the human imagination to create beauty and harmony out of chaos, no matter how mistaken its notion of these things may be, nor how clumsy its methods. It has conjured love out of the air, and seeks to preserve it by incantations; when she spoke a vow to love and honor her husband until death, she did a very reckless thing, for it is not possible by an act of the will to fulfill such an engagement. But it was the necessary act of faith performed in defense of a mode of feeling, the statement of honorable intention to practice as well as she is able the noble, acquired faculty of love, that very mysterious overtone to sex which is the best thing in it. Her hatred is part of it, the necessary enemy and ally.

[1948 — U.S.A.]

Questions

1. What is the effect of the first paragraph of this essay? Why, do you think, would an essayist find such an effect desirable?

2. "The Necessary Enemy" divides itself into three parts. Describe each part in a sentence or two. How do the first and second parts differ? Why did Porter put the first part first and the second part second? What is gained by Porter's beginning as she does (that is, with paragraphs 1–4)?

3. What metaphors are found in paragraphs 3 and 6? What is their effect?

4. What kind of structural element does Porter make use of in paragraph 5 and thereafter? How is this type of structuring related to her thesis?

5. What is that thesis? Where is it stated? What is the inherent paradox that it entails? Why is the "enemy" "necessary"? What does the essay teach about the nature of reality?

Writing Assignments

1. Why, according to Porter, is hate "necessary"? Write a paragraph addressing this matter, bringing your own experience to bear.

2. Porter holds that "we are all brought up on" romantic love, "especially in America." Is this true according to your experience? If so, write a paper in which you first define this amorphous concept and then discuss how you came by it. For example, how has your conception been influenced by the media, television, and the movies in particular? Conclude by stating whether you still believe in romantic love or have cast off the idea and why.

3. Write an essay in which you begin with and spend the first several paragraphs on a concrete example of something. Then, having established what that something is, analyze the example to make your point. Use "The Necessary Enemy" as your model.

✤ WORDSWORTH COUNTRY ✤

(A REVIEW OF DAVID B. PIRIE'S *WILLIAM WORDSWORTH: THE POETRY OF GRANDEUR AND OF TENDERNESS*)

Edward Proffitt

DESPITE ALL OF THE WORK DONE IN WORDSWORTH[1] STUDIES OVER   1
the last two decades, Wordsworth has remained largely
uncharted. Taking much of that work to task, David B. Pirie
provides us with an adequate map at last. No more shall we get
lost on the byways of debate over the two Wordsworths, or
Wordsworth and apocalypse, or Wordsworth and mortality.
With Pirie in hand, every reader should find ready passage to
Wordsworth in all his topological complexity.

Pirie takes his bearings from two lines from a manuscript   2
fragment of *The Prelude:*[2] "Two feelings have we also from the
first/Of grandeur and of tenderness." The grandeur is the
grandeur of the natural world, where "woods decay . . . ,
never to be decay'd," where, that is, one cannot distinguish the
trees from the forest, where each being is a cell in the one body
of life. Here we must live, and here we would feel at home. The
sense of grandeur, then, is a sense of being at home, of feeling
oneself part of the process of life. "But there's a Tree, of many,
one," says Wordsworth in the "Immortality Ode." It is also
human to separate out, to see the trees rather than the forest, to
become attached to particular things and especially to particular human beings. Such is the nature of human tenderness. Are
grandeur and tenderness then at strife?

"My own view," Pirie writes, "is that the unease of their   3
incompatibilities is what stirs [Wordsworth's] best verse to
greatness." I would put the matter somewhat differently. In the
Great Decade, Wordsworth had faith that he could marry mind
and world in a "spousal verse," as he puts it in the "Prospectus"

---

[1] *[William] Wordsworth:* (1770–1850) The great romantic landscape poet.
[2] *The Prelude:* Wordsworth's longest poem, an autobiography of the growth of his mind.

to *The Recluse,* and could do so by speaking of "nothing more than what we are." In full, this is his vision: of the possibility of the human mind to find the earth a home and yet remain human — in other words, to synthesize the dual impulses of grandeur and of tenderness. Much the same could be said of other Romantic poets (e.g., Coleridge and Keats), in whose work is a probing of the same ontological problem: how to be human in a non-reflecting, undifferentiating world, yet feel oneself to be part of that world. At any rate, having faith that a "unity of being," in Yeats's phrase, could be achieved, Wordsworth could explore the divisions and tensions of our beings "before the blissful hour arrives, . . . /Of this great consummation."

This difference is one of emphasis. I agree entirely with   4
Pirie that it is only after the Great Decade that Wordsworth fell into a comfortable union, or into assertion that the goal had been achieved. But Pirie's emphasis does lead him to misread, I think, at least one moment of joint grandeur and tenderness, "A Slumber Did My Spirit Seal." Taking the poem's "She" as alternately the poet's spirit and the dead loved one, Pirie forces the poem rather mechanically to yield what it must to support his thesis. He all but allegorizes the poem and thereby misses the rich complexity of its closure. "Rolled round in earth's diurnal course,/With rocks, and stones, and trees" — here, surely, grandeur and tenderness, nature's calm and human passion, are held together inextricably. The lines speak both consolation and grief simultaneously, attaining a kind of synthesis.

But quibbles aside, *yes:* "Wordsworth's best verse speaks to   5
both instincts. It insists that the strength of feeling which accompanies them proves that neither can be dismissed in favour of the other. At the most instinctual level, we recognize both the magnificence of the integrated universe *and* the preciousness of the few people that we set apart from it." And yes, Wordsworth's greatness lies in the singular honesty of his best work, in his refusal to manipulate his people toward the

desired end, in his tenacious exploration of the tensions between our needs. With these bearings of grandeur and tenderness, Pirie achieves the miraculous: intricate, delicate, and thoroughly convincing readings of nearly every major poem in the canon, readings that together give a detailed picture of the Wordsworthian terrain.

Most of Pirie's readings, full of fresh insights in and of 6 themselves, cumulate to impart the range of Wordsworth's endeavor — both psychological and linguistic. No one before has found such fullness of meaning in the language of this poet who so mistrusted language. To be sure, Wordsworth's diction and syntax have been treated well by earlier critics (e.g., William Empson, Donald Davie, Josephine Miles), but Pirie has a special touch. At every turn he reveals nuances in Wordsworth's language that have hitherto passed by the rest of us. Page by page, Pirie teaches us how careless we have been with Wordsworth and how careful Wordsworth was himself with words.

Thereby Pirie engenders a trust in this poet who of all great 7 poets has been the least trusted, even by his admirers. Also, as readable as many a recent book has been unreadable, Pirie's book — and especially his last chapter — dispels forever any notion that Wordsworth is in some vague way mystical or just soft-headed. Pirie details conclusively that at his best Wordsworth is a hard realist, exploring our existential dilemmas without allowing himself any easy outs. Oh, how bewildered (and sloppy) we have been! But no more. We now know the place — for the first time.

[1984 — U.S.A.]

Questions

1. An implicit metaphor is suggested by the essay's title and is extended in paragraph 1 and further in paragraphs 2, 5, and 7. What is that metaphor? What words and phrases in paragraph 1 accomplish the extension? What words extend the metaphor in paragraphs 2, 5, and 7? What functions does the metaphor have?

2. The one negative thing said about Pirie's book is in paragraph 4. Why here and not at the beginning or the end? Why is what is said in paragraph 4 called a "quibble" in paragraph 5?

3. Look at the end of each paragraph and the beginning of the next and point out what makes the movement coherent in each case.

Writing Assignments

1. In a paragraph or more, analyze the metaphor extended in this book review. What is it? How is it established? Where and how is it extended? What functions does it have? In what way is it apt in a discussion of Wordsworth?

2. Take a nonfiction book you have recently read — perhaps in connection with a course you have had — and write a book review. First state your reaction to the book; then try to convince your reader of the rightness of that reaction by an examination of the book's ideas and appropriate quotations from it.

----------✛ Is Sex Necessary? ✛----------
VIRGIN BIRTH AND OPPORTUNISM
IN THE GARDEN
David Quammen

Birds do it, bees do it, goes the tune. But the songsters, as usual, would mislead us with drastic oversimplifications. The full truth happens to be more eccentrically nonlibidinous: Sometimes they *don't* do it, those very creatures, and get the same results anyway. Bees of all species, for instance, are notable to geneticists precisely for their ability to produce offspring while doing *without*. Likewise at least one variety of bird — the Beltsville Small White turkey, a domestic dinner-table model out of Beltsville, Maryland — has achieved scientific renown for a similar feat. What we are talking about here is celibate motherhood, procreation without copulation, a phenomenon that goes by the technical name *parthenogenesis*. Translated from the Greek roots: virgin birth.

And you don't have to be Catholic to believe in this one.   2

Miraculous as it may seem, parthenogenesis is actually   3
rather common throughout nature, practiced regularly or
intermittently by at least some species within almost every
group of animals except (for reasons still unknown) dragonflies
and mammals. Reproduction by virgin females has been
discovered among reptiles, birds, fishes, amphibians, crusta-
ceans, mollusks, ticks, the jellyfish clan, flatworms, round-
worms, segmented worms; and among insects (notwithstanding
those unrelentingly sexy dragonflies) it is especially favored.
The order Hymenoptera, including all bees and wasps, is
uniformly parthenogenetic in the manner by which males are
produced: Every male honeybee is born without any genetic
contribution from a father. Among the beetles, there are
thirty-five different forms of parthenogenetic weevil. The
African weaver ant employs parthenogenesis, as do twenty-
three species of fruit fly and at least one kind of roach. The gall
midge *Miastor* is notorious for the exceptionally bizarre and
grisly scenario that allows its fatherless young to see daylight:
Miastor daughters cannibalize the mother from inside, with
ruthless impatience, until her hollowed-out skin splits open like
the door of an overcrowded nursery. But the foremost
practitioners of virgin birth — their elaborate and versatile
proficiency unmatched in the animal kingdom — are undoubtedly the aphids.

Now no sensible reader of even this book[1] can be expected,   4
I realize, to care faintly about aphid biology *qua* aphid biology.
That's just asking too much. But there's a larger rationale for
dragging you aphid-ward. The life cycle of these little nebbishy
sap-sucking insects, the very same that infest rose bushes and
house plants, not only exemplifies *how* parthenogenetic reproduction is done; it also very clearly shows *why*.

First the biographical facts. A typical aphid, which feeds   5
entirely on plant juices tapped off from the vascular system of
young leaves, spends winter dormant and protected, as an egg.

---

[1]*book: Natural Acts,* a book of essays by David Quammen.

The egg is attached near a bud site on the new growth of a poplar tree. In March, when the tree sap has begun to rise and the buds have begun to burgeon, an aphid hatchling appears, plugging its sharp snout (like a mosquito's) into the tree's tenderest plumbing. This solitary individual aphid will be, necessarily, a wingless female. If she is lucky, she will become sole founder of a vast aphid population. Having sucked enough poplar sap to reach maturity, she produces — by *live birth* now, and without benefit of a mate — daughters identical to herself. These wingless daughters also plug into the tree's flow of sap, and they also produce further wingless daughters, until sometime in late May, when that particular branch of that particular tree can support no more thirsty aphids. Suddenly there is a change: The next generation of daughters are born with wings. They fly off in search of a better situation.

One such aviatrix lands on an herbaceous plant — say a young climbing bean in some human's garden — and the pattern repeats. She plugs into the sap ducts on the underside of a new leaf, commences feasting destructively, and delivers by parthenogenesis a great brood of wingless daughters. The daughters beget more daughters, those daughters beget still more, and so on, until the poor bean plant is encrusted with a solid mob of these fat little elbowing greedy sisters. Then again, neatly triggered by the crowded conditions, a generation of daughters are born with wings. Away they fly, looking for prospects, and one of them lights on, say, a sugar beet. (The switch from bean to beet is fine, because our species of typical aphid is not inordinately choosy.) The sugar beet before long is covered, sucked upon mercilessly, victimized by a horde of mothers and nieces and granddaughters. Still not a single male aphid has appeared anywhere in the chain.

The lurching from one plant to another continues; the alternation between wingless and winged daughters continues. But in September, with fresh tender plant growth increasingly hard to find, there is another change.

Flying daughters are born who have a different destiny: They wing back to the poplar tree, where they give birth to a crop of wingless females that are unlike any so far. These latest girls know the meaning of sex! Meanwhile, at long last, the starving survivors back on that final bedraggled sugar beet have brought forth a generation of males. The males have wings. They take to the air in quest of poplar trees and first love. *Et voilà.* The mated females lay eggs that will wait out the winter near bud sites on that poplar tree, and the circle is thus completed. One single aphid hatchling — call her the *fundatrix* — in this way can give rise in the course of a year, from her own ovaries exclusively, to roughly a zillion aphids.

Well and good, you say. A zillion aphids. But what is the 9 point of it?

The point, for aphids as for most other parthenogenetic 10 animals, is (1) exceptionally fast reproduction that allows (2) maximal exploitation of temporary resource abundance and unstable environmental conditions, while (3) facilitating the successful colonization of unfamiliar habitats. In other words the aphid, like the gall midge and the weaver ant and the rest of their fellow parthenogens, is by its evolved character a galloping opportunist.

This is a term of science, not of abuse. Population ecologists 11 make an illuminating distinction between what they label *equilibrium* and *opportunistic* species. According to William Birky and John Gilbert, from a paper in the journal *American Zoologist:* "Equilibrium species, exemplified by many vertebrates, maintain relatively constant population sizes, in part by being adapted to reproduce, at least slowly, in most of the environmental conditions which they meet. Opportunistic species, on the other hand, show extreme population fluctuations; they are adapted to reproduce only in a relatively narrow range of conditions, but make up for this by reproducing extremely rapidly in favorable circumstances. At least in some cases, opportunistic organisms can also be categorized as colonizing organisms." Birky and Gilbert also emphasize that "The potential for rapid reproduction is the essential evolutionary ticket for entry into the opportunistic life style."

And parthenogenesis, in turn, is the greatest time-saving 12 gimmick in the history of animal reproduction. No hours or days are wasted while a female looks for a mate; no minutes lost to the act of mating itself. The female aphid attains sexual maturity and, bang, she becomes automatically pregnant. No waiting, no courtship, no fooling around. She delivers her brood of daughters, they grow to puberty and, zap, another generation immediately. If humans worked as fast, Jane Fonda today would be a great-grandmother. The time saved to parthenogenetic species may seem trivial, but it is not. It adds up dizzyingly: In the same time taken by a sexually reproducing insect to complete three generations for a total of 1,200 offspring, an aphid (assuming the *same* time required for each female to mature, and the *same* number of progeny in each litter), squandering no time on courtship or sex, will progress through six generations for an extended family of 318,000,000.

Even this isn't speedy enough for some restless opportun- 13 ists. That matricidal gall midge *Miastor*, whose larvae feed on fleeting eruptions of fungus under the bark of trees, has developed a startling way to cut further time from the cycle of procreation. Far from waiting for a mate, *Miastor* does not even wait for maturity. When food is abundant, it is the *larva*, not the adult female fly, who is eaten alive from inside by her own daughters. And as those voracious daughters burst free of the husk that was their mother, each of them already contains further larval daughters taking shape ominously within its own ovaries. While the food lasts, while opportunity endures, no *Miastor* female can live to adulthood without dying of mother-hood.

The implicit principle behind all this nonsexual reproduc- 14 tion, all this hurry, is simple: Don't argue with success. Don't tamper with a genetic blueprint that works. Unmated female aphids, and gall midges, pass on their own gene patterns virtually unaltered (except for the occasional mutation) to their daughters. Sexual reproduction, on the other hand, constitutes, by its essence, genetic tampering. The whole purpose of joining sperm with egg is to shuffle the genes of both parents and come up with a new combination that might perhaps be more advantageous. Give the kid something neither Mom nor Pop ever had. Parthenogenetic species, during their hurried phases at least, dispense with this genetic shuffle. They stick stubbornly to the gene pattern that seems to be working. They produce (with certain complicated exceptions) natural clones of themselves.

But what they gain thereby in reproductive rate, in great 15 explosions of population, they give up in flexibility. They minimize their genetic options. They lessen their chances of adapting to unforeseen changes of circumstance.

Which is why more than one biologist has drawn the same 16 conclusion as M. J. D. White: "Parthenogenetic forms seem to be frequently successful in the particular ecological niche which they occupy, but sooner or later the inherent disadvantages of their genetic system must be expected to lead to a lack of adaptability, followed by eventual extinction, or perhaps in some cases by a return to sexuality."

So it *is* necessary, at least intermittently (once a year, for 17 the aphids, whether they need it or not), this thing called sex. As of course you and I knew it must be. Otherwise surely, by now, we mammals and dragonflies would have come up with something more dignified.

[1982 — U.S.A.]

Questions

1. For what audience was this essay written? What in and about it tells you as much? How might it have differed had it been written for an audience of entomologists (bug scientists)?

2. What is remarkable about the diction here? What kind of tone does the essay's remarkable (that is, worthy of remark) diction help create? Why such diction and thence such a tone?

3. There are many figures of speech in this essay, especially explicit metaphors and examples of personification. Pick out some such figures for functional analysis. Why does Quammen use these figures? How do they combine with diction to create tone?

4. In paragraphs 5–8, Quammen sets forth the process of aphid reproduction. How is this section of the essay organized? What transitions highlight its structure?

5. What kind of beginning does this essay have? What is Quammen's purpose? What kind of exposition is the present essay an example of?

Writing Assignments

1. Write a paragraph using diction and figuration like Quammen's. Then write a second paragraph on the same topic, only this time use standard diction and no figuration. Observe the difference in tone and effect between the two paragraphs.
2. Write an essay setting forth the stages of some process you understand: cooking your favorite meal, developing photographs, making jewelry or making up your face, playing any kind of a game or sport, tuning up your bike or car, and so forth. Be sure to make clear the purpose of each step and to provide appropriate transitions as necessary.

✤ ON THE ART OF ✤ STEALING HUMAN RIGHTS
Rarihokwats (Jerry Gambill)

THE ART OF DENYING INDIANS THEIR HUMAN RIGHTS HAS BEEN 1 refined to a science. The following list of commonly used techniques will be helpful in "burglar-proofing" your reserves and *your rights*.

GAIN THE INDIANS' CO-OPERATION — It is much 2 easier to steal someone's human rights if you can do it with his OWN cooperation. SO. . . .

1. Make him a non-person. Human rights are for people. 3 Convince Indians their ancestors were savages, that they were pagan, that Indians are drunkards. Make them wards of the government. Make a legal distinction, as in the Indian Act, between Indians and persons. Write history books that tell half the story.

2. Convince the Indian that he should be patient, that these 4 things take time. Tell him that we are making progress, and that progress takes time.

3. Make him believe that things are being done for his own 5 good. Tell him that you're sure that after he has experienced your laws and actions that he will realize how good they have been. Tell the Indian he has to take a little of the bad in order to enjoy the benefits you are conferring on him.

4. Get some Indian people to do the dirty work. There are 6 always those who will act for you to the disadvantage of their own people. Just give them a little honor and praise. This is generally the function of band councils, chiefs, and advisory councils: They have little legal power, but can handle the tough decisions such as welfare, allocation of housing, etc.

5. Consult the Indian, but do not act on the basis of what you 7 hear. Tell the Indian he has a voice and go through the motions of listening. Then interpret what you have heard to suit your own needs.

6. Insist that the Indian "GOES THROUGH THE PROPER CHAN- 8 NELS." Make the channels and the procedures so difficult that he won't bother to do anything. When he discovers what the proper channels are and becomes proficient at the procedures, change them.

7. Make the Indian believe that you are working hard for 9 him, putting in much overtime and at a great sacrifice, and imply that he should be appreciative. This is the ultimate in skills in stealing human rights: When you obtain the thanks of your victim.

8. Allow a few individuals to "MAKE THE GRADE" and then point 10 to them as examples. Say that the "HARD WORKERS" and the "GOOD" Indians have made it, and that therefore it is a person's own fault if he doesn't succeed.

9. Appeal to the Indian's sense of fairness, and tell him that, 11 even though things are pretty bad, it is not right for him to make strong protests. Keep the argument going on his form of protest and avoid talking about the real issue. Refuse to deal with him while he is protesting. Take all the fire out of his efforts.

10. Encourage the Indian to take his case to court. This is very 12 expensive, takes lots of time and energy, and is very safe because the laws are stacked against him. The court's ruling will defeat the Indian's cause, but makes him think he has obtained justice.

11. Make the Indian believe that things could be worse, and 13 that instead of complaining about the loss of human rights, to be grateful for the human rights we do have. In fact, convince him that to attempt to regain a right he has lost is likely to jeopardize the rights that he still has.

12. Set yourself up as the protector of the Indian's human 14 rights, and then you can choose to act on only those violations you wish to act upon. By getting successful action on a few minor violations of human rights, you can point to these as examples of your devotion to his cause. The burglar who is also the doorman is the perfect combination.

13. Pretend that the reason for the loss of human rights is for 15 some other reason than that the person is an Indian. Tell him some of your best friends are Indians, and that his loss of rights is because of his housekeeping, his drinking, his clothing. If he improves in these areas, it will be necessary for you to adopt another technique of stealing his rights.

14. Make the situation more complicated than is necessary. 16 Tell the Indian you will have to take a survey to find out just how many other Indians are being discriminated against. Hire a group of professors to make a year-long research project.

15. Insist on unanimity. Let the Indian know that when all the 17 Indians in Canada can make up their minds about just what they want as a group, then you will act. Play one group's special situation against another group's wishes.

16. Select very limited alternatives, neither of which has much 18 merit, and then tell the Indian that he indeed has a choice. Ask, for instance, if he could or would rather have council elections in June or December, instead of asking if he wants them at all.

17. Convince the Indian that the leaders who are the most 19
    beneficial and powerful are dangerous and not to be
    trusted. Or simply lock them up on some charge like
    driving with no lights. Or refuse to listen to the real leaders
    and spend much time with the weak ones. Keep the people
    split from their leaders by sowing rumor. Attempt to get
    the best leaders into high-paying jobs where they have to
    keep quiet to keep their paycheck coming in.

18. Speak of the common good. Tell the Indian that you can't 20
    consider yourselves when there is the whole nation to think
    of. Tell him that he can't think only of himself. For
    instance, in regard to hunting rights, tell him we have to
    think of all the hunters, or the sporting-goods industry.

19. Remove rights so gradually that people don't realize what 21
    has happened until it is too late. Again, in regard to hunting
    rights, first restrict the geographical area where hunting is
    permitted, then cut the season to certain times of the year,
    then cut the limits down gradually, then insist on licensing,
    and then Indians will be on the same grounds as white
    sportsmen.

20. Rely on reason and logic (your reason and logic) instead of 22
    rightness and morality. Give thousands of reasons for
    things, but do not get trapped into arguments about what
    is right.

21. Hold a conference on HUMAN RIGHTS, have everyone blow off 23
    steam and tension, and go home feeling that things are well
    in hand.

[1968 — U.S.A.]

Questions

1. This piece was written and given as a speech. What in the piece itself
   indicates as much? What kind of actual audience is indicated?

2. Each section here begins with a verb in the imperative mood. Why?
   What is the rhetorical effect of this formal repetition?

3. What is the fictive audience of "On the Art of Stealing Human
   Rights"? What is the fictive stance of the speaker with respect to this

audience? How do both (the fictive audience and the fictive stance of the speaker) convey the satiric point?

4. The essay ends with a zinger (item 21). How so? Why is this especially ironic item saved till last?

Writing Assignments

1. In a paragraph or two, evaluate the effectiveness of this piece as a satirical essay. What is satirized? How and how well? Rarihokwats uses exaggeration and formal repetition here. Are these devices effective? Is the list structure effective? Why or why not?

2. Write an essay "after" "On the Art of Stealing Human Rights." That is, pretend that you are addressing an audience whose ideas and interests are the opposite of those of the audience you would actually be speaking to or writing for and, in the same kind of list structure (maybe ten items in all, with each item beginning in the imperative mood), make a satirical point by strategically exaggerating and otherwise distorting the position and/or the mode of operation of the butt of your satire. Some possible topics for this assignment are the art of stealing students' rights (spoken by a fictive dean, say, at a fictive conference of deans), the way to keep women in their place (spoken by a fictive male chauvinist at a fictive bachelor party), the strategies of keeping minorities where they belong (spoken by a fictive racist at a fictive KKK gathering). Remember, you will be arguing the opposite of what you really believe in such a way that it is clear that this is what you are doing.

✤ THE VINYL SANTA ✤
Lillian Ross

OUR LIGHTED FIREPROOF PLASTIC CHRISTMAS BELLS ARE STRUNG ALL   1
through the house, not a creature is stirring, and our mail-order
catalogues — now piled high on the back porch — have been
under surveillance since August, when they started coming in
from Atlantic City, New Jersey; Oshkosh, Wisconsin; Evan-
ston, Illinois; Chicago, Illinois; Falls Church, Virginia; Omaha,
Nebraska; Vineland, New Jersey; Northport, New York; New
York, New York; and elsewhere, including points across the
seas. We did our shopping during Indian summer, without
leaving our chair. Our house is full. Our task is completed. We
are ready.

On our front door is a "Deck the Door Knob of red-and-   2
green felt with touches of glittering gold that has three jingly
bells to say 'Hi! and Merry Christmas!' to all comers." On our
windows are "Press-On Window Scenes" of snowmen and
reindeer, and the windows are further ornamented with "Giant,
29-inch by 20-inch Personal Balls Artistically Hand-Lettered
with the Family Name." Mounted outside on the wall of the
house are "The Three Wise Men in Full Color in a Procession
of Heavy Weatherproof Methyl-methacrylate Plastic." Each
Wise Man is three feet tall and illuminated. A "Life-Size
Climbing Vinyl Santa" is on the rooftop, and on the front lawn
we have "3-D Thirty-Inch High Full Color Carollers of Strong
Vinylite Carolling 'Oh, Come All Ye Faithful!'" In place of our
regular doorbell we have a "glowing, jingling Santa stamped
with the family name with a cord that visitors pull that raises
Santa's arms in welcome, jingling bright brass bells." The
garage door is covered with a "Giant Door Greeter Five Feet
High and Six Feet Wide, Reading 'Merry Christmas.'"
Indoors, all our rooms have been sprayed either with "Bay-
berry Mist, the forest-fresh scent-of-Christmas" or with the
"pungent, spicy, exotic, sweet and rare frankincense-and-

myrrh spray — gift of the Magi to the newborn Babe." Each light switch is covered with a "Switchplate-Santa made of white felt with red bell-bedecked cap — the switch comes through his open mouth, the sight of which will make you feel jolly." The towels on the bathroom racks are hand-printed with designs of sleighs and candy canes. The rug next to the tub has "Jolly Old Santa centered in deep, soft, plushy, white pile, and he's wreathed in smiles and in cherries, too, for 'round his head is a gay, cherry wreath." All the mirrors in the house are plastered with red, green, and white pleated tissue cutouts of angels with self-adhesive backs. In the dining room, "Full Size Santa Mugs of Bright Red-and-White Glazed Ceramic are 'Ready' for a 'Spot' of Holiday Cheer." In the living room, we have a "giant holiday chandelier of metallic foil discs reflecting a rainbow of colors," and "giant four-foot electric candles in festive red-and-white candy stripes are glowing cheerfully from their rock-steady base to their dripping wax 'flame.' " On the hall table stands our "Electric Musical Church, five inches high, with inspirational strains of 'Silent Night' pealing reverently from behind lighted, colorfully stained windows."

The tree is trimmed, all the way from a "Perforated Golden 3 Star Making the Sun Envious of Its Brilliance, as though the Blazing Star of Bethlehem Were Pausing in Its Orbit at Your Home," down to the "Christmas Tree Bib Covered with a Profusion of Christmas Designs and Colors" on the floor. Reflecting the light of the Perforated Golden Star, which is made of anodized aluminum with "Hundreds of Holes through which the Light Twinkles just like a Real Star," hang dozens of "Personalized Tree Balls with Names of the Family Nicely Applied in Shimmering, Non-Tarnishing Glitter." Bare spots on the tree are filled in with "Luminous Tree Icicles of Plastic," "Luminous, Plastic, Heavenly Angel Babes Who Have Left the Milky Way," "Handcarved Wooden Angels Holding Hymnals on Gilded Hanging Strings," "Frosty White Pine Cones Lit with Colored Bulbs," "Miniature Felt Money Bags Gayly Trimmed in Assorted Designs of Yuletide," and "Yummy-Yum-Yum Santa Sweetest Holiday Lollipops."

On Christmas morning, there will be plenty of laughs when   4
everybody gets dressed. Dad will be wearing his "Personalized
Holiday Ringing Bell Shorts of White Sanforized Cotton with
Santa Claus Handpainted in All His Glory on One Side with a
Tinkling Bell on the Tassel of His Cap and Dad's name
embroidered in Contrasting Red on the Other." Big Sister will
have on "Bright Red Holiday Stretch Socks of Bright Red
Nylon Embossed with Contrasting White Holiday Motif."
Little Sister and Mom will have on matching "Candy Striped
Flannelette Housecoats." Brother will have on a "Clip-On Bow
Tie of Red Felt in a Holly Pattern" and also "The Host with the
Most Bright Red Felt Vest with Colorful Christmas Accent."
Auntie will have on "Ringing Bell Panties Boasting a Ribbon
Bedecked Candy Cane Handpainted in Brilliant Yuletide
Colors with a Real Tinkling Bell for Extra Cheer." And Shep
will have on his own "Personalized Dog Galoshes Embossed
with Dog Claus on the Toes." Odds and ends under the tree
will include a "Jingle Bell Apron that Plays a Merry Tune with
Every Movement," "Donner and Blitzen Salt and Pepper
Shakers," a set of "Holly Jewelry for the Holly-Days," a "Ten
Commandments Bookmark of Ten Radiant Gold-Plated
Squares that Look Like Ancient Scrolled Pages of the Old
Testament with the Commandments Etched Upon Them," and
"Hi-Fi Bible Stories on a Personalized Record." And our
Christmas dinner will be prepared with the help of the "No
Cooking Cookbook, with a Collection of Easy-To-Fix Recipes
for Busy Mothers that Turns Canned and Frozen Foods into a
Banquet of Gourmet Dishes."

[1966 — U.S.A.]

Questions

1. Why does Ross begin with a list of catalogues? What does the array
   of catalogues symbolically suggest?
2. A narrative of sorts, this essay tells a story. What story does it tell?
   How is it organized?
3. Syntactically, "The Vinyl Santa" is told mainly in the passive voice.
   Why?

4. Composed for the most part of advertising slogans and catalogue descriptions, the present essay is a satire not of Christmas but of. . . . Of what? What is Ross's satirical theme?

5. What do the allusion in paragraph 1 to "The Night Before Christmas" and the way the essay ends suggest? What is suggested by the kind of narrative voice Ross uses?

Writing Assignments

1. Changing the holiday, write an essay after "The Vinyl Santa." Amass objects and their catalogue descriptions (you may make these up yourself) associated with Thanksgiving, Easter, the Fourth of July. Then organize your objects and descriptions so as to make a satirical point without direct comment.

2. How does Ross get across her point? Write a paper analyzing her essay as to its satiric theme and how that theme is brought home to the reader.

✤ HOW I WRITE ✤
Bertrand Russell

I CANNOT PRETEND TO KNOW HOW WRITING OUGHT TO BE DONE, OR   1
what a wise critic would advise me to do with a view to improving my own writing. The most that I can do is to relate some things about my own attempts.

Until I was twenty-one, I wished to write more or less in   2
the style of John Stuart Mill.[1] I liked the structure of his sentences and his manner of developing a subject. I had, however, already a different ideal, derived, I suppose, from mathematics. I wished to say everything in the smallest number of words in which it could be said clearly. Perhaps, I thought, one should imitate Baedeker[2] rather than any more literary

---

[1]*John Stuart Mill:* (1806 – 1873) British economist and philosopher, whose style is rather cut and dry.

[2]*[Karl] Baedeker:* (1801 – 1859) Publisher of a series of European guidebooks, now called "Baedekers" after him.

model. I would spend hours trying to find the shortest way of saying something without ambiguity, and to this aim I was willing to sacrifice all attempts at aesthetic excellence.

At the age of twenty-one, however, I came under a new influence, that of my future brother-in-law, Logan Pearsall Smith.[3] He was at that time exclusively interested in style as opposed to matter. His gods were Flaubert[4] and Walter Pater,[5] and I was quite ready to believe that the way to learn how to write was to copy their technique. He gave me various simple rules, of which I remember only two: "Put a comma every four words," and "never use 'and' except at the beginning of a sentence." His most emphatic advice was that one must always rewrite. I conscientiously tried this, but found that my first draft was almost always better than my second. This discovery has saved me an immense amount of time. I do not, of course, apply it to the substance, but only to the form. When I discover an error of an important kind, I rewrite the whole. What I do not find is that I can improve a sentence when I am satisfied with what it means.

Very gradually I have discovered ways of writing with a minimum of worry and anxiety. When I was young each fresh piece of serious work used to seem to me for a time — perhaps a long time — to be beyond my powers. I would fret myself into a nervous state from fear that it was never going to come right. I would make one unsatisfying attempt after another, and in the end have to discard them all. At last I found that such fumbling attempts were a waste of time. It appeared that after first contemplating a book on some subject, and after giving serious preliminary attention to it, I needed a period of subconscious incubation which could not be hurried and was if anything impeded by deliberate thinking. Sometimes I would find, after a time, that I had made a mistake, and that I could not write the book I had had in mind. But often I was more fortunate.

[3]*Logan Pearsall Smith:* (1865–1946) American essayist and prose stylist.
[4]*[Gustave] Flaubert:* (1821–1880) The great French stylist, author of *Madame Bovary.*
[5]*Walter Pater:* (1839–1894) British essayist noted for the clarity of his style.

Having, by a time of very intense concentration, planted the problem in my subconsciousness, it would germinate underground until, suddenly, the solution emerged with blinding clarity, so that it only remained to write down what had appeared as if in a revelation.

The most curious example of this process, and the one 5 which led me subsequently to rely upon it, occurred at the beginning of 1914. I had undertaken to give the Lowell Lectures at Boston, and had chosen as my subject "Our Knowledge of the External World." Throughout 1913 I thought about this topic. In term time in my rooms at Cambridge, in vacations in a quiet inn on the upper reaches of the Thames, I concentrated with such intensity that I sometimes forgot to breathe and emerged panting as from a trance. But all to no avail. To every theory that I could think of I could perceive fatal objections. At last, in despair, I went off to Rome for Christmas, hoping that a holiday would revive my flagging energy. I got back to Cambridge on the last day of 1913, and although my difficulties were still completely unresolved I arranged, because the remaining time was short, to dictate as best as I could to a stenographer. Next morning, as she came in at the door, I suddenly saw exactly what I had to say, and proceeded to dictate the whole book without a moment's hesitation.

I do not want to convey an exaggerated impression. The 6 book was very imperfect, and I now think that it contains serious errors. But it was the best that I could have done at that time, and a more leisurely method (within the time at my disposal) would almost certainly have produced something worse. Whatever may be true of other people, this is the right method for me. Flaubert and Pater, I have found, are best forgotten so far as I am concerned.

Although what I now think about how to write is not so 7 very different from what I thought at the age of eighteen, my development has not been by any means rectilinear. There was a time, in the first years of this century, when I had more florid and rhetorical ambitions. This was the time when I wrote *A Free*

Man's Worship, a work of which I do not now think well. At that time I was steeped in Milton's prose, and his rolling periods reverberated through the caverns of my mind. I cannot say that I no longer admire them, but for me to imitate them involves a certain insincerity. In fact, all imitation is dangerous. Nothing could be better in style than the Prayer Book and the Authorized Version of the Bible, but they express a way of thinking and feeling which is different from that of our time. A style is not good unless it is an intimate and almost involuntary expression of the personality of the writer, and then only if the writer's personality is worth expressing. But although direct imitation is always to be deprecated, there is much to be gained by familiarity with good prose, especially in cultivating a sense for prose rhythm.

There are some simple maxims — not perhaps quite so 8 simple as those which my brother-in-law Logan Pearsall Smith offered me — which I think might be commended to writers of expository prose. First: never use a long word if a short word will do. Second: if you want to make a statement with a great many qualifications, put some of the qualifications in separate sentences. Third: do not let the beginning of your sentence lead the reader to an expectation which is contradicted by the end. Take, say, such a sentence as the following, which might occur in a work on sociology: "Human beings are completely exempt from undesirable behavior patterns only when certain prerequisites, not satisfied except in a small percentage of actual cases, have, through some fortuitous concourse of favorable circumstances, whether congenital or environmental, chanced to combine in producing an individual in whom many factors deviate from the norm in a socially advantageous manner." Let us see if we can translate this sentence into English. I suggest the following: "All men are scoundrels, or at any rate almost all. The men who are not must have had unusual luck, both in their birth and in their upbringing." This is shorter and more intelligible, and says just the same thing. But I am afraid any professor who used the second sentence instead of the first would get the sack.

This suggests a word of advice to such of my readers as may 9
happen to be professors. I am allowed to use plain English
because everybody knows that I could use mathematical logic if
I chose. Take the statement: "Some people marry their
deceased wives' sisters." I can express this in language which
only becomes intelligible after years of study, and this gives me
freedom. I suggest to young professors that their first work
should be written in a jargon only to be understood by the
erudite few. With that behind them, they can ever after say
what they have to say in a language "understood of the
people." In these days, when our very lives are at the mercy of
the professors, I cannot but think that they would deserve our
gratitude if they adopted my advice.

[1935 — Great Britain]

Questions

1. The statement of purpose (the second sentence of the first
   paragraph) suggests a way of structuring. What is that way? Is this
   the way of the essay at hand? How so?

2. Russell speaks of "the shortest way of saying something without
   ambiguity." This is the golden rule of good writing, at least writing
   directed toward an audience and aimed at communication. Why?
   But does this mean that all sentences should be short? What does the
   amendment "without ambiguity" suggest in this regard?

3. "I can[not] improve a sentence when I am satisfied with what it
   means," Russell states. What, then, is his criterion of judgment? Is
   this criterion good and worth adopting? Why or why not?

4. Russell uses, as an example of bad writing, a 55-word sentence
   (paragraph 8) whose diction and syntax are the same as those that
   Joan Didion (pages 184–89) and George Orwell (pages 402–16)
   deride. What are the damnable qualities of such diction and syntax?
   Russell restates the sentence in 28 words and concludes that "the
   shorter and more intelligible [statement] . . . says just the same
   thing." But this is not exactly the case, for the two sentences differ
   in pace, tone, voice, and ultimate stance. How so?

5. How does Russell's "advice" to "young professors" at the end of
   "How I Write" summarize his main point about good writing?

Writing Assignments

1. Russell's "maxims" (paragraph 8) are much like Orwell's "rules" in "Politics and the English Language" (page 415, paragraph 18). In a paragraph or more, compare these maxims and rules, concluding with a statement summarizing what both writers hold good writing to be.

2. Different writers write in different ways, and we each must find the way best suited at any given time to our own temperament and needs. Russell's title tacitly acknowledges this — "How I Write" and not "How to Write." Now, how do you write? Write an essay detailing how you go about writing an essay at this stage in your life, how you came to write in this manner, and how you hope to write in the future.

✤ THE NUCLEAR WINTER ✤
Carl Sagan

Into the eternal darkness, into fire, into ice.
— Dante, The Inferno

EXCEPT FOR FOOLS AND MADMEN, EVERYONE KNOWS THAT NUCLEAR   1
war would be an unprecedented human catastrophe. A more or less typical strategic warhead has a yield of 2 megatons, the explosive equivalent of 2 million tons of TNT. But 2 million tons of TNT is about the same as all the bombs exploded in World War II — a single bomb with the explosive power of the entire Second World War but compressed into a few seconds of time and an area 30 or 40 miles across . . .

In a 2-megaton explosion over a fairly large city, buildings   2
would be vaporized, people reduced to atoms and shadows, outlying structures blown down like matchsticks and raging fires ignited. And if the bomb were exploded on the ground, an enormous crater, like those that can be seen through a telescope on the surface of the Moon, would be all that remained where midtown once had been. There are now more than 50,000

nuclear weapons, more than 13,000 megatons of yield, deployed in the arsenals of the United States and the Soviet Union — enough to obliterate a million Hiroshimas.

But there are fewer than 3,000 cities on the Earth with 3 populations of 100,000 or more. You cannot find anything like a million Hiroshimas to obliterate. Prime military and industrial targets that are far from cities are comparatively rare. Thus, there are vastly more nuclear weapons than are needed for any plausible deterrence of a potential adversary.

Nobody knows, of course, how many megatons would be 4 exploded in a real nuclear war. There are some who think that a nuclear war can be "contained," bottled up before it runs away to involve many of the world's arsenals. But a number of detailed analyses, war games run by the U.S. Department of Defense and official Soviet pronouncements, all indicate that this containment may be too much to hope for: Once the bombs begin exploding, communications failures, disorganization, fear, the necessity of making in minutes decisions affecting the fates of millions and the immense psychological burden of knowing that your own loved ones may already have been destroyed are likely to result in a nuclear paroxysm. Many investigations, including a number of studies for the U.S. government, envision the explosion of 5,000 to 10,000 megatons — the detonation of tens of thousands of nuclear weapons that now sit quietly, inconspicuously, in missile silos, submarines, and long-range bombers, faithful servants awaiting orders.

The World Health Organization, in a recent detailed study 5 chaired by Sune K. Bergstrom (the 1982 Nobel laureate in physiology and medicine), concludes that 1.1 billion people would be killed outright in such a nuclear war, mainly in the United States, the Soviet Union, Europe, China, and Japan. An additional 1.1 billion people would suffer serious injuries and radiation sickness, for which medical help would be unavailable. It thus seems possible that more than 2 billion people — almost half of all the humans on Earth — would be destroyed in the immediate aftermath of a global thermonuclear war. This would represent by far the greatest disaster in the history of the human species and, with no other adverse effects, would probably be enough to reduce at least the Northern Hemisphere to a state of prolonged agony and barbarism. Unfortunately, the real situation would be much worse.

In technical studies of the consequences of nuclear weapons 6
explosions, there has been a dangerous tendency to underestimate the results. This is partly due to a tradition of conservatism which generally works well in science but which is of more dubious applicability when the lives of billions of people are at stake. In the Bravo test of March 1, 1954, a 15-megaton thermonuclear bomb was exploded on Bikini Atoll. It had about double the yield expected, and there was an unanticipated last-minute shift in the wind direction. As a result, deadly radioactive fallout came down on Rongelap in the Marshall Islands, more than 200 kilometers away. Almost all the children on Rongelap subsequently developed thyroid nodules and lesions, and other longterm medical problems, due to the radioactive fallout.

Likewise, in 1973, it was discovered that high-yield 7
airbursts will chemically burn the nitrogen in the upper air, converting it into oxides of nitrogen; these, in turn, combine with and destroy the protective ozone in the Earth's stratosphere. The surface of the Earth is shielded from deadly solar ultraviolet radiation by a layer of ozone so tenuous that, were it brought down to sea level, it would be only 3 millimeters thick. Partial destruction of this ozone layer can have serious consequences for the biology of the entire planet.

These discoveries, and others like them, were made by 8
chance. They were largely unexpected. And now another consequence — by far the most dire — has been uncovered, again more or less by accident.

The U.S. Mariner 9 spacecraft, the first vehicle to orbit 9
another planet, arrived at Mars in late 1971. The planet was enveloped in a global dust storm. As the fine particles slowly fell out, we were able to measure temperature changes in the

atmosphere and on the surface. Soon it became clear what had happened:

The dust, lofted by high winds off the desert into the upper 10 Martian atmosphere, had absorbed the incoming sunlight and prevented much of it from reaching the ground. Heated by the sunlight, the dust warmed the adjacent air. But the surface, enveloped in partial darkness, became much chillier than usual. Months later, after the dust fell out of the atmosphere, the upper air cooled and the surface warmed, both returning to their normal conditions. We were able to calculate accurately, from how much dust there was in the atmosphere, how cool the Martian surface ought to have been.

Afterwards, I and my colleagues, James B. Pollack and 11 Brian Toon of NASA's Ames Research Center, were eager to apply these insights to the Earth. In a volcanic explosion, dust aerosols are lofted into the high atmosphere. We calculated by how much the Earth's global temperature should decline after a major volcanic explosion and found that our results (generally a fraction of a degree) were in good accord with actual measurements. Joining forces with Richard Turco, who has studied the effects of nuclear weapons for many years, we then began to turn our attention to the climatic effects of nuclear war. [The scientific paper, "Global Atmospheric Consequences of Nuclear War," is written by R. P. Turco, O. B. Toon, T. P. Ackerman, J. B. Pollack, and Carl Sagan. From the last names of the authors, this work is generally referred to as "TTAPS."]

We knew that nuclear explosions, particularly ground- 12 bursts, would lift an enormous quantity of fine soil particles into the atmosphere (more than 100,000 tons of fine dust for every megaton exploded in a surface burst). Our work was further spurred by Paul Crutzen of the Max Planck Institute for Chemistry in Mainz, West Germany, and by John Birks of the University of Colorado, who pointed out that huge quantities of smoke would be generated in the burning of cities and forests following a nuclear war.

Groundbursts — at hardened missile silos, for example — 13 generate fine dust. Airbursts — over cities and unhardened military installations — make fires and therefore smoke. The amount of dust and soot generated depends on the conduct of the war, the yields of the weapons employed and the ratio of groundbursts to airbursts. So we ran computer models for several dozen different nuclear war scenarios. Our baseline case, as in many other studies, was a 5,000-megaton war with only a modest fraction of the yield (20 percent) expended on urban or industrial targets. Our job, for each case, was to follow the dust and smoke generated, see how much sunlight was absorbed and by how much the temperatures changed, figure out how the particles spread in longitude and latitude, and calculate how long before it all fell out of the air back onto the surface. Since the radioactivity would be attached to these same fine particles, our calculations also revealed the extent and timing of the subsequent radioactive fallout.

Some of what I am about to describe is horrifying. I know, 14 because it horrifies me. There is a tendency — psychiatrists call it "denial" — to put it out of our minds, not to think about it. But if we are to deal intelligently, wisely, with the nuclear arms race, then we must steel ourselves to contemplate the horrors of nuclear war.

The results of our calculations astonished us. In the 15 baseline case, the amount of sunlight at the ground was reduced to a few percent of normal — much darker, in daylight, than in a heavy overcast and too dark for plants to make a living from photosynthesis. At least in the Northern Hemisphere, where the great preponderance of strategic targets lies, an unbroken and deadly gloom would persist for weeks.

Even more unexpected were the temperatures calculated. 16 In the baseline case, land temperatures, except for narrow strips of coastline, dropped to minus 25° Celsius (minus 13° Fahrenheit) and stayed below freezing for months — even for a summer war. (Because the atmospheric structure becomes much more stable as the upper atmosphere is heated and the lower air is cooled, we may have severely *under*estimated how long the cold and the dark would last.) The oceans, a significant heat reservoir, would not freeze, however, and a major ice age would probably not be triggered. But because the temperatures would drop so catastrophically, virtually all crops and farm animals, at least in the Northern Hemisphere, would be destroyed, as would most varieties of uncultivated or undomesticated food supplies. Most of the human survivors would starve.

In addition, the amount of radioactive fallout is much more 17 than expected. Many previous calculations simply ignored the intermediate time-scale fallout. That is, calculations were made for the prompt fallout — the plumes of radioactive debris blown downwind from each target — and for the long-term fallout, the fine radioactive particles lofted into the stratosphere that would descend about a year later, after most of the radioactivity had decayed. However, the radioactivity carried into the upper atmosphere (but not as high as the stratosphere) seems to have been largely forgotten. We found for the baseline case that roughly 30 percent of the land at northern midlatitudes could receive a radioactive dose greater than 250 rads, and that about 50 percent of northern midlatitudes could receive a dose greater than 100 rads. A 100-rad dose is the equivalent of about 1,000 medical X-rays. A 400-rad dose will, more likely than not, kill you.

The cold, the dark, and the intense radioactivity, together 18 lasting for months, represent a severe assault on our civilization and our species. Civil and sanitary services would be wiped out. Medical facilities, drugs, the most rudimentary means for relieving the vast human suffering, would be unavailable. Any but the most elaborate shelters would be useless, quite apart from the question of what good it might be to emerge a few months later. Synthetics burned in the destruction of the cities would produce a wide variety of toxic gases, including carbon monoxide, cyanides, dioxins, and furans. After the dust and soot settled out, the solar ultraviolet flux would be much larger than its present value. Immunity to disease would decline. Epidemics and pandemics would be rampant, especially after the billion or so unburied bodies began to thaw. Moreover, the combined influence of these severe and simultaneous stresses on life are likely to produce even more adverse consequences — biologists call them synergisms — that we are not yet wise enough to foresee.

So far, we have talked only of the Northern Hemisphere. 19 But it now seems — unlike the case of a single nuclear weapons test — that in a real nuclear war, the heating of the vast quantities of atmospheric dust and soot in northern midlatitudes will transport these fine particles toward and across the Equator. We see just this happening in Martian dust storms. The Southern Hemisphere would experience effects that, while less severe than in the Northern Hemisphere, are nevertheless extremely ominous. The illusion with which some people in the Northern Hemisphere reassure themselves — catching an Air New Zealand flight in a time of serious international crisis, or the like — is now much less tenable, even on the narrow issue of personal survival for those with the price of a ticket.

But what if nuclear wars *can* be contained, and much less 20 than 5,000 megatons is detonated? Perhaps the greatest surprise in our work was that even small nuclear wars can have devastating climatic effects. We considered a war in which a mere 100 megatons were exploded, less than one percent of the world arsenals, and only in low-yield airbursts over cities. This scenario, we found, would ignite thousands of fires, and the smoke from these fires alone would be enough to generate an epoch of cold and dark almost as severe as in the 5,000-megaton case. The threshold for what Richard Turco has called the Nuclear Winter is very low.

Could we have overlooked some important effect? The 21 carrying of dust and soot from the Northern to the Southern Hemisphere (as well as more local atmospheric circulation) will certainly thin the clouds out over the Northern Hemisphere. But, in many cases, this thinning would be insufficient to render the climatic consequences tolerable — and every time it got better in the Northern Hemisphere, it would get worse in the Southern.

Our results have been carefully scrutinized by more than 22 100 scientists in the United States, Europe, and the Soviet

Union. There are still arguments on points of detail. But the overall conclusion seems to be agreed upon: There are severe and previously unanticipated global consequences of nuclear war — subfreezing temperatures in a twilit radioactive gloom lasting for months or longer.

Scientists initially underestimated the effects of fallout, 23 were amazed that nuclear explosions in space disabled distant satellites, had no idea that the fireballs from high-yield thermonuclear explosions could deplete the ozone layer, and missed altogether the possible climatic effects of nuclear dust and smoke. What else have we overlooked?

Nuclear war is a problem that can be treated only 24 theoretically. It is not amenable to experimentation. Conceivably, we have left something important out of our analysis, and the effects are more modest than we calculate. On the other hand, it is also possible — and, from previous experience, even likely — that there are further adverse effects that no one has yet been wise enough to recognize. With billions of lives at stake, where does conservatism lie — in assuming that the results will be better than we calculate, or worse?

Many biologists, considering the nuclear winter that these 25 calculations describe, believe they carry somber implications for life on Earth. Many species of plants and animals would become extinct. Vast numbers of surviving humans would starve to death. The delicate ecological relations that bind together organisms on Earth in a fabric of mutual dependency would be torn, perhaps irreparably. There is little question that our global civilization would be destroyed. The human population would be reduced to prehistoric levels, or less. Life for any survivors would be extremely hard. And there seems to be a real possibility of the extinction of the human species.

It is now almost forty years since the invention of nuclear 26 weapons. We have not yet experienced a global thermonuclear war — although on more than one occasion we have come tremulously close. I do not think our luck can hold forever. Men and machines are fallible, as recent events remind us. Fools and madmen do exist, and sometimes rise to power.

Concentrating always on the near future, we have ignored the long-term consequences of our actions. We have placed our civilization and our species in jeopardy.

Fortunately, it is not yet too late. We can safeguard the 27 planetary civilization and the human family if we so choose. There is no more important or more urgent issue.

[1983 – U.S.A.]

Questions

1. This essay divides itself into three broad sections plus the last paragraph. Indicate the inclusive paragraph numbers of each section and what each concerns. The second section divides itself into two sub-sections. What does each concern?

2. What is the function of paragraph 22? How does Sagan gain coherence in the essay as a whole?

3. "The Nuclear Winter" was originally published in *Parade*, a national Sunday supplement. Why did Sagan choose to publish the essay here? How did Sagan adapt his writing style to this audience?

4. How does Sagan establish his authority? Does he undercut it when he says, "Nuclear war is a problem that can be treated only theoretically" (paragraph 24)? Why or why not?

5. Of what does Sagan wish to persuade us? What is his thesis? What supports does he bring to bear in arguing it? What is his final purpose?

Writing Assignments

1. Write an essay evaluating "The Nuclear Winter." Consider, for instance, Sagan's reasons for being skeptical about the possibility of a "contained nuclear war." Are these reasons sound? Why or why not? Consider, too, the supports he brings to bear in arguing his thesis. Are they cogent? Are there arguments on the other side that he neglects? These are the kinds of question you should address in your evaluation.

2. Should there be a nuclear war, the final effects of the nuclear buildup will no doubt prove devastating. But many effects of this buildup can be witnessed here and now. The buildup certainly affects the national budget and deficit, for instance, and it has various psychological effects on each of us. What other effects can you think of? Research two or three of these immediate effects and write a paper detailing what the effects are and backing up what you say about each with solid support (like Sagan's).

——✤ The Rewards of Living ✤—— a Solitary Life

May Sarton

The other day an acquaintance of mine, a gregarious and 1 charming man, told me he had found himself unexpectedly alone in New York for an hour or two between appointments. He went to the Whitney and spent the "empty" time looking at things in solitary bliss. For him it proved to be a shock nearly as great as falling in love to discover that he could enjoy himself so much alone.

What had he been afraid of, I asked myself? That, 2 suddenly alone, he would discover that he bored himself, or that there was, quite simply, no self there to meet? But having taken the plunge, he is now on the brink of adventure; he is about to be launched into his own inner space, space as immense, unexplored, and sometimes frightening as outer space to the astronaut. His every perception will come to him with a new freshness and, for a time, seem startlingly original. For anyone who can see things for himself with a naked eye becomes, for a moment or two, something of a genius. With another human being present vision becomes double vision, inevitably. We are busy wondering, what does my companion see or think of this, and what do I think of it? The original impact gets lost, or diffused.

"Music I heard with you was more than music." Exactly. 3 And therefore music *itself* can only be heard alone. Solitude is the salt of personhood. It brings out the authentic flavor of every experience.

"Alone one is never lonely: the spirit adventures, walking/ 4 In a quiet garden, in a cool house, abiding single there."

Loneliness is most acutely felt with other people, for with 5 others, even with a lover sometimes, we suffer from our differences of taste, temperament, mood. Human intercourse often demands that we soften the edge of perception, or withdraw at the very instant of personal truth for fear of hurting, or of being inappropriately present, which is to say naked, in a social situation. Alone we can afford to be wholly whatever we are, and to feel whatever we feel absolutely. That is a great luxury!

For me the most interesting thing about a solitary life, and 6 mine has been that for the last twenty years, is that it becomes increasingly rewarding. When I can wake up and watch the sun rise over the ocean, as I do most days, and know that I have an entire day ahead, uninterrupted, in which to write a few pages, take a walk with my dog, lie down in the afternoon for a long think (why does one think better in a horizontal position?), read and listen to music, I am flooded with happiness.

I am lonely only when I am overtired, when I have worked 7 too long without a break, when for the time being I feel empty and need filling up. And I am lonely sometimes when I come back home after a lecture trip, when I have seen a lot of people and talked a lot, and am full to the brim with experience that needs to be sorted out.

Then for a little while the house feels huge and empty, and 8 I wonder where my self is hiding. It has to be recaptured slowly by watering the plants, perhaps, and looking again at each one as though it were a person, by feeding the two cats, by cooking a meal.

It takes a while, as I watch the surf blowing up in fountains 9 at the end of the field, but the moment comes when the world falls away, and the self emerges again from the deep unconscious, bringing back all I have recently experienced to be explored and slowly understood, when I can converse again with my hidden powers, and so grow, and so be renewed, till death do us part.

[1974 – U.S.A.]

Questions

1. What is the thesis of this essay? Where is it stated?
2. Sarton uses a number of metaphors here, some explicit and some implicit. What explicit metaphors are to be found in paragraphs 2 and 3? What is the effect of the metaphor in paragraph 3?

3. The quotation that forms paragraph 4 is dropped in without transition. Is transition needed here? Does paragraph 4 cohere with paragraphs 3 and 5? Why or why not? Is paragraph 4 effective? How so?

4. In the last paragraph there is a phrase that echoes a phrase in the first. What are the two phrases in question? What implicit metaphor do both entail? What is gained from this connection of the two paragraphs?

Writing Assignments

1. "Loneliness is most acutely felt with other people," Sarton holds. Do you agree or disagree? Write a paragraph or more on this subject — whether loneliness is more "acutely felt" in the company of others or when one is by oneself.

2. Sarton contrasts loneliness and solitude. Write an essay in which you define both and go on to contrast them yourself.

✤ HOMECOMING ✤
Eric Sevareid

My home town has changed in these thirty years of the American story. It is changing now, will go on changing as America changes. Its biography, I suspect, would read much the same as that of all other home towns. Depression and war and prosperity have all left their marks; modern science, modern tastes, manners, philosophies, fears and ambitions have touched my town as indelibly as they have touched New York or Panama City.

Sights have changed: there is a new precision about street and home, a clearing away of chicken yards, cow barns, pigeon-crested cupolas, weed lots and coulees, the dim and secret adult-free rendezvous of boys. An intricate metal "jungle gym" is a common backyard sight, the sack swing uncommon. There are wide expanses of clear windows, designed to let in the parlor light, fewer ornamental windows of colored glass designed to keep it out. Attic and screen porch are slowly vanishing and lovely shades of pastel are painted upon new houses, tints that once would have embarrassed farmer and merchant alike.

Sounds have changed: I heard not once the clopping of a 3 horse's hoof, nor the mourn of a coyote. I heard instead the shriek of brakes, the heavy throbbing of the once-a-day Braniff airliner into Minot, the shattering sirens born of war, the honk of a diesel locomotive which surely cannot call to faraway places the heart of a wakeful boy like the old steam whistle in the night. You can walk down the streets of my town now and hear from open windows the intimate voices of the Washington commentators in casual converse on the great affairs of state; but you cannot hear on Sunday morning the singing in Norwegian of the Lutheran hymns; the old country seems now part of a world left long behind and the old-country accents grow fainter in the speech of my Velva[1] neighbors.

The people have not changed, but the *kinds* of people have 4 changed: there is no longer an official, certified town drunk, no longer a "Crazy John," spitting his worst epithet, "rotten chicken legs," as you hurriedly passed him by. People so sick are now sent to places of proper care. No longer is there an official town joker, like the druggist MacKnight, who would spot a customer in the front of the store, have him called to the phone, then slip to the phone behind the prescription case, and imitate the man's wife to perfection with orders to bring home more bread and sausage and Cream of Wheat. No longer anyone like the early attorney, J. L. Lee, who sent fabulous dispatches to that fabulous tabloid, the *Chicago Blade,* such as his story of the wild man captured on the prairie and chained to the wall in the drugstore basement. (This, surely, was Velva's first notoriety; inquiries came from anthropologists all over the world.)

No, the "characters" are vanishing in Velva, just as they are 5 vanishing in our cities, in business, in politics. The "well-

---

[1]*Velva:* A small town in North Dakota.

rounded, socially integrated" personality that the progressive schoolteachers are so obsessed with is increasing rapidly, and I am not at all sure that this is good. Maybe we need more personalities with knobs and handles and rugged lumps of individuality. They may not make life more smooth; more interesting they surely make it.

They eat differently in Velva now; there are frozen fruits 6 and sea food and exotic delicacies we only read about in novels in those meat-and-potato days. They dress differently. The hard white collars of the businessmen are gone with the shiny alpaca coats. There are comfortable tweeds now, and casual blazers with a touch in their colors of California, which seems so close in time and distance.

It is distance and time that have changed the most and 7 worked the deepest changes in Velva's life. The telephone, the car, the smooth highway, radio and television are consolidating the entities of our country. The county seat of Towner now seems no closer than the state capital of Bismarck; the voices and concerns of Presidents, French premiers and Moroccan pashas are no farther away than the portable radio on Aunt Jessey's kitchen table. The national news magazines are stacked each week in Harold Anderson's drugstore beside the new soda fountain, and the excellent *Minot Daily News* smells hot from the press each afternoon.

Consolidation. The nearby hamlets of Sawyer and Logan 8 and Voltaire had their own separate banks and papers and schools in my days of dusty buggies and Model T's and marooned in the snowdrifts. Now these hamlets are dying. A bright yellow bus takes the Voltaire kids to Velva each day for high school. Velva has grown — from 800 to 1,300 — because the miners from the Truax coal mine can commute to their labors each morning and the nearby farmers can live in town if they choose. Minot has tripled in size to 30,000. Once the "Magic City" was a distant and splendid Baghdad, visited on special occasions long prepared for. Now it is a twenty-five minute commuter's jump away. So P. W. Miller and Jay Louis

Monicken run their businesses in Minot but live on in their old family homes in Velva. So Ray Michelson's two girls on his farm to the west drive up each morning to their jobs as maids in Minot homes. Aunt Jessey said, "Why, Saturday night I counted sixty-five cars just between here and Sawyer, all going up to the show in Minot."

The hills are prison battlements no longer; the prairies no 9 heart-sinking barrier, but a passageway free as the swelling ocean, inviting you to sail home and away at your whim and your leisure. (John and Helen made an easy little jaunt of 700 miles that week-end to see their eldest daughter in Wyoming.)

Consolidation. Art Kumm's bank serves a big region now; 10 its assets are $2,000,000 to $3,000,000 instead of the $200,000 or $300,000 in my father's day. Eighteen farms near Velva are under three ownerships now. They calculate in sections; "acres" is an almost forgotten term. Aunt Jessey owns a couple of farms, and she knows they are much better run. "It's no longer all take out and no put in," she said. "Folks strip farm now; they know all about fertilizers. They care for it and they'll hand on the land in good shape." The farmers gripe about their cash income, and not without reason at the moment, but they will admit that life is good compared with those days of drought and foreclosure, manure banked against the house for warmth, the hand pump frozen at 30 below and the fitful kerosene lamp on the kitchen table. Electrification has done much of this, eased back-breaking chores that made their wives old as parchment at forty, brought life and music and the sound of human voices into their parlors at night.

And light upon the prairie. "From the hilltop," said Aunt 11 Jessey, "the farms look like stars at night."

Many politicians deplore the passing of the old family-size 12 farm, but I am not so sure. I saw around Velva a release from what was like slavery to the tyrannical soil, release from the ignorance that darkens the soul and from the loneliness that corrodes it. In this generation my Velva friends have rejoined the general American society that their pioneering fathers left behind when they first made the barren trek in the days of the wheat rush. As I sit here in Washington writing this, I can feel their nearness. I never felt it before save in my dreams.

But now I must ask myself: Are they nearer to one another? 13 And the answer is no; yet I am certain that this is good. The shrinking of time and distance has made contrast and relief available to their daily lives. They do not know one another quite so well because they are not so much obliged to. I know that democracy rests upon social discipline, which in turn rests upon personal discipline; passions checked, hard words withheld, civic tasks accepted, work well done, accountings honestly rendered. The old-fashioned small town was this discipline in its starkest, most primitive form; without this discipline the small town would have blown itself apart.

For personal and social neuroses festered under this hard 14 scab of conformity. There was no place to go, no place to let off steam; few dared to voice unorthodox ideas, read strange books, admire esoteric art or publicly write or speak of their dreams and their soul's longings. The world was not "too much with us," the world was too little with us and we were too much with one another.

The door to the world stands open now, inviting them to 15 leave anytime they wish. It is the simple fact of the open door that makes all the difference; with its opening the stale air rushed out. So, of course, the people themselves do not have to leave, because, as the stale air went out, the fresh air came in.

Human nature is everywhere the same. He who is not 16 forced to help his neighbor for his own existence will not only give him help, but his true good will as well. Minot and its hospital are now close at hand, but the people of Velva put their purses together, built their own clinic and homes for the two young doctors they persuaded to come and live among them. Velva has no organized charity, but when a farmer falls ill, his neighbors get in his crop; if a townsman has a financial catastrophe his personal friends raise a fund to help him out. When Bill's wife, Ethel, lay dying so long in the Minot hospital and nurses were not available, Helen and others took their turns driving up there just to sit with her so she would know in her gathering dark that friends were at hand.

It is personal freedom that makes us better persons, and 17 they are freer in Velva now. There is no real freedom without privacy, and a resident of my home town can be a private person much more than he could before. People are able to draw at least a little apart from one another. In drawing apart, they gave their best human instincts room for expansion.

[1964 — U.S.A.]

Questions

1. Sevareid announces part of his thesis up front: "My home town has changed." But has it changed for the better or the worse? What more does the essay argue than the simple fact of change?

2. The first part of "Homecoming" concerns the less desirable aspects of the changes Sevareid details with examples. Where does the shift to the positive side come? Why this negative to positive order? What is the function of paragraph 11? In what way might what is noted in the paragraph 11 be symbolic?

3. What paragraphs are parallel in structure here? What establishes the parallelism? How does structural parallelism help Sevareid emphasize both the changes he observes and their causes?

4. The end of the essay (paragraph 17) rests on a paradox. What is it? What does the last paragraph serve to summarize? What, then, is Sevareid's position in full? How is that position made clear by his putting of the material of the last paragraph last?

Writing Assignments

1. Write a short paper about the changes you have witnessed in your old neighborhood, school, hangout, or whatever. In detailing these changes (use examples at all points, as Sevareid does), suggest the reasons for them and whether on balance they are for the better or the worse.

2. Write an essay in which you devote roughly half to negative observations about some perceived change (of change as loss) and the rest to a positive outlook (to how that change brings gains to offset the loss). You could take for a topic changing times, changing technology, changing values and mores, or changing stages as one grows. You might conclude with a statement as to whether loss or gain prevails on balance.

——✛ BLACK MEN AND PUBLIC SPACE ✛——
Brent Staples

Mʏ FIRST VICTIM WAS A WOMAN — WHITE, WELL DRESSED, PROBABLY   1
in her late twenties. I came upon her late one evening on a
deserted street in Hyde Park, a relatively affluent neighborhood in an otherwise mean, impoverished section of Chicago.
As I swung onto the avenue behind her, there seemed to be a
discreet, uninflammatory distance between us. Not so. She cast
back a worried glance. To her, the youngish black man —
a broad six feet two inches with a beard and billowing hair,
both hands shoved into the pockets of a bulky military
jacket — seemed menacingly close. After a few more quick
glimpses, she picked up her pace and was soon running in
earnest. Within seconds she disappeared into a cross street.

That was more than a decade ago. I was twenty-two years   2
old, a graduate student newly arrived at the University of
Chicago. It was in the echo of that terrified woman's footfalls
that I first began to know the unwieldy inheritance I'd come
into — the ability to alter public space in ugly ways. It was clear
that she thought herself the quarry of a mugger, a rapist, or
worse. Suffering a bout of insomnia, however, I was stalking
sleep, not defenseless wayfarers. As a softy who is scarcely able
to take a knife to a raw chicken — let alone hold one to a
person's throat — I was surprised, embarrassed, and dismayed
all at once. Her flight made me feel like an accomplice in
tyranny. It also made it clear that I was indistinguishable from
the muggers who occasionally seeped into the area from the
surrounding ghetto. That first encounter, and those that
followed, signified that a vast, unnerving gulf lay between
nighttime pedestrians — particularly women — and me. And I
soon gathered that being perceived as dangerous is a hazard in
itself. I only needed to turn a corner into a dicey situation, or
crowd some frightened, armed person in a foyer somewhere, or

make an errant move after being pulled over by a policeman. Where fear and weapons meet — and they often do in urban America — there is always the possibility of death.

In that first year, my first away from my hometown, I was 3 to become thoroughly familiar with the language of fear. At dark, shadowy intersections, I could cross in front of a car stopped at a traffic light and elicit the *thunk, thunk, thunk, thunk* of the driver — black, white, male, or female — hammering down the door locks. On less traveled streets after dark, I grew accustomed to but never comfortable with people crossing to the other side of the street rather than pass me. Then there were the standard unpleasantries with policemen, doormen, bouncers, cabdrivers, and others whose business it is to screen out troublesome individuals *before* there is any nastiness.

I moved to New York nearly two years ago and I have 4 remained an avid night walker. In central Manhattan, the near-constant crowd cover minimizes tense one-on-one street encounters. Elsewhere — in SoHo, for example, where sidewalks are narrow and tightly spaced buildings shut out the sky — things can get very taut indeed.

After dark, on the warrenlike streets of Brooklyn where I 5 live, I often see women who fear the worst from me. They seem to have set their faces on neutral, and with their purse straps strung across their chests bandolier-style, they forge ahead as though bracing themselves against being tackled. I understand, of course, that the danger they perceive is not a hallucination. Women are particularly vulnerable to street violence, and young black males are drastically overrepresented among the perpetrators of that violence. Yet these truths are no solace against the kind of alienation that comes of being ever the suspect, a fearsome entity with whom pedestrians avoid making eye contact.

It is not altogether clear to me how I reached the ripe old 6 age of twenty-two without being conscious of the lethality nighttime pedestrians attributed to me. Perhaps it was because in Chester, Pennsylvania, the small, angry industrial town where I came of age in the 1960s, I was scarcely noticeable against a backdrop of gang warfare, street knifings, and murders. I grew up one of the good boys, had perhaps a half-dozen fistfights. In retrospect, my shyness of combat has clear sources.

As a boy, I saw countless tough guys locked away; I have   7
since buried several, too. They were babies, really — a teenage cousin, a brother of twenty-two, a childhood friend in his mid-twenties — all gone down in episodes of bravado played out in the streets. I came to doubt the virtues of intimidation early on. I chose, perhaps unconsciously, to remain a shadow — timid, but a survivor.

The fearsomeness mistakenly attributed to me in public   8
places often has a perilous flavor. The most frightening of these confusions occured in the late 1970s and early 1980s, when I worked as a journalist in Chicago. One day, rushing into the office of a magazine I was writing for with a deadline story in hand, I was mistaken for a burglar. The office manager called security and, with an ad hoc posse, pursued me through the labyrinthine halls, nearly to my editor's door. I had no way of proving who I was. I could only move briskly toward the company of someone who knew me.

Another time I was on assignment for a local paper and   9
killing time before an interview. I entered a jewelry store on the city's affluent Near North Side. The proprietor excused herself and returned with an enormous red Doberman pinscher straining at the end of a leash. She stood, the dog extended toward me, silent to my questions, her eyes bulging nearly out of her head. I took a cursory look around, nodded, and bade her good night.

Relatively speaking, however, I never fared as badly as   10
another black male journalist. He went to nearby Waukegan, Illinois, a couple of summers ago to work on a story about a murderer who was born there. Mistaking the reporter for the killer, police officers hauled him from his car at gunpoint and but for his press credentials would probably have tried to book

him. Such episodes are not uncommon. Black men trade tales like this all the time.

Over the years, I learned to smother the rage I felt at so 11 often being taken for a criminal. Not to do so would surely have led to madness. I now take precautions to make myself less threatening. I move about with care, particularly late in the evening. I give a wide berth to nervous people on subway platforms during the wee hours, particularly when I have exchanged business clothes for jeans. If I happen to be entering a building behind some people who appear skittish, I may walk by, letting them clear the lobby before I return, so as not to seem to be following them. I have been calm and extremely congenial on those rare occasions when I've been pulled over by the police.

And on late-evening constitutionals I employ what has 12 proved to be an excellent tension-reducing measure: I whistle melodies from Beethoven and Vivaldi and the more popular classical composers. Even steely New Yorkers hunching toward nighttime destinations seem to relax, and occasionally they even join in the tune. Virtually everybody seems to sense that a mugger wouldn't be warbling bright, sunny selections from Vivaldi's *Four Seasons*. It is my equivalent of the cowbell that hikers wear when they know they are in bear country.

[1987 — U.S.A.]

Questions

1. How does this essay begin? Why is this way effective here?
2. What means of argumentation does Staples use? This is perhaps the most effective means he could use given the audience targeted and the nature of his topic. How so?
3. What means of support does Staples use primarily? What transitions indicate this means? Paragraphs 7 and 8 are the only paragraphs here lacking transition. Why? What is the effect of their rough juxtaposition?
4. This essay entails a character sketch of its author. Why is such a sketch necessary? What kind of person does Staples seem to be?

How do both the tone and voice of the essay contribute to our sense of what Staples is like?

5. What is the theme of "Black Men and Public Space"? How does the end of the essay underscore this theme?

Writing Assignments

1. a) In a paragraph, discuss Staples's use of anecdotes. How does he use them and to what effect?

   b) In a separate paragraph, discuss how you respond to this essay and why you respond thus.

2. Write a short paper in which you begin with an extended anecdote that leads to your point. Your anecdote might concern some situation in which you were misunderstood and suffered some consequence thereby through no fault of your own. Or it might concern something of this sort that happened to a friend. Or it might concern something else entirely. In any case, make sure you have a point and that your anecdote leads naturally to it. Then argue the point in the rest of the paper, perhaps referring back to your opening anecdote as you conclude.

———————— ❖ History Is Bunk ❖ ————————

Peter Steinfels

THERE HAVE RECENTLY BEEN COMPLAINTS THAT YOUNG PEOPLE ARE   1
not sufficiently interested in history, that they feel the study of the past to be "irrelevant" and with no connection to the problems we face today.

Of course these young people are absolutely right.   2

Let me give you an example. I have wasted (as it turns out)   3
a small but significant portion of my life studying the history of modern Germany. One of the most general conclusions of such study, reached by almost anyone who undertakes it for more than fifteen minutes, is that a nation can achieve the pinnacle of material, intellectual, and artistic civilization and yet, because of deep flaws in its political culture, perpetrate unthinkable

evils. Obviously that is the kind of lesson which has no relevance to us. You can see how my time has been wasted.

But let me illustrate the matter in more detail. Students of 4 German history are forced by their pedantic professors to pay attention to something known as the Prussian "Constitutional Crisis." This episode began in 1862 when the Prussian Chamber of Deputies, unhappy about King William I's proposed strengthening of the military and believing that the constitution meant what it said about the budget's having to be approved by the Chamber, refused to vote the funds the King's ministers requested. In turn, the feudal upper house, at the government's behest, threw out the Chamber's budget; and so there was no budget at all.

In a constitutional regime, one would think that the 5 government would then have resubmitted a compromise to the Chamber or simply have abided by the Chamber's will. But constitutional theorists are never at a loss for cleverness. Those in Prussia pointed out that, yes, the constitution did seem to insist on the Chamber's approval for the budget, but on the other hand the constitution also gave the government the right to collect the current taxes and duties until ordered otherwise. Therefore, a "gap" existed in the constitution; and necessity being the mother of invention for constitutional theorists as for everyone else, it was decided that in the unresolved situation created by the "gap," the necessity of maintaining the state implied the government could pretty much do what it pleased.

Such a conclusion was obviously not to everyone's taste, 6 and in the midst of the resulting tumult, the King called a brash, 47-year-old nobleman, politician, and diplomat to head the government. This was Otto von Bismarck.[1] (In the midst of this kind of useless study, it is nice to have a familiar personality on which to hang your hat.) Mr. Bismarck was not well received. He immediately defied the Chamber, proclaiming that power — blood and iron — would resolve the great questions of the

---

[1]*Otto von Bismarck:* (1815–1898) Called the "Iron Chancellor," Bismarck was the first chancellor of the German Empire.

day. The moderates and liberals replied that the legal and moral order was not violated with impunity. The historian Treitschke termed Bismarck's defiance a shallow and ridiculous vulgarity. But government without a budget continued.

Meanwhile, Bismarck dissolved the Chamber and called 7 new elections. In the intervening period, when there was no Chamber to counter his moves, he attacked the press, obtaining a royal order allowing the suppression of critical newspapers. He further maligned his opponents as unpatriotic and even as traitors. When the elected deputies wished to question Bismarck about a semi-secret agreement which allowed Russian troops to cross into Prussia to exterminate fugitive Polish rebels against the Czar, Bismarck refused even to explain his policy publicly.

By now, you must be convinced that none of these 8 ridiculous goings-on has the slightest relevance to our own politics;[2] but it is too late: you will have to hear the story out, so you will know exactly what we inflict upon our poor students.

None of these maneuvers — censorship, public disparage- 9 ment of the character and loyalty of his opponents, and even intimidation through the courts — had obtained for Bismarck the pliable legislative majority which he desired. The constitutional crisis remained unresolved.

But Bismarck was to find the solution in international 10 politics. He adroitly manipulated a series of international crises in a pyrotechnic display of diplomatics; waged two swift and successful wars, against Denmark and Austria; and successfully united all of northern Germany under the Prussian crown. He was the hero of the hour.

That part of the tale, I admit, possesses a certain melodrama 11 but now we descend to the truly dry-as-dust details: In the wake of his victory, Bismarck submitted to the Chamber an

---

[2]"History Is Bunk" appeared soon after Nixon began his second term and Watergate had started to unravel. See note 1 on page 574.

Indemnity Bill, legalizing his government's three years of illegal rule. Who could resist the successful Bismarck? Certainly not the German liberals. Had he not demonstrated that ruthlessness and toughness are crowned with success, whereas moral principles count for naught? Had he not stolen the cause of German unity from the liberals' own agenda, and even admitted the liberal principle of universal suffrage into the new constitution for the North German Confederation?

The liberals did more than vote Bismarck his indemnity. 12 They fell over themselves to recant the naive and impractical ideals of their former liberalism. They learned a new "realism" at Bismarck's school. "It does not become the German," wrote Treitschke, "to repeat the commonplaces of the apostles of peace . . . or to shut his eyes to the cruel truth that we live in an age of war."

The tale, as you can see, is not only boring and useless, it is 13 rather sad. The backbone of German liberalism, never much to boast about, was now broken for good. Bismarck was no Nazi; he accomplished his ends with a minimum of bloodshed, in a diplomatic performance which has been justly admired ever since. But the heritage he left Germany was one of submission to the strong and decisive leader, faith in power, cynicism about political principles, and contempt for public and parliamentary accountability. Brutality and force were rendered respectable, and adorned with a certain mystique. The opposition always cringed in fear of being branded disloyal. The results eventually were tragic for Germany, and for the rest of the world.

But the young people are right: none of this has anything to 14 do with us.

[1973 — U.S.A.]

Questions

1. Steinfels depends on irony to make and underscore his point. How so? What is ironic here? How is an ironic tone established?
2. What is his real point as distinguished from his ironic point? How is the former supported?

3. Why did Steinfels choose the example of Bismarck to suggest the relevance of history? What is the implied comparison between Bismarck and Nixon?

4. How is this essay organized by and large? What kind of a beginning does it have? What kind of an ending? Why is paragraph 2 printed as it is?

5. What is the tone of the essay's last sentence? Has Steinfels earned the right to this tone?

Writing Assignments

1. Write a short paper addressed to question 1 above. In analyzing the irony here, consider its effect as against that of a straightforward argument.

2. Write an essay in imitation of "History Is Bunk." That is, develop an ironic point the opposite of your real point; then argue the ironic point while making sure that your audience will recognize that it is ironic. Your tone will be crucial in this regard.

✤ A WELL IN INDIA ✤

Peggy and Pierre Streit

THE HOT DRY SEASON IN INDIA. . . . A CORROSIVE WIND DRIVES 1 rivulets of sand across the land; torpid animals stand at the edge of dried-up water holes. The earth is cracked and in the rivers the sluggish, falling waters have exposed the sludge of the mud flats. Throughout the land the thoughts of men turn to water. And in the village of Rampura these thoughts are focused on the village well.

It is a simple concrete affair, built upon the hard earth worn 2 by the feet of five hundred villagers. It is surmounted by a wooden structure over which ropes, tied to buckets, are lowered to the black, placid depths twenty feet below. Fanning out from the well are the huts of the villagers — their walls white from sun, their thatched roofs thick with dust blown in from the fields.

At the edge of the well is a semi-circle of earthen pots and, 3
crouched at some distance behind them, a woman. She is an
untouchable — a sweeper in Indian parlance — a scavenger of
the village. She cleans latrines, disposes of dead animals and
washes drains. She also delivers village babies, for this — like
all her work — is considered unclean by most of village India.

Her work — indeed, her very presence — is considered 4
polluting, and since there is no well for untouchables in
Rampura, her water jars must be filled by upper-caste villagers.

There are dark shadows under her eyes and the flesh has 5
fallen away from her neck, for she, like her fellow outcastes, is
at the end of a bitter struggle. And if, in her narrow world,
shackled by tradition and hemmed in by poverty, she had been
unaware of the power of the water of the well at whose edge she
waits — she knows it now.

Shanti, 30 years old, has been deserted by her husband, and 6
supports her three children. Like her ancestors almost as far
back as history records, she has cleaned the refuse from village
huts and lanes. Hers is a life of inherited duties as well as
inherited rights. She serves, and her work calls for payment of
one chapatty — a thin wafer of unleavened bread — a day from
each of the thirty families she cares for.

But this is the hiatus between harvests; the oppressive lull 7
before the burst of monsoon rains; the season of flies and dust,
heat and disease, querulous voices and frayed tempers — and
the season of want. There is little food in Rampura for anyone,
and though Shanti's chores have continued as before, she has
received only six chapatties a day for her family — starvation
wages.

Ten days ago she revolted. Driven by desperation, she 8
defied an elemental law of village India. She refused to make
her sweeper's rounds — refused to do the work tradition and
religion had assigned her. Shocked at her audacity, but united
in desperation, the village's six other sweeper families joined in
her protest.

Word of her action spread quickly across the invisible line 9
that separates the untouchables' huts from the rest of the

village. As the day wore on and the men returned from the fields, they gathered at the well — the heart of the village — and their voices rose, shrill with outrage: a *sweeper* defying them all! Shanti, a sweeper *and* a woman challenging a system that had prevailed unquestioned for centuries! Their indignation spilled over. It was true, perhaps, that the sweepers had not had their due. But that was no fault of the upper caste. No fault of theirs that sun and earth and water had failed to produce the food by which they could fulfill their obligations. So, to bring the insurgents to heel, they employed their ultimate weapon; the earthen water jars of the village untouchables would remain empty until they returned to work. For the sweepers of Rampura the well had run dry.

No water; thirst, in the heat, went unslaked. The embers of 10 the hearth were dead, for there was no water for cooking. The crumbling walls of outcaste huts went untended, for there was no water for repairs. There was no fuel, for the fires of the village were fed with dung mixed with water and dried. The dust and the sweat and the filth of their lives congealed on their skins and there it stayed, while life in the rest of the village — within sight of the sweepers — flowed on.

The day began and ended at the well. The men, their dhotis 11 wrapped about their loins, congregated at the water's edge in the hushed post-dawn, their small brass water jugs in hand, their voices mingling in quiet conversation as they rinsed their bodies and brushed their teeth. The buffaloes were watered, their soft muzzles lingering in the buckets before they were driven off to the fields. Then came the women, their brass pots atop their heads, to begin the ritual of water drawing: the careful lowering of the bucket in the well, lest it come loose from the rope; the gratifying splash as it touched the water; the maneuvering to make it sink; the squeal of rope against wooden pulley as it ascended. The sun rose higher. Clothes were beaten clean on the rocks surrounding the well as the women gossiped. A traveler from a near-by road quenched his thirst from a villager's urn. Two little boys, hot and bored, dropped pebbles into the water and waited for their hollow splash, far below.

As the afternoon wore on and the sun turned orange 12 through the dust, the men came back from the fields. They doused the parched, cracked hides of their water buffaloes and murmured contentedly, themselves, as the water coursed over their own shoulders and arms. And finally, as twilight closed in, came the evening procession of women, stately, graceful, their bare feet moving smoothly over the earth, their full skirts swinging about their ankles, the heavy brass pots once again balanced on their heads.

The day was ended and life was as it always was — almost. 13 Only the fetid odor of accumulated refuse and the assertive buzz of flies attested to strife in the village. For, while tradition and religion decreed that sweepers must clean, it also ordained that the socially blessed must not. Refuse lay where it fell and rotted.

The strain of the water boycott was beginning to tell on the 14 untouchables. For days they had held their own. But on the third their thin reserve of flesh had fallen away. Movements were slower; voices softer; minds dull. More and more the desultory conversation turned to the ordinary: the delicious memory of sliding from the back of a wallowing buffalo into a pond; the feel of bare feet in wet mud; the touch of fresh water on parched lips; the anticipation of monsoon rains.

One by one the few tools they owned were sold for food. A 15 week passed, and on the ninth day two sweeper children were down with fever. On the tenth day Shanti crossed the path that separated outcaste from upper caste and walked through familiar, winding alleyways to one of the huts she served.

"Your time is near," she told the young, expectant mother. 16 "Tell your man to leave his sickle home when he goes to the fields. I've had to sell mine." (It is the field sickle that cuts the cord of newborn babies in much of village India.) Shanti, the instigator of the insurrection, had resumed her ancestral duties; the strike was broken. Next morning, as ever, she waited at the well. Silently, the procession of upper-caste women approached. They filled their jars to the brim and without a word they filled hers.

She lifted the urns to her head, steadied them, and started 17
back to her quarters — back to a life ruled by the powers that
still rule most of the world: not the power of atoms or
electricity, nor the power of alliances or power blocs, but the
elemental powers of hunger, of disease, of tradition — and of
water.

[1959 — U.S.A.]

Questions

1. What is the structural mode of this essay once its narrative begins
   (paragraph 8)? What kind of transitions are used here? What are
   some examples of these transitions? Why is this structural mode
   appropriate?

2. What is the tone of the essay? Do the authors have a point of view
   as to the world they describe? If you think so, what is their point of
   view and how is it communicated? If you think not, why don't they?

3. Setting is especially important here. What first suggests as much?
   Why is the setting so highly particularized? Why do the Streits focus
   on and sketch in one character only — Shanti, the leader of the
   revolt?

4. Though hinted at earlier (at the end of paragraph 5), the thesis of "A
   Well in India" is not presented in full until the last sentence, where
   it acts as a conclusion. Why? Why is it effective for the thesis here
   to come last, after the world of the untouchables has been fully
   exposed? What allows the Streits to delay their thesis thus? That is,
   wanting a thesis, why do we keep on reading?

Writing Assignments

1. Does what the men say in paragraph 9 sound like anything said in
   our country now about the poor? If you think so, write a short paper
   beginning with a summary of Shanti's plight and the men's response
   and then moving to a consideration of our culture's attitudes about
   the poor. Be mindful that you will be working with an extended
   analogy.

2. In 1949, the Indian government made discrimination against
   untouchables illegal. But, as the Streits demonstrate, tradition dies
   hard. Write an essay illustrating from your first-hand knowledge
   how strong tradition can be, and how, sometimes disguised, it
   lingers on and controls people's lives long after its relevance has
   passed.

3. Write an essay "after" "A Well in India." That is, narrate a story about someone in a setting precisely described. Be sure to have a thesis in mind, but state it fully only at the end as a conclusion. Your detail will carry your reader on if it is rich and fully realized.

✤ THE HABIT ✤
William Styron

THE LAMENTABLE HISTORY OF THE CIGARETTE IS THAT OF A MORTALLY 1
corrupting addiction having been embraced by millions of people in the spirit of childlike innocence. It is a history which is also strikingly brief. Cigarettes began to be manufactured extensively around the turn of the century, but it was not until as recently as 1921 that cigarettes overtook chewing tobacco, as well as pipes and cigars, in per capita consumption, and the 1930s were well along before cigarette smoking became the accepted thing for ladies.

The popularity of cigarettes was inevitable and overwhelm- 2
ing. They were not offensive in close quarters, nor messy like pipes and cigars. They were easily portable. They did not look gross and unseemingly in a lady's mouth. They were cheap to manufacture, and they were inhalable. Unlike the great majority of pipe and cigar smokers, whose pleasure is predominantly oral and contemplative, most cigarette smokers inhale deep into their lungs with bladelike, rhythmic savagery, inflicting upon themselves in miniature a particularly abrasive form of air pollution. Further, the very fact of inhalation seems to enhance the cigarette's addictive power. Unhappily, few suspected the consequences in terms of health until long after cigarette smoking had gained its colossal momentum. That this type of auto-contamination is a major cause of lung cancer — that it is also a prime causative factor in deaths from coronary artery disease, bronchitis, asthma, emphysema, among other afflictions — was established, and for the first time well publicized, only a decade ago. The effect this knowledge has had upon the public consciousness may be suggested by the

fact that sales this year reached the galactic sum of one-half trillion cigarettes — one hundred billion more than in 1953. There is something historically intimidating in the idea that cigarette smoking as a mass diversion and a raging increase in lung cancer have both come about during the lifetime of those who are now no more than fifty years old. It is the very *recentness* of the phenomenon which helps make it so shocking. The hard truth is that human beings have never in such a brief space of time, and in so grand and guileless a multitude, embraced a habit whose unwholesome effects not only would totally outweigh the meager satisfactions but would hasten the deaths of a large proportion of the people who indulged in it. Certainly (and there seems little doubt that the Surgeon General's report will make this clear) only nuclear fallout exceeds cigarette smoking in gravity as a public health problem.

For its lucid presentation of the medical evidence alone, *The Consumers Union Report on Smoking* would be a valuable document. "The conclusion is inescapable," the *Report* begins, "and even spokesmen for the cigarette industry rarely seek to escape it: we are living in the midst of a major lung cancer epidemic. This epidemic hit men first and hardest, but has affected women as well. It cannot be explained away by such factors as improved diagnosis. And there is reason to believe that the worst is yet to come." Yet despite this minatory beginning the tone throughout is one of caution and reasonableness, and the authors — who manage an accomplished prose style rare in such collective undertakings — marshal their facts with such efficiency and persuasion that it is hard to imagine anyone but a fool or a tobacco lobbyist denying the close association between smoking and lung cancer. Yet, of course, not only lung cancer. The *Report* quotes, for instance, data based on an extensive study of smokers and nonsmokers among English physicians, where the death rate *from all causes* was found to be doubled among heavy cigarette smokers in the group of men past 65, and quadrupled in the group 35 to 44. And the *Report* adds, with the modest and constructive irony that makes the book, if not exactly a joy, then agreeable to read:

"These death rates among smokers are perhaps the least controversial of all the findings to date. For with respect to any particular disease there is always the possibility, however remote, that mistaken diagnosis and other conceivable errors may cast doubt on the statistics. But death is easily diagnosed."

In the end, however, what makes the *Report's* message 4
supportable to those distracted souls among the millions of American smokers who may wish to kick the habit — or who, having kicked the habit, may wonder if it is not too late — is a kind of muted optimism. For all present evidence seems to indicate that the common cocktail party rationalization ("I've smoked too long to stop now, the damage is done") has no real basis in fact. In research carried out by the American Cancer Society, microscopic studies of the lung tissues of ex-smokers have shown a process in which precancerous cells are dying out instead of flourishing and reproducing as in the tissues of continuing smokers. Here the *Report* states, in regard to a carefully matched group composed in equal numbers of nonsmokers, exsmokers and smokers: "Metaplastic cells with altered nuclei [i.e., precancerous cells] were found in 1.2 percent of the slides from the lungs of nonsmokers, as compared with 6.0 for ex-smokers — and *93.2 percent* for current smokers."

Certainly such evidence, combined with the fact that 5
ex-smokers have a lung cancer death rate which ranges down to one fifth of that of smokers who continue to smoke, should be of the greatest practical interest to anyone who ponders whether it may be worthwhile abandoning what is, after all, a cheerless, grubby, fumbling addiction. (Only the passion of a convert could provoke these last words. The *Report* was an aid to my stopping a two-pack-a-day habit which commenced in early infancy. Of course, stopping smoking may be in itself a major problem, one of psychological complexity. For myself, after two or three days of great flaccidity of spirit, an aimless oral yearning, aching moments of hunger at the pit of the stomach, and an awful intermittent urge to burst into tears, the problem resolved itself, and in less than a week all craving

vanished. Curiously, for the first time in my life, I developed a racking cough, but this, too, disappeared. A sense of smugness, a kind of flatness of soul, is the reward for such a struggle. The intensity of the addiction varies, however, and some people find the ordeal fearfully difficult, if not next to impossible. I do have an urgent suspicion, though, that the greatest barrier to a termination of the habit is the dread of some Faustian upheaval, when in fact that deprivation, while momentarily oppressive, is apt to prove not really cruel at all.)

But if the *Report* is splendidly effective as a caveat, it may be   6 read for its sociological insights as well. Certainly the history of commerce has few instances of such shameful abdication of responsibility as that displayed by the cigarette industry when in 1952 the "health scare," as it is so winsomely known in the trade, brought about the crisis which will reach a head in this month's report by the Surgeon General. It seems clear that the industry, instead of trying to forestall the inevitable with its lies and evasions, might have acquitted itself with some honor had it made what the *Report* calls the only feasible choices: to have urged caution on smokers, to have given money to independent research organizations, to have avoided propaganda and controversy in favor of unbiased inquiry. At the very least the industry might have soft-pedaled or, indeed, silenced its pitch to young people. But panic and greed dominated the reaction, and during the decade since the smoking-lung cancer link was made public, the official position of the industry has been that, in the matter of lung cancer, the villain is any and everything *but* the cigarette. Even the American Cancer Society is in on the evil plot and, in the words of one industry spokesman, "relies almost wholly upon health scare propaganda to raise millions of dollars from a gullible public."

Meanwhile, $200 million was spent last year on cigarette   7 ballyhoo, and during these last crucial ten years the annual advertising expenditure has increased 134 percent — a vast amount of it, of course, going to entice the very young. One million of these young people, according to the American Public Health Association, will die of smoking-induced lung cancer before they reach the age of seventy years. "Between the time a kid is eighteen and twenty-one, he's going to make the basic decision to smoke or not to smoke," says L. W. Bruff, advertising director of Liggett & Myers. "If he does decide to smoke, we want to get him." I have never met Mr. Bruff, but in my mind's eye I see him, poised like a cormorant above those doomed minnows, and I am amused by the refinement, the weight of conscience, the delicate interplay of intellectual and moral alternatives which go into the making of such a prodigious thought. As the report demonstrates, however, Mr. Bruff is only typical of the leaders of an industry which last year received a bounty of $7 billion from 63 million American smokers. Perhaps the tragic reality is that neither this estimable report nor that of the Surgeon General can measurably affect, much less really change, such awesome figures.

[1963 — U.S.A.]

Questions

1. The first sentence here is arresting. How so? Comment on its rhythm. How does its rhythm affect you? What of the rhythm of the first five sentences of paragraph 2? How is it created? Describe it and its effect.

2. "The Habit" divides itself into three sections. Indicate what paragraphs comprise each and sum up in a few words the focus of each.

3. How does Styron get from section to section? That is, what words, phrases, and sentences are transitional?

4. What kind of voice do you hear as you read this essay? How does the voice here projected help the author with respect to persuading an audience?

5. Styron conveys strong feelings but also a sense of objectivity. How does he accomplish the latter?

Writing Assignments

1. In two or three paragraphs, evaluate "The Habit" as to effectiveness. What techniques of persuasion does it incorporate? Are they used well? Are they persuasive? What kind of voice does the essay

establish? Does this voice help persuade the reader? Why? How persuasive is the essay overall? Is its argument rational or only a matter of opinion?

2. There are many harmful habits aside from smoking: alcohol, chocolate, television, gambling — each can be debilitating if carried to excess. Pick one such habit and write an essay designed to persuade readers to give it up or never to start it in the first place. Or you might read several reports on the habit you choose and turn this into a research assignment. In either case, argue rationally and in a voice likely to persuade readers.

✤ THE BUSY CLICHÉ EXPERT ✤
Frank Sullivan

Q: MR. ARBUTHNOT, AS AN EXPERT IN THE USE OF THE CLICHÉ, YOU   1
are a pretty busy man, aren't you?

A: Mr. Todd, you never spoke a truer word. Half the time   2
I don't know whether I'm coming or going. Why, taking care of
my livestock is a man's-size job in itself.

Q: Your livestock?   3

A: Yes, At least once every day I have to beard the lion,   4
keep the wolf from the door, let the cat out of the bag, take the
bull by the horns, count my chickens before they are hatched,
shoe the wild mare, and see that the horse isn't put behind the
cart or stolen before I lock the barn door. You'd think I'd be
rather fed up on dumb animals by this time, wouldn't you?

Q: It would seem likely, I must admit.   5

A: Well, I'm not. The more I see of men, the more I like   6
dogs. I dislike men, and do you know how I dislike them?

Q: No. How?   7

A: Cordially, to put it bluntly. Do you know how I treat   8
men?

Q: No.   9

A: With the contempt they so richly deserve.   10

Q: I'll warrant, Mr. Arbuthnot, that when you abandon,   11
you abandon lightly.

A: I do, and when cares weigh on me, they weigh heavily. 12
But I go my way. I grin and bear it.

Q: Well, I should think the chores you mentioned would be 13
exercise enough for any man, Mr. Arbuthnot.

A: Oh, that isn't my *exercise*. That's my work. 14

Q: What do you do for exercise? 15

A: I play the game. And hang up records. I sail a little. 16

Q: A skiff? 17

A: No, under false colors. I box some, too, hitting below the 18
belt, and I go in for dancing.

Q: What do you dance? 19

A: Attendance. I am also pretty good at putting my 20
shoulder to the wheel, sticking to my guns, pulling up stakes,
and champing at the bit.

Q: Doesn't all that exercise do you in? 21

A: I should say it does. Do you know how I sleep? 22

Q: How? 23

A: Like a log. When I don't sleep like a log, I sleep the sleep 24
of the just. In other words, I no sooner hit the hay than I'm in
the arms of Morpheus.

Q: What do you strike, Mr. Arbuthnot? 25

A: I strike bargains. I take advantage of propositions. I get 26
down to business. And to brass tacks. I enclose herewith, I beg
to remain, I suit the action to the word, and I laud to the skies.

Q: What do you speed? 27

A: I speed the day. 28

Q: What is it you settle, and what do you coin? 29

A: I settle hash and coin phrases. I beggar description. I 30
report progress. And I have quite a temper, too. Be careful, Mr.
Todd. If you poke fun at me, I'll fly off the handle, run amuck,
and hit the ceiling.

Q: In that case, I'll let well enough alone and not poke fun 31
at you.

A: I shudder to think what would happen if you did. 32

Q: What else do you do, Mr. Arbuthnot? 33

A: Well, let me see. I take into account, I go far enough, I 34
look for support, and I deem it a privilege. I put in an

appearance, I get the upper hand of, I bring the matter up, and I let the matter drop. I keep things humming, and I speak in terms of. I boast a finer collection, and feel under the weather. I think things out, and have it on good authority.

Q: Mr. Arb — 35

A: No, hear me out, Mr. Todd. You asked for it. I take to 36 task, I knuckle down, I buck up, I level criticism, I venture to predict, I inject a serious note, I lose caste, I am up to no good, I am down on my luck, I pass the time of day, I go down to posterity, I cast into the discard — that reminds me, do you realize why I am not wearing any pearls?

Q: Why not? 37

A: Swine got 'em. I steal marches, I beg the question, I 38 stand my ground, I turn over a new leaf. Why, Mr. Todd, I'm so busy I haven't got a minute I can call my own. I'm on the go from the moment I put in an appearance at the crack o' dawn. When I'm not playing second fiddle, I'm off to Newcastle with coals, or burying the hatchet, or attending to my oil business.

Q: You are in the oil business? 39

A: Well, rather, the troubled-waters business. I pour every 40 Tuesday from four to six. You must not fail to come to my show, Mr. Todd.

Q: You are having a show? 41

A: Yes, indeed. Advance showing of the autumn white 42 feathers. On top of all these things I have to watch my stones with eternal vigilance, to see that none are left unturned. Then I have my bones to pick, and my blacksmith shop.

Q: Good heavens, a blacksmith shop, too? 43

A: Oh, yes. I strike while the iron is hot. I find favor. I look 44 high and low. I stir my stumps. I nod approval. I bid farewell. I drop like flies, and I bend every effort. I pocket my pride and amass a fortune. If I don't pay the supreme penalty, I'll emerge unscathed.

Q: What is it you mince? 45

A: Words. I mark time. I face music. I fill the bill, answer 46 the purpose, say the word, and give pause. Do you wonder I have to have a girl come in by the day to mind my P's and Q's for me?

Q: No, I do not. But, Mr. Arbuthnot, in spite of your 47 versatility, there remains one thing you cannot do.

A: I admit it freely. I cannot make head or tail. But I can 48 stew in my own juice. You must grant me that. And I can shake a leg, and take a firm grip on myself. I can flatter myself, refresh my memory, bury my nose in a book, and put my best foot forward. I can gird my loins, give my right eye, save my face, elevate an eyebrow, wear a rapt expression, shoot a glance, use my head, knit my brows, fall down on my job, purse my lips, see eye to eye, keep a stiff upper lip, and a civil tongue in my head, without batting an eyelash. That's not doing so badly for a cliché expert, Mr. Todd.

Q: I should say not, Mr. Arbuthnot. I'd certainly like to see 49 you sometime when you are doing all those things together.

A: You mean at one and the same time. Well, rest assured, 50 I can do them. I speak the truth, the whole truth, and nothing but the truth. Good gracious, is that thunder I heard?

Q: Yes, I think that was a peal of thunder.   51

A: Then I must hurry. Good-by.   52

Q: But why not rest here until the storm has passed, Mr. 53 Arbuthnot?

A: I can't do it. I must go.   54

Q: But why?   55

A: I've got to brave the elements. Oh, dear, I hope the 56 lightning isn't forked or greased. Good- by.

[1934 — U.S.A.]

Questions

1. "The Busy Cliché Expert" is a satire. What is its satiric point?
2. How does the piece drive home its point? In what way is it an essay?
3. What questions of one's own speech and writing does Sullivan's "essay" make one ask? How effective is it at raising such questions in the reader (you)?

Writing Assignments

1. In a short essay (three to five paragraphs), discuss the deadening effect of clichés in a piece of prose. Why do they persist? Why should they be avoided?

2. Sullivan wrote many other essays in the same format — the cliché expert on this, that, and the other thing. Write an essay of this sort yourself "after" Sullivan. That is, using the same Q/A format, pick a topic (sports, love, medicine, the law) and give ironic voice to the many clichés your chosen field has given rise to.

✦ A Modest Proposal ✦

Jonathan Swift

for Preventing the Children of Poor People in Ireland from Being a Burden to Their Parents or Country, and for Making Them Beneficial to the Public

It is a melancholy object to those who walk through this great town, or travel in the country, when they see the streets, the roads and cabin-doors crowded with beggars of the female sex, followed by three, four, or six children, all in rags, and importuning every passenger for an alms. These mothers, instead of being able to work for their honest livelihood, are forced to employ all their time in strolling, to beg sustenance for their helpless infants, who, as they grow up, either turn thieves for want of work, or leave their dear native country to fight for the Pretender in Spain, or sell themselves to the Barbadoes.

I think it is agreed by all parties that this prodigious number of children, in the arms, or on the backs, or at the heels of their mothers, and frequently of their fathers, is in the present deplorable state of the kingdom a very great additional grievance; and therefore whoever could find out a fair, cheap, and easy method of making these children sound and useful members of the commonwealth would deserve so well of the public as to have his statue set up for a preserver of the nation.

But my intention is very far from being confined to provide 3 only for the children of professed beggars; it is of a much greater extent, and shall take in the whole number of infants at a certain age who are born of parents in effect as little able to support them as those who demand our charity in the streets.

As to my own part, having turned my thoughts for many 4 years upon this important subject, and maturely weighed the several schemes of other projectors, I have always found them grossly mistaken in their computation. It is true a child just dropped from its dam may be supported by her milk for a solar year with little other nourishment, at most not above the value of two shillings, which the mother may certainly get, or the value in scraps, by her lawful occupation of begging, and it is exactly at one year old that I propose to provide for them, in such a manner as, instead of being a charge upon their parents, or the parish, or wanting food and raiment for the rest of their lives, they shall, on the contrary, contribute to the feeding and partly to the clothing of many thousands.

There is likewise another great advantage in my scheme, 5 that it will prevent those voluntary abortions, and that horrid practice of women murdering their bastard children, alas, too frequent among us, sacrificing the poor innocent babes, I doubt, more to avoid the expense than the shame, which would move tears and pity in the most savage and inhuman breast.

The number of souls in Ireland being usually reckoned one 6 million and a half, of these I calculate there may be about two hundred thousand couples whose wives are breeders, from which number I subtract thirty thousand couples who are able to maintain their own children, although I apprehend there cannot be so many under the present distresses of the kingdom, but this being granted, there will remain an hundred and seventy thousand breeders. I again subtract fifty thousand for those women who miscarry, or whose children die by accident or disease within the year. There only remain an hundred and twenty thousand children of poor parents annually born: the question therefore is, how this number shall be reared, and provided for, which as I have already said, under the present situation of affairs is utterly impossible by all the methods hitherto proposed, for we can neither employ them in handicraft or agriculture; we neither build houses (I mean in the country), nor cultivate land: they can very seldom pick up a livelihood by stealing until they arrive at six years old, except where they are of towardly parts, although I confess they learn the rudiments much earlier, during which time they can however be properly looked upon only as probationers, as I have been informed by a principal gentleman in the County of Cavan, who protested to me that he never knew above one or two instances under the age of six, even in a part of the kingdom so renowned for the quickest proficiency in that art.

I am assured by our merchants that a boy or a girl before 7 twelve years old, is no saleable commodity, and even when they come to this age, they will not yield above three pounds, or three pounds and half-a-crown at most on the Exchange, which cannot turn to account either to the parents or the kingdom, the charge of nutriment and rags having been at least four times that value.

I shall now therefore humbly propose my own thoughts, 8 which I hope will not be liable to the least objection.

I have been assured by a very knowing American of my 9 acquaintance in London, that a young healthy child well nursed is at a year old a most delicious, nourishing and wholesome food, whether stewed, roasted, baked, or boiled, and I make no doubt that it will equally serve in a fricassee, or a ragout.

I do therefore humbly offer it to public consideration, that 10 of the hundred and twenty thousand children already computed, twenty thousand may be reserved for breed, whereof only one fourth part to be males, which is more than we allow to sheep, black-cattle, or swine, and my reason is that these children are seldom the fruits of marriage, a circumstance not much regarded by our savages, therefore one male will be sufficient to serve four females. That the remaining hundred thousand may at a year old be offered in sale to the persons of quality, and fortune, through the kingdom, always advising the mother to let them suck plentifully in the last month, so as to render them plump, and fat for a good table. A child will make two dishes at an entertainment for friends, and when the family dines alone, the fore or hind quarter will make a reasonable dish, and seasoned with a little pepper or salt will be very good boiled on the fourth day, especially in winter.

I have reckoned upon a medium, that a child just born will 11 weigh twelve pounds, and in a solar year if tolerably nursed increaseth to twenty-eight pounds.

I grant this food will be somewhat dear, and therefore very 12 proper for landlords, who, as they have already devoured most of the parents, seem to have the best title to the children.

Infant's flesh will be in season throughout the year, but 13 more plentiful in March, and a little before and after, for we are told by a grave author,[1] an eminent French physician, that fish being a prolific diet, there are more children born in Roman Catholic countries about nine months after Lent than at any other season; therefore reckoning a year after Lent, the markets will be more glutted than usual, because the number of Popish infants is at least three to one in this kingdom, and therefore it will have one other collateral advantage by lessening the number of Papists among us.

I have already computed the charge of nursing a beggar's 14 child (in which list I reckon all cottagers, labourers, and four-fifths of the farmers) to be about two shillings *per annum*, rags included, and I believe no gentleman would repine to give ten shillings for the carcass of a good fat child, which, as I have said, will make four dishes of excellent nutritive meat, when he hath only some particular friend of his own family to dine with him. Thus the Squire will learn to be a good landlord and grow popular among his tenants, the mother will have eight shillings net profit, and be fit for work until she produces another child.

Those who are more thrifty (as I must confess the times 15 require) may flay the carcass; the skin of which artifically dressed, will make admirable gloves for ladies, and summer boots for fine gentlemen.

---

[1]*author:* François Rabelais (1494? – 1553), a great French comic writer and satirist, author of *Gargantua and Pantagruel.*

As to our city of Dublin, shambles may be appointed for 16 this purpose, in the most convenient parts of it, and butchers we may be assured will not be wanting, although I rather recommend buying the children alive, and dressing them hot from the knife, as we do roasting pigs.

A very worthy person, a true lover of his country, and 17 whose virtues I highly esteem was lately pleased, in discoursing on this matter to offer a refinement upon my scheme. He said that many gentlemen of this kingdom, having of late destroyed their deer, he conceived that the want of venison might be well supplied by the bodies of young lads and maidens, not exceeding fourteen years of age, nor under twelve, so great a number of both sexes in every county being now ready to starve, for want of work and service: and these to be disposed of by their parents if alive, or otherwise by their nearest relations. But with due deference to so excellent a friend, and so deserving a patriot, I cannot be altogether in his sentiments. For as to the males, my American acquaintance assured me from frequent experience that their flesh was generally tough and lean, like that of our schoolboys, by continual exercise, and their taste disagreeable, and to fatten them would not answer the charge. Then as to the females, it would, I think with humble submission, be a loss to the public, because they soon would become breeders themselves: and besides, it is not improbable that some scrupulous people might be apt to censure such a practice (although indeed very unjustly) as a little bordering upon cruelty, which I confess, hath always been with me the strongest objection against any project, howsoever well intended.

But in order to justify my friend, he confessed that this 18 expedient was put into his head by the famous Psalmanazar, a native of the island Formosa, who came from thence to London, above twenty years ago, and in conversation told my friend that in his country when any young person happened to be put to death, the executioner sold the carcass to persons of quality, as a prime dainty, and that, in his time, the body of a plump girl of fifteen, who was crucified for an attempt to poison the emperor, was sold to his Imperial Majesty's Prime Minister of State, and other great Mandarins of the Court, in joints from the gibbet, at four hundred crowns. Neither indeed can I deny that if the same use were made of several plump young girls in this town who, without one single groat to their fortunes, cannot stir abroad without a chair, and appear at the playhouse and assemblies in foreign fineries, which they never will pay for, the kingdom would not be the worse.

Some persons of a desponding spirit are in great concern 19 about that vast number of poor people, who are aged, diseased, or maimed, and I have been desired to employ my thoughts what course may be taken to ease the nation of so grievous an encumbrance. But I am not in the least pain upon that matter, because it is very well known that they are every day dying, and rotting, by cold, and famine, and filth, and vermin, as fast as can be reasonably expected. And as to the younger labourers they are now in almost as hopeful a condition. They cannot get work, and consequently pine away from want of nourishment, to a degree that if at any time they are accidentally hired to common labour, they have not strength to perform it; and thus the country and themselves are in a fair way of being soon delivered from the evils to come.

I have too long digressed, and therefore shall return to my 20 subject. I think the advantages by the proposal which I have made are obvious and many, as well as of the highest importance.

For first, as I have already observed, it would greatly lessen 21 the number of Papists, with whom we are yearly over-run, being the principal breeders of the nation, as well as our most dangerous enemies, and who stay at home on purpose with a design to deliver the kingdom to the Pretender, hoping to take their advantage by the absence of so many good Protestants, who have chosen rather to leave their country than stay at home and pay tithes against their conscience to an idolatrous Episcopal curate.

Secondly, the poorer tenants will have something valuable 22 of their own, which by law may be made liable to distress, and help to pay their landlord's rent, their corn and cattle being already seized, and money a thing unknown.

Thirdly, whereas the maintenance of an hundred thousand 23 children, from two years old, and upwards, cannot be computed at less than ten shillings a piece *per annum*, the nation's stock will be thereby increased fifty thousand pounds *per annum*, besides the profit of a new dish, introduced to the tables of all gentlemen of fortune in the kingdom, who have any refinement in taste, and the money will circulate among ourselves, the goods being entirely of our own growth and manufacture.

Fourthly, the constant breeders, besides the gain of eight 24 shillings sterling *per annum*, by the sale of their children, will be rid of the charge of maintaining them after the first year.

Fifthly, this food would likewise bring great custom to 25 taverns, where the vintners will certainly be so prudent as to procure the best receipts for dressing it to perfection, and consequently have their houses frequented by all the fine gentlemen, who justly value themselves upon their knowledge in good eating; and a skilful cook, who understands how to oblige his guests, will contrive to make it as expensive as they please.

Sixthly, this would be a great inducement to marriage, 26 which all wise nations have either encouraged by rewards, or enforced by laws and penalties. It would increase the care and tenderness of mothers towards their children, when they were sure of a settlement for life, to the poor babes, provided in some sort by the public to their annual profit instead of expense. We should soon see an honest emulation among the married women, which of them could bring the fattest child to the market. Men would become as fond of their wives, during the time of their pregnancy, as they are now of their mares in foal, their cows in calf, or sows when they are ready to farrow, nor offer to beat or kick them (as it is too frequent a practice) for fear of a miscarriage.

Many other advantages might be enumerated. For instance, 27 the addition of some thousand carcasses in our exportation of barrelled beef; the propagation of swine's flesh, and improvement in the art of making good bacon, so much wanted among us by the great destruction of pigs, too frequent at our tables, are no way comparable in taste or magnificence to a well-grown, fat yearling child, which roasted whole will make a considerable figure at a Lord Mayor's feast, or any other public entertainment. But this and many others I omit, being studious of brevity.

Supposing that one thousand families in this city would be constant customers for infants' flesh, besides others who might have it at merry meetings, particularly weddings and christenings; I compute that Dublin would take off annually about twenty thousand carcasses, and the rest of the kingdom (where probably they will be sold somewhat cheaper) the remaining eighty thousand. 28

I can think of no one objection that will possibly be raised against this proposal, unless it should be urged that the number of people will be thereby much lessened in the kingdom. This I freely own, and it was indeed one principal design in offering it to the world. I desire the reader will observe, that I calculate my remedy *for this one individual Kingdom of* Ireland, *and for no other that ever was, is, or, I think, ever can be upon earth.* Therefore let no man talk to me of other expedients: *Of taxing our absentees at five shillings a pound: Of using neither clothes, nor household furniture, except what is of our own growth and manufacture: Of utterly rejecting the materials and instruments that promote foreign luxury: Of curing the expensiveness of pride, vanity, idleness, and gaming in our women: Of introducing a vein of parsimony, prudence, and temperance: Of learning to love our country, wherein we differ even from* Laplanders, *and the inhabitants of* Topinamboo: *Of quitting our animosities and factions, nor act any longer like the* Jews, *who were murdering one another at the very moment their city was taken: Of being a little cautious not to sell our country and consciences for nothing: Of teaching landlords to have at least one degree of mercy towards their tenants.* Lastly, *of putting a spirit of honesty, industry, and skill into our shopkeepers, who, if a resolution could now be taken to buy only our native goods, would immediately unite to cheat and* 29 *exact upon us in the price, the measure and the goodness, nor could ever yet be brought to make one fair proposal of just dealing, though often and earnestly invited to it.*

Therefore I repeat, let no man talk to me of these and the like expedients, till he hath at least a glimpse of hope that there will ever be some hearty and sincere attempt to put them in practice. 30

But as to myself, having been wearied out for many years with offering vain, idle, visionary thoughts, and at length utterly despairing of success, I fortunately fell upon this proposal, which as it is wholly new, so it hath something solid and real, of no expense and little trouble, full in our own power, and whereby we can incur no danger in disobliging England. For this kind of commodity will not bear exportation, the flesh being of too tender a consistence to admit a long continuance in salt, *although perhaps I could name a country which would be glad to eat up our whole nation without it.* 31

After all I am not so violently bent upon my own opinion as to reject any offer, proposed by wise men, which shall be found equally innocent, cheap, easy and effectual. But before some thing of that kind shall be advanced in contradiction to my scheme, and offering a better, I desire the author, or authors, will be pleased maturely to consider two points. First, as things now stand, how they will be able to find food and raiment for a hundred thousand useless mouths and backs? And secondly, there being a round million of creatures in human figure, throughout this kingdom, whose whole subsistence put into a common stock would leave them in debt two millions of pounds sterling; adding those who are beggars by profession, to the bulk of farmers, cottagers, and labourers with their wives and children, who are beggars in effect; I desire those politicians who dislike my overture, and may perhaps be so bold to attempt an answer, that they will first ask the parents of these mortals whether they would not at this day think it a great happiness to have been sold for food at a year old, in the manner I prescribe, and thereby have avoided such a perpetual scene of misfortunes as they have since gone through, by the 32 oppression of landlords, the impossibility of paying rent without money or trade, the want of common sustenance, with neither house nor clothes to cover them from the inclemencies of weather, and the most inevitable prospect of entailing the like, or greater miseries upon their breed for ever.

I profess in the sincerity of my heart that I have not the 33 least personal interest in endeavouring to promote this necessary work, having no other motive than the *public good of my country, by advancing our trade, providing for infants, relieving the poor, and giving some pleasure to the rich.* I have no children by which I can propose to get a single penny; the youngest being nine years old, and my wife past child-bearing.

[1729 — Great Britain]

Questions

1. What picture do we get of the speaker of "A Modest Proposal" from the first seven paragraphs? Why? What is Swift's purpose in painting the speaker thus?

2. Describe the mentality and character of the speaker in detail. What are his intellectual strengths? What might his profession be? What are his motives? What else do we learn about him? What is missing from his character? How does this lack affect the reader's reception of his argument?

3. The speaker moves into his proposal in paragraph 9. Where is it intimated earlier? Paragraph 8, which is transitional, and paragraph 9 maintain the tone of the opening paragraphs. What tone is that? What is the effect of its being maintained?

4. In paragraph 12, Swift shows through. How so? The phrase "already devoured most of the parents" suggests that the proposal itself is in part symbolic. What is symbolized?

5. The speaker suggests other policies that could be adopted to reduce poverty and starvation (paragraph 29) but goes on to dismiss them (paragraph 30). Why? What is satirized here?

6. In paragraph 17, Swift's speaker presents certain corollary ideas that, though rejected, seem to follow logically from the original premise (the proposal). Is the speaker's rejection convincing? Upon what basis does he reject his friend's ideas? What does this paragraph suggest about what generally happens when people start seriously to consider the unthinkable?

7. Readers frequently miss the irony of "A Modest Proposal." But from its title to its last sentence, it is ironic through and through. What specific ironies do you find? How is the essay overall ironic with regard to Swift's intention? But there is a deeper, more terrible irony yet. Given the conditions of life in Ireland as depicted in this essay, is not the speaker's argument persuasive and even rational? Consider "A Modest Proposal" from this perspective, bringing this final layer of irony to the surface.

Writing Assignments

1. In a short paper, evaluate the effectiveness of "A Modest Proposal," especially with regard to its layered irony. How effective is the essay (as opposed to its speaker) in persuading us that the British treatment of the Irish in Swift's day was inhumane and immoral?

2. Write a satiric piece proposing what should be done with ex-boy-friends or girlfriends, teachers, brothers or sisters. Try to be lightly ironic, indicating that you don't really believe what you say but that there is some truth in it after all.

3. Write an essay spoken by someone not yourself and whose position you actually hate. In doing so, remember that somehow or other your speaker must expose the foolishness or even insanity of his or her premise. Maintain a consistency of tone and voice throughout.

4. Research the living conditions of the Irish in Swift's day as well as Swift's connection with Ireland and the Irish. Then write a research paper on "A Modest Proposal," using your research to validate what you say about the essay.

✤ I WANT A WIFE ✤
Judy Syfers

I BELONG TO THAT CLASSIFICATION OF PEOPLE KNOWN AS WIVES. I AM   1
A Wife. And, not altogether incidentally, I am a mother.

Not too long ago a male friend of mine appeared on the   2
scene fresh from a recent divorce. He had one child, who is, of
course, with his ex-wife. He is looking for another wife. As I
thought about him while I was ironing one evening, it suddenly
occurred to me that I, too, would like to have a wife. Why do
I want a wife?

I would like to go back to school so that I can become   3
economically independent, support myself, and, if need be,
support those dependent upon me. I want a wife who will work
and send me to school. And while I am going to school I want
a wife to take care of my children. I want a wife to keep track
of the children's doctor and dentist appointments. And to keep
track of mine, too. I want a wife to make sure my children eat
properly and are kept clean. I want a wife who will wash the
children's clothes and keep them mended. I want a wife who is
a good nurturant attendant to my children, who arranges for
their schooling, makes sure that they have an adequate social
life with their peers, takes them to the park, the zoo, etc. I want
a wife who takes care of the children when they are sick, a wife
who arranges to be around when the children need special care,
because, of course, I cannot miss classes at school. My wife
must arrange to lose time at work and not lose the job. It may
mean a small cut in my wife's income from time to time, but I
guess I can tolerate that. Needless to say, my wife will arrange
and pay for the care of the children while my wife is working.

I want a wife who will take care of *my* physical needs. I   4
want a wife who will keep my house clean. A wife who will pick
up after my children, a wife who will pick up after me. I want
a wife who will keep my clothes clean, ironed, mended,
replaced when need be, and who will see to it that my personal

things are kept in their proper place so that I can find what I need the minute I need it. I want a wife who cooks the meals, a wife who is a *good* cook. I want a wife who will plan the menus, do the necessary grocery shopping, prepare the meals, serve them pleasantly, and then do the cleaning up while I do my studying. I want a wife who will care for me when I am sick and sympathize with my pain and loss of time from school. I want a wife to go along when our family takes a vacation so that someone can continue to care for me and my children when I need a rest and change of scene.

I want a wife who will not bother me with rambling complaints about a wife's duties. But I want a wife who will listen to me when I feel the need to explain a rather difficult point I have come across in my course of studies. And I want a wife who will type my papers for me when I have written them.

I want a wife who will take care of the details of my social life. When my wife and I are invited out by my friends, I want a wife who will take care of the babysitting arrangements. When I meet people at school that I like and want to entertain, I want a wife who will have the house clean, will prepare a special meal, serve it to me and my friends, and not interrupt when I talk about things that interest me and my friends. I want a wife who will have arranged that the children are fed and ready for bed before my guests arrive so that the children do not bother us. I want a wife who takes care of the needs of my guests so that they feel comfortable, who makes sure that they have an ashtray, that they are passed the hors d'oeuvres, that they are offered a second helping of the food, that their wine glasses are replenished when necessary, that their coffee is served to them as they like it. And I want a wife who knows that sometimes I need a night out by myself.

I want a wife who is sensitive to my sexual needs, a wife who makes love passionately and eagerly when I feel like it, a wife who makes sure that I am satisfied. And, of course, I want a wife who will not demand sexual attention when I am not in the mood for it. I want a wife who assumes the complete responsibility for birth control, because I do not want more children. I want a wife who will remain sexually faithful to me so that I do not have to clutter up my intellectual life with jealousies. And I want a wife who understands that *my* sexual needs may entail more than strict adherence to monogamy. I must, after all, be able to relate to people as fully as possible.

If, by chance, I find another person more suitable as a wife   8 than the wife I already have, I want the liberty to replace my present wife with another one. Naturally, I will expect a fresh, new life; my wife will take the children and be solely responsible for them so that I am left free.

When I am through with school and have a job, I want my   9 wife to quit working and remain at home so that my wife can more fully and completely take care of a wife's duties.

My God, who *wouldn't* want a wife?   10

[1971 — U.S.A.]

Questions

1. Given the gender of the author, what kind of title does this essay have? What audience do you suppose was it intended for? (The essay was first published in *Ms.*)

2. Not once does Syfers use the pronoun "she" to refer to "wife." Why? What is achieved by the repetition of the word "wife" and the phrase "I want a wife"? What is the theme of this essay?

3. What kind of rhythm does the essay's syntax, syntactical parallelism, and repetition produce? What tone does this rhythm in turn effect?

4. What are the topics of paragraphs 3, 4, 5, 6, and 7? These paragraphs move in an order of climax. How so and from whose perspective? How does the order reflect Syfers's theme?

Writing Assignments

1. This essay was published in 1971. How much has truly changed since then? Write a short paper arguing that a good deal has changed or not much at all. Be sure to be as specific as Syfers in her catalogues of wifely duties.

2. "I Want a Wife" is a satire of the cultural attitudes and fantasies of men vis-à-vis women. What of the reverse? What attitudes and fantasies do women have vis-à-vis men? Write an essay like Syfers's

on "I Want a Husband." Divide what you believe women's attitudes and fantasies to be into categories; then arrange your categories climactically. Use Syfers as your model as regards both structure and tone.

3. Read or reread Ellen Goodman's "The Just-Right Wife" (pages 253–55) and then write an essay comparing and contrasting it to "I Want a Wife." How are they thematically alike? How do they differ in tone? Both are ironic and satirical, yet the effects of their irony and satire differ. How so? Which is more likely to hold the attention of a general audience? Why?

❖ FITTING IN ❖
John Tarkov

Nom quite two miles and 30 years from the church where these thoughts came to me, is a small, graveled parking lot cut out of the New Jersey pines, behind a restaurant and a dance hall. On road signs, the town is called Cassville. But to the several generations of Russian-Americans whose center of gravity tipped to the Old World, it was known as Roova Farms. I think the acronym stands for Russian Orthodox Outing and Vacation Association. In the summers, the place might as well have been on the Black Sea.

One day during one of those summers, my old man showed up from a job, just off a cargo ship. He made his living that way, in the merchant marine. With him, he had a brittle new baseball glove and a baseball as yet unmarked by human error. We went out to that parking lot and started tossing the ball back and forth; me even at the age of 8 at ease with the motions of this American game, him grabbing at the ball with his bare hands then sending it back with an unpolished stiff-armed heave. It was a very hot day. I remember that clearly. What I can't remember is who put the first scuff mark on the ball. Either I missed it, or he tossed it out of my reach.

I chased it down, I'm sure with American-kid peevishness. 3
I wonder if I said anything. Probably I mouthed off about it.

Last winter, the phone call comes on a Saturday morning. 4
The old man's heart had stopped. They had started it beating
again. When I get to the hospital, he's not conscious. They let
me in to see him briefly. Then comes an afternoon of drinking
coffee and leaning on walls. Around 4 o'clock, two doctors
come out of coronary care. One of them puts his hand on my
arm and tells me. A nurse takes me behind the closed door.

Two fragments of thought surface. One is primitive and it 5
resonates from somewhere deep: *This all began in Russia long
ago.* The other is sentimental: *He died near the sea.*

I join the tips of the first three fingers of my right hand and 6
touch them to his forehead, then his stomach, then one side of
his chest, then the other. It's what I believe. I pause just briefly,
then give him a couple of quick cuffs on the side of his face, the
way men do when they want to express affection but something
stops them from embracing. The nurse takes me downstairs to
sign some forms.

He never did quite get the hang of this country. He never 7
went to the movies. Didn't watch television on his own. Didn't
listen to the radio. Ate a lot of kielbasa. Read a lot. Read the
paper almost cover to cover every day. He read English well,
but when he talked about what he'd read, he'd mispronounce
some words and put a heavy accent on them all. The paper was
the window through which he examined a landscape and a
people that were nearly as impenetrable to him as they were
known and manageable to me. For a touch of home, he'd pick
up Soviet Life. "I'm not a Communist," he used to tell me. "I'm
a Russian." Then he'd catch me up about some new hydroelec-
tric project on the Dnieper.

And so he vaguely embarrassed me. Who knows how many 8
times, over the years, this story has repeated itself: the
immigrant father and the uneasy son. This Melting Pot of ours
absorbs the second generation over a flame so high that the first
is left encrusted on the rim. In college, I read the

literature — Lenski on the three-generation hypothesis, stuff like that — but I read it to make my grades, not particularly to understand that I was living it.

When he finally retired from the ocean, he took his first real 9
apartment, on the Lower East Side, and we saw each other more regularly. We'd sit there on Saturday or Sunday afternoons, drinking beer and eating Chinese food. He bought a television set for our diversion, and, depending on the season, the voices of Keith Jackson and Ara Parseghian or Ralph Kiner and Lindsey Nelson would overlap with, and sometimes submerge, our own.

After the game, he'd get us a couple more beers, and we 10
would become emissaries: from land and sea, America and ports of destination. We were never strangers — never that — but we dealt, for the most part, in small talk. It was a son trying — or maybe trying to try — to share what little he knew with his father, and flinching privately at his father's foreignness. And it was a father outspokenly proud of his son, beyond basis in reason, yet at times openly frustrated that the kid had grown up unlike himself.

Every father has a vision of what he'd like his son to be. 11
Every son has a vision in kind of his father. Eventually, one of them goes, and the one remaining has little choice but to extinguish the ideal and confront the man of flesh and blood who was. Time and again it happens: The vision shed, the son, once vaguely embarrassed by the father, begins to wear the old man's name and story with pride.

Though he read it daily, the old man hated this newspaper. 12
Sometimes I think he bought it just to make himself angry. He felt the sports editor was trying to suppress the growth of soccer in America. So naturally, I would egg him on. I'd say things like: "Yeah, you're right. It's a conspiracy. The sports editor plus 200 million other Americans." Then we'd start yelling.

But when it came time to put the obituary announcements 13
in the press, after I phoned one in to the Russian-language

paper, I started to dial The Times. And I remembered. And I put the phone down. And started laughing. "O.K.," I said. "O.K. They won't get any of our business."

So he went out Russian, like he came in. Up on the hill, the 14 church is topped by weathered gold onion domes — sort of like back in the Old Country, but in fact just down the road from his attempt to sneak us both into America through a side door in New Jersey, by tossing a baseball back and forth on a hot, still, bake-in-the-bleachers kind of summer day.

I believe he threw the thing over my head, actually. It *was* 15 a throwing error, the more I think about it. No way I could have caught it. But it was only a baseball, and he was my father, so it's no big deal. I bounced a few off his shins that day myself. Next time, the baseball doesn't touch the ground.

[1985 — U.S.A.]

Questions

1. Describe the event mentioned in and the setting of the opening paragraphs. What do both intimate about father and son?
2. Tarkov uses colloquial language and even slang here and there. What are some examples of the latter? What does the diction of this essay say about father and son?
3. The theme of this essay is intimated in paragraph 8. What is it? What metaphor embodies this theme?

Writing Assignments

1. Write an essay in which you describe some aspect of your own heritage and how you have stayed true to it or departed from it. In either case, what are your feelings on this matter?
2. Write an essay on your relationship with your father. Find some point of focus (like baseball in Tarkov's essay) and, keeping your focus constant, try to convey the various feelings, some perhaps contradictory, that the thought of your father raises in you.

---------------✤ BEING A MAN ✤---------------
Paul Theroux

THERE IS A PATHETIC SENTENCE IN THE CHAPTER "FETISHISM" IN DR.   1
Norman Cameron's book *Personality Development and Psychopathology*. It goes, "Fetishists are nearly always men; and their commonest fetish is a woman's shoe." I cannot read that sentence without thinking that it is just one more awful thing about being a man — and perhaps it is an important thing to know about us.

I have always disliked being a man. The whole idea of   2
manhood in America is pitiful, in my opinion. This version of masculinity is a little like having to wear an ill-fitting coat for one's entire life (by contrast, I imagine femininity to be an oppressive sense of nakedness). Even the expression "Be a man!" strikes me as insulting and abusive. It means: Be stupid, be unfeeling, obedient, soldierly and stop thinking. Man means "manly" — how can one think about men without considering the terrible ambition of manliness? And yet it is part of every man's life. It is a hideous and crippling lie; it not only insists on difference and connives at superiority, it is also by its very nature destructive — emotionally damaging and socially harmful.

The youth who is subverted, as most are, into believing in   3
the masculine ideal is effectively separated from women and he spends the rest of his life finding women a riddle and a nuisance. Of course, there is a female version of this male affliction. It begins with mothers encouraging little girls to say (to other adults) "Do you like my new dress?" In a sense, little girls are traditionally urged to please adults with a kind of coquettishness, while boys are enjoined to behave like monkeys towards each other. The nine-year-old coquette proceeds to become womanish in a subtle power game in which she learns to be sexually indispensable, socially decorative and always alert to a man's sense of inadequacy.

Femininity — being lady-like — implies needing a man as 4
witness and seducer; but masculinity celebrates the exclusive
company of men. That is why it is so grotesque; and that is also
why there is no manliness without inadequacy — because it
denies men the natural friendship of women.

It is very hard to imagine any concept of manliness that 5
does not belittle women, and it begins very early. At an age
when I wanted to meet girls — let's say the treacherous years of
thirteen to sixteen — I was told to take up a sport, get more
fresh air, join the Boy Scouts, and I was urged not to read so
much. It was the 1950s and if you asked too many questions
about sex you were sent to camp — boy's camp, of course: the
nightmare. Nothing is more unnatural or prison-like than a
boy's camp, but if it were not for them we would have no Elks'
Lodges, no pool rooms, no boxing matches, no Marines.

And perhaps no sports as we know them. Everyone is 6
aware of how few in number are the athletes who behave like
gentlemen. Just as high school basketball teaches you how to
be a poor loser, the manly attitude towards sports seems to be
little more than a recipe for creating bad marriages, social
misfits, moral degenerates, sadists, latent rapists and just plain
louts. I regard high school sports as a drug far worse than
marijuana, and it is the reason that the average tennis
champion, say, is a pathetic oaf.

Any objective study would find the quest for manliness 7
essentially right-wing, puritanical, cowardly, neurotic and
fueled largely by a fear of women. It is also certainly philistine.
There is no book-hater like a Little League coach. But indeed
all the creative arts are obnoxious to the manly ideal, because at
their best the arts are pursued by uncompetitive and essentially
solitary people. It makes it very hard for a creative youngster,
for any boy who expresses the desire to be alone seems to be
saying that there is something wrong with him.

It ought to be clear by now that I have something of an 8
objection to the way we turn boys into men. It does not surprise
me that when the President of the United States has his
customary weekend off he dresses like a cowboy — it is both a

measure of his insecurity and his willingness to please. In many ways, American culture does little more for a man than prepare him for modeling clothes in the L. L. Bean catalogue. I take this as a personal insult because for many years I found it impossible to admit to myself that I wanted to be a writer. It was my guilty secret, because being a writer was incompatible with being a man.

There are people who might deny this, but that is because 9 the American writer, typically, has been so at pains to prove his manliness that we have come to see literariness and manliness as mingled qualities. But first there was a fear that writing was not a manly profession — indeed, not a profession at all. (The paradox in American letters is that it has always been easier for a woman to write and for a man to be published.) Growing up, I had thought of sports as wasteful and humiliating, and the idea of manliness was a bore. My wanting to become a writer was not a flight from that oppressive role-playing, but I quickly saw that it was at odds with it. Everything in stereotyped manliness goes against the life of the mind. The Hemingway personality is too tedious to go into here, and in any case his exertions are well-known, but certainly it was not until this aberrant behavior was examined by feminists in the 1960s that any male writer dared question the pugnacity in Hemingway's fiction. All the bullfighting and arm wrestling and elephant shooting diminished Hemingway as a writer, but it is consistent with a prevailing attitude in American writing: one cannot be a male writer without first proving that one is a man.

It is normal in America for a man to be dismissive or even 10 somewhat apologetic about being a writer. Various factors make it easier. There is a heartiness about journalism that makes it acceptable — journalism is the manliest form of American writing and, therefore, the profession the most independent-minded women seek (yes, it is an illusion, but that is my point). Fiction-writing is equated with a kind of dispirited failure and is only manly when it produces wealth — money is masculinity. So is drinking. Being a drunkard is another assertion, if misplaced, of manliness. The American male writer is traditionally proud of his heavy drinking. But we are also a very literal-minded people. A man proves his manhood in America in old-fashioned ways. He kills lions, like Hemingway; or he hunts ducks, like Nathanael West; or he makes pronouncements like, "A man should carry enough knife to defend himself with," as James Jones once said to a *Life* interviewer. Or he says he can drink you under the table. But even tiny drunken William Faulkner loved to mount a horse and go fox hunting, and Jack Kerouac roistered up and down Manhattan in a lumberjack shirt (and spent every night of *The Subterraneans* with his mother in Queens). And we are familiar with the lengths to which Norman Mailer is prepared, in his endearing way, to prove that he is just as much a monster as the next man.

When the novelist John Irving was revealed as a wrestler, 11 people took him to be a very serious writer; and even a bubble reputation like Eric *(Love Story)* Segal's was enhanced by the news that he ran the marathon in a respectable time. How surprised we would be if Joyce Carol Oates were revealed as a sumo wrestler or Joan Didion active in pumping iron. "Lives in New York City with her three children" is the typical woman writer's biographical note, for just as the male writer must prove he has achieved a sort of muscular manhood, the woman writer — or rather her publicists — must prove her motherhood.

There would be no point in saying any of this if it were not 12 generally accepted that to be a man is somehow — even now in feminist-influenced America — a privilege. It is on the contrary an unmerciful and punishing burden. Being a man is bad enough; being manly is appalling (in this sense, women's lib has done much more for men than for women). It is the sinister silliness of men's fashions, and a clubby attitude in the arts. It is the subversion of good students. It is the so-called "Dress Code" of the Ritz-Carlton Hotel in Boston, and it is the institutionalized cheating in college sports. It is the most primitive insecurity.

And this is also why men often object to feminism but are 13 afraid to explain why: of course women have a justified grievance, but most men believe — and with reason — that their lives are just as bad.

[1984 — U.S.A.]

Questions

1. This essay could have started with paragraph 2, its thesis paragraph. What, then, is the function of paragraph 1?

2. What is Theroux's thesis? How is it led to? In what way does it entail definition?

3. What kind of voice do you hear here? How does the voice established in the essay lend authority to its speaker and credence to his argument?

4. Where and to what effect does Theroux make use of comparison and contrast? How does the specific comparison and contrast he makes help persuade us that he is fair-minded and perceptive?

5. How does Theroux support his view of American "masculinity," or his definition thereof? What reasons — both general and personal — does he give that might persuade a reader of the merit of his case?

Writing Assignments

1. In Theroux's opinion, "It is very hard to imagine any concept of manliness that does not belittle women." If you disagree (or even if you agree), write a paragraph or more attempting such a definition. If you get stuck, then write a paragraph or more on why.

2. Write a short essay on your response to "Being a Man." Take up each of Theroux's points in succession and tell what your feelings are point by point and why you feel as you do.

✦ THE IKS ✦

Lewis Thomas

T HE SMALL TRIBE OF IKS, FORMERLY NOMADIC HUNTERS AND 1
gatherers in the mountain valleys of northern Uganda, have
become celebrities, literary symbols for the ultimate fate of
disheartened, heartless mankind at large. Two disastrously
conclusive things happened to them: the government decided to
have a national park, so they were compelled by law to give up
hunting in the valleys and become farmers on poor hillside soil,
and then they were visited for two years by an anthropologist
who detested them and wrote a book about them.

The message of the book is that the Iks have transformed 2
themselves into an irreversibly disagreeable collection of
unattached, brutish creatures, totally selfish and loveless, in
response to the dismantling of their traditional culture. Moreover, this is what the rest of us are like in our inner selves, and
we will all turn into Iks when the structure of our society comes
all unhinged.

The argument rests, of course, on certain assumptions 3
about the core of human beings, and is necessarily speculative.
You have to agree in advance that man is fundamentally a bad
lot, out for himself alone, displaying such graces as affection
and compassion only as learned habits. If you take this view,
the story of the Iks can be used to confirm it. These people seem
to be living together, clustered in small, dense villages, but they
are really solitary, unrelated individuals with no evident use for
each other. They talk, but only to make ill-tempered demands
and cold refusals. They share nothing. They never sing. They
turn the children out to forage as soon as they can walk, and
desert the elders to starve whenever they can, and the foraging
children snatch food from the mouths of the helpless elders. It
is a mean society.

They breed without love or even casual regard. They 4
defecate on each other's doorsteps. They watch their neighbors

for signs of misfortune, and only then do they laugh. In the book they do a lot of laughing, having so much bad luck. Several times they even laughed at the anthropologist, who found this especially repellent (one senses, between the lines, that the scholar is not himself the world's luckiest man). Worse, they took him into the family, snatched his food, defecated on his doorstep, and hooted dislike at him. They gave him two bad years.

It is a depressing book. If as he suggests, there is only   5
Ikness at the center of each of us, our sole hope for hanging on to the name of humanity will be in endlessly mending the structure of our society, and it is changing so quickly and completely that we may never find the thread in time. Meanwhile, left to ourselves alone, solitary, we will become the same joyless, zestless, untouching lone animals.

But this may be too narrow a view. For one thing, the Iks   6
are extraordinary. They are absolutely astonishing, in fact. The anthropologist has never seen people like them anywhere, nor have I. You'd think, if they were simply examples of the common essence of mankind, they'd seem more recognizable. Instead, they are bizarre, anomalous. I have known my share of peculiar, difficult, nervous, grabby people, but I've never encountered any genuinely, consistently detestable human beings in all my life. The Iks sound more like abnormalities, maladies.

I cannot accept it. I do not believe that the Iks are   7
representative of isolated, revealed man, unobscured by social habits. I believe their behavior is something extra, something laid on. This unremitting, compulsive repellence is a kind of complicated ritual. They must have learned to act this way; they copied it, somehow.

I have a theory, then. The Iks have gone crazy.   8

The solitary Ik, isolated in the ruins of an exploded culture,   9
has built a new defense for himself. If you live in an unworkable society you can make up one of your own, and this is what the Iks have done. Each Ik has become a group, a one-man tribe on its own, a constituency.

Now everything falls into place. This is why they do seem, 10
after all, vaguely familiar to all of us. We've seen them before.
This is precisely the way groups of one size or another, ranging
from committees to nations, behave. It is, of course, this aspect
of humanity that has lagged behind the rest of evolution, and
this is why the Ik seems so primitive. In his absolute selfishness,
his incapacity to give anything away, no matter what, he is a
successful committee. When he stands at the door of his hut,
shouting insults at his neighbors in a loud harangue, he is city
addressing another city.

·Cities have all the Ik characteristics. They defecate on 11
doorsteps, in rivers and lakes, their own or anyone else's. They
leave rubbish. They detest all neighboring cities, give nothing
away. They even build institutions for deserting elders out of
sight.

Nations are the most Iklike of all. No wonder the Iks seem 12
familiar. For total greed, rapacity, heartlessness, and irresponsibility there is nothing to match a nation. Nations, by law, are
solitary, self-centered, withdrawn into themselves. There is no
such thing as affection between nations, and certainly no nation
ever loved another. They bawl insults from their doorsteps,
defecate into whole oceans, snatch all the food, survive by
detestation, take joy in the bad luck of others, celebrate the
death of others, live for the death of others.

That's it, and I shall stop worrying about the book. It does 13
not signify that man is a sparse, inhuman thing at his center.
He's all right. It only says what we've always known and never
had enough time to worry about, that we haven't yet learned
how to stay human when assembled in masses. The Ik, in his
despair, is acting out this failure, and perhaps we should pay
closer attention. Nations have themselves become too frightening to think about, but we might learn some things by watching
these people.

[1973 — U.S.A.]

Questions

1. The first paragraph is structured anticlimactically. Why? What is the effect of the anticlimax? What tone does it help create?

2. What is Thomas's thesis? Where do you find it? Why didn't Thomas state it at the beginning? In what way did Thomas's intended audience perhaps influence the structure of the essay as a whole?

3. Does the analogy at the heart of this essay shed light primarily on the Iks or on group behavior or on both? What kind of an ending does "The Iks" have (reverse funnel, summary, conclusion, et cetera)? What thought are we left with?

Writing Assignments

1. Write a short paper explaining the degradation of the Iks according to a theory of your own devise. Structure your paper after Thomas's essay, ending with an observation of what the Iks have to teach us.

2. In an essay, compare and contrast "The Iks" with Stephen Jay Gould's "The Nonscience of Human Nature" (pages 262–68). They are alike, for instance, in that the thesis statement of each is delayed; they are alike in their views of human nature; they are alike in spirit. They differ, for instance, in final aim and in the nature of their conclusions. Having compared and contrasted the two essays, consider the value of each and whether or not they succeed as essays.

✚ CLEVER ANIMALS ✚
Lewis Thomas

SCIENTISTS WHO WORK ON ANIMAL BEHAVIOR ARE OCCUPATIONALLY 1
obliged to live chancier lives than most of their colleagues,
always at risk of being fooled by the animals they are studying
or, worse, fooling themselves. Whether their experiments
involve domesticated laboratory animals or wild creatures in
the field, there is no end to the surprises that an animal can
think up in the presence of an investigator. Sometimes it seems
as if animals are genetically programmed to puzzle human
beings, especially psychologists.

The risks are especially high when the scientist is engaged 2
in training the animal to do something or other and must bank
his professional reputation on the integrity of his experimental
subject. The most famous case in point is that of Clever Hans,
the turn-of-the-century German horse now immortalized in the
lexicon of behavioral science by the technical term, the "Clever
Hans Error." The horse, owned and trained by Herr von
Osten, could not only solve complex arithmetical problems, but
even read the instructions on a blackboard and tap out
infallibly, with one hoof, the right answer. What is more, he
could perform the same computations when total strangers
posed questions to him, with his trainer nowhere nearby. For
several years Clever Hans was studied intensively by groups of
puzzled scientists and taken seriously as a horse with something
very like a human brain, quite possibly even better than human.
But finally in 1911, it was discovered by Professor O. Pfungst
that Hans was not really doing arithmetic at all; he was simply
observing the behavior of the human experimenter. Subtle,
unconscious gestures — nods of the head, the holding of breath,
the cessation of nodding when the correct count was reached
— were accurately read by the horse as cues to stop tapping.

Whenever I read about that phenomenon, usually re- 3
counted as the exposure of a sort of unconscious fraud on the

part of either the experimenter or the horse or both, I wish Clever Hans would be given more credit than he generally gets. To be sure, the horse couldn't really do arithmetic, but the record shows that he was considerably better at observing human beings and interpreting their behavior than humans are at comprehending horses or, for that matter, other humans.

Cats are a standing rebuke to behavioral scientists wanting 4 to know how the minds of animals work. The mind of a cat is an inscrutable mystery, beyond human reach, the least human of all creatures and at the same time, as any cat owner will attest, the most intelligent. In 1979, a paper was published in *Science* by B. R. Moore and S. Stuttard entitled "Dr. Guthrie and Felis domesticus or: tripping over the cat," a wonderful account of the kind of scientific mischief native to this species. Thirty-five years ago, E. R. Guthrie and G. P. Horton described an experiment in which cats were placed in a glass-fronted puzzle box and trained to find their way out by jostling a slender vertical rod at the front of the box, thereby causing a door to open. What interested these investigators was not so much that the cats could learn to bump into the vertical rod, but that before doing so each animal performed a long ritual of highly stereotyped movements, rubbing their heads and backs against the front of the box, turning in circles, and finally touching the rod. The experiment has ranked as something of a classic in experimental psychology, even raising in some minds the notion of a ceremony of superstition on the part of cats: before the rod will open the door, it is necessary to go through a magical sequence of motions.

Moore and Stuttard repeated the Guthrie experiment, 5 observed the same complex "learning" behavior, but then discovered that it occurred only when a human being was visible to the cat. If no one was in the room with the box, the cat did nothing but take naps. The sight of a human being was all that was needed to launch the animal on the series of sinuous movements, rod or no rod, door or no door. It was not a learned pattern of behavior, it was a cat greeting a person.

The French investigator R. Chauvin was once engaged in a   6
field study of the boundaries of ant colonies and enlisted the
help of some enthusiastic physicists equipped with radioactive
compounds and Geiger counters. The ants of one anthill were
labeled and then tracked to learn whether they entered the
territory of a neighboring hill. In the middle of the work the
physicists suddenly began leaping like ballet dancers, terminat-
ing the experiment, while hundreds of ants from both colonies
swarmed over their shoes and up inside their pants. To
Chauvin's ethological eye it looked like purposeful behavior on
both sides.

Bees are filled with astonishments, confounding anyone   7
who studies them, producing volumes of anecdotes. A lady of
our acquaintance visited her sister, who raised honeybees in
northern California. They left their car on a side road, suited up
in protective gear, and walked across the fields to have a look
at the hives. For reasons unknown, the bees were in a furious
mood that afternoon, attacking in platoons, settling on them
from all sides. Let us walk away slowly, advised the beekeeper
sister, they'll give it up sooner or later. They walked until
bee-free, then circled the fields and went back to the car, and
found the bees there, waiting for them.

There is a new bee anecdote for everyone to wonder about.   8
It was reported from Brazil that male bees of the plant-
pollinating euglossine species are addicted to DDT. Houses
that had been sprayed for mosquito control in the Amazonas
region were promptly invaded by thousands of bees that
gathered on the walls, collected the DDT in pouches on their
hind legs, and flew off with it. Most of the houses were virtually
stripped of DDT during the summer months, and the residents
in the area complained bitterly of the noise. There is as yet no
explanation for this behavior. They are not harmed by the
substance; while a honeybee is quickly killed by as little as six
micrograms of DDT, these bees can cart away two thousand
micrograms without being discommoded. Possibly the euglossine bees like the taste of DDT or its smell, or maybe they are

determined to protect other insect cousins. Nothing about bees, or other animals, seems beyond imagining.

[1982 – U.S.A.]

Questions

1. What is Thomas's thesis and where is it stated? Study paragraph 1 carefully before answering.
2. Thomas demonstrates his thesis by way of exemplification. What are his examples? The first two seem somewhat different from the last three. How so?
3. What is the structural mode of this essay? What pattern if any do you find in the arrangement of paragraphs 2–3, 4–5, 6, 7, and 8? That is, why is the first block (2–3) first, the second second, and so on?
4. What accounts for the coherence of this essay, in which no obvious transitions are used between paragraphs? Or perhaps you feel that it could be more coherent. How would you make it so?
5. Is the ending effective with regard to the essay as a whole? Why or why not?

Writing Assignments

1. Do you have a pet? Does its behavior ever seem a mystery to you, or at least a remarkable adaption to living with human beings? If so, write a paragraph or short paper on that behavior, taking Thomas's thesis as your own. Supply concrete examples point by point.
2. The strangest behavior of all, of course, is that of human beings vis-à-vis animals. Write an essay that proceeds by exemplification on the oddities of human behavior with regard to animals, domesticated and/or wild.

✤ THE ATTIC OF THE BRAIN ✤
Lewis Thomas

Mᵧ parents' house had an attic, the darkest and strangest 1
part of the building, reachable only by placing a stepladder
beneath the trapdoor and filled with unidentifiable articles too
important to be thrown out with the trash but no longer suitable
to have at hand. This mysterious space was the memory of the
place. After many years all the things deposited in it became,
one by one, lost to consciousness. But they were still there, we
knew, safely and comfortably stored in the tissues of the house.

These days most of us live in smaller, more modern houses 2
or in apartments, and attics have vanished. Even the deep
closets in which we used to pile things up for temporary
forgetting are rarely designed into new homes.

Everything now is out in the open, openly acknowledged 3
and displayed, and whenever we grow tired of a memory, an
old chair, a trunkful of old letters, they are carted off to the
dump for burning.

This has seemed a healthier way to live, except maybe for 4
the smoke — everything out to be looked at, nothing strange
hidden under the roof, nothing forgotten because of no place
left in impenetrable darkness to forget. Openness is the new
lifestyle, no undisclosed belongings, no private secrets. Candor
is the rule in architecture. The house is a machine for living,
and what kind of a machine would hide away its worn-out,
obsolescent parts?

But it is in our nature as human beings to clutter, and we 5
hanker for places set aside, reserved for storage. We tend to
accumulate and outgrow possessions at the same time, and it is
an endlessly discomforting mental task to keep sorting out the
ones to get rid of. We might, we think, remember them later
and find a use for them, and if they are gone for good, off to the
dump, this is a source of nervousness. I think it may be one of
the reasons we drum our fingers so much these days.

We might take a lesson here from what has been learned 6 about our brains in this century. We thought we discovered, first off, the attic, although its existence has been mentioned from time to time by all the people we used to call great writers. What we really found was the trapdoor and a stepladder, and off we clambered, shining flashlights into the corners, vacuuming the dust out of bureau drawers, puzzling over the names of objects, tossing them down to the floor below, and finally paying around fifty dollars an hour to have them carted off for burning.

After several generations of this new way of doing things 7 we took up openness and candor with the febrile intensity of a new religion, everything laid out in full view, and as in the design of our new houses it seemed a healthier way to live, except maybe again for smoke.

And now, I think, we have a new kind of worry. There is 8 no place for functionless, untidy, inexplicable notions, no dark comfortable parts of the mind to hide away the things we'd like to keep but at the same time forget. The attic is still there, but with the trapdoor always open and the stepladder in place we are always in and out of it, flashing lights around, naming everything, unmystified.

I have an earnest proposal for psychiatry, a novel set of 9 therapeutic rules, although I know it means waiting in line.

Bring back the old attic. Give new instructions to the 10 patients who are made nervous by our times, including me, to make a conscious effort to hide a reasonable proportion of thought. It would have to be a gradual process, considering how far we have come in the other direction talking, talking all the way. Perhaps only one or two thoughts should be repressed each day, at the outset. The easiest, gentlest way might be to start with dreams, first by forbidding the patient to mention any dream, much less to recount its details, then encouraging the outright forgetting that there was a dream at all, remembering nothing beyond the vague sense that during sleep there had been the familiar sound of something shifting and sliding, up under the roof.

We might, in this way, regain the kind of spontaneity and 11 zest for ideas, things popping into the mind, uncontrollable and ungovernable thoughts, the feel that this notion is somehow connected unaccountably with that one. We could come again into possession of real memory, the kind of memory that can come from jumbled forgotten furniture, old photographs, fragments of music.

It has been one of the great errors of our time to think that 12 by thinking about thinking, and then talking about it, we could possibly straighten out and tidy up our minds. There is no delusion more damaging than to get the idea in your head that you understand the functioning of your own brain. Once you acquire such a notion, you run the danger of moving in to take charge, guiding your thoughts, shepherding your mind from place to place, *controlling* it, making lists of regulations. The human mind is not meant to be governed, certainly not by any book of rules yet written; it is supposed to run itself, and we are obliged to follow it along, trying to keep up with it as best we can. It is all very well to be aware of your awareness, even proud of it, but never try to operate it. You are not up to the job.

I leave it to the analysts to work out the techniques for 13 doing what now needs doing. They are presumably the professionals most familiar with the route, and all they have to do is turn back and go the other way, session by session, step by step. It takes a certain amount of hard swallowing and a lot of revised jargon, and I have great sympathy for their plight, but it is time to reverse course.

If after all, as seems to be true, we are endowed with 14 unconscious minds in our brains, these should be regarded as normal structures, installed wherever they are for a purpose. I am not sure what they are built to contain, but as a biologist, impressed by the usefulness of everything alive, I would take it for granted that they are useful, probably indispensable organs of thought. It cannot be a bad thing to own one, but I would no more think of meddling with it than trying to exorcise my liver, an equally mysterious apparatus. Until we know a lot more, it would be wise, as we have learned from other fields in medicine, to let them be, above all not to interfere. Maybe, even — and this is the notion I wish to suggest to my psychiatric friends — to stock them up, put more things into them, make *use* of them. Forget whatever you feel like forgetting. From time to time, practice *not* being open, discover new things *not* to talk about, learn reserve, hold the tongue. But above all, develop the human talent for forgetting words, phrases, whole unwelcome sentences, all experiences involving wincing. If we should ever lose the loss of memory, we might lose as well that most attractive of signals ever flashed from the human face, the blush. If we should give away the capacity for embarrassment, the touch of fingertips might be the next to go, and then the suddenness of laughter, the unaccountable sure sense of something gone wrong, and, finally, the marvelous conviction that being human is the best thing to be.

Attempting to operate one's own mind, powered by such a 15 magical instrument as the human brain, strikes me as rather like using the world's biggest computer to add columns of figures, or towing a Rolls-Royce with a nylon rope.

I have tried to think of a name for the new professional 16 activity, but each time I think of a good one I forget it before I can get it written down. Psychorepression is the only one I've hung on to, but I can't guess at the fee schedule.

[1982 — U.S.A.]

Questions

1. Thomas explores his thesis by way of a metaphorical analogy. What is that analogy? What is that thesis? Where is it stated? Why there?

2. Does Thomas's analogy help clarify his view of the brain? How so? What audience, do you think, did he intend? Does the way he presents the analogy (as distinguished from the analogy itself) work for or against clarity? How so?

3. What is the general tone of this essay? In answering, consider the last paragraph especially and such sentences as "I know it means waiting in line" (paragraph 9) and "Perhaps only one or two thoughts should be repressed each day" (paragraph 10). Is Thomas in earnest with respect to his basic premise? If so, why the humor?

4. Do you agree with paragraph 5? Or does it seem merely assertive? What of the essay as a whole? Are Thomas's statements supported with evidence or asserted only? In the case of this essay, does it matter?

Writing Assignments

1. "But it is our nature as human beings to clutter," Thomas holds (paragraph 5). Do you agree or disagree? In either case, write a short paper defending your view. Use examples and, if possible, an extended analogy like Thomas's.

2. Read or reread Nancy Hill's "Teaching as Mountaineering" (pages 310–14), which, like "The Attic of the Brain," entails an extended analogy. Then write a paper evaluating the two essays as to how the central analogy of each is presented and developed. You will first need to establish the likenesses and/or differences of the two essays with regard to the central analogy of each; then move to your evaluation, playing one essay off against the other.

✛ Late Night Thoughts ✛ on Listening to Mahler's Ninth Symphony
Lewis Thomas

I CANNOT LISTEN TO MAHLER'S NINTH SYMPHONY WITH ANYTHING   1
like the old melancholy mixed with the high pleasure I used to take from this music. There was a time, not long ago, when what I heard, especially in the final movement, was an open acknowledgment of death and at the same time a quiet celebration of the tranquillity connected to the process. I took this music as a metaphor for reassurance, confirming my own strong hunch that the dying of every living creature, the most natural of all experiences, has to be a peaceful experience. I rely on nature. The long passages on all the strings at the end, as close as music can come to expressing silence itself, I used to hear as Mahler's idea of leave-taking at its best. But always, I

have heard this music as a solitary, private listener, thinking about death.

Now I hear it differently. I cannot listen to the last 2 movement of the Mahler Ninth without the door-smashing intrusion of a huge new thought: death everywhere, the dying of everything, the end of humanity. The easy sadness expressed with such gentleness and delicacy by that repeated phrase on faded strings, over and over again, no longer comes to me as old, familiar news of the cycle of living and dying. All through the last notes my mind swarms with images of a world in which the thermonuclear bombs have begun to explode, in New York and San Francisco, in Moscow and Leningrad, in Paris, in Paris, in Paris. In Oxford and Cambridge, in Edinburgh. I cannot push away the thought of a cloud of radioactivity drifting along the Engadin,[1] from the Moloja Pass to Ftan, killing off the part of the earth I love more than any other part.

I am old enough by this time to be used to the notion of 3 dying, saddened by the glimpse when it has occurred but only transiently knocked down, able to regain my feet quickly at the thought of continuity, any day. I have acquired and held in affection until very recently another sideline of an idea which serves me well at dark times: the life of the earth is the same as the life of an organism: the great round being possesses a mind: the mind contains an infinite number of thoughts and memories: when I reach my time I may find myself still hanging around in some sort of midair, one of those small thoughts, drawn back into the memory of the earth: in that peculiar sense I will be alive.

Now all that has changed. I cannot think that way 4 anymore. Not while those things are still in place, aimed everywhere, ready for launching.

This is a bad enough thing for the people in my generation. 5 We can put up with it, I suppose, since we must. We are moving along anyway, like it or not. I can even set aside my private fancy about hanging around, in midair.

---

[1]*Engadin:* A valley in eastern Switzerland.

What I cannot imagine, what I cannot put up with, the 6
thought that keeps grinding its way into my mind, making the
Mahler into a hideous noise close to killing me, is what it would
be like to be young. How do the young stand it? How can they
keep their sanity? If I were very young, sixteen or seventeen
years old, I think I would begin, perhaps very slowly and
imperceptibly, to go crazy.

There is a short passage near the very end of the Mahler in 7
which the almost vanishing violins, all engaged in a sustained
backward glance, are edged aside for a few bars by the cellos.
Those lower notes pick up fragments from the first movement,
as though prepared to begin everything all over again, and then
the cellos subside and disappear, like an exhalation. I used to
hear this as a wonderful few seconds of encouragement: we'll
be back, we're still here, keep going, keep going.

Now, with a pamphlet in front of me on a corner of my 8
desk, published by the Congressional Office of Technology
Assessment, entitled *MX Basing,* an analysis of all the alternative strategies for placement and protection of hundreds of
these missiles, each capable of creating artificial suns to
vaporize a hundred Hiroshimas, collectively capable of destroy-
ing the life of any continent, I cannot hear the same Mahler.
Now, those cellos sound in my mind like the opening of all the
hatches and the instant before ignition.

If I were sixteen or seventeen years old, I would not feel the 9
cracking of my own brain, but I would know for sure that the
whole world was coming unhinged. I can remember with some
clarity what it was like to be sixteen. I had discovered the
Brahms symphonies. I knew that there was something going on
in the late Beethoven quartets that I would have to figure out,
and I knew that there was plenty of time ahead for all the
figuring I would ever have to do. I had never heard of Mahler.
I was in no hurry. I was a college sophomore and had decided
that Wallace Stevens[2] and I possessed a comprehensive
understanding of everything needed for a life. The years

---

[2]*Wallace Stevens:* (1879–1955) An American poet, considered to be of major stature.

stretched away forever ahead, forever. My great-great grand-father had come from Wales, leaving his signature in the family Bible on the same page that carried, a century later, my father's signature. It never crossed my mind to wonder about the twenty-first century; it was just there, given, somewhere in the sure distance.

The man on television, Sunday midday, middle-aged and 10 solid, nice-looking chap, all the facts at his fingertips, more dependable looking than most high-school principals, is talking about civilian defense, his responsibility in Washington. It can make an enormous difference, he is saying. Instead of the outright death of eighty million American citizens in twenty minutes, he says, we can, by careful planning and practice, get that number down to only forty million, maybe even twenty. The thing to do, he says, is to evacuate the cities quickly and have everyone get under shelter in the countryside. That way we can recover, and meanwhile we will have retaliated, incinerating all of Soviet society, he says. What about radioactive fallout? he is asked. Well, he says. Anyway, he says, if the Russians know they can only destroy forty million of us instead of eighty million, this will deter them. Of course, he adds, they have the capacity to kill all two hundred and twenty million of us if they were to try real hard, but they know we can do the same to them. If the figure is only forty million this will deter them, not worth the trouble, not worth the risk. Eighty million would be another matter, we should guard ourselves against losing that many all at once, he says.

If I were sixteen or seventeen years old and had to listen to 11 that, or read things like that, I would want to give up listening and reading. I would begin thinking up new kinds of sounds, different from any music heard before, and I would be twisting and turning to rid myself of human language.

[1982 — U.S.A.]

Questions

1. This essay is structured on a contrast of then and now. Which paragraphs concern "then" and which "now"? How does the contrast help make the essay coherent? What pattern emerges from how the contrast proceeds?

2. As well as the structural contrast just mentioned, "Late Night Thoughts" incorporates a fine rhythmic contrast. In this regard, contrast paragraphs 1 and 6, say. How do they differ syntactically? What differences in rhythm does the syntactical difference create? In what way are these contrasting rhythms part of the meaning?

3. Thomas describes himself as "a solitary, private listener" (paragraph 1). He is also a very personal writer, depending on his feelings and personal experience to make his points. (This is true of all four essays by him in this book, especially of "The Attic of the Brain" and "Late Night Thoughts"). How effective is his use of a limited, personal perspective? What are the limitations of this stance?

4. The movement from paragraphs 9 to 10 is entirely incoherent. Why? What does the deliberate incoherence here suggest dramatically with regard to the theme of this essay? What is that theme, which here serves to unify Thomas's disparate materials by its inclusiveness with respect to those materials? In answering, consider paragraph 10 in particular.

Writing Assignments

1. Have you observed and been affected by some drastic change within your lifetime? If so, write a paper about it, telling what it is and especially what you felt before the change and what you now feel, or how the change in question has altered your general perspective on things. Make this a personal essay, like Thomas's.

2. Write a short paper taking off from the following formula: time of day/thoughts on listening to a piece of music. Try to suggest the effect of the time of day on your mood and the thoughts and feelings the piece of music stirs up in you.

3. Read or reread all four essays by Thomas in this book (beginning at page 521). They're all short, so take heart. Then write a review of the four essays together. Point out Thomas's characteristics as a writer — of style, voice, stance (see question 3 in this regard), and so forth — and evaluate the effectiveness of his rhetoric and the worth of his work, at least of the four essays you've read.

---------✤ IT'S JUST TOO LATE ✤---------
Calvin Trillin

Knoxville, Tennessee
March 1979

UNTIL SHE WAS SIXTEEN, FANEE COOPER WAS WHAT HER PARENTS   1
sometimes called an ideal child. "You'd never have to correct
her," FaNee's mother has said. In sixth grade, FaNee won a
spelling contest. She played the piano and the flute. She seemed
to believe what she heard every Sunday at the Beaver Dam
Baptist Church about good and evil and the hereafter. FaNee
was not an outgoing child. Even as a baby, she was uncomfortable when she was held and cuddled. She found it easy to
tell her parents that she loved them but difficult to confide in
them. Particularly compared to her sister, Kristy, a cheerful,
open little girl two and a half years younger, she was reserved
and introspective. The thoughts she kept to herself, though,
were apparently happy thoughts. Her eighth-grade essay on
Christmas — written in a remarkably neat hand — talked of the
joys of helping put together toys for her little brother, Leo, Jr.,
and the importance of her parents' reminder that Christmas is
the birthday of Jesus. Her parents were the sort of people who
might have been expected to have an ideal child. As a boy, Leo
Cooper had been called "one of the greatest high-school
basketball players ever developed in Knox County." He went
on to play basketball at East Tennessee State, and he married
the homecoming queen, JoAnn Henson. After college, Cooper
became a high-school basketball coach and teacher and,
eventually, an administrator. By the time FaNee turned
thirteen, in 1973, he was in his third year as the principal of
Gresham Junior High School, in Fountain City — a small Knox
County town that had been swallowed up by Knoxville when
the suburbs began to move north. A tall man, with curly black

hair going on gray, Leo Cooper has an elaborate way of talking ("Unless I'm very badly mistaken, he has never related to me totally the content of his conversation") and a manner that may come from years of trying to leave errant junior-high-school students with the impression that a responsible adult is magnanimous, even humble, about invariably being in the right. His wife, a high-school art teacher, paints and does batik, and created the name FaNee because she liked the way it looked and sounded — it sounds like "Fawn-*ee*" when the Coopers say it — but the impression she gives is not of artiness but of soft-spoken small-town gentility. When she found, in the course of cleaning up FaNee's room, that her ideal thirteen-year-old had been smoking cigarettes, she was, in her words, crushed. "FaNee was such a perfect child before that," JoAnn Cooper said some time later. "She was angry that we found out. She knew we knew that she had done something we didn't approve of, and then the rebellion started. I was hurt. I was very hurt. I guess it came through as disappointment."

Several months later, FaNee's grandmother died. FaNee 2 had been devoted to her grandmother. She wrote a poem in her memory — an almost joyous poem, filled with Christian faith in the afterlife ("Please don't grieve over my happiness/Rejoice with me in the presence of the Angels of Heaven"). She also took some keepsakes from her grandmother's house, and was apparently mortified when her parents found them and explained that they would have to be returned. By then, the Coopers were aware that FaNee was going to have a difficult time as a teenager. They thought she might be self-conscious about the double affliction of glasses and braces. They thought she might be uncomfortable in the role of the principal's daughter at Gresham. In ninth grade, she entered Halls High School, where JoAnn Cooper was teaching art. FaNee was a loner at first. Then she fell in with what could only be considered a bad crowd.

Halls, a few miles to the north of Fountain City, used to be 3 known as Halls Crossroads. It is what Knoxville people call "over the ridge" — on the side of Black Oak Ridge that has always been thought of as rural. When FaNee entered Halls High, the Coopers were already in the process of building a house on several acres of land they had bought in Halls, in a sparsely settled area along Brown Gap Road. Like two or three other houses along the road, it was to be constructed basically of huge logs taken from old buildings — a house that Leo Cooper describes as being, like the name FaNee, "just a little bit different." Ten years ago, Halls Crossroads was literally a crossroads. Then some of the Knoxville expansion that had swollen Fountain City spilled over the ridge, planting subdivisions here and there on roads that still went for long stretches with nothing but an occasional house with a cow or two next to it. The increase in population did not create a town. Halls has no center. Its commercial area is a series of two or three shopping centers strung together on the Maynardville Highway, the four-lane that leads north into Union County — a place almost synonymous in east Tennessee with mountain poverty. Its restaurant is the Halls Freezo Drive-In. The gathering place for the group FaNee Cooper eventually found herself in was the Maynardville Highway Exxon station.

At Halls High School, the social poles were represented by   4 the Jocks and the Freaks. FaNee found her friends among the Freaks. "I am truly enlighted upon irregular trains of thought aimed at strange depots of mental wards," she wrote when she was fifteen. "Yes! Crazed farms for the mental off — Oh! I walked through the halls screams & loud laughter fill my ears — Orderlys try to reason with me — but I am unreasonable! The joys of being a FREAK in a circus of imagination." The little crowd of eight or ten young people that FaNee joined has been referred to by her mother as "the Union County group." A couple of the girls were from backgrounds similar to FaNee's, but all the boys had the characteristics, if not the precise addresses, that Knoxville people associate with the poor whites of Union County. They were the sort of boys who didn't bother to finish high school, or finished it in a special program for slow learners, or got ejected from it for taking a swing at the principal.

"I guess you can say they more or less dragged us down to their level with the drugs," a girl who was in the group — a girl who can be called Marcia — said recently. "And somehow we settled for it. It seems like we had to get ourselves in the pit before we could look out." People in the group used marijuana and Valium and LSD. They sneered at the Jocks and the "prim and proper little ladies" who went with the Jocks. "We set ourselves aside," Marcia now says. "We put ourselves above everyone. How we did that I don't know." In a Knox County high school, teenagers who want to get themselves in the pit need not mainline heroin. The Jocks they mean to be compared to do not merely show up regularly for classes and practice football and wear clean clothes; they watch their language and preach temperance and go to prayer meetings on Wednesday nights and talk about having a real good Christian witness. Around Knoxville, people who speak of well-behaved high-school kids often seem to use words like "perfect," or even "angels." For FaNee's group, the opposite was not difficult to figure out. "We were into wicked things, strange things," Marcia says. "It was like we were on some kind of devil trip." FaNee wrote about demons and vultures and rats. "Slithering serpents eat my sanity and bite my ass," she wrote in an essay called "The Lovely Road of Life," just after she turned sixteen, "while tornadoes derail and ever so swiftly destroy every car in my train of thought." She wrote a lot about death.

FaNee's girl friends spoke of her as "super-intelligent." Her English teacher found some of her writing profound — and disturbing. She was thought to be not just super-intelligent but super-mysterious, and even, at times, super-weird — an introverted girl who stared straight ahead with deep-brown, nearly black eyes and seemed to have thoughts she couldn't share. Nobody really knew why she had chosen to run with the Freaks — whether it was loneliness or rebellion or simple boredom. Marcia thought it might have had something to do with a feeling that her parents had settled on Kristy as their perfect child. "I guess she figured she couldn't be the best," Marcia said recently. "So she decided she might as well be the worst."

Toward the spring of FaNee's junior year at Halls, her   7
problems seemed to deepen. Despite her intelligence, her grades were sliding. She was what her mother called "a mental dropout." Leo Cooper had to visit Halls twice because of minor suspensions. Once, FaNee had been caught smoking. Once, having ducked out of a required assembly, she was spotted by a favorite teacher, who turned her in. At home, she exchanged little more than short, strained formalities with Kristy, who shared their parents' opinion of FaNee's choice of friends. The Coopers had finished their house — a large house, its size accentuated by the huge old logs and a great stone fireplace and outsize "Paul Bunyan"-style furniture — but FaNee spent most of her time there in her own room, sleeping or listening to rock music through earphones. One night, there was a terrible scene when FaNee returned from a concert in a condition that Leo Cooper knew had to be the result of marijuana. JoAnn Cooper, who ordinarily strikes people as too gentle to raise her voice, found herself losing her temper regularly. Finally, Leo Cooper asked a counsellor he knew, Jim Griffin, to stop in at Halls High School and have a talk with FaNee — unofficially.

Griffin — a young man with a warm, informal manner —   8
worked for the Juvenile Court of Knox County. He had a reputation for being able to reach teenagers who wouldn't talk to their parents or to school administrators. One Friday in March of 1977, he spent an hour and a half talking to FaNee Cooper. As Griffin recalls the interview, FaNee didn't seem alarmed by his presence. She seemed to him calm and controlled — Griffin thought it was something like talking to another adult — and, unlike most of the teenagers he dealt with, she looked him in the eye the entire time. Griffin, like some of FaNee's friends, found her eyes unsettling — "the coldest, most distant, but, at the same time, the most knowing eyes I'd ever seen." She expressed affection for her parents, but she didn't

seem interested in exploring ways of getting along better with them. The impression she gave Griffin was that they were who they were, and she was who she was, and there didn't happen to be any connection. Several times, she made the same response to Griffin's suggestions: "It's too late."

That weekend, neither FaNee nor her parents brought up 9 the subject of Griffin's visit. Leo Cooper has spoken of the weekend as being particularly happy; a friend of FaNee's who stayed over remembers it as particularly strained. FaNee stayed home from school on Monday because of a bad headache — she often had bad headaches — but felt well enough on Monday evening to drive to the library. She was to be home at nine. When she wasn't, Mrs. Cooper began to phone her friends. Finally, around ten, Leo Cooper got into his other car and took a swing around Halls — past the teenage hangouts like the Exxon station and the Pizza Hut and the Smoky Mountain Market. Then he took a second swing. At eleven, FaNee was still not home.

She hadn't gone to the library. She had picked up two girl 10 friends and driven to the home of a third, where everyone took five Valium tablets. Then the four girls drove over to the Exxon station, where they met four boys from their crowd. After a while, the group bought some beer and some marijuana and reassembled at Charlie Stevens's trailer. Charlie Stevens was five or six years older than everyone else in the group — a skinny, slow-thinking young man with long black hair and a sparse beard. He was married and had a child, but he and his wife had separated; she was back in Union County with the baby. Stevens had remained in their trailer — parked in the yard near his mother's house, in a back-road area of Knox County dominated by decrepit, unpainted sheds and run-down trailers and rusted-out automobiles. Stevens had picked up FaNee at home once or twice — apparently, more as a driver for the group than as a date — and the Coopers, having learned that his unsuitability extended to being married, had asked her not to see him.

In Charlie's trailer, which had no heat or electricity, the 11
group drank beer and passed around joints, keeping warm with
blankets. By eleven or so, FaNee was what one of her friends
has called "super-messed-up." Her speech was slurred. She was
having trouble keeping her balance. She had decided not to go
home. She had apparently persuaded herself that her parents
intended to send her away to some sort of home for incorrigi-
bles. "It's too late," she said to one of her friends. "It's just too
late." It was decided that one of the boys, David Munsey, who
was more or less the leader of the group, would drive the
Coopers' car to FaNee's house, where FaNee and Charlie
Stevens would pick him up in Stevens's car — a worn Pinto
with four bald tires, one light, and a dragging muffler. FaNee
wrote a note to her parents, and then, perhaps because her
handwriting was suffering the effects of beer and marijuana and
Valium, asked Stevens to rewrite it on a large piece of paper,
which would be left on the seat of the Coopers' car. The
Stevens version was just about the same as FaNee's, except that
Stevens left out a couple of sentences about trying to work
things out ("I'm willing to try") and, not having won any
spelling championships himself, he misspelled a few words, like
"tomorrow." The note said, "Dear Mom and Dad. Sorry I'm
late. Very late. I left your car because I thought you might need
it tomorrow. I love you all, but this is something I just had to
do. The man talked to me privately for one and a half hours and
I was really scared, so this is something I just had to do, but
don't worry, I'm with a very good friend. Love you all. FaNee.
P.S. Please try to understand I love you all very much, really I
do. Love me if you have a chance."

At eleven-thirty or so, Leo Cooper was sitting in his living 12
room, looking out the window at his driveway — a long gravel
road that runs almost four hundred feet from the house to
Brown Gap Road. He saw the car that FaNee had been driving
pull into the driveway. "She's home," he called to his wife, who
had just left the room. Cooper walked out on the deck over the
garage. The car had stopped at the end of the driveway, and the
lights had gone out. He got into his other car and drove to the

end of the driveway. David Munsey had already joined Charlie Stevens and FaNee, and the Pinto was just leaving, travelling at a normal rate of speed. Leo Cooper pulled out on the road behind them.

Stevens turned left on Crippen Road, a road that has a field 13 on one side and two or three small houses on the other, and there Cooper pulled his car in front of the Pinto and stopped, blocking the way. He got out and walked toward the Pinto. Suddenly, Stevens put the car in reverse, backed into a driveway a hundred yards behind him, and sped off. Cooper jumped in his car and gave chase. Stevens raced back to Brown Gap Road, ran a stop sign there, ran another stop sign at Maynardville Highway, turned north, veered off onto the old Andersonville Pike, a nearly abandoned road that runs parallel to the highway, and then crossed back over the highway to the narrow, dark country roads on the other side. Stevens sometimes drove with his lights out. He took some of the corners by suddenly applying his hand brake to make the car swerve around in a ninety-degree turn. He was in familiar territory — he actually passed his trailer — and Cooper had difficulty keeping up. Past the trailer, Stevens swept down a hill into a sharp left turn that took him onto Foust Hollow Road, a winding, hilly road not much wider than one car.

At a fork, Cooper thought he had lost the Pinto. He started 14 to go right, and then saw what seemed to be a spark from Stevens's dragging muffler off to the left, in the darkness. Cooper took the left fork, down Salem Church Road. He went down a hill, and then up a long, curving hill to a crest, where he saw the Stevens car ahead. "I saw the car airborne. Up in the air," he later testified. "It was up in the air. And then it completely rolled over one more time. It started to make another flip forward, and just as it started to flip to the other side it flipped back this way, and my daughter's body came out."

Cooper slammed on his brakes and skidded to a stop up 15 against the Pinto. "Book!" Stevens shouted — the group's equivalent of "Scram!" Stevens and Munsey disappeared into the darkness. "It was dark, no one around, and so I started yelling for FaNee," Cooper has testified. "I thought it was an eternity before I could find her body, wedged under the back end of that car. . . . I tried everything I could, and saw that I couldn't get her loose. So I ran to a trailer back up to the top of the hill back up there to try to get that lady to call to get me some help, and then apparently she didn't think that I was serious. . . . I took the jack out of my car and got under, and it was dark, still couldn't see too much what was going on . . . and started prying and got her loose, and I don't know how. And then I dragged her over to the side, and, of course, at the time I felt reasonably assured that she was gone, because her head was completely — on one side just as if you had taken a sledgehammer and just hit it and bashed it in. And I did have the pleasure of one thing. I had the pleasure of listening to her breathe about the last three times she ever breathed in her life."

David Munsey did not return to the wreck that night, but Charlie Stevens did. Leo Cooper was kneeling next to his daughter's body. Cooper insisted that Stevens come close enough to see FaNee. "He was kneeling down next to her," Stevens later testified. "And he said, 'Do you know what you've done? Do you really know what you've done?' Like that. And I just looked at her, and I said, 'Yes,' and just stood there. Because I couldn't say nothing." There was, of course, a legal decision to be made about who was responsible for FaNee Cooper's death. In a deposition, Stevens said he had been fleeing for his life. He testified that when Leo Cooper blocked Crippen Road, FaNee had said that her father had a gun and intended to hurt them. Stevens was bound over and eventually indicted for involuntary manslaughter. Leo Cooper testified that when he approached the Pinto on Crippen Road, FaNee had a strange expression that he had never seen before. "It wasn't like FaNee, and I knew something was wrong," he said. "My concern was to get FaNee out of the car." The district attorney's office asked that Cooper be bound over for reckless driving, but the judge declined to do so. "Any father would have done what he did," the judge said. "I can see no criminal act on the part of Mr. Cooper."

Almost two years passed before Charlie Stevens was 17 brought to trial. Part of the problem was assuring the presence of David Munsey, who had joined the Navy but seemed inclined to assign his own leaves. In the meantime, the Coopers went to court with a civil suit — they had "uninsured-motorist coverage," which requires their insurance company to cover any defendant who has no insurance of his own — and they won a judgment. There were ways of assigning responsibility, of course, which had nothing to do with the law, civil or criminal. A lot of people in Knoxville thought that Leo Cooper had, in the words of his lawyer, "done what any daddy worth his salt would have done." There were others who believed that FaNee Cooper had lost her life because Leo Cooper had lost his temper. Leo Cooper was not among those who expressed any doubts about his actions. Unlike his wife, whose eyes filled with tears at almost any mention of FaNee, Cooper seemed able, even eager to go over the details of the accident again and again. With the help of a school-board security man, he conducted his own investigation. He drove over the route dozens of times. "I've thought about it every day, and I guess I will the rest of my life," he said as he and his lawyer and the prosecuting attorney went over the route again the day before Charlie Stevens's trial finally began. "But I can't tell any alternative for a father. I simply wanted her out of that car. I'd have done the same thing again, even at the risk of losing her."

Tennessee law permits the family of a victim to hire a 18 special prosecutor to assist the district attorney. The lawyer who acted for the Coopers in the civil case helped prosecute Charlie Stevens. Both he and the district attorney assured the jurors that the presence of a special prosecutor was not to be construed to mean that the Coopers were vindictive. Outside the courtroom, Leo Cooper said that the verdict was of no importance to him — that he felt sorry, in a way, for Charlie Stevens. But there were people in Knoxville who thought Cooper had a lot riding on the prosecution of Charlie Stevens.

If Stevens was not guilty of FaNee Cooper's death — found so by twelve of his peers — who was?

At the trial, Cooper testified emotionally and remarkably 19 graphically about pulling FaNee out from under the car and watching her die in his arms. Charlie Stevens had shaved his beard and cut his hair, but the effort did not transform him into an impressive witness. His lawyer — trying to argue that it would have been impossible for Stevens to concoct the story about FaNee's having mentioned a gun, as the prosecution strongly implied — said, "His mind is such that if you ask him a question you can hear his mind go around, like an old mill creaking." Stevens did not deny the recklessness of his driving or the sorry condition of his car. It happened to be the only car he had available to flee in, he said, and he had fled in fear for his life.

The prosecution said that Stevens could have let FaNee out 20 of the car when her father stopped them, or could have gone to the commercial strip on the Maynardville Highway for protection. The prosecution said that Leo Cooper had done what he might have been expected to do under the circumstances — alone, late at night, his daughter in danger. The defense said precisely the same about Stevens: he had done what he might have been expected to do when being pursued by a man he had reason to be afraid of. "I don't fault Mr. Cooper for what he did, but I'm sorry he did it," the defense attorney said. "I'm sorry the girl said what she said." The jury deliberated for eighteen minutes. Charlie Stevens was found guilty. The jury recommended a sentence of from two to five years in the state penitentiary. At the announcement, Leo Cooper broke down and cried. JoAnn Cooper's eyes filled with tears; she blinked them back and continued to stare straight ahead.

In a way, the Coopers might still strike a casual visitor as an 21 ideal family — handsome parents, a bright and bubbly teenage daughter, a little boy learning the hook shot from his father, a warm house with some land around it. FaNee's presence is there, of course. A picture of her, with a small bouquet of flowers over it, hangs in the living room. One of her poems is displayed in a frame on a table. Even if Leo Cooper continues to think about that night for the rest of his life, there are questions he can never answer. Was there a way that Leo and JoAnn Cooper could have prevented FaNee from choosing the path she chose? Would she still be alive if Leo Cooper had not jumped into his car and driven to the end of the driveway to investigate? Did she in fact tell Charlie Stevens that her father would hurt them — or even that her father had a gun? Did she want to get away from her family even at the risk of tearing around dark country roads in Charlie Stevens's dismal Pinto? Or did she welcome the risk? The poem of FaNee's that the Coopers have displayed is one she wrote a week before her death:

> I think I'm going to die
> And I really don't know why.
> But look in my eye
> When I tell you good-bye.
> I think I'm going to die.

[1979 — U.S.A.]

Questions

1. The story Trillin narrates, which first appeared in *The New Yorker,* is not really newsworthy. So what, do you think, did Trillin's highly literate audience expect of this essay? Does he deliver?

2. Describe the narrative voice of "It's Just Too Late." Is it, for instance, warm, distanced, cold, intimate, personal, objective? How does Trillin create the kind of voice he does? Is this kind of voice effective here? Why or why not?

3. What does paragraph 1 focus on? Trillin could easily have broken this long paragraph into three shorter paragraphs. Why didn't he? What does the paragraph as it stands suggest? Though Trillin assigns no blame directly, he has a bias, which comes out subtly in the details he presents concerning Leo Cooper. How so?

4. What is the structural mode here? The physical setting described in paragraph 3 could be taken as symbolizing one reason for FaNee's behavior, or an important effect of its basic cause. How so? What is the basic cause suggested by Trillin? What is the essay's theme?

5. Why does Trillin ask questions at the end without answering them? Is this an effective way to end? What is implied by the quotation at the very end from FaNee's poetry? How does this ending qualify and augment the essay's theme as pointed to in question 4?

Writing Assignments

1. In a journalistic voice, narrate some rebellious act of your own or of someone you know. Try to characterize the people involved in detail and, perhaps, to *suggest* the meaning of the act through your choice and arrangement of details.

2. Read or reread Lewis Thomas's "Late Night Thoughts" (pages 533–36) with an eye especially to voice and stance. Then write a paper contrasting Thomas and Trillin as to both and justifying the disparate methods of each author by showing how voice and stance are integrally related in each essay to content.

3. Reviewing Trillin's book *Killings*, in which the present essay was reprinted, one critic held: "When suspense should be building in 'It's Just Too Late,' . . . it cannot because we know that FaNee is going to die" (*N.Y. Times Book Review*, Feb. 19, 1984). Write a critique of Trillin's essay judging this and other such matters (for example, is Trillin at fault for not telling us what Jim Griffin told FaNee? — see paragraph 8 and the end of paragraph 11). Come to a judgment also as to the efficacy of the essay overall. In this regard, consider both its narrative voice and its theme.

✤ THE HISTORIAN AS ARTIST ✤
Barbara Tuchman

I WOULD LIKE TO SHARE SOME GOOD NEWS WITH YOU. I RECENTLY   1
came back from skiing at Aspen, where on one occasion I shared the double-chair ski-lift with an advertising man from Chicago. He told me he was in charge of all copy for his firm in all media: TV, radio, *and* the printed word. On the strength of this he assured me — and I quote — that "Writing is coming back. *Books* are coming back." I cannot tell you how pleased I was, and I knew you would be too.

Now that we know that the future is safe for writing, I want   2
to talk about a particular kind of writer — the Historian — not just as historian but as artist; that is, as a creative writer on the same level as the poet or novelist. What follows will sound less immodest if you will take the word "artist" in the way I think

of it, not as a form of praise but as a category, like clerk or laborer or actor.

Why is it generally assumed that in writing, the creative 3 process is the exclusive property of poets and novelists? I would like to suggest that the thought applied by the historian to his subject matter can be no less creative than the imagination applied by the novelist to his. And when it comes to writing as an art, is Gibbon[1] necessarily less of an artist in words than, let us say, Dickens? Or Winston Churchill less so than William Faulkner or Sinclair Lewis?

George Macaulay Trevelyan, the late professor of modern 4 history at Cambridge and the great champion of literary as opposed to scientific history, said in a famous essay on his muse that ideally history should be the exposition of facts about the past, "in their full emotional and intellectual value to a wide public by the difficult art of literature." Notice "wide public." Trevelyan always stressed writing for the general reader as opposed to writing just for fellow scholars because he knew that when you write for the public you have to be *clear* and you have to be *interesting* and these are the two criteria which make for good writing. He had no patience with the idea that only imaginative writing is literature. Novels, he pointed out, if they are bad enough, are *not* literature, while even pamphlets, if they are good enough, and he cites those of Milton, Swift, and Burke, [2] are.

The "difficult art of literature" is well said. Trevelyan was 5 a dirt farmer in that field and he knew. I may as well admit now that I have always *felt* like an artist when I work on a book but I did not think I ought to say so until someone else said it first (it's like waiting to be proposed to). Now that an occasional reviewer here and there has made the observation, I feel I can talk about it. I see no reason why the word should always be

---

[1] *[Edward] Gibbon:* (1737–1794) British historian, author of *The Decline and Fall of the Roman Empire.*

[2] *[Edmund] Burke:* (1729–1797) British statesman and philosopher who, like Milton and Swift before him, wrote eloquent political tracts (pamphlets).

confined to writers of fiction and poetry while the rest of us are lumped together under that despicable term "Nonfiction" — as if we were some sort of remainder. I do not feel like a Non-something; I feel quite specific. I wish I could think of a name in place of "Nonfiction." In the hope of finding an antonym I looked up "Fiction" in Webster and found it defined as opposed to "Fact, Truth and Reality." I thought for a while of adopting FTR, standing for Fact, Truth, and Reality." I thought for a while of adopting FTR, standing for Fact, Truth, and Reality, as my new term, but it is awkward to use. "Writers of Reality" is the nearest I can come to what I want, but I cannot very well call us "Realtors" because that has been pre-empted — although as a matter of fact I would like to. "Real Estate," when you come to think of it, is a very fine phrase and it is exactly the sphere that writers of nonfiction deal in: the real estate of man, of human conduct. I wish we could get it back from the dealers in land. Then the categories could be poets, novelists, and realtors.

I should add that I do not entirely go along with Webster's   6 statement that fiction is what is distinct from fact, truth, and reality because good fiction (as opposed to junk), even if it has nothing to do with fact, is usually *founded* on reality and *perceives* truth — often more truly than some historians. It is exactly this quality of perceiving truth, extracting it from irrelevant surroundings and conveying it to the reader or the viewer of a picture, which distinguishes the artist. What the artist has is an *extra* vision and an *inner* vision plus the ability to express it. He supplies a view or an understanding that the viewer or reader would not have gained without the aid of the artist's creative vision. This is what Monet does in one of those shimmering rivers reflecting poplars, or El Greco in the stormy sky over Toledo, or Jane Austen compressing a whole society into Mr. and Mrs. Bennet, Lady Catherine, and Mr. Darcy. We realtors, at least those of us who aspire to write literature, do the same thing. Lytton Strachey perceived a truth about Queen Victoria and the Eminent Victorians, and the style and form which he created to portray what he saw have changed the whole approach to biography since his time. Rachel Carson perceived truth about the seashore or the silent spring, Thoreau about Walden Pond, De Tocqueville and James Bryce about America, Gibbon about Rome, Karl Marx about Capital, Carlyle about the French Revolution.[3] Their work is based on study, observation, and accumulation of fact, but does anyone suppose that these realtors did not make use of their imagination? Certainly they did; that is what gave them their extra vision.

Trevelyan wrote that the best historian was he who 7 combined knowledge of the evidence with "the largest intellect, the warmest human sympathy and the highest imaginative powers." The last two qualities are no different than those necessary to a great novelist. They are a necessary part of the historian's equipment because they are what enable him to *understand* the evidence he has accumulated. Imagination stretches the available facts — extrapolates from them, so to speak, thus often supplying an otherwise missing answer to the "Why" of what happened. Sympathy is essential to the understanding of motive. Without sympathy and imagination the historian can copy figures from a tax roll forever — or count them by computer as they do nowadays — but he will never know or be able to portray the people who paid the taxes.

When I say that I felt like an artist, I mean that I constantly 8 found myself perceiving a historical truth (at least, what *I* believe to be truth) by seizing upon a suggestion; then, after careful gathering of the evidence, conveying it in turn to the reader, not by piling up a list of all the facts I have collected, which is the way of the Ph.D., but by exercising the artist's privilege of selection.

Actually the idea for *The Proud Tower* evolved in that way 9 from a number of such perceptions. The initial impulse was a line I quoted in *The Guns of August* from Belgian Socialist poet

---

[3]Among the people referred to in this paragraph are two painters (Monet, El Greco), a novelist (Jane Austen, with reference to her novel *Pride and Prejudice*), two essayists (Carson, Thoreau), a political and economic theorist (Marx), and four historians (Alexis De Tocqueville, James Bryce, Edward Gibbon, and Thomas Carlyle).

Emile Verhaeren. After a lifetime as a pacifist dedicated to the social and humanitarian ideas which were then believed to erase national lines, he found himself filled with hatred of the German invader and disillusioned in all he had formerly believed in. And yet, as he wrote, "Since it seems to me that in this state of hatred my conscience becomes diminished, I dedicate these pages, with emotion, to the man I used to be."

I was deeply moved by this. His confession seemed to me so poignant, so evocative of a time and mood, that it decided me to try to retrieve that vanished era. It led to the last chapter in *The Proud Tower* on the Socialists, to Jaurès the authentic Socialist, to his prophetic lines, "I summon the living, I mourn the dead," and to his assassination as the perfect and dramatically right ending for the book, both chronologically and symbolically. 10

Then there was Lord Ribblesdale. I owe this to *American Heritage*, which back in October 1961 published a piece on Sargent and Whistler[4] with a handsome reproduction of the Ribblesdale portrait. In Sargent's painting Ribblesdale stared out upon the world, as I later wrote in *The Proud Tower*, "in an attitude of such natural arrogance, elegance and self-confidence as no man of a later day would ever achieve." Here too was a vanished era which came together in my mind with Verhaeren's line, "the man I used to be" — like two globules of mercury making a single mass. From that came the idea for the book. Ribblesdale, of course, was the suggestion that ultimately became the opening chapter on the Patricians. This is the reward of the artist's eye: It always leads you to the right thing. 11

As I see it, there are three parts to the creative process: first, the extra vision with which the artist perceives a truth and conveys it by suggestion. Second, medium of expression: language for writers, paint for painters, clay or stone for sculptors, sound expressed in musical notes for composers. Third, design or structure. 12

---

[4]*Sargent and Whistler:* John Singer Sargent (1856–1925) and James Whistler (1834–1903), both well-known American painters.

When it comes to language, nothing is more satisfying than 13
to write a good sentence. It is no fun to write lumpishly, dully,
in prose the reader must plod through like wet sand. But it is a
pleasure to achieve, if one can, a clear running prose that is
simple yet full of surprises. This does not just happen. It
requires skill, hard work, a good ear, and continued practice, as
much as it takes Heifetz to play the violin. The goals, as I have
said, are clarity, interest, and aesthetic pleasure. On the first of
these I would like to quote Macaulay, a great historian and
great writer, who once wrote to a friend, "How little the all
important art of making meaning pellucid is studied now!
Hardly any popular writer except myself thinks of it."

As to structure, my own form is narrative, which is not 14
every historian's, I may say — indeed, it is rather looked down
on now by the advanced academics, but I don't mind because
no one could possibly persuade me that telling a story is not the
most desirable thing a writer can do. Narrative history is
neither as simple nor as straightforward as it might seem. It
requires arrangement, composition, planning just like a
painting — Rembrandt's "Night Watch," for example. He did
not fit in all those figures with certain ones in the foreground
and others in back and the light falling on them just so, without
much trial and error and innumerable preliminary sketches. It
is the same with writing history. Although the finished result
may look to the reader natural and inevitable, as if the author
had only to follow the sequence of events, it is not that easy.
Sometimes, to catch attention, the crucial event and the
causative circumstance have to be reversed in order — the event
first and the cause afterwards, as in *The Zimmermann Telegram*.
One must juggle with time.

In *The Proud Tower*, for instance, the two English chapters 15
were originally conceived as one. I divided them and placed
them well apart in order to give a feeling of progression, of
forward chronological movement to the book. The story of the
Anarchists with their ideas and deeds set in counterpoint to
each other was a problem in arrangement. The middle section

of the Hague chapter on the Paris Exposition of 1900 was originally planned as a separate short centerpiece, marking the turn of the century, until I saw it as a bridge linking the two Hague Conferences, where it now seems to belong.

Structure is chiefly a problem of selection, an agonizing 16 business because there is always more material than one can use or fit into a story. The problem is how and what to select out of all that happened without, by the very process of selection, giving an over- or under-emphasis which violates truth. One cannot put in everything: The result would be a shapeless mass. The job is to achieve a narrative line without straying from the essential facts or leaving out any essential facts and without twisting the material to suit one's convenience. To do so is a temptation, but if you do it with history you invariably get tripped up by later events. I have been tempted once or twice and I know.

The most difficult task of selection I had was in the 17 Dreyfus[5] chapter. To try to skip over the facts about the *bordereau* and the handwriting and the forgeries — all the elements of the Case as distinct from the Affair — in order to focus instead on what happened to France and yet at the same time give the reader enough background information to enable him to understand what was going on, nearly drove me to despair. My writing slowed down to a trickle until one dreadful day when I went to my study at nine and stayed there all day in a blank coma until five, when I emerged without having written a single word. Anyone who is a writer will know how frightening that was. You feel you have come to the end of your powers; you will not finish the book; you may never write again.

There are other problems of structure peculiar to writing 18 history: how to explain background and yet keep the story moving; how to create suspense and sustain interest in a

---

[5] *[Alfred] Dreyfus* (1859–1935): A French army officer wrongly convicted of treason and subsequently (1906) acquitted. The case became notorious and had wide political repercussions.

narrative of which the outcome (like who won the war) is, to put it mildly, known. If anyone thinks this does not take creative writing, I can only say, try it.

Mr. Capote's *In Cold Blood*,[6] for example, which deals with 19 real life as does mine, is notable for conscious design. One can see him planning, arranging, composing his material until he achieves his perfectly balanced structure. That is art, although the hand is too obtrusive and the design too contrived to qualify as history. His method of investigation, moreover, is hardly so new as he thinks. He is merely applying to contemporary material what historians have been doing for years. Herodotus [7] started it more than two thousand years ago, walking all over Asia Minor asking questions. Francis Parkman went to live among the Indians: hunted, traveled, and ate with them so that his pages would be steeped in understanding; E. A. Freeman, before he wrote *The Norman Conquest,* visited every spot the Conqueror had set foot on. New to these techniques, Mr. Capote is perhaps naïvely impressed by them. He uses them in a deliberate effort to raise what might be called "creative" journalism to the level of literature. A great company from Herodotus to Trevelyan have been doing the same with history for quite some time.

[1966 — U.S.A.]

Questions

1. In the first paragraph, Tuchman three times refers to "you," meaning her audience. At whom do you think Tuchman aimed her essay? How does the intended audience account for the essay's diction? What else does this audience account for?

2. This essay contains many arresting metaphors. Pick out two or three. What is the function of each in its context? Why does each work well in communicating the idea it was intended to communicate?

---

[6]*In Cold Blood:* A novel by Truman Capote that is based on an actual murder case and that stays close to the facts of that case.

[7]*Herodotus* (fifth century B.C.): A Greek historian often called the "father of history."

3. What is Tuchman's thesis and where is it stated? Why is it not stated in the first paragraph? What is the function of paragraph 1?

4. The present essay is finely coherent, in part because of the transitions supplied by Tuchman. Look through the essay and bracket all transitional words, phrases, sentences, and paragraphs. Sometimes transitions are not needed because the material coheres of its own accord. Where is this true in the essay at hand? Explain why.

5. Tuchman makes use of all four means of support we have looked at (exemplification, definition, appeal to authority, and analogy) and three of the five structural elements we have considered (chronology, enumeration, and comparison and contrast). Locate an instance of each kind of support and each kind of element. In what way do these various types of support and structure serve Tuchman with respect to her final goal (to communicate to her audience and to persuade us of the validity of her thesis)?

6. "The Historian as Artist" contains many good ideas about writing and gives insight into the writing process. What are some of those ideas? What have you learned from the essay about the writing process?

7. According to Tuchman, good writing must be *"clear* and . . . *interesting."* Does Tuchman's essay fulfill these criteria? How so? Is her essay thereby persuasive? Why or why not?

Writing Assignments

1. In a paragraph or two, enumerate the ideas about writing that you find in "The Historian as Artist" and evaluate their worth to you.

2. This essay contains many diverse parts, yet it is thoroughly coherent. Write a short paper analyzing how Tuchman made the parts cohere into a comprehensible whole. Be specific and use examples throughout.

3. Go to the library and read an essay by Oscar Wilde entitled "The Critic as Artist," which Tuchman almost assuredly had in mind in titling her work. Then write an essay comparing the two as to point, focus, and overall design.

✤ ON OUR BIRTHDAY ✤
— AMERICA AS IDEA
Barbara Tuchman

THE UNITED STATES IS A NATION CONSCIOUSLY CONCEIVED, NOT ONE   1
that evolved slowly out of an ancient past. It was a planned idea
of democracy, of liberty of conscience and pursuit of happiness.
It was the promise of equality of opportunity and individual
freedom within a just social order, as opposed to the restrictions
and repressions of the Old World. In contrast to the militarism
of Europe, it would renounce standing armies and "sheathe the
desolating sword of war." It was an experiment in Utopia to
test the thesis that, given freedom, independence, and local
self-government, people, in Kossuth's words, "will in due time
ripen into all the excellence and all the dignity of humanity." It
was a new life for the oppressed, it was enlightenment, it was
optimism.

Regardless of hypocrisy and corruption, of greed, chica-   2
nery, brutality, and all the other bad habits man carries with
him whether in the New World or Old, the founding idea of the
United States remained, on the whole, dominant through the
first hundred years. With reservations, it was believed in by
Americans, by visitors who came to aid our Revolution or later
to observe our progress, by immigrants who came by the
hundreds of thousands to escape an intolerable situation in their
native lands.

The idea shaped our politics, our institutions, and to some   3
extent our national character, but it was never the only
influence at work. Material circumstances exerted an opposing
force. The open frontier, the hardships of homesteading from
scratch, the wealth of natural resources, the whole vast
challenge of a continent waiting to be exploited, combined to
produce a prevailing materialism and an American drive bent as
much, if not more, on money, property, and power than was
true of the Old World from which we had fled. The human

resources we drew upon were significant: Every wave of immigration brought here those people who had the extra energy, gumption, or restlessness to uproot themselves and cross an unknown ocean to seek a better life. Two other factors entered the shaping process — the shadow of slavery and the destruction of the native Indian.

At its Centennial the United States was a material success. 4 Through its second century the idea and the success have struggled in continuing conflict. The Statue of Liberty, erected in 1886, still symbolized the promise to those "yearning to breathe free." Hope, to them, as seen by a foreign visitor, was "domiciled in America as the Pope is in Rome." But slowly in the struggle the idea lost ground, and at a turning point around 1900, with American acceptance of a rather half-hearted imperialism, it lost dominance. Increasingly invaded since then by self-doubt and disillusion, it survives in the disenchantment of today, battered and crippled but not vanquished.

What has happened to the United States in the twentieth 5 century is not a peculiarly American phenomenon but a part of the experience of the West. In the Middle Ages plague, wars, and social violence were seen as God's punishment upon man for his sins. If the concept of God can be taken as man's conscience, the same explanation may be applicable today. Our sins in the twentieth century — greed, violence, inhumanity — have been profound, with the result that the pride and self-confidence of the nineteenth century have turned to dismay and self-disgust.

In the United States we have a society pervaded from top 6 to bottom by contempt for the law. Government — including the agencies of law enforcement — business, labor, students, the military, the poor no less than the rich, outdo each other in breaking the rules and violating the ethics that society has established for its protection. The average citizen, trying to hold a footing in standards of morality and conduct he once believed in, is daily knocked over by incoming waves of venality, vulgarity, irresponsibility, ignorance, ugliness, and trash in all senses of the word. Our government collaborates abroad with the worst enemies of humanity and liberty. It wastes our substance on useless proliferation of military hardware that can never buy security no matter how high the pile. It learns no lessons, employs no wisdom, and corrupts all who succumb to Potomac fever.

Yet the idea does not die. Americans are not passive under   7 their faults. We expose them and combat them. Somewhere every day some group is fighting a public abuse — openly and, on the whole, notwithstanding the FBI, with confidence in the First Amendment. The U.S. has slid a long way from the original idea. Nevertheless, somewhere between Gulag Archipelago and the featherbed of cradle-to-the-grave welfare, it still offers a greater opportunity for social happiness — that is to say, for well-being combined with individual freedom and initiative — than is likely elsewhere. The ideal society for which mankind has been striving through the ages will remain forever beyond our grasp. But if the great question, whether it is still possible to reconcile democracy with social order and individual liberty, is to find a positive answer, it will be here.

[1976 — U.S.A.]

Questions

1. This essay contains much parallelism. Locate a few examples and be ready to explain their effect.
2. "On Our Birthday" divides itself into three parts. What paragraphs constitute each? What is the main idea of each part?
3. The three parts that comprise this structurally elegant essay move dialectically, from statement to counterstatement to a synthesis of the two. Which of the three comprises Tuchman's thesis? What is that thesis? Why is it placed where it is?
4. A dialectical structure, such as we have here, is particularly suited to the expression of opposing or ambivalent attitudes and emotions. What ambivalence on Tuchman's part does the present essay reveal? Is the ambivalence resolved at the end of the essay? How so?

Writing Assignments

1. Write a paragraph on any topic in imitation of the first paragraph of "On Our Birthday." That is, compose your paragraph entirely of sentences that exhibit internal parallelism and parallelism from sentence to sentence.

2. Write an essay "after" Tuchman — that is, an essay that moves from statement to counterstatement to final synthesis. For a topic you might choose conflicting attitudes or emotions of your own, discussing one and then its converse on your way to a possible harmonizing of the two. Your thesis could be presented at the beginning, but in this case you might try saving it for the third part of your essay — "synthesis."

------------------- ✤ TARZAN REVISITED ✤ -------------------
Gore Vidal

THERE ARE SO MANY THINGS THAT PEOPLE WHO TAKE POLLS NEVER GET   1
around to asking. Fascinated as we all are to know what our countrymen think of great issues (approving, disapproving, don't-knowing, with that native shrewdness which made a primeval wilderness bloom with Howard Johnson signs), the pollsters never get around to asking the sort of interesting personal questions our new Romans might be able to answer knowledgeably. For instance, how many adults have an adventure serial running in their heads? How many consciously daydream, turning on a story in which the dreamer ceases to be an employee of IBM and becomes a handsome demigod moving through splendid palaces, saving maidens from monsters (or monsters from maidens: this is a jaded time). Most children tell themselves stories in which they figure as powerful figures, enjoying the pleasures not only of the adult world as they conceive it but of a world of wonders unlike dull reality. Although this sort of Mittyesque[1] daydreaming is supposed to

---

[1]*Mittyesque:* Refers to James Thurber's character Walter Mitty, an inveterate daydreamer.

cease in maturity, I suggest that more adults than we suspect are dazedly wandering about with a full Technicolor extravaganza going on in their heads. Clad in tights, rapier in hand, the daydreamers drive their Jaguars at fantastic speeds through a glittering world of adoring love objects, mingling anachronistic historic worlds with science fiction. "Captain, the time-warp's been closed! We are now trapped in a parallel world, inhabited entirely by women with three breasts!" Though from what we can gather about these imaginary worlds, they tend to be more Adlerian than Freudian:[2] the motor drive is the desire not for sex (other briefer fantasies take care of that) but for power, for the ability to dominate one's environment through physical strength, best demonstrated in the works of Edgar Rice Burroughs, whose books are enjoying a huge revival.

When I was growing up, I read all twenty-three Tarzan   2 books, as well as the ten Mars books. My own inner story-telling mechanism was vivid. At any one time, I had at least three serials going as well as a number of tried and true reruns. I mined Burroughs largely for source material. When he went to the center of the earth à la Jules Verne (much too fancy a writer for one's taste), I immediately worked up a thirteen-part series, with myself as lead and various friends as guest stars. Sometimes I used the master's material, but more often I adapted it freely to suit myself. One's daydreams tended to be Tarzanish pre-puberty (physical strength and freedom) and Martian post-puberty (exotic worlds and subtle *combinazione*[3] to be worked out). After adolescence, if one's life is sufficiently interesting, the desire to tell oneself stories diminishes. My last serial ran into sponsor trouble when I was in the Second World War, and it was never renewed.

Until recently I assumed that most people were like myself: 3 daydreaming ceases when the real world becomes interesting

---

[2]*Adlerian than Freudian:* Alfred Adler (1870–1937) and Sigmund Freud (1856–1939). Adler held the drive for power to be central to the unconscious, whereas Freud believed sex to be.

[3]*combinazione:* Free associations.

and reasonably manageable. Now I am not so certain. Pondering the life and success of Burroughs leads one to believe that a good many people find their lives so unsatisfactory that they go right on year after year telling themselves stories in which they are able to dominate their environment in a way that is not possible in the overorganized society.

According to Edgar Rice Burroughs, "Most of the stories I   4 wrote were the stories I told myself just before I went to sleep." He is a fascinating figure to contemplate, an archetypal American dreamer. Born in 1875 in Chicago, he was a drifter until he was thirty-six. He served briefly in the U.S. Cavalry; then he was a gold miner in Oregon, a cowboy in Idaho, a railroad policeman in Salt Lake City; he attempted several businesses that failed. He was perfectly in the old-American grain: the man who could take on almost any job, who liked to keep moving, who tried to get rich quick but could never pull it off. And while he was drifting through the unsatisfactory real world, he consoled himself with an inner world where he was strong and handsome, adored by beautiful women and worshiped by exotic races. His principal source of fantasy was Rider Haggard.[4] But even that rich field was limited, and so, searching for new veins to tap, he took to reading the pulp magazines, only to find that none of the stories could compare for excitement with his own imaginings. Since the magazine writers could not please him, he had no choice but to please himself, and the public. He composed a serial about Mars and sold it to *Munsey's*. The rest was easy, for his fellow daydreamers recognized at once a master dreamer.

In 1914 Burroughs published *Tarzan of the Apes* (Rousseau's   5 noble savage reborn in Africa),[5] and history was made. To date the Tarzan books have sold over twenty-five million copies in fifty-six languages. There is hardly an American male of my generation who has not at one time or another tried to master

---

[4]*Rider Haggard:* (1856–1925) A British novelist, author of *King Solomon's Mines.*

[5]*Rousseau's:* Jean Jacques Rousseau (1712–1778). A French author and philosopher who coined the phrase "noble savage."

the victory cry of the great ape as it issued from the
androgynous chest of Johnny Weissmuller, to the accompaniment of thousands of arms and legs snapping during attempts to
swing from tree to tree in the backyards of the Republic.
Between 1914 and his death in 1950, the squire of Tarzana,
California (a prophet more than honored in his own land),
produced over sixty books, while enjoying the unique status of
being the first American writer to be a corporation. Burroughs
is said to have been a pleasant, unpretentious man who liked to
ride and play golf. Not one to compromise a vivid unconscious
with dim reality, he never set foot in Africa.

With a sense of recapturing childhood, I have just reread   6
several Tarzan books. It is fascinating to see how much one
recalls after a quarter century. At times the sense of *déjà vu*[6] is
overpowering. It is equally interesting to discover that one's
memories of *Tarzan of the Apes* are mostly action scenes. The
plot had slipped one's mind . . . and a lot of plot there is. The
beginning is worthy of Conrad. "I had this story from one who
had no business to tell it to me, or to any other. I may credit the
seductive influence of an old vintage upon the narrator for the
beginning of it, and my own skeptical incredulity during the
days that followed for the balance of the strange tale." It is
1888. The young Lord and Lady Greystoke are involved in a
ship mutiny ("there was in the whole atmosphere of the craft
that undefinable something which presages disaster"). The peer
and peeress are put ashore on the west coast of Africa, where
they promptly build a tree house. Here Burroughs is at his best.
He tells you the size of the logs, the way to hang a door when
you have no hinges, the problems of roofing. One of the best
things about his books is the descriptions of making things. The
Greystokes have a child, and conveniently die. The "man-child"
is discovered by Kala, a Great Ape, who brings him up as a
member of her tribe. As anthropologist, Burroughs is pleasantly
vague. His apes are carnivorous, and they are able, he darkly
suspects, to mate with human beings.

---

[6]*déjà vu:* The feeling that something in the present has happened before.

Tarzan grows up as an ape, kills his first lion (with a full 7
nelson), teaches himself to read and write English by studying
some books found in the cabin. The method he used, sad to say,
is the currently fashionable "look-see." Though he can read and
write, he cannot speak any language except that of the apes. He
also gets on well with other members of the animal kingdom,
with Tantor the elephant, Ska the vulture, Numa the lion
(Kipling was also grist for the Burroughs dream mill). Then
white folks arrive: Professor Archimedes Q. Porter and his
daughter Jane. Also, a Frenchman named D'Arnot who
teaches Tarzan to speak French, which is confusing. By an
extraordinary coincidence, Jane's suitor is the current Lord
Greystoke, who thinks the Greystoke baby is dead. Tarzan
saves Jane from an ape. Then he puts on clothes and goes to
Paris, where he drinks absinthe. Next stop, America. In
Wisconsin, he saves Jane Porter from a forest fire: only to give
her up nobly to Lord Greystoke, not revealing the fact that *he*
is the real Lord Greystoke. Fortunately in the next volume, *The
Return of Tarzan*, he marries Jane and they live happily ever
after in Africa, raising a son John, who in turn grows up and
has a son. Yet even as a grandfather, Tarzan continues to have
adventures with people a foot high, with descendants of
Atlantis, with the heirs of a Roman legion who think that Rome
is still a success. All through these stories one gets the sense that
one is daydreaming, too. Episode follows episode with no
particular urgency. Tarzan is always knocked on the head and
taken captive; he always escapes; there is always a beautiful
princess or high priestess who loves him and assists him; there
is always a loyal friend who fights beside him, very much in that
Queequeg[7] tradition which, Professor Leslie Fiedler assures us,
is the urning[8] in the fuel supply of the American psyche. But no
matter how difficult the adventure, Tarzan, clad only in a

---

[7] *Queequeg:* The savage friend of Ishmael, the protagonist of Herman Melville's novel *Moby-
Dick.*

[8] *urning:* A homosexual.

loincloth with no weapon save a knife (the style is comforting to imitate), wins against all odds and returns to his shadowy wife.

Stylistically, Burroughs is — how shall I put it? — uneven. He has moments of ornate pomp, when the darkness is "Cimmerian"; of redundancy, "she was hideous and ugly"; of extraordinary dialogue: "Name of a name," shrieked Rokoff. "Pig, but you shall die for this!" Or Lady Greystoke to Lord G.: "Duty is duty, my husband, and no amount of sophistries may change it. I would be a poor wife for an English lord were I to be responsible for his shirking a plain duty." Or the grandchild: "Muvver," he cried, "Dackie doe? Dackie doe?" "Let him come along," urged Tarzan. "Dare!" exclaimed the boy, turning triumphantly upon the governess, "Dackie do doe yalk!" Burroughs use of coincidence is shameless even for a pulp writer. In one book he has three sets of characters shipwrecked at exactly the same point on the shore of Africa. Even Burroughs finds this a bit much. "Could it be possible [muses Tarzan] that fate had thrown him up at the very threshold of his own beloved jungle?" It was possible since anything can happen in a daydream. 8

Though Burroughs is innocent of literature and cannot reproduce human speech, he does have a gift very few writers of any kind possess: he can describe action vividly. I give away no trade secrets when I say that this is as difficult for a Tolstoi as it is for a Burroughs (even William).[9] Because it is so hard, the craftier contemporary novelists usually prefer to tell their stories in the first person, which is simply writing dialogue. In character, as it were, the writer settles for an impression of what happened rather than creating the sense of the thing happening. In action Tarzan is excellent. 9

There is something basic in the appeal of the 1914 Tarzan which makes me think that he can still hold his own as a daydream figure, despite the sophisticated challenge of his two 10

---

[9] *(even William):* William Burroughs (1914–   ), an American novelist.

young competitors, James Bond and Mike Hammer. For most adults, Tarzan (and John Carter of Mars) can hardly compete with the conspicuous consumer consumption of James Bond or the sickly violence of Mike Hammer, but for children and adolescents the old appeal continues. All of us need the idea of a world alternative to this one. From Plato's Republic to Bondland, at every level, the human imagination has tried to imagine something better for itself than the existing society. Man left Eden when he got up off all fours, endowing his descendants with nostalgia as well as chronic backache. In its naïve way, the Tarzan legend returns us to that Eden where, free of clothes and the inhibitions of an oppressive society, a man is able, as William Faulkner put it in his high Confederate style, to prevail as well as endure. The current fascination with LSD and nonaddictive drugs — not to mention alcohol — is all a result of a general sense of boredom. Since the individual's desire to dominate his environment is not a desirable trait in a society that every day grows more and more confining, the average man must take to daydreaming. James Bond, Mike Hammer, and Tarzan are all dream selves, and the aim of each is to establish personal primacy in a world that, more and more, diminishes the individual. Among adults, the current popularity of these lively fictions strikes me as a most significant and unbearably sad phenomenon.

[1963 — U.S.A.]

Questions

1. What kind of a beginning does this essay have? What kind of a movement does the first paragraph exhibit generally? Specify its movement from topic to topic.

2. For whom was this review-essay written? What tells you as much? Taking this audience into account, judge whether the long account of Burroughs's life and especially the even longer plot summary of *Tarzan of the Apes* are necessary or whether they merely dilute any point Vidal is making.

3. Full of information, "Tarzan Revisited" is something like a scholarly article. But it is nothing like such an essay in terms of diction, pace,

and tone. How would you describe these elements here? What effect do they have on the reader?

4. In this essay, Vidal tries to make two points. What are they? Where is the first taken up and where the second? Is it a good or bad idea to try to make two points at once? Why?

Writing Assignments

1. a) In a paragraph, evaluate "Tarzan Revisited" as to its presenting two points in a single essay.

   b) In a separate paragraph, discuss your response to this essay, stating what that response is and detailing why you respond thus.

2. In paragraph 3, Vidal expresses uncertainty as to whether or not adults have daydream fantasies. What do you think on this score? Write a paper arguing one side of the issue or the other. For evidence, use your own daydreams (if you have them), and/or those of someone you know, and/or such cultural phenomena as soap operas and fantasy movies (for instance, the *Star Wars* movies).

✤ Drugs ✤

Gore Vidal

It is possible to stop most drug addiction in the United States 1 within a very short time. Simply make all drugs available and sell them at cost. Label each drug with a precise description of what effect — good and bad — the drug will have on the taker. This will require heroic honesty. Don't say that marijuana is addictive or dangerous when it is neither, as millions of people know — unlike "speed," which kills most unpleasantly, or heroin, which is addictive and difficult to kick.

For the record, I have tried — once — almost every drug 2 and liked none, disproving the popular Fu Manchu theory that a single whiff of opium will enslave the mind. Nevertheless many drugs are bad for certain people to take and they should be told why in a sensible way.

Along with exhortation and warning, it might be good for 3 our citizens to recall (or learn for the first time) that the United

States was the creation of men who believed that each man has the right to do what he wants with his own life as long as he does not interfere with his neighbor's pursuit of happiness. (That his neighbor's idea of happiness is persecuting others does confuse matters a bit.)

This is a startling notion to the current generation of 4 Americans. They reflect a system of public education which has made the Bill of Rights, literally, unacceptable to a majority of high school graduates (see the annual Purdue reports) who now form the "silent majority" — a phrase which that underestimated wit Richard Nixon took from Homer who used it to describe the dead.

Now one can hear the warning rumble begin: If everyone 5 is allowed to take drugs everyone will and the GNP will decrease, the Commies will stop us from making everyone free, and we shall end up a race of zombies, passively murmuring "groovy" to one another. Alarming thought. Yet it seems most unlikely that any reasonably sane person will become a drug addict if he knows in advance what addiction is going to be like.

Is everyone reasonably sane? No. Some people will always 6 become drug addicts just as some people will always become alcoholics, and it is just too bad. Every man, however, has the power (and should have the legal right) to kill himself if he chooses. But since most men don't, they won't be mainliners either. Nevertheless, forbidding people things they like or think they might enjoy only makes them want those things all the more. This psychological insight is, for some mysterious reason, perennially denied our governors.

It is a lucky thing for the American moralist that our 7 country has always existed in a kind of time-vacuum: We have no public memory of anything that happened before last Tuesday. No one in Washington today recalls what happened during the years alcohol was forbidden to the people by a Congress that thought it had a divine mission to stamp out Demon Rum — launching, in the process, the greatest crime wave in the country's history, causing thousands of deaths from bad alcohol, and creating a general (and persisting) contempt among the citizenry for the laws of the United States.

The same thing is happening today. But the government 8 has learned nothing from past attempts at prohibition, not to mention repression.

Last year when the supply of Mexican marijuana was 9 slightly curtailed by the Feds, the pushers got the kids hooked on heroin and deaths increased dramatically, particularly in New York. Whose fault? Evil men like the Mafiosi? Permissive Dr. Spock? Wild-eyed Dr. Leary? No.

The Government of the United States was responsible for 10 those deaths. The bureaucratic machine has a vested interest in playing cops and robbers. Both the Bureau of Narcotics and the Mafia want strong laws against the sale and use of drugs because if drugs are sold at cost there would be no money in it for anyone.

If there was no money in it for the Mafia, there would be no 11 friendly playground pushers, and addicts would not commit crimes to pay for the next fix. Finally, if there was no money in it, the Bureau of Narcotics would wither away, something they are not about to do without a struggle.

Will anything sensible be done? Of course not. The 12 American people are as devoted to the idea of sin and its punishment as they are to making money — and fighting drugs is nearly as big a business as pushing them. Since the combination of sin and money is irresistible (particularly to the professional politician), the situation will only grow worse.

[1970 — U.S.A.]

Questions

1. This essay begins with its thesis statement. What is the effect here and in general of this way of beginning? How would you describe the pace of "Drugs"? How do its beginning, type of syntax, and paragraphing help create this pace?

2. What is the essay's tone? How does its pace affect its tone? What else goes into the making of tone here? What kind of voice do you hear overall?

3. Vidal establishes authority (or seems to attempt to) in two quite different ways. What are they? Are they effective? Why or why not?
4. In that Vidal admits that his proposal stands no chance of being legislated (paragraph 12), what was his purpose in writing "Drugs"? Why else might one write an essay like this if not to persuade through authority and reasoning?

Writing Assignments

1. Write a paper evaluating Vidal's proposal that "all drugs" should be made available and sold at cost. What good effects might this idea have if adopted by Congress? What bad effects might it have? Which outweighs the other? How so? Which, therefore, should be our course of action?
2. If not to persuade, why would someone write an essay like "Drugs"? In a paragraph or more, suggest what other motives people might have for writing such a controversial essay. You could conclude by suggesting what other motives you detect in "Drugs" itself.
3. Do some research into Prohibition and its consequences. Then write an essay either refuting Vidal's analogy (paragraph 7) or elaborating on it and affirming its aptness. Provide examples and be concrete.

✥ NUCLEAR MADNESS: ✥ WHAT YOU CAN DO
Alice Walker

NUCLEAR MADNESS IS A BOOK YOU SHOULD READ IMMEDIATELY.   1
Before brushing your teeth. Before making love. Before lunch. Its author is Helen Caldicott (with the assistance of Nancy Herrington and Nahum Stiskin), a native Australian, pediatrician, and mother of three children. It is a short, serious book about the probability of nuclear catastrophe in our lifetime, eminently thoughtful, readable, and chilling, as a book written for nuclear nonexperts, as almost all Americans are, would have to be.

Caldicott was six years old when the atomic bomb was   2
dropped on Hiroshima, and calls herself a child of the atomic

age. She grew up, as many of us did, under the threat of nuclear war. She recalls the fifties, when students were taught to dive under their desks at the sound of the air-raid siren and Americans by the thousands built underground fallout shelters.

During the sixties, political assassinations, the Civil Rights 3 Movement, and the Vietnam War turned many people away from concern about atomic weapons and toward problems they felt they could do something about. However, as Caldicott states, the Pentagon continued resolutely on its former course, making bigger and "better" bombs every year.

Sometime during the sixties Robert McNamara, then 4 Secretary of Defense, said that between the United States and the Soviet Union there already existed some four hundred nuclear bombs, enough to kill millions of people on both sides, a viable "deterrent," in his opinion, to nuclear war. The Pentagon and the Kremlin, however, apparently assumed this was not enough, and so today between the two "superpowers" there are some *fifty thousand* bombs.

What this means is that the U.S. and the U.S.S.R. literally 5 have more bombs than they know what to do with: so they have targeted every city in the Northern Hemisphere with a population of at least twenty-five thousand with the number of bombs formerly set aside to wipe out whole countries. So even as you squeeze out your toothpaste, kiss your lover's face, or bite into a turkey sandwich, you are on the superpowers' nuclear hit list, a hit list made up by people who have historically been unable to refrain from showing off every new and shameful horror that they make.

For several years Caldicott has been on leave from her 6 work at the Harvard Medical Center, and spends all her time practicing what she calls "preventative medicine," traveling across the Earth attempting to make people aware of the dangers we face. Like most medicine, hers is bitter, but less bitter, she believes, than watching helplessly while her child patients suffer and die from cancer and genetic diseases that are directly caused by the chemical pollutants inevitably created in the production of nuclear energy.

The nuclear industry, powerful, profit-oriented, totally 7
unconcerned about our health, aided and abetted by a
government that is its twin, is murdering us and our children
every day. And it is up to us, each one of us, to stop it. In the
event of a nuclear war all life on the planet will face extinction,
certainly human beings. But even if there is no war we will face
the same end — unless we put an end to the nuclear-power
industry itself — only it will be somewhat slower in coming, as
the air, the water, and the soil become too poisoned from
nuclear waste (for which there is no known safe disposal) to
support life.

What can we do? Like Caldicott, but even more so, I do not 8
believe we should waste any time looking for help from our
legal system. Nor do I have faith in politicians, scientists, or
"experts." I have great faith, however, in individual people: you
with the toothbrush, you in the sack, and you there not letting
any of this shit get between you and that turkey sandwich. If it
comes down to it, I know one of us *individuals* (just think of
Watergate)[1] may have to tackle the killer who's running to
push the catastrophe button, and I even hope said tackle will
explain why so many of us are excellent football players. (Just
as I hope *something* will soon illustrate for us what our brothers
learned of protecting life in Vietnam.)

As individuals we must join others. No time to quibble 9
about survival being "a white issue." No time to claim you don't
live here, too. Massive demonstrations are vital. Massive civil
disobedience. And, in fact, massive anything that's necessary to
save our lives.

Talk with your family; organize your friends. Educate 10
anybody you can get your mouth on. Raise money. Support

---

[1]*Watergate:* Refers to the break-in at Democratic headquarters (located in a building
complex known as "Watergate") ordered by Republican higher-ups and the subsequent
attempt by Richard Nixon, the 37th president of the United States, to cover up the truth.
Brought to light by two crusading individuals (Bob Woodward and Carl Bernstein, both
reporters for *The Washington Post*), the scandal resulted in the resignation of Nixon, the only
president ever to resign.

those who go to jail. Write letters to those senators and congressmen who are making it easy for the nuclear-power industry to kill us: tell them if they don't change, "cullud" are going to invade their fallout shelters. In any case, this is the big one. We must save Earth, and relieve those who would destroy it of the power to do so. Join up with folks you don't even like, if you have to, so that we may all live to fight each other again.

But first, read Caldicott's book, and remember: the good 11 news may be that Nature is phasing out the white man, but the bad news is that's who She thinks we all are.

[1982 — U.S.A.]

Questions

1. Who is the "you" of the first sentence here? That is, who comprises Walker's intended audience? (See the end of paragraph 8 and the beginning of paragraph 9.) Why does Walker address her audience as personally as she does?

2. As this essay moves on, the personal mode of address seems almost symbolic, symbolizing the need for. . . . What?

3. The very sentence structure of paragraphs 9 and 10 suggests the sense of urgency that Walker would impart. How so? What is the rhythmic feel of these paragraphs?

4. What is Walker's thesis? Where is it stated? What effect does its positioning have?

Writing Assignments

1. Write a short essay in which you "target" an audience — young people, say, or college students — and try to persuade your targeted audience to do something that you think they should be doing at this point in history.

2. Taking a book you have recently read, write a review of it in which you try to persuade your reader not only to read the book but to take it to heart and act on its main thesis. You might try using your title as your thesis statement.

✤ A Sweet Devouring ✤
Eudora Welty

When I used to ask my mother which we were, rich or poor, 1
she refused to tell me. I was then nine years old and of course
what I was dying to hear was that we were poor. I was reading
a book called *Five Little Peppers* and my heart was set on baking
a cake for my mother in a stove with a hole in it. Some version
of rich, crusty old Mr. King — up till that time not living on our
street — was sure to come down the hill in his wheelchair and
rescue me if anything went wrong. But before I could start a
cake at all I had to find out if we were poor, and poor *enough;*
and my mother wouldn't tell me, she said she was too busy. I
couldn't wait too long; I had to go on reading and soon Polly
Pepper got into more trouble, some that was a little harder on
her and easier on me.

Trouble, the backbone of literature, was still to me the 2
original property of the fairy tale, and as long as there was
plenty of trouble for everybody and the rewards for it were
falling in the right spots, reading was all smooth sailing. At that
age a child reads with higher appetite and gratification, and
with those two stars sailing closer together, than ever again in
his growing up. The home shelves had been providing me all
along with the usual books, and I read them with love — but
snap, I finished them. I read everything just alike — snap. I
even came to the *Tales from Maria Edgeworth* and went right
ahead, without feeling the bump — then. It *was* noticeable that
when her characters suffered she punished them for it, instead
of rewarding them as a reader had rather been led to hope. In
her stories, the children had to make their choice between being
unhappy and good about it and being unhappy and bad about
it, and then she helped them to choose wrong. In *The Purple Jar,*
it will be remembered, there was the little girl being taken
through the shops by her mother and her downfall coming
when she chooses to buy something beautiful instead of

something necessary. The purple jar, when the shop sends it out, proves to have been purple only so long as it was filled with purple water, and her mother knew it all the time. They don't deliver the water. That's only the cue for stones to start coming through the hole in the victim's worn-out shoe. She bravely agrees she must keep walking on stones until such time as she is offered another choice between the beautiful and the useful. Her father tells her as far as he is concerned she can stay in the house. If I had been at all easy to disappoint, that story would have disappointed me. Of course, I did feel, what is the good of walking on rocks if they are going to let the water out of the jar too? And it seemed to me that even the illustrator fell down on the characters in that book, not alone Maria Edgeworth, for when a rich, crusty old gentleman gave Simple Susan a guinea for some kind deed she'd done him, there was a picture of the transaction and where was the guinea? I couldn't make out a feather. But I liked *reading* the book all right — except that I finished it.

My mother took me to the Public Library and introduced me: "Let her have any book she wants, except *Elsie Dinsmore.*" I looked for the book I couldn't have and it was a row. That was how I learned about the Series Books. The *Five Little Peppers* belonged, so did *The Wizard of Oz,* so did *The Little Colonel,* so did *The Green Fairy Book.* There were many of everything, generations of everybody, instead of one. I wasn't coming to the end of reading, after all — I was saved.

Our library in those days was a big rotunda lined with shelves. A copy of *V.V.'s Eyes* seemed to follow you wherever you went, even after you'd read it. I didn't know what I liked, I just knew what there was a lot of. After *Randy's Spring* there came *Randy's Summer, Randy's Fall* and *Randy's Winter.* True, I didn't care very much myself for her spring, but it didn't occur to me that I might not care for her summer, and then her summer didn't prejudice me against her fall, and I still had hopes as I moved on to her winter. I was disappointed in her whole year, as it turned out, but a thing like that didn't keep me from wanting to read every word of it. The pleasures of reading itself — who doesn't remember? — were like those of a Christmas cake, a sweet devouring. The "Randy Books" failed chiefly in being so soon over. Four seasons doesn't make a series.

All that summer I used to put on a second petticoat (our librarian wouldn't let you past the front door if she could see through you), ride my bicycle up the hill and "through the Capitol" (shortcut) to the library with my two read books in the basket (two was the limit you could take out at one time when you were a child and also as long as you lived), and tiptoe in ("Silence") and exchange them for two more in two minutes. Selection was no object. I coasted the two new books home, jumped out of my petticoat, read (I suppose I ate and bathed and answered questions put to me), then in all hope put my petticoat back on and rode those two books back to the library to get my next two.

The librarian was the lady in town who wanted to be it. She called me by my full name and said, "Does your mother know where you are? You know good and well the fixed rule of this library: *Nobody is going to come running back here with any book on the same day they took it out.* Get both those things out of here and don't come back till tomorrow. And I can practically see through you."

My great-aunt in Virginia, who understood better about needing more to read than you *could* read, sent me a book so big it had to be read on the floor — a bound volume of six or eight issues of *St. Nicholas* from a previous year. In the very first pages a serial began: *The Lucky Stone* by Abbie Farwell Brown. The illustrations were right down my alley: a heroine so poor she was ragged, a witch with an extremely pointed hat, a rich, crusty old gentleman in — better than a wheelchair — a runaway carriage; and I set to. I gobbled up installment after installment through the whole luxurious book, through the last one, and then came the words, turning me to *un*lucky stone: "To be concluded." The book had come to an end and *The Lucky Stone* wasn't finished! The witch had it! I couldn't believe this infidelity from my aunt. I still had my secret childhood feeling that if you hunted long enough in a book's pages, you could find what you were looking for, and long after I knew books better than that, I used to hunt again for the end of *The Lucky Stone*. It never occurred to me that the story had an existence anywhere else outside the pages of that single greenbound book. The last chapter was just something I would have to do without. Polly Pepper could do it. And then suddenly I tried something — I read it again, as much as I had of it. I was in love with books at least partly for what they looked like; I loved the printed page.

In my little circle books were almost never given for 8 Christmas, they cost too much. But the year before, I'd been given a book and got a shock. It was from the same classmate who had told me there was no Santa Claus. She gave me a book, all right —*Poems by Another Little Girl*. It looked like a real book, was printed like a real book — but it was *by her. Homemade* poems? Illusion-dispelling was her favorite game. She was in such a hurry, she had such a pile to get rid of — her mother's electric runabout was stacked to the bud vases with copies — that she hadn't even time to say, "Merry Christmas!" With only the same raucous laugh with which she had told me, "Been filling my own stocking for years!" she shot me her book, received my Japanese pencil box with a moonlight scene on the lid and a sharpened pencil inside, jumped back into the car and was sped away by her mother. I stood right where they had left me, on the curb in my Little Nurse's uniform, and read that book, and I had no better way to prove when I got through than I had when I started that this was not a real book. But of course it wasn't. The printed page is not absolutely everything.

Then this Christmas was coming, and my grandfather in 9 Ohio sent along in his box of presents an envelope with money in it for me to buy myself the book I wanted.

I went to Kress's. Not everybody knew Kress's[1] sold books, 10 but children just before Christmas know everything Kress's ever sold or will sell. My father had showed us the mirror he was giving my mother to hang above her desk, and Kress's is

---

[1]*Kress's:* A five and dime that rivaled Woolworth's.

where my brother and I went to reproduce that by buying a mirror together to give her ourselves, and where our little brother then made us take him and he bought her one his size for fifteen cents. Kress's had also its version of the Series Books, called, exactly like another series, "The Camp Fire Girls," beginning with *The Camp Fire Girls in the Woods*.

I believe they were ten cents each and I had a dollar. But 11 they weren't all that easy to buy, because the series stuck, and to buy some of it was like breaking into a loaf of French bread. Then after you got home, each single book was as hard to open as a box stuck in its varnish, and when it gave way it popped like a firecracker. The covers once prized apart would never close; those books once open stayed open and lay on their backs helplessly fluttering their leaves like a turned-over June bug. They were as light as a matchbox. They were printed on yellowed paper with corners that crumbled, if you pinched on them too hard, like old graham crackers, and they smelled like attic trunks, caramelized glue, their own confinement with one another and, over all, the Kress's smell — bandannas, peanuts and sandalwood from the incense counter. Even without reading them I loved them. It was hard, that year, that Christmas is a day you can't read.

What could have happened to those books? — but I can tell 12 you about the leading character. His name was Mr. Holmes. He was not a Camp Fire Girl: he wanted to catch one. Through every book of the series he gave chase. He pursued Bessie and Zara — those were the Camp Fire Girls — and kept scooping them up in his touring car, while they just as regularly got away from him. Once Bessie escaped from the second floor of a strange inn by climbing down a gutter pipe. Once she escaped by driving away from Mr. Holmes in his own automobile, which she had learned to drive by watching him. What Mr. Holmes wanted with them — either Bessie or Zara would do — didn't give me pause; I was too young to be a Camp Fire Girl; I was just keeping up. I wasn't alarmed by Mr. Holmes — when I cared for a chill, I knew to go to Dr. Fu Manchu, who had his own series in the library. I wasn't fascinated either. There was one thing I wanted from those books, and that was for me to have ten to read at one blow.

Who in the world wrote those books? I knew all the time 13 they were the false "Camp Fire Girls" and the ones in the library were the authorized. But book reviewers sometimes say of a book that if anyone else had written it, it might not have been this good, and I found it out as a child — their warning is justified. This was a proven case, although a case of the true not being as good as the false. In the true series the characters were either totally different or missing (Mr. Holmes was missing), and there was too much time given to teamwork. The Kress's Campers, besides getting into a more reliable kind of trouble than the Carnegie Campers, had adventures that even they themselves weren't aware of: the pages were in wrong. There were transposed pages, repeated pages, and whole sections in upside down. There was no way of telling if there was anything missing. But if you knew your way in the woods at all, you could enjoy yourself tracking it down. I read the library "Camp Fire Girls," since that's what they were there for, but though they could be read by poorer light they were not as good.

And yet, in a way, the false Campers were no better either. 14 I wonder whether I felt some flaw at the heart of things or whether I was just tired of not having any taste; but it seemed to me when I had finished that the last nine of those books weren't as good as the first one. And the same went for all Series Books. As long as they are keeping a series going, I was afraid, nothing can really happen. The whole thing is one grand prevention. For my greed, I might have unwittingly dealt with myself in the same way Maria Edgeworth dealt with the one who put her all into the purple jar — I had received word it was just colored water.

And then I went again to the home shelves and my lucky 15 hand reached and found Mark Twain — twenty-four volumes, not a series, and good all the way through.

[1957 — U.S.A.]

Questions

1. "A Sweet Devouring" is a narrative. What is its structural type? There are some fine, organic transitions here. What, for instance, supplies transition between paragraphs 1 and 2?

2. What is the significance of Welty's reference to Mark Twain at the end of the essay? What is her theme? How does her theme account for the organizational mode of the essay?

3. With what does Welty begin the essay? That is, what are we given in paragraph 1? Why is this a good way for her to begin? How does the essay proceed after the first paragraph? Why does it proceed thus?

4. The title, "A Sweet Devouring," provides a metaphor that is extended over the course of the essay. What is the metaphor? In what ways is it appropriate here? Where is it extended?

5. Their drama heightened by the paragraphing, paragraphs 9 and 15 are dramatic in terms of content. How so? Paragraph 15 points to the future as it brings the essay to a close. Why is such an ending satisfying?

Writing Assignments

1. Titles can do a good deal of work. A title can even state the thesis of an essay, as is the case with the essay before this — "Nuclear Madness: What You Can Do." As to Welty's essay, its title establishes its dominant metaphor. Write a paragraph or more on that metaphor: what it is, how it is extended, and how it bears on the meaning of the essay.

2. Find a point of focus in your own childhood, as reading is Welty's, and discuss your childhood in relation to this event, sequence of events, or whatever. Try to end with a suggestion of the future (that is, from the perspective of you as child).

3. Choose whatever topic and thesis (or theme) you will and write an essay "after" "A Sweet Devouring" with respect to metaphor. Establish a metaphor — perhaps in your title — and then extend it by bringing it back and back again in one way or another. Use Welty's essay as your model. To do so, you must answer question 4 above with care.

✤ THE GASTROPODS ✤
E. B. White

Q: I HAVE AN AQUARIUM, AND I GOT A SNAIL FOR IT BECAUSE THEY   1
told me it would keep the water clean, and the snail
unexpectedly bore young, although it was in there all alone. I
mean there weren't any other snails in there, only fish. How
could it have young, very well?

A: THE SNAIL IN YOUR AQUARIUM IS A MOLLUSK. IT IS QUITE LIKELY   2
an hermaphrodite, even though it came from a reputable
department store. For being hermaphroditic, nobody can blame
a snail. We cannot tell you everything we know about the
gastropods because we know, possibly, more than is good for
us. In the absence of specific information to the contrary, we
would say that the snail in your aquarium had been going
around a good deal with other snails before you got him (her).
Some mollusks (not many) can have children merely by sitting
around and thinking about it. Others can have children by
living in a state of reciprocity with other hermaphrodites. Still
others are like us, dioecious, possessed of only one sexual
nature but thankful for small favors.

The shellfish and the snails are a great group, though it is   3
a pose with many people to consider them dull. Usually the
people who find mollusks dull are dull themselves. We have met
mollusks in many parts of the world: in gardens in France, on
the rocks at low tide on Long Island Sound, in household
aquaria, on the sidewalks of suburban towns in the early
mornings, in restaurants, and in forests. Everywhere we found
them to be sensitive creatures, imaginative and possessed of a
lively sense of earth's pleasant rhythm. Snails have a kind of
nobility. Zoologists will tell you that they occupy, in the animal kingdom, a position of enviable isolation. They go their
own way.

We can understand your curiousity about sex in snails. 4
Mollusks are infinitely varied in their loves, their hates, and
their predilections. They have a way of carrying out ideas they
get in their head. They are far from cold, as many people
suppose them; indeed, one of the most fascinating love stories
we ever read was in the *Cambridge Natural History*, in which was
described the tryst kept by a pair of snails on a garden wall. We
have never forgotten the first sentence of that romantic and
idyllic tale, nor have we forgotten the name of the snail, L.
Maximus. The story started: "L. Maximus has been observed
at midnight to ascend a wall or some perpendicular surface." It
then went on to relate how, after some moments spent greeting
each other, crawling round and round, the snails let themselves
down on a little ladder of their own devising, and there,
suspended in the air ten inches or so from the top of the wall,
they found love.

Often very fecund, mollusks are rarely too busy to give 5
attention to their children after birth, or to prepare for their
coming. There is, in Algeria, a kind of mollusk whose young
return for shelter to the body of their mother, somewhat in the
manner of little kangaroos. There is, in the Philippines, a snail
who is so solicitous for her expected babies that she goes to the
trouble of climbing, with infinite pains and no little discomfort,
to the top of a tall tree, and there deposits her eggs in a leaf,
folding the leaf adroitly for protection. Another kind of
mollusk, having laid her eggs upon a stone, amuses herself by
arranging them like the petals of a rose, and hatches them by
holding her foot on them. Mollusks tend to business.

Sometimes different species intermarry, but this is rare. 6
The interesting point about it is that such unions generally take
place when the air is heavily charged with electricity, as before
a storm, or when great rains have made the earth wet. The
Luxembourg Garden in Paris is a place snails go to for
clandestine matches of this sort. H. Variabilis goes there, and
Pisana. The moisture, the electricity, the fragrant loveliness of
a Paris night, stir them strangely.

Probably, if you know so little of the eroticism of snails, 7
you have not heard of the darts some of them carry — tiny
daggers, hard and sharp, with which they prick each other
for the excitement it affords. These darts are made of carbon-
ate of lime. The Germans call them *Liebespfeil*, "love shaft."
Many British mollusks are without them, but that's the way
it goes.

We could tell much more. We could tell about mollusks that 8
possess the curious property of laying their eggs on the outside
of their own shell, and of the strange phenomenon of the
Cephalopod, who, when he takes leave of his lady, leaves one
of his arms with her, so that she may never lack for an embrace.
But we feel we have answered your question.

[1942 — U.S.A.]

Questions

1. What is the main figure of speech used here?
2. How would you describe the diction of this piece?
3. What effects does the essay's main figure of speech together with its
   diction have on its tone? What is its tone?
4. In part, "The Gastropods" is satirical. Of what?
5. Who might White have imagined his audience to be? Would you
   include yourself in this group? How does the essay's tone strike
   you?

Writing Assignments

1. In a paragraph, write a quick critique of "The Gastropods." Do you
   like the essay? Does it succeed in its satire? Or does its tone put you
   off and make you feel a degree of hostility toward the essay? In
   either case, why?
2. Write an essay in which you compare and contrast "The Gastropods" with Isak Dinesen's "The Iguana" (pages 214–15). How are
   they alike in subject matter and focus? How do they differ in aim
   and treatment? Which is the better essay?

————— ✛ CALCULATING MACHINE ✛ —————

E. B. White

A PUBLISHER IN CHICAGO HAS SENT ME A POCKET CALCULATING 1
machine by which I may test my writing to see whether it is
intelligible. The calculator was developed by General Motors,
who, not satisfied with giving the world a Cadillac, now dream
of bringing perfect understanding to men. The machine (it is
simply a celluloid card with a dial) is called the Reading-Ease
Calculator and shows four grades of "reading ease" — Very
Easy, Easy, Hard, and Very Hard. You count your words and
syllables, set the dial, and an indicator lets you know whether
anybody is going to understand what you have written. An
instruction book came with it, and after mastering the simple
rules I lost no time in running a test on the instruction book
itself, to see how *that* writer was doing. The poor fellow! His
leading essay, the one on the front cover, tested Very Hard.

My next step was to study the first phrase on the face of the 2
calculator: "How to test Reading-Ease of written matter."
There is, of course, no such thing as reading ease of written
matter. There is the ease with which matter can be read, but
that is a condition of the reader, not of the matter. Thus the
inventors and distributors of this calculator get off to a poor
start, with a Very Hard instruction book and a slovenly phrase.
Already they have one foot caught in the brier patch of English
usage.

Not only did the author of the instruction book score badly 3
on the front cover, but inside the book he used the word
"personalize" in an essay on how to improve one's writing. A
man who likes the word "personalize" is entitled to his choice,
but I wonder whether he should be in the business of giving
advice to writers. "Whenever possible," he wrote, "personalize
your writing by directing it to the reader." As for me, I would
as lief simonize my grandmother as personalize my writing.

In the same envelope with the calculator, I received another 4
training aid for writers — a booklet called "How to Write

Better," by Rudolf Flesch. This, too, I studied, and it quickly demonstrated the broncolike ability of the English language to throw whoever leaps cocksurely into the saddle. The language not only can toss a rider but knows a thousand tricks for tossing him, each more gay than the last. Dr. Flesch stayed in the saddle only a moment or two. Under the heading "Think Before You Write," he wrote, "The main thing to consider is your *purpose* in writing. Why are you sitting down to write?" And Echo answered: Because, sir, it is more comfortable than standing up.

Communication by the written word is a subtler (and more beautiful) thing than Dr. Flesch and General Motors imagine. They contend that the "average reader" is capable of reading only what tests Easy, and that the writer should write at or below this level. This is a presumptuous and degrading idea. There is no average reader, and to reach down toward this mythical character is to deny that each of us is on the way up, is ascending. ("Ascending," by the way, is a word Dr. Flesch advises writers to stay away from. Too unusual.)

It is my belief that no writer can improve his work until he discards the dulcet notion that the reader is feebleminded, for writing is an act of faith, not a trick of grammar. Ascent is at the heart of the matter. A country whose writers are following a calculating machine downstairs is not ascending — if you will pardon the expression — and a writer who questions the capacity of the person at the other end of the line is not a writer at all, merely a schemer. The movies long ago decided that a wider communication could be achieved by a deliberate descent to a lower level, and they walked proudly down until they reached the cellar. Now they are groping for the light switch, hoping to find the way out.

I have studied Dr. Flesch's instructions diligently, but I return for guidance in these matters to an earlier American, who wrote with more patience, more confidence. "I fear chiefly," he wrote, "lest my expression may not be *extra-vagant* enough, may not wander far enough beyond the narrow limits of my daily experience, so as to be adequate to the truth of which I have been convinced. . . . Why level downward to our dullest perception always, and praise that as common sense? The commonest sense is the sense of men asleep, which they express by snoring."

Run that through your calculator! It may come out Hard, 8 it may come out Easy. But it will come out whole, and it will last forever.

[1942 – U.S.A.]

Questions

1. Comment on the diction of this essay. How does it differ from that of the last essay ("The Gastropods")?

2. What is the tone of the first four paragraphs here? What is the tone of the last four?

3. What is the thesis of "The Calculating Machine"? Where is it stated? What is the function of the paragraphs that come before the thesis statement?

4. What is the purpose of the quotation in paragraph 7 from Thoreau? What is the effect of the short paragraph that ends the essay?

Writing Assignments

1. In two or more paragraphs contrast the two halves of "The Calculating Machine" (paragraphs 1–4 and 5–8) as to tone. What is the tone of each half? How is the tone of each established? How does the contrast function in the essay?

2. Write a paper in imitation of the structure of "The Calculating Machine." In your first few paragraphs, present a topic humorously, leading thereby to your thesis statement. Then state your thesis and argue it in full earnestness by analysis, analogy, and appeal to authority.

✦ READING, WRITING ✦
AND RATIONALITY
George Will

NEIL POSTMAN OF NEW YORK UNIVERSITY IS NOT AMUSED. HE HAS 1
seen television and has decided it is the cause of the decline and
fall of just about everything. He announces this, fortissimo,[1] in
his book *"Amusing Ourselves to Death: Public Discourse in the Age of
Show Business."* Postman is professor of "communication arts
and sciences." Remember when professors taught philosophy,
history, mathematics — stuff like that?

Orwell warned[2] about a regime that would control through 2
hate and pain. But what is upon us, says Postman, is Huxley's
nightmare,[3] the perfumed oppression of control through
pleasure — through "man's almost infinite appetite for distrac-
tions." People are rendered passive as the truth is drowned in
a sea of amusing irrelevance. People become entertained slaves
of technologies that destroy their ability to think. Until the
1840s, information could move about 35 miles an hour — as fast
as a train. The telegraph, Postman says, began an information
glut that has culminated in a world made incoherent by
broadcast journalism.

Postman has decided that a Gresham's law of communi- 3
cation dictates that television and print cannot coexist: books
are doomed. He has decided that television will always over-
whelm words with pictures, and will debase such language as
it uses. "Television," says Postman, "does not ban books, it
simply displaces them." Actually, there often is a healthy syn-
ergism between media. The writings of Isak Dinesen (Karen
Blixen) have a new audience created by the movie "Out of
Africa."

---

[1]*fortissimo:* Very loudly.
[2]The reference is to George Orwell's novel *1984.*
[3]The reference is to Aldous Huxley's novel *Brave New World.*

Still, Postman's preference for print is sensible. Anyone 4 professionally engaged in mass communications through both print and broadcast — for the eye and for the ear — understands the advantages of print. Postman rightly says the process of reading encourages rationality. A printed page, containing a narrative or argument that unfolds line by line, encourages a more coherent view of the world than does a slam-bang broadcast of quickly changing, high-impact images — flood, fire, terrorism, a congressional hearing, now off to a denture-adhesive commercial, now back to war, the stock market, etc. Reading is active: it requires the discipline of bodily stillness and mental attention. Absorbing television is an essentially passive experience. Were broadcasting to supplant rather than just supplement print, much — civilization in fact — would be lost. But were television to vanish, the people who today read almost nothing would still read almost nothing, or would read the sort of printed matter that would cause Johannes Gutenberg to regret his invention of movable type. Besides, print is doing nicely, thank you.

True, it is not what it was when it had the field to itself. 5 Postman says that in 1776 Thomas Paine sold more than 100,000 copies of "Common Sense" in two months, which is equivalent to selling 8 million copies of a book in two months today. "Uncle Tom's Cabin" sold 305,000 in one year, comparable to 4 million today. And when Charles Dickens toured America in 1842 his celebrity was Springsteenian. Books and authors do not now have such megatonnage. But the reading public is large, growing and remarkably receptive to seriousness.

Postman says we are witnessing the debasing of public 6 discourse by entertainment values. Alas, his book is occasionally evidence for his argument. When he says most newscasters "spend more time with their hair dryers than with their scripts," he is being entertaining rather than accurate. He says that when the printing press was dominant, public discourse was "generally coherent, serious and rational." But before saying that television has "devastated political discourse," he should reread the yellow press of the gilded age or examine the "I drink hard cider" campaign that won the White House for Harrison in 1840. Postman says that most of the first 15 presidents would not have been recognized if they had walked among average citizens. But the run of presidents from 7 through 15 (Jackson through Buchanan) hardly establishes the superiority of an information system essentially without pictures. Postman, who seems to think the 1984 election was decided by a Reagan joke in the second debate, says it is highly unlikely that 300-pound William Howard Taft could be a candidate today. Does Postman mean that in the Age of Television only glamorous people win nomination (Johnson? McGovern? Nixon? Ford? Mondale?)? Who is Postman to call Americans "quite likely the least well-informed people in the Western world"?

Postman's analysis resembles Galbraith's in *The Affluent* 7 *Society*. That 1958 best seller beat up on another of the intellectuals' favorite villains — advertising. It said: the mindless masses (not me or you, discerning readers) are enervated, manipulated victims. Galbraith's book, like Postman's, was published after the voters had had the bad manners to re-elect a conservative president disdained by most intellectuals.

While we are speaking, as I gather we are, about 8 "communication arts and sciences," note that Postman uses jargon ("decontextualize"), uses "disappear" as a transitive verb (a politics of imagery "may disappear history"), confuses "captivation" with capture ("radio's captivation by the music industry") and repeatedly misuses the adjective "massive" ("a massive reorientation"; television's "damage is especially massive to youthful viewers"), which properly applies to things with mass. And the book begins: "We were keeping our eye on 1984. When the year came and the prophecy didn't. . . . He does not mean "prophecy," he means "that which was prophesied."

Postman is right to insist that media technologies are not 9 neutral in their effects on discourse, and a world that does not read well will not think well. However, he should heed an axiom from the pretelevision age: physician, heal thyself.

[1986 — U.S.A.]

Questions

1. Will's attitude about the book he reviews is clear from the tone of paragraph 1 alone. What is that tone? How is it established?

2. The thesis of a book review need not be stated overtly. Why? What is Will's thesis? How do you know?

3. In paragraph 8, Will attacks Postman on a fairly personal basis. (This kind of attack is called *"ad hominem,"* meaning "the man rather than the argument.") Is this attack fair? Is it relevant? Is it persuasive?

4. What can be learned from Will's review that might help you, should you write a book, avoid such a negative reception?

Writing Assignments

1. Choose a book, preferably one you hate (negative reviews are always easier to write than positive), and write a review of it. If you dislike the book, then Will's review should prove a perfect model.

2. Is Will's criticism in paragraph 8 fair or does it strike below the belt? Whichever you conclude, write an essay defending your judgment. Your argument should entail a discussion of the relation of the person and the idea. That is, consider whether a person's limitations invalidate that person's ideas or whether the two are separate issues, in which case the ideas of an individual must be judged on their own merit entirely.

✤ TELEVISION AND VIOLENCE: ✤
A NEW APPROACH
Marie Winn

THE SUBJECT OF TELEVISION VIOLENCE AND ITS POTENTIAL EFFECT ON   1
children has long been a source of controversy. Congressional
studies were carried out in 1954, 1961, 1964, and 1970. When
the Surgeon General's *Report on Television and Social Behavior* was
published in 1972, four of the five volumes were devoted to
studies dealing with the effects of viewing violent television
programs. Indeed, most seminars, articles and studies considering the effects of television on children focus on this single
issue.

The intense interest in the effects of television violence   2
upon children is understandable: the number of juveniles
arrested for serious and violent crimes increased *1600 percent*
between the years 1952 and 1972, according to FBI figures.[1]
Since this is the very period in which television became
ascendant in the lives of American children, and since the
programs children watch are saturated with crime and destruction, it has long seemed reasonable to search for a link between
the two.

And yet this link continues to elude social scientists and   3
researchers, in spite of their great efforts to demonstrate its
existence. The truly repugnant, sadistic, amazingly various
violence appearing on home screens must surely have subtle
effects upon children's behavior, but it clearly does not cause
them to behave in seriously antisocial ways. After all, the
majority of American children are regularly exposed to those
violent programs that have been proposed as a causative factor
in the increase of juvenile violence, and yet the children
involved in the FBI statistics are but a small proportion of the

---

[1]"Skyrocketing Juvenile Crime," *The New York Times*, February 21, 1975. [All notes here
are the author's.]

viewing population. And while a number of research studies *do* indicate a relationship between viewing violence on television and subsequent aggressive behavior, that behavior as seen in the research laboratory obviously does not involve rape or murder, the serious crimes included in the FBI report, but rather ordinary childish aggression — pushing, shoving, hitting, and so on.

Common sense balks at the idea that television violence will   4 lead normal children to become juvenile delinquents. Indeed, it is the intuitive certainty that watching violent programs will not turn their children into rapists and murderers that permits parents to be lax about their children's indulgence in their favorite, invariably violent, programs in spite of the earnest advice of psychologists and educators.

It is particularly hard for parents to buy the idea that   5 television instigates aggressive behavior when its function in the home is so different. There, television keeps children quiet and passive, cuts down on loud and boisterous play, prevents outbursts between brothers and sisters, and eliminates a number of potentially destructive household "experiments" children might be indulging in were they not occupied by "Kung Fu" or "Batman."

Selma Fraiberg gives a sensible reason for rejecting a direct   6 connection between normal children's viewing of violent programs and an epidemic of violence:

> I do not mean . . . that the vulgar fiction of television is capable of turning our children into delinquents. The influence of such fiction on children's attitudes and conduct is really more subtle. We need to remember that it is the parents who are the progenitors of conscience and that a child who has strong ties to his parents will not overthrow their teachings more easily than he could abandon his parents themselves. I do not think that any of us here needs to fear this kind of corruption of our children. [2]

---

[2] Quoted from address to Child Study Association of America, 1961.

A further flaw in the argument that violence on television 7 might cause children to behave more violently has been stated by a television critic who points out that if this were true, there would be a concomitant effect produced by the inevitable moralistic and "good" aspects of those same violent programs:

> If indeed the cumulative watching is turning us all, gradually, into depraved beings, then the cumulative watching of good must be turning us all, gradually, into saints! You cannot have one without the other. That is, unless you are prepared to demonstrate that evil is something like cholesterol — something that slowly accumulates and clogs the system, while good is something like spinach, easily digested and quickly excreted.[3]

But if it is not the violent content of television programs 8 that leads to violent behavior, is it merely a coincidence that the entry of television into the American home brought in its wake one of the worst epidemics of juvenile violence in the nation's history? As a professor of law and sociology stated in response to the suggestion that television is a contributing factor to juvenile violence: "I'm not suggesting a direct connection [with television] but it's inconceivable that there is no effect.[4]

There are indeed reasons to believe that television is deeply 9 implicated in the new upsurge of juvenile aggression, particularly in the development of a new and frightening breed of juvenile offender, but those searching for a direct link between violent programs and violent actions are on a wrong tack. The *experience* of television itself (regardless of content) and its effects upon a child's perception of reality may be a more profitable line of inquiry.

In trying to understand the relationship between television 10 viewing and violent behavior, one must first confront the

---

[3]Edith Efron, "Does Television Violence Really Affect TV Viewers?" *TV Guide,* June 14, 1975.

[4]Enid Nemy, "Violent Crime by Young People: No Easy Answers," *The New York Times,* March 17, 1975.

curious fact that television today is dominated by violent programs. This was not always the case. It is noteworthy that between 1951 and 1953 there was a 15 percent increase in violent incidents on the television screen. And between 1954 and 1961 the percentage of prime-time programming devoted to action adventures featuring violence went from an average of 17 percent to about 60 percent of all programs. By 1964, according to the National Association for Better Radio and Television, almost 200 hours a week were devoted to crime scenes, with over 500 killings committed on the home screen! This reflects a 20 percent increase of violence on television over 1958 programming, and a 90 percent increase since 1952.[5]

Why did television, relatively nonviolent at its start, 11 gradually become the hotbed of crime and mayhem it now is? Are people more fond of violence today than they were in 1950?

The answer to the first question is simple: people *want* 12 violence on television. The rating system that effectively controls what appears on national television indicates that the public regularly chooses violent programs over more peaceful alternatives. Clearly there exists no evil conspiracy of wicked advertisers and network executives to destroy American morals and values by feeding citizens a steady diet of death and destruction. To the contrary, the advertisers meekly protest they would gladly give the public "Pollyanna" round the clock if that's what people would watch. But the rating system shows that people won't watch "Pollyanna" when they can watch "Dragnet." Advertisers want to make sure that the greatest number of people will watch *their* program, and they have learned that their chances are better if their program is action-packed.

The answer to *why* people choose to view violence on 13 television, and why there has been an increase in violent programming in spite of periodic outcries from government investigating commissions, educators, and parents' coalitions,

---

[5]*Crime on Television: A Survey Report* (Los Angeles: National Association for Better Radio and Television, 1964).

lies, as do all the answers to basic questions about television viewing, in the very nature of the television experience — in its essential passivity.

In viewing television the grown-up, as well as the child, is 14 taking advantage of an easily available opportunity to withdraw from the world of activity into the realm of nondoing, nonthinking, indeed, temporary nonexisting. But the viewer does not choose to watch soothing, relaxing programs on his television set, though his main purpose in watching is often to be soothed and relaxed. Instead he opts for frantic programs filled with the most violent activities imaginable — deaths, tortures, car crashes, all to the accompaniment of frenzied music. The screen is a madhouse of activity as the viewer sits back in a paradoxical state of perfect repose.

By choosing the most active programs possible, the viewer 15 is able to approximate a *feeling* of activity, with all the sensations of involvement, while enjoying the safety and security of total passivity. He is enjoying a *simulation* of activity in the hope that it will compensate for the actuality that he is involved in a passive, one-way experience.

Once the attraction of television violence is recognized as a 16 compensation for the viewer's enforced passivity, the gradual increase of violence on television within the last two decades becomes understandable. For during that period not only did television ownership increase enormously, but people began to spend more of their time watching television. Between 1950 and 1975, for instance, television household use increased from 4 hours and 25 minutes per day to 6 hours and 8 minutes per day.[6] Apparently, as television viewing increases in proportion to more active experiences in people's lives, their need for the pseudo-satisfactions of simulated activity on their television screens increases as well. A quiet, contemplative, slow-paced program might only underscore the uncomfortable fact that they are not really having any experiences at all while they are watching television.

---

[6]*Nielsen Television Index* (A. C. Nielsen Co., Hackensack, N.J.).

The idea that television experiences can lead to a feeling of 17
activity, that a person can somehow be deceived into feeling
that he is *actually experiencing* those television happenings, raises
a most important question about the television experience:
what effect does the constant intake of simulated reality have
upon the viewer's perceptions of actual reality?

Two professors at the Annenberg School of Communica- 18
tions at the University of Pennsylvania, Larry Gross and
George Gerbner, have studied some of the effects of television
"reality" upon people's ideas and beliefs pertaining to the real
world. The results of their investigations suggest that the
television experience impinges significantly upon viewers'
perceptions of reality.

Gerbner and Gross asked heavy television viewers and 19
light television viewers certain questions about the real world.
The multiple-choice quiz offered accurate answers together
with answers that reflected a bias characteristic of the television
world. The researchers discovered that heavy viewers of
television chose the television-biased answers far more often
than they chose the accurate answers, while light viewers were
more likely to choose the correct answers.

For example, the subjects were asked to guess their own 20
chances of encountering violence in any given week. They were
given the possible answers of 50-50, 10-1, and 100-1. The
statistical chances that the average person will encounter
personal violence in the course of a week are about 100-1, but
heavy television viewers consistently chose the answers 50-50
or 10-1, reflecting the "reality" of television programs where
violence prevails. The light viewers chose the right answer far
more consistently.

The heavy viewers answered many other questions in a way 21
revealing that what they saw on television had altered their
perceptions of the world and society. They were more likely
than light viewers to overestimate the U.S. proportion of the
world population, for instance. They also overestimated the
percentages of people employed as professionals, as athletes,
and as entertainers in the "real world," just as television
overemphasizes the importance of these groups.

Education played no significant role in ameliorating the 22 distortions of reality produced by heavy television watching. In most cases college-educated subjects were just as likely as those with only a grade-school education to choose the television-biased answers.[7]

The viewers' incorrect notions about the real world do not 23 come from misleading newscasts or factual programs. The mistaken notions arise from repeated viewing of *fictional* programs performed in a realistic style within a realistic framework. These programs, it appears, begin to take on a confusing reality for the viewer, just as a very powerful dream may sometimes create confusion about whether a subsequent event was a dream or whether it actually happened. After seeing violence dealt out day after day on television programs, the viewer incorporates it into his reality, in spite of the fact that while he watches he *knows* that the programs are fictional. The violent television world distorts the viewer's perceptions of the real world, and his expectations of violence in life reflect his exposure to violence on television.

But once television fantasy becomes incorporated into the 24 viewer's reality, the real world takes on a tinge of fantasy — or dullness because it fails to confirm the expectations created by televised "life." The separation between the real and the unreal becomes blurred; all of life becomes more dreamlike as the boundaries between the real and the unreal merge. The consequences of this merger appear in our daily papers and on the news:

People attending a real parade find it dull and say, "We 25 should have stayed home and watched it on television. It would have been more exciting."[8]

A woman passes a burning building and says to her friend, 26 "Don't worry, they're probably making a TV movie."[9]

---

[7]Larry Gross, "The 'Real' World of Television," *Today's Education*, January-February, 1974.

[8]Kurt Lang and Gladys Engel Lang, "The Unique Perspective of Television and Its Effects — A Pilot Study," *American Sociological Review*, February, 1953.

[9]*Mainliner Magazine*, July, 1974.

Members of a real California family live out their lives in 27
weekly installments as part of a television series, with infidelity,
discovered homosexuality, and divorce happening before the
viewers' very eyes, happening "for real" on TV.[10]

Thirty-seven people see a young woman murdered in their 28
courtyard and look on passively without coming to her aid as if
it were a television drama.[11]

A seventeen-year-old boy who lived through a devastating 29
tornado says, "Man, it was just like something on TV."[12]

A disturbing possibility exists that the television experience 30
has not merely blurred the distinctions between the real and the
unreal for steady viewers, but that by doing so it has dulled
their sensitivities to real events. For when the reality of a
situation is diminished, people are able to react to it less
emotionally, more as spectators.

An experiment devised by Dr. Victor Cline at the Univer- 31
sity of Utah Laboratories compared the emotional responses of
two groups of boys between the ages of 5 and 14 to a
graphically violent television program.[13] One group had seen
little or no television in the previous two years. The other group
had watched a great deal of television, an average of 42 hours
a week for at least two years.

As the two groups of boys watched an eight-minute 32
sequence from the Kirk Douglas movie about boxing, _Cham-
pion,_ their emotional responses were recorded on a physio-
graph, an instrument not unlike an elaborate lie detector that
measures heart action, respiration, perspiration, and other body
responses.

---

[10]See Roger Rosenblatt's "Residuals on an American Family," _New Republic_, November 23,
1974; for a discussion of the Loud family and their appearance on "An American Family."
[11]See _The New York Times_, April 12, 1964, for an account of the Kitty Genovese murder.
[12]Quoted by Edmund Carpenter in _Oh What a Blow That Phantom Gave Me_ (New York:
Holt, Rinehart, Winston, 1972).
[13]Victor Cline, _The Desensitization of Children to Television Violence_ (Bethesda, Md.: National
Institute of Health, 1972).

According to their reactions as measured on the physio- 33 graph, the boys with a history of heavy television viewing were significantly less aroused by what they saw. They had, the researchers concluded, become so habituated to emotion-arousing events on television that their sensitivities had become blunted. Since they had inevitably watched many violent television programs in the course of their 42 hours of viewing a week, the researchers assumed their desensitization was an effect of constant exposure to violent content. The brunt of the author's subsequent writings has been against violence on television. In an article entitled "Television Violence: How It Damages Your Children," Cline concludes his warnings about the dangers of television violence with a plea for better programming, and even includes a few words of praise for programs like "The Waltons."[14]

And yet the children upon whose diminished emotional 34 reactions he based his conclusions watched 42 hours of television a week or more, while the children whose reactions were undulled watched almost no television at all. Common sense suggests that 42 hours a week of *any* television program might tip the balance from reality to unreality in a child's life sufficiently to lower his arousal level. Six hours daily of "The Waltons" seems just as likely to affect a child's ability to respond normally to human realities as an equal amount of "Mod Squad" or "Adam-12" or any of the other programs that Cline and others are exercised about.

Dr. Cline's experiment requires a sensitive instrument to 35 measure the emotional responses, or lack of them, in his young subjects. The effects of television viewing upon normal children's perceptions of and responses to real-life situations are surely subtle and measurable only with a finely calibrated machine, if at all. A different situation obtains with disturbed

---

[14]Victor Cline, "Television Violence — How It Damages Your Children," *Ladies' Home Journal*, February, 1975.

children, or children from pathological backgrounds. Watching television may affect such children far more profoundly.

A child therapist notes: 36

"I find that watching television is most destructive for psychotic children. The very thing I want to help them to understand is the real world, to increase their awareness of reality, of cause and effect. This is very much shattered by the illogic of cartoon characters being able to fly through the air, for instance, or the other fantastic things that seem so real on television. Some of these children have omnipotent fantasies. They think they can fly, too. They see someone going *zap* with his hand and making another person disappear and their omnipotent fantasy is only reinforced. Of course, the concept of one person making another disappear is also terrifying to a psychotic child, because that's what he deeply believes anyhow."

The observation that television distorts reality far more for 37 a disturbed child than for a normal child may bear a relation to the epidemic of juvenile crime in the last two decades. For there is no doubt that the children involved in serious crimes today are not normal. Their histories reveal without exception a background of poverty, degradation, neglect, scholastic failure, frustration, family pathology . . . and heavy television viewing. But while poverty and family pathology did not appear for the first time in American society in the decades between 1952 and 1972, a frightening new breed of juvenile offender did. "It is as though our society had bred a new genetic strain," writes a reporter in *The New York Times*, "the child-murderer who feels no remorse and is scarcely conscious of his acts."[15]

Almost daily the newspapers report juvenile crimes that fill 38 the hearts of normal readers with horror and disbelief: ten- and twelve-year-old muggers preying on the elderly, casually torturing and murdering their helpless victims, often for small gains; youths assailing a bicyclist in the park and beating him to

---

[15]Ted Morgan, "They Think 'I Can Kill Because I'm 14,' " *The New York Times Magazine*, January 19, 1975.

death with a chain before escaping with his bike; kids breaking into an apartment and stomping an elderly man or drowning a woman in her bathtub.[16]

Law officers and authorities frequently blame lenient laws 39 for the incidence of these crimes. Since in most states lawbreakers under the age of 16 are handled by a family court whose guiding philosophy is rehabilitation rather than punishment or detention for the protection of society, these young criminals need not be deterred by the fear of severe punishment: the harshest action facing a youth under 16 who commits murder in many states is confinement for up to 18 months in a public or private institution. But there is something new about these children, something that cannot be explained away as an arrogant belief that the law will be lenient toward them, that they can literally get away with murder.

"The law says a child should be treated differently, because 40 he can be rehabilitated," says a Brooklyn police officer, "but kids weren't committing the types of crimes you see now . . . kids have changed."[17]

The common factor characterizing these "changed" kids 41 who kill, torture, and rape seems to be a form of emotional detachment that allows them to commit unspeakable crimes with a complete absence of normal feelings such as guilt or remorse. It is as if they were dealing with inanimate objects, not with human beings at all. "It's almost as though they looked at the person who got killed as a window they were going to jimmie, as an obstacle, something that got in their way," says Charles King, director in charge of rehabilitation of New York State's Division for Youth.[18]

Today certain courts are even beginning to place juveniles 42 in secure facilities in response to "the new type of child who is coming into the system." A psychiatrist connected with the

---

[16]See "Youthful Violence Grows," *The New York Times,* November 4, 1974; and "Tale of a Young Mugger," *The New York Times,* April 11, 1976.
[17]Quoted by Morgan, *op. cit.*
[18]Quoted in "Youthful Violence Grows," *The New York Times,* November 4, 1974.

Brooklyn Family Court describes these children as showing "a total lack of guilt and lack of respect for life. To them another person is a thing — they are wild organisms who cannot allow anyone to stand in their way."[19]

If, indeed, a new breed of juvenile offender has appeared in 43 the last two decades, can this be accounted for by the great new element that has been introduced into children's lives within that time span — television? Poverty, family pathology, leading to severe personality disorders, neglect, inadequate schools, all these, alas, are old and familiar afflictions for certain portions of American society.

But the five, six, seven hours a day that troubled children 44 spend watching television, more hours than they spend at any other real-life activity, is a distinctly new phenomenon. Is it possible that all these hours disturbed children spend involved in an experience that dulls the boundaries between the real and the unreal, that projects human images and the *illusion* of human feelings, while requiring no human responses from the viewer, encourages them to detach themselves from their antisocial acts in a new and horrible way?

If it is, then the total banishment of violence from the 45 television screen will not mitigate the dehumanizing effects of long periods of television viewing upon emotionally disturbed children. For the problem is not that they learn *how* to commit violence from watching violence on television (although perhaps they sometimes do), but that television conditions them to deal with real people as if they were on a television screen. Thus they are able to "turn them off," quite simply, with a knife or a gun or a chain, with as little remorse as if they were turning off a television set.

[1977 — U.S.A.]

---

[19]Dr. Denise Shine, head of the Rapid Intervention psychiatrists' office in Brooklyn Family Court, quoted in Morgan, *op. cit.*

Questions

1. Paragraphs 1–9 of this long essay form a funnel beginning. What is Winn's governing thesis? How does she funnel down to it (for instance, by a movement from the general to the particular)? Why did Winn choose this way of moving?

2. This essay brings much disparate material together coherently. How does it do so? In answering, look at the transitions supplied between paragraphs as well as phrasing that precludes the need for more formal transitions.

3. How does paragraph 11 (a transitional paragraph) set the pattern for paragraphs 12–16? What is the structural mode of this section?

4. What kind of evidence is used in each of the following sections: paragraphs 17–23, 24–29, 30–34, 36, 37, and 38–42? Why does Winn use several different types of evidence? Which kind do you find most persuasive?

5. Paragraphs 43 and 44 repeat what is said in paragraph 37. Why? What kind of an ending does this essay have? How does paragraph 45 relate to paragraph 9?

Writing Assignments

1. Using yourself as your own guinea pig, write a short paper analyzing the effects of television on you that you can isolate. Further, try to pinpoint what it is about television that could give rise to such effects. Refer to Winn's essay whenever (and if) appropriate.

2. Since 1977, when Winn's essay was first published, the issue of the effects of television has continued to be debated. (See, for instance, George Will, "Reading, Writing and Rationality," pages 589–591). Do some research in this area — two or three articles, say, as well as a chapter or two in a book or two — and then write an essay on the focus of the debate since Winn. What conclusions do more recent commentators come to? What causes for what effects are now postulated? How is Winn's analysis now regarded? As always, quote and note according to standard practice (see "Appendix 2: A Brief Guide to the Use and Documentation of Sources").

3. Along with television, such recent cultural phenomena as rock music, rock videos, and sports violence have been identified as causes of various ill effects in society at large. Choose one of these phenomena, or take some other like phenomenon if you have one in mind; do some research on it (look at magazine articles, for example, and newspaper editorials); get a thesis (for instance, that sports

violence has detrimental effects on fans); and write a paper arguing your thesis, using your research to back you up, as Winn uses hers to support her contention about television. Try to avoid the obvious and to present well-grounded evidence to support your view.

✤ A KILLING ✤
Larry Woiwode

O<small>NCE IN THE MIDDLE OF A</small> W<small>ISCONSIN WINTER</small> I <small>SHOT A DEER</small>, <small>MY</small>   1 only one, while my wife and daughter watched. It had been hit by a delivery truck along a country road a few miles from where we lived and one of its rear legs was torn off at the hock; a shattered shin and hoof lay steaming in the redbeaded snow. The driver of the truck and I stood and watched as it tried to leap a fence, kicked a while at the top wire it was entangled in, flailing the area with fresh ropes of blood, and then went hobbling across a pasture toward a wooded hill. Placid cows followed it with a curious awe. "Do you have a rifle with you?" the driver asked. "No, not with me. At home." He looked once more at the deer, then got in his truck and drove off.

I went back to our Jeep where my wife and daughter were   2 waiting, pale and withdrawn, and told them what I was about to do, and suggested that they'd better stay at home. No, they wanted to be with me, they said; they wanted to watch. My daughter was three and a half at the time. I got my rifle, a .22, a foolishly puny weapon to use on a deer but the only one I had, and we came back and saw that the deer was lying in some low brush near the base of the hill; no need to trail its blatant spoor. When I got about a hundred yards off, marveling at how it could have made it so far in its condition through snow that came over my boot tops, the deer tried to push itself up with its front legs, then collapsed. I aimed at the center of its skull, thinking, *This will be the quickest,* and heard the bullet ricochet off and go singing through the woods.

The deer was on its feet, shaking its head as though stung,   3 and I fired again at the same spot, quickly, and apparently missed. It was now moving at its fastest hobble up the hill, broadside to me, and I took my time to sight a heart shot. Before the report even registered in my mind, the deer went down in an explosion of snow and lay struggling there, spouting blood from its stump and a chest wound. I was shaking by now. Deer are color-blind as far as science can say, and as I went toward its quieting body to deliver the coup de grace, I realized I was being seen in black and white, and then the deer's eye seemed to home in on me, and I was struck with the understanding that I was its vision of approaching death. And then I seemed to enter its realm through its eye and saw the countryside and myself in shades of white and grey. *But I see the deer in color,* I thought.

A few yards away, I aimed at its head once more, and there   4 was the crack of a shot, the next-to-last round left in the magazine. The deer's head came up, and I could see its eye clearly now, dark, placid, filled with an appeal, it seemed, and then felt the surge of black and white surround and subsume me again. The second shot, or one of them, had pierced its neck; a grey-blue tongue hung out over its jaw; urine was trickling from below its tail; a doe. I held the rifle barrel inches from its forehead, conscious of my wife's and daughter's eyes on me from behind, and as I fired off the final and fatal shot, felt myself drawn by them back into my multicolored, many-faceted world again.

[1975 — U.S.A.]

Questions

1. What type of structure marks this essay? Why is this type appropriate to the kind of essay it is?

2. What does such a detail as "Placid cows followed it with a curious awe" (paragraph 1) add to the essay? Why did Woiwode include details of this sort and this detail specifically?

3. Why does Woiwode stress *his* view of the doe and what he can construe her view of him must be? (See the ends of paragraphs 3 and 4.) Yet he empathizes with her. What, then, is the theme of the essay?

Writing Assignments

1. Rewrite Woiwode's description of the death of the doe from her point of view (imagined, of course), starting with her being hit by a truck and ending with her last breath. Let your description in its vividness say what it is you have to say.

2. Write an essay "after" "A Killing." That is, narrate an experience of nature of your own from which you learned something unexpected. Be concrete in your rendering of details (as is Woiwode), embodying what you have to say (your theme) in such concretions as imagery.

---❖ FEMALE ATHLETES: ❖---
THEY'VE COME A LONG WAY, BABY
P. S. Wood

THERE HAS BEEN AN EXPLOSION IN WOMEN'S COMPETITIVE SPORTS. IF   1
women have not yet achieved equal time on the playing fields of America, or equal space in the halls of fame, they have come a long way, and are moving up fast. For example:

> Thirty-three percent of all high-school athletes are female, a six-fold increase since the early 1970s, according to figures supplied by the Women's Sports Foundation. In colleges, the figure is 30 percent, an increase in ten years of 250 percent.
>
> Since 1970, the number of women tennis players in the country has jumped from about 3 million to 11 million, the number of golfers from less than a half million to more than 5 million. According to one survey, of the nation's 17.1 million joggers, well over one-third are women — in 1970, there were too few to count.
>
> In 1980, according to six sports federations (tennis, golf, bowling, skiing, racquetball, basketball), financial rewards for female athletes topped more than $16 million, up from less than $1 million a decade ago.

As women rush into athletic competition, certain questions   2
are being raised: How good are women as athletes? How do they compare with men? Are women's bodies strong enough, tough enough, to take the battles?

New research on the physical and athletic differences 3 between men and women shows that in some respects women may be at least as tough as men. Some evidence suggests that women's endurance may be equal or perhaps even superior to men's. Women's bodies are constructed so that certain crucial organs are better guarded from injury; ovaries, for instance, lie inside the pelvic cavity, far better placed for protection than the testicles.

Furthermore, the folk wisdom that other elements of the 4 female anatomy make women athletes more vulnerable seems incorrect. The suspicion that severe bruises cause breast cancer is not borne out; breasts are less susceptible to injury than knees or elbows, whether male or female. And the old idea that, at certain times of the month, women do not operate at peak performance is generally not true for athletes. World and Olympic records have been set by women in all stages of their menstrual cycles. Moreover, at certain intense levels of training, menstruation conveniently turns off for many women, a phenomenon that has been linked in some studies to a reduction in body fat, in other studies to physical and emotional stress.

The point is that, if concern for safety is a determining 5 factor, women should have the same opportunities to participate in competitive athletics as men. And, by and large, they have the same reasons for wanting to do so. Says tennis star Billie Jean King: "Athletics are an essential part of education for both sexes. Girls and boys are going to grow up easier in each other's company."

No one suggests now that equal experience is going to lead 6 to equal performance in all things athletic. Men are bigger and stronger, can run faster, throw and jump farther. But the fact that women are genetically ordained through most of life to compete with less powerful bodies, far from tarnishing their performance, makes it more worthy.

Actually, boys and girls start out with nearly identical 7 equipment so far as fitness for sports goes. If anything, girls, because they mature faster, may have an edge, as youth soccer-league coaches, for example, are finding out.

At puberty, the situation abruptly changes. Estrogen levels 8
begin to build in the female body. There is a growth spurt
which peaks at about 12 years, then tapers off by 14 or 15.
Most boys begin to mature sexually a year and a half to two
years later than girls, and then keep on developing much
longer, in some cases up to six years longer.

On the average, men end up ten percent bigger. They have 9
longer bones, providing better leverage; wider shoulders — the
foundation for a significant advantage in upper-body strength
— and bigger hearts and lungs. In addition, while the body of
the female adolescent is preparing for childbirth by storing up
fat reserves, the male body is growing muscle. And this occurs
quite apart from exercise. Exercise adds strength and endurance, and increases the size of the muscles. But on average, men
have more muscle fibers than women; and they have an added
advantage in the hormone testosterone, which adds bulk to
those fibers.

When the Army first accepted women at West Point in 10
1976, it found it necessary to quantify the strength differences
of the incoming plebes. The upshot of numerous tests indicated
that women had approximately one-third the strength of men in
the upper body and two-thirds the strength of men in the legs,
and about the same amount of strength as men in the abdomen.
The implications are obvious for those American games that
have dominated the sports pages for years: women are no
match for men in football, baseball and basketball, all of which
place a high premium on upper-body strength. Tennis, too,
illustrates the female disadvantage. Tracy Austin has mastered
the basic strokes of the game every bit as well as most of the top
male players. But she simply cannot match them in the serve,
which demands upper-arm strength and happens to be the key
stroke of the game.

Sometimes the special combination of female traits works to 11
women's advantage. Ever since Gertrude Ederle swam the
English Channel in 1926, two hours faster than any man had
ever done it, women have dominated the sport of long-distance
swimming. Women generally have ten percent more fat than

men. This appears not only in the characteristic deposits on the thighs, buttocks and breasts, but in an overall layer of subcutaneous fat. The result is that women are more buoyant than men and better insulated against cold. An added edge is their narrower shoulders, which offer less resistance through the water.

Another advantage long-distance swimmers may share with 12 other well-trained female athletes is the ability to call on reserves of energy perhaps unavailable to men. Running the marathon, women get tired, but few report "hitting the wall," an expression for the sudden pain and debilitating weakness that strike many male runners after about two hours, when most of the glycogen that fuels their muscles is gone. The training necessary to run the marathon conditions the body to call directly on fats after the glycogen is used up. One controversial theory is that women, because of hormonal differences, utilize their fat more efficiently than men. Another is that, since women have more stored fat than men, their staying power is greater.

Beyond physical characteristics, past social attitudes have 13 had a substantial influence on the sex factor in athletics. The old attitude was epitomized in the expression "throwing like a girl." At first glance there does appear to be a certain innate awkwardness in the way girls throw a ball. But Prof. Jack Wilmore of the University of Arizona, in researching female and male relative athletic ability, had a number of right-handed men throw lefty: the men proved equally awkward. Wilmore said it seemed apparent from his studies that throwing is an acquired trait. The broader shoulders and bigger muscles of men give them an advantage in speed or distance, but not, innately, in grace.

The effect of such subtle forces on women's competitive 14 athletics seems clear. A coach at an Ivy League university says, "Women have taken up athletics so recently that they don't understand what it takes to be good. They are greener and they lack competitive experience. Beyond that, and the greater strength and speed of men, there is no fundamental difference.

Girls make the same mistakes boys do — and have the same youthful enthusiasm. It will just take time."

It already has taken time, but the first step may have been 15 the hardest: shucking the encumbering skirts and petticoats in which Western women had been trapped. Another early milestone was the introduction around 1900 of the "safety bicycle," the basic two-wheeler used today. It is credited with getting women actively out on their own in large numbers for the first time. Then came World War II and the opportunity for Rosie the Riveter[1] and her sisters to prove themselves.

Shortly thereafter, the communist world began to score 16 propaganda points in the Olympics with the formidable showing of its female athletes. Eastern-bloc sports factories turned out such superior goods that when at Rome, in 1960, a hitherto unknown American sprinter named Wilma Rudolph ran off with three gold medals, she became an instant national hero. The vehicle that carried Rudolph to her fame was television — and from that year on, the upstart medium, with its voracious appetite for sporting events, would find ample fare in women's sports.

In the past decade, more milestones went by. In 1972, 17 Congress passed Title IX of the Education Amendments of 1972, providing that "no person in the United States shall, on the basis of sex, be excluded from participation in any education program or activity receiving federal financial assistance." It took most of the remainder of the '70s for the Department of Health, Education and Welfare to define the law, and for schools across the country to begin to comply.

In 1973, New Jersey ruled that qualified girls must be 18 allowed to play Little League baseball. Male coaches across the country screamed that the sky was falling. The following year, Little League changed its bylaws to include girls.

---

[1]*Rosie the Riveter:* A symbol of the women who, replacing the men off fighting the war, worked in factories during World War II.

Even so, as the '80s begin, Donna Lopiano, director of 19 women's athletics at the University of Texas at Austin, assesses women athletes as still ten years from realizing their potential. "The kids we think are super now," she says, "are going to be the rule, not the exception. We are just starting to get kids who are good already, who have received coaching from the age of 15."

Some believe the day is coming when women will compete 20 head to head with men in more and more sports events, particularly in track and swimming events of longer distance. Australian scientist K. F. Dyer sees the difference between some men's and women's track and swimming records closing so fast he expects it to disappear altogether in the not too distant future.

There are predictions, too, that women will eventually 21 surpass men in the super-marathons — those of 50 miles or more. Lyn Lemaire, a 29-year-old Harvard law student, proved that last year when she joined a field of 15 for the Iron Man Triathlon, a 140.6-mile non-stop race around the Hawaiian island of Oahu, combining swimming, cycling and a final, conventional 25-mile marathon. Of the 12 finishers, Lyn Lemaire placed fifth. The event may have to be renamed.

[1980 — U.S.A.]

Questions

1. What does Wood allude to in his subtitle? Why?
2. What is the thesis of this essay? Why is it stated twice?
3. What structural mode marks the three examples presented in paragraph 1? What is the function of paragraphs 2 and 6? How are paragraphs 7 and 8 organized?
4. What is the structural mode of paragraphs 9–10 and 11–12? Why is the material of 11–12 put after that of 9–10? Paragraph 13 moves in a new direction. How does Wood signal the move?
5. What is the structural mode of paragraphs 15–21? What transitions are used in keeping with this mode? The type of organization here leads naturally to the last paragraph and a very effective ending. How so?

Writing Assignments

1. Like athletic records, sexual stereotypes in sports are being shattered with increasing rapidity. But what of other fields and areas of endeavor? Write a paper analyzing women's advances or lack thereof in business, say, or college teaching, law, medicine, and so forth. You may wish to do some research in connection with this assignment, but make the viewpoint of the paper your own.

2. In what ways did cultural attitudes in the past impede women and keep them from growing fully? In what ways do those attitudes persist? Write an essay comparing and contrasting the present and the past with respect to women and women's rights. Because time is involved here, consider chronology as a possible organizational mode especially on the paragraph level.

✤ THE DEATH OF THE MOTH ✤
Virginia Woolf

Moths that fly by day are not properly to be called moths; 1 they do not excite that pleasant sense of dark autumn nights and ivy-blossom which the commonest yellow-underwing asleep in the shadow of the curtain never fails to rouse in us. They are hybrid creatures, neither gay like butterflies nor sombre like their own species. Nevertheless the present specimen, with his narrow hay-coloured wings, fringed with a tassel of the same colour, seemed to be content with life. It was a pleasant morning, mid-September, mild, benignant, yet with a keener breath than that of the summer months. The plough was already scoring the field opposite the window, and where the share had been, the earth was pressed flat and gleamed with moisture. Such vigour came rolling in from the fields and the down beyond that it was difficult to keep the eyes strictly turned upon the book. The rooks too were keeping one of their annual festivities; soaring round the tree tops until it looked as if a vast net with thousands of black knots in it had been cast up into the air; which, after a few moments sank slowly down upon the trees until every twig seemed to have a knot at the end of it. Then, suddenly, the net would be thrown into the air again in a wider circle this time, with the utmost clamour and vociferation, as though to be thrown into the air and settle slowly down upon the tree tops were a tremendously exciting experience.

The same energy which inspired the rooks, the ploughmen, 2 the horses, and even, it seemed, the lean bare-backed downs, sent the moth fluttering from side to side of his square of the window-pane. One could not help watching him. One was, indeed, conscious of a queer feeling of pity for him. The possibilities of pleasure seemed that morning so enormous and so various that to have only a moth's part in life, and a day moth's at that, appeared a hard fate, and his zest in enjoying his meagre opportunities to the full, pathetic. He flew vigorously to one corner of his compartment, and, after waiting there a second, flew across to the other. What remained for him but to fly to a third corner and then to a fourth? That was all he could do, in spite of the size of the downs, the width of the sky, the far-off smoke of houses, and the romantic voice, now and then, of a steamer out at sea. What he could do he did. Watching him, it seemed as if a fibre, very thin but pure, of the enormous energy of the world had been thrust into his frail and diminutive body. As often as he crossed the pane, I could fancy that a thread of vital light became visible. He was little or nothing but life.

Yet, because he was so small, and so simple a form of the 3 energy that was rolling in at the open window and driving its way through so many narrow and intricate corridors in my own brain and in those of other human beings, there was something marvellous as well as pathetic about him. It was as if someone had taken a tiny bead of pure life and decking it as lightly as possible with down and feathers, had set it dancing and zigzagging to show us the true nature of life. Thus displayed one could not get over the strangeness of it. One is apt to forget all about life, seeing it humped and bossed and garnished and cumbered so that it has to move with the greatest circumspection and dignity. Again, the thought of all that life might have been had he been born in any other shape caused one to view his simple activities with a kind of pity.

After a time, tired by his dancing apparently, he settled on 4 the window ledge in the sun, and, the queer spectacle being at an end, I forgot about him. Then, looking up, my eye was caught by him. He was trying to resume his dancing, but seemed either so stiff or so awkward that he could only flutter to the bottom of the window-pane; and when he tried to fly across it he failed. Being intent on other matters I watched these futile attempts for a time without thinking, unconsciously waiting for him to resume his flight, as one waits for a machine, that has stopped momentarily, to start again without considering the reason of its failure. After perhaps a seventh attempt he slipped from the wooden ledge and fell, fluttering his wings, on to his back on the window sill. The helplessness of his attitude roused me. It flashed upon me that he was in difficulties; he could no longer raise himself; his legs struggled vainly. But, as I stretched out a pencil, meaning to help him to right himself, it came over me that the failure and awkwardness were the approach of death. I laid the pencil down again.

The legs agitated themselves once more. I looked as if for 5 the enemy against which he struggled. I looked out of doors. What had happened there? Presumably it was mid-day, and work in the fields had stopped. Stillness and quiet had replaced the previous animation. The birds had taken themselves off to feed in the brooks. The horses stood still. Yet the power was there all the same, massed outside indifferent, impersonal, not attending to anything in particular. Somehow it was opposed to the little hay-coloured moth. It was useless to try to do anything. One could only watch the extraordinary efforts made by those tiny legs against an oncoming doom which could, had it chosen, have submerged an entire city, not merely a city, but masses of human beings; nothing, I knew, had any chance against death. Nevertheless after a pause of exhaustion the legs fluttered again. It was superb this last protest, and so frantic that he succeeded at last in righting himself. One's sympathies, of course, were all on the side of life. Also, when there was nobody to care or to know, this gigantic effort on the part of an insignificant little moth, against a power of such magnitude, to retain what no one else valued or desired to keep, moved one strangely. Again, somehow, one saw life, a pure bead. I lifted the pencil again, useless though I knew it to be. But even as I did so, the unmistakable tokens of death showed themselves. The body relaxed, and instantly grew stiff. The struggle was over. The insignificant little creature now knew death. As I looked at the dead moth, this minute wayside triumph of so great a force over so mean an antagonist filled me with wonder. Just as life had been strange a few minutes before, so death was now as strange. The moth having righted himself now lay most decently and uncomplainingly composed. O yes, he seemed to say, death is stronger than I am.

[1942 — Great Britain]

Questions

1. What is the primary figurative mode of this essay? In what way is this mode appropriate to the essay?
2. A meditation, "The Death of the Moth" achieves a kind of definition of. . . . Of what? What is the essay's theme?
3. What is the purpose of the description in paragraph 2 of what the speaker can see through the window? How does the description relate to the essay's theme?
4. What unifies "The Death of the Moth" and gives it focus?

Writing Assignments

1. There are many little happenings in nature that one could focus on in a paper — for example, a bee banging on a window to get out, even though the window is open. Take this or some other phenomenon and write a short paper, beginning with a description of the phenomenon and seeking definition.
2. Choose something — event, person, natural phenomenon — as a point of focus for meditation. Then, having let your mind play around this focal point, write a coherent essay in which you attempt to capture the essence and texture of your meditation.

❖ PROFESSIONS FOR WOMEN ❖
Virginia Woolf

W HEN YOUR SECRETARY INVITED ME TO COME HERE,[1] SHE TOLD ME   1
that your Society is concerned with the employment of women
and she suggested that I might tell you something about my
own professional experiences. It is true I am a woman; it is true
I am employed; but what professional experiences have I had?
It is difficult to say. My profession is literature; and in that
profession there are fewer experiences for women than in any
other, with the exception of the stage — fewer, I mean, that are
peculiar to women. For the road was cut many years ago — by
Fanny Burney, by Aphra Behn, by Harriet Martineau, by Jane
Austen, by George Eliot — many famous women, and many
more unknown and forgotten, have been before me, making the
path smooth, and regulating my steps. Thus, when I came to
write, there were very few material obstacles in my way.
Writing was a reputable and harmless occupation. The family
peace was not broken by the scratching of a pen. No demand
was made upon the family purse. For ten and sixpence one can
buy paper enough to write all the plays of Shakespeare — if one
has a mind that way. Pianos and models, Paris, Vienna and
Berlin, masters and mistresses, are not needed by a writer. The
cheapness of writing paper is, of course, the reason why women
have succeeded as writers before they have succeeded in the
other professions.

But to tell you my story — it is a simple one. You have only   2
got to figure to yourselves a girl in a bedroom with a pen in her
hand. She had only to move that pen from left to right — from
ten o'clock to one. Then it occurred to her to do what is simple
and cheap enough after all — to slip a few of those pages into an
envelope, fix a penny stamp in the corner, and drop the
envelope into the red box at the corner. It was thus that I

---

[1]*here:* This essay was delivered to The Women's Service League in 1931.

became a journalist; and my effort was rewarded on the first day of the following month — a very glorious day it was for me — by a letter from an editor containing a cheque for one pound ten shillings and sixpence. But to show you how little I deserve to be called a professional woman, how little I know of the struggles and difficulties of such lives, I have to admit that instead of spending that sum upon bread and butter, rent, shoes and stockings, or butcher's bills, I went out and bought a cat — a beautiful cat, a Persian cat, which very soon involved me in bitter disputes with my neighbours.

What could be easier than to write articles and to buy   3 Persian cats with the profits? But wait a moment. Articles have to be about something. Mine, I seem to remember, was about a novel by a famous man. And while I was writing this review, I discovered that if I were going to review books I should need to do battle with a certain phantom. And the phantom was a woman, and when I came to know her better I called her after the heroine of a famous poem, The Angel in the House.[2] It was she who used to come between me and my paper when I was writing reviews. It was she who bothered me and wasted my time and so tormented me that at last I killed her. You who come of a younger and happier generation may not have heard of her — you may not know what I mean by the Angel in the House. I will describe her as shortly as I can. She was intensely sympathetic. She was immensely charming. She was utterly unselfish. She excelled in the difficult arts of family life. She sacrificed herself daily. If there was chicken, she took the leg; if there was a draught she sat in it — in short she was so constituted that she never had a mind or a wish of her own, but preferred to sympathize always with the minds and wishes of others. Above all — I need not say it — she was pure. Her purity was supposed to be her chief beauty — her blushes, her great grace. In those days — the last of Queen Victoria — every house had its Angel. And when I came to write I encountered

---

[2]*The Angel in the House:* A long Victorian poem about the progress of love that is true and "pure" through courtship and marriage. The heroine is a clergyman's daughter.

her with the very first words. The shadow of her wings fell on my page; I heard the rustling of her skirts in the room. Directly, that is to say, I took my pen in my hand to review that novel by a famous man, she slipped behind me and whispered: "My dear, you are a young woman. You are writing about a book that has been written by a man. Be sympathetic; be tender; flatter; deceive; use all the arts and wiles of our sex. Never let anybody guess that you have a mind of your own. Above all, be pure." And she made as if to guide my pen. I now record the one act for which I take some credit to myself, though the credit rightly belongs to some excellent ancestors of mine who left me a certain sum of money — shall we say five hundred pounds a year? — so that it was not necessary for me to depend solely on charm for my living. I turned upon her and caught her by the throat. I did my best to kill her. My excuse, if I were to be had up in a court of law, would be that I acted in self-defence. Had I not killed her she would have killed me. She would have plucked the heart out of my writing. For, as I found, directly I put pen to paper, you cannot review even a novel without having a mind of your own, without expressing what you think to be the truth about human relations, morality, sex. And all these questions, according to the Angel of the House, cannot be dealt with freely and openly by women; they must charm, they must conciliate, they must — to put it bluntly — tell lies if they are to succeed. Thus, whenever I felt the shadow of her wing or the radiance of her halo upon my page, I took up the inkpot and flung it at her. She died hard. Her fictitious nature was of great assistance to her. It is far harder to kill a phantom than a reality. She was always creeping back when I thought I had despatched her. Though I flatter myself that I killed her in the end, the struggle was severe; it took much time that had better have been spent upon learning Greek grammar; or in roaming the world in search of adventures. But it was a real experience; it was an experience that was bound to befall all women writers at that time. Killing the Angel in the House was part of the occupation of a woman writer.

But to continue my story. The Angel was dead; what then 4 remained? You may say that what remained was a simple and common object — a young woman in a bedroom with an inkpot. In other words, now that she had rid herself of falsehood, that young woman had only to be herself. Ah, but what is "herself"? I mean, what is a woman? I assure you, I do not know. I do not believe that you know. I do not believe that anybody can know until she has expressed herself in all the arts and professions open to human skill. That indeed is one of the reasons why I have come here — out of respect for you, who are in process of showing us by your experiments what a woman is, who are in process of providing us, by your failures and successes, with that extremely important piece of information.

But to continue the story of my professional experiences. I 5 made one pound ten and six by my first review; and I bought a Persian cat with the proceeds. Then I grew ambitious. A Persian cat is all very well, I said; but a Persian cat is not enough. I must have a motor car. And it was thus that I became a novelist — for it is a very strange thing that people will give you a motor car if you will tell them a story. It is a still stranger thing that there is nothing so delightful in the world as telling stories. It is far pleasanter than writing reviews of famous novels. And yet, if I am to obey your secretary and tell you my professional experiences as a novelist, I must tell you about a very strange experience that befell me as a novelist. And to understand it you must try first to imagine a novelist's state of mind. I hope I am not giving away professional secrets if I say that a novelist's chief desire is to be as unconscious as possible. He has to induce in himself a state of perpetual lethargy. He wants life to proceed with the utmost quiet and regularity. He wants to see the same faces, to read the same books, to do the same things day after day, month after month, while he is writing, so that nothing may break the illusion in which he is living — so that nothing may disturb or disquiet the mysterious nosings about, feelings round, darts, dashes and sudden discoveries of that very shy and illusive spirit, the imagination. I suspect that this state is the same both for men and women. Be that as it may, I want you to imagine me writing a novel in a state of trance. I want you to figure to yourselves a girl sitting with a pen in her hand, which for minutes, and indeed for hours, she never dips into the inkpot. The image that comes to my mind when I think of this girl is the image of a fisherman lying sunk in dreams on the verge of a deep lake with a rod held out over the water. She was letting her imagination sweep unchecked round every rock and cranny of the world that lies submerged in the depths of our unconscious being. Now came the experience, the experience that I believe to be far commoner with women writers than with men. The line raced through the girl's fingers. Her imagination had rushed away. It had sought the pools, the depths, the dark places where the largest fish slumber. And then there was a smash. There was an explosion. There was foam and confusion. The imagination had dashed itself against something hard. The girl was roused from her dream. She was indeed in a state of the most acute and difficult distress. To speak without figure[3] she had thought of something, something about the body, about the passions which it was unfitting for her as a woman to say. Men, her reason told her, would be shocked. The consciousness of what men will say of a woman who speaks the truth about her passions had roused her from her artist's state of unconsciousness. She could write no more. The trance was over. Her imagination could work no longer. This I believe to be a very common experience with women writers — they are impeded by the extreme conventionality of the other sex. For though men sensibly allow themselves great freedom in these respects, I doubt that they realize or can control the extreme severity with which they condemn such freedom in women.

These then were two very genuine experiences of my own. 6 These were two of the adventures of my professional life. The first — killing the Angel in the House — I think I solved. She died. But the second, telling the truth about my own experi-

---

[3]*without figure:* That is, to speak in literal language rather than figurative (her mode up until this point).

ences as a body, I do not think I solved. I doubt that any woman has solved it yet. The obstacles against her are still immensely powerful — and yet they are very difficult to define. Outwardly, what is simpler than to write books? Outwardly, what obstacles are there for a woman rather than for a man? Inwardly, I think, the case is very different; she has still many ghosts to fight, many prejudices to overcome. Indeed it will be a long time still, I think, before a woman can sit down to write a book without finding a phantom to be slain, a rock to be dashed against. And if this is so in literature, the freest of all professions for women, how is it in the new professions which you are now for the first time entering?

Those are the questions that I should like, had I time, to ask 7 you. And indeed, if I have laid stress upon these professional experiences of mine, it is because I believe that they are, though in different forms, yours also. Even when the path is nominally open — when there is nothing to prevent a woman from being a doctor, a lawyer, a civil servant — there are many phantoms and obstacles, as I believe, looming in her way. To discuss and define them is I think of great value and importance; for thus only can the labour be shared, the difficulties be solved. But besides this, it is necessary also to discuss the ends and the aims for which we are fighting, for which we are doing battle with these formidable obstacles. Those aims cannot be taken for granted; they must be perpetually questioned and examined. The whole position, as I see it — here in this hall surrounded by women practising for the first time in history I know not how many different professions — is one of extraordinary interest and importance. You have won rooms of your own in the house hitherto exclusively owned by men. You are able, though not without great labour and effort, to pay the rent. You are earning your five hundred pounds a year. But this freedom is only a beginning; the room is your own, but it is still bare. It has to be furnished; it has to be decorated; it has to be shared. How are you going to furnish it, how are you going to decorate it? With whom are you going to share it, and upon what terms? These, I think, are questions of the utmost importance and interest. For the first time in history you are able to ask them; for the first time you are able to decide for yourselves what the answers should be. Willingly would I stay and discuss those questions and answers — but not to-night. My time is up; and I must cease.

[1942 — Great Britain]

Questions

1. Who comprised Woolf's immediate audience? How does this essay reflect its intended audience? In this regard, comment on Woolf's use of narrative.

2. What Woolf says about herself is meant to be taken as an analogy for the experience of all women in the professions. Where is this made clear? What common difficulties, according to Woolf, do women share?

3. In addition to metaphors (for example, the metaphor entailing the "fisherman lying sunk in dreams" in paragraph 5), Woolf uses no less than four symbols central to her thought. What are they? What do they mean? What is their effect?

4. What kind of impression do you get of the speaker here, with her love of Persian cats and cars? In other words, what kind of tone do you hear and what kind of voice? Voice is particularly important with regard to effect here. How so?

5. Analyze the diction (which includes figurative language) and syntax of this essay. Taking both into account, characterize Woolf's style.

6. In that the present essay was drafted as a speech, paragraphing was of no concern. But one might question the paragraphing of the text as it appears in print — namely, that of paragraphs 3, 5, and 7. How might all three be broken up into shorter units? Be ready to justify your reparagraphing here. Could a case be made for Woolf's paragraphing? What?

Writing Assignments

1. "It is far harder to kill a phantom than a reality," Woolf states toward the end of paragraph 2. What does this mean? Write a short paper explaining the meaning of this sentence by way of a narrative recounting of your struggle with a phantom in the past or at present. Be sure to suggest why your phantom was (is) harder to deal with than an occurrence of substance in the everyday world. You might both begin and end with Woolf's observation.

2. Choose a profession and write an essay on the obstacles that loom before a woman (trying to be a doctor, say, or a college professor) or a man (hoping to enter nursing, perhaps, or to become a grade school teacher) with regard to entering that profession. What angel and what rock does the one or the other face? That is, what internal blocks (absorbed from the culture) and what external impediments (actual hindrances blocking the way) must be overcome? When writing this essay, you might try to use (that is, speak in terms of) and develop one or two of Woolf's symbolic images — the angel, perhaps, and/or the rock.

✣ SIMPLICITY ✣

William Zinsser

CLUTTER IS THE DISEASE OF AMERICAN WRITING. WE ARE A SOCIETY 1 strangling in unnecessary words, circular constructions, pompous frills and meaningless jargon.

Who really knows what the average businessman is trying 2 to say in the average business letter? What member of an insurance or medical plan can decipher the brochure that tells him what his costs and benefits are? What father or mother can put together a child's toy — on Christmas Eve or any other eve — from the instructions on the box? Our national tendency is to inflate and thereby sound important. The airline pilot who wakes us to announce that he is presently anticipating experiencing considerable weather wouldn't dream of saying that there's a storm ahead and it may get bumpy. The sentence is too simple — there must be something wrong with it.

But the secret of good writing is to strip every sentence to 3 its cleanest components. Every word that serves no function, every long word that could be a short word, every adverb that carries the same meaning that is already in the verb, every passive construction that leaves the reader unsure of who is doing what — these are the thousand and one adulterants that weaken the strength of a sentence. And they usually occur, ironically, in proportion to education and rank.

During the late 1960's the president of Princeton Univer- 4
sity wrote a letter to mollify the alumni after a spell of campus
unrest. "You are probably aware," he began, "that we have
been experiencing very considerable potentially explosive
expressions of dissatisfaction on issues only partially related."
He meant that the students had been hassling them about
different things. As an alumnus I was far more upset by the
president's syntax than by the students' potentially explosive
expressions of dissatisfaction. I would have preferred the
presidential approach taken by Franklin D. Roosevelt when he
tried to convert into English his own government's memos,
such as this blackout order of 1942:

> Such preparations shall be made as will completely obscure
> all Federal buildings and non-Federal buildings occupied by
> the Federal government during an air raid for any period of
> time from visibility by reason of internal or external
> illumination.

"Tell them," Roosevelt said, "that in buildings where they 5
have to keep the work going to put something across the
windows."

Simplify, simplify. Thoreau said it, as we are so often 6
reminded, and no American writer more consistently practiced
what he preached. Open *Walden* to any page and you will find
a man saying in a plain and orderly way what is on his mind:

> I love to be alone. I never found the companion that was so
> companionable as solitude. We are for the most part more
> lonely when we go abroad among men than when we stay in
> our chambers. A man thinking or working is always alone, let
> him be where he will. Solitude is not measured by the miles
> of space that intervene between a man and his fellows. The
> really diligent student in one of the crowded hives of
> Cambridge College is as solitary as a dervish in the desert.

How can the rest of us achieve such enviable freedom from 7
clutter? The answer is to clear our heads of clutter. Clear
thinking becomes clear writing: one can't exist without the
other. It is impossible for a muddy thinker to write good
English. He may get away with it for a paragraph or two, but

soon the reader will be lost, and there is no sin so grave, for he will not easily be lured back.

Who is this elusive creature, the reader? He is a person 8 with an attention span of about twenty seconds. He is assailed on every side by forces competing for his time: by newspapers and magazines, by television and radio and stereo, by his wife and children and pets, by his house and his yard and all the gadgets that he has bought to keep them spruce, and by that most potent of competitors, sleep. The man snoozing in his chair with an unfinished magazine open on his lap is a man who was being given too much unnecessary trouble by the writer.

It won't do to say that the snoozing reader is too dumb or 9 too lazy to keep pace with the train of thought. My sympathies are with him. If a reader is lost, it is generally because the writer has not been careful enough to keep him on the path.

This carelessness can take any number of forms. Perhaps a 10 sentence is so excessively cluttered that the reader, hacking his way through the verbiage, simply doesn't know what it means. Perhaps a sentence has been so shoddily constructed that the reader could read it in any of several ways. Perhaps the writer has switched pronouns in mid-sentence, or has switched tenses, so the reader loses track of who is talking or when the action took place. Perhaps Sentence B is not a logical sequel to Sentence A — the writer, in whose head the connection is clear, has not bothered to provide the missing link. Perhaps the writer has used an important word incorrectly by not taking the trouble to look it up. He may think that "sanguine" and "sanguinary" mean the same thing, but the difference is a bloody big one. The reader can only infer (speaking of big differences) what the writer is trying to imply.

Faced with these obstacles, the reader is at first a 11 remarkably tenacious bird. He blames himself — he obviously missed something, and he goes back over the mystifying sentence, or over the whole paragraph, piecing it out like an ancient rune, making guesses and moving on. But he won't do this for long. The writer is making him work too hard, and the reader will look for one who is better at his craft.

The writer must therefore constantly ask himself: What am 12
I trying to say? Surprisingly often, he doesn't know. Then he
must look at what he has written and ask: Have I said it? Is it
clear to someone encountering the subject for the first time? If
it's not, it is because some fuzz has worked its way into the
machinery. The clear writer is a person clear-headed enough to
see this stuff for what it is: fuzz.

I don't mean that some people are born clear-headed and 13
are therefore natural writers, whereas others are naturally
fuzzy and will never write well. Thinking clearly is a conscious
act that the writer must force upon himself, just as if he were
embarking on any other project that requires logic: adding up
a laundry list or doing an algebra problem. Good writing
doesn't come naturally, though most people obviously think it
does. The professional writer is forever being bearded by
strangers who say that they'd like to "try a little writing some
time" when they retire from their real profession. Good writing
takes self-discipline and, very often, self-knowledge.

Many writers, for instance, can't stand to throw anything 14
away. Their sentences are littered with words that mean
essentially the same thing and with phrases which make a point
that is implicit in what they have already said. When students
give me these littered sentences I beg them to select from the
surfeit of words the few that most precisely fit what they want
to say. Choose one, I plead, from among the three almost
identical adjectives. Get rid of the unnecessary adverbs.
Eliminate "in a funny sort of way" and other such
qualifiers — they do no useful work.

The students look stricken — I am taking all their wonder- 15
ful words away. I am only taking their superfluous words away,
leaving what is organic and strong.

"But," one of my worst offenders confessed, "I never can 16
get rid of anything — you should see my room." (I didn't take
him up on the offer.) "I have two lamps where I only need one,
but I can't decide which one I like better, so I keep them both."
He went on to enumerate his duplicated or unnecessary objects,
and over the weeks ahead I went on throwing away his

duplicated and unnecessary words. By the end of the term — a term that he found acutely painful — his sentences were clean.

"I've had to change my whole approach to writing," he told 17 me. "Now I have to *think* before I start every sentence and I have to *think* about every word." The very idea amazed him. Whether his room also looked better I never found out. I suspect that it did.

[1976 — U.S.A.]

Questions

1. The two sentences that compose paragraph 1 could be reversed. Why did Zinsser put his thesis sentence first? What is gained thereby? And why did he state the thesis as it is stated?

2. What is the function of paragraph 2?

3. Contrast the quotation at the end of paragraph 4 with paragraph 5 as to diction and syntax. Why did Zinsser make Roosevelt's sentence a separate paragraph?

4. What is the function of the quotation from Thoreau in paragraph 6? How does the quotation help Zinsser exemplify his point?

5. Paragraph 10 begins with an implicit metaphor. What is it? What does it imply? The word "bloody" at the end of the same paragraph is particularly apt. How so? (Look up "sanguine" and "sanguinary" before answering.)

6. In "How I Write," Bertrand Russell states: "What I do not find is that I can improve a sentence when I am satisfied with what it means" (page 455, paragraph 3). How is this statement analogous to Zinsser's central tenet that "clear thinking becomes clear writing" (paragraph 7)?

Writing Assignments

1. "Our national tendency is to inflate," says Zinsser (paragraph 2). Find an example of inflated, cluttered prose — in an editorial, perhaps, or a political speech, or possibly even in this book — and then, in a paragraph or more, analyze your example, pointing out why it is cluttered and how it could be pared down.

2. Take a paragraph of your own that you now feel is cluttered, pare it down, and then write a paper contrasting the original and the rewrite.

3. Write a paper comparing Zinsser with Didion (pages 178–207), Orwell (pages 402–23), or Russell (pages 454–58) as to what Zinsser and the writer you choose say about using the English language. Or you might take the essays of all four authors, abstract the principles of good writing found therein, and, after your introduction, devote a paragraph or two to a discussion of each principle.

4. Write an essay "after" Zinsser. Begin immediately with your thesis sentence, then draw your reader in by relating what you have to say to common experience, and then argue your thesis by examples and apt quotations. For a topic, you might take some other area of human endeavor (other than writing) in which simplicity should be the rule but clutter actually is. Or you could choose some other aspect of writing (other than clutter) that could be addressed as Zinsser addresses clutter in his essay.

APPENDIX 1:
USING METAPHORS

METAPHOR IS NOT JUST A WAY OF SAYING THINGS; PRIMARILY, IT IS A mode of thought that is fundamental to how we conceive the world and that underlies all of our conceptions of it (see Lakoff and Johnson, "Concepts We Live By," pages 358–60). But our interest here is in *using* metaphors, so I will speak only of metaphor as a verbal tool, one with which the unknown can be defined *succinctly* in terms of the known, the abstract in terms of the concrete. Take, for instance, this marvelous metaphor from May Sarton's "The Rewards of Living a Solitary Life": "Solitude is the salt of personhood" (page 468, paragraph 3). Solitude is a pure abstraction and, because people have very different attitudes toward it, an unknown (that is, just what Sarton means by the word is an unknown). Salt, on the other hand, is entirely concrete and absolutely known: we all know what salt is, how it tastes, and what it is used for. The coupling of solitude and salt, then, tells us a good deal about Sarton's conception or definition of solitude and gives us a way of concretely understanding what without the metaphor would be only an abstract idea. Such is the power of metaphor.

But what, exactly, is metaphor? As I state in the section on "Figuration" in Chapter 2, a metaphor is an analogy between two *unlike* terms — solitude and salt, for instance. The terms must be essentially dissimilar for a phrase to be metaphorical (figurative as opposed to literal). If they are not, then we have nothing but a simple analogy: The two brothers are a lot alike. Further, there are four basic types of metaphor: explicit and implicit, discrete and extended. An *explicit metaphor* is just that, a metaphor so stated that both terms of the anology are present in the verbal formula: "*Solitude* is the *salt*," "the *man* is a *dynamo*," "My *love* is like a red, red *rose*" (this last is a simile, which is simply an explicit metaphor underscored by the use of "as" or "like"). An *implicit metaphor* is a metaphor one of whose terms is not present in the verbal formula but somehow immediately implied: every time we speak of "feeding the computer," we are making an implicit analogy between it and a living creature; when we speak of "spending time," we are making an implicit analogy between time and money (which we know are linked by the explicit metaphor "time is money"); and should you feel "wounded" by something someone has said, what was said is implicitly a knife, say, or a gun. A *discrete metaphor* is any metaphor used once and not returned to; when I speak of "metaphor as a verbal tool" in paragraph 1, for instance, I am using a discrete metaphor, for I don't return to the second term ("tool") as I proceed. Just the opposite is true of *extended metaphor*. That is, an extended metaphor is one developed over a passage of some length or even over a whole essay.

All metaphors help a writer gain succinctness and clarity of definition. Extended metaphors can also help structure a piece of prose and thus give it a sense of order as well as a sense of forward motion. To take an example, in Chapter 1, I use and extend a metaphor involving writing and sports:

> But take heart: the more one writes, the less difficult writing becomes, just as the more time one puts in practicing a sport, the less difficult the sport becomes and the greater one's facility. One must know the ground rules to begin with, of course, as well as the purposes of and ways of handling whatever equipment the sport entails. The same is true of writing. To continue the analogy, this whole chapter is aimed at acquainting you with the ground rules of exposition. As to equipment, we

have the types of exposition, each type being a different piece of equipment you need to learn how to handle. [A discussion of the types of exposition follows — pages 14–15.]

Promoting succinctness, the metaphor here is used to define something about writing in terms that you (my intended audience) most likely understand and thus will be able to relate to, for it is probable that you know more about sports than about writing. (Writing, in any case, is conceptual rather than perceptual.) The metaphor makes the discussion concrete and so more immediate and memorable than it would be without the metaphor. Used judiciously, then, metaphors can help a writer to be succinct and concrete, and to define vividly and with effect. As to extension, by virtue of its extension, the sports metaphor gives the quoted passage a sense of order and forward momentum, as it leads directly into the next section of the chapter. It also lends, I think, a certain lightness and playfulness (the play of the mind) that make the passage livelier than it would be without the extension. These, too, are qualities that metaphor can effect.

Explicit or implicit, discrete or extended, metaphor can be a great aid to writing well. However, it can also backfire if not thought through carefully. Metaphors can go wrong in many ways, and therefore you should be alert to many things when using it. For one thing, expunge any trite metaphors that creep into your writing. Called *dead metaphors* because they have been used so often as no longer to do anything other than deaden one's prose, such metaphors as "clear as crystal," "white as a sheet," and "ran like the wind" do the opposite of what metaphors should do. Pale and worn, they are so familiar that they lend no verbal force at all. Also, avoid metaphors that are strained or that call undue attention to themselves: for example, "like a boiling lobster, the sky turned from black to red." Not only is this metaphor strained, but it brings up feelings and associations that are not relevant to a simple description of the changing colors of a sky and that work against the desired mood. All of the implications of a metaphor — like boiling to death here — must be taken into account when one is using metaphor, and metaphors often must be discarded because of aberrant implications in a given context.

Then, be on the lookout for *mixed metaphor* — that is, the piling up of discrete metaphors that don't fit well together: "Now is the time to take a stand in the public eye"; "Afraid that she would never reach the top of the heap, Elsa dived into her studies, determined not to give up before the first round even began." In the first instance, the poor public is having its eye put out; in the second, Elsa, a very agile girl indeed, dives from a heap while boxing. When visualized, these metaphors are ludicrous in context with each other. Because metaphors have a way of linking up, one must watch what happens between them. The result of not doing so is usually a descent into nonsense. The same is true of extended metaphors, which can easily become mixed. When extending a metaphor, make sure that you stay to the same area for all metaphorical terms. The following goes wrong because the area from which the third metaphorical term is drawn is different from that of the first two terms: "Their struggle for power was like a championship fight between two heavyweights, and when the governor lowered his guard, the senator scored the deciding goal." For the metaphor to work, it must be extended thus: "the senator delivered the knockout punch."

Finally, be alert to the little quirks of language and, because of odd linkages, avoid using metaphor at all in certain contexts: for example, "Consumers beware! The water company is trying to bleed us dry!"; "Mrs. Johnson married an old flame, who managed to burn down her house on their wedding night." These sentences, both from newspapers, don't contain mixed metaphors as such; but a literal statement in context with a figurative statement can sometimes be ludicrous — as are the linkages of "water" and "bleed," "flame" and "burn." Both sentences would have been far better if the metaphor in each had been restated in literal language. I can't resist quoting two more like sentences, which further exemplify the need for caution when using figurative language: "It is indeed an honor to sit beside the giants upon whose shoulders we stand"; " 'As a student,' Professor Marsh said, 'Maynard was in a class by himself.' "

In sum, there is a logic to metaphor that must be respected. When constructing or extending a metaphor, the writer must think out all the implications of every metaphorical term and make sure that no aberrant implications make the metaphor(s) ineffectual or even nonsensical; the writer must also check that discrete metaphors don't clash, making nonsense when taken together; that there are no odd linkages between metaphors and other words in a passage; and, when extending, that all of the metaphorical terms are drawn from the same area. Again, there are many possible pitfalls for the unwary with regard to metaphor. But nothing can pack as much power as the right metaphor in the right place.

Appendix 2: A Brief Guide to the Use and Documentation of Sources and Related Matters

Using Sources

Plagiarism

Plagiarism is the unacknowledged use — whether intentional or not — of another person's words or ideas. What you should know first about the use of source material is that anything not your own in a paper will be considered plagiarized if it is not attributed properly. Every direct quotation must be either put within quotation marks or blocked and indented, and a citation must be given referring to a Works Cited list at the end of your paper. Summaries and paraphrases also call for citations. If you cite your sources appropriately, there will be no problem. If you don't, your theft — for that is what it will be — will most likely be caught. Plagiarism usually shouts its presence, especially if the student has lifted something from a published text. Even if the instructor does not know the source, plagiarism can be recognized on stylistic or ideational grounds alone. And how silly plagiarism is. It insults the intelligence of the reader and shows that the student has completely misunderstood the purpose of research. When you do research, proudly show the work you have done by your citations. What is impressive is how you use your sources to buttress *your* ideas.

Referring to Titles

The way titles are quoted is simple: as a general rule, the title of something published in a longer work with a title of its own is put within quotation marks; the title of anything published as an independent unit is italicized (underlined in a typed text). For instance, the title of any essay in this book should be put in quotation marks: "My Wood" or "Salvation" or "Politics and the English Language." Should you refer to the book as a whole, underline its title: Prose in Brief: Reading and Writing Essays. The titles of books, newspapers, and magazines are underlined; the titles of chapters within books, articles in magazines, short stories and lyric poems, and so forth are put in quotation marks. Incidentally, just as quotation marks and italics (underlining) are not used in titles of the works themselves, you should use neither when you place your own title at the head of your paper. However, if your paper title *includes* a story or book title, these should be put in quotation marks or underlined, as appropriate. Here are two examples of paper titles containing titles of published works:

Extended Metaphor in "A Sweet Devouring"

The use of the Elements of Exposition as Defined in

    Prose in Brief: Reading and Writing Essays

Remember that your *whole* title should not have quotation marks around it or be underlined (unless, of course, your title consists of nothing but the title of the work you are writing about — a practice almost always to be discouraged).

Continuous vs. Blocked Quotations

When quoting from a source, you must make a decision depending upon what is being quoted and how much of it. That is, one or two lines of verse and up to four lines of prose should be put in quotation marks and typed so as to be continuous with your text. The following exemplifies this mode of quotation and the way it looks: I began this paragraph by saying, "When quoting from a source, you must make a decision depending upon what is being quoted and how much of it." However, more than four lines of prose (or more than two lines of verse) should be blocked and indented — that is, separated from the lines of your own writing and indented from the left ten spaces. Such quotations are often introduced by a clause ending in a colon, though other punctuation, or even none, may sometimes serve, depending on how the beginning of the quoted text flows grammatically from your own text. The following blocked quotation illustrates these points.

Of British Imperialism, P. T. Moon says in his chapter entitled "Conclusions":

> The British Empire reached its pinnacle with the crowning of Victoria as Empress of India. Before that, the Empire had taken up the slack of a rapidly expanding industrial giant; but once the industrial complex was in place, the Empire only bled the nation of its talent and skill. To manage it, just as to manage any colossal enterprise, required enormous energy, energy that should have gone into solving pressing domestic problems. We have lived to see that the price of empire is too dear, ultimately more costly for the rulers than the ruled.

```
Such, of course, is exactly Forster's point in "My
Wood."
```

This is the look of a blocked quotation. (It would be followed by a parenthetical citation, but we will consider such documentation later in this appendix.) Note that there are no quotation marks around the material blocked; the blocking itself signals quotation. Another note of caution: do not use long quotations to excess. Summarize or paraphrase whenever possible. Use your sources for evidence, not padding.

A quotation within a blocked quotation — that is, something being quoted by the author of your source — is put within normal (double) quotation marks (" "). In continuous quotations, such an interior quotation goes within single quotation marks, as in the following sentences quoted from E. M. Forster's "My Wood": "Property pushes itself in as a substitute," Forster holds, "saying, 'Accept me instead — I'm good enough for all three.' It is not enough. It is, as Shakespeare said of lust, 'The expense of spirit in a waste of shame': it is 'Before, a joy proposed; behind, a dream.' " Observe the punctuation here. In American English, periods and commas go *inside* the closing quotation marks thus: "Property pushes itself in as a substitute." Semicolons and colons go *outside*. Exclamation points and question marks go inside if they are part of the quotation and outside if they are your own.

CHANGING PUNCTUATION

There are, then, two minor changes of punctuation that you can and often must make with respect to continuous quotations: (1) if quotation marks are found *within* the material you are quoting, change those quotation marks from double (" ") to single (' ') ones; (2) if necessary to make the quotation fit smoothly into your sentence, use a comma (or ellipsis dots — see the next subsection) within the closing quotation marks even though the original may have had no mark of punctuation there or some other mark, such as a period, that you will be replacing with the comma. Consider, for instance, the punctuation changes that have to be made in order for me to incorporate Forster's sentences quoted above as part of the following sentence of my own:

```
" 'Accept me instead--I'm good enough for all
three,' " Forster's personified "property" pleads, but
Forster answers emphatically, "It is not enough," and
then goes on to quote from Shakespeare's sonnet begin-
ning, "The expense of spirit in a waste of shame is
lust in action."
```

Here Forster's double quotation marks around the words of his personified "property" *—Accept me instead — I'm good enough for all three—* have been changed to single quotation marks; the periods that in the original come after "enough for all three" and "It is not enough" have been changed to commas to make these sentences fit into the new structure; and the colon that in Foster's essay comes after "lust in action" has been changed to a period. (You will find Forster's original sentences in paragraph 5 of "My Wood," page 8.)

Ellipsis and Square Brackets

Quotations must be exact, except for the two minor changes of punctuation we have just mentioned in connection with continuous quotations. However, quotations need not be complete. You can quote anything you like, from a paragraph or more down to a phrase or even a word. You can also leave words out of a quotation or add words of your won. The first is accomplished by ellipsis. Consider this sentence from the blocked quotation a few pages back and then two versions of it shortened by ellipsis:

```
To manage it, just as to manage any colossal enter-
prise, required enormous energy, energy that should
have gone into solving pressing domestic problems.
```

```
To manage it . . . required enormous energy, energy
that should have gone into solving pressing domestic
problems.
```

```
To manage it . . . required enormous energy . . . .
```

Not used at the beginning of a quotation (for the reader knows that your quotation is an excerpt), ellipsis entails the use of three spaced dots to show that something from the source has been left out (only three dots, note, except when the ellipsis comes at the end of a sentence, in which case the period is also required).

If you wish to insert words of your own into a quotation for some reason — to make the quotation fit more smoothly with the structure of your sentence as a whole, perhaps, or to comment on something within the quotation — you can do so by the use of square brackets. Here, for example, is how you might add a comment of your own in brackets if you were quoting the sentence just used to illustrate ellipsis:

```
To manage it . . . required enormous energy, energy
that should have gone into solving domestic [as op-
posed to colonial] problems.
```

FITTING QUOTATIONS WITH CONTEXTS

A quotation must be exact, yet — as we have noted — it must also fit smoothly into the context in which you are putting it. Often the context, the quotation, or both must be adjusted to make the necessary accommodation. A quotation can be adjusted by ellipsis, by additions in brackets, and by paraphrase (that is, what does not grammatically fit your context can be restated in your own words and the rest quoted). Your own context can also be adjusted. For instance, if you were quoting from my discussion of "My Wood" in Chapter 1, you would not want to write:

```
In reconsidering "My Wood," Proffitt states that he
"find no reason to change my mind."
```

The quotation is exact but, in its new context, ungrammatical and confusing. The problem can be solved in various ways. One way would be to change your sentence by adding the word *can* (which fits grammatically with the quotation's first word, *find*) and by making a bracketed insertion in the quotation itself to change *my* to *his* (the brackets alert the reader that the word is yours and not in the original source):

```
In reconsidering "My Wood," Proffitt states that he
can "find no reason to change [his] mind."
```

INTRODUCING QUOTATIONS

In your remarks introducing a quotation, you will usually want to incorporate the name of the person being quoted, and in any case you will want to make sure that the reason for your quotation is immediately clear. If the reason may not be clear, introduce the quotation by briefly suggesting why you are using it in the present context. For instance, let's say that in a paper on "My Wood" you write:

```
Forster's third point is that property engenders
pseudocreativity and that our proper carnality gets
entangled with the desire for ownership. " 'Possession
is one with loss.' "
```

You would need to revise this statement and introduce the quotation, for here it just sits, a puzzlement to the reader and so an obstacle to your achieving your purpose. Note how, in the following revision, the quotation is introduced in a way that clarifies why it is quoted here:

```
Forster's third point is that property engenders
pseudocreativity and that our proper carnality gets
entangled with the desire for ownership. He sums up
this point with a line from Dante: " 'Possession is
one with loss.' "
```

In both versions, of course, you would need to add a citation to your source — a procedure we will consider shortly.

Quotation, Summary, and Paraphrase

Quotation is not the only way, or always the best way, to present the ideas of another. Often a summary or a paraphrase will prove more effective. A summary is a condensation of someone else's thinking down to the core of that person's idea. For instance, the paragraph headed "Fitting Quotations with Contexts" on page 642 could be summarized as follows: Proffitt emphasizes that quotations must fit smoothly into their new contexts (642). A paraphrase is more elaborate but is still a condensation in that it restates someone else's thought in brief. A paraphrase of the paragraph on context that we just summarized would be something like this: As Proffitt emphasizes, in order to make a quotation fit smoothly into its new context — and it is important for the writer to do so — the context itself can be adjusted by, for instance, the use of paraphrase, and the quotation can be adjusted by ellipsis or by addition in square brackets (642).

Observe that the paraphrase, like the summary, is restricted to the ideas in the source and that the paraphrase follows its sequence of ideas. Be sure to be alert and recognize that you are summarizing or paraphrasing if you are. Then provide the proper citations.

Sources: Primary and Secondary

Sources can be divided into *primary* and *secondary*. A primary source is just that: it is a work that comes *first*. In a paper on "The Road Not Taken," for instance, "The Road Not Taken" would be a primary source. So would any document by Frost — a letter, say, or a journal in which he wrote about the poem. Secondary sources include works of commentary, criticism, history, and so forth. What you need to remember is that primary sources are direct evidence and secondary sources are not. One uses secondary sources to bolster an argument and to lend authority to one's views. But just because so and so said such and such in a published book or periodical does not make it so. Finally, the only valid evidence is the primary source, and secondary sources should not be used to substitute for the grappling with a primary text that alone can give rise to a worthwhile paper.

CITING SOURCES

Whether you are quoting directly, summarizing, or paraphrasing, you must provide an appropriate citation in your text. The dual purpose of any citation is to acknowledge your borrowing as smoothly and concisely as possible within the text and to enable your reader to locate full information about your source in a list called *Works Cited,* which should be arranged alphabetically by authors' last names and placed at the end of your paper. Thus the key element of a citation within your paper is the author's last name, together with the specific page number(s) on which the cited material appears in the source.

Put the author's last name and the page reference (the page or pages on which the material you are quoting, summarizing, or paraphrasing can be found) in parentheses at the end of every quotation, summary, or paraphrase:

"Whether you are quoting directly, summarizing, or paraphrasing, you must provide an appropriate citation in your text" (Proffitt 645).
Quotations must fit smoothly into their new context (Proffitt 642).

Often it is smoother, however, to mention the author's name in introducing the summary, paraphrase, or quotation, in which case you need not repeat the name in the parenthetical citation; the page reference alone is then enough:

As Proffitt says, "Whether you are quoting directly, summarizing, or paraphrasing, you must provide an appropriate citation in your text" (645).

Proffitt stresses that quotations must fit smoothly in their new context (642).

Parenthetical citation is used for books, stories, articles, and newspapers alike, with more detailed information left for the Works Cited list put at the end of a paper (we shall take up this matter shortly).

Citing Continuous vs. Blocked Quotations

There is one small difference between citations coming after continuous quotations and those coming after blocked quotations. When citations for continuous quotations come at the ends of sentences (as they most often do), the sentence period comes *after* the citation as in the following example:

The essay reaches its most eloquent moment with the plea, "Shoot not the iguana" (Dinesen 215).

With blocked quotations, the period comes at the end of the quotation, and the citation stands alone two spaces to the right of the period. Here, for instance, are the first sentences of the previous subsection as they would appear and be cited in a blocked quotation:

> Whether you are quoting directly, summarizing, or paraphrasing, you must provide an appropriate citation in your text. The dual purpose of any citation is to acknowledge your borrowing as smoothly and concisely as possible within the text and to enable your reader to locate full information about your source in a list called Works Cited, which should be arranged alphabetically by authors' last names and placed at the end of your paper. (Proffitt 645)

THREE PROBLEM SPOTS

There are a few other matters concerning citation that you will
need to know when doing a properly documented paper. If you
have parenthetical citations for two or more works by the same
author, then each citation must include not only the author's last
name but also a short form of the title of the work (followed, of
course, by the page reference). For instance, in a paper that
contained the following sentences referring to two different essays
by Joan Didion in this book, "On Morality" and "Miami: The
Cuban Presence," here is how the citations would be treated:

```
The first sentence of "On Morality" makes one feel hot
and uncomfortable: "As it happens I am in Death Val-
ley, in a room at the Enterprise Motel and Trailer
Park, and it is July, and it is hot" (Didion,
"Morality" 178).
But the most revealing insight in Didion's essay is
"that assimilation would be considered by most Cubans
a doubtful goal" ("Miami" 200).
```

Without the short-title designations in the citations, the reader
would not be able to tell which of the two works by Didion is
being quoted in each case. (Note: The second example does not
contain the name "Didion" in the citation because the name is
used in introducing the quotation.)

A somewhat similar problem is that of two or more authors
having the same last name. In this case, each citation must include
a first name or initial, as follows: (Glenn Gould 256), (Stephen
Jay Gould 262).

Further, in citing an anonymous work such as a news report,
use instead of the author's name the first word or phrase (omitting
initial articles *A*, *An*, or *The*) of the title of the piece, followed by
the page reference: ("Myth" 112) for a citation to page 112 of an
article entitled "Myth and the Mythic Mind" in *The Book of All
Mythologies*. The reader will be able to locate the full reference in

the Works Cited list because anonymous works are alphabetized by the first word of their titles. Finally, a special case of the anonymous work is an article in an encyclopedia or other reference volume in which the articles are arranged alphabetically. When you cite these articles, no page reference is required because the reader can quickly look the article up in its alphabetical location. In sum, use common sense. The main purpose of parenthetical citation is to allow the reader to use the appended Works Cited list with ease. Everything done should serve this purpose.

THE WORKS CITED LIST

At the end of your paper, on its own page, should be a list called Works Cited containing an entry for each of the sources you have used. As we have seen, the information in the citations within your paper is abbreviated. In Works Cited you list your sources alphabetically by the last name of each author (or the title if there is no author indicated) and give your reader complete information for each source so that the reader can go to the source to confirm its validity or to study the subject further. There are a great many possible kinds of entries and so, naturally, a great many possible complications in getting a Works Cited list into shape. However, for our purposes — and, in fact, for the purposes of most people most of the time — only a few types of entry need be considered. We will examine here the most common types, especially those that will be valuable to you in using this book. A Works Cited list including all the examples discussed in this appendix appears at the conclusion (pages 654–56). The style followed here, as throughout this appendix, is the one most commonly used in literature and composition courses, that of the Modern Language Association of America. (Some other styles are used in other disciplines.) Should you happen to need information beyond what is presented here, consult Joseph Gibaldi and Walter S. Achtert, *MLA Handbook for Writers of Research Papers*, 3rd ed., New York: MLA, 1988, which is sure to be in your college library.

BOOKS AND JOURNAL ARTICLES

The works most frequently cited are books and articles. An entry for a book should include the name of the author, last name first (if a work has two or more authors, names of authors after the first are straightforward); the full title of the work, including subtitle (separated from the title by a colon), underlined; the edition, if other than the first edition; and finally the city of publication followed by a colon, a shortened form of the publisher's name, and the date of publication. Here are two examples:

Brooks, Cleanth, R. W. B. Lewis, and Robert Penn Warren. American Literature: The Makers and the
Making. Shorter ed. New York: St. Martin's,
1974.

Forster, E. M. Aspects of the Novel. New York: Harcourt, 1954.

When a work has more than three authors, give only the first author's name, followed by a comma and the phrase "et al." (not in quotation marks), which is Latin for "and others." For instance, had the first book listed above had four authors rather than three, the author would have been given as follows: Brooks, Cleanth, et al.

For articles, treat the author's name exactly as for a book. Then comes the title of the article in quotation marks; next, the name of the journal, underlined; and finally the volume number, issue number, date of publication, and the inclusive page numbers of the article (not the page reference for your specific citation, which appears in parentheses in the text of your paper). For a daily, weekly, or monthly periodical, however, omit volume and issue numbers and give the specific date instead. Following are two typical entries:

Funey, James. "E. M. Forster: A Study in Tone."
Journal of Exposition 18.2 (1984): 23–41.

Staggs, Lemual. "Isak Dinesen." Publishers Weekly.
15 June 1987: 62–63.

In the entry for the Funey article, the volume number of the journal is 18, and the issue number is 2 (with this information, only the year of publication, 1984, is given); the article runs from page 23 to page 41. Because the Staggs entry is for a weekly publication, the specific date replaces the volume and issue number.

Observe the spacing in all four entries above: two spaces are used after each discrete item of information that is followed by a period — after the author's name, for example, and again after the title of the book or article, and still again after the edition, as in the entry for Brooks, Lewis, and Warren. The same would be true of other discrete items of information, such as the name of an editor or translator (as other examples in this appendix will show). Note, too, that the first line of an entry is not indented and the rest of the lines are indented five spaces.

ANTHOLOGIES

For an anthology, give the editor's name, last name first (as for an author), followed by a comma, a space, and the abbreviation "ed." Then give the title and the rest of the information as for any other book. Such an entry looks like this:

```
Proffitt, Edward, ed.   Prose in Brief: Reading and
     Writing Essays.   San Diego: Harcourt: 1991.
```

In a paper in which, for instance, you compare two stories found in the present text, this would be your main entry. How the individual stories would be entered in the list is covered in the next subsection.

A WORK IN AN ANTHOLOGY

For a story or other selection found in an anthology for which you have provided a main entry as shown just above, begin with the author of the selection (in the usual way). Next give the selection title, followed by a period, in quotation marks (exception: titles of plays are underlined); if the selection is a translation, next give the translator's name preceded by "Trans."; and finally give the last name of the anthology's editor and the inclusive page numbers of the story or other selection as it appears in the anthology. Here are two examples:

Dinesen, Isak. "The Iguana." Trans. Isak Dinesen.
    Proffitt 214–15.
Didion, Joan. "Bureaucrats." Proffitt 184–89.

This kind of entry, referring to main entry for the anthology itself (in this case the main entry for Proffitt shown in the preceding subsection), is convenient if you cite more than one selection from the same anthology; it saves you the trouble of repeating all the information about the anthology in the entry for each selection. However, if you refer to only one selection from the anthology, you will find it more efficient simply to use one full entry as follows:

Didion, Joan. "Bureaucrats." Prose in Brief: Reading
    and Writing Essays. Ed. Edward Proffitt. San
    Diego: Harcourt, 1991, 184–89.

REFERENCE BOOKS AND ANONYMOUS MATERIAL

Treat a *signed* article in an encyclopedia or other reference book as you would an article or story in a collection, except don't include the name of the editor of the reference work:

Edel, Leon. "Henry James and His Followers." Ency-
    clopaedia Britannica: Macropaedia. 1974 ed.

If the article is not signed or if you are listing a book with no author given, the name of the book or article should appear alphabetically thus:

The Times Atlas of the World. 5th ed. New York: New
    York Times, 1975.
"Swift, Jonathan." The Columbia Encyclopedia. 1950
    ed.

Titles beginning with "A," "An," or "The" are alphabetized according to the second word of the title. Note, too, how an edition is indicated, and observe that if the materials within the source volume are arranged alphabetically you may omit volume and page numbers.

A NEWSPAPER ARTICLE

To list an article from a newspaper, begin with the writer's name if specified (if not, begin with the title of the article), followed by the title of the article (the major headline) in quotation marks, the name of the paper (excluding initial "A," "An," or "The") underlined, the complete date, the edition if an edition, and the section letter, if the paper is divided into sections, along with the inclusive page numbers if the article is continuous (see first example to follow) or the first page number followed by plus sign if the article is continued after skipping pages (see second example).

Crane, Stephen.   "Captain Murphy's Shipwrecked Crew."

   Florida Times Union 5 Jan. 1897: 1—2.

"The Literate and the Damned."   Bar Harbour Post Dis-

   patch 12 July 1953, late ed.: B17+

The second entry tells us that the article begins on page 17 of section B and then skips to a page farther back, as often happens in magazines and newspapers. Note, incidentally, that the names of all months except May, June, and July (in other words, all months with names more than four letters long) are abbreviated in Works Cited entries (*Jan.* in the first entry above but *July* in the second).

TWO OR MORE WORKS BY THE SAME AUTHOR

For two or more works by the same author, give the author's name for the first work and then, for the other works, use three typed hyphens in place of the author's name (the hyphens are followed by a period, as is the author's name). Arrange the words alphabetically by title.

```
Gould, Stephen Jay.  "In a Jumbled Drawer."  Proffitt
     280-92.
---.  "The Nonscience of Human Nature."  Proffitt
     262-68.
---.  The Panda's Thumb.  New York: Norton, 1980.
```

When different books are involved, a full citation for each is necessary, though the author's name is still indicated by the three typed hyphens for the second and subsequent works in the list.

SAMPLE WORKS CITED LIST AND SAMPLE MANUSCRIPT

On the next page is a typewritten Works Cited list in the proper MLA format, listing representative works referred to in the preceding discussions. Study it carefully and be sure that you understand the entries individually and also the reasons for the order in which they are presented. Following this sample list is the sample essay on Forster's "My Wood" from Chapter 1 (pages 5–8), now revised to incorporate documented sources and typewritten in MLA format so that you can see how margins, spacing, page numbering, and other such matters are handled.

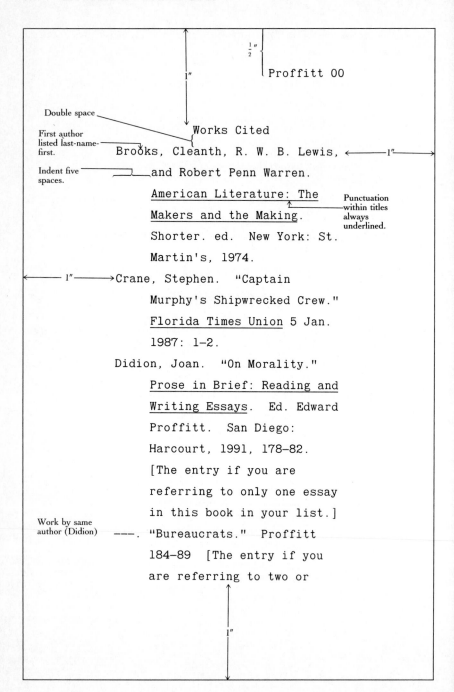

Double space

First author listed last-name-first.

Indent five spaces.

Punctuation within titles always underlined.

Work by same author (Didion)

Proffitt 00

Works Cited

Brooks, Cleanth, R. W. B. Lewis, and Robert Penn Warren. American Literature: The Makers and the Making. Shorter. ed. New York: St. Martin's, 1974.

Crane, Stephen. "Captain Murphy's Shipwrecked Crew." Florida Times Union 5 Jan. 1987: 1–2.

Didion, Joan. "On Morality." Prose in Brief: Reading and Writing Essays. Ed. Edward Proffitt. San Diego: Harcourt, 1991, 178–82. [The entry if you are referring to only one essay in this book in your list.]

———. "Bureaucrats." Proffitt 184–89 [The entry if you are referring to two or

Proffitt 00

more essays in this book in
your list.]

Dinesen, Isak. "The Iguana."

    Trans. Isak Dinesen.

            Proffitt 214–15.

Edel, Leon. "Henry James and

    His Followers."

    <u>Encyclopedia Britannica:</u>

    <u>Macropaedia</u>. 1974 ed.

Forster, E. M. <u>Aspects of the</u>

    <u>Novel</u>. New York: Harcourt,

    1954.

———. "My Wood." Proffitt 5–8.

Funey, James. "E. M. Forster: A

    Study in Tone." <u>Journal of</u>

    <u>Exposition</u> 18.2 (1984): 23–

    41.

Gibaldi, Joseph, and Walter S.

    Achtert. <u>MLA Handbook for</u>

    <u>Writers of Research Papers</u>.

    3rd ed. New York: MLA,

    1988.

List authors' names in order in which they are cited on title page of book.

Major elements separated by periods plus two spaces.

Proffitt 00

Gould, Stephen Jay. "In a
        Jumbled Drawer." Proffitt
        280–92.

———. "The Nonscience of Human
        Nature." Proffitt 262–68.

———. The Panda's Thumb. New
        York: Norton, 1980.

"The Literate and the Damned."
        Bar Harbor Post Dispatch.
        12 July 1953, late ed.:
        B17+.

Proffitt, Edward, ed. Prose in
        Brief: Reading and Writing
        Essays. San Diego:
        Harcourt, 1989.

Staggs, Lemual. "Isak Dinesen."
        Publishers Weekly. 15 June
        1987: 62–63.

"Swift, Jonathan." The Columbia
        Encyclopedia. 1950 ed. The
        Times Atlas of the World.
        5th ed. New York: New York
        Times, 1975.

Anonymous article alphabetized by title (ignoring "The")

Full citation necessary for different book by same author. Three dashes still replace author's name.

Article skips pages after beginning on page B17.

No page numbers required for article in alphabetized reference work.

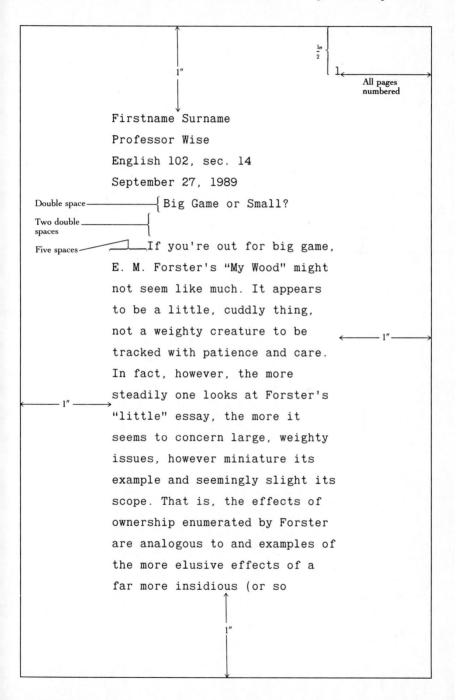

½″
2

1

All pages
numbered

Firstname Surname

Professor Wise

English 102, sec. 14

September 27, 1989

Double space ——————{ Big Game or Small?

Two double
spaces

Five spaces ————⌐——If you're out for big game,
E. M. Forster's "My Wood" might
not seem like much. It appears
to be a little, cuddly thing,
not a weighty creature to be
tracked with patience and care.
In fact, however, the more
steadily one looks at Forster's
"little" essay, the more it
seems to concern large, weighty
issues, however miniature its
example and seemingly slight its
scope. That is, the effects of
ownership enumerated by Forster
are analogous to and examples of
the more elusive effects of a
far more insidious (or so

1″

1″

1″

Last name precedes page number on pages after the first.

Surname 2

Forster would move the reader to feel) type of ownership on the British public.

The date of the essay and a knowledge of its intended audience are key to an understanding of its full range. Dating from the 1930s (when the British Empire was still intact) and aimed at literate Britishers, the essay assumes that its targeted readers would be concerned with the issue of Empire——"a pressing political

Author's name (Hoyle) not needed here because given in text leading to the reference.

concern in the '30's," according to Michael Hoyle (52)——and would grasp that Forster's novel A Passage to India is the book alluded to in the first paragraph. The intended audience would also have known that this novel——Forster's most widely

Surname 3

celebrated single work—depicts
British imperialism and its
adverse effects on the British
themselves. Once understood,
this allusion alone suggests
that "My Wood" concerns
something rather more embracing
than the ownership of a small
patch of woods in some byway in
Great Britain. It suggests that
the wood and the effects on the
speaker of his ownership as
described in the essay should be
taken as part of an unstated
analogy: that his wood is to
Forster what the Empire is to
the British. So the essay
concerns "the effect of property
upon the character" (Forster 6)
not only of the individual but
of the nation at large.

        The effects enumerated by

Surname 4

Forster of his owning a piece of
property, therefore, are also to
be understood as the effects he
sees in the British of their
possession of colonies. Like
him, they have become heavy,
heavy by being weighed down by
an empire--"if you have a lot of
things you cannot move around a
lot" (Forster 6)--and heavy by
having become like the rich man
in Christ's parable referred to
by Forster ("It is easier for a
camel to go through the eye of a
needle, than for a rich man to
enter into the kingdom of God").
Physical heaviness here is
symbolic of spiritual heaviness,
of a pompous and self-satisfied
state of soul, or what one
critic of the Empire called
"spiritual inertia" (Thomas 27).

Author's name
included here
because not
mentioned in
text leading to
this citation.

Citations to
specific pages
where
quotations
appear.

Periods and
commas go
inside quotation
marks *unless*
citation
intervenes.

Surname 5

It is this that Forster sees in
his countrymen—a profound
spiritual heaviness stemming
from their colonial power and
rule.

    As indirectly depicted by
Forster, the British are also
seen as expansionist and all but
damnably acquisitive. Such is
what his analogy suggests with
respect to the second effect of
owning property enumerated: just
as Forster would extend the
boundaries of his wood,
acquiring property without end,
so the British actually did
extend the boundaries of the
Empire in their avariciousness.
The reference to Ahab, the
infidel Old Testament king who
married Jezebel, suggests that
the desire to expand—whether on

Surname 6

the part of an individual or a
nation--is as treacherous and
immoral as Ahab and Jezebel
themselves (the reference is to
1 Kings 21.1-7).

The third charge against
colonization is exemplified by
Forster's desire to "express"
his personality through doing
something to his piece of
property. Most suburbs bear
witness to this expressive
fallacy in their proliferating
lawn ornaments, not to mention
the lawns themselves and the
energy wasted in a vain attempt
at self-expression through lawn

Ellipsis signals
an intentional
omission.

maintenance. Property surely
does "push . . . itself in as a
substitute" for true "creation
and enjoyment" (Forster 7-8). The
implication of this expressive

Surname 7

fallacy when extended to the
Empire is that the energies of
the British have been
misdirected into and sapped by
their colonial expansion.
Thoreau's dictum that "The more
one has, the less one is" (25)
applies to mighty nations no
less than to private citizens.

     Finally, there is
selfishness--whether with regard
to blackberries or colonies. Put
in climactic order, this evil in
particular redounds against the
property owner or colonist by
making them petty and
mean-spirited. Such is what
Forster's last example declares,
as subtly does his title if we
put the stress on its first
word. The "sweets of property,"
whether a wood or an empire, are

Surname 8

the sweets of sin, which turn in
the end to destroy the sinner.
The irony of this turning is
implicit in Forster's phrase
"the sweets of property" (8).
Speaking of British imperialism,
P. T. Moon makes the same point,
only overtly, in his chapter
entitled "Conclusions"

Blocked quotation indented ten spaces.

(513-566):

Regular double space before (and after) blocked quotation.

The British Empire
reached its pinnacle
with the crowing of
[Queen] Victoria as
Empress of India.
Before that, the
Empire had taken up
the slack of a rapidly
expanding industrial
giant; but once the
industrial complex was

Surname 9

in place, the Empire
only bled the nation
of its talent and
skill. To manage it
. . . required
enormous energy,
energy that should
have gone into solving
pressing domestic
problems. We have
lived to see that the
price of empire is too
dear, ultimately more
costly for the rulers
[here is the irony]
than the ruled. (565)
To be sure, Forster does
not refer to the British Empire
directly; except for the pointed
comment about "A rocket
containing a Union Jack"
attaining "universal dominion"

Square brackets
show that
words not in
original source
have been
added

Citation after
blocked
quotation *follows*
the final period.

Two spaces

Surname 10

(7), he tells us only about
himself and his wood. But his
various references--to the
Bible, for instance, and to
Dante--intimate that he has
something bigger in mind,
something of the scope of those
references, and that the effects
detailed of the ownership of a
small piece of property
exemplify something more
far-reaching. No, Forster does
not take us after small game. It
is big game he's after. In the
course of his essay, that is,
his little wood comes to stand
for the British Empire itself
and, further, for the very idea
of possession; and the
enumerated effects of Forster's
ownership come to be those of
the colonies on the British and

Surname 11

of ownership in general. Through
his concrete example, then,
Forster shows us the full
meaning of the sentence he
quotes from Dante: " 'Possession
is one with loss' " (8).

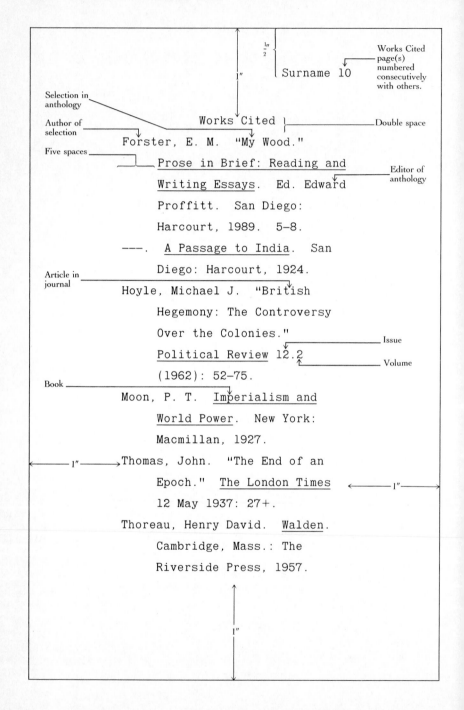

GROUPINGS BY THEME/THESIS AND MODE

The Brain

See "The Mind/The Brain."

Changing Times

Comedy/Satire

Death

Education

The Family

Growth / Identity / Regression

Guns and Drugs

History

Informational Essays (Selected)

Justice

Men and Women

Morality

Nature/Human Nature/Civilization

The Nuclear Threat

Other Peoples

Personal Essays (Selected)

Persuasive Essays (Selected)

Progress

Relationships

Religion

Satire

See "Comedy/Satire."

Science [See also "Technology."]

Social Issues

[Fully half of the essays in the text touch on issues of social importance. The titles that follow are representative.]

Wildlife/Ecology

Women's Issues

Writing/Language/The Writing Process

GROUPINGS BY ELEMENTS AND OTHER FORMAL FEATURES

Authority (Appeal to)

Beginnings

See "Thesis Positions."

Character Sketch

Chronology

Classification

Comparison and Contrast

Definition

Diction

Exemplification and Other Concretions (Excluding Figuration)

[Exemplification and other types of concretion (imagery, descriptive detail, and so forth) are to be found in virtually all of the essays in this book. The essays that follow were selected because such concretions are a prominent means in each.]

Figuration

[All entries are for discrete metaphor unless otherwise noted.]

Flaws (Essays with Instructive Problems)

Narration/Narrator

Order of Climax/Anti-Climax

Paragraphing — For Special Effect

Paragraphing — Transitional Paragraphs

Parallelism (Grammatical, Structural, Ideational)

Rhythm and Sound

Setting

Spatial Sequence

Style

See "Diction" and "Syntax."

Symbol/Symbolism

Syntax

Theme (*Essays with a Theme Rather than a Thesis*)

Thesis Position

At the Beginning

Funnel Position

Thesis Up Front *(Title or First Sentence)*

Thesis as Conclusion

Titles (Vis-à-vis Thesis)

Tone

Transitional Paragraphs

See "Paragraphing — Transitional Paragraphs."

Voice

GLOSSARY

Note: Terms printed in **bold type** have entries of their own, to which the reader may wish to refer.

abstraction Any word that denotes a concept, a quality, a feeling, a classification, or whatever, without stimulating in the mind a particular sensation — for example, "refraction" as opposed to "green, red, and blue." Contrast **concretion.** See pages 76, 79–80 and 631.

allusion An *indirect* reference to something assumed to be known by the listener or reader — for instance, the phrase "a mighty white whale, large enough to swallow a boat" alludes to both Melville's *Moby Dick* and the biblical story of Jonah. Compare **reference.**

analogy The exemplifying, explaining, or interpreting of something by way of its similarities to something else. There are two broad types of analogy, *literal* and *figurative.* Involving comparison between things that are essentially alike — American men and Arab men, for instance — literal analogy is a means of support (though not a proof). Involving comparison between things that are essentially un-alike — for example, American men and lions — figurative analogy is the basis of **metaphor.** See pages 41–42, 90.

analytic prose Prose in which a subject is divided into its component parts and examined accordingly. See pages 515–16.

audience An element of expository prose, many features of which are conditioned by the type of audience addressed. See pages 13–14, 69–70.

authority, appeal to A means of **support** that entails the use of what authorities in a given field have said or statistics or personal experience as evidence backing up a contention or point. See pages 40–41, 92–93, 537–38.

centrifugal exposition A kind of exposition, usually having an overtly stated **thesis,** in which the focus is outward — on ideas, events, or whatever, in the external world. Contrast **centripetal exposition.** See page 100.

centripetal exposition   A kind of exposition, usually entailing an unstated **theme,** in which the focus is inward — on the self and its history, musings, and so forth. Contrast **centrifugal exposition.** See page 100.

character sketch   A type of essay, or any portion thereof, entailing a portrait of a given individual. See pages 76–77.

chronological organization   The organization of a paragraph or an essay according to some time sequence. For instance, a paragraph or paper that moves from "at first" to "later" to "still later" to "at the last" would be organized chronologically. See pages 21, 94.

classification   The breaking of something into its classes or types — for example, the six types of title, the two broad classes of the essay — for the purposes of **definition.** Classification always proceeds by the **enumeration** of types one by one. See pages 37, 95.

coherence   The sense that the relationship of parts in a piece of writing is logical and clear. See pages 59–64.

comparison and contrast   A prime way of understanding, comparison and contrast is also a tool of analysis and a mode of organization. It entails the focusing on the likenesses or differences or both between two or more things in order to see at least one of them with heightened clarity. See pages 22–25, 37–38, 96.

concretion   Any word, phrase, or aspect of a text that has immediate sensory effect — for example, the phrase "a juicy steak" is concrete because we can visualize the steak and imagine its smell and taste. Contrast **abstraction.** See pages 76, 79–80, 631.

context   The passage or the essay, poem, or whatever as a whole in which a given detail is found and from which it gains its meaning.

dead metaphor   Any metaphor that, through overuse, no longer has metaphorical effect: "sly as a fox," "feed the computer." See page 633.

definition   A means of **support,** often entailing **classification** and **exemplification,** that involves the delineation of the meaning of a word or concept, the traits of a person, or whatever. See pages 40, 91–92.

diction   The choice of words, or the kind of words chosen, in a given passage or utterance. A few possible distinctions as to diction are abstract/concrete; denotative/connotative; formal/colloquial; general/specific; technical/common. Diction is a prime element of **style.** See pages 76, 87–90.

discourse/discursive   *Discourse* refers to verbal expression in speech or writing. *Discursive* refers specifically to that type of verbal expression that proceeds according to the principles and goals of **expository prose.**

discrete metaphor   A metaphor used once and once only in a given **context.** Contrast **metaphorical extension.** See page 632

discrete paragraph   A paragraph that is self-contained, that stands alone as a short composition in itself. See pages 18–21.

enumeration   A way of organizing material that falls into distinct parts, stages, or whatever. If, for instance, there are three reasons for believing something, then one can proceed by enumeration —first, second, and third. See pages 26–27, 96.

exemplification   A prime means of **support** that entails the illustration of theoretical statements, abstractions, and so forth, with concrete instances. See pages 37–39, 79–80, 90–91.

explicit metaphor   A kind of metaphor in which both the defining term and the term being defined are expressed overtly — for instance, "Solitude [the term being defined] is the salt [the defining term] of personhood." Compare **metaphor.** See page 632.

expository prose   Writing designed to explain something in a clear, precise manner. The essay is a chief form of expository prose, or exposition. Essays, which may support a **theme** or argue a **thesis,** are aimed at communicating thoughts with clarity and, ideally, with pleasure. See pages 14–15.

extended metaphor   See **metaphorical extension.**

figurative language   Any use of words not meant to be taken literally. Any expression involving **metaphor,** for instance, or **hyperbole** or **personification** is figurative: "Harold the ox" (if said of a human being rather than an ox), "I won by a mile" (when literally the win was by a few feet), "the long arm of the law." Often, whether something is literal or figurative depends on the **context.** Contrast **literal language.** See pages 80–83, 631–32.

figure of speech   Any expression that is **figurative** as opposed to **literal.** Common figures of speech are **hyperbole, understatement, personification,** and **metaphor.**

genre   The category into which a piece of writing falls by virtue of its style, form, and purpose. The essay, for instance, is a genre.

hyperbole   A **figure of speech** entailing exaggeration — for example, "I won by a mile" or "by a nose," when in fact the win was by a few feet in both cases. Contrast **understatement.**

image/imagery   Images are verbal **concretions** (words that call sensations to mind) used to convey feelings and states of mind through sense impression. Often, imagery is used to form metaphors and symbols, thus reinforcing or determining the meaning of a work.

implicit metaphor   A kind of metaphor in which the defining word or the word defined or both are not overtly expressed but are somehow immediately implied — for instance, "biting words," which implies that the words (the word being defined) are teeth (the defining word implied by "biting"). Compare **metaphor.** See page 632.

informational prose   Prose whose purpose is to convey information. For example, the consequences of British imperialism in India could be the subject of an informational essay. See page 15.

irony   Refers to an incongruity felt between, for instance, what is said and what is meant (sarcasm, for example), or between what seems to be and what actually is, or between what someone believes and what is actually true. Whatever the kind, irony always entails a sense of discrepancy.

literal language   Any use of words meant to be taken strictly at face value — for instance, "It's time to get to work" as opposed to "It's time to get hopping." Contrast **figurative language.**

metaphor   Any **figurative** expression entailing an analogy — whether explicit or implicit — between essentially unlike things (it is the essential unlikeness of its terms that makes the expression figurative in the first place). The object of metaphor is definition: definition of one term of the verbal construction by way of the other — for example, "He [word being defined] is an ox [defining word]." See **analogy, explicit metaphor, implicit metaphor,** and **simile.** See also pages 82–83, 631–32.

metaphorical extension   The sustaining of some prime metaphor over a passage (from a sentence to a paragraph or more) or even over the length of an entire essay. Metaphors are extended by a writer's staying to the same area for all defining terms. For instance, "You *light* up my life: you are a *candle* in my *darkness*, the *rays* of my hope, the *sun* of all my days." See pages 632–33.

mixed metaphor   Metaphors that in combination or extension do not work well together — for example, "It's time to take a firm stand in the public eye." See page 634.

narration/narrative/narrator   Any essay or portion thereof that tells a story (*narration* means *story*) is *narrative*. When a whole essay is narrative — as, for instance, are most autobiographical essays — its **speaker** is often referred to as the *narrator*. There are two basic types of narration and narrator: first-person and third-person. First-person narrators narrate stories about themselves (autobiography); third-person narrators tell us about other people and times (biography and history). See pages 71–73.

order of climax   The movement of a sentence, paragraph, or paper from less important details or support to more important. Order of climax is so important psychologically that whatever other type of order a paragraph or paper may follow, order of climax should be respected and violated only for special purpose. See pages 27–28, 95–96.

overstatement   See **hyperbole.**

pace   The rapidity or slowness of an utterance or passage, and thus a prime constituent of its **rhythm.**

paradox   Any statement that seems self-contradictory but that, upon analysis, turns out to have validity — for example, "And death once dead, there's no more dying then."

parallelism   Primarily, the grouping of like thoughts into identical syntactical patterns: "of the people, by the people, for the people." A matter of both grammar and syntax, parallelism is an aspect of **style.** Critics also speak of structural and ideational parallelism, meaning that two paragraphs, say, are parallel in structure or that two paragraphs present parallel ideas. See pages 88–89.

personification   A **figure of speech** in which some human quality is attributed to an abstraction, an inanimate object, an animal, or whatever — for example, "Let justice *decide*"; "the *fury* of the gale"; "the *hopeful* robin's song." See pages 80–81.

persuasive prose   Prose designed chiefly to persuade the reader of the rightness of the writer's judgment. See pages 16–17.

proofreading   Reading over a piece of writing in order to correct errors in spelling, agreement, punctuation, and so forth. The final proofreading is for typographical errors. See page 67.

reference   *Overt* mention of someone or something in our cultural past or present to evoke a certain meaning or set of associations in the mind of the reader. For instance, to say "He is the Babe Ruth of songwriters" would suggest a writer with so many big "hits" as to be legendary. Compare **allusion.**

rhythm   The way words move (*rhythm* comes from a Greek word meaning "to flow") when put together — for instance, fast or slow, ponderously or light-heartedly, evenly or haltingly. Prose rhythms, which in large measure are created by **syntax,** are apparent particularly with regard to special effects and closure. See pages 83–87.

sarcasm   A type of **irony** used to show scorn.

satire   Writing, usually comic, that holds a subject up to ridicule.

setting   Location as to time or place, or both. Setting in essays can help to create mood, and often a setting is used symbolically. See pages 78–79.

simile   A type of **explicit metaphor** in which the comparison is emphasized by the introduction of *as* or *like.* For instance: "My love is *like* a red, red rose." See page 632.

spatial sequence   The organization of a paragraph or an essay according to the spatial relationship of the parts of the subject being considered. For instance, one might describe the motor of a car from top to bottom. If a subject lends itself to spatial treatment, one must let the reader know how one is going to proceed and then follow through. See pages 22, 94.

speaker   Used to refer to the person whose voice we hear when reading an essay, whether that of the author or (and especially) a character whom we are meant to imagine as addressing us.

style   The sum of the choices a writer makes as to the selection of words **(diction)** and type of sentence structure **(syntax).** Style tends to be characteristic of a writer, though every writer adjusts style to fit the particular circumstance. See pages 87–90.

subordination   The combining of ideas so that one is made grammatically dependent on the other by being cast into a phrase or a subordinate clause. The purpose of subordination is to gain

coherence as well as to reinforce a sense of **unity** by making prime information stand out. See pages 56–57, 60–62.

support   The material used to demonstrate the validity of a thesis. One can subdivide support material into *major* and *minor,* minor support backing up major support, which in turn backs up the governing thesis of paragraph or essay. The prime *means of support* are **analogy, authority, definition,** and **exemplification.** See pages 19–20, 37–42.

symbol   Anything in a text that conveys meaning different from (though usually related to) its literal meaning. The desert setting in Joan Didion's "On Morality" (pages 178–82), for instance, symbolizes the hostility of nature. See page 81.

syntax   The relationship of the position of words in sentences to meaning, as well as the way in which words are put together to form various sentence patterns. In English, meaning is primarily determined by syntax: for instance, "Dog bites man" versus "Man bits dog." As to sentence patterns, the two main types are *loose* (with the main information coming at the head) and *periodic* (with the main information coming last in the sentence). Along with **diction,** syntax is a prime constituent of **style.** See pages 87–90.

theme   The controlling attitude, insight, or point *implied* in a thematic essay. Compare **thesis.** See pages 98–101.

thesis   The main point of a piece of **expository prose** when, as is usually the case, that point is stated *overtly* (the thematic essay, which develops a **theme** that is *implied,* is the exception): that which is demonstrated, exemplified, and argued in the body of such a piece. A thesis, it should be noted, is not a topic. A *topic* is what a thesis makes a statement about. "Cats" is a topic; "Cats are man's best friend" is a thesis — something that someone could conceivably argue against. See pages 11–12, 98–101.

tone   The way something is said as that way reveals the feelings or attitude of a **narrator** or **speaker** of an essay. Tone is created especially by **diction.** See pages 73–76.

topic   See **thesis.**

transition   Anything in a piece of writing that facilitates the movement from one segment to another. See pages 52–58.

understatement   A **figure of speech** in which emphasis is gained by a deliberate underplaying of the magnitude or effect of what is being described. For instance, "Last week I saw a woman flayed, and you

will hardly believe how much it altered her person for the worse"
(Swift). Contrast **hyperbole.**

unity   The sense that everything in a piece of writing works to one end,
or relates to one central idea. A lack of unity results from the
presence of extraneous material or material that seems unrelated to
the central idea because the writer has failed to make the
relationship clear. See pages 59–64.

voice   The quality or flavor of a spoken utterance in a piece of writing;
the sense of a person speaking when we read and the qualities of the
voice we hear. Voice is created especially by **diction** and **tone.** See
pages 73–76.

COPYRIGHTS AND ACKNOWLEDGMENTS

BROOKS ATKINSON   "The Warfare in the Forest Is Not Wanton." Copyright ©
1968 by The New York Times Company. Reprinted by permission.

RUSSELL BAKER   "The Plot Against People" and "Little Red Riding Hood
Revisited." Copyright © 1968, 1980 by The New York Times Company.
Reprinted by permission.

WENDELL BERRY   "Horse-Drawn Tools and the Doctrine of Labor Saving."
Exerpted from *The Gift of Good Land*, copyright © 1981 by Wendell Berry.
Published by North Point Press and reprinted by permission.

SANDRA CALVI   "My Dog." Reprinted by permission of the author.

BRUCE CATTON   "Grant and Lee: A Study in Contrasts." Copyright U.S. Capitol
Historical Society. Reprinted with permission.

JOHN CIARDI   "Of Writing and Writers." From *Saturday Review*, April 18, 1964.
Reprinted by permission of Omni Publications International Ltd.

ELDRIDGE CLEAVER   "The Blood Lust." From *Soul on Ice* by Eldridge Cleaver.
Copyright 1967 by McGraw-Hill Publishing Co. Reprinted by permission.

ALLAN COOPER   "REMark: Software Wildcats." Reprinted with permission of
PC WORLD from Volume 3, Issue 7.

THOMAS COTTLE   "Overcoming an Invisible Handicap." From *Psychology Today*,
January 1980. Reprinted by permission.

NORMAN COUSINS   "Who Killed Benny Paret?" From *Saturday Review*, 1987.
Reprinted by permission of Omni Publications International Ltd.

ALLAN DERSHOWITZ   "Discrimination by Creed." From *San Francisco Chronicle*,
November 16, 1986. Copyright © 1986 by United Feature Syndicate, Inc.
Reprinted by permission.

JOAN DIDION   "On Morality." From *Slouching Towards Bethlehem* by Joan Didion.
Copyright © 1965, 1968 by Joan Didion. Reprinted by permission of Farrar,
Straus and Giroux, Inc. "Bureaucrats" and "In Bed." Both from *The White Album*
by Joan Didion. Copyright © 1976, 1979, 1989 by Joan Didion. Reprinted by
permission of Farrar, Straus and Giroux, Inc. "Miami: The Cuban Presence."
From *The New York Review of Books*, May 28, 1987. Copyright © 1987 by Joan
Didion. Reprinted by permission of Simon & Schuster, Inc.

ANNIE DILLARD   "Living like Weasels." From *Teaching a Stone to Talk* by Annie
Dillard. Copyright © 1982 by Annie Dillard. Reprinted by permission of Harper
& Row, Publishers, Inc.

Isak Dinesen   "The Iguana" and "Pooran Singh." Both from *Out of Africa* by Isak Dinesen. Copyright © 1937 by Random House, Inc. and renewed 1965 by Rungstedlundfonden. Reprinted by permission of Random House, Inc.

Jane Doe   "I Wish They'd Do It Right." Copyright © 1977 by The New York Times Company. Reprinted by permission.

Lisa Donofrio   "The Guidette." Reprinted by permission of the author.

Annette Dula   "No Home in Africa." Copyright © 1975 by The New York Times Company. Reprinted by permission.

Flora Mancuso Edwards   "Elvira's Story." From *The City Today*, edited by George L. Groman. Copyright © 1978 by Harper & Row, Publishers, Inc. Reprinted by permission of Harper & Row, Publishers, Inc.

Peter Elbow   "Desperation Writing." From *Writing Without Teachers* by Peter Elbow. Copyright © 1973 by Oxford University Press, Inc. Reprinted by permission.

Peter Farb   "How to Talk about the World." From *Word Play: What Happens When People Talk* by Peter Farb. Copyright © 1973 by Peter Farb. Reprinted by permission of Alfred A. Knopf, Inc.

E. M. Forster   "My Wood." From *Abinger Harvest*. Copyright 1936 and renewed 1964 by Edward Morgan Forster. "Tolerance." From *Two Cheers for Democracy*. Copyright 1951 by Edward Morgan Forster and renewed 1979 by Donald Parry. Both reprinted by permission of Harcourt Brace Jovanovich, Inc.

Barry Goldwater   "Why Gun-Control Laws Don't Work." Reprinted by permission from the December 1975 *Reader's Digest*. Copyright © 1975 by The Reader's Digest Assn., Inc.

Ellen Goodman   "The Just-Right Wife." Copyright © 1984, Washington Post Writers Group/Boston Globe Newspaper Company. Reprinted with permission.

Glenn Gould   "Music and Technology." From *The Glenn Gould Reader*, edited by Tim Page. Copyright © 1984 by Estate of Glenn Gould and Glenn Gould Ltd. Reprinted by permission of Alfred A. Knopf, Inc.

Stephen Jay Gould   "The Nonscience of Human Nature." Reprinted from *Ever Since Darwin: Reflections in Natural History*, by Stephen J. Gould, by permission of W. W. Norton & Company, Inc. Copyright © 1977 by Stephen J. Gould. Copyright © 1973, 1974, 1975, 1976, 1977 by The American Museum of Natural History. "Sex, Drugs, Disasters, and the Extinction of the Dinosaurs." From *The Flamingo's Smile: Reflections in Natural History* by Stephen J. Gould. Reprinted by permission of the author. "In a Jumbled Drawer." Reprinted with permission from *Natural History*, Vol. 97, No. 8. Copyright The American Museum of Natural History, 1988.

Jeff Greenfield   "The Black and White Truth about Basketball." First appeared in *Esquire* magazine. Reprinted by permission of Sterling Lord Literistic, Inc. Copyright © 1975 by Jeff Greenfield (and 1984 by Jeff Greenfield).

Dick Gregory   "If You Had to Kill Your Own Hog." From *The Shadow That Scares Me* by Dick Gregory. Copyright © 1968 by Dick Gregory. Used by permission of Doubleday, a division of Bantam, Doubleday, Dell Publishing Group, Inc.

GERALD GROW   "How to Write 'Official.'" Reprinted with permission from *Simply Stated*, the newsletter of the Document Design Center, American Institute for Research.

S. I. HAYAKAWA   "What Does It Mean to Be Creative?" From *Through the Communication Barrier* by S. I. Hayakawa. Reprinted by permission of the author.

NANCY K. HILL   "Teaching as Mountaineering." Copyright © 1980, *The Chronicle of Higher Education*. Reprinted with permission.

JANE HOWARD   "Families." Copyright 1978 by Jane Howard. Reprinted by permission of Simon & Schuster, Inc.

EDWARD HOYT   "Party Buddies." Reprinted by permission of the author.

LANGSTON HUGHES   "Salvation." From *The Big Sea* by Langston Hughes. Copyright © 1940 by Langston Hughes. Renewal copyright © 1968 by Arna Bontemps and George Houston Bass. Reprinted by permission of Hill and Wang, a division of Farrar, Straus and Giroux, Inc.

MARK HUNTER   "The Beat Goes Off: How Technology Has Gummed Up Rock's Grooves." Copyright © 1987 by *Harper's Magazine*. All rights reserved. Reprinted from the May issue by special permission.

ZORA NEALE HURSTON   "How It Feels to Be Colored Me." From *I Love Myself When I Am Laughing: A Zora Neale Hurston Reader*, edited by Alice Walker. Reprinted by permission of the Estate of Zora Neale Hurston.

BARBARA HUTTMANN   "A Crime of Compassion." Reprinted by permission of the author.

ALDOUS HUXLEY   "Waterworks and Kings." From *The Olive Tree* by Aldous Huxley. Copyright 1937 by Aldous Huxley; copyright © renewed 1965 by Laura Huxley. Reprinted by permission of Harper & Row, Publishers, Inc.

EDWARD M. KENNEDY   "The Need for Handgun Control." From *The Los Angeles Times*, April 15, 1981. Reprinted by permission of the author.

MARTIN LUTHER KING, JR.   "I Have a Dream." Reprinted by permission of Joan Daves. Copyright © 1963 by Martin Luther King, Jr.

GEORGE LAKOFF AND MARK JOHNSON   "Concepts We Live By." From *Metaphors We Live By* by George Lakoff and Mark Johnson. Copyright 1980 by University of Chicago Press. Reprinted by permission.

LAURA LALAINA   "Organizational Cultures: A Contrast." Reprinted by permission of the author.

C. S. LEWIS   "We Have No Right to Happiness." From *God in the Dock* by C. S. Lewis. Copyright © C. S. Lewis Pte Ltd. 1970. Reproduced by permission of Curtis Brown, London.

BARRY LOPEZ   "Buffalo." Reprinted with permission of Charles Scribner's Sons, an imprint of Macmillan Publishing Company, from *Winter Count* by Barry Lopez. Copyright © 1981 by Barry Holstun Lopez.

BEN MARSH   "A Rose-Colored Map." Copyright © 1977 by *Harper's Magazine*. All rights reserved. Reprinted from the July issue by special permission.

M. T. MASUCCI   "Three Months with the Aboto." Reprinted by permission of the author.

MARYANN MCCARRA   "Dialectical Spirituality." Reprinted by permission of the author.

CLAIRE MCMAHON   "My Summer Job." Reprinted by permission of the author.

MÁIRÉAD MENSCHING   "My Car." Reprinted by permission of the author.

JESSICA MITFORD   "Behind the Formaldehyde Curtain." From *The American Way of Death* by Jessica Mitford. Copyright © 1963, 1978 by Jessica Mitford. Reprinted by permission of Simon & Schuster, Inc.

HAROLD J. MOROWITZ   "Drinking Hemlock and Other Nutritional Matters." From *The Wine of Life and Other Essays on Society, Energy and Living Things* by Harold J. Morowitz. Copyright © 1979 by Harold J. Morowitz. Reprinted by permission of St. Martin's Press, Inc., New York.

TERENCE MULGREW   "Entertaining a Child." Reprinted by permission of the author.

LIANE ELLISON NORMAN   "Pedestrian Students and High-Flying Squirrels." From *Center Magazine*, Jan.–Feb. 1978. Reprinted by permission.

WILLIAM O'CONNELL   "Court Day." Reprinted by permission of the author.

GEORGE ORWELL   "Politics and the English Language" and "A Hanging." From *Shooting an Elephant and Other Essays* by George Orwell. Copyright 1950 by Sonia Brownell Orwell and renewed 1978 by Sonia Pitt-Rivers. Reprinted by permission of Harcourt Brace Jovanovich, Inc.

JO GOODWIN PARKER   "What Is Poverty?" From *America's Other Children*, edited by George Henderson. Copyright © 1971 by the University of Oklahoma Press.

KATHERINE ANNE PORTER   "The Necessary Enemy." From *The Collected Essays and Occasional Writings of Katherine Anne Porter*. Copyright © 1948, 1976 by Katherine Anne Porter. Reprinted by permission of Isabel Bayley, Literary Trustee, Estate of Katherine Anne Porter.

EDWARD PROFFITT   "Wordsworth Country." First appeared in *Southern Humanities Review* (summer 1984), Auburn University, Auburn, Ala. Reprinted by permission.

DAVID QUAMMEN   "Is Sex Necessary? Virgin Birth and Opportunism in the Garden." From *Natural Acts* by David Quammen. Reprinted by permission of David Quammen. All rights reserved. Copyright © 1982 by David Quammen.

LILLIAN ROSS   "The Vinyl Santa." From *Talk Stories* (Simon & Schuster). Reprinted by permission. Copyright © 1962 The New Yorker Magazine, Inc.

BERTRAND RUSSELL   "How I Write." Extract taken from *Portraits from Memory* by Bertrand Russell. Copyright 1953. Reproduced by kind permission of Unwin Hyman Ltd.

CARL SAGAN   "The Nuclear Winter." Copyright © 1983 by Carl Sagan. All rights reserved. First published in *Parade*. Reprinted by permission of the author.

MAY SARTON   "The Rewards of Living a Solitary Life." Copyright © 1974 by The New York Times Company. Reprinted by permission.

ERIC SEVAREID   "Homecoming." From *This Is Eric Sevareid* by Eric Sevareid. Reprinted by permission of Don Congdon Associates, Inc. Copyright © 1964 by Eric Sevareid.

BRENT STAPLES   "Black Man and Public Space." Reprinted by permission of the author.

PETER STEINFELS   "History Is Bunk." Copyright © Commonweal Foundation. Reprinted by permission.

PEGGY AND PIERRE STREIT   "A Well in India." Copyright © 1959 by The New York Times Company. Reprinted by permission.

WILLIAM STYRON   "The Habit." From *This Quiet Dust* by William Styron. Copyright © 1982 by William Styron. Reprinted by permission of Random House, Inc.

FRANK SULLIVAN   "The Busy Cliché Expert." From *A Pearl in Every Oyster* by Frank Sullivan. Used by permission of the Historical Society of Saratoga Springs, New York.

JUDY SYFERS   "I Want a Wife." Copyright 1971 by Judy Syfers. Reprinted by permission.

JOHN TARKOV   "Fitting In." Copyright © 1985 by The New York Times Company. Reprinted by permission.

PAUL THEROUX   "Being a Man." From *Sunrise with Seamonsters* by Paul Theroux. Copyright © 1985 by Cape Cod Scriveners Company. Reprinted by permission of Houghton Mifflin Company.

LEWIS THOMAS   "The Iks." From *The Lives of a Cell* by Lewis Thomas. Copyright © 1974 by Lewis Thomas. All rights reserved. "Clever Animals," "The Attic of the Brain," and "Late Night Thoughts on Listening to Mahler's Ninth Symphony." From *Late Night Thoughts on Listening to Mahler's Ninth Symphony* by Lewis Thomas. Copyright © 1982 by Lewis Thomas. All rights reserved. All reprinted by permission of Viking Penguin, a division of Penguin USA Inc.

CALVIN TRILLIN   "It's Just Too Late." From *Killings* by Calvin Trillin. Copyright © 1984 by Calvin Trillin. Reprinted by permission of Houghton Mifflin Company.

BARBARA TUCHMAN   "The Historian as Artist" and "On Our Birthday — America as Idea." From *Practicing History* by Barbara Tuchman. Copyright © 1981 by Alma Tuchman, Lucy T. Eisenberg and Jessica Tuchman Matthews. Reprinted by permission of Alfred A. Knopf, Inc.

GORE VIDAL   "Tarzan Revisited." From *Reflections Upon a Sinking Ship* by Gore Vidal. Reprinted by permission of William Morris Agency, Inc. on behalf of the author. Copyright © 1963 by Gore Vidal. "Drugs." Reprinted from *Homage to Daniel Shays: Collected Essays* by Gore Vidal, by permission of Random House, Inc.

ALICE WALKER   "Nuclear Madness: What You Can Do." Copyright 1982 by Alice Walker, in her volume *In Search of Our Mothers' Gardens.* Reprinted by permission of Harcourt Brace Jovanovich, Inc.

EUDORA WELTY   "A Sweet Devouring." From *The Eye of the Story: Selected Essays and Reviews* by Eudora Welty. Copyright © 1978 by Eudora Welty. Reprinted by permission of Random House, Inc.

E. B. WHITE   "The Gastropods." Copyright 1929 by Harper & Row, Publishers, Inc. Copyright © renewed 1957 by E. B. White and James Thurber. "Calculating Machine." Copyright 1951 by E. B. White. From *Poems and Sketches of E. B. White.* Copyright 1981 by E. B. White. Both reprinted by permission of Harper & Row, Publishers, Inc.

GEORGE WILL   "Reading, Writing and Rationality." From *Newsweek,* March 17, 1986. Copyright © 1986, Newsweek, Inc. All rights reserved. Reprinted by permission.

MARIE WINN   "Television and Violence: A New Approach." From *The Plug-In Drug* by Marie Winn. Copyright © 1977 by Marie Winn Miller. All rights reserved. Reprinted by permission of Viking Penguin, a division of Penguin Books USA Inc.

LARRY WOIWODE   "A Killing." Copyright 1975 by Larry Woiwode. First appeared in *Esquire* Magazine. Reprinted by permission of Donadio & Ashworth, Inc.

P. S. WOOD   "Female Athletes: They've Come a Long Way, Baby." Copyright © 1980 by The New York Times Company. Reprinted by permission.

VIRGINIA WOOLF   "The Death of the Moth" and "Professions for Women." From *The Death of the Moth and Other Essays* by Virginia Woolf. Copyright 1942 by Harcourt Brace Jovanovich, Inc. and renewed 1970 by Marjorie T. Parsons, Executrix. Reprinted by permission of the publisher.

WILLIAM ZINSSER   "Simplicity." From *On Writing Well* by William Zinsser. Copyright © 1976 by William K. Zinsser. Reprinted by permission of the author.

INDEX OF AUTHORS AND TITLES

A 0
B 1
C 2
D 3
E 4
F 5
G 6
H 7
I 8
J 9